Great Reading from

LIFE

Great Reading from

LIFE

A Treasury of the Best Stories and Articles
Chosen by the Editors

BONANZA BOOKS
New York

This 1987 edition is published by Bonanza Books, distributed by Crown Publishers, Inc., 225 Park Avenue South, New York, New York 10003, by arrangement with Harper & Row Publishers, Inc.

Printed and Bound in the United States of America

Library of Congress Cataloging in Publication Data

Great reading from Life.

I. Life (Chicago, Ill.)
AC5.G692   1987   081   87-9354
ISBN: 0-517-63208-X

h g f e d c b

ACKNOWLEDGMENTS

Grateful acknowledgment is made for permission to reprint the following selections:

ONCE ABOARD THE "RELUCTANT." Reprinted with the permission of Houghton Mifflin Company from *Mr. Roberts*. Copyright 1946 by Thomas Heggen.

MR. BLANDINGS BUILDS HIS DREAM HOUSE. Reprinted with the permission of Simon and Schuster, Inc., and Messrs. Michael Joseph, Ltd., from *Mr. Blandings Builds His Dream House*. Copyright 1946 by Eric Hodgins.

A NICE LITTLE BANK TO ROB. From *A Nice, Busy Little Bank That Should Be Robbed*. Copyright © 1959 by Evan McLeod Wylie.

HOW SUCCESS RUINED A WOULD-BE BUM. Reprinted with the permission of Harcourt, Brace and Company, Inc., and Messrs. Victor Gollancz, Ltd., from *Subways Are for Sleeping*. Copyright 1957 by Edmund G. Love.

"LET YOUR KIDS ALONE." Copyright 1958 by Robert Paul Smith.

THE DARK WINE OF GENIUS. Copyright 1951 by Robert Coughlan.

THE ART OF EL GRECO. Reprinted with the permission of Harper & Brothers and Chatto & Windus, Ltd., from *Themes and Variations*. Copyright 1950 by Aldous Huxley.

"THE PRIVATE WORLD OF WILLIAM FAULKNER. Copyright 1954 by Robert Coughlan.

"THE END OF A DARK AGE IN RUSSIA. From *The End of a Dark Age Ushers in New Dangers* by Whittaker Chambers. Copyright © 1956 by Time Inc.

A DIVIDED SOUTH SEARCHES ITS SOUL. Reprinted with the permission of Random House, Inc. Condensed from *Segregation: The Inner Conflict in the South*. Copyright © 1956 by Robert Penn Warren.

CONTENTS

V: MAKERS OF HISTORY

VI: ORDEALS

VII: MEMORIES

VIII: RELIGIONS

IX: WARS

X: WORLDS

INTRODUCTION

    Topical writing—the kind "he that runs may read"—sometimes seems to get embalmed in the cliché, "dead as yesterday's newspaper." Yet Mark Twain's *The Innocents Abroad* started as a series of news reports for the *Daily Alta Californian*, and William White became famous for an editorial called "What's the Matter with Kansas?" during the 1896 election. People who have forgotten all about the Populists remember the Emporia editor's stinging jibe at that "old mossback Jacksonian who snorts and howls because there is a bathtub in the State House." In 1941 a prophetic challenge, "The American Century," was written by LIFE's Editor-in-Chief, Henry R. Luce, and is still being quoted today. The article appears in *Great Reading from* LIFE and its timeliness is illustrated by this paragraph:

    America as the dynamic center of ever-widening spheres of enterprise, America as the training center of the skillful servants of mankind, America as the Good Samaritan, really believing again that it is more blessed to give than to receive, and America as the powerhouse of the ideals of Freedom and Justice—out of these elements surely can be fashioned a vision of the twentieth century to which we can and will devote ourselves in joy and gladness and vigor and enthusiasm.

Why great *reading*? Didn't the same Mr. Luce say, "The photograph is not the newest but it is the most important instrument of journalism which has been invented since the printing press"? Yes, but LIFE, in addition to being the pioneer in photo-journalism, has also been dedicated to good writing—good topical writing which, far from being dead the next day or the next week, has the validity of history recorded as history is being made. This is history that doesn't have to be stuffy or forbidding—and isn't. It represents the many aspects of an era—warmth and humor, dramatic events and folklore, fact and philosophy, sharp on-the-spot reporting and thoughtful reminiscenses. This, I think, is what the reader will find in these adaptations of seventy articles and stories selected from LIFE's first twenty-four years.

There are the writings of the men who themselves made and are making world history—Winston S. Churchill, Dwight D. Eisenhower, Harry S. Truman, John F. Kennedy and Richard M. Nixon. There are selections by men who make literary history, like Bruce Catton, A. B. Guthrie, Jr., John Hersey and Robert Penn Warren. There is the satisfying work of trained observers, anonymous reporters and name writers of LIFE's staff, who record great and small (but also important) events with the trained skill of the professional.

In point of time the selections range from the yesterday of "The Earth Is Born" and "The Norman Conquest" to the tomorrow of "What It's Like to Fly into Space." In style they range from Churchill's eloquence to Harry Truman's plain but serviceable prose. And in subject matter they go from the subfinite, "How Success Ruined a Would-Be Bum," to "The World, the Flesh and the Devil" and "The Starry Universe"—the infinite.

EDWARD K. THOMPSON
Editor, LIFE

I
ADVENTURES

Noel Sickles

THE CONQUEST
OF MT. EVEREST

by Sir Edmund Hillary

JULY 13, 1953

> *On May 29, 1953, a British expedition, led by Sir John Hunt, conquered Mt. Everest, earth's highest point, whose gale-swept peak had defied—and fascinated—mountain climbers for decades. Two teams of two men each made the final assault on the peak. The first pair, Charles Evans and Tom Bourdillon, were turned back 300 feet short of the summit. Then Edmund Hillary, a New Zealand beekeeper, and Tenzing Norkey, a Sherpa tribesman, made their way successfully to the top. Here Hillary describes the last stages of his perilous ascent.*

At 4 A.M. the weather looked perfect and when I opened the tent door the view was indescribably beautiful, with all the icy peaks far below us glowing clearly in the early morning light as they towered above their still dark and sleeping valleys. Tenzing gleefully pointed out the monastery of Thyangboche, faintly visible on its dominant spur sixteen thousand feet below us. We started up our cooker and in a determined effort to prevent the weaknesses arising from dehydration, we drank large quantities of lemon juice and sugar and followed this with our last tin of sardines on biscuits.

I dragged our oxygen sets into the tent, cleaned the ice off them

3

and then completely rechecked and tested them. Over our eiderdown clothing we donned our windproofs and on our hands we pulled three pairs of gloves—silk, woolen and windproof. Finally at 6:30 A.M. we crawled out of our tent into the snow, hoisted our thirty pounds of oxygen gear onto our backs, connected up our masks and turned on the valves to bring life-giving oxygen into our lungs. A few good deep breaths and we were ready to go.

Tenzing moved off and kicked a deep line of steps away from the rock bluff which protected our tent into the steep powder snow slope to the left of the main ridge. The ridge was now all bathed in sunlight and we could see our first objective—the south summit—far above us. Tenzing, moving purposefully, kicked steps in a long traverse back toward the ridge. We reached its crest just where it forms a great distinctive snow bump at about twenty-eight thousand feet.

From here the ridge narrowed to a knife edge and I took over the lead. We were moving slowly but steadily with plenty in reserve. Soft, unstable snow on the crest of the ridge made a route on it both uncomfortable and dangerous so I moved a little down on the steep left side where the wind had produced a thin crust. This sometimes held our weight but more often than not gave way with a sudden knock which had disturbing effects on our balance and morale. After several hundred feet of this the ridge suddenly eased and in a tiny hollow we came upon the two oxygen bottles left on the earlier attempt by Evans and Bourdillon. I scraped the ice off the gauges and was greatly relieved to find that they still contained several liters of oxygen—sufficient to get us down to the South Col if used sparingly.

I continued on up the ridge which soon steepened and broadened out into the very formidable snow face which formed the last four hundred feet of the south summit. Snow conditions on this face were, we felt, distinctly dangerous, but as no alternative route seemed available we persisted in our strenuous and uncomfortable efforts to beat a trail up it. It was with some relief that we finally reached some firmer snow higher up and then chipped steps up the last steep slopes and cramponed onto the south summit. It was now 9 A.M.

We looked with some interest at the virgin ridge ahead of us. Both Bourdillon and Evans had been depressingly definite about its problems and difficulties and we realized it could form an almost insuperable barrier. At first glance it was certainly impressive and even rather frightening. On the right great contorted cornices, overhanging masses of ice and snow, thrust out like twisted fingers over the twelve-thousand-foot drop of the Kangshung face. Any move into these cornices could only bring disaster. From the cornices the ridge dropped steeply to the left until the snow merged with the great rock face sweeping up from the Western Cwm. Only one encouraging feature was apparent. The steep snow slope between the cornices and the rock precipices seemed to be composed of firm hard snow. If we could cut a trail of steps along this slope we could make some progress at least.

Our first partly full bottles of oxygen were now exhausted so we disconnected them and threw them aside. We turned on our remaining full bottles—eight hundred liters of oxygen which should give us four and a half hours' going at three liters per minute. Our apparatus was now much lighter, weighing only about nineteen pounds, and as I cut steps down off the summit I felt a distinct sense of freedom and well being. As my ice ax bit into the first steep slope my highest hopes were realized. The snow was crystalline and firm. Two or three rhythmical blows of the ice ax produced a step large enough even for our oversized high altitude boots. And best of all, a firm thrust of the ice ax would sink it halfway up the shaft, giving a solid and comfortable belay.

We moved one at a time. I would cut a forty-foot line of steps, with Tenzing belaying me as I worked. Then in turn I would sink my ax, put a few loops of the rope around it and Tenzing—protected against a breaking step—would move up to me. Several of the cornices were particularly large and in order to escape them I cut a line of steps down to where the snow met the rocks. Half scrambling on the rocks and cutting handholds in the snow, we managed to shuffle past these difficult positions.

On one of these occasions I noted that Tenzing seemed to be breathing with difficulty and stopped to examine his oxygen set. I found that his exhaust tube, some two inches in diameter, was blocked with ice. I was able to clear it out and give him much needed relief. On checking my own set I found the same thing was occurring and from then on kept a much closer eye on this problem.

The weather for Everest was practically perfect. This did not mean that it would be an ideal day for the beach, but equipped as we were in all our eiderdown clothing and windproofs we suffered no discomfort from cold or wind. However, on the one occasion on which I removed my snow glasses in order to examine more closely a tricky section, I was very soon blinded by fine snow drawn by the cool wind. I hastily replaced my glasses.

After an hour's steady step cutting we reached the foot of the most formidable-looking problem on the ridge, a forty-foot vertical rock step. We had seen this step through the binoculars from far-away Thyangboche and realized that at this altitude it might well spell the difference between success and failure. The rock itself, smooth and almost holdless, might have been an interesting Sunday afternoon problem to a group of expert rock climbers in England's Lake District, but here it was a barrier far beyond our feeble strength to overcome.

But once again a possibility of tackling it remained. On its east side was another great cornice and running up the full forty feet of the step was a narrow crack between the cornice and the rock. Leaving Tenzing to belay me as best he could, I moved into this crack. Then, kicking backward with my crampons, I gained a purchase on the frozen snow behind me and levered myself off the ground. Taking advantage of every little rock hold and of all the friction of knee, shoulders and arms I could muster, I literally cramponed backward up the crack, with the fervent prayer that the cornice would remain attached to the rock. My progress was slow but steady and as Tenzing paid out the rope I inched my way upward until I could finally reach over the top of the rock and drag myself out of the crack onto a wide ledge. For a few moments I lay still, regaining my breath. For the first time I really felt the fierce determination that nothing now could stop our reaching the top.

When I had recovered I took a firm stance and commenced towing in the rope as Tenzing in his turn wiggled his way up the crack. He collapsed exhausted at the top like a giant fish that had just been hauled from the sea after a terrible struggle. I checked our remaining

6

oxygen and roughly calculated our flow rates. Everything was going well. Tenzing had been moving rather slowly but was still climbing safely and well. His only comment when I inquired about his condition was to smile and wave along the ridge. The ridge continued as before—giant cornices on the right, steep slopes on the left. I went on cutting steps. We had no idea where the top was. The ridge curved away to the right and as I cut around the back of one hump another higher one would swing into view. Time was passing and the ridge seemed never-ending.

To save time I tried cramponing without cutting steps but quickly realized our margin of safety on these steep slopes at this altitude was too small and so went on step cutting. I was starting to tire a little now. Tenzing was moving very slowly. As I chipped steps around still another corner, I wondered rather dully just how long we could keep it up. Then I realized that the ridge ahead, instead of still rising, now dropped sharply away and far below I could see the East Rongbuk Glacier! I looked upward to see a narrow snow ridge running up to a sharp point. A few more whacks of the ice ax in the firm snow and we stood on the summit.

My initial feelings were of relief—relief that there were no more steps to cut, no more ridges to traverse and no more humps to tantalize us with hopes of success. Despite the knitted helmet, goggles and oxygen mask, all crusted with icicles, that concealed Tenzing's face, there was no disguising his infectious grin of pure delight as he looked all around him. We shook hands and then, casting those Anglo-Saxon formalities aside, Tenzing threw his arms around my shoulders and we thumped each other on the back until forced to stop from lack of breath.

I glanced at my watch: 11:30 A.M. The ridge had taken us two and a half hours, but it seemed more like five. I checked our oxygen again—yes, the slow rate seemed to be pretty constant. But if we intended to remain on three liters, we were going to have to waste no time on the return as we had only two hours' more endurance. In this time we had to return along the ridge and descend the dangerous slopes of the south summit to the two partly filled bottles waiting for us far below.

I turned off my oxygen and removed my set. I then produced my camera and set to work to photograph everything in sight. First of all some photographs of Tenzing waving a string of flags—Nepalese, British, United Nations and Indian. Then I endeavored to take photographs down all the ridges of Everest. I had little hope of the results being particularly successful, as I had a lot of difficulty in holding the camera steady in my clumsy gloves, but I felt they would at least serve as a record. After some ten minutes of this I realized I was becoming rather clumsy-fingered and slow-moving. I quickly replaced my oxygen set and experienced once more the stimulating effect of even a few liters of oxygen.

While I had been taking these photographs Tenzing had made a little hole in the snow and in it placed various articles of food, a bar of chocolate, a packet of biscuits and a handful of hard candy—small offerings indeed, but at least a gift of some sort as a token offering to the gods that devout Buddhists believe have their home on this lofty summit.

After fifteen minutes we turned to go. The whole world around us lay spread out like a giant relief map and I could take in with a glance country that we had spent months mapping and exploring on previous trips. Reaction was setting in and we must get off our mountain. Already, as the spur of ambition died under the glow of success, we felt weakness in our limbs and shortage of breath. I moved down off the summit. Wasting no time, we cramponed along our tracks, spurred by the urgency of diminishing oxygen.

Bump followed bump in rapid succession. In what seemed almost miraculous time we reached the top of the rock step. Now, with the almost casual indifference of familiarity, we kicked and jammed our way down it again. We were tired out but not too tired to be careful. We scrambled cautiously over the rock traverses, moved one at a time over shaky snow sections and finally cramponed on our steps and back onto the south summit. Only one hour back from the top! We were holding our own against time. A swig of sweetened lemonade refreshed us and we turned down again.

As I led the way down the great snow slope, I hacked each step with as much care as if our lives depended on it—as well they might. Every step down was a step nearer safety and, when we finally moved off the slope onto the ridge below, we both looked at each other and almost visibly shrugged off the sense of fear that had been with us all day.

We were now very tired but moved automatically down to the two oxygen cylinders cached on the ridge. We were only a short distance from camp, so we loaded the cylinders onto our frames, continued down our tracks and reached our tent on its crazy platform at 2 P.M. Already the moderate winds of the afternoon had wrenched the tent loose from some of its fastenings and it presented a forlorn sight.

We were very thirsty and still had to get down to the South Col. Tenzing lit the kerosene stove and started to make a lemonade drink heavily sweetened with sugar. I changed our oxygen sets onto the last partly filled bottles and cut down our flow rates to two liters a minute. Far below on the South Col we could see minute figures and knew that Lowe would be eagerly waiting for our descent.

We slowly packed up our sleeping bags and air mattresses and strapped them onto our frames. Then, with a last look at the camp that had served us so well, we turned downward with dragging feet and set ourselves to the task of safely descending the ridge. With our numbed faculties the time seemed to pass as in a dream, but finally we reached the site of the Swiss ridge camp and branched off down into the great couloir.

There an unpleasant surprise greeted us. The strong wind which was now blowing had completely wiped out all steps and only a steep, hard surface greeted our weary eyes. There was nothing to do but start cutting again. For two hundred feet I chipped steps laboriously downward. Gusts of driving wind almost tore us from our steps. Tenzing took over the lead and cut down another one hundred feet, then moved onto softer snow and kicked a track right down the couloir.

Two figures came toward us and met us a couple of hundred feet above camp. They were Lowe and Noyce, laden with hot soup and emergency oxygen. We were too tired to make any response to Lowe's enthusiastic acceptance of our news. We stumped down to the col and slowly ground our way up the short rise to the camp. Off came our oxygen and into the tent we crawled and with a sigh of pure delight collapsed into our sleeping bags, while the tents flapped and shook under the perpetual South Col gale.

Yes, the South Col might be the worst spot in the world, but to us at the moment—with the Primus stove humming and our friends Lowe and Noyce fussing about us—it was home.

When Everest's conquerors came down from the mountain, they received a swelling welcome from the proud, excited people of Nepal—and as many foreigners as could get there. LIFE's India Correspondent James Burke, striking out alone from press headquarters at Katmandu, the capital city, was the first reporter to meet Tenzing, whose name was ringing in a chanting cheer throughout the city. As night fell they sat down on a grassy hill above the city. Tenzing held the flashlight while Burke wrote down verbatim his broken-phrased story of the victory.

Everest place my home. My people name Everest Chomolungma. That mean mountain birds cannot fly over. I think good name, don't you? Sometimes I climb ridge above Nanpa La [a nineteen-thousand-foot pass near Tenzing's home village of Thami] for better view Chomolungma. Then I sit think what lamas at Thyangboche [the main Tibetan Buddhist monastery in the area] say. They say Buddha god live there on top and they make worship to mountain. I have feeling for climbing to top and making worship more close to Buddha god. Not same feeling like English sahibs who say want "conquer" mountain. I feel more making pilgrimage.

Everest no hardest climb. Everest no easy but Nanda Devi with French expedition 1951 most dangerous for me. On ice fall ice very raw. Steep drop both sides. I climb slowly one inch one time. No place hold. Very small put foot. Ice very slippery.

On Swiss expedition [to Everest] last year we get 27,550 feet. So cold give boxing blows keep warm. When spit it become ice, fall like stone. Breathing become snow and stick to hair on face. One small tent no sleeping bag. Next morning oxygen no work because freezing. I try pump but after cannot pumping, throw away and leave there. We go climbing without oxygen to 28,215 feet. This highest point. Can no go much higher. No food no drink for twenty-four hour. If have one cup tea think can climb top. We fail but everyone so happy we climb highest point. But no flower that high so sahibs make sausage garland give us. We dance happy.

After second Swiss expedition 1952 I get sick. First I think no go again. Then think must try again. Must get top Chomolungma. Then I begin feel stronger. When I get on mountain [on the British expedition] maybe halfway up I no more feel hungry thirsty. Also forget family and no think afraid. Only think must get top. Up 27,900 feet where Hillary and I stop for night no sleep much. Maybe one two hours then wake up. Throat feel choking. But keep thinking must get top.

On top I no think anything at first. Then I look at Hillary. He hold out hand for shake. I shake then throw arms around him and we hit other on back. Very happy. I look every side. Good day, no much wind. All hills below look like Buddha gods. I can see very far. North in Tibet I see Rongbuk Gompa [monastery] and North Col where old expedition come. That way look very hard. In west I see Thyangboche and I think lamas praying there. I put little offering in snow. I feel very good. I have make worship close to Buddha god like think when I am boy on ridge above Nanpa La.

Hillary ask me hold up flags on ax handle. I hold up British, Nepal and U.N. flags for picture, also Indian. Friend in Darjeeling give me Indian flag, I ask Colonel Hunt if all right take it to top and he say "good."

Next day back at camp I get Sherpa write letter my family [Tenzing can neither read nor write, except for his own name]. It say, "This letter is from Tenzing. Myself along with one Sahib reached summit Everest on 29th May. Hope you will feel happy. Cannot write more. May I be excused."

PARACHUTING FOR FUN

by Loudon Wainwright

AUGUST 10, 1959

You can drop 10,500 feet in a minute, go 125 mph, or fly like the birds—if so inclined—in the new sport of parachuting. Although LIFE Staff Writer Loudon Wainwright preferred to keep his feet on the ground while working on this article, he lets the reader experience the risks and the exuberance of "falling free" in the air.

If you are between the ages of sixteen and forty-five and are bored with drag racing, motorcycling, skin diving, mountain climbing and bullfighting, the chances are good that you could recapture some of the old zip by taking a parachute jump, preferably one involving a long free fall, say for about thirty seconds from the time you leave the airplane until you pull the rip cord.

The view from the plane at 7,000 feet is marvelous. The fall itself, at a top speed of 125 mph, is exciting without being taxing. The time is passed pleasantly in barrel rolls and loops as the patchwork of the ground slowly expands before your eyes and the actual open-

12

ing—if the man back in the rigging shed has done his job conscientiously—is gentle. The final swinging descent takes place in blessed silence as you deftly manipulate your 28-foot-diameter, undie-thin nylon for a dead-center landing on the target. Of course, it is perfectly permissible to shout in jubilation on the way down and you are almost sure to be wearing a silly expression when, after a one-and-a-half-mile drop, you land with the delicate shock of a man who has jumped from a four-foot wall.

Most parachutists, whether novices or veterans, wear the same expression: the cheeks are flushed, the eyes are shining, the mouth trembles. It is a look compounded of joy, lust and, for the novice, enormous relief, and it plainly states that you are a jumper and you are alive and it's all a hell of a kick.

Most people, whose fear of heights and falling probably dates back to their first infant plunge to the floor of the nursery, understandably feel that a parachute is a horrifying emergency device used to get from up to down only when there is no other way out. The thesis therefore that parachuting is a restorative and fun besides amounts to apparent insanity. Surely, they think, the heart would stop, the cord would fail, the chute would rip and the jumper would fall, screaming and kicking all the way, straight into the ground—where his remains would approximate the status of a quivering aspic.

Yet there is a growing, if still exclusive, coterie of serious-minded and responsible young men in the U.S. who devoutly believe in the manifold physical and spiritual benefits of parachuting. Not only that, they believe that it is utterly safe—though they would deem a leap like the one described above inadvisable without considerable practice and training. These men, when they are not falling out of airplanes themselves, are busily spreading their exhilarating gospel, which is that practically everybody can and should jump.

Astonishingly enough, their message appears to be having some effect, indicating that there are more relaxed people around than one might suppose. While it is still possible to jump almost anywhere without falling into another chutist, the sport is definitely on the increase around the country. There are weekend parachuting clubs in Seattle, Cincinnati, San Francisco, New Orleans and seventy other

U.S. localities. Several colleges have clubs that compete against one another. Military paratroopers whose daily business is jumping have formed free-time chuting groups at posts in North Carolina, Kentucky and California. At all of these places the membership is rising—or rather floating downward—in ever greater numbers. It is estimated that whereas last year there were only fifteen hundred organized jumpers in the U.S., there are now as many as three thousand—a slightly larger number than the French total, but still well below the estimated figure of six thousand sport jumpers in the Soviet Union.

The new leapers are generally not the sort of thrill-seekers for whom a long fall is the only thing left. Business executives, doctors, lawyers, lady librarians and teachers are some of the more respectable types who are parachuting these heady days, and in Philadelphia there is an honor-roll college student with the odd distinction of never having gone up in a plane that he has not left in mid-air.

The anti-catapedaphobic center of the nation is a country airport ringed by green hills in Orange, Massachusetts. On a clear day with light winds there is rarely a moment when the sky above Orange is not dotted with the blossoms of brightly colored chutes gently lowering their enthusiastic cargoes to the ground. In the three months since the Sport Parachuting Center there first opened, more than 700 jumpers, 175 of them initiates, have taken advantage of its unique facilities. The worst injury to a parachutist in that period has been a slight ankle sprain, although there was an awful moment one gusty Saturday in June when a tiny lady in an oversized chute appeared actually to be climbing for a while immediately after she left the plane, soaring like Dorothy in the opening cyclone in *The Wizard of Oz*. Normal time of descent after opening is about two minutes. Four minutes elapsed before this lady arrived harmlessly in the woods.

Small planes carrying prospective jumpers drop into Orange from Boston, New York and as far away as Kansas City. Young men who arrive in their own cars are continually walking into the center's office and inquiring, somewhat shamefacedly, "Is this the place where people jump?" Others come with their families. It is a startling commonplace at Orange to see mothers and fathers calmly munching hot dogs while they wait for Junior to come plunging out of that airplane high above them.

The proprietor of the Orange facility is a thirty-year-old French-born American named Jacques André Istel, who drove cars at enormous speeds and worked for his father's investment firm before he became the Billy Graham of parachuting. Istel is an uncompromising evangelist for his sport. For Istel, parachuting is a high form of human expression, like writing poetry, and a parachutist, particularly one who has dropped about five thousand feet through space before opening his canopy, is a man who has glimpsed his greatest potential. "The parachutist has a sense of purpose, a sense of conquest impossible for most people to achieve in other ways," says Istel. "There are too many restrictions in modern life. A young man can't do anything without breaking some law. In parachuting he has complete freedom, including freedom of the choice to save his own life. If he fouls up, he is dead." Being dead, Istel would want it quickly understood, is a state no parachutist, unless he is a very old parachutist, need contemplate.

Although accuracy in landing is a key requirement of sport jumping, it must be obvious that everything depends on what seems the ultimate madness: leaving the plane in the first place. By this it is not intended to conjure up images of reluctant jumpers losing their nerve, fighting off their jumpmasters and demanding to be taken back to earth the way the Wright brothers intended—by plane. Actually this almost never happens, although every novice is afraid that it will. However reluctant he may be at the last moment, the jumper has already made his decision before he leaves the ground. Though he is frightened and often wonders what wild combination of stupidity and bravado got him into this dreadful spot, he goes when he is told to go. His ego demands it. One first jumper who was asked how he felt as he was about to climb into the plane summed up the dilemma of a man caught between sober contemplation and pride: "It all seems very unlikely."

When the most unlikely moment of all arrives, it is not enough just to fling oneself out of the plane. At the jumpmaster's command to stand by, the chutist must swing his feet out of the open side of the plane (it is usually a high-wing monoplane) and place them carefully on a step which extends about eighteen inches out from the cabin. When the instructor says "Go," the jumper rises to his feet on this step and reaches outside for the strut which supports the wing. This maneuver completed, he is standing entirely outside the cabin, facing the direction in which the plane is going. In goggles and helmet, with the wind whipping at his coveralls and the chute packs around his body, he looks in his crouched stance like a throwback to the golden days of cinematic wing-walking. Though he is often a fearful man wondering how he is possibly going to do what he has to do next, he looks unmistakably like Richard Arlen waiting for just the proper time to drop off and fall straight into the cockpit of the enemy plane beneath him.

At this biggest of all possible moments the jumper is supposed to leave immediately. This is not an attractive time. Although the plane has slowed for his departure, the wind is still tearing at him at about 80 mph, and there are very large quantities of open space beneath him. "When I got out there," said one novice, "I forgot absolutely everything. But it seemed a poor time for further questions, so I just let go."

Letting go is one way to do it, but the best take-off requires a more concentrated effort. The jumper should lean forward against the strut, then kick vigorously back and up with his feet and push off with his hands. If he does all this properly, he finds himself in mid-air, parallel to earth, back arched, head thrown back and arms flung wide in the swan dive to end all swan dives.

This mid-air, spread-eagle stance, curiously known in the trade as the "stable position," is crucial for a smooth, relatively uneventful flight. If the novice does not maintain it until his opening chute pulls him into an upright position, he is very likely to start an uncontrolled tumbling and looping called "disorderly fall." For the experienced parachutist this phrase has exactly the same derogatory connotation that disorderly conduct has for a night court magistrate.

It would seem that virtually nothing could call for more sheer resolve than just bailing out and letting the static line take care of the opening. Yet experienced jumpers scorn it for themselves. They tend to look on the novice's jumping altitude of 2,400 feet as a sort of kiddie pool in the sky. Parachuting to them means long free falls from high altitudes. During these falls they perform truly astonishing gyrations and, although they are only wingless bodies ultimately powerless against gravity, they actually fly. This is sky diving, without question the world's most exacting and exciting sport.

A first-rate sky diver—there are probably only 50 of them in the U.S., including Istel and his three instructors at Orange—is in most cases a man who has made 100 or more jumps, the great majority of them free falls with delays of up to 60 seconds before opening the chute. To bring off a 60-second "delay" successfully, the jumper has to bail out at 12,500 feet; when he finally pulls the rip cord a minute later, he is 2,000 feet from the ground. (The world's free fall record, established by Nikolai Nikitine of Russia in 1957, is 47,953 feet. The women's free fall record—as might be expected, parachuting is not a male monopoly—is held by a Russian lady named Valentina Kouliche.)

If the sheer span of time and distance covered in these falls stirs wonderment in the breasts of groundlocked laymen, it is really what takes place on the way down that counts. The free-falling parachutist can perform a wide variety of controlled acrobatics through subtle movements of his arms, legs and even hands. A good jumper can do flat horizontal turns, loops and barrel rolls under perfect control. His greatest danger is not that he will whirl into unconsciousness but that he will simply get carried away by the fun of it all.

Such bemusement is dangerous for a simple but startling reason: there is very little feeling in falling. When he first leaves the airplane, a man drops like a stone and picks up speed rapidly, but around ten or twelve seconds after he has jumped he is traveling between 120 and 125 mph and never goes any faster. At this rate, which many hot-rodders and Jaguar drivers with one anxious eye on the rearview mirror achieve almost daily, he can feel the wind tearing at his helmet and raising his goggles slightly from his face, but there is no other sensation of falling. Lew Sanborn, an instructor at Orange, says, "It's like floating in an ocean of air." Another instructor, Nate Pond, comments, "You can get over on your back and stabilize there and it's just like being in a great big featherbed with all of your arms and legs and body resting against the air." Losing track of time and altitude in such comfortable surroundings can be fatal: the feathers reach only to the ground.

There are safeguards against this. Most experienced jumpers wear both stop watches and altimeters to keep track of both seconds and feet so that they can pull their cords in ample time. French jumpers have devised a buzzer, like a kitchen timer, that sounds inside their helmets at the right moment. But it is all too easy to forget to look at the instruments.

Aside from not jumping at all, the best way to eliminate these dangers is by training and experience. Istel's group, like other parachuting clubs around the country, takes great pains to insure a jumper's readiness before allowing him to sample the heady magic of free fall. At Orange the novice gets a brief lecture on parachuting theory, and he is shown the proper way to exit from the plane and to steer his open canopy. Then he is put through a rigorous course on the right way to make a tumbling fall when he finally hits the ground. Only after this does the student go up for his first static line jump.

Beginners are accompanied by a jumpmaster, who sees to it that the static line is properly hooked up, gauges the wind and directs the pilot to the proper jump point. The jumpmaster studies the novice carefully as he leaves the plane. His written reports on the poorer exits, given later to the student, make enlightening reading. "Thrashed," "Tumbled," "Very weak exit, flopped on the wheel before clearing," "Eyes shut" and "Remained on the step too long" are some of the candid comments. They indicate not only the jumper's performance but something of the extraordinary tension most first leapers experience when it is really time to go.

Parachuting is mostly an individual performance, but at times it becomes positively congenial. There are five-man drops in international competition, and a particularly companionable form of jumping takes place when two parachutists make their delayed falls together, swooping, rolling, diving in close to each other and then pulling apart again. This sight makes it clear that the human body, in the midst of its inevitable plunge to earth, is able to fly. Even without artificial wings, which most parachutists deplore as dangerous aberrations, the body is a primitive airfoil. Slight movements can affect its attitude, direction and even its rate of fall.

The single most astonishing act performed by two parachutists is the baton pass, which is rather like the engineer of one train trying to pass a flag to the engineer of another train as they go by in opposite directions at high speed. Last month at Orange it was attempted by Instructor Lew Sanborn and Bradford Straus, a twenty-two-year-old Harvard graduate. The men were to leave the airplane at seven thousand feet. Straus, who was going first, would be carrying a foot-long wooden baton. Sanborn would follow about a second later. His job was to overtake Straus in the air and get the baton. A small group of watchers, some with binoculars, others shielding their eyes against the afternoon glare, looked on from the ground.

Straus leaped, a tiny black figure against the washed-out blue of the sky. He fell spread-eagled, stomach to earth, the baton in his outstretched hand. Sanborn followed almost immediately. He kept his head down, arms in against his sides, streamlining his body as much as possible in an effort to overtake Straus in the sky. He began to catch up with Straus, who, after four seconds of free fall, was more than fifty feet ahead.

In twelve seconds, after both jumpers had reached top speed, it was possible to see that Sanborn had reached Straus's level. They were now about five thousand feet above the ground and almost half their margin of time was gone. Horizontally, the two chutists were about sixty feet apart.

Suddenly, at what appeared to be great speed, they veered in toward one another. From the ground it seemed certain that they would collide. The two black figures merged and then broke apart again. One of the watchers who had been following the whole jump with binoculars, groaned. "They missed," he said. "Too fast." Twenty seconds had passed since the chutists had left the plane. Very little time was left.

Wide apart again, Sanborn and Straus renewed their approach, more cautiously this time. The tense crowd on the ground watched silently now. The men were only three thousand feet up; they had five seconds left. With what seemed agonizing slowness they drew close to each other. They were almost together, and then Sanborn veered and passed over Straus's body. It was possible to see that they had made contact: both bodies seemed to tumble for an instant. And as the man with binoculars cheered, "He got it!" the two jumpers drifted apart, and from their packs the two parachutes, one red, the other red, white and blue, bloomed simultaneously in the bright afternoon sky. Sanborn landed standing up, collapsed his chute and waved happily to his partner with the baton he had seized in mid-air.

Such work can be particularly hazardous. Men working together can get even more preoccupied than on an individual jump. There are two people cluttering up a relatively small patch of sky, and quite often baton passers bump each other hard.

The question remains: why do people jump? Why, in a culture whose proudest ornament is the moderate with his feet planted firmly on the ground, does anybody feel obliged to strap on a parachute and take his chances with half a mile or more of literal space? Why bother?

There are many first jumpers who go because it seems the most dangerous thing they could possibly do with any reasonable degree of safety. They go because the thought of it scares them to death but also because they know the chances of survival are really very good. In jumping they are proving at a minimal cost that they can face fear. But this does not mean that the strain on these jumpers is minimal. As they ride up to bail-out altitude beside the yawning open door their gaze becomes fixed, their faces sweat, they only nod numbly in response to the cheerful chatter of the jumpmaster.

But the great majority of first jumpers seem to be those who for some reason genuinely want the experience: the leap, the fall, the opening, the gentle, lonely ride back to earth under the full canopy of the extended parachute. These people, though almost invariably nervous, listen carefully to Istel and the other instructors and take their jump rides with a look of calm anticipation on their faces.

A most articulate initiate to parachuting is Dustin Smith, a blond, bright nineteen-year-old who works at the center. He jumps every time Istel or the other instructors will let him, and he is now working on sky-diving turns.

"In this country there's nothing to do," says Smith, who once spent some time living in Greenwich Village and trying with indifferent success to be a beatnik. "You can wear your coat collar up or put on sunglasses at night, but it's really hard to express yourself. I'd tried hitchhiking and for a while I wanted to go to Europe to learn bullfighting. Then I heard about this, and it sounded like something.

"The first time you go on a free fall is the weirdest. It's like a first date. You have no idea what's going to happen. You are terrified on the step. Then you look down, like God. And the ultimate is going away from the plane. In this you're free and you're purely responsible for yourself. The first time I packed my own chute, I was afraid to close it up but I finally did. There's a real moment of truth when you reach for the cord. You come down absolutely elated. You've done something that in one way is ridiculous—and in another way makes great sense."

Ridiculous or sensible, parachuting will doubtless remain, with its component ingredients of excitement and danger, a taunt to the adventurous, a challenge to the challengeable.

Jacques Istel himself best expresses the absorption, even the addiction, a real parachutist feels for his sport. Early one summer evening recently Istel, who had just completed his second jump of the day, was stretched out on the sandy ground near the huge target circle waiting for the last planeload of the fading day to drop its human cargo. The evening was still; there was no wind and the sun had just dropped behind the hills to the west of the airport. It still shone orange on the wings of the plane passing slowly overhead.

Lying flat in the sand with his hands behind his head, Istel stared up at the plane. Suddenly a black dot appeared beneath it, seemed almost to hang suspended for a moment before the long thin line of the unfilled chute trailed out behind it. The chute opened, a sudden red and white, and the tiny figure, its fall interrupted, swung almost gaily in the harness. In a few seconds the sound of the chute's opening report, like a sheet snapping once on a distant clothesline, reached the earth. "It looked like a good exit," Istel said. "He held his position well. He might even make a parachutist." He stopped talking and looked up at the sky. "Oh, it's a perfect day," he said. Then he added, "Of course, any day you've had a couple of jumps is a perfect day."

WHAT IT'S LIKE
TO FLY
INTO SPACE

by Warren R. Young

APRIL 13, 1959

> *After successfully enduring an exacting series of physical and psychological tests, potential space pilots for the U.S. Air Force are known as "Tigers." (Those who fail are referred to as "Bunnies.") In preparation for this article, LIFE Science Editor Warren R. Young underwent the total "Tiger" experience. Among other things, he was jolted, roasted, frozen, spun about and floated weightless in air. When it was all over he was a bit shaken, but well qualified to write about the training of our future astronauts.*

When I had floated about two feet above the floor, I gave a gentle push against the rear bulkhead with my toes. Immediately, like a miniature dirigible, I was literally and completely weightless. Suddenly a feeling of elation and triumph engulfed me. It was as if I had overcome the heavy grasp of gravity all by myself and had passed magically through a secret door to an alien world, a world of new dimensions and mysterious delights.

I was taking part, as a journalistic observer, in a series of space tests conducted by scientists of the Air Force, Navy and National Aeronautics and Space Administration. Some of these tests were recently used by NASA to select the little group of men for Project Mercury, the U.S. program to rocket a man into orbit around the earth. The tests will also solve some of the medical problems that still stand in the way of our sending men into space—and later to the moon and planets.

From past experiments and discoveries we already know that when the first man-shoot comes—whether performed by Americans or Russians—the space pilot will be menaced by a cacophony of sound capable of producing both disorientation and body damage, by a buffet of shocks and shakes, by devastating extremes of heat and cold and total vacuum, by the terrors and hallucinations of prolonged isolation and by the various crushing, dizzying and floating effects of wildly varying gravitational forces.

Into this horrendous environment the space scientists, who already have had trouble launching payloads of robot instruments, will soon catapult the most fragile and vulnerable package of all, the human body. To compound their problem, this package is likely to insist on a fair chance not only of functioning during the trip but of returning to the earth alive on the first try. When a man is aboard, there can be no "partially successful" rocket shoots.

Ideally, experts in the "human factors" would like to put human test subjects into one colossal, mechanical, ground-borne space simulator and simultaneously bombard them with all the known hazards of space travel. Unfortunately no such machine yet exists. But an ingenious assortment of devices *has* been built, each capable of reproducing almost exactly one or two of the stresses that will be encountered in space.

These are the machines I rode (although only to limits presumed to be safe for an editor who has grown somewhat out-of-condition and overweight since his air cadet days). My purpose was to experience and record the different sensations produced by the stresses of space; sensations unknown to most people but now being borne day after day to vastly more grueling degrees by the dedicated, inquisitive and over-modest band of U.S. space experimenters.

The first and by far the most delightful of the experiments that I was allowed to sample was weightlessness, officially known as the zero gravity experiment. I became weightless in a modified Convair 131-B transport plane named *How High the Moon,* in which experiments are conducted by Major Edward L. Brown, a psychologist and pilot at the Aero Medical Laboratory of Wright Field, Ohio. In a satellite, man will become weightless as soon as he goes into orbit because the centrifugal force throwing him outward, the result of his enormous velocity, will exactly balance the inward pull of gravity. To duplicate this situation, at least briefly, *How High the Moon* is put through a precise maneuver. First it is power-dived from about 12,000 feet until it reaches an air speed of 285 mph. Then it is sharply pulled up into a steep 30° climb. For the next 15 seconds the plane arcs through the air like a lobbed tennis ball, as weightlessly as if in orbit. Inside, everybody and every object that is not securely tied down (as the pilots are) rises eerily and floats aimlessly about.

Lying face-down on the padded floor of the plane as it began to pull up from its dive, I was pressed flat by a force of 2½ G's (2½ times the force of gravity), which made my body "weigh" 500 pounds. I remember wishing the G's would go away. I felt as if I were a lizard to whom the feat of rising to an upright posture must seem just barely possible but not worth the effort. Then, gradually, the heavy hand of gravity relaxed its pressure until it vanished. Gently, inexorably, I floated off the floor.

I was astonished to find that the world of weightlessness actually feels more natural than our customary gravity-controlled realm. Free floating at zero G seems to give simultaneous buoyancy to both body and spirit. I remember grinning ridiculously at the others in the plane as I discovered the new world. It was hard to remember or to care which was "up" and which was "down." Never again will ceilings be the same for me.

In this weightless world time seems to stretch like a rubber band. Over and over, as the plane finally pulled out of the maneuver and I sank to the floor with regained weight, it seemed as if minutes had passed. Yet each time it had been only fifteen seconds.

In time, as its delights become known, weightlessness will doubtless be pursued by large numbers of people. Before many years we can expect to hear that a new fountain pen is capable of writing while weightless, that history's first weightless wedding ceremony has been performed, or that some wealthy and thoughtful host has thrown the first weightless cocktail party.

Weightlessness is only one aspect of the menace of altered gravity. During his launch in a rocket and his re-entry through the earth's atmosphere, the space pioneer is sure to undergo rapid acceleration and deceleration, both of which will multiply his weight several times. Centrifuges, which whirl men around at the end of long booms, are among the best devices used to study this problem.

At Wright Field I climbed onto a weblike chair mounted at the end of a centrifuge's twenty-foot arm. I held control sticks in each hand. I had been told that as the centrifuge turned, a light would be flicked on repeatedly in front of my eyes. Each time, with a button on my right-hand control stick, I was supposed to turn out the light as a signal to the operators that I was neither unconscious nor blinded by the force of the G's. With the left-hand joy-stick I was supposed to test my co-ordination while undergoing G stresses by keeping two needles centered on the face of a standard aircraft instrument.

With a powerful whine like a subway train starting away from a station, the centrifuge began whipping me around in a circle. Within seconds I had achieved 3½ G's. I found that I could still lift my feet and head, although with great difficulty. When the centrifuge stopped and my pulse proved normal, the scientists agreed to give me a faster ride at 5 G's. This time the additional acceleration and resulting pressure was very noticeable. I could no longer lift my head, which now weighed 50 pounds. At this point my total weight was more than half a ton. In order to breathe I had to force my diaphragm up and down consciously, for the centrifugal force pinned my chest, preventing my lungs from expanding. Everything in front of me was a meaningless blur, except for a small area directly before my eyes. To my surprise, it was now easier to concentrate on the aircraft instrument, and the added weight of my arm made it easier to stabilize the joy-stick. (I learned later that my "score" at 5 G's was about as good as when standing still—and far better than at 3 G's.) When he called to me I could hear the voice of the operator, who was standing on the central hub of the centrifuge, but the sound seemed to come from far away. I did not answer, for I was afraid that, if I got my mouth open, it might be forced shut on my tongue. The sensation was as if I were being crushed at the bottom of a well. But despite the inconvenience of weighing so much, there was no pain.

The absolute limits of human tolerance to G's, I learned, are determined not so much by the crushing effect of the over-all force as by the distortion of various body parts. Oddly enough, the most important distortion is not that of a breakable organ but of the blood, which tends to collect in stagnant pools in the legs and lungs. Aside from the pain in chest and limbs, this prevents the blood from carrying oxygen to the head, causing blackout of the eyes, then unconsciousness and finally brain damage.

In actual rocket travel, the worst G stresses of all may not be long-sustained force but the violent shaking and vibration that may occur during launch or re-entry. I rode two devices intended to test human tolerance of vibration. By comparison they make even the most antique commuter trains feel like air-sprung chariots. At the Navy's Bethesda, Maryland, laboratories I was invited to sit on the same shake table which tested the squirrel monkey, Old Reliable, before he rode a Jupiter-C rocket out over the Atlantic to fame and a watery grave. "Test animals sometimes die after ten minutes on this table," I was matter-of-factly informed. "The vibration seems to make various organs hemorrhage. But we'll reduce the amplitude for you so that it will be only about as jolting as the worst broncho ride in a rodeo."

The comparison proved to be apt. After less than 30 seconds of being kicked in the posterior at the rate of 180 times a minute my bouncing got out of phase with the table. I was coming down when it was going up. Suddenly I noticed a peculiar puffing noise like the explosive wheeze of an air compressor. Air from my own lungs was causing this sound. As I struggled to retain my seat on the bouncing table, I was pulled sharply down with each vibration at the same moment that my liver was still rising upward because of the previous jolt. My liver banged into my diaphragm, compressing my lungs and forcing out the air in sudden bursts. My breathing was entirely at the mercy of the machine, as if I were in an iron lung that some madman had adjusted to pump three times a second.

Soon the Navy scientists switched off the vibrator—long enough to announce that its speed would now be increased to 600 vibrations per minute. Strangely, the faster tempo made the ride more tolerable.

At Pensacola, Florida, I was one of the first persons to ride inside a unique new contraption called the Human Disorientation Device, which was developed by the Naval School of Aviation Medicine at a cost of some $1 million. The H.D.D. looks and acts something like a tremendous automatic cocktail shaker, a huge metal barrel that spins horizontally and also vertically. Its purpose is to help scientists study the effect of multiple rotational movements on our sense of balance. It duplicates some situations in a rocket that is spinning and tumbling end over end in space. After I had been inside its whirling belly several seconds, the bulkhead in front of me—which actually was moving right along with me—appeared to rock dizzily back and forth. The rotation had completely disoriented my sense of balance.

Besides being shaken, floated and spun, space medicine experimenters are roasted, frosted, pressurized, exhausted on treadmills, and blasted with shattering sounds. Standing in front of Wright Field's huge sirens while they roared at 157 decibels, I could feel my elbows vibrating as if they were wineglasses responding to the correct musical note. For the rest of the day, so I imagined, I could hear the back of my skull ringing with a pure, bell-like sound. Later, sealed into a room-size oven, I tried out a temperature of 130°. After twenty-five minutes I was sweating profusely but the only real discomfort was caused by the seventeen thermocouples and electrocardiogram electrodes taped to various parts of my body including one big toe, and the rubber cuff wrapped around my arm for blood-pressure readings. Every few minutes the doctor in charge would signal to me through the window ten feet away, then inflate the cuff by remote control. Through a stethoscope which extended through the oven wall, he listened to my pulse. Apparently he heard nothing interesting, for he granted my request to turn the oven up to 160°.

At the high point I felt even hotter than I had once during an attack of heat prostration. An egg, which I had thoughtfully broken on a metal plate to see whether the egg or I would stand the heat better, began to congeal.

The cold-tolerance test looked much less impressive. It involved nothing but a pan of water in which ice cubes were floating to keep the water at a temperature of exactly 32°. I was supposed to soak my feet in it for a mere seven minutes. To my amazement, as I prepared to dunk my feet, I saw that everybody in the area—flight surgeons, physiologists, test pilots and noncoms—gathered around me in a curious little semicircle, all wearing expectant grins. "Please don't sock me too hard," said a doctor sitting beside me with a sly but enigmatic smile. A bit uncertain at all this extraordinary interest, I put my feet in the ice water and asked, "Is this all?"

I soon found that it was. For the first thirty seconds the water felt cool but not unpleasant. Then my ankles began to ache. After two minutes my legs ached up to the knees with the same intensity caused by a minor bone fracture. There were still five minutes to go and a flight surgeon chuckled, "He'll never make it." After three minutes the ache subsided. My legs were numb. But then an exquisite little pain began to assert itself in the toes, as if a gentle torturer were carefully cutting off the tips with a sharp sliver of glass.

At last I understood why this test may be used as a measure of both physical and psychological endurance to help the Air Force choose a group known as the Tigers, or potential "candidates for unusual missions"—*i.e.*, space pilots. Those who fail are referred to as "bunnies." When I pulled out my frosted feet after the appointed seven minutes, they were deep scarlet below the water line. But I had lasted it out, and I was flattered when I heard one of the scientists remark—even though I knew he was joking—"Well, he's a Tiger."

My delusion of triumph soon vanished on the treadmill. Extraordinary muscular prowess will not be necessary for space pilots, but good physical condition is an obvious requisite for any explorer who will be exposed to abnormal rigors. One of the simplest indications of over-all condition is the number of minutes a man can run uphill on an old-fashioned treadmill that is raised progressively to steeper angles. I stayed on it for only 4½ minutes. At that point my heart was pounding away at 160 beats per minute, double the normal rate, and I ran out of energy completely. A trained athlete or fit pilot, by contrast, would have shown almost no reaction to this brief sprint.

"Many of these tests will not tell us who would make the best pilot or spaceman," a flight surgeon said to me, "but they will enable us to screen out a lot of unsuitable people—for instance otherwise perfect candidates who cannot tolerate cold. And we're looking for human standards by which we can choose groups of top candidates for difficult missions, and endurance standards that will determine how elaborate the cockpit equipment will have to be to protect the men."

"The ideal way to go into space," says Colonel John Paul Stapp, director of Wright Field's Aero Medical Laboratory, "is the way the Navy went under the North Pole. They didn't go in a two-man submarine and die. They went in the *Nautilus*. Their answer was fine engineering, with all the hazards overcome in advance."

If this is the standard, I asked Stapp, when will it be a reasonable risk to send a man out by rocket through crushing G's, the wild world of weightlessness and the shattering terrors of noise, vibration, cold, heat and vacuum? "This is just my own scientific opinion," he said, "but after three successive, successful experiments with chimpanzees, we'll be ready for a man."

II
FOIBLES AND JESTS

Whitney Darrow Jr.

ONCE ABOARD
THE "RELUCTANT"

by Thomas Heggen

OCTOBER 7, 1946

> *One of the few good fiction writers produced by World War II, the late Thomas Heggen is remembered for his best-selling novel* Mister Roberts. *This selection, although complete in itself, is a chapter from that novel. In it Heggen tells what happened to a new ensign when he tried to spring Navy regulations on his fellow officers and the rugged crew of the cargo ship* Reluctant.

Nothing in Ensign Keith's background and early training had adequately conditioned him for duty aboard the *Reluctant*. He was not a prude, but he had deeply acquired a certain correctness of outlook which resembled prudishness and which, for a time, warred vigorously with his new milieu. From early Bostonian childhood he had been taught that certain truths were self-evident: that the Democratic party was incorrigibly evil; that a long engagement was essential to a happy marriage; that solitary drinking makes a drunkard, and that breeding and character were what counted in life. When he had finished two years at Bowdoin, the Navy came along, made him an officer and issued him a few more Truths: that an officer was, *ipso facto*, a gentleman; that a commission in the Navy was a sacred trust; that an officer must not fraternize with enlisted men, and the one to the effect that an officer enjoys special privileges by virtue of his added responsibilities. Young Keith came aboard equipped with a full set of these excellent, if sometimes impractical, Truths, and it took Boatswain's Mate Dowdy and the boys the better part of a month to get, as Dowdy put it, "Mr. Keith squared away."

His arrival on board the *Reluctant,* or rather the manner of it, was a genuine event. Keith caught the ship while it lay at anchor in the bay of "Tedium" Island. The day was typically hot and sticky, and the lightest shirt was uncomfortable. The captain was ashore, and the gangway watch had relaxed accordingly. Ed Pauley, the officer-of-the-deck, was reading an Ellery Queen story, and Farnsworth, the messenger, was poring over a comic book when Farnsworth saw this most remarkable thing. A boat from the beach was making the gangway and an officer, lugging heavy baggage, was climbing aboard. He was wearing blues! "Holy Jesus!" croaked Farnsworth, "Mr. Pauley!"

Pauley got to his feet just in time to see a young ensign stand rigidly at the head of the gangway, salute the colors, step aboard, salute him and announce with great positiveness, "Request permission to come aboard, sir. Ensign Keith reporting for duty." The face of Ensign Keith was a fiery red and steaming with perspiration; at his armpits and at his back, wide, black stains were spreading, his trousers hung like wet washrags and his white shirt was sweated to a solid gray. In a kind of trance Pauley, who was wearing faded khakis, dirty trousers and an almost buttonless shirt, returned the salute and mumbled, "Sure, sure . . . my name's Pauley." It took Pauley a minute or two to collect himself, and then he led the new arrival in to see the executive officer.

Mr. LeSueur was an outspoken man. He was sitting at his desk when Pauley, trailed by Keith, appeared. For a moment he just stared, popeyed; then, before Pauley could say a word, before Keith could even state his business, he shouted, "What in the hell are you doing in those things?"

Ensign Keith was visibly upset. At midshipmen's school they had taught that reporting aboard ship was a very formal business. "I'm Ensign Keith," he said as well as he could. "Reporting for duty, sir."

Mr. LeSueur pounded the desk. "That doesn't answer my question! What in the hell are you doing in blues?"

Ensign Keith, who was standing at rigid attention, turned even redder. "When reporting for duty, blue baker is the uniform prescribed by Navy Regs, sir," he said stiffly.

Mr. LeSueur passed a hand over his face. "Blue baker," he muttered. "Navy Regs." Finally he got up and shook hands with Keith. "And for Christ's sake get out of those things in a hurry!" he told him. He turned to Pauley, "Take him to your room, Ed. You'll live with Mr. Pauley." Without another word he sat down and returned to his work.

If the way to enter cold water is to dive headfirst, then perhaps Ensign Keith's ungentle immersion into his new life was for the best. In the next few days he was buffeted with surprises like a non-stop punching bag. Almost everything he saw and heard, contradicted, refuted, ignored, or scorned one of the impregnable Truths he had learned so well. His new roommate, Ed Pauley, didn't get up at seven o'clock, when an officer should; he slept until noon. He didn't shave daily as an officer should; he was growing a shaggy red beard. The officers lounged all day in the sacrosanct wardroom. They kept their hats on in the wardroom, a scandalous violation of naval etiquette. Some of them even sat with their feet on the tables. None of them seemed to do any work. None used the title "sir" in addressing each other, but other more vigorous and colloquial titles were freely used. Coarse, extramarital exploits were discussed openly at the dinnertable. Some of the officers drank: Keith was sure he had smelled liquor on Ed Pauley's breath. He had heard any number of the officers addressing the enlisted men by their first names or by nicknames. With his own ears he had heard various officers speak seditiously of the ship and the Navy and, worst of all, of the captain. He had even heard one officer threaten to commit a piece of shocking mischief against the captain. And they didn't refer to him as the captain at all; they called him "stupid." Or worse than that.

Young Keith was shocked. He could scarcely have been more shaken had his own mother gone out and robbed the Kenmore Trust and Savings. In all of his twenty and a half years nothing like this had ever happened. When the roots of a man's faith are torn out and examined, he can do one of two things: he can bind them to himself all the more fiercely, or he can let them go. For a few days Ensign Keith was very quiet and it wasn't clear which course he would take. Then, consciously or not, he seemed to make a decision.

The first time Keith stood a watch, it became clear which way he would go. It was Dowdy, the boatswain's mate, who brought this to light. Dowdy was over on the beach one day, ostensibly on ship's business. Actually he had another purpose. He had heard of a Seabee who would part with beer for a price. This Seabee wanted, and got, $2 a bottle, and Dowdy bought six bottles which he concealed in a light cardboard box. It had been four months since he had had beer and he thought with almost unbearable affection of his cargo.

As he stepped aboard, Dowdy threw the usual perfunctory salute to the colors and started aft. He noticed, more or less in passing, the officer of the deck—it was that new kid, what was his name?—but he didn't bother saluting. Dowdy was pretty much of a personage on the ship, and all the officers either respected him or left him alone. He had gotten perhaps ten feet when he heard someone call, "Where do you think you're going?" and he turned around and saw this boot ensign standing there, giving him the dirtiest kind of look. Dowdy was all set to put the kid in his place, but before he could say a word Ensign Keith shot a question that absolutely floored him, "How long have you been in the Navy?"

Well, Dowdy had eleven years in, and to hear this question from a brand-new ensign was too much. Dowdy just stood there and his mouth worked like a fish and no sound came out.

"When you come aboard you salute the officer of the deck," Ensign Keith explained acidly. "Now go back and come aboard properly!"

It was a moment before Dowdy could even move. Then in a kind of idiotic sleepwalk he went back and came aboard properly; he saluted Ensign Keith.

"That's better," said Ensign Keith bitingly. "Watch it after this." He looked Dowdy up and down coldly. He noticed the box under

Dowdy's arm. "What's that?" he asked suspiciously.

Dowdy stared stupidly at the box, as though seeing it for the first time.

"Let me see," said Ensign Keith. And Dowdy's will was so paralyzed that he handed him the priceless box, a thing he never would have done in his right mind.

Ensign Keith tore open the box. Then his eyes went wide and his voice got shrill. "Beer!" he shouted. "Beer! Bringing liquor on board a Navy ship! Don't you know that's a general court-martial offense? How long have you been in the Navy anyhow?" And before Dowdy's helpless, pleading, agonized eyes he flung the box over the side. The gift of movement returned to Dowdy then, and he rushed to the rail just in time to witness a scene of incredible waste: six bottles of irreplaceable beer sinking in eight fathoms of water. The sight brought tears to his eyes. For a brief, burning moment of insanity he thought of strangling Ensign Keith, but his will for even that pleasurable task was gone before he could act. A broken man, Dowdy stumbled off to the compartment. A boot ensign! Dowdy felt like crying.

Young Keith's reputation was made right there. From the obscure "new ensign" he was transformed overnight into the best-known officer on the ship. News of the gangway incident spread like a kerosene fire: let alone, it would certainly have attained a fabulous, legendary character. But Ensign Keith didn't let it stand alone; he added to it. He added to it the very next morning when he put the messenger on report for sneaking below to smoke without his permission. He added to it that same afternoon when he put two men on report for appearing on deck without their shirts. Every day and every way he added to it. He was hell on wheels. He banished all reading matter from the gangway desk. He demanded that his messengers stand their watches in immaculate dungarees. He seemed to be trying, singlehanded, to restore the ship to the Navy, from whence it had strayed.

One morning in port on the four-to-eight watch he decided that the crew wasn't turning out for reveille. He was very right. Chief Johnson made reveille at 6:30 and at a quarter of seven Ensign Keith went down in the compartment and found it loaded with sleeping bodies. He summoned his most resolute voice and addressed the bodies, "All right! Get up here! Get out of those sacks. Every man who's not out of here in five minutes goes on report!" Not a sound. Not a movement. Here and there an eyelid cracked ever so slightly to peer at the intruder; that was all. Suddenly from the far, after corner of the compartment a clear, unstuttering voice sounded: "Get out of here, you son-of-a-bitch. I'm warning you!" Dowdy lived in that corner, but the voice could have been anyone's. Ensign Keith jumped. "Who was that?" he demanded weakly. Silence. Heavy breathing. Not a movement. Ensign Keith repeated his previous threat: "I'll be back here in five minutes. Everyone who's not out goes on report." It didn't sound at all convincing. He didn't come back either.

A wise man would have profited from that experience, and perhaps it left a mark on young Ensign Keith; but nothing that was immediately apparent. He went on much as before, only he didn't try to make a personal reveille again. The report list stayed as long as ever. He gave the crew a thoroughly bad time. If he were embarked upon a deliberate program of self-destruction, he could not have chosen a more likely means to achieve this end.

The compartment at night buzzed with talk of the new ensign, and in the dark corners little sinister groups would gather and plot and threaten and scheme. A quite wise man, Dowdy listened to this talk and gauged it, and when he became convinced of its serious intent, he went to his friend, Lieutenant Roberts: "Mr. Roberts," he said, "if he doesn't knock it off, that new ensign is going to wake up some day with a marlinespike through his skull. Can you pound some sense in his head?" Roberts promised to talk with Ensign Keith.

The talk wasn't very successful. Roberts found Keith alone in his room and in a very nice, tactful way tried to explain a few things. Then he asked Keith very politely if he didn't think he could ease up just a little.

Ensign Keith listened with the respect due his senior officer, then he answered formally: "I appreciate your interest, sir, but I feel that I'm just doing my duty. The regulations which I'm trying to enforce were made by the fathers of our Navy and they've lasted a long time." That was the failure of mediation, and Ensign Keith continued on his implacable way. It seemed then that there was no solution short of the marlinespike. His life expectancy dropped lower and lower, and just when it seemed nil, a solution came to pass of such aptness, happiness and general satisfaction that Ensign Keith was completely forgiven his transgressions and restored in full standing to the community of good will, from which he never strayed again. It happened one night at sea.

Under way, young Keith stood junior O.O.D. watches under Ed Pauley. The J.O.O.D. was the battery officer and he was also, nominally, the security officer. At least once a watch he was supposed to make the rounds of the ship and determine that everything was safe, peaceful, and reasonably quiet. On this night Keith was standing the eight-to-twelve watch with Pauley. It was perhaps ten o'clock when he left the bridge to make the rounds. He went through the compartment, through the galley and the mess hall, around past the refrigeration spaces and the storerooms and the offices, down into the 'tween-decks spaces along the starboard side and back again on the port side, past more storerooms and the barber shop and the armory. At the armory he stopped. A crack of light was showing under the door, and inside he could hear voices and a rattling sound. There was a funny smell, too. Ensign Keith pushed the door open.

A startled group looked up at him from the deck. Dowdy was there, and Olson, and Dolan, and Vanessi, the storekeeper, and Stefanowski, the machinist's mate, and over in the corner by the rifle racks, holding a glass in one hand and with the other trying to force a record onto the turntable of the portable phonograph was Schaffer, another gunner's mate. The air in the armory was thick with smoke and this other smell. On the deck beside Olson was a large pewter crock from the galley, and the men had glasses beside them. The group on the deck was huddled kneeling before the after bulkhead, and Dowdy had just thrown a pair of dice against the bulkhead. Each man had a pile of bills beside him, and in the middle of the cleared space there were other piles.

Ensign Keith shut the door behind him. He looked quickly and accusingly around the room. "You men are gambling," he announced.

No one spoke. No one affirmed or denied the charge. No one moved. Six pairs of sullen, menacing eyes watched Ensign Keith.

"Don't you know," he demanded, "that gambling is a general court-martial offense?"

A look of craftiness came to Dowdy's face. "Oh, we ain't gambling, sir," he said kindly, as though Keith had made a perfectly natural mistake. "We're just shooting a little crap for fun. It's not for money."

"Then what's the money doing out there?" Keith asked triumphantly.

Dowdy smiled and dismissed it with his hand. "Oh, that's just to keep score with. We figure out that way who has the most points and then at the end of the game we give it all back." He smiled disarmingly at the officer. "It's the best way I've found yet to keep score." He added righteously, "No, sir, we can't none of us afford to gamble. We've found that gambling never pays."

Ensign Keith stood there, doubt and anger and uncertainty chasing each other across his face. He lifted his cap and replaced it on his head. He pinched his nose. He looked suspiciously around the room and saw the glasses and the pewter crock, and he smelled the funny smell.

"What's that?" he demanded. "In that jar there? What are you drinking?"

Dowdy looked over at the crock. "That?" he said soothingly. "Oh, that's some fruit juice. That's some pineapple juice we got from the galley. That's all that is."

Ensign Keith wasn't satisfied. "Let me see," he said to Olson.

Olson shot a quick, questioning glance at Dowdy.

Dowdy smiled benevolently. "Sure," he said. "Give Mr. Keith a drink of fruit juice. Here's a glass."

At any given time there were apt to be brewing on the ship fifteen different batches of jungle juice, but it was agreed that Olson made the most distinctive brand. His jungle juice had *character*, everyone said. For one thing, through influential connections among the mess cooks, he had access to more ingredients than his competitors. Olson would take an empty ten-gallon water breaker, fill it half up with raisin mash, add whatever fruit juices—orange, pineapple, grapefruit, it didn't matter—the mess cooks had been able to provide, add sugar, stir well, and stow the breaker in an unlikely corner of number two hold. After a week to ten days of turmoil, the mixture was ready for tapping. It was as unpredictable as a live volcano. In taste it was as deceptively tranquil as sloe gin, and one or two glasses would creep up on the uninitiated like a well-wielded hand-billy.

It was ten o'clock when Ensign Keith left the bridge. At eleven, Ed Pauley had occasion to call the flying bridge, and Keith's absence was reported to him. Pauley was irritated, but more than irritated he was surprised that Keith was doping off: it wasn't at all consistent. He sent the messenger around to find Keith, and when, after a thorough fifteen-minute search, the messenger reported negatively, he became slightly worried. He considered the vigorous feeling against Keith. He remembered the threats he had heard. He wondered if it wasn't just possible that something had happened.

Pauley took Bergstrom, his quartermaster, and set out. Bergstrom carried a flashlight. Pauley fully expected to find Keith down in the bilges with a marlinespike in his back—if he found him at all. They went through the crew's compartment and looked in every bunk. They opened storerooms and even opened the refrigerator spaces. They looked in the Chief's quarters. They looked in the boatswain's locker. They even looked in the spud locker. Glumly, Pauley led the way through the 'tween-decks spaces on his way to the holds. This was a hell of a thing. If he didn't find him in the holds, he'd have to call the Old Man. There'd be hell to pay for this. As he passed the armory, Pauley heard music and voices. He stopped, for the loudest of the voices was clearly Keith's.

Pauley had prepared himself for almost anything, but not for what he found in the armory. Dowdy and Keith and Olson were standing against the workbench. Dowdy and Olson had their arms flung about Keith, simultaneously supporting him and leaning on him. Loudly and with much stress on certain words the three were singing a thoroughly obscene tune called "Violate me in the Violet time in the Vil-est way that you know." Within the compass of his two supporters, Keith was flopping his arms about to no discernible rhythm. His eyes were glassy and a huge white grin was pasted on his face. The phonograph beside them was unobtrusively playing a Strauss waltz. Over by the bulkhead Vanessi and Stefanowski teetered on their haunches and peered nearsightedly at the dice on the deck. They argued noisily about what the dice read. In the corner, lying on his back, cradled on two life jackets, Schaffer slept soundly. His mouth was open and a marshmallow was propped in it. There were at least two broken glasses on the deck and the air was fragrant with the smell of jungle juice. Everyone, less Schaffer, greeted Pauley hilariously.

When he had recovered a little, Pauley pointed at Keith: "Who's that?" he asked.

Dowdy peered into Keith's face to find out. He shook him by the shoulder and Keith's head bobbed back and forth. "That?" said Dowdy. "That's old Jim Keith. You know old Jim Keith."

Keith nodded his head solemnly and grinned some more. "This is old Jim Keith," he echoed. "You know old Jim Keith."

Dowdy winked widely at Pauley. He continued to shake Keith's shoulder. "Yessir," he announced, "old Jim's a good son-of-a-bitch."

Keith nodded heavy approval. "Yessir," he mumbled, "old Jim's a good son-of-a-bitch." Then without a sound, a surprised look on his face, as though the idea had just occurred to him, he slipped easily to the deck, sound asleep.

It turned out he was right about being a good son-of-a-bitch. His old rectitude collapsed like a pricked balloon. He never gave the boys trouble again. He took to sleeping until noon and sitting around the wardroom with his feet in bedroom slippers propped on a table. Until the captain put a stop to it, he wore for a while a tan polo shirt that was screamingly nonregulation. He and his messenger would spend the gangway watches playing checkers on a miniature board, and at sea Keith would sit on a ready box and listen to the stories that fanned from his gun crews. He turned out to be a nice, good-natured kid. As Dowdy said, it just took a little while to get him squared away.

MR. BLANDINGS
BUILDS
HIS DREAM HOUSE

by Eric Hodgins

APRIL 29, 1946

> *This is the woeful tale of a man who started out to build a house and ended up, buffeted and bilked, spending three times what he had planned. Eric Hodgins' novel* Mr. Blandings Builds His Dream House, *from which this* LIFE *article was adapted, was a best seller in 1946 and one of the most popular movies of 1948. It was followed by a sequel,* Blandings Way, *in 1950. Eric Hodgins was a vice president of Time Inc., who resigned as an officer of the company because he preferred to be a writer and an editor. He likes writing so much that he now devotes all his time to it.*

Said Samuel Johnson, "To build is to be robbed."

The sweet old farmhouse burrowed into the upward slope of the land so that you could enter either its bottom or middle floor at ground level. In front of it, rising and spreading along the whole length of the house, was the vastest lilac tree that Mr. and Mrs. Blandings had ever seen. When the house was new, the lilac must have been a shrub planted in the dooryard—and house and shrub had gone on together, side by side, since then. That was 170 years ago this April.

Using a penknife as a key, the real-estate man unlocked a lower door. As it swung back, the top hinge gave way and splashed in a red

43

powder on the floor. The door lurched against Mr. Blandings and gave him a sharp crack on the forehead, but the damage was repaired in an instant and Mr. Blandings, a handkerchief at his temple and his wife by his side, stood looking out through one of the amethyst window lights at a view that made them both cry out.

"On a clear day you can see the Catskills," said the real-estate man.

Mr. and Mrs. Blandings were not such fools as to exclaim at this revelation. But by the way the two of them said, "Uh-hum?" with a rising inflection in perfect unison, the real-estate man knew that his sale was made. Not today, of course; the offer might not come for a fortnight. But it would come. He computed 5 per cent of $10,275 rapidly in his head and turned to the chimney footing.

"You'd have to do a little pointing up here," he said, indicating a compact but disorderly pile of stone, in which a blackened hollow suggested a fireplace that had been in good working order at the time of the Treaty of Ghent. Mrs. Blandings, looking at the rubble, saw instead the kitchen of the Wayside Inn: a tempered scale of copper pans and skillets near the oven wall, a bootjack in the corner, a shoat glistening on the spit.

What Mr. Blandings saw broke through into speech: "With a flagstone floor in here it would be a nice place for a beer party on a Saturday night. You'd put the keg right in that corner."

"You could at that," said the real-estate man, as if he had just heard a brilliant revision of the atomic theory. He quickly did 5 per cent of $11,550 in his head; aloud he said, "Let's go upstairs and then let's take a look at your orchard. There's a very interesting story connected with . . ."

The effect of the plural possessive pronoun was as a fiery liquor in Mr. and Mrs. Blandings' veins.

Thus it came about that Mr. and Mrs. Blandings bought—for $11,550—the old Halleck place.

"Let's say your land'll cost you $10,000 in round numbers," the real-estate man had said the day before it had actually cost $11,550. "And let's say it'll cost you $10,000 to restore that farmhouse. So you've made a $20,000 investment that'll stand you all the rest of your life." This lyric passage had served the Blandingses in lieu of thought for several months, until one evening Mrs. Blandings had looked up from her mending.

"Do you suppose it's worth our while to remodel that old house?" she had asked in a faraway voice.

If she had flatly announced the illegitimacy of the two Blandings children she could scarcely have had a more thunderous effect on her husband.

Eventually Mr. Blandings came to believe that he himself had had this prudent idea. He asked his lawyer friend Bill Cole to dig him up an engineer—a good practical fellow who wouldn't be carried away by *anything*. As a result Mr. Giobatta Appolonio, engineer, did indeed visit the old Halleck place some days later. In his black shoes, dark business suit and derby he made an odd picture among the rolling hills, particularly compared with Mr. Blandings in his slightly aggressive rural tweeds.

Mrs. Blandings had expected Mr. Appolonio to bring a bag of instruments along like a physician. But Mr. Appolonio's only instrument was a foot rule. He merely stood looking at the house for five minutes from about a hundred feet away. He then went up to it and kicked it on one corner. Mr. and Mrs. Blandings winced in unison when something unidentified fell off. Mr. Appolonio returned to his clients and spoke to them in a soft voice.

"You should tear it down," he said.

"I wish you wouldn't drink so when you're upset," said Mrs. Blandings. She and her husband were back in their city apartment. The train trip home with Mr. Appolonio had been very trying. Once home, Mr. Blandings had written out a check for his $50 fee and mailed it to him instantly with a curt, correct note. But now Mr. Blandings was alone with God and Mrs. Blandings, and there was no concealing from either one that Mr. Blandings had paid a considerable sum, above land cost alone, for a structure that he had now been advised (for $50 more) to destroy. He could see no recourse from either of them, or from the real-estate man, or from Ephemus W. Halleck.

"Don't act surprised when the children grow up to be guttersnipes, hearing words like that in their own living room," said Mrs. Blandings.

"We can fix up that old house," said Mr. Simms, the new architect. "Of course we can. But it will cost you as much as building a new house. My advice is to start afresh."

Starting afresh sounded to Mr. and Mrs. Blandings like what they wanted most in all the world to do.

The Blandingses had begun their home-building career with the assumption that they had $20,000 to spend. When the real-estate man had pointed out to them that $10,000 for land and the old house, plus $10,000 for "restoration" came to this precise figure, the logic and arithmetic had seemed very simple indeed. It was somewhat more clouded now, but not hopelessly so—not hopelessly so by a long shot, Mr. Blandings kept saying to himself. Manifestly, with some $14,000 invested so far, you couldn't skimp on the building by putting up a mere $6,000 bungalow. No—the house the Blandingses would have to build was that $10,000 house they had in mind from the beginning. Prices were somewhat higher now, of course, so an adjusted figure would probably be something nearer $12,500. That was the figure to shoot at anyway; it might come out a little on the high side, but still. . . . And suppose it even turned out to be $15,000, when you included everything, as of course it wouldn't. . . .

What the Blandingses wanted was simple enough: a two-story house in quiet, modern, good taste; frame and whitewashed brick veneer, to blend with the older architectural examples that dotted the hills about them. They wanted a good-sized living room, a dining room and kitchen on the first floor; four bedrooms and accompanying baths on the second; a roomy cellar, a good attic, plenty of closets and a couple of nice porches. And that was all.

A week or so later Mr. Simms said, "It's beginning to look more like a $22,000 house than anything else," and for the first time the word "mansion" was used in conversation—facetiously, of course.

It was apparent at last that the plans would soon be finished. Mr. Blandings, having missed several sessions between his wife and Mr. Simms, had fallen seriously behind the procession and had the uneasy feeling that his house was now beyond his control. He would discover his wife and his architect discussing in familiar terms the breezeway, of which he had never heard. Matters of cabinets, shelving, random-width floor boards, gutters, dry wells, olive-knuckle butts, flues, muntins, mullions, tiles, shakes, ranges, pitches and reveals came at him in unexpected ways and from unanticipated angles.

"I sometimes wonder if you people know what you're heading into," Mr. Simms said one night as he packed up to go home, but he and the Blandingses were in a relaxed mood, with highballs in their hands. It was a bad evening for warnings.

When Mr. Simms, after going into a monastic seclusion for three weeks, emerged again, it was with a set of drawings and specifications that floored the Blandingses: the simple plans and elevations that they had seen grow on the drafting board were superseded now by section drawings, framing plans, wiring diagrams; everything had become so dense with dimensions as to be undecipherable except to experts. It was time to ask for bids.

Mr. Simms arrived on a Saturday morning, looking a little constricted about the mouth, but brisk. "We've got all our bids," he said. "I've summarized them on the top sheet."

Mr. Blandings opened the manila folder and leaped upward as from a bayonet thrust through the chair bottom.

"Good God!" cried Mr. Blandings, and let the folder slip from his grasp. Mrs. Blandings, a stouter soul, bent her gaze and read:

ESTIMATES BLANDINGS JOB—BALD MOUNTAIN

Antonio Doloroso,	Julius Akimbo & Co. $37,500.00
Builders $32,117.00	Zack, Tophet & Payne $28,920.50
Caries & Plumline .. $34,265.00	John Retch & Sons .. $30,852.00

"There are a couple of things to be noted from this," said Mr. Simms, speaking in an even, level, slightly rapid voice. "In the first place, Julius Akimbo obviously doesn't want the job or he wouldn't have put in any round-figure bid that size. As for that bid from Zack, Tophet & Payne I wouldn't touch it with a ten-foot pole. They have a reputation for bidding low and then loading on the extras. That sort of gives us three to choose between. They're all good builders; John Retch is as good as any and with that low figure I don't think you'll go wrong on him. Even as it is, I think we'll have to get to work and cut some of our costs."

This, Mr. Blandings thought in a blurred way, was putting it mildly. The cost-cutting job began then and there. What Mr. Blandings now discovered was that you could no more reverse the growth process of the house than you could shrink an adolescent back into last year's clothes. But there were, of course, some things to be done. Bronze casement windows changed to steel of the lightest cross-section made. Red brass piping became galvanized iron. A whole flagged terrace disappeared. The house would now be insulated only to the eaves—and to hell with having a cool attic in summer. The plumbing fixtures became notably less Pompeian.

Even so, it was slow, dispiriting work. It depressed Mr. Blandings deeply to observe that the elimination of the big flagged terrace on which he had already, in anticipation, had a few delicious drinks, saved him, on Mr. Retch's figures, only $172.50. "If I was *adding* the terrace it wouldn't cost me a cent less than $700," said Mr. Blandings savagely. But he said it to himself, for he no longer had anyone to talk to. He was being cheated, he was being bilked, he was being made a fool of, but he could not find the villain, because everyone was a villain—his wife, Mr. Simms, the local bank, John Retch and his burly, ugly, insolent sons, Mr. Appolonio, Ephemus Halleck and the real-estate man—all, all had made him the butt and victim of a huge conspiracy, clever and cruel.

"There!" he heard Mrs. Blandings saying to Mr. Simms a fortnight later. "We've got Mr. Retch's figures down to $26,991.17. That's more like it."

"I think we've pared it down as far as it will go," said Mr. Simms tactfully. "Retch is an honest builder, and that's about what your house will cost you *if* you don't start getting into extras with him."

With one voice, but from deeply differing emotions, Mr. and Mrs. Blandings assured Mr. Simms that there would be *no* extras.

Mr. Blandings' ego, scarred by forces too vast to identify, was powerfully restored a week later on his visit to the big, impressive savings bank in the industrial city of Seagate. Thither Mr. Blandings and his friend and attorney Bill Cole had gone to seek the mortgage. In no more than an hour's conversation the bank agreed to advance Mr. Blandings $18,000 at 5 per cent, the loan to be amortized over twenty years, anticipation of repayments permitted. (That left plenty for Mr. Blandings to raise by other means, but he knew where he could hock the stock he held in his own company.) Mr. Blandings could have a wad of cash as soon as the bank's title attorneys completed their search on the Halleck property.

This last puzzled Mr. Blandings but did not disturb him. "I thought we'd done that," he said to Bill Cole as they left the bank together. "What did I pay old Judge Quondam $125 for when I bought the property from Halleck originally?"

Bill Cole explained that that had been a title search, all right. "It would have satisfied the local bank if you'd done business with them," he said. "But Seagate-Proletarian has $5,000,000 out in mortgages in a hundred communities besides yours and they have to have their own guarantees and satisfactions, naturally. It won't amount to much. Their title attorneys are Barratry, Lynch & Replevin; they'll soak you $200 but it'll be worth it to have their stamp of approval."

On a crisp autumn morning the steam shovel arrived. Mr. and Mrs. Blandings, Mr. Simms and John Retch himself were present for the ground breaking, and Mrs. Blandings was delighted with the rugged honesty and great good humor of Mr. Retch—"A rough diamond with a heart of gold," she said. Mrs. Blandings was also happy that Mr. Blandings seemed himself again, as indeed he was. Any man who can raise $18,000 in an hour's conversation with one of the biggest savings banks in the east has certainly no call to be so jumpy about finances as Mr. Blandings could now see, looking back on it all, he had permitted himself to become.

"I wonder why the steam shovel isn't working," said Mrs. Blandings. It had been more than an hour now since they had last heard its snortings come drifting down the hill.

"He's been at it five hours," said Mr. Blandings, speaking of the villainous-looking man who had turned out to be the excavating subcontractor. "Let's see what things look like."

Hand in hand, the Blandingses, like happy children, climbed the hill—*their* hill, as Mrs. Blandings put it. On the summit Mr. Attilio Campobasso's steam shovel rested unevenly on its treads. From the south portion of the staked-out ground it had dug a hole that went down six feet. Toward the north end the excavation was ragged and uneven and, while the shovel operator sat in his cab and smoked, three men with hand shovels were at work with the earth. As they worked, Mr. and Mrs. Blandings could see growing the outlines of what appeared to be a mammoth, ossified whale.

"Looka that," said Mr. Campobasso.

"Boulder?" asked Mr. Blandings.

"Boulder!" said Mr. Campobasso, uttering an unmusical laugh. "Atsa no boulder. Atsa *ledge*. We go home now, come back next week, start blasting, keep on blasting plenty, yes *sir*."

EXCERPTS FROM MRS. BLANDINGS' DIARY

Oct. 7: Mr. Campobasso's blasting foreman wanted to know if we had liability insurance: a sharp piece of rock apparently fell on one of old Mr. Lange's chickens half a mile down the road and he was very nasty about it. Blasting probably to go on another two weeks, at least. Nervous headache.

Oct. 10: I don't understand trouble over the title and I don't think Bill Cole does either. The title lawyers say they have nothing to show them that Mr. Halleck was entitled to act as the administrator of *his father's estate,* from which it seems we bought, not from Mr. Halleck himself. Mr. Dolliver at First National Bank was *gleeful* when he bumped into me this morning, said anybody but a dumb city bank would know that of course Ephemus was his father's administrator and had always "been so accepted" since the old man died in 1922.

Oct. 22: Mr. Retch asked for some money today. He got Campobasso to compromise his blasting bill at a flat $1,900! A nasty man, if I ever saw one. Jim put up most of his Amalgamated stock to borrow $15,000 to tide us over until the bank loan comes through. We have to get something called a "waiver of lien" from every one of Mr. Retch's subcontractors before the bank gives us a penny and there must be at least twenty of them!

Nov. 4: It *would* freeze in November so hard the concrete man can't pour any of the forms for the cellar walls!

Nov. 5: A man came around and wanted to sell us a tennis court this afternoon. There were also three tree salesmen on the premises. I didn't know trees *had* salesmen.

Nov. 15: What are we going to do with all the rock that Campobasso man excavated for the cellar? Nobody will take any responsibility for it; even Mr. Simms just shrugs his shoulders and changes the subject. But there it is, a mountain of it, right in front of where the front door is supposed to be. I *insist* it be carted away.

Nov. 27: Glory be! Bill Cole says the bank and its lawyers are ready for "the closing." This means now we get our money at last. All Jim has to do is give the law firm $500 "in escrow" in case anything should go wrong with those wretched "waivers of lien" from those filthy subcontractors. Jim turned purple at the idea of giving Barratry, Lynch another $500, but he wrote out a check just the same. Five toilets arrived today and they're lying all around the field. It looks *unspeakably* vulgar!

All work on the house now came to a stop. The window casements had not come.

The truck had left the factory and would be on the site tomorrow. No, the truck had not left, the windows had been shipped by freight. No, the windows would be shipped by truck *when* they were ready, which would not be for another three weeks. No, the windows must be there and mislaid by the contractor. No, an order for the windows had never been received, but "we would give your valued custom promptest attention should we be so favored."

Mr. Blandings actually felt a sense of triumph when, after a while, roughly half of the windows arrived and the truckmen dumped them in a disorderly pile in the roadway. Several days later, two window installers arrived, very drunk, looked at the windows and roamed away again, never to return. Mr. Blandings ventured to inquire of Mr. Retch why some work could not go forward even in the absence of the remaining windows or any crew to install them. This inquiry struck Mr. Retch as in the most flagrant bad taste. In coarse tones he explained to Mr. Blandings that (a) the mason subcontractor was stalled since he could not complete his brick courses around the missing frames; (b) the heating subcontractor could make no further progress until the house was closed in; (c) the tiler hired for the bathrooms could affix no tile; (d) not even the subfloors could be laid when the house was still open to rain and snow; (e) it was manifest that plastering could never be started now until spring, if at all, and (f) the electrical subcontractor's workmen refused to run any more BX cable around wet joists and columns. He ended by confidently predicting that the whole house would shortly burn down from one of the temporary oil stoves the workmen insisted on using to keep their hands warm enough to hold a hammer, and whose fault would the whole blinking business be then?

Suddenly enough windows arrived to build a biscuit factory.

When Mr. and Mrs. Blandings resumed their visits to Bald Mountain it was in the flowering spring. They saw the house and a cry escaped them. It was a cry of joy. There it stood in its gleaming whiteness, more lovely than the fairest drawings that ever Mr. Simms had drawn. The house seemed to await them as a girl would wait with downcast eyes for her lover's first shy kiss.

The entrance to the citadel was not accomplished with ease; the house appeared, on closer examination, to be floating placidly on a sea of mud where the new grading had been liquefied by the warm rains. But once across this ten-foot moat, the Blandingses removed their ruined shoes and stood with reverence in their stocking feet upon the gleaming oaken floors. . . .

The Blandingses had built a good house—a very fine house indeed. Only Mr. Blandings *really* knows how much money he spent on it. But no one would go wrong if he took something like $51,000 as a basic figure.

A NICE LITTLE
BANK TO ROB

by Evan McLeod Wylie

JUNE 3, 1957

*This fantastic but absolutely true story of a bungling
trio who stole $188,784 in cash shows how amateurs in
recent years have helped to cause a dramatic rise in
the number of bank holdups. Evan McLeod Wylie's
article for* LIFE *was later made into a movie.*

Although bank robbing has traditionally been regarded as the most
exacting of all crimes, to be attempted only by fiendishly clever
operators like Willie Sutton or hardened, desperate thugs like the
gang that pulled the Brinks job, the field has recently become overrun by slaphappy amateurs.

For sheer, outrageous success in the face of fantastic ineptitude,
however, no robbery could possibly equal the one brought off by the
three men who in 1956 held up a drive-in bank in Port Chester, New
York. The story which can now be put together of their exploits is
worth telling because it shows how, like so many other amateurs, they

received the unstinted, though unknowing, co-operation of the police, the bank's employees and local residents.

The Port Chester affair was one of the biggest bank robberies in U.S. history. It took the bandits ten hours to loot the little bank. They were such bungling amateurs that it was a wonder they escaped with one dollar, let alone an astonishing $188,784.51. Their planning was horribly haphazard. Their conduct was totally disorganized. Their names were Artie, Angie and Frankie.

Arthur Paisner, through circumstances mostly beyond his control, played the most prominent role. He is a short, balding, roly-poly individual who exudes good humor. From World War II until shortly before he became a bank robber, he had been a law-abiding topflight mechanic in a big garage in New Rochelle, New York, ten miles down U.S. Route No. 1 from Port Chester. The men who still work there recall him as a jovial, generous-natured fellow who loved to make friends.

Artie's private life was exemplary. He lived at home with his widowed mother but spent most of his time romancing a neighborhood girl who, in this account, shall be called Ida. He indulged a love of animals by bringing home stray cats, giving puppies to his friends and owning a cocker spaniel. Also, as he has since said, "I was interested in a particular end of horses—the betting end."

When a huge trotting track opened in nearby Yonkers, New York, Artie began to spend his evenings "at the trots." He began to bet heavily and lose the same way. Presently he left the big garage to open his own gas station a few miles away in Larchmont. The new enterprise quickly reflected the personality and interests of its proprietor. Puppies tussled in the window. A radio blared track results. The station became a hangout for local bookmakers and followers of the races. Soon Artie had two new friends.

One was Angelo P. John, a tall, thin, darkly handsome individual who had suffered a setback in his effort to become a race horse trainer when he flunked the written examination for trainer in New York State. While waiting to take the test again Angie was making a living dispensing sandwiches and coffee to workers at construction projects from the back of a station wagon. He was a rather moody individual whose manner ranged from petulance to gloomy silence.

The other new friend usually put in an appearance behind the wheel of a long, sleek convertible. His name was Rocco Frank Tateo. His stocky build was draped in sharply tailored suits. He combed his long brown locks with care, wore tinted sunglasses and flashed a bulging bankroll.

Frankie's place of business was a bedraggled yellow taxi in which he transported horseplayers to the race track. While a fee was charged for this service, Frankie's main interest was accepting wagers on the horses from the riders. This practice is against the law. Because of his taste for convertibles, he more often was referred to as "Frankie the Convertible Driver" or simply as Frankie Convertible.

The distractions represented by his new friends soon brought trouble to Artie—and irritated Ida. The gas station failed. Artie put money in Angie's sandwich business and that failed too. The autumn of 1954 found both facing a financial crisis. At this point Artie and Angie became part of the amateur crime wave.

Shortly before 8 A.M. on September 24, two bandits held up a small drive-in branch of the County Trust Company in Mount Vernon, a few miles from New Rochelle. They tied up four bank employes and spent half an hour in the bank before escaping with $97,000.

The bandits were Artie and Angie. They promptly used their proceeds to become owners of a racing stable. With $7,000 in crisp bills they purchased a hapless gelding named Battleover, whose grandfather was Man o' War, and shipped him to Florida for the winter racing season. Angie, having meanwhile passed the examination, became his trainer. Artie circulated amiably about the paddocks, patting the horses with the air of a man whose dream had come true.

In the first race in which he was entered Battleover threw his jockey. Then he went lame for several weeks. The new partners relaxed in palm-shaded motels, sported in Miami nightclubs and dawdled at the dog races. Ida, still laboring away at a typewriter in an office in snowbound Manhattan, received a stream of optimistic postcards from Artie, assuring her the racing business would soon make marriage possible.

Now Frankie Convertible came to call on Artie and Angie. Suspicious of his two friends' sudden departure for the sunny South, he had broken into an empty store in which Artie kept his mechanic's tools and found a pile of coin bags from the Mount Vernon bank. The next day he boarded an air coach for Miami.

Instead of congratulating Angie and Artie on their exploit, Frankie ungraciously demanded to be cut in on the loot. The ensuing discussion, which Artie subsequently recalled as "not pleasant," ended when Frankie was given $7,000 to keep his mouth shut.

Most disgusted with Artie's equine enterprise was his girl Ida. She refused to have anything to do with the track and she was still seething over her memory of the pistol episode. This had come about because she had let Artie use her car one morning during the summer while his was in the repair shop. That evening she was surprised to find herself charged with illegal possession of a revolver. It had been found by a policeman who had been searching the car's trunk for ownership clues after Artie had absent-mindedly left the car parked illegally.

Artie apologetically admitted the gun was his. A Florida racetrack friend had given it to him, he told Ida, and he hastened to clear her name by going to court and paying a $100 fine.

In November, Artie and Angie sent Battleover to an elegant horse farm near New Rochelle for a rest cure. They visited him daily. So did Frankie Convertible, who astonished the horsemen by arriving in his old yellow taxi to renew old acquaintance.

To refinance their bankrupt stable, Artie and Angie had decided to knock over another bank. This time Frankie Convertible was to be an active partner. The visits to the horse farm gave the three an opportunity to meet and talk and also look for a suitable target. "We would drive around," Artie has since said, "and one of us would say, 'Now there's a nice little bank and it looks as if it had a lot of money in it.'"

One February afternoon they stopped in nearby Port Chester for hamburgers. As they got back into their car, there fell into their line of vision an attractive one-story tapestry brick building with white columns and a white picket fence. It was the Irving Avenue branch of the bank which had already provided such bounty—the County

Trust Company. One of the first drive-in banks in the east, it had attracted so many new customers that workmen at that very moment were putting the finishing touches on a new wing. Artie, Angie and Frankie sat staring at it with rapt fascination. "It seemed," Artie recalled later, "like a nice, busy little bank that should be robbed."

The spur-of-the-moment decision was followed by casual preparations that would have appalled an oldtime bank robber. Instead of studying the target scientifically, the three men merely sat in the car in a nearby municipal parking lot in broad daylight and observed the bank's operations. Angie deposited in the Irving Avenue drive-in some of the money he had stolen from the bank's Mount Vernon branch. This gave him reason to drift in and out and gain a clearer picture of the internal workings.

Very shortly, their interest centered on Mary Kostolos, a gentle brunette who had been a teller with County Trust for twenty-eight years. She was, they noted, the first to arrive in the morning and the last to leave at night, using a key to unlock the front door. Anyone with such responsibilities, it was decided, probably would also know how to open the bank vault. She was a widow who lived alone.

One morning they drove to the railroad station in Larchmont, New York, and stole a green Oldsmobile sedan belonging to a commuter. This would be the getaway car. Frankie Convertible, assuming his new responsibilities as an active partner, volunteered to equip it with stolen license plates.

In the green car they now proceeded to trail Mary Kostolos around Port Chester, observing her habit of shopping downtown on Thursday evenings before returning around 10 P.M. to her apartment. "We were happy to find that the woman lived in a nice, quiet, secluded neighborhood," says Artie, "and we all agreed that was the best place to pick her up."

Their preparations continued to be casual. Their horse barn conferences were interrupted by grooms with buckets and pitchforks. Several times Angie was late to the meetings because he had been detained at home to boil bottle nipples and mix formula for a new baby. Artie had developed a painful lump in the region where Battleover had kicked him.

The irksome ailment bedeviled Artie so much that he finally confided to Ida that he was sure he had cancer. In practical feminine fashion she insisted he see her doctor, which he did a few days before the planned bank job. After one glance the physician diagnosed it as a nonmalignant cyst. Arrangements were made for a surgeon to remove it the following Monday.

On Thursday evening the three conspirators rendezvoused at a local Howard Johnson's restaurant. After a round of hamburgers they drove Artie's car and the green Oldsmobile to the parking lot of an A & P supermarket a few blocks from the bank, parked Artie's car, got into the stolen green car and drove to Mary Kostolos' house. For more than one hour they sat there waiting.

At 10:15 P.M. Mrs. Kostolos drove up, turned into the garage, switched out her headlights and reached for her parcels. In a flash two men, one from each side, were with her in the front seat. The two were Artie and Frankie. Admonishing her to be quiet, Artie shot the car backward into the street and drove rapidly up the block. Angie followed in the green car.

Mrs. Kostolos found herself being driven down dark streets in her own automobile, wedged in between two menacing male strangers. In a confusion of terror she shrank away from them, gasping, "Let me go! Oh, let me go!" as Artie urged quietly, "Now sit still, lady. You're going to be all right. All we want is the money down at your bank."

"But I can't get that money," she cried.

"Don't try to fool us," said Artie. "We know you've got a key to that bank and you're going to open the vault for us just like you do every morning."

"I've never opened a vault in my life!" cried Mary. "I swear to you I don't know the combination. It's always opened by someone from the main office at eight o'clock in the morning!"

A strangled gasp gave hint of the impact of this news on Frankie Convertible. Artie, the leader, was less perturbed. With Angie still following in the green car he cruised around Port Chester for a bit and then stopped in a side street. Leaving Frankie to guard the petrified Mrs. Kostolos, he strolled back to inform Angie.

Angie took the news of the 8 A.M. vault opening even harder than

Frankie. Wishing Artie the best of luck, he drove the green car home, moped around the kitchen mixing baby formula and finally went to bed.

For the next two hours, while Port Chester slept, Mary Kostolos was driven up one street and down another. Though her blue Hudson was well known in town, no notice was taken of its wanderings. As time passed, Artie casually plied Mary with questions about the bank and attempted to coax her into conversation. To Frankie Convertible, who was crouching uncommunicatively in the back seat, it became appallingly evident that Artie was out to make another friend. He got jumpier by the minute.

Toward 1 A.M. Artie drove boldly up to the bank but bright lights and juke box music still emanated from the bar and grill across the street. "We'll have to wait for the drunks to go home," he observed cheerfully. Presently Mary declared that she thought she was going to faint.

"We'll find you a nice rest room," Artie replied. He drove until he found a closed gas station, opened the door to the ladies room and ushered Mrs. Kostolos inside.

This was too much for Frankie Convertible. Bank robbery as conducted by Artie had worn him to a frazzle. "*You* can take all kinds of chances," he cried, waving his arms, "but this is ridiculous!" For his part, he had decided, like Angie, that he wanted to go home.

At this point, Artie recalled later, he himself had been reduced to low spirits and was ready to abandon the whole project. But as he and Mrs. Kostolos passed the bank he noticed the bar and grill was finally closed and Irving Avenue dark and deserted. He drew up to the curb about thirty feet from the front gate of the bank.

Artie assisted Mrs. Kostolos from her car, guided her up the front walk of the bank and unlocked its front door with her key.

The time was now about 4 A.M. For nearly all of the next three hours Mrs. Kostolos remained huddled in a chair, still wearing the cloth coat and gloves in which she had gone shopping the evening before, weeping silently into a handkerchief. Occasionally she glimpsed Artie's bulky, swarthy figure in blue-green jacket, slacks, floppy gray hat and horn-rimmed spectacles scrutinizing the street through a crack in the blinds or dropping to his hands and knees to scuttle across the lobby. She did not know how many other accomplices were waiting outside the bank. She did not know whether their plans called for her to be killed or carried away with them as a hostage. What she never suspected, of course, was that Artie did not know either.

Thanks to the defection of his two partners, Artie had no idea how he was going to get out of the bank safely. It was with blinking astonishment, therefore, that peeking out of a window a little after 7 A.M. Artie saw the green getaway car cruise slowly by the bank and then, like a rescue ship passing up a castaway, disappear up the block. Angie and Frankie had decided to return to Port Chester to keep track of his progress though obviously neither felt the need to assist him. It confirmed the conclusion Artie had already reached, that "on this job I was the Patsy."

Port Chester meanwhile, was stirring out of its slumbers. Tires swished on wet asphalt as a steady stream of commuters poured past the bank to the railroad station. Toward 7:30 A.M. Artie came back to Mrs. Kostolos and said, "I want you to walk around the lobby and do what you always do first thing in the morning. And don't try to give anybody any signals or you'll be sorry."

He stood out of sight of the windows as she tottered weakly around lighting lamps. At 7:40 A.M. she admitted a young teller named Ernest Marino who, along with Mary, was quickly escorted to the lavatory by Artie. He had just finished binding them both with white plastic clothesline when Purdy Ungemack, assistant treasurer of the County Trust in Port Chester, pulled into a parking space across the street. According to a rotating system, it was his turn to stop by the drive-in branch and open the vault.

Ordinarily Ungemack's wife drove him to work and waited while he signaled from the window that all was well. But this morning she was ill and so Ungemack was alone.

"As I stepped inside," he remembers, "he came out of the washroom, pointing the gun and saying, 'All right, let's lock up that door.'"

Ungemack glimpsed Marino tied in the washroom, and hearing Mary Kostolos' sobs presumed her to be guarded by one or more other men. He backed away from Artie, who said, "Now get over there and open that vault and don't set off any alarms or I'll blow your brains out."

The time was now 7:47 and at police headquarters the vault alarm had automatically disconnected. Ungemack obediently set its dials to the proper combination and opened the outer door. Artie reached in and scooped about $10,000 of ready cash for the teller drawers into a cardboard box he had brought with him.

"Open the inside door too," he ordered.

"I can't," Ungemack replied tensely. "There's a safety timer on it. It won't release for fifteen minutes."

"We'll wait for it," Artie answered decisively. "Just face the wall, if you don't mind."

Inside the bank it now became deathly quiet save for the cheerful ticking of the vault timer and Mary's muted crying. Outside, horns indicated commuting traffic was reaching its peak. From the other side of a partition just a few feet away came the clatter of workboxes as carpenters arrived to complete the bank's new wing.

The police car detailed to guard the bank during its opening had nosed around the corner. Its usual parking space was blocked by the workmen's cars and the lone policeman inside settled for a spot a little farther down the block, sitting back in his seat and watching the bank's early customers gathering on its front step. As the village eight o'clock whistle blew, they began to rattle the front door and Mary Kostolos murmured, "Oh, my God, something awful is going to happen now!" Two more incredibly long minutes passed before the vault timer stopped ticking.

"Now?" asked Artie.

Ungemack nodded and swung open the inner door. Exposed to view lay nearly $180,000. As the customers continued impatiently to try the front door, Artie crammed as much cash as he could into his cardboard box. Then he crossed the lobby with casual relaxed steps, obtained a trash basket from beneath a table, filled it and covered it with a couple of paper towels from the lavatory. He then said to Ungemack, "Pick up the box. We're going out to the car. Tell those people outside you'll be back in a minute."

Ungemack was certain that someone among the customers, workmen, storekeepers or police would perceive what was happening and he recalls thinking numbly, "Here we go. Here's where the shooting starts."

But when the door opened the customers merely stepped aside grumpily and Ungemack found himself proceeding to the street with the box containing upwards of $100,000. Inside the empty bank Mary and Ernie Marino, who had steeled themselves for shouts and shots, heard only a resounding silence.

Ungemack reached the sidewalk. Across the street a shopkeeper waved him a cordial good morning. The police officer still sat in his car. The robber said, "Up to the blue car," and Ungemack realized that Mary's car was to be the getaway car.

Artie quickly tossed his wastebasket in the back seat. He said to Ungemack, "Put that box in front," and, as soon as he had done so, remarked cordially, "Well, thanks. So long now," ran around the front of the car, leaped into the driver's seat, pulled out into the traffic and shot up the hill.

Ungemack dazedly looked around for the rest of the robbers. Suddenly realizing there were none, he vainly scanned the street for the police car, which was now obscured by parked cars and then rushed back into the bank to telephone police headquarters.

Artie speeded to the A & P lot. His car was still there. As he hurriedly transferred box and wastebasket to his own car, Frankie and Angie materialized beside him, staring goggle-eyed at the haul. "Artie," they cried. "Here we are to help you!"

"I was not," Artie observed later, "interested in anything they had to say."

Snarling at them to keep away from him, he sped out of the lot. Angie and Frankie suddenly perceived that he had left them with (a) Mary Kostolos' blue Hudson, which would certainly be pounced upon by the police at any moment, and (b) the stolen green Oldsmobile. It was a moment for a quick decision and Angie made one. He got into his own car, which he had brought along that morning, and drove off. Frankie had dropped the green car's keys and was too nervous to look for them. He hailed a passing taxi carrying two girls to the railroad station and boarded a train for New York.

Artie reached home unhindered. But by 4 P.M. he realized that it would be necessary to negotiate a price of silence from his faint-hearted partners and by telephone arranged a meeting at Frankie's apartment. After permitting himself the luxury of denouncing them both, he asked whether they had the nerve to expect him to give them any of the money. Frankie hesitantly replied that one third to each would be satisfactory.

Bellowing that he would burn the money or go to jail before he would agree to such a holdup, Artie picked up his box and basket of $188,784.51 and prepared to walk out. But Angie, stepping in as arbiter, declared that rather than see an unfortunate argument develop, he and Frankie would accept a lesser amount.

Artie thereupon sulkily handed over $35,000 to Frankie and $30,000 to Angie and went back home to nurse his cyst. On Sunday night he entered a hospital in preparation for his operation the next day.

Newspapers said the bandits were professionals who had made a clean getaway in a "perfectly executed, movielike robbery."

An FBI field office was set up in the Port Chester Municipal Building and a large-scale manhunt was begun. A general teletype alarm alerted seventy thousand police in thirteen states and FBI field offices as far away as Alaska and Hawaii.

Port Chester itself was saturated with teams of agents and detectives, and by suppertime Friday their search had yielded results. One man's story seemed particularly interesting. A few minutes after eight that morning he had noticed two strangers arguing in a corner of the A & P lot. Though he knew nothing of the robbery this alert citizen had taken the trouble to memorize the first four digits of the license plate of the car in which one of the strangers drove away. He recalled them as "WS-45."

The FBI men also learned that their check on a green Oldsmobile apparently abandoned in the A & P parking lot had established that it was a stolen car. A key case found nearby seemed to indicate that the car had been abandoned in haste. Two girls reported that a stranger had popped into their taxi outside the A & P lot that morning and ridden with them to the railroad station.

There seemed good reason to learn more about all the ninety-nine automobile owners whose plates began with WS-45, and at 10 P.M. Saturday one team of agents, checking out the eightieth "WS-45" owner, one Arthur Paisner, ran across the fact that he had been fined $100 the previous August for illegal ownership of a revolver found in the car of a Miss Ida B. of the Bronx. Agents had traced the key case found near the stolen green Oldsmobile to a Mamaroneck, New York, dealer. By the purest coincidence this man had sold a car to one Arthur Paisner the year before. He had heard it had been driven to Florida. Soon agents in Miami were reporting that an Arthur Paisner had raced horses in Miami the previous winter and had had as a partner one Angelo P. John of 121 North Broadway, White Plains, New York. This was a tasty morsel of news since still other agents had found that the little license plate date tag of the stolen green Olds had been removed from a car parked just two doors from Angie's address.

On Monday an FBI artist added the spectacles and gray hat worn by the bank bandit to the rogues gallery photo for which Artie had posed at the time of the pistol charge. It was shown to Mrs. Kostolos, Purdy Ungemack and the man who had noted "WS-45" leaving the A & P lot. Their unanimous reaction was "Why, that's him!"

Still the FBI made no arrests, lest the $188,784.51 be lost or destroyed. Also it was discovered that Artie was not at home.

At this point in the manhunt Ida was being treated as a major suspect because of the gun found in her car the previous summer. Perhaps, it was speculated, she would turn out to be the gun-toting brains of the whole robbery. By Monday afternoon, only four days after the robbery, the manhunt was reaching a climax that would have made a movie director ecstatic.

As Ida departed from her New York job she became undoubtedly the most closely observed office worker in Manhattan. Agents in subways, on street corners and in radio cars spotted strategically about the city delivered minute-to-minute reports on her progress toward the Bronx.

Simultaneously, in White Plains, Sheriff Hoy's men discreetly surrounded Angie's apartment. Detectives crouched in cellars and observed his movements from the windows of neighboring apartments. Still more teams watched at the horse farms. Miami agents hopefully set traps for Artie in Florida and Pinkerton men looked for him at the racetracks and in racing stables across the nation.

The silent, never-slackening watch continued throughout Monday night and all day Tuesday. That evening agents again shadowed Ida home from work and after supper followed as she drove to a hospital in the Bronx. They tagged along as she went up to a second-floor semiprivate room. And there was Artie, now minus his cyst and helplessly recumbent in a hospital bed.

Still seeking the money, the FBI waited until the next day to confront Artie. He seemed astonished. "You're crazy," he protested. "I'm no robber." The agents asked if Artie would mind if they searched his home.

"Go right ahead. Search it," he answered generously.

The FBI men thus knew immediately that the money was not in Artie's apartment, but with characteristic nosiness they went over and rummaged around anyway. One agent looked in the back of a bureau and discovered an old bill from a garage on Tremont Avenue in the Bronx. The government men went to the garage, found Artie's car, opened the trunk and found themselves staring at a sea of bank notes.

Artie confessed. Angie and Frankie were arrested and all but $2,500 of the bank money recovered. Ida was completely cleared; the FBI accepted her declaration that if she had ever known what Artie was up to she would have "crowned him, but good."

Although he had been briefly one of the most spectacularly successful bank robbers in American history, Artie remained an unaffected, friendly fellow. At the conclusion of their trial the judge sentenced Angie and Frankie, who had been sullenly unco-operative throughout the trial, to 25 years and 22½ years respectively. To Artie, who had co-operated amicably with the prosecution, he gave only 18 years and this comment: "I have a feeling, deep inside of me, Paisner, that somehow or other you are going to keep out of trouble from now on."

And so far, at least, he certainly has.

HOW SUCCESS
RUINED
A WOULD-BE BUM

by Edmund G. Love

OCTOBER 7, 1957

A college graduate and former schoolteacher, Edmund G. Love was driven by personal problems to spend more than three years leading the life of a vagrant bum, largely in New York City. During this period he gained an unusual insight into the little-known world of human derelicts. This article, which is adapted from Mr. Love's book Subways Are for Sleeping, deals with one of these derelicts. Although a true story, names and certain details are masked.

George Spoker was a medium-sized man with thin lips and rimless spectacles. He always wore a blue workingman's shirt and a dark red bow tie to set off a somewhat crumpled old herringbone tweed suit. He claimed that he was a bum and he lived like one for seven years. He sat on a bench in New York City's Madison Square and consorted with other bums. He slept in flophouses and doorways and spent as little as possible for food. But in certain respects, Spoker was different from most derelicts. He was always asking questions about the way the others lived and, although he rarely found fault with the answers he received, he always left the impression that he did not necessarily believe them. He acted like a small-town banker who knew exactly how much money all his customers had.

The comparison of George Spoker with a banker is not at all inappropriate. He had been one for a good many years in a city near San Francisco. One day the examiners had found a shortage in his books, and shortly thereafter he had been sent to San Quentin prison for two and a half years.

Spoker never went home after serving his sentence. During his prison term his wife had divorced him and his possessions had been liquidated. None of his friends had visited him. He once told someone why he went to New York: "I was a bum to everybody and I made up my mind if that's what people were going to think of me, I might just as well be one. I wanted to be the dirtiest, raggedest, most foul-mouthed specimen of manhood that ever lived."

As authorities on such matters know, the one hallmark of a bum is aimlessness. From the start a lack of aimlessness differentiated Spoker from his chosen colleagues.

There was another big difference between George Spoker and the mine run of bums. He had money. While he had been in prison his grandmother died, leaving him a monthly income of $78. Just as this comparative affluence set him off from the usual derelict, so did his ingenuous, fastidious approach to the bum's life. When he first arrived in New York, Spoker felt that as a bum he must live in a flop-house. He tried a few on the Bowery but could not stand the bugs, so eventually he established himself farther uptown on Third Avenue, where lodgings cost 50¢ a night instead of 25¢. He tried eating at restaurants like Beefsteak John's, but he could not stand the sight of three or four kinds of food all heaped together in one pile. He transferred to Nedick's and the Automat. Since one of the keystones of his bumdom involved being a drunken stiff, he very carefully budgeted his money so that he would have enough to get good and drunk every Saturday night.

The getting drunk part of it was the thing that made George Spoker aware of his shortcomings as a bum. He fell into the habit of patronizing one bar all the time. It was a place called Beanie's Tavern on 14th Street. It was a stand-up bar, and the mirror was covered by signs that were faintly reminiscent of a supermarket. About the only thing that Beanie's never ran was a one-cent sale. There were weekly specials on brands of whisky that the Internal Revenue Service had never heard of, and the inside of the place was filled with disreputable-looking men lapping up the bargains. Outside on the sidewalk there were invariably ten or twenty homeless men gazing hungrily through the windows. It was easy to see that Beanie's Tavern was populated by real bums. Among them, George soon came to feel like a National Guard recruit in a group of battle-scarred veterans just back from Korea.

The realization that he was a failure in the thing that he had set out to do made Spoker more determined than ever and this purposefulness set him even further from his goal. He made up his mind to try living like these models with whom he had become acquainted. He began to carry a notebook and each time he heard of a new place to sleep he wrote it down. Then he set out to try every one of them. But he soon discovered that sleeping on a park bench is hard work, and after a while he found himself gravitating back to the flophouses. Each time this happened he became more disgusted with himself and eventually reached the astonishing conclusion that he did not have the guts to be a bum. There was only one way he could be sure of not giving up. That was to give away his money. He began by having it changed into quarters which he handed out at random.

It was at this point in his life that George Spoker's true nature reasserted itself. As a banker, orderliness and system had been ingrained into him. And he could not bear to give away something for nothing. In order to satisfy both of these inclinations, he decided that he would trade his quarters for information. Each time he gave one away to a fellow bum, he asked the recipient to tell him where he had slept lately. This information was carefully entered in the little notebook. When one notebook was filled up, Spoker got a bigger one. It was not long before he discovered that his informants would talk just as much for a dime as they would for a quarter, so he reduced his unit of charity.

The information that went into George Spoker's notebooks comprised a curious marginal note on life in New York. Vacant buildings were listed, as were tunnel excavations, used-car lots and encampments of Jehovah's Witnesses. For over a year George Spoker slept in a different place every night. Those he did not sleep in, he investigated. Pertinent information included the habits of guards or police, means of ingress and egress, and the best times of night for use of the premises. One day George met a bearded old character who insisted that he had been sleeping in a Roman sarcophagus in the Metropolitan Museum for ten years, off and on. George checked this claim and found it plausible but never quite got up the nerve to spend the night there.

One afternoon George was accosted by a vagrant who had once added something to the notebook. The man said he had been trying to find Spoker because he had been evicted from his customary sleeping place and needed a new one. He was willing to pay 25¢ for a look at the places George must have available. George did well by the petitioner. He told him about a spot he guaranteed for two weeks of undisturbed slumber.

This encounter revolutionized Spoker's life. The thought that he could sell back for a quarter the same information he had received for a dime had not occurred to him before. In order to take full advantage of the possibilities he began telling the men he interviewed that if they ever wanted to find him, he would be in a certain place every day at one o'clock in the afternoon. At first this place was Union Square, but Spoker later moved to Madison Square, where things were less hectic. Soon he was selling information on sleeping arrangements to seven or eight vagrants a day. By then he had a list of between two thousand and three thousand hideaways.

Spoker also received a lot of information that had nothing whatsoever to do with shelter. Bums often mentioned that they had eaten free at some mission or other, or that a certain charitable institution in town was a phony enterprise, no use at all to a bum. Spoker knew of dishwashing jobs in restaurants, of bowling alleys that needed pin boys, and who was hiring men to carry sandwich boards in any given week. He put it all in his notebook. With all this information in his possession, George soon became something of a one-man sociological movement. There is a spirit of helpfulness among vagrants in New

York, and word soon got around that anybody who wanted a little money in his pocket should go see Spoker. Spoker would not furnish any money himself, but he could furnish tips as to where it could be found. He himself could be found, as everyone now knew, on the bench in Madison Square.

One hot evening as he strolled leisurely around the square, Spoker stopped to talk to a man he found sitting on a chair outside the entrance to one of the office buildings. It turned out that he was a night watchman who had worked in the vicinity in one capacity or another since he was a young man. Spoker began asking about some of the events he had come across in his reading and the old man was only too happy to recall the past. It soon became George's habit to drop by and chat with his new friend every night.

On one particularly rainy evening the old man suggested that his visitor stay in the subbasement all night. He even rounded up some burlap bags to make a comfortable bed. From that time on Spoker lived in Madison Square. His friend soon introduced him to other night watchmen and night engineers, and by winter George was as much a fixture in the neighborhood as the statues in the park. He even bought a sleeping bag and blankets which he moved from one basement to another.

In the fall of 1948 George Spoker stumbled onto something good. While going over his notebooks in the park one September day, he was suddenly assailed by a thundershower. As was his practice during such forced curtailments of activity, Spoker spent his time loitering in the lobby of one of the buildings, chatting idly with the elevator starter, who was an acquaintance. When the shower had passed and he was about to leave the building, Spoker casually guessed he would saunter over to 23rd Street for a cup of coffee. The starter wondered if George would mind bringing back a cup for him.

"I thought about it all the way across the park," Spoker remembers. "The man had given me a quarter to pay for his coffee and had intimated that I could keep the change. This looked like it might be a good business. I bought six cups of coffee instead of one and saw to it that each of the elevator operators got one of them. They all paid me, and they all tipped me."

When he had pocketed his tips, Spoker began asking questions. He found out that no one was bringing coffee into the building. Within a week he had received permission from the building superintendent to bring snacks to all the building employes at regular intervals. He had also asked to be allowed to solicit a similar privilege from all the firms in the building, where more than 600 people were employed. Mathematically speaking, Spoker was no slouch. He estimated that there were 25,000 to 30,000 workers employed within a one-block radius of Madison Square. They would drink 12,000 cups of coffee or partake of that many snacks on an average day. At a nickel a snack, somebody who took advantage of the possibilities could make $600 a day in tips. George Spoker made up his mind to be the somebody.

By this time, bums seeking lodgings or employment were coming to him in great numbers. The Spoker Aid Society, as he used to call it, became the key to George's new business, and the business became the key to the Aid Society. Beginning in the winter of 1948-49, Spoker carefully organized a catering service in the buildings around Madison Square. In each building he would talk to the heads of the various businesses and lay out a route that would keep a man occupied for a full eight-hour day and pay between $10 and $15 in tips. Then he turned the route over to one of the bums who came to him for help, taking $3 of the tips for himself. Eventually Spoker had about twenty men working for him.

It took George almost three years to reach the apex of his career. By that time he had branched out considerably. Initially, he and his men had filled the coffee orders at one or another of the numerous lunch counters in the area. But after the business became bigger, he rented the cheapest basement he could find and set up his own kitchen to take care of the orders. His profits soon reached about $600 a week.

In 1952 ex-convict George Spoker, now a carefully honest citizen, filed a federal income tax return for $31,000. At that time he was still sitting on his park bench in Madison Square and sleeping every night in any one of about twenty subbasements in the neighborhood. He was still wearing his blue shirt, red bow tie and the crumpled old suit he had brought to New York. And he was still keeping most of his records in one of ten or eleven notebooks he kept beside him on his bench.

Spoker was careful to let most of his men go after ten or twelve weeks. So long as he did not pay any one man more than $600 a year, George felt that he did not have to bother with withholding taxes. No one found fault with any of these arrangements. The employes were all bums to begin with and they recognized George as a benefactor who had given them a little time to get on their feet.

It was a woman who caused George Spoker to give up his career. After fencing his way through two newspaper interviews without saying anything important, he was suddenly faced one morning with a good-looking, red-haired woman of about thirty who told him a simple and rather commonplace New York story. Her name was Sarah Haddon and she had come to town to be an actress. She had not found enough work, and that morning when she came back to her room from breakfast, she found that she had been locked out. A friend of hers had told her that he had gone to Spoker in a similar emergency, so here she was. Sarah Haddon was actually a newspaperwoman who intended to write down everything that George Spoker said and did, then put it in the Sunday magazine section.

"I'd been in Madison Square for five years," Spoker once said in discussing Sarah, "and she was the first woman who ever came to me for help. I can usually spot a bum a mile away, but I suddenly realized while she was talking that I'd never even *seen* a woman bum. It was quite a challenge."

What he did was go out and rent an apartment for Miss Haddon. He knew of a small flat on East 27th Street that was vacant, so he paid a month's rent and even stocked it with $20 worth of groceries. Spoker's motivation in renting this apartment was strictly charitable. Miss Haddon was simply the X in an equation that had to be solved at once and George took great pride in solving problems. When Miss Haddon returned to the bench in Madison Square that afternoon, he took her by the arm and led her triumphantly to her new place of residence, showed her inside, demonstrated how the stove worked and left her alone.

Miss Haddon, as might have been expected, already possessed a perfectly good apartment of her own, and the presentation of this new set of living quarters put her in a difficult position. She was slightly aghast at what she had done. For the moment she decided that she had better accept the charity to keep George's feelings from being hurt.

There ensued a period of several weeks in which she spent a good part of every evening at the 27th Street place talking with Spoker, who got into the habit of dropping around every night after dinner to see how she was making out. Each time he came he brought some little thing in the way of flowers or food to make her drab world a pleasanter place in which to live. Miss Haddon stayed around the apartment until he left for one of his subbasements, and then she went home to her roommate with a new supply of groceries. Toward the end of the third month Miss Haddon seems to have decided that she had better live in the apartment that was being furnished for her. She moved in, bag and baggage.

By the time Sarah Haddon decided to accept George Spoker's full hospitality, romance had begun to show through the charity. Despite his own appraisal of himself, Spoker was not entirely without charm and Sarah Haddon was certainly attractive. They fell in love. When George and Sarah were married, the secret of Spoker's true life could be hidden no longer. When she found it out, his wife moved her new husband to a home in Connecticut. She never wrote the story the paper had assigned her to do.

Every day now Spoker took a train to Manhattan. He continued to sit on his park bench in Madison Square, running his catering service and maintaining the fiction that he was a bum. No one will ever know how much money he was worth by that time, but it was a lot. One rumor had it that he had built up an income of around $10,000 or $12,000 a year from investments alone. By now it must have been hard for George to keep from admitting, even to himself, that he was not a bum.

Finally, in January, 1954, he gave up. He sold out his business to a large catering company at a huge profit and retired to the country. It was a combination of Sarah Haddon and weariness that made him leave his park bench.

"There is nothing the matter with being a bum," he told one of his friends, "but when you have to commute fifty miles every day to do it, there's just no percentage in it."

A TREASURY
OF ECCENTRICS

by Nigel Dennis

DECEMBER 2, 1957

*Continental Europeans go mad and are put away;
Americans find an analyst. Englishmen in similar states of
mental confusion are often regarded as merely eccentric.
Novelist Nigel Dennis contends that English eccentricity
is here to stay because it advances the happiness of
humanity. But times are changing. What with inflation
and high taxation, few English eccentrics can now afford
to go it alone. So they incorporate, striving for the
greatest happiness of the greatest number of eccentrics.*

Englishmen are notorious defenders of tradition. But while defending
it, they have always been careful to maintain among themselves a
proper number of those strange souls who deliberately defy it: the
eccentrics. Consequently, each time a leading eccentric dies, normal
Englishmen suddenly feel unbalanced. They would rather lose the
Archbishop of Canterbury, the Lord Chief Justice and the editor of
the *New Statesman*. After all, England can always replace her dignitaries, but only nature can replace her eccentrics.

A case in point was the sudden death in 1957 of Charles K.
Ogden. Well known among scholars as the inventor of a language-

simplifying scheme called Basic English, this mild scholar of the college community of Cambridge was also one of the greatest eccentrics of our time, and his passing affected Englishmen deeply. Even the usual question, "Who will step into his shoes?" stopped observers cold. For one thing, many eccentrics absolutely refuse to wear shoes at all. Ogden wore nothing but suede shoes with square toes. Who, indeed, would step into them?

Visitors to Ogden's college rooms used to be greeted by a hat rack suspended over the staircase well, far out of reach of anyone who wished to hang his hat on it. Nonetheless, two hats always hung there, a bowler and a straw. Often it was a long time before his visitors realized the hats were made to fit the undersized heads of a non-existent breed, midway between men and midgets.

An old friend of Ogden's, Lance Sieveking, once described the first time he pressed past the hatty Scylla and Charybdis and entered the presence of Ogden himself. The great man rose from the floor, where he had been seated with friends eating from saucers of sweets, nuts and bananas, and in a whispering voice offered his visitor a cigarette of herbs. Sieveking noted the high, domed forehead, the deepset twinkling eyes, the suit of a bluish shade seemingly unknown to the color spectrum, the flannel shirt with a collar so capacious that, in the event of wishing to scratch his chest, Ogden could thrust his arm through and down without detriment to his neck. It was a memorable vision.

Ogden was a great collector. He collected masks, books, clocks and music boxes up to six feet in length. When all his clocks and boxes were ticking, chiming and tinkling, Ogden's home was a noisy place to be in, the more so if Ogden himself were singing and dancing too. But he detested any noise that was made by someone else. He was a vigorous supporter of the Anti-Noise League and did his utmost to prevent street cries and traffic sounds from entering his house. When they succeeded in doing so, he would turn up his radio full blast so that no particle of foreign sound intruded upon his private din. Thus isolated from the clamor of the world, he would work happily all night, breaking off at sunrise for dinner.

Such foibles were eccentric without a doubt, but they tell us little of what lay at the heart of the wizard whom hundreds knew affectionately as "Og." To find the real, underlying "Og" we must study his two most important endeavors.

The first is his invention of Basic English. Like most eccentrics Ogden was maddened by the folly he saw in the lives of other people. Most of them, he believed, went through life with no idea of what they were doing and were totally unable to express themselves clearly. Ogden's solution was to boil the English language down to 850 simple words. Ogden argued that if everyone in the world learned to operate his 850 words, everyone would have a clear, common means of communication. This would soon lead to international amity. It has not worked out this way.

The second of Ogden's masterworks was a complete success. It was at his suggestion that the embalmed body of the great nineteenth-century English philosopher, Jeremy Bentham, which sits fully dressed in a common room of London's University College, had its underwear changed for the first time since Bentham was mummified in 1832. Later we can go into the question of *why* Bentham became a mummy at all. At the moment, what interests us is: why should Ogden have been worried about the mummy's underwear? The answer—of crucial importance to the understanding of English eccentricity—is that Ogden and Bentham were bound by ties far stronger than the mere clip-knots and buttons of underclothing. In the field of ideas Ogden was Bentham's heir, and the changing by the one of the most intimate garments of the other was not really an act of eccentricity at all. It was the sort of thing any son might do for a respected father who was not disposed to do it for himself.

Mere burial to Bentham was a silly, wasteful act which brought the least possible happiness to the least possible number. A good corpse, he argued, could be put to sundry uses. For example, embalmed, fully dressed, its visage painted with copal varnish to keep out the wet, it could be stood near the house as an object of veneration. Why, asked Bentham, plant rows of trees along the driveways of stately homes when rows of varnished forebears might line the way, each with white and woolly stockings falling about its ankles, each topped by its grotesque straw? What could be more sensible, more useful—in a word, more basically English?

From Bentham's unorthodox life and death we can see that all English eccentricity is an offshoot of English philosophy. Furthermore, all English philosophy, from Sir Francis Bacon to Ogden, has been governed by two questions: Is this idea a useful one? Will it advance the happiness of humanity? Britain is almost the only country in the world where philosophers think along these lines; and that is why eccentricity there can go about its business feeling that the whole nation is behind it to the last man. It is also why continental Europeans go mad and are shut up, while Englishmen are deemed merely eccentric and go their way unhampered from the cradle to the mummy.

One sure test of eccentricity is whether it sits comfortably on its owner and causes surprise only among others. A true eccentric always presses on, ignoring his own surprising effects but often angry that his effects should seem surprising at all. The late eighteenth-century writer and Free-Thinker, John Fransham, condemned daily bedmaking as "the height of effeminacy" and hoped to see the day when once a week would become the national norm. This interesting utilitarian fooled many people into thinking that he was childish and neurotic, not just eccentric. They could accept as an infallible sign of eccentricity his having once burned his oboe in order to boil his teakettle. But they dismissed as unforgivably silly his playing with a toy named a "bilbo-catch," persevering "until he had caught the ball on the spike exactly 666,666 times." The truth is that Fransham's act was even more useful, and thus more eccentric, than the burning of the oboe. Six hundred and sixty-six is "the perfect number" of numerology. By duplicating it Fransham was getting as close as thought could bring him to the grand ideal of the greatest happiness of the greatest number.

This episode teaches us how difficult, but how important, it is to distinguish between an eccentric's eccentricities and his mere jokes, worries and daily work. Let us therefore study an English eccentric of real stature and note when he was trying his hardest to be useful and when he was merely relaxing. Let us look at the eminent nineteenth-century naturalist, Squire Charles Waterton, the greatest and best-loved eccentric of them all.

Waterton liked to crouch on all fours behind the hangings of his entrance hall, and when his guests came in to hang up their coats he would make a noise like a snarling dog and sink his teeth deep into their ankles. In South America he rode an alligator bareback, keeping it under control by twisting its forelegs. But such acts were mere jests. They served no useful purpose and brought little happiness to any number. Waterton's real eccentricities went far deeper. An ardent Roman Catholic, he spent much of his life trying to exterminate black rats from England, arguing that they were foreigners who had been smuggled into England by Hanoverian Protestants.

Waterton was one of the greatest British taxidermists, and when one of his cargoes of South American birds was held up by British customs he retaliated nobly. Disemboweling and preserving a howler monkey, he dressed it in fashionable clothes, gave its face a resemblance to the chief of customs and set it up in the hall of a London club as an example to others (the link with Bentham is obvious). Waterton once established a bird sanctuary for carrion crows, buzzards and magpies, arguing quite rightly that these creatures were discriminated against.

He would stop at nothing in his pursuit of useful information, and his *Wanderings in South America* contains a noble account of how he let his bare toes dangle night after night from his jungle hammock in the hope that vampire bats would suck his blood. The refusal of the bats to do so may be explained by the revulsion they must have felt on seeing Waterton's feet, for the naturalist thought that shoes should only be worn indoors and invariably walked the jungle barefooted, cutting stones, insects and bad bits of flesh from his feet with a clasp knife. Waterton claimed that no man could climb trees properly in boots, and he seems to have taken for granted, as eccentrics are prone to do, that other people shared his passion for shinning up trees and hopping up and down on the tops of high walls on one foot.

Only once in the long history of this primal eccentric do we find a trace of compromise creeping in. That occurred during a trip to the U.S. when he sprained his ankle. Remembering how speedily he had cured a previous sprain by putting his ankle under a pump, he decided to cure this sprain more speedily yet by putting it into Niagara Falls. "As I held my leg under the fall," he wrote, "I tried to meditate on the immense difference there was betwixt a house pump and this tremendous cascade of nature . . . but the magnitude of the subject was too overwhelming and I was obliged to drop it."

When Britons look back on such giant predecessors as Waterton and compare them with the men of today, they sigh for a type that seems to have disappeared. But close observation shows no diminution whatever in eccentric English behavior today. The author of this article, for instance, was only the other day complaining to an old friend of the weakness of modern pockets. The friend, who had never before shown any sign of eccentricity save that of being caught up a tree during the army's retreat to Dunkirk, studying a Lesser Spotted Woodpecker, answered at once: "Yes. The modern pocket is a national disgrace. That is why *my* pockets are always made out of old money bags from the Midland Bank." One can instantly recognize eccentricity's true note. Here, as of old, the utilitarian chord is struck immediately. Back goes the mind at once over the long centuries—to sporting Jemmy Hirst, a retired tanner of the nineteenth-century, who, astride a bull, went shooting with pigs because they were hardier than pointers; to Orator John Henley, an eighteenth-century preacher who was the first to see that the best way to make shoes was to buy boots and cut the tops off them; to Benjamin Stillingfleet, the noted eighteenth-century naturalist, who fostered modesty by always writing of himself with a small "i."

Nonetheless there has been a change—not in English partiality to eccentric behavior but in the manner in which it is conducted. In recent years every English eccentric has had to face the hard fact that heavy taxation is proving too much for his pocket, even when the pocket is an old money bag. Today's eccentric is in the same position as the family grocer, the small farmer and the small businessman. He must incorporate or die.

Luckily, most English eccentrics have not hesitated to make this decisive move. Where formerly they fought alone, each for his whim, they now band together in competitive groups, each group striving in its own way for the greatest happiness of the greatest number. Eccentric clubs and groups are now flourishing in England as never before. There are groups which mix herbs in cows' horns and empty them into compost heaps at a certain phase of the moon, and there are groups which diagnose illnesses by swinging plumb lines over charts marked with the parts of the body. The trouble with all such organizations is, of course, their inability to agree on what is useful. They are convinced that other groups are simply hotheaded. For instance, the very idea that atomic energy contains only "evil forces," as some groups maintain, is anathema to The Atomic Energy Association of Great Britain, whose patron, Mrs. Ronald Copeland, insists that atomic energy ripens crops. "If we can use it to ripen all the corn people need," Mrs. Copeland predicts, "then we can banish war."

Meanwhile the aim of "AT-EN," as it is called, is to put space-time and atomic energy within reach of the man in the street. Accordingly AT-EN has tried to invent a sort of Basic English that will make the meaning of the new universe absolutely clear. On one occasion at a London hotel AT-EN staged a gala pantomime named *Isotopia*. The act of nuclear fission was demonstrated by a lady dressed in a black lace tunic and carrying a banner marked ELECTRON, who danced rapidly between and around two other ladies labeled PROTON and NEUTRON. But the big hit of the evening was the playing by the late Muriel, Lady Anderson of her new symphony, *Atomica*. A marked advance on the composer's previous work (a song called "What a Lovely Girl You Are," presented in a vaudeville theater), *Atomica* consisted chiefly of loud, heavy chords, which indicated atomic bombs, and springing, tinkling passages which reflected the extreme surprise and alarm of the human race.

Such splendid group efforts should provide great encouragement to the uneasy. With the death of C. K. Ogden we may well, as some people fear, have lost the last great eccentric to "go it alone," the last to leave a powerful individual impression. But with clubs like AT-EN flourishing, no one need feel any alarm over the survival of English eccentricity.

"LET YOUR KIDS ALONE"

by Robert Paul Smith

JANUARY 27, 1958

> All that "Big Brother" parents do, says Robert Paul Smith,
> is mess up their children's world. In this article he
> delivers some strong-minded opinions on the mistakes he
> thinks today's parents are making in the process of bringing
> up their children. Mr. Smith is best remembered for
> that delightful 1957 best seller Where Did You Go? Out.
> What Did You Do? Nothing.

When I was a kid, the way we got to play baseball was this: school
was out, we ran home and hooked a handful of cookies, hollered,
"I'm home, goin' out on the block," grabbed a beat-up fielder's glove,
went out on the block and met a friend who had an old first baseman's
mitt and a ball, went down the block a little and hollered at the kid
who had the bat. So we proceeded until we had rounded up all those
kids who were not chained to piano practice, making model airplanes,
lying on their backs studying the ceiling, feeding their rabbits or
writing out one thousand times, "I will not put blotting paper in the
inkwell." We went to the vacant lot and played a game resembling

major league baseball only in that it was played with a bat and bases. It was fun.

My kid went to play soccer the other day. The way you play soccer now is this: you bring home from school a mimeographed schedule for the Saturday morning soccer league. There are six teams, named after colleges, and the schedule is so arranged that at the end of the season, by a mathematical process of permutations and combinations that would take me six weeks to figure out, every team has played every other team and every kid has shown up at the right hour the right number of times. There are always exactly eleven men on each team, the ball is regulation size, the games are played on a regulation-size field with regulation-size soccer goals, and there is a regulation-size adult to referee.

After the game I asked my kid, "Was it fun?" "Yes," he said, but he didn't sound sure. "We lost 3–0." When I was a kid, we lost 3–0 too— and also 16–2 and 135–3 at soccer or baseball or kick-the-can—but by the time we had fought about where the strike zone was, what was out of bounds and who was offside, we could wind up winning the argument, if not the game.

Because, you see, it was *our* game. I think that my kid was playing someone else's game. I think he was playing Big Brother's game.

Big Brother, in this case, is all the parents who cannot refrain from poking their snoots into a world where they have no business to be, into the whole wonderful world of a kid, which is wonderful precisely because there are no grownups in it. In come today's parents, tramping down the underbrush, cutting down the trees, driving away the game, making the place hideous with mimeographed sheets and names and regulations. They are into everything. They refuse to let anything alone if there is a kid connected with it. They have invented a whole new modern perversion: child-watching.

There are two main groups of child-watchers. The first, which includes the PTA's and the child study leagues and the children's mental hygiene groups, watches but does not touch. These are the peepers through one-way glass, the keepers of notebooks, the givers of tests.

The second group watches *and* touches—and also coaches and uniforms and proliferates rulebooks. This group manages such things as the soccer leagues and the Little Leagues and the Cub Scouts and the Boy Scouts and the Girl Scouts and the Brownies and the Sea Scouts and the Explorer Scouts and, I'd bet, the Satellite Scouts. These are the getters down on all fours, the spies in the children's world, the ones who cannot be sure whether they wish the kids to be as grownup as themselves, or wish themselves to be as childish as the kids.

All this child-watching and child-helping and child-pushing has made it tough for the kids to do anything without a complete set of instructions. Of course, once in a while they do break through the instruction barrier. The afternoon following the soccer game, my kid went off on his own business. This consisted of assembling an arrangement of batteries and resistors and what I have learned are called capacitors (not condensers), which makes five tiny neon tubes blink in a manner I can only describe as infuriating. Obviously this was fun for him. There are no plans for constructing such a machine. Indeed, it may be the first time such a machine has been built. So he built it. But he did not go outside and do the idle footling of a soccer ball which I used to do because the kid next door happened to have a soccer ball, and he did not play one-o-cat or throw a football around or even watch squirrels.

He did not do this because, although Big Brother has organized every league known to man and issued a rule book therefor, he has not yet put out a mimeographed sheet of instructions on watching squirrels. There are no books on how to be a lousy right fielder (it came to me natural), and in no book does it say that when you go to make a tackle, of course you shut your eyes and lie about it later. No doubt these books are being written.

Perhaps the finest single example of an organization that is devoted to not leaving the kids alone is the Scouts. It is not my intention to knock the Scouts as a whole. It is a well-meaning organization devoted to salutary works. I am sure that its officials are high-principled, admirable people. I merely wish to point out that the name of the organization is the *Boy* Scouts. It is for *boys*. And yet there is a small, wallet-sized card printed by the Boy Scouts of America entitled "The Scout Parent's Opportunity." Among the exhortations on this card are these:

"Be a companion to your own son." "Weave Cub Scouting into

home-life pattern." "Use the program to draw the family closer." "Be with your son at all pack meetings." "Work closely with the Den Mother."

The day an organization, *any* organization, tells me how to be a companion to my son is the day I am going to take a good hard look at that organization, and if they mean it for real, I am going to prepare to mount the barricades. I find "The Scout Parent's Opportunity" a terrifying document, but it is as nothing compared to another communiqué from the same organization. This is a sheet of yellow paper headed HERE ARE THE THINGS YOU DO TO BECOME A BOBCAT.

Well, the very first thing you do to become a Bobcat is learn and take the Cub Scout promise: "I promise to DO MY BEST to do my DUTY to GOD and my COUNTRY, to be SQUARE, and to OBEY the Law of the Pack." (The capital letters are *not* mine.) Only after you have said you will OBEY the Law of the Pack do you find out what the Law of the Pack is. The very first article of the Law is, "The Cub Scout FOLLOWS Akela." Then you hear that "Akela means 'Good Leader'—your mother and father, your teacher, your Cubmaster, and many other people who have shown that they are the kind of people who are able and willing to help you." Follow this reasoning carefully: first you say you will do something; then you find out what it is that you have promised to do; and then you find out what the thing you have promised to do means.

Before I let my kid subscribe to this, he is going to have a little talk with OLD FATHER, who is going to HOLLER at him GOOD AND LOUD. And what OLD FATHER is going to TELL him is never sign a BLANK CHECK, and before he goes off following Akela, he better take a GOOD HARD LOOK at all these people who have shown that they are "able and willing" to help him and find out where they are able and willing to lead him TO.

Bobcats, I have news for you. I know who Akela is, and he is not all those people. He is the old leader of the wolves in Kipling's Mowgli stories, and during wolf meetings he lies quietly on the Council Rock, interpreting the law and keeping order by means of dignity and aloofness. He spends a great deal of time keeping his mouth shut and he spends absolutely no time at all down in the grass with the young cubs playing Pin the Tail on the Hartebeest or Ring Around the Cobra.

I know a father in Connecticut whose kid FOLLOWED Akela to a Den, and after several sessions the kid wanted out. He did not know how to convey this horrible intelligence to Akela, so instead he went to his father. Apparently he thought quitting the Scouts was like breaking with the Communist party, or trying to get away from George Raft and being cut down by a machine gun at the corner of Fifth and Main.

The thing that drove this boy away from the Cub Scouts grew out of the little joker in one corner of the Bobcats' contract. It is called the "Parents' O.K." and it says: "We have had an active part in our son's first Cub Scout experience—becoming a Bobcat. We have tried to see things through his eyes and not expect too much. On the other hand, we haven't been too easy. We have helped him complete all the Bobcat requirements and we are satisfied that he has done his best."

This sounds mawkish but fairly harmless. The way my friend from Connecticut tells it, it isn't harmless at all. "Your kid brings you a book called the Wolf Cub Scout Book. If, Lord help us, you're a Good Scout Dad, you read a little of the book. On page 18 is something called 'Feats of Skill,' and your kid has to do any three of them to pass. He can choose a frontward, backward and falling somersault, or playing catch with someone twenty feet away, or climbing at least twelve feet up a tree, or swimming thirty feet in shallow water, or walking a two-by-four forward, sideways and backward. Now I'm for this, so I watch my kid practice. He tries and he doesn't get anywhere near twelve feet up the tree. I say, 'No, that's about five feet. You didn't do it.' When he tries to walk backward on the two-by-four, he falls off, so I say, 'Give it a little more work.' After all, I'm the one who's got to sign a paper saying he passed the test."

I could see why my friend was concerned: when he signs contracts, he fulfills them.

"So there's this pack meeting," my friend continued, "and they start giving kids badges because they have done their feats of skill. After a while, my boy and I see this one kid from our block who we *know* can't find his bottom with both hands in the dark, and he's getting a badge because he did the feats of skill. It's 'proven.' His mother signed the pledge. My kid looks at me. Something is very fishy here, is what he is thinking. That goof climbed twelve feet up a tree? Then why can't he climb stairs very good? It didn't take my kid long to figure it out: mothers lie and scoutmasters believe them. So he quit.

"That summer my kid took a look at an island in the middle of a lake at a kind of farm he goes to. He was the littlest kid there. He swam out and back and wrote a letter home, and in the envelope was a weed from the island. I didn't have to tell him it was a feat of skill and the weed was a badge. He knew it."

I suggested to my friend that he tell his kid that Akela—Mr. Kipling's Akela—would have known it, too, and so would Dan Beard, whose concern in helping found the Boy Scouts was to get kids out on their own in the country where they could learn to be independent.

I hear that things are bad in the Brownie world too. One Boston mother complains that she was required to learn to do everything her daughter had to learn to do to become a Brownie. At what cost to her self-esteem she cannot say, she even had to learn to sing, with gestures, the "Brownie Smile Song," which includes the words, "I have something in my pocket." And what mother has in her pocket is a smile, which she takes out and puts on her face. I ask you.

A New York City mother swears that when her daughter was "invested" in the Brownies, all the mothers had to be invested too. "I went to the investiture," this mother says, "and before I knew it, I and all the other mothers were standing up in a line, reciting the Brownie oath and having badges pinned on us."

Well, what's the point? The real point is that this kind of jazz doesn't fool anyone but the parents. The kids know that any grownup who gets down on all fours and makes mudpies with them is either a spy or a fool. Not that kids don't like spending time with grownups, but what they want is for the grownup to take them into his world. They are familiar with the child's world, they can handle themselves there. But a grownup can take them to a new place, an exciting world of cigars and restaurants with linen napkins and automobiles and tall people. But do parents do this today? No, they are too busy being Real Dandy Scout Dads and True Blue Brownie Moms.

The Scouts, of course, are only an example. This same attitude is found everywhere that parents and children get together. Anybody who thinks that the kids don't understand what is going on is living in a dream. These kids watch their parents making spectacles of themselves, and they reach conclusions. All parents who are now, or ever have been, down on all fours should give careful thought to the conclusions that they invite their kids to reach.

It seems to me that we are doing things we do not really want to do for kids who do not really want to have them done. Perhaps the saddest proof of all is provided by the town of Proctor, Minnesota, where members of the Duluth, Missabe and Iron Range Railway Employees Association actually go out on the street to try to get kids to use their bowling alleys, golf course, ball park, football field, rifle range, skating rink and tennis courts. No sale. The Proctor Moose Lodge offered to give away quarters to all the children of its 450 members on the Fourth of July. All the kids had to do was show up and hold out their hands. The first year only 50 kids bothered to show and the next year fewer than 25. The project was abandoned. And when Proctor sponsored a safety contest open to all the school kids in town, only one boy entered. Naturally he won first prize, a watch, but since he already had a watch he asked for $10 instead.

For reasons of their own the kids of Proctor don't want to use the bowling alleys, don't want to walk that far for a quarter, don't care very much about safety. I suspect that the main reason is that they never asked for any of these things and would rather be left alone. What is true for the kids of Proctor is going to be true for the kids of San Francisco and Chicago and New York and Ashtabula. The thing to do, I think, is for us to stop pestering them.

To this end I have formed an organization called Modern Parents Anonymous, or MPA (not under any circumstances to be confused with a recently formed Seattle organization known as PPPTA, or Proud Papas of the Parent-Teachers Association). MPA got its start one night when four supposedly adult persons—my wife and I and another couple—were sitting in moderately comfortable chairs in our moderately well-heated, well-lighted living room. All four of us read books and magazines, we have minds to think with and an enormous world to think about. So for two hours we talked about—children.

The actions of our children seemed more sensible to me than our own. They had looked into the living room some time before, seen that grownups were in tedious conclave, said hello and good-by and left. They were not wasting their time talking about us. The moment I realized this, MPA was born.

The principal goal of MPA is to encourage parents to think and worry and talk about something other than their own offspring. I have a list of things that might be talked about: freedom, liberty, the mating habits of Eskimos, the difference between Conté crayon and charcoal, the difference between voltage and amperage, religion, Ralph De Palma, the inflation of a basketball, the principle of a two-stroke engine, money, marbles and chalk. These intelligent areas of discourse I obtained from my kids. The care and handling of parents is not, of course, on their list. They stay away from this topic with consummate ease.

Last year I wrote a book which suggested, in the mildest possible ways, that if people remembered what a nuisance grownups were when they were kids, perhaps now that they were in turn presumably grownups they might like to get off the kids' backs. The mail has been fantastic, all in agreement, and most fantastic of all have been the communications from PTA groups asking me to come and holler at them.

I am booked for one such PTA talk in the near future, and I have a letter on the subject from the program chairman. "We need you, Mr. Smith," the letter says. "We want to stimulate our parents to think seriously about the probable risk of too many set designs for living and about the possible triumphs of unstressed, unconformist ways of growing."

Translating from the PTA-ese, I take this to mean that they want me to tell them how to leave their kids alone to grow up in peace. Well, I will go, and if I do not lose my nerve I will tell them that the way to leave kids alone is to leave them alone.

THE "CLAN"
IS THE MOST

by Paul O'Neil

DECEMBER 22, 1958

> *In Hollywood there is no Frank but Frank (Sinatra).*
> *Frank is king of the clan and only the clan matters.*
> *When its members gather at Frank's, Hollywood society*
> *(nonclan) is expected to suffer attacks of the most*
> *excruciating envy. And it does, Daddy, it does. Staff*
> *Writer Paul O'Neil went out to Hollywood to survey*
> *Frank and the clan. As you can see, he more than*
> *held his own.*

For decades after Rudolph Valentino vanished into legend and the
white Duesenberg ceased to be the pumpkin coach of stardom, the
social climate of Hollywood remained essentially unchanged. Hollywood's attitudes suggested both Louis XIV and Barnum & Bailey, its
"royalty" was seated and unseated by combers of fan mail, its definitive
social event was the première, and its hopes and dreams were reflected
in the haggislike prose of Louella O. Parsons. But all that is suddenly
changed. Nonconformity is now the key to social importance, and
that Angry Middle-Aged Man, Frank Sinatra, is its prophet—and
the reigning social monarch. Under the new order, society falls into

four classifications: the squares, the clan, the mouse pack and the coffee drinkers. But only the clan (composed of those on whom Frank smiles) *really matters.*

The squares are the types who reigned in the old days. Studio tycoons are obviously squares, since they know bankers and may even wear vests. But so are many famous actors and actresses. Jimmy Stewart is regarded as a square by the clan and so are Gregory Peck and Clark Gable. "What," asked one clansman, "would we say to *them? They go hunting.*" While they are squares, however, Stewart, Peck and Gable are harmless squares and thus not finks. Finks are treacherous squares (squares who might call Hedda Hopper and say something unpleasant about Frank). Even finks are more important than members of the mouse pack, for finks at least have money, power and scheming minds, and—nonconformity or not—these elements of life remain all-important in Hollywood. The mouse pack is a group of young actors and actresses who emulate Frank but can only afford Chevrolets. The coffee drinkers are the lowest group of all: theatrical beatniks who wear sweat shirts and blue jeans.

The uninitiated sometimes refer to the clan as the rat pack. It is a natural mistake, for Frank, in a sense, is the heir of the late Humphrey Bogart. It was Bogie, a man with a gravelly sense of the ridiculous and a hatred of phonies, who first demonstrated that a genuinely talented actor could spit in the eye of Hollywood custom and get away with it. He formed his friends and admirers into what he jocularly called the Holmby Hills Rat Pack, and some of the present clan, including Frank himself, were members.

Actress Lauren Bacall, Bogie's sultry and sharp-tongued widow, now insists that the rat pack was much the superior group. "The rat pack," she says, with only a half-humorous glint of the cheetahlike Bacall eye, "really *stood* for something. We had officers. Bogie was Director of Public Relations and I was the Den Mother. We had principles. You *had* to stay up late and get drunk, and all our members were against the P.T.A. We had *dignity.* And woe betide anyone who attacked one of our members. We *got* them."

But all this is simply a discussion of the past. The rat pack is no more; it died with Bogie. Today there is no Frank but Frank, and any former rats who may have become his liegemen now cry that "Frank is the *most!*" As paramount chieftain and head witch doctor of the clan (a word used only as a casual reference and never as a formal name since both the Rotary and Kiwanis clubs have names), Frank personifies its nonconformist attitude: a public and aggressive indifference, not only to what the customers expect of their movie stars but also to what Hollywood expects of its own citizens. He is known, variously, among the faithful as The Pope, The General or The Dago. Dean Martin, who is next in influence (and who also calls meetings), is known as The Admiral.

Martin's relative eminence is dramatized by his choice of automobiles. Frank drives a Dual-Ghia, a hot-looking automobile with an Italian body and a Dodge engine. Eddie Fisher, one of Frank's most ardent emulators, also drives a Dual-Ghia. So does English actor Peter Lawford, whose wife Pat (a daughter of Boston's millionaire ex-Ambassador Joseph P. Kennedy) is one of the clan's proudest exhibits. Tony Curtis tells his friends, "I've *got* to get a Dual-Ghia like Frank." But Martin is perfectly content with a Thunderbird and a Cadillac.

This group, plus Sammy Davis, Jr., comprises the hard core of the clan and is sometimes referred to as the cell. Actor Ernie Kovacs is a partial or poker-playing member of the cell, and he is much prized because he holds a cigar with its lighted end down, a position in which it can be extinguished, while he is staring at his hand, if a full highball glass is cautiously raised beneath it. Actor David Niven, an ex-member of the rat pack, and Milton Berle are also positioned on the immediate periphery of the cell. So are Lyricist Sammy Cahn and Tunesmith Jimmy Van Heusen, both of whom write material for Frank and Dean. Judy Garland, Debbie Reynolds and a new young actress, Shirley MacLaine, are the females whose talent the clan admires most. The clan also includes what Director Billy Wilder calls "groupies," knots of acceptable nonsquares who are welcomed to its larger convocations and camp meetings but who also lead separate social lives of their own. George Burns, whom the clan considers "the funniest man in the world," has this status, and so do Agent Irving Lazar and millionaire studio executive William Goetz.

Most members of this group are at least forty years old and either live or aspire to live in $250,000 houses. Their nonconformity must obviously be of an especially tailored type. In the period during which their personalities have been aerated and activated by Frank, a good many members have borrowed from the vocabularies of the cop-hater, the union agent and the beatnik, but they have no trouble with cops, they quarrel with their employers only through their agents, and they never, never wear sweat shirts. While vibrantly emancipated, most of them patronize Hollywood tailor Sy Devore, who will produce a seersucker jacket for $125 (New Yorkers can buy a seersucker jacket, with pants, at high-style Brooks Brothers for $28.75). The cell is made up largely of saloon entertainers, heaved into prominence by the industrial anarchy which followed the advent of television. A good deal of their rebelliousness is simply a belligerent insistence on doing The Act their own way, the free and easy way.

While they stand amazed at their own dialogue ("You gotta have your brains ready when you're with us"), they are essentially performers rather than wits, and their sharpest repartee involves a fragmentary use of old gags. Since all concerned know the "feed lines," they speak only the "boffo lines" and thus achieve a curious kind of communication which makes baffled outsiders feel uneasy. Much of their nonconformity, too, involves the ancient grudges of the entertainer. They die for publicity but distrust reporters and the press in general. They live for applause but bitterly resent the intrusion of rubes, punks, jerks and creeps who stare at them, crowd around them and thrust scraps of paper under their noses. Emboldened by independence, success and the heady example of Frank, whom they admire as ballplayers admire Ted Williams, the clan strives hard to give the outer world the back of its collective hand.

Frank says, "If they'd only quit tugging at my sleeve." Lyricist Cahn explains, "You don't know how it is. Frank can't even eat in a restaurant without some guy pulling up a chair, sitting down and breathing on him." Says Dean Martin, "You'd be crazy to walk down Fifth Avenue without a long black overcoat and a false beard." Says Sammy Davis, Jr., "As soon as I go out the front door of my house in the morning, I'm on, Daddy, I'm on! But when I'm with the group I can relax. We trust each other.

"We're in Las Vegas a lot, but only when we work or go to cheer one of our own who is working there. Frank and Dean and I are in demand. We pull in the *'shtarkers'*—the heavies, the gamblers. Frank's got 2 per cent of the Sands [Hotel] and Dean's got one-half of 1 per cent and I'm going to get a per cent of a per cent too. But that's just a sort of bonus. They let us buy in because we're faithful. The Riviera offered me $37,500 a week. Crazy! I turned it down. We gamble. There's nothing else to do in Vegas. Man, it's like Baghdad. You can't sleep. All the chicks are after loot. So you sing, and what else do you do? Sometimes Dean and Frank sit in for the dealers. It must cost the house $1,000 every time. They see a little old schoolteacher making a bet and they slip her the good cards and let her win big. You gotta know about Frank to know about us. Frank is the most generous man in the world. He's restless. He can't sleep. He says what he thinks. But he's pertinent! There's nobody, absolutely nobody, who won't like Frank if Frank wants them to. Frank has a lot of chicks, but nobody is more gentlemanly around women. And if you're his friend, that's *it*. If you need him, *Daddy, he . . . is . . . there!*"

This sentimentality and a kind of ingrown, theatrical flamboyance are continually being expressed with gifts. Members of the clan present them to each other on every possible occasion: cuff links, cigarette lighters, huge silver cigarette boxes with long messages of esteem or concern engraved on their lids, initialed bedroom slippers imported from London.

When Frank and Director Billy Wilder recently started speaking to each other after a two-year tiff, they engaged in a ceremony known as "Making Up and Exchanging Gifts." One is unthinkable without the other.

Wilder, as a reconstituted member of the clan, thereafter received an accolade which publicly marked him as nonsquare. Because the director had patiently endured weeks of insubordination from Marilyn Monroe while filming *Some Like It Hot,* Tony Curtis secretly arranged a stunt calculated to express the cast's—and, by implication, the clan's—admiration. In the picture's big scene, a papier-mâché cake is wheeled into a gangster banquet and Edward G. Robinson, Jr., jumps out of it, machine gun in hand, and mows down the dinner-jacketed mobsters. But the first time Wilder ordered it filmed, a naked woman jumped out instead and gave the startled—though delighted —director a big kiss.

Frank, being a bachelor and a restless type, calls a good many of the clan meetings on the spur of the moment. His secretary, Gloria, telephones the appointed ones and simply says, "Frank is having a gathering of the clan at seven o'clock. He wants you to come." Sometimes the boys play poker. Sometimes Frank runs off a movie or two (borrowed from some ever-obliging studio) for both husbands and wives. Birthdays, christenings and holidays are celebrated with similar informal convocations at Frank's big house in Coldwater Canyon, Martin's big house in Beverly Hills or Curtis' big house in Bel Air. The assembled performers spend hours singing to each other or playing their latest albums amid appropriate exclamations of affection and joy. On weekends they often retire to other expensive houses at Palm Springs for similar activity.

But if the clan's delights are simple, its refusal to share them with the world devastates the brash Hollywood soul. The clan never eats out in public if it can help it (although members often dine at Frank's restaurant, Villa Capri, or Dean Martin's restaurant, Dino's Lodge, where they can be protected from the herd). The clan never gives the sort of huge, fancy, dress-up parties which, historically, have been the key to swank and glory in Hollywood. Frank, in fact, decided to call off a New Year's shindig at "the Springs" because he felt it might be too *big*. All clan members are agreed upon a long list of squares whom they do *not* invite to parties, a startling innovation calculated to give everyone else in town the same doubtful status Northerners must endure in Charleston, South Carolina. Hollywood is expected to experience the pangs of envy when the Dual-Ghias gather at Frank's. And it does, Daddy, it does.

YOU, TOO, CAN OWN A RACE HORSE

by Ernest Havemann

JULY 21, 1958

> *Yes, and you, too, can become rich if your horse doesn't develop weak knees, weak ankles, bowed tendons, dislocated stifles, synovial deposits, osselets or sufferings from a score of other possible troubles. These can mar an owner's bliss, also his pocketbook, as Ernest Havemann found out. A former* TIME *editor and* LIFE *staff writer who has written extensively on subjects ranging from psychoanalysis to the business expense account, he now free-lances, works on a novel—and follows his own horses.*

In late 1956, when I was in Pittsburgh on a *Life* assignment, I took a day off and went to the races at Wheeling Downs, a half-mile track fifty-six miles away in West Virginia. It was the most foolish move I ever made. Not only did I pick nine straight losers but that evening, seeking some solace before starting home, I went to a saloon in Wheeling and sat down, as fate would have it, next to a horse trainer.

I have been a confirmed horse player since I was twelve years old —got it from my father, who ran away from home when he was a kid in an unsuccessful attempt to become a jockey—but I had never before met a trainer. I considered him a very glamorous person, especially when I learned that he had saddled Living High, longest priced winner of the day at $23.40.

"It must be wonderful to own horses," I said. "But I guess it's strictly the Sport of Kings."

The trainer looked at me curiously. "Nowadays it's the sport of anybody with the price of a used car," he said. "And for what a Cadillac costs, you can buy three horses."

"You mean anybody can own a horse?"

"Sure."

"Me too?"

"You too."

A few weeks later I, too, owned a race horse.

It happened with deceptive ease. The trainer, whose name is Raymond Ardell Horner, or Dell for short, moved his horses to Sunshine Park on the west coast of Florida. I met him over in Miami and we went to an auction of two-year-olds at Hialeah Park. Two-year-olds are the babies of racing, just starting their careers. Nobody knows how good they are, and sometimes you can pick up a bargain. On the other hand you may buy one that will never, as horsemen like to say, outrun your grandmother. I decided to risk $1,500 and hope for the best.

A filly named Believer approached the auction ring. Studying her page in the catalogue, Dell Horner said, "Look at all that black type!"

Black type, as I gathered from his tone, is the best. The sales catalogues list all the parents, grandparents and great-grandparents of the horse going under the hammer, and all the brothers, sisters, half-brothers, half-sisters, uncles, aunts, great-uncles, great-aunts and other relatives who have done anything commendable at the races. (The failures on the family tree are discreetly omitted.) If any of the near or distant kin have won a stakes race, such as the Kentucky Derby or the Preakness, their names are set in blackface type to make them stand out from the common run of horse which might have attained success in, say, the first and cheapest race of the day at a minor track like Wheeling.

Believer had plenty of black type in her pedigree. Besides, she was described as a cribber. At the time I thought this was good, most likely meaning that she was happy to remain in bed all day and cause no trouble. I bid $1,000 hoping that Believer would not mind the insult. A long silence followed. The auctioneer tried hard for $1,100, gave up and pointed a portentous finger at me. "She's yours," he cried, and my doom was sealed.

Owning one race horse is like eating one peanut. As I sat there, watching the rest of the auction and seeing many grand-looking animals go for what seemed like ridiculously low prices, illusions of financial acumen began racing through my brain. Anybody who has ever read the *Daily Racing Form* knows that most young horses never get to the Derby. Buying one of them is like buying a lottery ticket, just a stab in the dark. Why not improve the odds by buying *two* lottery tickets?

A filly named Miss Glade was led into the ring. She was a magnificent coal black. I started the bidding at $500, which after all was still left over from my original $1,500 commitment. Somebody bid $600. Just for fun, I bid again. Before I knew it, I had said $1,600 and the auctioneer was pointing the finger at me again.

After the auction Dell and I went back to the stables to look at my purchases. Like most $2 bettors, I had never really been close to a horse before. I had to screw up my courage for quite a while before venturing near these two beasts, who looked much larger in close-up than they had in the ring. Miss Glade promptly bit the little finger of my right hand, creating a bone crease which I can feel to this day.

Believer did not bother to bite, chiefly because she had her teeth clamped on the edge of the stall door and was making strange noises with her windpipe.

"What's that?" I asked.

"She's cribbing," Dell said. "That's what they mean by a cribber. She holds like that with her teeth and sucks air into her stomach. Boy, is she a cribber!"

I felt a sudden alarm. "Is that bad?"

"How fast do you think you could run," Dell asked, "if you swallowed a couple of balloons beforehand?"

After Dell had been training the two fillies for a few days at Sunshine Park, he gave me the worst news of all. "I thought from what the sales catalogue said that all these two-year-olds were supposed to be ready for the races. But I guess these two are the exceptions. As near as I can tell, they're barely used to the saddle. I figure they need at least sixty to ninety days of training before they can go to the post."

By this time I had discovered that even little girl horses have tremendous appetites and consume enormous quantities of oats, hay, carrots, bran, greens, vitamin powders and anything else that they can get their teeth into. I had also learned that a set of shoes cost $16 and up and that an exercise boy charges $2 for a morning workout. "That's a long time without purses," I said.

"You're right. But if we run the horses now, we won't win any purses anyway—and we'll just ruin their future chances."

What can you do in a situation like this? Once you have been bitten by the bug, there is only one answer. To pay the upkeep, you buy another horse—one that is ready to race right away.

I bought Wedding Ring. She was a beautiful bright chestnut filly and she belonged to another customer of Dell's. She was in top form but had to be sold because of financial problems (I used to wonder, in those days of my horse-owning youth, why so many owners had financial problems).

I cashed some government bonds and called an old horse-playing friend of mine named George Love. George was delighted to find that he, too, could own a race horse—or a piece of one. I told him to join me at Sunshine Park and bring money.

Wedding Ring was to run one final time for her old owner. The morning of the race Dell Horner told George and me, "I don't see how this filly can lose today. If you feel like making a good bet—maybe big enough to pay for her—go ahead. I guarantee she'll win by three lengths."

This was a tempting thought. But we hardly knew Dell. For all we knew, he might have been the world's worst handicapper. We decided to watch how much of his own money he risked and be guided accordingly.

We walked with him from the stable to the paddock that afternoon and watched him saddle the horse. Immediately afterward he led us to a spot in the grandstand. Far from making a big bet himself on Wedding Ring, he did not bet at all. George looked at me and made a little gesture, pointing his thumb at the ground. I nodded.

We never went near the betting windows. Wedding Ring took the lead at the start, won by three lengths and paid $15.60.

Afterward I asked Dell, "How come *you* didn't bet on her if you were so sure?"

"I never bet," he answered. "A couple of years ago I put $500 on one of my horses and found out later, on pretty good authority, that the jockey who rode for me had $500 of *his* money on a different horse. Naturally my horse finished up the track and I haven't made a bet since."

A week later Wedding Ring ran in the Havemann-Love colors, bright yellow and black. To anybody who has ever done any serious horse playing, there is no thrill in the world like watching your own silks parade to the post for the first time. Fascinated by the sight, George and I made several more trips to the betting windows than we had planned. We weren't going to let Wedding Ring get away from us again, especially not on this historic day.

She broke indifferently, never got anywhere near the front and finished ninth, beaten a good ten lengths. Don't ask me why. Owners know no more than the $2 bettors about the mysterious reasons that cause a horse to run its head off one day and barely get up a gallop the next time.

It is amazing how quickly one can become an expert at telling a jockey how to ply his trade. The second time Wedding Ring ran in the Havemann-Love colors, I stood in the paddock and without shame or embarrassment told my trainer (who had saddled a thousand horses in his time) and my jockey (Bobby Wall, who had ridden several thousand) just how to make the horse win. It was my judgment that she should not be used up setting the pace but should be reserved to make her run down the stretch. Dell and Bobby nodded gravely, apparently greatly impressed by my analysis of

Wedding Ring and her competition.

When the gate opened, Bobby pushed Wedding Ring right into the lead. It was a six-furlong race and another horse tried to run with her. Bobby kept her going in front and shook off the other horse around the turn. Coming into the stretch three other horses began to move up to her and they all crossed the wire abreast. The photo of the finish showed Wedding Ring in front by part of a nose.

In my first month I had my first winner, a thrill for which many owners have to wait for many months and sometimes years. Naturally I was delighted, although a little puzzled by the way she had cut out the pace.

"To tell you the truth," Dell admitted as we walked down to have our picture taken in the winner's circle, "I gave the jockey his instructions this morning. I just can't go along with your idea that this filly will come from behind. I wanted to see you get a purse, so I told him to take her right out in front and keep her there as long as he could."

If you should ever buy a horse, never let yourself be deluded that you are now the boss. In the horse business the owner is just a necessary evil. The trainer runs the show. He will listen to you respectfully, he will compliment you sincerely on your knowledge and judgment, but he will do exactly what he has intended to do all along. I now know several millionaires who own horses. Some of them have trainers who never went past the fourth grade and are completely unable to speak a grammatical sentence. Yet these owners cannot get their advice accepted even on such simple matters as what brand of oats to buy, much less on how often and how fast to work the horses in the morning. They could, of course, fire the trainer and get a new man. They never do because they know from experience that the new man would be even more stubborn.

At any rate I had a winner. I was in business. Wedding Ring had cost me and my partner only $4,000 and in two weeks had earned a purse of $950 for us. All this at a lesser track, where the purses were quite small. What would Wedding Ring do when we got on the summer circuit? How long had this been going on?

Dell and I walked back to the stable area where Wedding Ring was cooling out. She was noticeably lame in the left front leg.

This—unknown to most $2 bettors and unknown to me until I learned the hard way—is the hazard that makes owning horses the craziest business in the world. The modern race horse, inbred for speed, carrying the maximum amount of muscle on the minimum amount of bone structure, is as frail as a pastry shell. Next time you go to the track, notice those front legs, especially from the knee down. They are almost as slender as a woman's wrist, but they have to support the full shock of a twelve-hundred-pound animal coming down against a hard race track after a twenty-foot stride made at a speed which at times exceeds forty mph.

Among the troubles that can befall a horse are: weak knees, weak ankles, bowed tendons, strained suspensories, dislocated stifles, popped splints, cracked splints, broken sesamoids, bucked shins, bone chips, bone spurs, ring bone, calcium deposits, synovial deposits, osselets, quarter cracks, sore shoulders and sore feet, as well as a host of ailments such as thrush, laminitis, navicular disease, coughs, colic, shipping fever and rheumatism, not to mention knee spavin, bog spavin, bone spavin and blood spavin.

The training bills are high but predictable. A smalltime owner has to turn his horses over to the trainer of a public stable, a man who will train for anybody who cares to pay the fee. The fee runs from $7 a day at the smaller tracks to $12 a day in New York and New Jersey, plus 10 per cent of all purses earned by the horse. In addition the owner pays for shoeing, veterinary services and vanning the horse from track to track, north in the summer and south in the winter (about $400 to $500 for horses that race the year around). He also pays the jockey, who gets a fee of $15 and up just for getting on the horse, plus 10 per cent of the purse if he wins.

All this sounds expensive—and it is—but a horse can pay its own way at a small track by earning $4,500 a year in purses, at a big track by earning $7,000 a year. For a horse that gets to the post twenty or thirty times a year, this is not too difficult. Anything above the break-even point goes for amortization and profit.

Thus the theoretical chance of making money is pretty favorable, and the more horses you own the better. If you own enough horses, say six or more, you can even hire a trainer on a salary and eliminate the middleman's profit. If you are a good businessman with a hard-working trainer—a man like Dell Horner who thinks nothing of starting his work day at 6 A.M., ending it at 7 P.M. and then going to his hotel room to study the *Racing Form*—you may be able to hold your annual costs per horse to around $3,500. Practically any horse with four legs can earn more than that nowadays.

The only trouble is that so few horses have four legs. Wedding Ring, that day she won for me at Sunshine Park, broke a splint bone. We did not know it at the time because we were trying to save money on such frills as X-rays. The pictures were taken a few months later at Randall Park in Cleveland, where she smashed the sesamoid bones in her other front leg. Wedding Ring will never run again and is retired to a farm in Kentucky, where I hope she is in the process of becoming mother to the winner of 1962's Kentucky Derby. (The odds are about one in 10,000, that being the number of thoroughbred foals dropped every year.)

Believer proved to be one of the least ambitious race horses on record. The standard method of training a young horse is to send it out to jog or gallop around the race track every morning with the exercise boy simply sitting still. Sooner or later, as the horse's muscles are developed by this daily workout, it does what horsemen call "take hold of the bit"—that is to say, it begins to want to see how fast it can go. Believer jogged lazily around the track for three months before she ever showed any such curiosity. The first time she seemed to display any interest she popped a splint.

More than a year passed before we got her to the post. Then, though she showed a lot of speed, she proved to be a hard-luck horse. Sometimes she was unprepared at the start. Sometimes she was caught on the outside of the field and had to lose too much ground on the turns. In her last race, which was at the end of May, she did some kind of damage to a stifle and to her right ankle. At the moment she can barely walk, and the vet says we may as well figure we have another brood mare.

Miss Glade developed along different lines. She soon learned to take hold of the bit. But the stronger and faster she got, the meaner she got. Although she was just a two-year-old filly, supposedly of a kind and gentle age and sex, the grooms were afraid to enter her stall. Bad-tempered or not, she could run. She was third in her first start and first in her third start, against a good field at Delaware Park.

After that race we figured she was probably worth $10,000. In her next workout she damaged a knee. The vet said she needed at least six months of rest on a farm. We gladly gave it to her. Last January we brought her back to the races. Her knee was greatly improved but her disposition was worse than ever. She now had the habit of dawdling in the starting gate and letting the field get twenty lengths ahead of her before she started to give chase. A sort of poor man's Silky Sullivan, she made up worlds of ground once she got going, but she always got going too late.

In her last start she not only dawdled but then wheeled, dumping her jockey over her neck. She is now under temporary suspension pending evidence of reform. If she would only start running again she would still be worth $10,000, maybe more. But how do you bring mental hygiene to a race horse? As things stand now, we are simply doomed to school her at the gate every morning and hope for a miracle. The trouble is that it costs $8 a day to hope.

I have been unlucky—I think. I know other owners (I hate them) who borrowed money to buy a horse for $3,000 and watched it win, place or show in its next dozen races—at the end of which they had the original cost and all training expenses paid, a nice profit banked and the free and clear ownership of a good sound horse that was still ready to keep running and winning indefinitely.

If such is your ambition, you, too, can own a race horse. As Dell pointed out to me in the long, long ago, you can buy one as cheap as a used car. If you are lucky, you will never have to shell out another cent. Indeed, you will immediately start to reap profits. But watch out for those splint bones, sesamoids, hocks, stifles and mental disturbances. Without all these I, too, would be rich. Or at least solvent.

THE SCARY, SAPPY LIFE OF SKI MANIACS

by Marshall Smith

FEBRUARY 2, 1959

> *Skiing—a health-giving, body-building, exhilarating winter sport? Not on your life, says* Life *Sports Editor Marshall Smith. On the contrary, the nation's ski slopes are becoming a shambles. Rising casualty lists suggest it is less a sport than a menace, although broken bones remain a badge of honor among ski addicts. Perhaps the reason Marshall Smith can analyze this situation with compassionate detachment is that he does not ski himself.*

The hand-crank telephone connecting strategic points in the area jangled to life. "Summit," a voice said, "there's a crack-up on the Canyon." The voice was cool and matter of fact, obviously that of a professional making a routine announcement. A second voice cut in on the line. "We got you," it said. The first voice continued, "Location just above the road . . . looks pretty bad . . . send one man and I'll swing up from here."

At the rescue center an occupant stirred. "I'll take this one," he said, and strapped on his leather first-aid pouch. Within five minutes the rescue team was at the scene, unloading a Thomas splint (for traction cases) and a box splint (for simple breaks). Within ten minutes the victim had been wrapped securely in blankets to prevent shock and placed head downward on a crude but effective conveyance. Expertly maneuvered by the rescuers, it moved rapidly over rough terrain. On reaching the first-aid station, the patient was examined, then transferred to a waiting ambulance which delivered him to a doctor. The voice on the telephone droned, "Mark on the board that the meat wagon is out."

The operation described above is neither a Strategic Air Command rescue nor a mop-up after a peacetime paratroop drop. Rather it is a routine occurrence at the ski resort of Mt. Snow, Vermont, and it happens day in and day out between December and April at any well-run ski slope in the U.S. The rescuers are members of a ski patrol. The conveyance used to bring in the wounded is a toboggan. The victim could be any one of about twelve thousand cheerful martyrs who will show up in classrooms and offices this winter, brandishing casts, slings and crutches.

If any other supposedly peaceful pursuit required such elaborate machinery for bringing in the wounded, it would be banned forthwith in the name of public safety. Not skiing. The fanatics who strap boards to their feet and defy the laws of gravity and common sense have a self-perpetuating lobby. They defend their obsession on the grounds that it is healthy and invigorating, and the skiing wounded are the first to insist that skiing is really less hazardous than picnicking and only slightly more dangerous than reading in bed.

Furthermore, they go around trying to talk other people into taking up skiing. Once in the fold, the convert in turn becomes a fanatic and sets out to win new converts. At present the number of such zealots in the U.S. has reached three million and is swelling at the frightening rate of 200,000 a year.

Skiing proselyters begin with the most unsuspecting people—little children, innocent spouses, trusting friends—and then go after total strangers. Once a victim has taken the fatal step of investing $150 or more in ski equipment, there is seldom any retreat, and the ski slopes are thus kept supplied with fresh victims.

Two basic come-ons are used to enlist new skiers. Both are destructive, but no skier is ever deterred by destruction.

Approach *A* lures the beginner with a sugar-coated vision of a gala weekend: fresh air and fun on the mountaintop, hot-buttered rum afterward, and girls—man, you have to beat 'em off with ski poles. This approach prompted one eligible male to set off with his friend and tempter for Stowe, Vermont.

The first morning the friend took him to the top of the Nose Dive, a serpentine of snow so precipitous that even experts approach it warily. The new recruit, standing insecurely on his new skis, studied the trail that dropped down steeply for about fifty yards and then veered out of sight to the right. "What do I do when I get to that turn?" he asked. The friend reassured him: "You've ice-skated, haven't you? Well, just turn sideways and dig in your skis."

The recruit shoved off and picked up speed. The cold air nipped at his face. His stomach had a weightless feeling he had experienced in rapidly descending elevators and roller coasters. Boy, was this living! When he came to the turn he dug in his skis like ice skates, just as he had been told—and all hell broke loose. It was two years before he skied again. It took that long for a cracked rib, a broken shoulder and his confidence to heal. The man, whose name is Ray O'Connell, is now not only a hopeless addict but even an enthusiastic stockholder in a ski resort.

Approach *B* is the love trap. It is deadly for either sex. A case in point is the story of a college lad whose betrothed was a honey-haired coed. The only barrier in the way of connubial bliss was the fact that she skied and he did not. So she took him to the slopes to teach him herself, the lesson beginning at the base of the T-bar lift.

A T-bar, which carries skiers to higher altitudes, is usually mounted while it is moving, and this got the beginner off to a bad start. The T-bar caught his ladylove just right but dumped him on his face in the snow. By the time he got himself untangled, she was far up the mountain. Undaunted, he latched onto another bar and set out in pursuit.

About halfway up he got interested in the scenery and forgot to keep the bar tucked firmly under his behind. Suddenly it slithered up over his back, and only by a heroic lunge was he able to catch it in his arms. Hanging on in this fashion, he was dragged upward for another hundred yards, at which point one ski came off and he lost his hold from sheer exhaustion. A passing lift-rider grabbed his wayward ski and shouted that he would leave it at the top.

Our hero was now abandoned on the mountain with only one ski and no knowledge of how to use it. Painfully wallowing onward and upward, he sank to the hips with every step, until at last he reached the top and found his beloved. "Where the hell have you been?" she demanded angrily. "I could have made two runs in the time I've waited for you. Come on, let's go."

It so happened that the snow that day was of the "blue ice," or extremely fast, variety. Every time the beginner started to move he would reach what seemed like terminal velocity in what seemed like one-fifth of a second, then fall on the back of his head. On the first run downhill he fell forty-nine times. The only good thing about the situation was that with each spill he slid a few feet closer to warmth and safety.

He endured all the self-tortures that new skiers must face. His ski boots crushed his feet like Iron Maidens, cutting off circulation. His arches ached terribly and his thighs, bruised and scraped on the outside, were seized by cramps. He was sweating inside his clothes but was afraid to touch his semifrozen ears for fear they would snap off. He was frightened, frustrated, humiliated and, above all, mad. He was mad at all the smug athletes who kept rocketing past him down the slope. The only logical thing to do on reaching the base shelter was to throw his skis in the open fire and give up the whole thing. But he did not. He gave up the girl instead—and is now an ardent skier.

Why do skiers, who seem rational enough in between times, persist in such madness? One veteran doctor in New Hampshire, who stopped keeping score on broken bones after setting his first thousand, maintains that most skiers are troubled people. "They suspect a deficiency in themselves," he declares. "They are out to justify themselves, to prove that they have what they think they have."

When disaster strikes a true skier, there is usually no whimpering. The male skier's first words to the doctor are almost invariably, "When can I ski again?" The female skier is likely to be more concerned about her skintight stretch pants ($49.95 at Saks Fifth Avenue) than about the shattered leg they cover. A doctor approaching a wounded female often hears: "If you have to cut my ski pants, cut along the seam." The ski wound is treasured like a dueling scar. It becomes a merit badge, and its proud possessor may send off $5 to the Broken Bone Club for the skier's equivalent of the Purple Heart, a small silver pin bearing the replica of a fractured tibia.

The only way to protect most skiers is to put them in a strait jacket from December to April. But for those few who will listen to reason there are some points to bear in mind. The first is that disaster can strike anyone, novice or expert, at any time and in any manner. A ski patrolman at Aspen bent over to pick up a clipboard while standing stock still, lost his balance and fell, fracturing his leg in four places. It is not even necessary to be on snow. One beginner, too proud to look like a beginner his first time on skis, strapped the boards to his feet in the quiet of his hotel room, just to get the feel of walking around on them. Immediately he caught a tip under the door, fell and broke his leg.

On every mountain it is possible to say precisely where most accidents will occur, and it is seldom on trails bearing such foreboding names as Shincracker, Suicide Six or The Jaws of Death. At Sun Valley the place to beware is Dollar Mountain, a hill for novices. Winter Park in Colorado keeps a pin map of its trails with accident locations marked. The greatest concentration of pins is right at the bottom of the practice slope.

Overconfidence is the most grievous of the sins which lead to skiing accidents. It bubbles up within skiers at an alarming rate on the most ideal days, particularly with a bright sun shining on new powder snow. Then they all get to feeling frisky and acting like winterized hot-rodders. "There isn't much we can do about it," says Hal Hartman, head of the Aspen ski patrol, "except to bring 'em down after they crack up."

Doctors and ski patrolmen can almost set their watches by the time the casualties start rolling in. The worst time is right after lunch, before the skier gets a second wind and while he is still logy from eating. Later on pure fatigue sets in, compounded by fading light and a drop in temperature which makes the snow deceptively faster. But nothing prevents the skier from taking that perilous "last run."

Skiing's chief concession toward self-preservation in the past ten years has been the introduction of "safety" bindings. This innovation, now standard equipment with 65 per cent of all skiers, releases the ski from the foot when any unorthodox pressure is applied, thus reducing the possibility of fracture. One leading manufacturer of bindings, Earl Miller, goes around demonstrating his product by taking all seventy-two types of spills possible in skiing without harming himself. But he refuses to call his wares "safety" bindings. "Anything to do with skiing," says Miller, "should not contain the word safety."

Nothing clears a slope quite so quickly as the cry, "Runaway ski!" People dive headlong into the trees and take cover behind stumps and ledges. A runaway ski went right through a dog on the south slope at Cranmore Mountain, New Hampshire, one day, and others have afflicted humans with everything from a broken foot to the loss of an eye.

Only slightly less terrifying are runaway skis with people still on them. "It's getting like driving," mourns one veteran of the good old days. "You got to look both ways before coming to an intersection." With new recruits swarming the already overcrowded slopes, the wonder is that there are not still more collisions—and collisions, says Willy Schaeffler of the Olympic ski committee, are seldom little accidents.

Some are caused by courteous skiers who are legitimately out of control. But the growing menace of the slope is the hit-and-run artist who creates vast chaos and consternation. His warning cry is a wild yell, and on his mad run down the mountain he terrifies beginners by cutting across their paths. He sideswipes people, scatters small groups, discombobulates ski classes—and never stops to say "sorry." In this country he is called a "basher." In the Bavarian Alps he is called a "ski pig" and there is actually a law against him. Ski policemen issue him a summons wherever they find him, even if he is a stretcher-case being carried off the mountain.

In the next decade, to safeguard skiers from themselves, cops on ski-bikes will undoubtedly patrol U.S. slopes. And if a safety movement ever gets started, it could go all the way. Then all skiers would be required to pass physical fitness tests. Lifts would operate only on cloudy days, and then only until lunchtime. There would be traffic control booths with caution blinkers marking critical points and leading down to them a series of trailside signs, Burma Shave-style, spelling out the legend: "Danger Ahead!—Watch Out!—This Means You!"

III
GENIUS

David Fredenthal

THE MAGIC
OF TOSCANINI

by Winthrop Sargeant

JANUARY 17, 1944

A legend in his lifetime, Toscanini sometimes reduced music critics to windy incoherence. This cool and precise appraisal of the Maestro results from the fact that Winthrop Sargeant was a second violinist in the New York Phil-harmonic Symphony before he turned to music criticism. He has known the whiplash of Toscanini's baton. As a LIFE editor and writer, Winthrop Sargeant wrote on music, art, the movies and other subjects. He is now music critic of The New Yorker.

Twenty-five years ago the name Toscanini referred to an able but relatively obscure and already middle-aged Italian opera conductor whose principal triumphs had been won in the orchestra pits at La Scala and the Metropolitan Opera House. Today Arturo Toscanini, who will be seventy-seven years old in March [1944], is the most celebrated musician in the world. He is, Mussolini and the Pope excepted, the most famous living Italian.

Musicians have reverently collected the splintered batons that he breaks and throws away when he is angry. One New York woman treasures a piece of ruptured paneling that he once broke when, in a temper, he thrust his fist through a door in his Carnegie Hall dressing room. A reverent Italian court once acquitted him of responsibility for accidentally injuring a hapless fiddler whose bow he broke in a rage over an imperfect note. Legends about his amazingly accurate ear and his phenomenal memory have approached the incredible. Critics have been known to lose their analytical wits at his performances and come away mumbling (and writing) incoherent gibberish instead of criticism.

The man thus prematurely immortalized is a sharp-eyed, white-haired, extremely wiry Italian whose bare five feet of height usually come as a surprise to those who meet him off the stage. He dresses with prim severity, nearly always in black. Socially he is surprisingly shy. He loves the company of pretty women, hugely enjoys the floor show of a Manhattan night club. But he always looks vaguely out of place in any gathering he cannot lead with a baton. He has a reputation for childish helplessness in practical affairs and is said to be incapable of finding his own collar buttons or getting his hair cut without the help of his sedate, capable-looking wife. But he is shrewd enough to bargain closely over his concert and broadcast fees. In private life he is alternately fussy and playful, headstrong in both his enthusiasms and his hatreds, intolerant of anything in the way of opposition. To many, his celebrated tiffs with Europe's Nazi and Fascist authorities have made him a symbol of democratic idealism. A fervent nationalist like most of his countrymen, he is politically an avowed and tested liberal. He has recently gone on record favoring a democratic postwar Italy and opposing not only Fascism but the House of Savoy as well. But Toscanini is, both professionally and by temperament, an absolute dictator. He is also deeply and matter-of-factly convinced that he is the greatest conductor in the world.

Many people agree with him. In an age of virtuosos, Arturo Toscanini is, in fact, the biggest virtuoso of them all. His arrival at Rockefeller Center in New York City for his weekly broadcasts is as carefully prepared for as an official reception. In his dressing room several dress suits, complete from tie to socks, are carefully laid out, awaiting his intermission rubdown and change of clothing. A bowl of watermelon balls, which he likes to eat following the concert, lies cooling for him in a refrigerator. Pictures of his wife and family and favorite composers, without which he will refuse to conduct, are tastefully arranged on his dressing table. A punctual half hour before broadcast time, Toscanini's chauffeur-driven Chevrolet arrives at the Forty-ninth Street entrance of the RCA Building from his rented home in Riverdale. Toscanini steps into an elevator and is carefully whisked to the eighth floor. The hundred men of the NBC Symphony, already seated and tuned up, are waiting in nervous silence.

Toscanini is one of the most functional of all conductors. Everything he does, from the most towering tantrum to the merest flick of an eyebrow, has a definite musical purpose. During rehearsals he speaks little, and most of his verbal admonitions take the form of curses, prayers, or rapid, impatient descriptive adjectives. He deals with the music in musical terms, usually singing snatches of melody instead of explaining. And with the emotional substance of music he deals emotionally, playing directly upon the sensibilities of his men, angering, cajoling, pacifying them with a thousand subtle, mercurially changing moods, causing them to play exactly what he wants by controlling their emotions rather than their conscious minds. His contact with his musical material seems as immediate as the contact of a sculptor with a handful of soft clay.

There are, however, compensations for the player who sweats under this omniscience. Toscanini has a way of intuitively sensing the potentialities, failings and even the momentary emotional states of the men who are playing under him. He seldom tyrannizes over a nervous man, and he never picks a flaw or throws a tantrum arbitrarily. Nor does he seek, as lesser conductors sometimes do, to bamboozle experienced orchestra players with meaningless and transparent sleight of hand in order to impress them with his knowledge. The knowledge, fortified by the famous Toscanini memory, is there. It needs no herald trumpeting to get itself noticed. Any mistake, except one due to carelessness or downright stupidity, generally meets with encouragement and patient drilling. Though he is relentless in exposing any laxity, the Maestro's attitude toward the music and toward his men is one of open, almost childlike, sincerity. Moreover, orchestra players will tell you that it is actually more difficult to make a mistake under Toscanini than under any other conductor. His erratic, paddling beat is so enormously expressive that even an unimportant player who is temporarily at sea can tell, just by watching it, exactly where and how to make his entrances.

Every rehearsal sees a thousand moods rise and subside in the "old man," a thousand ways of getting what he wants out of the hundred-odd men under him. Completely absorbed in his complicated task, he seems as transparent and unself-conscious as a four-year-old child gravely making mud pies. While he is conducting he sings continuously—or rather, wails like a disembodied banshee—apparently quite oblivious to the fact that his piping, cracked-sounding voice can often be heard above the music by the first few rows of the audience. Sometimes, like a possessed dervish he will take to praying and swearing, trying to bring forth a performance by a species of incantation. An obstinately repeated error will suddenly rouse him to furious sarcasm: "*Io credo . . .*" he will begin with fiery deliberation. "I think, that there is an accent over that F sharp. But," he will continue, biting off each word and glaring at the culprit, "I am only Toscanini, and I am probably wrong. *Vediamo!*" Calling for a copy of the score, he will rustle impatiently through the pages, holding them within three or four inches of his near-sighted eyes. Then, finding the passage in question, he will elaborately pretend to be thunderstruck. "Ah, no, *Signori*. Imagine! I am right! Mozart has written an accent there." With an impatient whip stroke and a murderous-sounding grunt, the scene will be finished and the culprit, who has been staring guiltily at the accent all the time, will thank his stars that his temporary moment in the spotlight is over.

Catlike in his fastidiousness, Toscanini reacts physically to every sound, seeming almost to purr with responsiveness or to lay back his ears in apprehension over what is going on. He will close his eyes the better to apprehend some minute, distant, half-perceived flaw. Something is not satisfactory, but he doesn't know consciously what it is. He will ruffle slightly as if his fur has been stroked the wrong way. The closed eyes will pucker malignantly; the forehead will wrinkle. Then, all at once, every feature will contract acidly and a microscopic convulsion will quiver through his whole body.

The baton, whipping furiously, comes in contact with the music stand and is broken off short. He discards it and, trembling with rage, selects another from the supply he always keeps on hand. Still unappeased, he deliberately snaps the new baton in half between his fingers, throws the pieces over his shoulder, precipitates the score into the orchestra pit and kicks over the music stand. After that anything may happen. Perhaps the rehearsal is over. Perhaps, after much persuasion on the part of the players, a tremendous effort at self-control and a third brand-new baton, he will continue where he left off.

Not all of Toscanini's efforts are so purely emotional. It is true that he seldom bothers to explain anything logically. But he will sometimes illustrate things by quick, graphic, visual analogies.

Some time ago the Maestro was getting Debussy's *Iberia* ready for performance. A smoothly singing passage for three trombones struck him as being too coarse, though it was played in a manner that would have passed muster with nearly any other conductor. Swearing and praying were of no avail. The trombones sounded too much like trombones; not ethereal, not supple enough. Finally the "old man" stopped his exclamations and bowed his head for a moment in thought. Then he pulled a large silk handkerchief from his pocket and, holding it suspended for an instant, allowed it to float gently down through the air, catching it with his other hand. That was what he wanted. The trombones had to float through the passage like a bit of fine-spun silk in mid-air. The trombonists got the idea. Their tooting became as smooth and elastic as the cantilena of a master cellist.

Toscanini's two most fabled gifts are his remarkable accuracy of ear and his amazingly retentive memory. The "old man" can pick out and correct an individual fiddler's intonation in the midst of a heavily orchestrated score, or detect instantly the absence of a minute shading in the third-clarinet part while the rest of the orchestra is playing full blast. The memory is not only a valued gift; it is an absolute necessity to him because of his defective eyesight. Though he can see objects at a distance as well as anybody and can detect the presence of a good-looking girl a block away, Toscanini cannot read a score on the music stand before him.

Toscanini claims that he never has to make a deliberate effort to memorize anything. A few readings (with the score pressed within three inches of his little foxlike eyes) seem sufficient to fix the most complicated score indelibly in his mind. From that point on, Toscanini is not only prepared to conduct a performance from memory (a trick almost any conductor can do after a few hours of study), but to rehearse every detail of each player's individual part, correcting with photographic accuracy, minutiae that most conductors miss even with the scores in front of them. He needs no more than a weekend to commit the most elaborate scores (including those of whole operas) to memory. And once memorized, they evidently stick for years. In his head he is said to preserve, ready for immediate reference, the scores of about one hundred operas and two hundred symphonic compositions. A bassoon player once approached him in ·a state of hysteria before a concert, explaining that he couldn't go on. He had broken the E-flat key on his instrument. Toscanini concentrated a minute and then reassured him: "Don't worry. The note E flat doesn't occur in the bassoon part of any of the scores we are playing this evening."

Though he is modest almost to the point of shyness in private life, Toscanini, as a public personality, is as fiercely independent as an emperor. His lordly refusals to knuckle down to the Fascists in Italy and the Nazi administrators of the Bayreuth and Salzburg festivals are now a matter of history. They have, in fact, made the "old man" a political hero to millions who never would have paid him homage merely as a musician. Aside from a few painful incidents like the famous face-slapping scene in Bologna, the "old man" has enjoyed his fight, especially when he had a chance to make the enemy look ridiculous. When the Philharmonic played in Turin in the spring of 1930 before an audience including the Princess of Piedmont, Toscanini had one of these chances. A legal and temperamental *impasse* had been produced by three conflicting rules: the first was the traditional Italian rule that when royalty is present at a concert the Italian national anthem must be played. The second was Mussolini's rule that when the national anthem is played it must be immediately followed by the Fascist Party anthem "Giovinezza." The third was Toscanini's own private rule that he never would under any circumstances conduct "Giovinezza," which he had once described as musical trash unworthy of his baton. The authorities pleaded, but Toscanini was firm. The Princess could have her ceremonial national anthem; but no "Giovinezza" for Mussolini. Finally, after much negotiation, a solution was found. While the Philharmonic waited on the stage, formal and stiff in evening dress, a ragged-looking local brass band, dressed in what looked like street cleaners' uniforms, filed out furtively in front of the footlights and gave both the Italian anthem and Mussolini's "Giovinezza" performances that sounded almost homicidal. During the whole proceeding Toscanini, with a perfectly straight face, stood with folded arms before the orchestra. When the anthems were over and the scared-looking band had filed out again, the concert began.

Yet there have been occasions when the Maestro has been perfectly willing to sacrifice his own reputation for the sake of a nervous or harassed player's comfort. The first concert of the New York Philharmonic's 1930 European tour was given at the Paris Opera House. The ten-day Atlantic crossing, without opportunity for adequate practice, had left many of the players soft from inactivity. This was particularly true of the brass section where lips quickly lose their strength when there is any letdown from work. On the program there was one of the most exposed and difficult horn parts in the symphonic repertory—the solo part of the Nocturne from Mendelssohn's *Midsummer Night's Dream* music. The Philharmonic's first horn player, Bruno Jaenicke, was a man widely and justly regarded as one of the finest in the world, but even he suffered somewhat from the abnormal conditions preceding the performance. The solo of the Nocturne ends in a long, sustained note, and by the time the horn player reached it he was close to the limit of his endurance. Toscanini perceived immediately what the situation was and cut the note short considerably before its just point of expiration. The result was a glaring error of musical taste which must have irked the Maestro greatly. But the horn player was saved a nasty experience which might have ended in a humiliating breakdown.

Integrity in all his relations with his musicians has won the conductor the universal respect of orchestra players. Resting as it does on a complete understanding of musicians and their problems, it contributes much to that quality of personal leadership which, in the last analysis, constitutes the essence of Toscanini's genius as a conductor. Musicianship, taste, sense of style, sensitiveness of ear, photographic knowledge of the score, all contribute to the objective side of his interpretations. But there is another factor in Toscanini's conducting without which none of these qualities would achieve practical significance—his psychological grip on the men who play under him. The ability to control an orchestra is by no means unique with Toscanini. Most really good conductors possess the quality of leadership. But the depth to which this control penetrates in Toscanini's case, the amount of musical detail that it directly affects, is probably greater than with any conductor now before the public. And the uncanny faculty which permits this degree of control is primarily neither a matter of musicianship nor of personal prestige, but of intuitive sensibility in dealing with persons.

A few years ago Wagner's *Tannhäuser* Bacchanale was to be played in Carnegie Hall. Toward the end of this operatic excerpt, in its concert version, there is a passage where four solo violins delicately echo the music of the Venusberg maidens. The passage is an exposed and ticklish one, and is usually assigned to the concertmaster and his assistants of the first two desks of violins. Toscanini, with the idea of intensifying the off-stage effect of this passage (which in the opera is sung by a chorus in the wings), directed that it should be played by the *last* two desks of the first violins. Now, violinists in the rear ranks of a section, however competent they may be, are not used to playing solo passages, and are likely to shudder with apprehension at such a prospect. But Toscanini was determined to have it so, and so it was. Rehearsals turned out to be fairly satisfactory. At the performance, however, everyone was apprehensive. The chaotic, orgiastic surge of the music unwound itself in the usual manner and subsided at the end into its customary, and on this occasion somewhat frightening, calm. The place for the entrance of the four lone violinists finally arrived. The violinists, jittery with fright, launched into their solos like reluctant waders in an ice-cold brook. Their bows began to wobble and stagger down their strings. Before a note had passed it was obvious that the whole thing was likely to end in a catastrophe. At this point, Toscanini stopped conducting altogether and, pulling out his handkerchief, started coughing violently into it. The effect was instantaneous. Seeing the "old man" himself in difficulties, the four violinists suddenly realized that it was up to them to save the show on their own heroic initiative. All trace of nervousness immediately disappeared in the face of the overwhelming emergency. Their performance was magnificent. Many of the men thought the coughing fit was genuine. But, by a strange coincidence, similar fits had a way of cropping up in similar emergencies. The foxy old Maestro had probably used the recipe on many a jittery soprano during his long years in the opera house. It was a very unorthodox piece of conducting. But it got results.

Through his innate musicality, his native feeling for the dramatic, his remarkable sense of musical proportion, Toscanini can build a symphony into a wonderfully logical edifice of perfect detail and telling dramatic emphasis, giving each phrase a quality of suspense that holds the most indifferent audience spellbound. In these qualities Toscanini is probably unequaled. And they are so impressive that people are apt, in their enthusiasm, to overlook certain of Toscanini's weaknesses and limitations. Most of the limitations are those of personal outlook, of temperament. They boil down, on analysis, to the quality of Toscanini's mind, to the type of man Toscanini is.

Arturo Toscanini has a classical, Mediterranean mind. His interpretations are as lucid, sharply defined and brightly lit as if the warm sun of his native Parma were seeking out and illuminating every musical nook and cranny. He worships logic, clarity and polish, abhors everything enigmatic, diffuse, rough-hewn or boisterous. This classical attitude of mind probably has something to do with the wonderful clarity and polish that he gets into his interpretations. But it also affects his taste in choosing programs and the quality of his conducting in certain types of music. His passion for clarity will lead him to prefer music that is clear, but intrinsically cheap, to music that is profound but awkward and lumbering. His fine Italian hand refines a great deal of the plain-spoken vigor out of symphonies like those of Bruckner, Brahms and Sibelius, though it must be admitted that he does a crystal-clear job with them. Tchaikovsky and the contemporary

Russians he has only recently learned to like. A notorious hater of the more violent and cacophonous types of modern music, he has nevertheless recently taken a polite interest in modern American composers like Samuel Barber, Roy Harris and Gershwin (whose *Rhapsody in Blue* he conducts manfully but, by general consensus, badly).

Although he has been a symphony conductor for twenty years, Toscanini's conducting still occasionally betrays the habits of the opera house. His eye, or ear, is always on the main melody, the main climax, the main point of emphasis. He can chisel a lyric melody, or a driving rhythm, with a precision and clarity few contemporaries can equal. But he is not altogether at home in chiaroscuro or in the multicolored weft of Romantic counterpoint. With Toscanini, what musicians call "inner voices" are apt to lack independence and variety of color. His orchestral passages are invariably clear and brilliant, but often as monochromatic as a steel engraving.

With all his mastery of the technique of symphonic performance, Toscanini has one technical weakness. This weakness is a curious tendency to get befuddled in eccentric rhythms. He has been known to get off balance while rehearsing the rhythmic complexities of Ravel's second suite from *Daphnis et Chloé* or syncopated passages in Strauss's *Till Eulenspiegel*. The passages are short, and Toscanini invariably recovers himself adroitly. In another conductor such a shortcoming would be one among many. In Toscanini's case it is all the more striking because he seems to have no other technical weakness whatever.

A curious phenomenon often noted in connection with Toscanini's conducting is his tendency to "wear out" an orchestra. After a few brilliant seasons under the "old man" the finest orchestras seem to go to pot. No other conductor can bring them back into first-class working order again. The most noted example of this was the slump that occurred in the performances of the New York Philharmonic Symphony as soon as he left it in 1936. More than any conductor of his generation, Toscanini is an autocrat. He carries on his own shoulders the responsibility for every musical decision, every detail of phrasing, every breath drawn or movement made by the hundred-odd men under him. This works brilliantly as long as the hypnotic Toscanini is at the helm. But once the hypnotism is withdrawn and a less totalitarian maestro takes over, the machine loses its power of co-ordination. The Philharmonic, in 1936, lost not its physical or emotional vitality, but the will that had galvanized its smallest components into co-ordinated activity. The will had been Arturo Toscanini's.

But if Arturo Toscanini cannot be all things to all listeners, he can be more things to most of them than any other contemporary maestro. And if he occasionally leaves a symphony orchestra as limp as a discarded ventriloquist's dummy, most concertgoers agree that the show he has put on has been worth it. In the early Italianate Teutonic classics—Haydn and Mozart—he is the supreme master of brilliance, polish and aristocratic style. He is probably, all in all, the greatest living conductor of Beethoven. In works of the clearer, more lyric Romantic composers—Schubert, Weber, Schumann, Mendelssohn— he has few rivals. He is the greatest of all contemporary Wagner conductors. And he can play the works of the great French Impressionist Debussy with a sense of atmosphere equaled by few and a pliancy and dramatic intensity equaled by none.

Again and again Toscanini has been criticized for unearthing some tawdry little operatic overture or piece of ballet music and performing it on a serious symphonic program. But even his severest critics have had to admit that he always managed to make these trivial items seem like polished gems before he was through with them. There is perhaps a grain of truth in the popular anecdote that has Toscanini meeting the Italian composer, Respighi, on a street corner in Italy: "Have you heard me conduct your *Pines of Rome*?" inquires the Maestro. "No, I haven't," admits Respighi. "You really should," replies Toscanini dryly. "It's wonderful. You wouldn't recognize it."

EUGENE O'NEILL COMES BACK TO BROADWAY

by Tom Prideaux

OCTOBER 14, 1946

> *When Eugene O'Neill returned to Broadway with* The
> Iceman Cometh, *his first play in twelve years,* Tom
> *Prideaux,* LIFE's *drama critic, wrote this review of O'Neill's
> contribution to the American theater. Prideaux had been
> having lunch in O'Neill's apartment when the dramatist
> suddenly reached in his inside pocket and handed him,
> for exclusive publication, the quotation from* Long
> Day's Journey into Night *which concludes the article.
> At that time O'Neill said the play could not be published
> for twenty-five years. As things turned out, however, it
> did appear in Sweden in 1956 and subsequently won a
> Pulitzer Prize.*

Eugene Gladstone O'Neill is, with the sole exception of William
Shakespeare, the most widely read playwright in the history of the
theater. Although no Broadway event is more glittering than an
O'Neill première, he is honored even more abroad than at home.
Audiences from Stockholm to Shanghai have suffered over the woes of
Anna Christie and *The Emperor Jones*. Twenty O'Neill plays have
been performed in Japan, for which the author received no payment
other than some brocade from a polite translator. Repertory companies
have barnstormed his plays all over South America.

In such imposing textbooks as Morrison and Commager's *Growth of the American Republic* we read that O'Neill "is indubitably the most distinguished of American dramatists, imaginative, original, profound." He is the first American to win three Pulitzer Prizes and the only American playwright to cop the Nobel Prize (1936).

Eugene Gladstone O'Neill was born on October 16, 1888, in a respectable family hotel, the Barrett House on Forty-third Street and Broadway. The building was recently demolished. His Irish father, James O'Neill, was a noted romantic actor; his Irish mother, Ella Quinlan, a convent-bred girl from Cleveland. There was a brother, James, Jr., who was ten years older and played bit parts in the father's company.

James, Sr., was famous for one role, Edmond Dantès in the *Count of Monte Cristo*. For sixteen years he toured the country in it, the infant Eugene usually tagging along with his parents. They were not the traditional poor actors with their baby cradled in a trunk. In good years the elder O'Neill made as much as $50,000 and always provided his son with a nurse. Still, Eugene was brought up in the theater. Night after night, backstage, he beheld the rip-roaring melodrama. "I can still see my father," he says, "dripping with salt and sawdust, climbing on a stool behind the swinging profile of dashing waves. It was then that the calcium lights in the gallery played on his long beard and tattered clothes as he declared with outstretched arms, 'The world is mine!' "

Despite the luxuries which his family could afford, there were hardships in being an actor's son. It was the heyday of the traveling stock company when even the best actors played one-night stands and moved on, sometimes at dawn. O'Neill developed an almost pathological hatred of hotels. He recalls the terrible food, the endless dusty train rides and his longing for some kind of security. But O'Neill loved the theater. And though he looked down on the Victorian stage conventions of his father's day, he always looked up to his father's showmanship that wowed the gallery from Boston to New Orleans.

O'Neill's yearning for security was hardly satisfied by his schooling, which separated him from his family. It began during his eighth year at a Catholic Sisters' boarding school on the Hudson. Three years later he entered a military school in New York City and then, in 1902, transferred to Betts Academy at Stamford, Connecticut, from which he graduated in 1906. Summers were spent at the family headquarters in New London. There his father owned a large home and in later years became owner of a small enterprise romantically entitled the Monte Cristo Garage.

On his visits to New York O'Neill was often under the wing of brother James. While Eugene was shy and moody, James was happy-go-lucky. He aspired to be a big-city newspaperman. He knew most of the girls in show business, and when Eugene visited him in New York, James took care that he was well entertained. "The girls in those days," says O'Neill, "were less ambitious and more fun. While other boys were shivering themselves into a fit of embarrassment at the mere thought of a show girl, I really was a wise guy." As a self-confessed wise guy, O'Neill entered Princeton in the fall of '06.

As the result of a drunken prank, O'Neill was suspended for two weeks in the spring of '07. At the end of his freshman year he was dropped from Princeton because he had flunked three of his midyear exams and all of his finals. After his college fiasco and in a mood of youthful defiance O'Neill cherished a romantic ambition to become a "royal tramp." He was glad to go alone on a trip, financed by his father, to prospect for gold in Honduras along a jungle-bordered river. On the eve of sailing he hastily and somewhat absent-mindedly married a New York girl, Kathleen Jenkins, who bore him a son in his absence. The gold turned out to be illusory. O'Neill did not live with his wife and in 1912 she divorced him.

O'Neill soon realized that he felt at home only when he was away from home. In 1910 he boarded a Norwegian square-rigger for Buenos Aires. He still speaks of the nights when he used to lie on the bowsprit as of a deep religious experience. "As I watched the spray beating against the ship and looked back at the big moonlit sails," he recalls, "I felt synchronized with the rhythm of life."

The rhythm of life in Buenos Aires was less inspiring. He worked briefly for a sewing-machine company and an electrical firm, then took a job as a stevedore and shipped twice to South Africa on a cattleboat. But it was not time wasted. By the year he would have graduated from Princeton he had made the South Atlantic his campus.

His fraternity brothers were sailors, stokers, dock hands and beach-combers. As young Americans are supposed to, he was making "good contacts" during his schooling. They proved useful to him in his future profession.

Drifting back to New York in 1911, he lived off and on at Jimmy, the Priest's, a longshoreman's saloon, sleeping on the hickory-topped tables when he was too broke to afford $3 a week for a room upstairs. One of his roommates was a broken-down English newspaperman who always believed that he would really reform—tomorrow. O'Neill wrote about him in the only fiction he ever published, a short story called "Tomorrow," and he used him again as Jimmy Tomorrow in *The Iceman Cometh*. The real Jimmy was found dead one day beneath his own window. O'Neill believes he committed suicide because he lost hope—"His tomorrows finally gave out."

With his sea fever still running high, O'Neill shipped once to Southampton in 1912 and proudly returned with an able-bodied sea-man's rating. After treating his shipmates to a bountiful champagne party at the old Astor bar, he awoke to find himself on a train headed for New Orleans.

In New Orleans he ran into his father who was touring the Orpheum Circuit in a short vaudeville version of *Monte Cristo*. He had always wanted the boy to become an actor. Impelled by a press-ing financial need, young O'Neill joined the show and played a jailor until the troupe reached Ogden, Utah. There his father re-marked, "Sir, I am not satisfied with your performance." Said the son, "Sir, I am not satisfied with your play." A few weeks later he went back home to Connecticut and got a job as a cub reporter on the New London *Telegraph*.

Though he claims he was "a bum reporter," O'Neill was happy on his job. It consisted mainly of writing doggerel verse for a biweekly column called *Laconics*. The editor was impressed by O'Neill's "mod-esty, his native gentlemanliness, his wonderful eyes and his literary style." But his happiness was brief. A doctor informed him that he had tuberculosis and on Christmas Eve, 1912, he entered the Gaylord Sanatorium at Wallingford, Connecticut.

O'Neill managed to triumph over the disaster and even turned it to profit. He read all of Ibsen and Strindberg. After he left the sanatorium, completely cured, he wrote several one-act plays. In 1914 he took his first manuscript, *Thirst,* a collection of one-act plays, to a Boston publisher on the strength of his father's promise that he would pay the printing bill if the plays did not sell. They didn't and his father paid.

His father also paid for a year's study in Professor Baker's famous play-writing course at Harvard where, O'Neill says, he benefited chiefly by Baker's faith in him. The following summer (1915) O'Neill elected to continue his writing on Cape Cod. There he met a little group of serious amateurs called the Provincetown Players. They provided O'Neill with a laboratory where he could try out his most radically experimental plays.

The first O'Neill play, a one-acter called *Bound East for Cardiff,* was given on an old fish wharf built on piles over the ocean. It dramatized the fears and bewilderment of an injured sailor dying in his bunk. Structurally it was hardly a play at all, but it struck a new note of realism in American drama.

In the fall of 1916, O'Neill followed the Provincetowners to New York. Eventually they settled in an old stable on Macdougal Street where the audience sat on hard, wooden benches and the actors elbowed each other on a tiny stage. A new era was beginning in the theater. It was serious and sometimes arty but always interesting. First-string critics gladly took the long trip downtown and bruised their haunches in order to stimulate their brains. Nobody made any money. Nine of O'Neill's one-act plays were produced, for which he received no royalties. Other small groups were springing up with similar artistic aims. The Washington Square Players were soon to become the Theatre Guild. In the midst of all this theatrical ferment O'Neill met Kenneth Macgowan and Robert Edmond Jones, who later were to produce his plays. Jones designed the settings for many of them and worked with him on *The Iceman.*

In and out of the group passed an odd assortment of such future notables as Edna St. Vincent Millay, Ann Harding, Paul Robeson, Susan Glaspell, James Light and Wilbur Daniel Steele. They argued art, ate art, slept art and on occasion ventured to drink art, in a saloon called the Hell Hole, among such nonartists as truck drivers, petty racketeers and the remnants of a notorious gang called the Hudson Dusters. O'Neill was in good standing among the regulars at the Hell Hole. They never suspected he was a playwright, not even when he got tight one night and recited, in one of his rare moments of verbosity, Francis Thompson's poem, "The Hound of Heaven"—all of its 182 sad lines.

The impulse that drove poets and dramatists into low dives was part of the same revolution in American culture that was producing the outspoken novels of Theodore Dreiser and Carl Sandburg's apostrophe to Chicago, the "Hog Butcher for the World." It was part of the same revolt against prettified art which produced the "Ash Can" school of painters with their interest in city streets, McSorley's saloon and prize fights. O'Neill was a close friend of the painter George Bellows, and accompanied him to prize fights where he first made sketches for such ringside classics as "Stag at Sharkeys." In his efforts to depict life as he really saw it, O'Neill was in the spirit of his time. Only in a backward field like the commercial theater did he seem ahead of his time.

Though O'Neill's short sea plays were winning him a limited fame in theatrical circles, his first real acclaim came in 1917 when he sent three one-act plays to *The Smart Set,* a leading literary magazine. Its energetic young editors, George Jean Nathan and H. L. Mencken, hailed them with delight and published all three. Describing O'Neill at the start of their long friendship, Nathan wrote, "When I first knew him O'Neill—or Gladstone as it is my facetious custom personally to address him—exuded all the gay warmth of an Arctic winter. Life to him . . . was indistinguishable from a serial story consisting entirely of bites from mad dogs, fatal cancers and undertakers in love."

In 1918, however, O'Neill exuded enough gay warmth to marry Miss Agnes Boulton, a young short-story writer, but appended a cautious codicil to the ceremony, "Until love do us part." They had two children, Shane and Oona. During the first year of their marriage he wrote *Beyond the Horizon,* a full-length play of marital misery. They were divorced in 1929.

His father lived to witness the première of *Beyond the Horizon*. From his box seat the old man beheld a somber drama of two brothers falling in love with the same girl. The brother who won her was a poetic type. He let the farm run to seed and died of consumption. The other brother, a more practical sort, lost his self-respect when he turned from wheat raising to wheat gambling. The audience did not cheer as they used to when Monte Cristo rose from the waves, but the old man could see that the show was going over. When he met his son after the curtain, he grumbled, "Are you trying to send the audience home to commit suicide?" But he was proud and excited, and there were tears in his eyes. A few months later, before he died, he knew that his son's play had won the Pulitzer Prize for being the season's most distinguished drama.

For the next twenty years O'Neill worked hard, usually sticking to his desk from eight in the morning to 1:30 P.M., seven days a week. For relaxation he turned to the sea. In his Cape Cod days he used to paddle far offshore in an Eskimo kayak. In the city he liked prize fights, baseball games, six-day bicycle races. He hated large social gatherings. Of his saloon habits he says, "When I say I drank hard, I mean hard." But that was usually in New York. When he settled down to work in the country it was another story. "I never try to write a line when I'm not strictly on the wagon."

Not satisfied with straight realistic plays, O'Neill ventured into new fields. With the Provincetown group willing to gamble as producers, O'Neill offered *The Emperor Jones* (1920), the first modern play to present a Negro as a tragic hero. Brutus Jones was a misfit. He had committed murder and fled to the West Indies, where he was caught between civilization and the jungle, and bedeviled by his own superstitions. Symbolic of his undoing was an offstage thumping of tom-toms that grew louder and faster for a solid hour until both the audience and Jones were driven frantic, and he was shot down by his pursuers. As a stage device the tom-toms were more hair-raising than anything in *Monte Cristo*.

O'Neill's next hit was *Anna Christie* (1921), which told how an embittered old Swedish sea captain drove his beloved daughter into prostitution just to save her from "Dat Ole Davil Sea." Written in

O'Neill's best water-front idiom, it somehow managed to end happily and for years has given stage actresses, from Pauline Lord to Ingrid Bergman, a wonderfully meaty part. It brought O'Neill his second Pulitzer Prize.

Another tormented leading character was Yank in *The Hairy Ape* (1922). As a stoker on a luxury liner, Yank gloried in his brute strength until a rich girl called him a "filthy beast." Here again O'Neill has revealed his compassion for misfits and underdogs, and again, in the semirealistic scenes of a ship's stokehole jammed with half-naked, cursing stokers shoveling coal into a row of blazing furnaces, he had achieved a maximum of stage excitement. O'Neill was delighted to receive a note from one of his old seagoing friends who had seen *The Hairy Ape*. It read, "I liked the show a lot, but for God's sake tell that No. 4 stoker to stop leaning his prat against that red-hot furnace."

No synopses can do justice to O'Neill's many hits and flops or even suggest their variety. Year after year he experimented with masks, whirring dynamos, choral chants. In *Desire under the Elms* he wrote about hard-bitten New Englanders, and in *Marco Millions* he dramatized the conflict between Oriental mysticism and the Western businessman. In all of his plays he deplored the evils of too much materialism, too many repressions and too little faith. O'Neill had rejected the formal Catholic faith of his parents, but he was a strong defender of spiritual values.

One of his most radical experiments was *Strange Interlude* (1928), which took a year to write and four hours to perform. Stripped of its cosmic implications about the female soul, *Strange Interlude* was simply a sensational sex drama—one of the best ever written. Its heroine had three lovers, all of whom she needed to give her a sense of fulfillment. To intensify the drama O'Neill required all of his characters to speak aloud their innermost thoughts, apparently unheard by anyone else on the stage. Though this was a development of the old-fashioned "aside," its effect was new and startling. As one critic remarked, "It seemed to rip the bandages from souls in torment." *Interlude* was produced by the Theatre Guild, which undertook it purely for prestige value, expecting to lose $25,000. It netted $500,-

ooo apiece for the Guild and O'Neill, and brought him his third Pulitzer Prize.

O'Neill had an even more ambitious experiment in mind when in 1928 he embarked on a long voyage. It was a thirteen-act tragedy to be named *Mourning Becomes Electra*, based on the Greek trilogy written by Aeschylus in 458 B.C. O'Neill transplanted the action to New England at the end of the Civil War.

Eager to settle in France and work on his new play, O'Neill rented a château near Tours and took with him his third wife, Carlotta Monterey, whom he married in Paris, July, 1929. After nearly three years of writing and rewriting, O'Neill produced his tragedy of "brooding, fateful intensity," packed with murder, suicide and hints of incest. As presented on Broadway in 1931 it was acclaimed as a masterpiece of austere beauty. One of the few dissenting comments came from the late Robert Benchley, who praised the show but confessed that five hours in one seat had made him "cushion-conscious."

At the peak of his fame O'Neill directed his quest for tranquillity to Sea Island Beach, Georgia, where he built a seaside home. There he turned out two normal-length plays, *Days Without End*, a quick flop on Broadway, and *Ah, Wilderness!*, his only comedy. Surprisingly, as a spinner of homely humor about a happy New England family, O'Neill scored one of his biggest hits.

Humor and happiness were new notes for O'Neill. Taking stock about this time, Barrett H. Clark in his book *Eugene O'Neill, the Man and His Work*, wrote that of the thirty-six O'Neill plays he had seen or read, there were only five in which there was no murder, death, suicide or insanity. In the others he found a total of eight suicides and one unsuccessful attempt, twelve important murders, twenty-three deaths, nearly all due to violence, and seven cases of insanity.

In 1932 the O'Neills sold their new home in Georgia and migrated to the West Coast, where they thought the year-around climate would be more conducive to work. Near San Francisco they built "Tao House," named after Taoism, the Chinese philosophy of wisdom and peace, and O'Neill dug in to work on a herculean project. It was to be a nine-play cycle of American life from 1775 to 1932, entitled *A Tale of Possessors Self-Dispossessed*. He became virtually a recluse and sometimes for three months at a stretch saw nobody but his wife. He completed several plays, but by 1943 his health and the state of the wartime world so upset him that he was forced to abandon his cycle. His serenity was further disrupted by the news that his daughter, Oona, had married Charlie Chaplin, thus giving O'Neill a son-in-law only one year younger than himself. O'Neill disapproved of the marriage.

O'Neill has always eluded any cut-and-dried assessment. One of his oldest friends, Robert Edmond Jones, attributes the complexity of his genius to the diversity of its composing elements. There is, says Jones, an Irish O'Neill, a New England O'Neill, a Catholic O'Neill, a Monte Cristo O'Neill and a dozen other O'Neills. O'Neill's critics often discover that they are not even talking about the same man.

During a mass interview, before the opening of *The Iceman,* O'Neill came as close as he ever has to stating the core of his philosophy. "If the human race is so damned stupid," he said, "that in two thousand years it hasn't had brains enough to appreciate that the secret of happiness is contained in one simple sentence which you'd think any school kid could understand and apply, then it's time we dumped it down the nearest drain and let the ants have a chance. That simple sentence is, 'For what shall it profit a man if he shall gain the whole world, and lose his own soul.' "

O'Neill's last play, *Long Day's Journey into Night,* like the first plays of his career, is overlaid with the mysticism that the sea always held for him—the element that made him, as a young sailor aboard a square-rigger, feel "synchronized with the rhythm of life." *Life* is here privileged to quote for the first time [in 1946] a significant passage from the manuscript, spoken by a leading character, Edmund:

"You've just told me some high spots in your memories. Want to hear mine? They're all connected with the sea. Here's one. When I was on the Squarehead square-rigger, bound for Buenos Aires. Full moon in the Trades. The old hooker driving 14 knots. I lay on the bowsprit, facing astern, with the water foaming into spume under me, the masts, with every sail white in the moonlight, towering high above me. I became drunk with the beauty and singing rhythm of it, and for a moment I lost myself—actually lost my life.

I was set free! I dissolved in the sea, became white sails and flying spray, became beauty and rhythm, became moonlight and the ship and the high dim-starred sky! I belonged, without past or future, within peace and unity and a wild joy, within something greater than my own life, or the life of Man, to Life itself! To God, if you want to put it that way . . . and several other times in my life, when I was swimming far out, or lying alone on the beach, I have had the same experience. Became the sun, the hot sand, green seaweed anchored to a rock, swaying in the tide. Like a saint's vision of beatitude. Like the veil of things as they seem drawn back by an unseen hand. For a second you see—and, seeing the secret, are the secret. For a second there is meaning! Then the hand lets the veil fall and you are alone, lost in the fog again, and you stumble on towards nowhere, for no good reason! (*He grins wryly.*) It was a great mistake my being born a man. I would have been much more successful as a sea gull or a fish. As it is, I will always be a stranger who never feels at home, who does not want and is not really wanted, who can never belong, who must always be a little in love with death!"

THE DARK WINE
OF GENIUS

by Robert Coughlan

JANUARY 16, 1950

> *The story of Maurice Utrillo, a debauched alcoholic who painted some of the most serene yet arresting pictures of the modern era, appeared in* LIFE *a few years before Utrillo died. Although* LIFE *Staff Writer Robert Coughlan never met his subject, his re-creation of Utrillo, his family and his times shows what can be accomplished by skillful use of good research. Coughlan's study of Utrillo, which won several awards, was later expanded into a book.*

On December 26, 1883, in a room on the Rue du Poteau in a haphazard neighborhood of Montmartre, an eighteen-year-old girl called "Suzanne" Valadon gave birth to an illegitimate child. Montmartre then was still almost a suburb of Paris, with gardens and vineyards tucked away among the twisted old streets. But at the top of the hill in the area known as the Butte, where the streets fork off from an open square and interlace the upper slopes, the artists had established themselves in dozens of little courtyard studios. Here the girl had come each day, climbing up the hillside to pose and often staying on into the night to take part in the life of the district. She was beautiful and

135

undisciplined, a *gamine* of the streets; and somewhere on the Butte, with some man who has never been finally identified, she formed the liaison that resulted in the birth of her child. The baby was named Maurice. For years he had no surname but then was given one as casually as he had been conceived. A Spanish journalist named Miguel Utrillo, a friend of Suzanne's, offered his own out of sympathy for her, and it was duly recorded on the official register of the district: "Maurice Utrillo."

This child, so literally a product of the Montmartre art colony, grew up into a career exactly appropriate to his origin. For forty years he has been one of the important figures of modern art. His paintings hang in every gallery that pretends to cover the modern era and in leading private collections throughout Europe and the Americas. They hang also, in the form of reproductions, in many thousands of Main Street sitting rooms, for Utrillo's work is popular among ordinary people who simply like to look at something pleasant on a wall. Mostly they are scenes of Montmartre streets, squares or vistas. Sometimes they contain no human figures at all, and there rarely are more than a few, usually women, crudely painted, as static as wooden dolls, big-hipped and dressed in the fashion of forty years ago. It is the streets and buildings themselves that interest Utrillo; the physical Montmartre of ancient, stained walls, cafés with colored signs, red-tipped chimney pots, pitched roofs and the living geometry made by the little buildings set like children's blocks on the crooked streets. He paints them with love and respect and devotion, giving them a warmth of color and a dignity which they do not possess in fact. Above all, the pictures have an air of luminous peace, of quiet and strength.

That is an extraordinary thing about them. For Utrillo is a tormented man. In a milieu where neuroticism is almost a necessary card of admission, and where lunacy has so often accompanied genius that there is a tendency to confuse the two, he very early established his own legend. He was a drunkard at the age of thirteen. By the time he was eighteen he was a dipsomaniac and was ready to be sent off to an institution for the first of a series of "cures." The greater part of his life has been spent in the murky world of the alcoholic; and the record, like his life, is blurred. Now and then a scene looms into the foreground. . . .

1913, Montmartre. In the small hotel of his friend M. Gay. Utrillo has asked Gay to lock him in a back room on an upper story with his paints and canvases and not to let him out. All goes well until nightfall; then Utrillo begins to call from the room, to knock loudly, to beat and kick on the door. Gay holds to his promise. Utrillo shouts and then screams, careening around the room, upsetting paints, canvases, furniture. A crowd gathers outside. At last Utrillo breaks open the windows, jumps, lands unhurt and runs off into the night to search for a drink.

1921, a street in Paris. A drunken man lurches out of a *pissoir.* His clothing is dirty and disarrayed, his hair is matted and he is unshaven. He waves a half-empty bottle in one hand and shouts insults at the passers-by. It is Utrillo. The police come and take him away.

1924, No. 12 Rue Cortot, Montmartre. At the studio where Utrillo lives with his mother, grandmother and stepfather. He has been gone for two nights and a day, and Suzanne, fearing that he has had an accident, has spent the night looking for him. On the morning of the second day the police bring him. He is sober but half dead. His face is raw, his scalp is laid open and there is a bloody cloth around his head. The police say that they picked him up from a gutter and took him to jail, and there in his cell he beat his head against the walls and tried to kill himself.

Yet, to be set against such scenes as these, there are the pictures, more than two thousand of them, mostly of Montmartre, almost all with the soft and nearly classic serenity that no one has quite been able to imitate. Usually art reflects the personality of the artist; but there is no easy connection between Utrillo and his work. Nor is it enough to ask why he paints in a certain spirit, for the method of his art is equally surprising. Living in the time and place where modern art was born, among those who created it, he is perhaps the least "modern" of the important living painters. It is a mystery, the solution of which would perhaps furnish the key to the larger mystery of Utrillo's personality.

If no final solution may be ventured, there are at any rate certain pieces of evidence and certain clues. Some go back to Utrillo's birth, and others even further back, into the womb of modern art itself.

There is no accurate way to explain—or predict—the appearance of a great period in art. There have been only a few such times in the Western world. We seem to be at the tag end of one of them now. It is a period that has lasted just about eighty-five years, or not much more than the combined life span of Utrillo and his mother. Her life does much to explain his, and both reflect the era.

Marie-Clémentine ("Suzanne") Valadon was born in 1865 in the village of Bessines near Limoges, the illegitimate child of a peasant woman named Madeleine Valadon and an unknown father. Her mother soon moved to Paris, where she found work as a scrubwoman and seamstress, and settled with the child in Montmartre. Marie-Clémentine was left largely to grow up as she might, for the mother had to be out all day and a good part of the night to make their living.

Marie-Clémentine had blue eyes, a delightful figure and impudent manners, and since artists do not spend all their time thinking about theory, she soon became a popular model. Toulouse-Lautrec twice did her portrait. She worked a great deal for both Puvis de Chavannes and Renoir and is the subject of several of the latter's studies of nudes. She would pose for him naked in his garden, hidden by the big lilac bushes from the sight of passers-by.

One day she was late. Renoir became worried about her and walked down to her home to investigate. He found her with crayons, pastel sticks and a nearly finished self-portrait. In surprise and amusement he said, "You, too?" She was embarrassed and tried to put the picture away, but Renoir took it and then, with greater surprise, said, ". . . And you *hide* it?" The picture was good—amazingly good, considering that Marie-Clémentine had never had a lesson in drawing. It hangs now in the Museum of Modern Art in Paris.

At this time she was probably already pregnant with the child who was to become Maurice Utrillo. In the legend that has grown up about her and Utrillo a number of men—including Renoir, Degas, Puvis de Chavannes and Miguel Utrillo himself—have been named as the father.

Maurice grew into a strange little boy. He was attractive to look at, with a dark, sweet, almost girlish face, but he was intensely shy and very soon began to show the symptoms of emotional instability. He had temper tantrums, smiled rarely and stayed a good deal by himself; and when he met opposition he would threaten, "I'll break everything," or "I'll jump out of the window and kill myself." His grandmother Madeleine was puzzled. "He's a sweet darling," she would say, "but I wonder what he has in his blood. He frightens me sometimes."

When Maurice was seven his mother began an affair with a man named Paul Mousis, a well-to-do lawyer who worked for an importing company but who had many friends among the Montmartre artists and intellectuals. Mousis talked of marrying Suzanne—and five years later finally did so—but while he was kind to Maurice, he made it clear that he would never allow the boy to bear his name. Suzanne was distressed. The symbolic value of a "legitimate" surname for the child was important to her. To save her feelings, and at the same time oblige his friend Mousis with an easy gesture, Miguel Utrillo stepped forward with the solution already mentioned. A journalist, essayist, painter and architect of aristocratic Spanish lineage and high intellectual quality, Miguel Utrillo was one of the most respected of the Montmartre group. No name could have been better.

The arrangement pleased everyone but the boy. He saw little enough of his mother but was devoted to her, almost frantically so, and he could not bear to have a name different from hers. He went on calling himself Maurice Valadon. Eleven years later, when he began to paint, he signed his canvases with that name. For a while he compromised on M. U. Valadon and then settled on the invention, "Maurice Utrillo, V."—the V. for Valadon—the signature used on the great bulk of his work.

When he was twelve he was sent off to the Rollin *collège*, a preparatory school, and he traveled back and forth on the train every day like any commuter. He showed some flair for mathematics but for the most part did poorly. He preferred to spend his time across the street at the Café des Oiseaux where, with his liberal allowance, he could play host to his few friends. He drank wine, but as he grew older he found ways to get cognac and absinthe. Finally absinthe, a drink so deteriorating that its sale was finally prohibited in France, became his favorite. Mousis took him out of the Rollin *collège* and got him a job in a bank. He did well enough at the work, but his drinking and erratic behavior —once he broke an umbrella over a superior's head—made it impossible to keep him on. At eighteen the first serious signs of mental degeneration set in: he had tantrums during which he screamed with fury. At Mousis's insistence Suzanne put him in the nearby Ste. Anne asylum.

It was a Dr. Ettinger, a friend, who suggested that Maurice might be helped by an occupational therapy such as painting. After two months at Ste. Anne he was released, supposedly cured. But soon he began to drink again, and Suzanne remembered Dr. Ettinger's advice.

Maurice would do anything for her—except stop drinking. Disliking the idea, he nevertheless tried painting. He showed no particular talent for it. He went on in order to please her, however, and little by little began to find the rudiments of technique. He did not stop drinking, but his habits improved as he became more immersed in these experiments, and within two years he seemed well enough that he was allowed to go and live in Suzanne's studio on the Rue Cortot in Montmartre.

Although apartment buildings have replaced some of the old landmarks, the Rue Cortot is much the same now as it was then, a little, twisting street of cobblestones and plaster houses with doors that open into charming courtyards. For Maurice it evoked bittersweet, elusive memories. He could stand at a given corner and review all the scenes of his early childhood: down there the roofs of the Rue du Poteau, where he was born; that other street led to the elementary school where he had gone every day in his high-laced shoes, dark suit, cape and muffler and hard little black hat. Over there across from the vineyard was the Lapin Agile (Agile Rabbit), the café-restaurant where Valadon had met Renoir and where she had taken Maurice when he was five. Somewhere, in one of these studios or hotels or the back room of some café—he never knew where—he himself had been conceived. He began to paint the streets of Montmartre.

By that time other young men had already discovered the post-impressionists and were setting off to imitate and outdo them. Van Gogh had died thirteen years before, and in 1901 his work had been brought together in a retrospective show that caused great excitement among some of the young artists. Led by Matisse, Vlaminck, Roualt, Derain and Braque, they banded together under the name of *fauves* ("wild beasts") and began to paint with a distorted violence that made the mad Dutchman's work seem conservative. They lived and worked mostly in Montmartre, and Utrillo came to know them and even to be friends of a sort with a few of them.

But he remained outside their artistic orbit. They were theorists, who painted in their several ways because of thought-out convictions about form, composition, color values and the function-of-the-artist. He knew little about theory and painted because of a deep necessity to express something that he could not consciously define. Moreover he was in no condition to be swept up by a cause, for he was drinking again. He gave way gradually but surely, until at last, after a few years on the Butte, he was again a chronic alcoholic. He would drink anything. At some of the cafés it became an accepted sport to buy him wine and then, when he was too drunk to notice, to empty pipe ashes into his glass. Sometimes he carried a smoked red herring in his pocket to nibble at and increase his thirst.

One of his drinking friends was André Utter, an artist three years younger than he. They had met in 1904, when Maurice was visiting at Pierrefitte and Utter had gone to the same village for a holiday. Utter has described him as he was then: "Already he had that familiar look of a mountebank Hamlet, with his emaciated face and his disheveled hair. He gesticulated as he walked, talking loudly, clearly subject to some congenital nervous excitement which could not be appeased." After drinking awhile Maurice might begin to stare around the room, at the artists and the paintings and the girls, and suddenly begin to shout and break glasses.

When he was sober he was tractable enough—very shy, with an air of perpetual anxiety, but unassuming and even rather sweet in disposition. Up to a point, alcohol was a useful crutch to his personality. He could laugh and be companionable and look people in the face. Then, at a certain stage, something happened inside his mind, and he became capable of the most terrible violence. For a while he had a phobia against pregnant women, and when he saw them in the street he would chase them and pull their hair and try to kick them in the stomach.

Drunk or sober, however—and usually it was an intermediate point between the two—he went on painting, and gradually he worked out a style. Owing something to the impressionists in its use of color harmonies, something to the postimpressionists in its air of solidity, it nevertheless was his own individual and often masterful style. About 1909 he began his "white period," which lasted until 1914. It was so called because of his abundant use of zinc white —sometimes blended with white plaster—to record the luminous effect of sunlight on the white plaster houses and the stone and marble churches that he liked most to paint. The best of these pictures are valued now at about $8,000. At the time Utrillo disposed of them for whatever they would bring—often for a meal or a bottle of wine.

One of the first dealers to notice him was a former baker named Sagot, otherwise known as Sagot-the-Madman, who in 1905 began to buy a few paintings from him for prices ranging from a few sous to five francs (a franc was then worth twenty cents). In 1909 he was given a very small monthly retainer by another dealer named Louis Libaude, a former horse auctioneer who has been described as having "the air of a cardsharper in a hearse." In 1910 he took an armload of paintings over to the important Galerie Druet. He was half-drunk, and when M. Druet glanced at them and turned them down he had the courage and impudence to go into the street and try to hawk them to the passers-by. A critic named Francis Jourdain was there that day, however, and saw something in the paintings that Druet did not. He went to see more of them at Libaude's and later he brought friends. The word spread on the Butte that Utrillo had to be taken seriously as a painter.

By that time Suzanne Valadon was in her early forties. Although Mousis was not a demanding husband, he and the paraphernalia of conventional marriage took time, and she was becoming bored. Moreover her beauty was going: she had begun to drink a good deal, and the eroding effects of alcohol, the secret affairs she carried on and age itself had begun to show in her face. Through Maurice she had met Utter. He was young—twenty-one years younger than she— handsome, an artist and a thorough Bohemian. She began an affair with him in 1909. In 1911 she left Mousis entirely and, accompanied by her mother, went to live with Utter at the studio he shared with Utrillo in Montmartre. A few months later the four of them moved over to the Rue Cortot near her old studio, and there they settled. Utrillo drank and drank and drank and by the spring of 1912 he was in a sanitarium at Sannois.

The pattern was set and, with variations, it would repeat itself grotesquely over the next decade. Utrillo was soon released—"cured" again—and after a summer in Brittany came back to the Rue Cortot. In 1913 Libaude gave him a one-man show, and in the same year he was returned for a few months to Ste. Anne's. In 1914 Utter was drafted for the Army—Utrillo was of course rejected—and in a fit of sentiment Suzanne married him before he left for the front. In 1915 Grandmother Madeleine died at the age of eighty-five. The following year Utrillo was in another institution, this time an asylum for the really insane where he slept in a barred cell and where some of the other inmates, when they could, snatched his tubes of paint and ate them, thinking they were colored creams. He was released after eight months and went back to Montmartre, then again committed, again released and so on until by 1921 he had been in and out of institutions eight times since his first release from Ste. Anne's.

During this time he was not—except perhaps briefly—clinically insane. His behavior was strange and he always drank too much and was wholly irresponsible when drunk, but neither eccentricity nor alcoholism was a stigma on the Butte, so he was always welcomed back. Those garbled years, in fact, supplied some of the happiest human relationships of his life. His best friend was named César Gay, and it was not strange that he was a former police sergeant. Utrillo understandably had been on bad terms with the police during his earlier years, but the passage of time had bred mutual understanding. The police stopped mistreating him, and he learned always to go along with them peacefully. Once he even painted a picture of himself being led away. He kept a supply of paints and materials on hand at the station house, and the police, many of whom had become amateur artists themselves due to long association with the inhabitants of Montmartre, established the rule that he could not be released until he had done a picture or two for their collection. At last the chief had so many Utrillos that he used their backs for scratch pads.

Another great friend was the painter, Modigliani, as prodigious a drinker as he. Modigliani moved in 1910 from Montmartre to Montparnasse, on the Left Bank, where an artists' colony was forming—a colony that in time was to replace Montmartre as the chief center of modern painting. Utrillo would wander over now and then to make the rounds with him or, if both lacked money, to join him in peeling vegetables at Rosalie's restaurant for food and wine. Their climactic meeting occurred in 1919. Utrillo had escaped from a sanitarium and, knowing he would be looked for in Montmartre, had headed instead for Montparnasse. There he ran into his old friend, who happened to have money. They toured the cafés together, picking up a gallery as they went along. Modigliani would introduce Utrillo at each stop as, "The greatest painter in the world. He can drink more than anybody." Utrillo would reply modestly, "No, no, you are the greatest. You can drink more." During the evening they collected Zborowski, a dealer who had taken an interest in both of them, and the three ended near dawn in Modigliani's studio to sleep. When the others awoke, Utrillo was gone. So, it developed, was Modigliani's coat, which Utrillo had taken to sell so they could buy more wine. Zborowski finally found him after he had drunk up the coat and was about to sell his own coat and vest. After retrieving the pawned coat, he took him off to a hotel room in Montmartre. There he kept him hidden for several months, safe from the authorities, and supplied him with food, wine and materials while he painted. Modigliani died only a year later of drugs, alcohol and tuberculosis.

Of all the good friends Utrillo had in those days the best was an imagined one. She was Joan of Arc. He had had no religious training at all, but like every French schoolchild he had learned her story:

the protector and patron saint of France, the national symbol of chaste and noble womanhood. In these tormented years he became addicted to her. He found a small gold-plated statuette of her in a bazaar and thereafter carried it everywhere with him in his pocket. He would take it out and talk to it, telling it his troubles, and at night he would put it beside his bed.

During all this time—in and out of institutions, sometimes hiding from the police, his mother and Utter, or his own demons—he painted. Indeed his output would have been extraordinary for anyone in the best health, and for one in his condition it was fantastic. During the four war years he produced about a thousand paintings and drawings, an average of one every day and a half. It was not important to him where he happened to be. He had an extraordinary visual memory, and he had besides a carefully collected file of postcards, snapshots and newspaper pictures. They gave him the factual substance of his scenes, which he then molded and colored to suit himself. He painted some wonderful pictures of churches, some of streets in Paris and in nearby villages, but his favorite subject, the one he painted obsessively and insistently, remained Montmartre.

And at last real recognition began to come. In 1921 there was an exhibition of his and Valadon's works at the well-known Weill gallery, and later that year Francis Carco published a little book about him in a series called "New French Painters." Soon all the dealers were after him, skillfully egged on by André Utter, whose real *forte* was business. The money began to pour in. Utter, blandly telling of his own role later, referred to Utrillo as "the best commercial deal that had come up in half a century."

By 1924 he was famous. He was also back in a sanitarium. He spent the whole spring in one at Ivry, then again he was released and came back to the Rue Cortot. It was a few months later that the police delivered him to Suzanne bloody and near death and told her how he had tried to beat his brains out against the cell walls.

He had never tried suicide before. Now, at the moment of his first great triumph and deepest despair, Suzanne resolved to save him if she could. The year before, she and Utter had traded some of Utrillo's paintings for the Château de Saint-Bernard near Lyons,

250 miles south of Paris. She decided to go there with him and Utter to live. The autumn they put Utrillo in a car, his head still bandaged, and moved south. Thereafter, for a number of years, he disappeared from public notice. He still painted, though at a slower rate than before. In his bare room, furnished only with an iron bed, a straw-bottomed chair, an easel and his gilded statuette of St. Joan, he painted the remembered scenes of Montmartre.

Suzanne did her best to take proper care of him. But she was incapable of consistency. Her own paintings had become successful, and the role of the martyr mother could not attract her for long. She kept the studio on the Rue Cortot and she and Utter went back often, leaving Utrillo under the close guard of the servants. Now and again she would bring Utrillo back from the château, and they would all join in a family reunion. Gradually Utrillo was allowed to spend the winter months in Paris. And as her own alcoholism increased Suzanne became a less reliable guardian for him, until at last something resembling the previous state of affairs developed. Utrillo did not drink as much, but Suzanne and Utter drank more.

Into this demented atmosphere, one day in 1929, stepped Lucie Pauwels. She is now Mme. Utrillo: a rather short, stout woman of dynamic and forceful personality, endowed with endless energy and loquacity. She tells her own part of the story well.

"My husband collected paintings—he had exquisite taste—and he had some Utrillos. In the winter of 1929 M. Pauwels and I went up to Montmartre to look for Suzanne Valadon and Utrillo. We didn't know where they lived, so my husband went one way and I another. I had taken only a few steps when I saw approaching me a tiny little woman, looking a little like a jockey, with a portfolio of drawings under her arm. I said, 'Excuse me, Madame, but are you not the painter, Suzanne Valadon?' She smiled very warmly and replied, 'I am.' I quickly called my husband and we went together to the studio on the Rue Cortot.

"When we entered, Maurice was in that familiar pose of his—the elbow on the knee, face in palm of hand, eyes staring at the floor. When he looked up I could see a flash of admiration go over his face. But he was too well-bred to do anything about it. When we left that night Maurice said to his mother, his eyes filling with longing, 'Send me, send me a wife like Mme. Pauwels!' After that I used to go and see Suzanne Valadon often, and we became very good friends. I saw Maurice occasionally and I could tell how enamored of me he was, by my grace and beauty, but of course I was married." (The incomparable M. Pauwels died in 1933.)

One day in 1935 she received word that Suzanne Valadon was seriously ill at the American Hospital in Paris and was calling for her. "I hurried over to her. She was in a very bad condition. Her recovery took a long time, and I went to see her almost every day. While she was still in danger of death she said to me, 'What will happen to my poor Maurice if I die? Who will take care of him?' "

From then on Lucie took things into her capable hands. Utrillo invited her out to dinner and before the evening was over he had proposed. He had to produce his military card in order to get a license, and it developed that Suzanne had thrown it out long ago. Luckily he remembered the date and serial number, and Mme. Pauwels soon got a duplicate. She wanted a church wedding as well as a civil one, but Utrillo had never been baptised. In short order he was baptised and confirmed. Due to Suzanne's wild way with finances, Utrillo had no money for an engagement present or wedding ring, but Lucie managed that too. She found a metalsmith who traded a silver cigarette case and the rings for a small painting. Utrillo's clothes were a disgrace, for although he had plenty of them, everything was soiled and in disrepair. Lucie cleaned and mended the pants of the suit he was married in. The wedding took place in May, 1935, in Lucie's home town of Angoulême.

Suzanne Valadon died three years later. The two events, the marriage and his mother's death so soon afterward, revolutionized Utrillo's manner of life. Lucie kept him at Angoulême, where she devoted herself to the functions of wife and police matron. She let him paint only a little and meantime allowed none of his paintings to be sold. The result was that existing Utrillos quadrupled in value, and when finally she began to release new ones she got such good prices that she was able to buy a substantial villa at Le Vésinet, a rich suburb of Paris. Here she established Utrillo in an ironclad and antiseptic regimen that rarely varied.

To anyone who knew the Utrillo of old this is an astonishing place, with the air of a combined fortress, museum, pet market, seed company display, shrine and lovers' retreat. It is called La Bonne Lucie. The house, of confectioner's pink stucco with dove-gray trim, sits at the foot of a garden of neat rectangular lawns, potted plants, small trees and crushed stone walks, decorated with lifelike ceramics of frogs and turtles and two large marble statues of classic figures. On one side of the garden is a dog run for the prize Pekinese that Mme. Utrillo raises. On the other is a large aviary containing fifty parakeets of a variety developed by M. Pauwels in his days as a bird fancier. The house furnishings are ornate and varied, with sumptuous use of gilding, carving and tapestry. The main sitting room is dominated by two large murals of Montmartre by Utrillo and a three-foot granite statue of Joan of Arc. Here and there on the walls, printed in gold leaf, is a series of mottoes and sentiments such as, "It is here that they have linked in love their two lives, in the shadow of genius."

The house contains several dozen paintings by Utrillo and an almost equal number by Mme. Utrillo, who began to paint a few years ago. She signs her canvases "Lucie Valore," her stage name, and customarily refers to herself in that way. "Lucie Valore, Maurice Utrillo, Suzanne Valadon—none of them had any training in painting," she sometimes says. "It is truly incredible!" She paints in a "primitive" style—with crudely drawn figures and bright, flat colors—and her work is widely unappreciated. She knows how often great talent goes unnoticed, however, and is not discouraged.

She supervises every detail of Utrillo's business affairs and has handled them so well that he is wealthy now. In contrast to the time when he had no money for the wedding rings, he has been able to buy her a double rope of pearls and several extraordinarily large dia-mond-crusted rings. Her clothes come from the leading couturiers of Paris—not, Lucie explains, because of any vanity on her part but because, "I must dress in keeping with my name as the wife of the greatest painter in France."

The whole scene pleases Lucie almost beyond her powers to

148

express. "How wonderful it is for him here," she said recently. "What a change for the Master, my little Maurice, my genius! And it is I, Lucie Valore, who has done it all. I am the Joan of Arc!"

At first Utrillo sometimes seemed rebellious under her care. He would slip away to the village to look for wine, but scouting parties always found him before much damage was done. Once, in 1941, he escaped entirely. Lucie recalls this with emotion: "I looked all over the house and began to call, 'Maurice! Maurice! Maurice!' but there was no answer. We searched every place for him, the servants and I and the two English ladies next door, and called the police and all the cafés in the surrounding towns. To no avail! Finally I went to bed in such a terrible state. I felt that I would never see the Master, my wonderful genius, never again." But toward the end of the next morning Utrillo turned up, escorted by an officer of the private protective service that guards the neighborhood. He had been found wandering in the town. He had gotten drunk and, he told Lucie, had lost his way home and spent the night in an abandoned cabin in the nearby woods. After that heavy doors were put up at the front entrance, and Utrillo was given no more pocket money.

At sixty-six [in 1950] Maurice Utrillo is a small husk of a man with the tottering walk, the rheumy eyes, the skin folds and nervous tics and emaciated look of a Bowery character. He seems to live much of the time in a semicoma; again, the mists partly clear and he becomes almost animated, perhaps to make an ironical little joke, perhaps to raise his voice in a weak, hoarse shout and stamp his foot against some action or suggestion from Lucie or others around him. He lives by a minute routine imposed from without and within. He has become obsessively religious and every morning and evening spends an hour in the little chapel that has been built for him in back of the house. He has memorized the names of all the Saints' Days and pays his respects to each in series around the calendar. St. Joan still is his favorite. He has made pilgrimages both to Domremy, her birthplace, and to Orléans. He still has the little gilded statuette of her and has added other statues and medals. "Every day, many times, I kiss all my Joans of Arc," he told a visitor. "It's hard work but it's saintly work." On Sundays, after the regular services are over and the people have left, he is driven to the nearby church of St. Pauline, where a large statue of St. Joan stands on a side altar. He sits in a chair directly in front of it and spends an hour in solitary devotion.

The day of Suzanne Valadon's death he spends in his chapel, praying until he passes into a state of exhaustion. A room in the house has been made into a memorial for her and is hung with her drawings and paintings. He goes there every morning to spend time among the relics of this "noble woman, as beautiful as she is good," as he once described her in a poem, "this superwoman in human form."

He still drinks—but it is heavily watered wine and in quantities carefully supervised by Lucie and the three servants. Like many old alcoholics, he has reached the state where even a small amount makes him mildly intoxicated.

And he still paints. He has a little back room that faces the chapel and there, surrounded by his Joans of Arc and other religious objects, he works for about two hours each afternoon and for several hours each night. When he sits at the easel a transformation takes place, and the decrepit old man gives way to the confident artist. His hands are steady, and the long thin fingers, as clean and scrubbed as a surgeon's, apply the strokes without hesitation. He finishes about twenty pictures a year. Some of them are poor imitations of himself, but others are as deft and lovely as anything he has done since the white period. They are almost always scenes of Montmartre.

Recently he was asked whether he would like to live in Montmartre again. "The people there are all idiots—idiots!" he said. Then later: "There's not an hour that I don't think of it." And a little later: "I'm shut in out here and they won't let me go. I would rather be there than anywhere."

THE ART
OF EL GRECO

by Aldous Huxley

APRIL 24, 1950

Best known for his novels Point Counter Point *and* Brave
New World, *Aldous Huxley is also a biographer and a
versatile man of letters who has written discerningly
on painting and painters. His article on El Greco, the
mysterious Greek who was belatedly recognized as a
giant in art and the forerunner of modern painters, was
originally written for* LIFE. *It was later included in Huxley's
book of essays* Themes and Variations.

A century ago the man whom we now accept unquestioningly as an
Old Master was either completely ignored or, if known at all, despised.
For some critics El Greco was merely an incompetent who had never
learned drawing and did not know how to tell a story dramatically.
Others, with a more "scientific" turn of mind, explained him away as
a lunatic who suffered from uncorrected astigmatism and was there-
fore unable to see the world as it really is. Among English visitors
to Spain one of the few who genuinely admired El Greco was George
Borrow, traveler and linguist, author of the famous *The Bible in
Spain*. When, in 1837, Borrow first visited Toledo, he saw a picture

representing "the burial of the Count of Orgaz, the masterpiece of Domenico the Greek, a most extraordinary genius. . . . Could it be purchased, I should say it would be cheap at £5,000." In that year of Queen Victoria's accession the pound was a thing of fine gold, stuffed with purchasing power and still completely immune from income tax. To say that a painting was worth five thousand of these glorious objects was to express an admiration only just this side of idolatry. Even as late as 1890 one of the artist's few French admirers could say that there were not more than ten people in all Paris who cared for his work. It is only within the last forty years that El Greco has finally come into his own. Contemporary critics now recognize him for what, among other and odder things, he undoubtedly was—one of the most powerful painters of his day, and the lonely, the profoundly original precursor of what we now call "modern art."

Domenico Theotocopuli, whom we know by his Spanish nickname of El Greco, "the Greek," was born in 1541 near Candia, on the island of Crete.

Young Domenico presumably received a sound Greek education and studied painting under the best masters of the island. Not, however, for very long. Sometime in his early twenties he set sail for Venice. When he left that city a few years later he was described as "a pupil of Titian," who was then a very old man, but painting as well as, or even better than, he had ever done in his youth. Does this signify that El Greco actually worked as a pupil in Titian's studio? We cannot say. All that is certain is that he made a thorough study of Venetian art and that, having worked for a time according to its principles, he found it unsatisfactory. It could hardly have been otherwise. For his taste Venetian art was too pagan, too voluptuous, too decorative, too much concerned with appearances, insufficiently inward and serious. In search of an art more conformable to his own nature and ideals El Greco migrated in 1570 to Rome. But Rome, alas, proved to be no less disappointing than Venice. Her great masters of the Renaissance were all dead, and their successors were second-rate mannerists, incapable of creating anything new, and living parasitically upon the achievements of the past.

At some date prior to 1577 El Greco undertook yet another migration, this time to Spain. Here his wanderings came to an end. He settled in Toledo. With his Spanish wife, Jerónima de las Cuebas, and his son, Jorge Manuel, he remained there until his death in 1614. Of his life in Spain we know only a very little more than we know of his life in Crete and Italy—that is to say, next to nothing. Here are some of the scanty odds and ends of information that have come down to us:

Professionally, El Greco was successful. Many commissions came his way and he was well paid for his work. On several occasions he went to law with his ecclesiastical patrons in order to get his price. He had the reputation of spending his money with a lordly extravagance, and it was said that he paid an orchestra to make music while he ate his meals. His apartment on the verge of the great canyon of the Tagus River contained twenty-four rooms, most of which, however, were left almost completely unfurnished. Of his own genius he had no doubts. He knew that he painted superlatively well and he was quite ready to say so in public. Moreover, when Philip II and certain of the clergy objected to his pictures on the ground that they did not respect the norms of ecclesiastical art, he steadfastly refused to compromise and went on painting exactly as he thought fit. Like Tintoretto, he modeled small clay figures, with the aid of which he studied effects of lighting and foreshortening. Pacheco, the father-in-law of the great painter Velásquez, saw a whole cupboardful of these figures when he visited El Greco shortly before the latter's death.

Among the painter's friends were poets, men of learning, eminent ecclesiastics. His library, as we know from the inventory which was made after his death, contained, among other Greek works, the *Concerning Mystic Theology* of Dionysius the Areopagite. In the light of this fact, a curious anecdote recorded by Giulio Clovio, one of El Greco's Roman friends, takes on a special significance. "Yesterday," wrote Clovio in a letter which is still extant, "I called at [El Greco's] lodgings to take him for a walk through the city. The weather was very fine. . . . But on entering the studio I was amazed to find the curtains so closely drawn that it was hardly possible to see anything. The painter was sitting in a chair, neither working nor sleeping, and declined to go out with me on the ground that the light of day disturbed his inward light." From this it would appear that El Greco took more than a theoretical interest in the mystical states described by Dionysius and the Neo-Platonists: he also practiced some form of meditation.

Of El Greco's appearance we know nothing for certain. The so-called "Self-portrait" may perhaps represent the painter's features, but the evidence is inconclusive. At every turn the man eludes us. Only the pictures remain.

Like most of his predecessors and contemporaries, El Greco was mainly a religious painter, a teller of old familiar stories from the Gospels and the legends of the saints.

A picture that "tells a story" we call representational. It may tell the story, for example, of the Nativity, the story of Mars and Venus, the story of a certain landscape or a certain person as it or he appeared at a certain moment of time. But this story is never the whole story. A picture always expresses more than is implicit in its subject. Every painter who tells a story tells it in his own manner, and that manner tells another story superimposed, as it were, upon the first—a story about the painter himself, a story about the way in which one highly gifted individual reacted to his experience of our universe. The first story is told deliberately; the second tells itself independently of the artist's conscious will.

El Greco told religious stories in his own peculiar manner, and his manner tells another story, so enigmatic that we pore over it in fascinated bewilderment.

In looking at any of the great compositions of El Greco's maturity we must always remember that the intention of the artist was neither to imitate nature nor to tell a story with dramatic verisimilitude. Like the postimpressionists three centuries later, El Greco used natural objects as the raw material out of which, by a process of calculated distortion, he might create his own world of pictorial forms in pictorial space under pictorial illumination. Within this private universe he situated his religious subject matter, using it as a vehicle for expressing what he wanted to say about life.

And what *did* El Greco want to say? The answer can only be inferred; but to me it seems clear. Those faces with their uniformly rapturous expression, those hands clasped in devotion or lifted toward heaven, those figures stretched out to the point where the whole inordinately elongated anatomy becomes a living symbol of upward aspiration—all these bear witness to the artist's constant preoccupation with the ideas of mystical religion. His aim was to assert the soul's capacity to come, through effort and through grace, to ecstatic union with the divine spirit. This idea of union was more and more emphatically stressed as the painter advanced in years. The frontier between earth and heaven, which is clearly defined in such works as "The Burial of Count Orgaz" and "The Dream of Philip II," grows fainter in later works, and finally disappears altogether. Thus, in El Greco's final version of "The Baptism of Christ" there is no separation of any kind. The forms and colors flow continuously from the bottom of the picture to the top. The two realms are totally fused.

Does this mean that El Greco actually found a perfect pictorial expression for what his contemporary, St. Theresa of Avila, called "the spiritual marriage"? I think not. For all their extraordinary beauty, these great paintings are strangely oppressive and disquieting. Consciously El Greco was telling two stories—a story from the Gospels or the legends of the saints, and a story about mystical union with the divine. But, unconsciously, he told yet another story, having little or nothing to do with the two he knew he was telling. All that is disquieting in El Greco pertains to this third story and is conveyed to the spectator by his highly individual manner of treating space and the forms by which that space is occupied.

His pictures are neither flat nor fully three-dimensional. There is depth in his private universe, but only a very little of it. From the picture plane to the remotest object in the background there is, in most cases, an apparent distance of only a few feet. On earth as in heaven there is hardly room to swing a cat. Moreover, unlike Tintoretto and the baroque artists of the seventeenth century, El Greco never hints at the boundlessness beyond the picture frame. His compositions are centripetal, turned inward on themselves. He is the painter of movement in a narrow room, of agitation in a prison. This effect of confinement is enhanced by the almost complete absence from his paintings of a landscape background. The whole picture space is tightly packed with figures, human and divine, and where any chink is left between body and body, we are shown only a confining wall of cloud as opaque as earth, or of earth as fluidly plastic as the clouds. So far as El Greco is concerned, the world of nonhuman nature is practically nonexistent.

No less disquieting than the narrowness of El Greco's universe is the quality of the forms with which he filled it. Everything here is organic, but organic on a low level, organic to a point well below the limit of life's perfection. That is why there is no sensuality in these paintings, nothing of the voluptuous. In a work of art we are charmed and attracted by forms which represent or at least suggest the forms of such objects as we find attractive in nature—flowers, for example, fruits, animals, human bodies in their youthful strength and beauty. In life we are not at all attracted by protoplasm in the raw or by individual organs separated from the organism as a whole. But it is with forms suggestive precisely of such objects that El Greco fills his pictures. Under his brush the human body, when it is naked, loses its bony framework and even its musculature, and becomes a thing of ectoplasm—beautifully appropriate in its strange pictorial context, but not a little uncanny when thought of in the context of real life. And when El Greco clothes his boneless creatures, their draperies become pure abstractions, having the form of something indeterminately physiological.

A painter or a sculptor can be simultaneously representational and nonrepresentational. In their architectural backgrounds and, above all, in their draperies, many works even of the Renaissance and the baroque incorporate passages of a most unadulterated abstraction. These are often expressive in the highest degree. Indeed, the whole tone of a representational work may be established, and its inner meaning expressed, by those parts of it which are most nearly abstract.

In some of El Greco's paintings a third, a half, even as much as two-thirds of the entire surface is occupied by low-level organic abstractions, to which, because of their representational context, we give the name of draperies, or clouds, or rocks. These abstractions are powerfully expressive and it is through them that, to a considerable extent, El Greco tells the private story that underlies the official subject matter of his paintings.

Within his own Byzantine-Venetian tradition El Greco combined representation with abstraction in a manner which we are now accustomed to regard as characteristically modern. His peculiar treatment of space and form seems to tell a story of obscure happenings in the subconscious mind—of some haunting fear of unlimited extension, some dream of security in the imagined equivalent of a womb. The conscious aspiration toward union with the divine spirit, which is what El Greco was trying to express, is overridden by a subconscious longing for the consolations of some ineffable uterine state. In these paintings there is no redemption of time by eternity, no transfiguration of matter by the spirit. On the contrary, it is the low-level organic that has engulfed the spiritual and transformed it into its own substance.

When we think of it in relation to the great world of human experience, El Greco's universe of swallowed spirit and visceral rapture seems, as I have said, curiously oppressive and disquieting. But considered as an isolated artistic system, how strong and coherent it seems, how perfectly unified, how fascinatingly beautiful! El Greco was supremely a painter, and a reproduction cannot do justice to the richness of his textures and his astonishing use of color. His career as a colorist was a progress from Venetian warmth toward a frigid brilliance, whose astounding apotheosis is seen in the great "Assumption of the Virgin." Here, as usual, heaven is only a few feet deep; but it is no Black Hole of Calcutta. Call it rather an "iridescent hole," cold and bright as one of those caves of ice at the foot of a glacier.

El Greco's antipathy to warm tones is manifest in most of his later paintings. No warmth of local color is ever permitted to creep into the shadows which, in the portraits, are produced (so far as one can see) by lightly scumbling black into the pale flesh tints. In his color, as in his drawing, in his treatment of space and in the quality of his forms, El Greco remains strictly himself, with none but a collateral artistic ancestry and no direct artistic descendants. There he stands alone, the strangest and the most solitary figure in the whole history of European painting.

THE PRIVATE
WORLD OF
WILLIAM FAULKNER

by Robert Coughlan

SEPTEMBER 28, 1953

In this article by LIFE *Staff Writer Robert Coughlan, the
literary output of Novelist William Faulkner is examined
against the background of the melodramatic events and
the passionatae people who inspired it. In 1949
Faulkner won the Nobel Prize for Literature, the fourth
American writer to be so honored.*

Jefferson, the county seat of Yoknapatawpha County, in northern
Mississippi, is a pretty town with an old brick courthouse, pillared and
porticoed, on a big central square, and a number of big, white-pillared
houses set in broad lawns, although some of the finest homes were lost
when General Smith partially burnt the town in 1864. Jefferson has
practically no manufacturing but lives on, and in turn nourishes, the
surrounding countryside, which is given over largely to cotton and
lumbering. A passing stranger would find little to distinguish the town
and the county from many such towns and counties in Mississippi or
in all that area of the deep South. Nor is it likely that he would think

the people different from others in that domain. If the stranger were a Southerner he would feel very much at home there.

Given omniscience, however—the literary omniscience of a novelist, for instance—and suspended from a large gas bag (also useful equipment for novelists) so as to obtain a wide view of the countryside, he would discover that the peaceful aspect was an illusion. Indeed, looking into the hearts and minds and studying the actions of most of the adult white population, he would be appalled at what he saw.

Peering down on Frenchman's Bend, a hamlet in the southeast part of the county, he would find a man named Flem Snopes cheating and manipulating his neighbors until at last he controlled them all, marrying the daughter of his most important victim, swindling and driving a farmer insane with a nonexistent buried treasure and moving on to Jefferson with his tribe of decadent relatives to corrupt that town. At this same hamlet years later (the omniscient aerialist can also telescope time as novelists do) he would see a college girl named Temple Drake falling into the hands of a gunman named Popeye, who rapes her in a macabre way and afterward installs her in a Memphis house of prostitution and engages a friend to violate her further, whereupon she becomes a victim of passion. Popeye eventually is executed for a crime he did not commit and Temple's father takes her to Paris.

Drifting away from Frenchman's Bend, the aerialist would study with horrified interest the tribulations of the Bundren family. Addie Bundren, a hill woman, dies and her coffin is built. On the long trip by wagon to the cemetery at Jefferson, accompanied by her shiftless husband, her pregnant unmarried daughter and her four sons, her body putrefies and attracts vultures. The coffin is swept away in a flooded river but is recovered, nearly burns in a barn fire but is saved, and is buried at last. One son is led from the graveside to a lunatic asylum. Another, the youngest, believes his mother is a fish. The father, having cheated a third son of his horse, and his daughter of the money her lover had given her for an abortion, buys new false teeth and marries a woman from whom he had borrowed some shovels to dig his wife's grave. She has a phonograph, and the eldest boy thinks it will be nice to have music in the home.

Bearing north over the pine hills and eroded cotton land until he neared Jefferson, the aerialist would arrive over Compson's Mile and would be shocked to see the situation to which this once-great plantation and once-great family had fallen. There are the parents and their four children: the father alcoholic, the mother neurasthenic, the daughter pregnant with a stranger's child, one son an idiot, another selfish and villainous, still another proud, romantic but weak. He would see this last-named boy, Quentin, pretend that he had committed incest with his sister and commit suicide; see the idiot brother castrated and sent to an institution; see the sister marry, divorce and give herself to lovers; see the wicked brother hound her illegitimate daughter and drive her away, sell the old plantation house and use the proceeds to establish himself as a cotton broker and to acquire a mistress, a Memphis prostitute.

Farther north there is the sound of gunfire. The aerialist swings in a favoring current and views a wild scene: horsemen galloping, Negroes stampeding toward a river, an old woman burying treasure, boys crouched in the bushes shooting at a Yankee soldier, the old woman being shot, the same boys tracking her assassin, flaying him and nailing his skin to the door of a cotton compress. But amidst all the tumult the overpowering figure of Colonel John Sartoris is seen in actions of amazing initiative and gallantry. He raises a regiment in Jefferson and gallops off to Manassas; demoted by his own men, who elect an upstart named Sutpen to his command, he returns to Jefferson, raises a new troop and gallops off again, this time to serve with General Forrest's raiders. The Civil War over, he disciplines the carpetbaggers, builds a railroad the length of the county and is shot dead by a scoundrel.

The colonel's heirs live on in the shadow of his memory. His son becomes president of the bank in Jefferson and dies of heart failure brought on by the reckless driving of his great-grandson. His grandson is scarcely seen, living only long enough to marry and produce this great-grandson and his twin brother, both of whom are pilots in the First World War. One twin is killed in France. The other, obsessed with this event and blaming himself for it, lives in spiritual torment and at last kills himself testing an experimental airplane.

Off to the northwest there is a commotion in the forest: wild, naked Negroes felling trees, heaving and sweating, dragging huge logs, sawing them into boards, at last rearing a splendid house surrounded by a lovely park and sweeping fields. A big, grim-faced man gallops about on horseback: he is Sutpen, the same who would (later) oust Colonel Sartoris from the command of the regiment. He must build a dynasty and this great house to shelter it but his plans are doomed. Sutpen disowns his first son when he discovers that there is Negro blood in the mother's family. The son falls in love with Sutpen's daughter by a second marriage and is killed by his half-brother who becomes a fugitive. Coming home years later, the half-brother dies in a fire that consumes the house. Sutpen meantime, ruined by the Civil War but still hoping for a son to whom he can pass his name and ambitions, seduces the granddaughter of a squatter and is killed by him.

In the far north of the county there is the wilderness. Indians can be seen in their villages, then the Indians disappear and white men and boys come and set up camps and hunt for game (especially for one huge, crafty old bear), and then the wilderness itself disappears as the timber companies move in. The aerialist drifts south again and hovers over Jefferson, that deceptively quiet town. There Temple Drake can be seen, married now and working out a tortured sequel to her earlier mishaps. Here and there on the streets is a Compson or a Sartoris or a friend of those families, an Edmonds, De Spain or McCaslin, but the town seems to be overrun with Snopeses. The Snopeses are everywhere, even in the Sartoris bank. Odd and terrible things are happening. Joe Christmas, illegitimate and probably part Negro, is put in an orphanage, then adopted by a stern and righteous farmer and his wife. Joe beats the farmer and steals the wife's savings, has an affair with the spinster descendant of Yankees, kills her and is pursued around the county and captured. His own grandfather incites a mob to lynch him. But he escapes, only to be hunted down by a patriotic young man named Percy Grimm who shoots and mutilates him.

Meantime a girl named Lena Grove, pregnant by Christmas' partner in the bootlegging business, has journeyed on foot from Alabama to find him so he can claim the child. But he flees and she goes to Tennessee with her baby.

Here too is seen Lucas Beauchamp, an old Negro accused of murder and about to be lynched. But he is saved by the courage of a white boy, a Negro boy and an old maid. And here also, among many other scenes of horror and bravery, can be found an old woman who, fearing that her husband would leave her, has killed him and has dressed him in his best and laid him on his bed and keeps him thus until he becomes a mummy.

The aerialist is, of course, imaginary, but so are Jefferson and Yoknapatawpha County. The town and county—it can be said with relief—are the literary invention of William Faulkner, who is their "sole proprietor." The stories sketched above in briefest outline form part of the subject matter of these of his works, in order: *The Hamlet, Sanctuary, As I Lay Dying, The Sound and the Fury, The Unvanquished, Sartoris, Absalom, Absalom!, The Bear, Requiem for a Nun, Light in August, Intruder in the Dust,* and his most famous short story, "A Rose for Emily".

If Jefferson and Yoknapatawpha County bear a resemblance in many details to Lafayette County, Mississippi, and its county seat of Oxford, where Faulkner lives, it is still true, however one may feel about the events he makes happen there, that in inventing them he has achieved one of the most impressive feats of imagination in modern literature. His accomplishment was recognized most notably in 1950 when he received the Nobel Prize for literature. He has been given many other honors, among them the William Dean Howells Medal of the American Academy of Arts and Letters and the rank of Officer in the French Legion of Honor.

William Faulkner is a small, wiry man of fifty-six [in 1953] with close-cropped iron-gray hair, an upswept mustache of a darker color, a thin, high-bridged aquiline nose, heavy-lidded and deeply set brown eyes in which melancholy, calculation and humor variously are reflected, and a face tanned and webbed, especially near the eyes, with the creases and lines and tiny tracings of advancing middle age and the erosion of many days spent in the open in all weathers. He is entirely self-possessed, with a manner easy, courteous, speculative and deadly. He is a quiet man; yet when he is at ease, with his short legs out-stretched and a blackened pipe in his thin lips, and perhaps a drink at his elbow, he is like a somnolent cat who still in the wink of an eye could kill a mouse. Faulkner does not look or act like what he is. He acts like a farmer who has studied Plato and looks like a river gambler. In his appearance there is something old-fashioned, even archaic.

Oxford, like Faulkner's imaginary town of Jefferson, lies in the northern part of Mississippi and has a population of about four thou-sand. It is intensely and unmistakably a town of the deep South, not only in its appearance but in its smells, its manners and morals, the speech and properties of its citizens. Faulkner lives in one of its most beautiful houses, built circa 1840 by an Irish planter remembered as Colonel Shegog. It had fallen into terrible decay, but Faulkner grad-ually has restored it since he bought it in 1930 and now it is in good shape, although several rooms remain to be done over.

It seems to a visitor that Oxford, the house and the physical aspect of Faulkner himself are a continuum, that they have the organic relationship of a bird in a tree in a woods or a frog on a log in a swamp. The town in turn is organic to the state, and Mississippi, undoubtedly, is organic to the South. Faulkner in his setting is thus like a good if romantic painting in which every element is conceived in proportion and with harmony of line and color.

Where the continuum breaks is in the character and personality of William Faulkner himself. He prefers to be an enigma and one can believe that he will always remain one, even to himself, for his in-consistencies go beyond artistic license or mere eccentricity. His is not a split personality but rather a fragmented one, loosely held together by some strong inner force, the pieces often askew and sometimes painfully in friction. It is to ease these pains, one can guess, that he escapes periodically and sometimes for periods of weeks into alcohol-ism, until his drinking has become legendary in the town and in his profession, and hospitalization and injections have on occasion been necessary to save his life. After one of these episodes he returns for a relatively long period to an existence of calm sobriety: he is not an alcoholic but perhaps more accurately an alcoholic refugee, self-pursued.

The war within can be seen in many aspects. He is thoughtful of others and oblivious of others; he is kind and he is cruel; he is courtly and he is cold; he is a philosopher at large who has no integrated philosophy; he loves the South and feels revulsion for the South; he is a self-effacing but vain man who longed for recognition and rebuffed it when it came; a man of integrity who has contributed to a false legend about himself. Of much more serious importance, he is a great writer and a bad writer. His best work ranks with the best in the world, and his worst ranks, if not with the worst, then with the merely mediocre, with the potboilers and self-conscious effusions of experimental Art—"flagpole sitting," as he had called it—which he (or one part of him) scorns.

One of the virtues of Faulkner's best work is its sense of the past, so that every event is seen in deep perspective, colored and shaded like a forest floor, where today's growth feeds and blooms on the refuse of the past and will itself become food for the future. This derives from his own sense of the past: the past of the South, of his county and town and especially of his family. For the Sartoris family, whose exploits and agonies occupy one novel and one volume of short stories and who appear as leading or supporting characters in many of the other works, have a basis in reality. They are, in fact, the Falkners (or Faulkners), as seen from William Faulkner's point of view and as molded by him to suit the needs of fiction.

Like any contemporary Sartoris, William Faulkner can be comprehended only in relation to far-off events, not simply those of his own childhood but of generations preceding. He is the product and to some extent the victim of circumstances whose beginning can be dated in 1839 with a characteristic scene of Faulknerian violence.

In that year (as it is told in the Falkner family) William Cuthbert Faulkner, his great-grandfather, then aged fourteen, quarreled with his younger brother James, bloodied his head with a hoe, and was so severely whipped by his father that he ran away from home (this was in Missouri, whither the parents had migrated from Tennessee) to Ripley, Mississippi. There he had an uncle, a schoolteacher named

John Wesley Thompson. He arrived after many difficulties to find that his uncle was in jail at Pontotoc, the county seat, charged with murder.

At Pontotoc his uncle arranged for the boy to be fed and lodged until the trial was over. Thompson was acquitted and took William into his home at Ripley and treated him as his son. While in jail Thompson had read law and afterward set himself up as a lawyer. William worked as his clerk, studied law and finally became his uncle's partner. He married a Knoxville girl named Holland Pearce and they had a son, John Wesley Thompson Faulkner. But Holland Pearce soon died and when the Mexican War came William volunteered as a private. He was a captain when he came back at the war's end.

With the outbreak of the Civil War William raised a volunteer regiment, the 2nd Mississippi, and rode off at its head to take part in the first Battle of Bull Run. Evidently he was a daring soldier, but the same hot temper that had started his adventures remained unchecked and he made enemies among his men. At the yearly election of officers they chose another leader and demoted him from command. Thereupon he rode back to Ripley, raised another regiment of volunteers, the 7th Mississippi Cavalry, and galloped off, again a colonel, to serve with gallantry under the command of Nathan Bedford Forrest.

Afterward he came back to his law practice and took a leading part in the reconstruction of Ripley and its surrounding Tippah County. Soon—by 1868—he had conceived the idea which was to dominate the rest of his life and which eventually would cause his death. He decided to build a railroad to link Ripley with the commerce of the middle South, up to Middleton, Tennessee, and with that purpose enlisted a partner named Richard J. Thurmond, a local banker and lawyer. In 1872 the road was finished.

Probably it was about this time—the family records are not clear —that the colonel changed the spelling of his name. There were, so the story goes, "some no-good people named Faulkner down around Pontotoc" and, as Colonel Faulkner's prestige grew, so did his irritation at being asked if he were related to them. Finally he dropped the "u," becoming Falkner, to put an end to it.

To his already full life he now added authorship. In 1880 he produced *The White Rose of Memphis,* a melodramatic novel that became one of the great popular successes of its era: it sold 160,000 copies and ran through 35 editions, and was reissued in 1952. Two years later he wrote *The Little Brick Church,* designed as "an answer to *Uncle Tom's Cabin* from the South." In 1884 he brought out *Rapid Ramblings in Europe.*

Writing was only a pastime, however. The railroad remained his preoccupation, becoming finally almost an obsession. In 1887-88 he and Thurmond had extended the line south to Pontotoc. His ultimate goal was Gulfport, far to the southeast. Thurmond objected and, since he was as strong-willed and short-tempered as the colonel, their argument developed into a rancorous feud. It was finally agreed that they would draw lots, the winner to buy out the loser at the latter's own price. Thurmond lost and set his price so high that no one imagined Falkner could pay it. But he sent couriers around the town and county to all the members of his old 7th Cavalry. From their small private caches, from fruit jars, strongboxes and secret chimney recesses came enough so that, together with the money he could borrow in New York against his own half-interest, he could meet the payment, with less than a thousand dollars to spare. Soon afterward he ran for the state legislature so that he could steer a rate increase bill through its course.

Thurmond filed against him for the legislature and lost. A few hours after the election results were announced, Falkner was passing Thurmond's office. Just outside the door he was stopped by several of Thurmond's henchmen. They said they wanted to congratulate him. He chatted with them for a few moments and then (according to the Falkner family version) turned to see Thurmond standing inside the doorway leveling a pistol at him. The shot struck him in the mouth and the ball lodged in his throat. He died that night.

Thurmond was tried for murder but pleaded self-defense and produced witnesses to swear that Colonel Falkner had drawn first. The town considered this credible, as he had shot and killed other men over antagonisms less deep than he felt for Thurmond. The trial resulted in acquittal and Thurmond moved to North Carolina, where he made a new fortune in textiles.

William Faulkner's readers will have no difficulty in identifying Colonel Falkner as the Colonel John Sartoris of *Sartoris, The Unvanquished* and various other novels and stories. It is all there, colored and modeled, naturally, in the interests of fiction and magnified to heroic proportions, so that Colonel Sartoris becomes the quintessence of his time and class, yet perhaps no more magnified in the fiction than in the Falkner family.

William Faulkner descends from him through the line of John Wesley Thompson Falkner, the only child of Holland Pearce. John was known as "the young colonel," an honorary title which, it is explained in the Falkner family, he "inherited" from his father, who is referred to as "the old colonel." John Wesley Thompson Falkner married Sallie Murry and had three children, a girl named Holland and known as "Antee" (pronounced Aunt T), a boy named John Wesley Thompson Falkner ("J. W. T. II," now Judge Falkner of Oxford), and Murry. The latter married Maud Butler of Oxford ("Miss Maud") and became the father of four sons, among whom the first was William Faulkner, born on September 25, 1897, at New Albany, Union County, about thirty-five miles from Oxford.

How the Falkners moved from New Albany to Oxford, an event of considerable importance in literary history—since otherwise, presumably, the Jefferson of the stories would resemble New Albany and would be populated by a different cast of characters—forms still another epic of Sartoris-Falkner derring-do.

The first home in Oxford was a fine old house on Van Buren Avenue, with stained glass in the windows and huge oak trees on a long expanse of green lawn. When William was about five they moved to a house on South Lamar, a few doors away and across from the young colonel's mansion; near also to the house where Miss Maud now lives; and near the Oldhams, whose eldest daughter Estelle was to become William's youthful sweetheart and later his wife. In this house he passed his boyhood. At school, when the teacher would ask the children to stand up and tell the class what they wanted to be when they grew up, Billy—Leo Calloway, his seat mate in the third grade, now a rural mail carrier, remembers that it was always the same—would rise and say, "I want to be a writer like my great-granddaddy."

And looking back now, his family can see, as his uncle J. W. T. II says, "He never *was* nothin' but a writer." The quality that is called creativeness in a writer is closely akin to lying and, in turn, to what in children is called "imagination." Billy was a storyteller of such precocity that even then he could use the gift to avoid unpleasant work: his playmates did his chores while he entertained them with tales. His cousin Sally, Antee's daughter, remembers, "It got so that when Billy told you something, you never knew if it was the truth or just something he'd made up." Perhaps the real world and the world of imagination have never since that time been really separated in Faulkner's mind, and what might be exaggeration or broken promises or even lying in others can be equated in him, as undoubtedly he equates it, with personal honesty.

This imagination could not fail to be deeply stirred by the stories of the old colonel; nor, later, could it be unmoved by the contrast between the present and the past, a contrast not only in the physical aspect of the land and forests, and not only in the spirit that marked the old colonel's time and his own, but in the situation of his family. The young colonel (the elder Bayard Sartoris of the stories) was a venerable figure of Faulkner's childhood, a dignified and also an exceptionally stubborn man of whom it has been said, "When he was sot, a meetin' house wasn't no sotter." He improved and extended the railroad and branched out in Oxford as a local capitalist, becoming president of the First National Bank. When he lost control of it to a shrewd back-country financier named Joe Parks (Bayard's loss of the Sartoris bank to Flem Snopes is mentioned in several stories), he withdrew all his money and, so the legend goes, put it in a water bucket, carried it across the courthouse square and deposited it in the rival bank.

In his younger son Murry, William Faulkner's father, the fire that drove the old colonel had burnt itself almost to an ash. He dropped out of his class at Ole Miss, worked fitfully at a number of jobs, excelling at none, and became a conductor on the family railroad. This was his job at the time William was born.

Looking around him at other Oxford families, William Faulkner could see that this was not unusual, that what had happened to the Faulkners evidently was part of a larger socio-historical event. To a considerable extent his books seem to be an attempt to grope through to an explanation of this event.

It has been a process often inconsistent in purpose, in method, in thought and in the literary quality of its results. Reading the books is a good deal like mining for gold. The finest ones are *The Sound and the Fury, As I Lay Dying, Light in August* and *The Hamlet*. The worst are *Mosquitoes, Pylon* and the novelette called *The Wild Palms*. The intervening strata are occupied by *Soldier's Pay* and *Sartoris*, both competent but undistinguished; *Absalom, Absalom!* a long, undisciplined and difficult novel with patches of splendid writing; *Sanctuary*, Faulkner's most famous book, roughly half gold and half dross; its sequel, *Requiem for a Nun*, mostly trash; *Intruder in the Dust*, a good mystery story badly confused by Faulkner's theories on the race problem in the South; *The Bear*, a fine symbolic nature story marred by a turgid and discursive ending; *Old Man*, another novelette, a great story of a convict adrift on a Mississippi flood; and the many short stories, some of them, like "A Rose for Emily" and "Red Leaves", as superb in their medium as his best novels, some others pointless or dull or both.

In Faulkner's writing, life has no meaning except to the individual. There is no moral law beyond what in an older day might have been called "the code of the gentleman": "courage and honor and pride, and pity and love of justice and of liberty." But to keep this code brings no rewards beyond self-respect, it brings no salvation, no protection, for the "good" and "bad" characters are damned impartially to futility. The rare exceptions are made usually for "bad" people, who triumph over what, in any ordinary lexicon, would be called virtue.

Yet, while so often rewarding the "bad" and penalizing or frustrating the "good," Faulkner usually leaves no doubt as to who is who. A substantial part of his work is concerned with the theme of Sartoris *vs*. Snopes. The Sartoris family and their like are the leaders of the old South, sometimes weak and sometimes wrong but fundamentally good, noble and brave, while the Snopeses and their allies have arisen largely from the former poor whites, who by deceit and greed have gradually taken the power that the Sartorises once maintained. It is not, however, a simple contest between good and evil, for the Sartorises themselves are stained. It was they who brought slavery to the South and this great sin, in Faulkner's mystical reckoning, has had to be expiated: their defeat in the Civil War, the ordeal of Reconstruction, the emotional and moral decadence that has overtaken them, leaving them helpless before the onslaught of the Snopeses, are all beads of penance on a rosary that has no end.

Faulkner has occasionally seemed to have intimations of God, but these are so vague in his work that evidently they have no relevance to any major theme. Instead it is the land itself that has imposed the penance. Slavery put a curse on the land, and the land put a curse on the Sartorises which can be lifted only (if ever) by generations of damnation. Meantime what Faulkner calls the "legal fiction" of ownership of the land has fallen to the Snopeses, who cut its forests, let its farms erode and its rivers silt, take everything from it and give nothing, until, for instance, Mississippi has become the poorest state per capita in the Union. But the land takes its retribution against the Snopeses, by making them hollow men and women, as impotent emotionally and spiritually as Popeye, the Snopesian city gunman in *Sanctuary*, is impotent physically.

Thus the land itself, the living earth, is hero, God and protagonist in Faulkner's work as a whole. "People don't own land," one of his characters says, "It's the land that owns the people." If Faulkner has a philosophy this may be its distillation, although it is less a philosophy than a mystique, a kind of religious revelation.

The grandiose exploits of the early Sartorises, as well as the decay of the younger ones, the growth of the disease of Snopesism, the cannibalizing of both Sartorises and inattentive Snopeses by aggressive Snopeses, the stories of hill families and dedicated barbers, animals and children and Negroes, college girls and sheriffs, convicts and preachers, lawyers and gamblers and bootleggers and sewing machine salesmen and hunters and all the other immense cast of characters Faulkner has assembled, and the rape, robbery, incest, murder, suicide, fratricide, dope addiction, alcoholism, idiocy, insanity, grave robbery, miscegenation, necrophilia, adultery, fornication, prostitution, lynching, treachery, selfishness, ingratitude, horror, gallantry and courage which embellish his plots are not the recordings of a naturalist, but are the symbolic expressions of Faulkner's outrage and revulsion at what he conceived to be the tragedy of William Faulkner, of the South and of Man.

Charles Gary Solin

THE AMERICAN CENTURY

by Henry R. Luce

FEBRUARY 17, 1941

> *The reader should note well the date of authorship of this article—nearly a year before Pearl Harbor. At that time President Roosevelt was assuring the public that "your boys are not going to be sent into any foreign wars"; and scarcely a politician or editor disputed him.*
>
> *"The American Century" predicted that the United States would and must go into the war; would win it; would undertake the reconstruction of the postwar world and be the generator of the great human ideas of freedom and justice. Says the author today: "The great ideas have not yet prevailed on a world scale; that is part of the prediction and of the advocacy that still hangs in the balance."*

We Americans are unhappy. We are not happy about America. We are not happy about ourselves in relation to America. We are nervous —or gloomy—or apathetic.

As we look out at the rest of the world we are confused; we don't know what to do. "Aid to Britain short of war" is typical of halfway hopes and halfway measures.

As we look toward the future—our own future and the future of other nations—we are filled with foreboding. The future doesn't seem to hold anything for us except conflict, disruption, war.

There is a striking contrast between our state of mind and that of the British people. On September 3, 1939, the first day of the war in England, Winston Churchill had this to say: "Outside the storms of war may blow and the land may be lashed with the fury of its gales, but in our hearts this Sunday morning there is Peace."

Since Mr. Churchill spoke those words the German Luftwaffe has made havoc of British cities, driven the population underground, frightened children from their sleep, and imposed upon everyone a nervous strain as great as any that people have ever endured. Readers of *Life* have seen this havoc unfolded week by week.

Yet close observers agree that when Mr. Churchill spoke of peace in the hearts of the British people he was not indulging in idle oratory. The British people are profoundly calm. There seems to be a complete absence of nervousness. It seems as if all the neuroses of modern life had vanished from England.

In the beginning the British government made elaborate preparations for an increase in mental breakdowns. But these have actually declined. There have been fewer than a dozen breakdowns reported in London since the air raids began.

The British are calm in their spirit not because they have nothing to worry about but because they are fighting for their lives. They have made that decision. And they have no further choice. All their mistakes of the past twenty years, all the stupidities and failures that they have shared with the rest of the democratic world, are now of the past. They can forget them because they are faced with a supreme task—defending, yard by yard, their island home.

With us it is different. We do not have to face any attack tomorrow or the next day. Yet we are faced with something almost as difficult. We are faced with great decisions.

We know how lucky we are compared to all the rest of mankind. At least two-thirds of us are just plain rich compared to all the rest of the human family—rich in food, rich in clothes, rich in entertainment and amusement, rich in leisure, rich.

And yet we also know that the sickness of the world is also our sickness. We, too, have miserably failed to solve the problems of our epoch. And nowhere in the world have man's failures been so little excusable as in the United States of America. Nowhere has the contrast been so great between the reasonable hopes of our age and the actual facts of failure and frustration. And so now all our failures and mistakes hover like birds of ill omen over the White House, over the Capitol dome and over this printed page. Naturally, we have no peace.

But, even beyond this necessity for living with our own misdeeds, there is another reason why there is no peace in our hearts. It is that we have not been honest with ourselves.

In this whole matter of War and Peace especially, we have been at various times and in various ways false to ourselves, false to each other, false to the facts of history and false to the future.

In this self-deceit our political leaders of all shades of opinion are deeply implicated. Yet we cannot shove the blame off on them. If our leaders have deceived us it is mainly because we ourselves have insisted on being deceived. Their deceitfulness has resulted from our own moral and intellectual confusion. In this confusion, our educators and churchmen and scientists are deeply implicated.

Journalists, too, of course, are implicated. But if Americans are confused it is not for lack of accurate and pertinent information. The American people arc by far the best informed people in the history of the world.

The trouble is not with the facts. The trouble is that clear and honest inferences have not been drawn from the facts. The day-to-day present is clear. The issues of tomorrow are befogged.

There is one fundamental issue which faces America as it faces no other nation. It is an issue peculiar to America and peculiar to America in the twentieth century—now. It is deeper even than the immediate issue of War. If America meets it correctly, then, despite hosts of dangers and difficulties, we can look forward and move forward to a future worthy of men, with peace in our hearts.

If we dodge the issue, we shall flounder for ten or twenty or thirty bitter years in a chartless and meaningless series of disasters.

The purpose of this article is to state that issue, and its solution, as candidly and as completely as possible. But first of all let us be completely candid about where we are and how we got there.

Where are we? We are *in* the war. All this talk about whether this or that might or might not get us into the war is wasted effort. We are, for a fact, *in* the war.

Of course, we are not technically at war, we are not painfully at war, and we may never have to experience the full hell that war can be. Nevertheless the simple statement stands: we are *in* the war. The irony is that Hitler knows it—and most Americans don't. It may or may not be an advantage to continue diplomatic relations with Germany. But the fact that a German embassy still flourishes in Washington beautifully illustrates the whole mass of deceits and self-deceits in which we have been living.

Perhaps the best way to show ourselves that we are in the war is to consider how we can get out of it. Practically, there's only one way to get out of it and that is by a German victory over England. If England should surrender soon, Germany and America would not start fighting the next day. So we would be out of the war. For a while. Except that Japan might then attack in the South Seas and the Philippines. We could abandon the Philippines, abandon Australia and New Zealand, withdraw to Hawaii. And wait. We would be out of the war.

We say we don't want to be in the war. We also say we want England to win. We want Hitler stopped—more than we want to stay out of the war. So, at the moment, we're in.

WE GOT IN VIA DEFENSE

. . . But what are we defending?

Now that we are in this war, how did we get in? We got in on the basis of defense. Even that very word, defense, has been full of deceit and self-deceit.

To the average American the plain meaning of the word defense is defense of American territory. Is our national policy today limited to the defense of the American homeland by whatever means may seem wise? It is not. We are *not* in a war to defend American territory. We are in a war to defend and even to promote, encourage and incite so-called democratic principles throughout the world. The average American begins to realize now that that's the kind of war he's in. And he's halfway for it. But he wonders how he ever got there, since a year ago he had not the slightest intention of getting into any such thing. Well, he can see now how he got there. He got there via "defense."

Behind the doubts in the American mind there were and are two different picture-patterns. One of them stressing the appalling consequences of the fall of England leads us to a war of intervention. As a plain matter of the defense of American territory is that picture necessarily true? It is not *necessarily* true. For the other picture is roughly this: while it would be much better for us if Hitler were severely checked, nevertheless, regardless of what happens in Europe it would be entirely possible for us to organize a defense of the northern part of the Western Hemisphere so that this country could not be successfully attacked. You are familiar with that picture. Is it true or false? No man is qualified to state categorically that it is false. If the entire rest of the world came under the organized domination of evil tyrants, it is quite possible to imagine that this country could make itself such a tough nut to crack that not all the tyrants in the world would care to come against us. And of course there would always be a better than even chance that, like the great Queen Elizabeth, we could play one tyrant off against another. Or, like an infinitely mightier Switzerland, we could live discreetly and dangerously in the midst of enemies. No man can say that that picture of America as an impregnable armed camp is false. No man can honestly say that as a pure matter of defense—defense of our homeland—it is necessary to get into or be in this war.

The question before us then is not *primarily* one of necessity and survival. It is a question of choice and calculation. The true questions are: Do we *want* to be in this war? Do we *prefer* to be in it? And, if so, for what?

WE OBJECT TO BEING IN IT

. . . Our fears have a special cause

We are in this war. We can see how we got into it in terms of defense. Now why do we object so strongly to being in it?

There are lots of reasons. First, there is the profound and almost universal aversion to all war—to killing and being killed. But the reason which needs closest inspection, since it is one peculiar to this war and never felt about any previous war, is the fear that if we get into this war, it will be the end of our constitutional democracy. We are all acquainted with the fearful forecast—that some form of dictatorship is required to fight a modern war, that we will certainly go bankrupt, that in the process of war and its aftermath our economy will be largely socialized, that the politicians now in office will seize complete power and never yield it up, and that what with the whole trend toward collectivism, we shall end up in such a total national socialism that any faint semblances of our constitutional American democracy will be totally unrecognizable.

We start into this war with huge government debt, a vast bureaucracy and a whole generation of young people trained to look to the government as the source of all life. The party in power is the one which for long years has been most sympathetic to all manner of socialist doctrines and collectivist trends. The President of the United States has continually reached for more and more power, and he owes his continuation in office today largely to the coming of the war. Thus, the fear that the United States will be driven to a national socialism, as a result of cataclysmic circumstances and contrary to the free will of the American people, is an entirely justifiable fear.

BUT WE WILL WIN IT

... The big question is how

So there's the mess—to date. Much more could be said in amplification, in qualification and in argument. But, however elaborately they might be stated, the sum of the facts about our present position brings us to this point—that the paramount question of this immediate moment is not whether we get into war but how do we win it?

If we are in a war, then it is no little advantage to be aware of the fact. And once we admit to ourselves we are in a war, there is no shadow of doubt that we Americans will be determined to win it—cost what it may in life or treasure.

WHAT ARE WE FIGHTING FOR?

... And why we need to know

Having now, with candor, examined our position, it is time to consider the larger issue which confronts us. Stated most simply, that issue is: What are we fighting for?

Each of us stands ready to give our life, our wealth and all our hope of personal happiness, to make sure that America shall not lose any war she is engaged in. But we would like to know what war we are trying to win—and what we are supposed to win when we win it.

This questioning reflects our truest instincts as Americans. But more than that. Our urgent desire to give this war its proper name has a desperate practical importance. If we know what we are fighting for, then we can drive confidently toward a victorious conclusion and, what's more, have at least an even chance of establishing a workable Peace.

Furthermore—and this is an extraordinary and profoundly historical fact which deserves to be examined in detail—America and only America can effectively state the war aims of this war.

Almost every expert will agree that Britain cannot win complete victory—cannot even, in the common saying, "stop Hitler"—without American help. Therefore, even if Britain should from time to time announce war aims, the American people are continually in the position of effectively approving or not approving those aims. On the contrary, if America were to announce war aims, Great Britain would almost certainly accept them. And the entire world including Adolf Hitler would accept them as the gauge of this battle.

Americans have a feeling that in any collaboration with Great Britain we are somehow playing Britain's game and not our own. Whatever sense there may have been in this notion in the past, today it is an ignorant and foolish conception of the situation. In any sort of partnership with the British Empire, Great Britain is perfectly willing that the United States of America should assume the role of senior partner. This has been true for a long time. Among serious Englishmen, the chief complaint against America (and incidentally their best alibi for themselves) has really amounted to this—that America has refused to rise to the opportunities of leadership in the world.

Consider this recent statement of the London *Economist*:

"If any permanent closer association of Britain and the United States is achieved, an island people of less than 50 millions cannot expect to be the senior partner. . . . The center of gravity and the ultimate decision must increasingly lie in America. We cannot resent this historical development. We may rather feel proud that the cycle of dependence, enmity and independence is coming full circle into a new interdependence."

We Americans no longer have the *alibi* that we cannot have things the way we want them so far as Great Britain is concerned. With due regard for the varying problems of the members of the British Commonwealth, what we want will be okay with them.

The important point to be made here is simply that the complete opportunity of leadership is *ours*. If we don't want it, if we refuse to take it, the responsibility of refusal is also ours, and ours alone.

Admittedly, the future of the world cannot be settled all in one piece. But if our trouble is that we don't know what we are fighting for, then it's up to us to figure it out. Don't expect some other country to tell us. Stop this Nazi propaganda about fighting somebody else's war. We fight no wars except our wars. "Arsenal of Democracy"? We may prove to be that. But today we must be the arsenal of America and of the friends and allies of America.

Friends and allies of America? Who are they, and for what? This is for us to tell them.

DONG DANG OR DEMOCRACY

> . . . *But whose Dong Dang, whose Democracy?*

But how can we tell them? And how can we tell ourselves for what purposes we seek allies and for what purposes we fight? Are we going to fight for dear old Danzig or dear old Dong Dang?* Or, if we cannot state war aims in terms of vastly distant geography, shall we use some big words like Democracy and Freedom and Justice? Yes, we can use the big words. The President has already used them. And perhaps we had better get used to using them again. Maybe they do mean something—about the future as well as the past. Some amongst us are likely to be dying for them—on the fields and in the skies of battle.

But is there nothing between the absurd sound of distant cities and the brassy trumpeting of majestic words? And if so, whose Dong Dang and whose Democracy? Is there not something a little more practically satisfying that we can get our teeth into? Is there no sort of understandable program? A program which would be clearly good for

---

*Dong Dang, a border hamlet in what was then French Indochina, was an entry point for the Japanese army invading China. U.S. isolationists enjoyed chanting: "We'll die for dear old Dong Dang."—ED.

America, which would make sense for America—and which at the same time might have the blessing of the Goddess of Democracy and even help somehow to fix up this bothersome matter of Dong Dang?

Is there none such? There is. And so we now come squarely and closely face to face with the issue which Americans hate most to face. It is that old, old issue with those old, old battered labels—the issue of Isolationism versus Internationalism.

We detest both words. We spit them at each other with the fury of hissing geese. We duck and dodge them.

Let us face that issue squarely now.

In the field of national policy, the fundamental trouble with America has been, and is, that whereas their nation became in the twentieth century the most powerful and the most vital nation in the world, nevertheless Americans were unable to accommodate themselves spiritually and practically to that fact. Hence they have failed to play their part as a world power—a failure which has had disastrous consequences for themselves and for all mankind. And the cure is this: to accept wholeheartedly our duty and our opportunity as the most powerful and vital nation in the world and in consequence to exert upon the world the full impact of our influence, for such purposes as we see fit and by such means as we see fit.

"For such purposes as we see fit" leaves entirely open the question of what our purposes may be or how we may appropriately achieve them. Emphatically our only alternative to isolationism is not to undertake to police the whole world nor to impose democratic institutions on all mankind.

America cannot be responsible for the good behavior of the entire world. But America is responsible, to herself as well as to history, for the world environment in which she lives. Nothing can so vitally affect America's environment as America's own influence upon it, and therefore if America's environment is unfavorable to the growth of American life, then America has nobody to blame so deeply as she must blame herself.

In its failure to grasp this relationship between America and America's environment lies the moral and practical bankruptcy of any and all forms of isolationism. It is most unfortunate that this virus of isolationist sterility has so deeply infected an influential section of the Republican party. For until the Republican party can develop a vital philosophy and program for America's initiative and activity as a world power, it will continue to cut itself off from any useful participation in this hour of history. And its participation is deeply needed for the shaping of the future of America and of the world.

But politically speaking, it is an equally serious fact that for seven years Franklin Roosevelt was, for all practical purposes, a complete isolationist. He was more of an isolationist than Herbert Hoover or Calvin Coolidge. The fact that Franklin Roosevelt has recently emerged as an emergency world leader should not obscure the fact that for seven years his policies ran absolutely counter to any possibility of effective American leadership in international co-operation. There is of course a justification which can be made for the President's first two terms. It can be said, with reason, that great social reforms were necessary in order to bring democracy up to date in the greatest of democracies. But the fact is that Franklin Roosevelt failed to make American democracy work successfully on a narrow, materialistic and nationalistic basis. And under Franklin Roosevelt we ourselves have failed to make democracy work successfully. Our only chance now to make it work is in terms of a vital international economy and in terms of an international moral order.

This objective is Franklin Roosevelt's great opportunity to justify his first two terms and to go down in history as the greatest rather than the last of American Presidents.

Without our help he cannot be our greatest President. With our help he can be. Under him and with his leadership we can make isolationism as dead an issue as slavery, and we can make a truly *American* internationalism something as natural to us in our time as the airplane or the radio.

In 1919 we had a golden opportunity, an opportunity unprecedented in all history, to assume the leadership of the world. We did not understand that opportunity. Wilson mishandled it. We rejected it. The opportunity persisted. We bungled it in the 1920's and in the confusions of the 1930's we killed it.

To lead the world would never have been an easy task. To revive the hope of that lost opportunity makes the task now infinitely harder than it would have been before. Nevertheless, with the help of all of us, Roosevelt must succeed where Wilson failed.

THE TWENTIETH CENTURY IS THE AMERICAN CENTURY

. . . Some facts about our time

Consider the twentieth century. It is ours not only in the sense that we happen to live in it but ours also because it is America's first century as a dominant power in the world. So far, this century of ours has been a profound and tragic disappointment. No other century has been so big with promise for human progress and happiness. And in no one century have so many men and women and children suffered such pain and anguish and bitter death.

It is a baffling and difficult and paradoxical century. No doubt all centuries were paradoxical to those who had to cope with them. But, like everything else, our paradoxes today are bigger and better than ever. Yes, better as well as bigger—inherently better. We have poverty and starvation—but only in the midst of plenty. We have the biggest wars in the midst of the most widespread, the deepest and the most articulate hatred of war in all history. We have tyrannies and dictatorships—but only when democratic idealism, once regarded as the dubious eccentricity of a colonial nation, is the faith of a huge majority of the people of the world.

And ours is also a revolutionary century. Revolutionary, of course, in science and in industry. And also revolutionary, as a corollary, in politics and the structure of society. But to say that a revolution is in progress is not to say that the men with either the craziest ideas or the angriest ideas or the most plausible ideas are going to come out on top. The Revolution of 1776 was won and established by men most of whom appear to have been both gentlemen and men of common sense.

Clearly a revolutionary epoch signifies great changes, great adjustments. And this is only one reason why it is really so foolish for people to worry about our "constitutional democracy" without worrying or, better, thinking hard about the world revolution. For only as we go out to meet and solve for our time the problems of the world revolution, can we know how to re-establish our constitutional democracy for another fifty or one hundred years.

This twentieth century is baffling, difficult, paradoxical, revolutionary. But by now, at the cost of much pain and many hopes deferred, we know a good deal about it. And we ought to accommodate our outlook to this knowledge so dearly bought. For example, any true conception of our world of the twentieth century must surely include a vivid awareness of at least these four propositions.

First: our world of two billion human beings is for the first time in history one world, fundamentally indivisible. Second: modern man hates war and feels intuitively that, in its present scale and frequency, it may even be fatal to his species. Third: our world, again for the first time in human history, is capable of producing all the material needs of the entire human family. Fourth: the world of the twentieth century, if it is to come to life in any nobility of health and vigor, must be to a significant degree an American Century.

As to the first and second: in postulating the indivisibility of the contemporary world, one does not necessarily imagine that anything like a world state—a parliament of men—must be brought about in this century. Nor need we assume that war can be abolished. All that it is necessary to feel—and to feel deeply—is that terrific forces of magnetic attraction and repulsion will operate as between every large group of human beings on this planet. Large sections of the human family may be effectively organized into opposition to each other. Tyrannies may require a large amount of living space. But Freedom requires and will require far greater living space than Tyranny. Peace cannot endure unless it prevails over a very large part of the world. Justice will come near to losing all meaning in the minds of men unless Justice can have approximately the same fundamental meanings in many lands and among many peoples.

As to the third point—the promise of adequate production for all mankind, the "more abundant life"—be it noted that this is characteristically an American promise. It is a promise easily made, here and elsewhere, by demagogues and proponents of all manner of slick schemes and "planned economies." What we must insist on is that the abundant life is predicated on Freedom—on the Freedom which has created its possibility—on a vision of Freedom under Law. Without Freedom, there will be no abundant life. With Freedom, there can be.

And finally there is the belief—shared let us remember by most men living—that the twentieth century must be to a significant degree an American Century. This knowledge calls us to action now.

AMERICA'S VISION OF OUR WORLD

. . . How it shall be created

What can we say and foresee about an American Century? It is not enough merely to say that we reject isolationism and accept the logic of internationalism. What internationalism? Rome had a great internationalism. So had the Vatican and Genghis Khan and the Ottoman Turks and nineteenth-century England. After the First World War, Lenin had one in mind. Today Hitler seems to have one in mind. But what internationalism have we Americans to offer?

Ours cannot come out of the vision of any one man. It must be the product of the imaginations of many men. It must be a sharing with all peoples of our Bill of Rights, our Declaration of Independence, our Constitution, our magnificent industrial products, our technical skills. It must be an internationalism of the people, by the people and for the people.

No narrow definition can be given to the American internationalism of the twentieth century. It will take shape, as all civilizations take shape, by the living of it, by work and effort, by trial and error, by enterprise and adventure and experience.

And by imagination!

As America enters dynamically upon the world scene, we need most of all to seek and to bring forth a vision of America as a world power which is authentically American and which can inspire us to live and work and fight with vigor and enthusiasm. And as we come now to the great test, it may yet turn out that in all our trials and tribulations of spirit during the first part of this century we as a people have been painfully apprehending the meaning of our time, and now in this moment of testing there may come clear at last the vision which will guide us to the authentic creation of the twentieth century—our Century.

Consider four areas of life and thought in which we may seek to realize such a vision:

First, the economic. It is for America and for America alone to determine whether a system of free economic enterprise—an economic order compatible with freedom and progress—shall or shall not prevail in this century. We know perfectly well that there is not the slightest chance of anything faintly resembling a free economic system prevailing in this country if it prevails nowhere else. What then does America have to decide? Some few decisions are quite simple. For example: we have to decide whether or not we shall have for ourselves and our friends freedom of the seas—the right to go with our ships and our ocean-going airplanes where we wish, when we wish and as we wish. The vision of America as the principal guarantor of the freedom of the seas, the vision of America as the dynamic leader of world trade, has within it the possibilities of such enormous human progress as to stagger the imagination. Let us not be staggered by it. Let us rise to its tremendous possibilities. Our thinking of world trade today is on ridiculously small terms. For example, we think of Asia as being worth only a few hundred million a year to us. Actually, in the decades to come Asia will be worth to us exactly zero—or else it will be worth to us four, five, ten billions of dollars a year. And the latter are the terms we must think in, or else confess a pitiful impotence.

Closely akin to the purely economic area and yet quite different from it, there is the picture of an America which will send out through the world its technical and artistic skills. Engineers, scientists, doctors, movie men, makers of entertainment, developers of airlines, builders of roads, teachers, educators. Throughout the world, these skills, this training, this leadership is needed and will be eagerly welcomed, if only we have the imagination to see it and the sincerity and good will to create the world of the twentieth century.

But now there is a third thing which our vision must immediately be concerned with. We must undertake now to be the Good Samaritan of the entire world. It is the manifest duty of this country to undertake to feed all the people of the world who as a result of this worldwide collapse of civilization are hungry and destitute—all of them, that is, whom we can from time to time reach consistently with a very tough attitude toward all hostile governments. For every dollar we spend on armaments, we should spend at least a dime in a gigantic effort to feed the world—and all the world should know that we have dedicated ourselves to this task. Every farmer in America should be encouraged to produce all the crops he can, and all that we cannot eat—and perhaps some of us could eat less—should forthwith be dispatched to the four quarters of the globe as a free gift, administered by a humanitarian army of Americans, to every man, woman and child on this earth who is really hungry.

But all this is not enough. All this will fail and none of it will happen unless our vision of America as a world power includes a passionate devotion to great American ideals. We have some things in this country which are infinitely precious and especially American— a love of freedom, a feeling for the equality of opportunity, a tradition of self-reliance and independence and also of co-operation. In addition to ideals and notions which are especially American, we are the inheritors of all the great principles of Western civilization—above all Justice, the love of Truth, the ideal of Charity. The other day Herbert Hoover said that America was fast becoming the sanctuary of the ideals of civilization. For the moment it may be enough to be the sanctuary of these ideals. But not for long. It now becomes our time to be the powerhouse from which the ideals spread throughout the world and do their mysterious work of lifting the life of mankind from the level of the beasts to what the Psalmist called a little lower than the angels.

America as the dynamic center of ever-widening spheres of enterprise, America as the training center of the skillful servants of mankind, America as the Good Samaritan, really believing again that it is more blessed to give than to receive, and America as the powerhouse of the ideals of Freedom and Justice—out of these elements surely can be fashioned a vision of the twentieth century to which we can and will devote ourselves in joy and gladness and vigor and enthusiasm.

Other nations can survive simply because they have endured so long—sometimes with more and sometimes with less significance. But this nation, conceived in adventure and dedicated to the progress of man—this nation cannot truly endure unless there courses strongly through its veins from Maine to California the blood of purposes and enterprise and high resolve.

Throughout the seventeenth century and the eighteenth century and the nineteenth century, this continent teemed with manifold projects and magnificent purposes. Above them all and weaving them all together into the most exciting flag of all the world and of all history was the triumphal purpose of freedom.

It is in this spirit that all of us are called, each to his own measure of capacity, and each in the widest horizon of his vision, to create the first great American Century.

RUSSIA
BY THIRDS

A LIFE *Editorial*

DECEMBER 16, 1946

> *When this editorial was written, soon after World War II, the Cold War was in its early stages and just beginning to be identified as such. This appraisal of what has remained a political hot potato is still timely and, Mr. Khrushchev notwithstanding, still valid.*

The friendliness of the American people toward Russia reached a high point in 1945 and has been declining ever since. So say the Gallup and Roper polls. By September, 1946, a Gallup poll found 62 per cent of Americans confessing that their feelings toward Russia had become less friendly than a year ago.

That was a year in which the Soviets suppressed political freedom in eastern Europe, stirred up trouble in Iran, looted Manchuria, made tedious and insulting speeches in Paris and generally threw wrenches into the peace machinery. Hence this "less friendly" feeling for Russia is not surprising. It may be accounted as a step in the education of the American people in world affairs. It is not a very long step, however, and if we leave it at that it may even turn out to be a step backward. For there is something naïve about this easy personification of nations, this readiness to classify them as friendly and unfriendly, the way high-school kids classify each other as droopy or solid. Different nations have different characteristics just as people do, but they are not that simple. The next step toward sophistication in our public opinion on Russia is to be clear on just what we like or dislike about it, what we fear and what we hope.

Some Englishmen, with their customary forehandedness, have already taken a stance toward the Russians which seems the very essence of sophistication but is actually even blinder than our own cloudy and generalized mistrust. This stance may be called the aristocratic, and it has a strong snob appeal to certain kinds of American ("My dear Lady Decies, I couldn't agree more"). It starts out with a parable (a little shopworn by now):

Three people in evening clothes are playing cards after an excellent dinner when gradually, through the glass door to the kitchen, they become aware that a bearded, dirty and powerful tramp is looting the refrigerator. What should they do? Ignore him? Chase him away? Or invite him to sit down with them and make a fourth? The latter is supposed to be the civilized course. You are reminded, with quotations from Kipling, that Adam-zad ("the bear that walks like a man") is not the easternmost European but the westernmost Oriental; that he is an uncouth bounder, just a peasant really, but terribly sensitive and anxious to join our Anglo-Saxon club; that if we are patient with his inferiority complex, he will soon learn good manners just by association with us. After all, as the London *Economist* quotes the gossip, Madame Gromyko never wore shoes until she was sixteen. So don't let us lose our tempers. *Noblesse oblige.*

This aristocratic stance is tempting because it flatters us. But it does not flatter the Russians, and it is based on a very superficial reading of their national character and the character of their regime. It makes no distinctions between Russia past and Russia present, nor between the

Russian people and their rulers. Yet to make distinctions is just what we should do.

There are three main things to distinguish: the Russian government, the Russian nation and the Russian people. Toward the first, the American people must for the present be hostile; toward the second, neutral, but the third are our friends.

The Russian government is a more pervasive tyranny than the czar's ever was. Is it any of our business what form of government another country gets? It cannot be our State Department's business, for we have diplomatic relations with the Soviets and it is very bad diplomacy to come between a people and their government. But it can be our business as American citizens to condemn the methods and principles of this regime. Two Soviet policies in particular have repeatedly obstructed the growth of real peace between America and Russia. The first is Communist messianism, which has exaggerated enormously and unnecessarily our few real conflicts with the legitimate aspirations of the Russian nation. The second is Communist isolationism, which has drawn an iron curtain between the Russian and American people.

The Russian nation is of course no newcomer to the game of power politics and no mere tramp in the kitchen. Her diplomats have had their victories no less renowned than her generals, from Prince Potemkin to Count Witte; and *much nineteenth-century history* revolved around the great diplomatic duel between Russia and Britain. Since 1939 Russia has annexed 274,000 square miles of Europe and Asia and brought eight independent countries within her sphere of influence. Practically all that square mileage represented the recovery of lands held by Russia before 1918; and most of the new spheres of influence were either controlled or ogled by many a czar. Thus there is a continuity in much Russian "imperialism" which gives it an almost legitimate cast—as legitimate as power politics can ever be. European diplomats have long recognized that Russia really needs a warm water port, for instance, and that the Montreux Convention governing the Dardanelles was not divinely inspired.

But what if, in pressing these "legitimate" Russian claims, the Soviets turn them into instruments of social disruption? It is not just

Russia that is expanding; it is a messianic dream whose prophet Lenin (echoed by Stalin) said most explicitly that he sought the worldwide overthrow of capitalism. Who declared this holy war? Not Russia, but a handful of fanatics. Russia is their vehicle, their Trojan horse, just as their Communist parties abroad are Russia's. Today there is virtually no distinguishing between the two. In the name of human liberty, America is bound to resist the spread of Communism. In doing so we must perforce resist Russia. Perhaps we should have had to resist Russia anyway in some places (such as Manchuria) for the same balance-of-power reasons that motivated the British in their long and relatively peaceful duel. But we have had no chance to try our hand at that kind of peace-waging, for the Soviets will not let us separate the Russian interest from the supposed interest of the world proletariat. This we must hold against the Soviet government; it has made it well-nigh impossible for us to feel correctly neutral toward the Russian nation.

Far more serious than this, however, is the Soviet government's isolation of its own people. For they are a people who can teach us much, who can learn much from us, and whom we need to know. As Woodrow Wilson said about the German people, we have no quarrel with them.

The Soviet censorship is even worse now than during the war. This was not the idea of the Russian people. When *Life*'s Richard Lauterbach crossed Russia on the Trans-Siberian last summer, he was twice challenged by police who wanted to seize his camera. Each time his fellow passengers came to his rescue by shouting, "Let him alone, the war's over." The Russian people, though they frankly envy American wealth, are not at all ashamed of what they have already accomplished in twenty-five years of trying to catch up. Their natural feeling toward America is one of friendly and unsatisfied curiosity. When Ilya Ehrenburg lectured on his American trip in Moscow last month, the room was jammed with standees who listened intently for two hours.

Among his hearers, we may be sure, were the same variety of human types that have always made up Russia. A Gogol, if the censors would let him, could still find among them plenty of petty graft and vanity to satirize, and a Dostoevsky could still embrace their 169 ethnic groups in his tremendous categories of saintly Alyoshas, passionate Dmitris, brain-ruled Ivans. This is not the place for a character analysis of the Russian people. But the state of the world requires that we remind ourselves that they *are* people—human beings not too different from ourselves.

Throughout Soviet history the average Russian's patriotism has been kept at fever pitch by mental pictures of what Russia would be like tomorrow, and tomorrow, and tomorrow. As our own Wobblies used to say, it was pie in the sky. And whenever there was a slight payoff, as in the consumer goods boom of 1933–36, the Russian people took the pie joyfully. During the war they were sustained by an uncomplicated dream of peace, more building, more "culture"—cultural bathrooms, cultural fountain pens, cultural fifty-kopek ice cream for all. That is what the Russian people wanted. It does not seem too much.

Instead there is another purge and a new deferment of consumer industries for the sake of military strength and new arrivals in the concentration camps. Yet the Russian people love freedom, and they love their fellowman with a passion almost unique among all peoples. They swarm easily but they are not barbarians; they are poor but they are not tramps. They are victims of a system against which their only weapon is patience and their incorruptible humanity. They need our trust. Let us never answer their need with anger or scorn.

A WEEK
OF SHOCK
AND DECISION

by LIFE's *editorial staff*

FEBRUARY 13, 1950

> *As the week began, President Truman pondered*
> *how to announce the hydrogen bomb. A young physicist*
> *named Klaus Fuchs went apparently unnoticed about*
> *his top-secret business. For some people it was National*
> *Kraut & Frankfurter Week; for others, National Youth*
> *Week. As usual, everybody paid closest attention to what*
> *concerned him most. But as the week drew on, certain*
> *forces, already in motion, were to result in decisions*
> *of deep meaning to millions. We are still living*
> *in the shadow of that week, here summarized in*
> *the combined writing of a group of LIFE correspondents*
> *and editors.*

Out in Denver an interviewer asked a man what he thought about the atomic bomb now. "I just feel better," the man said uncomfortably, speaking for millions, "when I don't think about it." He wasn't being complacent or putting his head in the sand, but it did seem to be pretty useless to worry about something that, like tomorrow's sunrise, was entirely out of his hands. But for anybody who read the papers or listened to the radio or couldn't afford a desert island, it was getting harder all the time not to worry and to avoid thinking about it.

As the week went on it became harder. First there was that week-end speech of Dr. Harold C. Urey to shudder over. As the discoverer of heavy hydrogen, which made the building of an H-bomb possible, and as a man not given to loose talk, he could hardly be brushed off as an alarmist. Because of a "curious prejudice" on the part of government advisers against certain kinds of atomic development, Dr. Urey said, "we may have already lost the armaments race." Since the race was on in earnest, "I am very unhappy to conclude that the hydrogen bomb should be developed and built." If the Russians built it first, he foresaw an ultimatum so effective as to make the bomb's use unnecessary. If we built it first, since ultimatums are out of character for the Western nations, Urey asked, "then what do we do next?" And if both got it, there would be a dangerously unstable equilibrium. The only solution would be an Atlantic Union so strong as to overwhelmingly tip the balance of power in our favor.

The speech was still sinking in when President Truman made it even harder to avoid thinking about atoms. In a 127-word statement he said he had "directed the Atomic Energy Commission to continue its work on all . . . atomic weapons, including the so-called hydrogen or superbomb." There would have been greater cause for alarm had the President said anything else, but there was hardly cause for complacency in the thought that we were off on a search for something not just one thousand times as destructive as the atomic bomb but *limitlessly* destructive.

Then two days later Brien McMahon (D., Connecticut), chairman of the Joint Congressional Committee on Atomic Energy and a deeply troubled man, made a bold, persuasive speech to the Senate. The U.S. had a choice, as he saw it, of (1) "resigning ourselves to a generation of waging the cold war . . . pouring out our substance to stay ahead in the weapons competition even after the Kremlin becomes armed with hydrogen bombs," or (2) "moving heaven and earth to stop the atomic armaments race . . . [and] tap to the roots the resources of our ingenuity and imagination."

What he offered was a super-Marshall Plan, to cost $10 billion a year for five years, or two-thirds our present military budget, to be matched by two-thirds of other nations' military budgets and to be dedicated to giving a decent life to the two-thirds of the world's peoples who "live continuously at the margins of starvation." Somehow

Russia would have to go along, and as a persuader the senator suggested a vast step-up in the Voice of America, to give it thundering amplification behind the Iron Curtain. Reported the slightly awe-struck *New York Times,* "Mr. McMahon, who is aware of many atomic 'secrets' by virtue of his position, held many of his Senate colleagues in a sort of chilly suspense as he described the potentialities of the hydrogen bomb." When the suspense was over, he was congratulated on all sides. His hope that the Russians could be coaxed aboard the bandwagon might be far-fetched, but his daring approach would certainly be explored. And, as propaganda, it might have a profound effect on the Russian people.

The week's greatest blow to complacency, however, was not the Truman announcement, nor the McMahon word picture of "chunks of the sun" being used to incinerate fifty million Americans in a matter of minutes. Nor was it Defense Secretary Louis Johnson's saber-rattling pronouncement that he was getting the U.S. ready "to lick hell out of her" if Russia broke the peace. It was, rather, something that none of the three knew about when he spoke.

In London's Shell-Mex House, home of the British Atomic Energy Commission, a policeman walked up to one of the agency's brightest brains and arrested him as a spy. He was Dr. Klaus Fuchs, German-born, but a British citizen. He was accused of having twice, in 1945 and 1947, given away atomic secrets that could be useful to an enemy.

The long trail that led to Fuchs was picked up last fall when British intelligence found a serious leak at Harwell. Counterespionage agents kept running into secrets in Russian hands that could only have come from someone familiar with American atomic installations. The British called in the FBI, which sent some of its smartest operatives to London. Together they built up a file to construct a theoretical picture of the unknown spy and by a painstaking process of elimination narrowed the field to one man: Klaus Fuchs. From that point to his arrest last week their quarry was under intense surveillance.

Although his British bosses never knew it, Fuchs had been a Communist almost since his naturalization in 1942. For three years, while working in America on the Manhattan Project, he had had access to the highest of secrets. And as Lieutenant General Leslie Groves, who headed the project, told the stunned Joint Committee later in the week, that may have included hydrogen-bomb secrets. Fuchs's aid to the Russians was no small thing, said General Groves; between Fuchs and the traitorous scientist Dr. Alan Nunn May they may have given the U.S.S.R. "well over a year's advantage" in its frantic race to build an atomic bomb. From FBI Director J. Edgar Hoover senators got the impression that the FBI might be on the trails of still other important spies.

After all this shocking news it was almost an anticlimax when Professor Frederick Seitz, of the University of Illinois, told fellow members of the American Physical Society that Russia's atomic development has moved "at least five times greater" than our own rate of advance since the war. Fuchs may have helped, said Dr. Seitz, but the big reason for Russia's speed was her concentration of probably more than half her national income on military development. He urged that it would be immoral for the U.S. not to speed up too: "Who among us will feel sinless," he asked, "if he has remained passively by while Western culture was being overwhelmed?"

THE END
OF A DARK AGE
IN RUSSIA

by Whittaker Chambers

APRIL 30, 1956

> With a sigh of overdue relief, the world welcomed
> the death of Stalin, which brought to an end one of
> the bloodiest epochs of personal rule in history.
> But Whittaker Chambers, himself a one-time Communist
> who has long fought Communism with his brilliant
> pen, warned that Communist aggression against the
> West would not end with Stalin. Rather, it would develop
> new and subtler forms for the conquest of mankind.
> He was right.

There are two stories about the Twentieth Congress of the Soviet Communist party. One is about what is happening now, at this moment, throughout international Communism and within the Communist empire (including the dissolution of the Cominform). The other is about the political meaning of those events for the West. The first is the latest act of a bloody tragedy that has not its like in history. The second has momentous meanings for us all. Together they spell peril for the West. But the peril is blurred because the political meanings of the second story are in danger of becoming lost in the sensational developments of the first.

The first is the story of the "reverse purge"—the posthumous liquidation of Stalin and Stalinism—proclaimed at the Twentieth Congress. Within the three decades, 1920 to 1950, roughly from the Tenth Congress of the Soviet Communist party to the Communist mop-up of mainland China, Communism's will to change history was personified in one man—the late Josef Stalin. To become the embodiment of the revolutionary idea in history Stalin had to corrupt Communism absolutely. He justified his acts by the necessities of that history and the needs of that infallible party which all Communists serve. In their name he asserted that what was true was a lie and what was a lie was truth. He sustained this corruption by a blend of cunning and brute force. History knows nothing similar on such a scale.

This great turn in Communist tactics, which takes the form of the liquidation of Stalinism, opens an unparalleled struggle for men's minds. Communism is bidding for the allegiance of all those in the West who are in any way affected by its doctrine, its power or its spell. The West could make no greater mistake than to exaggerate first impressions or read into this move simply another scramble for personal power among the Kremlin masters.

The Communists are realists. They will count on the long pull. And the pull will presently be intense in the minds of millions. With Stalin down, the force of Communist attraction will be great, on many levels, and with a play of appeals that the West will not readily understand.

How did it happen that this great zigzag came in the year 1956, at the Twentieth Congress of the Soviet Communist party? The answers have to do with an international situation that is reasonably open to survey, and an internal Soviet situation, including a power struggle in the Kremlin, where lack of exact information, or conflicting information, takes us into the realm of astrology. Everybody is guessing. I would guess, too, if there seemed any urgent reason to. I prefer to center on the international situation, that dealing directly with the West, since it has seemed to me from the first that it was chiefly that the zigzag at the Twentieth Congress was meant to deal with. First, a word about congresses and zigzags.

Nothing is any longer decided *at* these great Communist congresses.

They simply register important decisions, taken in the highest Communist echelons, out of sight and sound of the party masses, and probably some time before they are announced.

This is especially necessary because of the frequent zigzags of the party line. Zigzags are much misunderstood. But there is nothing inherently irrational about them. Communism has one fixed purpose: to take over the rest of the world. That purpose never changes. Only the tactics for effecting it change. Given the fixed purpose, the tactics can change endlessly, can change, at need, into the very opposite of what they have been, and sometimes overnight, or so it seems.

A violent zigzag in the party line is a sign that Communism, in its perpetual assessment of the balance of forces, the power pattern in the world, has concluded that the power pattern has changed in such a way as to indicate that a rather definite stage of history is ending and a new one is beginning. A new power pattern commonly calls for new tactics in order for Communism to work successfully in it.

The Twentieth Congress met at what Communists suppose to be an ultimate, or penultimate, stage of this century's history. It met to register the general line of a new tactic whose end result, if successful, would foreclose that stage of history in a world wholly Communist, or on the point of becoming so. New tactics were enjoined by the new power pattern, the changed balance of force between Communism and the West. This new balance of forces was revealed—but not caused—by the Geneva conferences of 1955. The actual shift in the power balance had occurred several years before. But after the Geneva conferences a zigzag in the party line became a certainty.

On many in the West these Geneva conferences had an almost physically stunning effect. Of the two, the first (Summit) conference, which fed the illusion of "the Geneva spirit," was more stunning than the second conference which seemed to bury it. Except in fairly limited circles, the shock was not due to the fact that President Eisenhower lent the prestige of his presence to the Summit conference. As statesman he had little choice. The bull market in popular illusion showed clearly enough how narrow had been his margin of practical maneuver.

Geneva disclosed how little, vis-à-vis the Communist empire, the West had left to bargain with. The West had nothing that the Communists wanted enough (short of total or piecemeal submission), nothing they feared enough (short of total atomic war). And total atomic war they knew they need not really fear.

Western diplomacy, not through stupidity but because of a new adverse balance of real power in the world, found itself obliged to treat with Communism at a level no higher than that of a family dealing with kidnapers for its stolen children. Yet the meaning of this shift in power balance, which in history is of somewhat the same order as the sinking of land masses into the sea would be in nature, seemed scarcely to dent the West's awareness.

Behind the shift lay two interlocking situations, one technological, one political. The technological one was the open secret, which the Geneva conferences dramatized, that the atom bomb is no longer, at least in the sense that Sir Winston Churchill meant, the shield of the free world. Both sides possessed retaliatory power deadly enough to make resort to atomic war mutually suicidal.

But behind the deadlocked weapons situation lay a political situation ultimately much graver for the West. The key to this situation had been China.

"My statesmanship," wrote Henry Adams in 1903 (the date is noteworthy), "is still all in China, where the last struggle for power is to come. . . . The only country now on the spot is Russia, and if Russia organizes China as an economical power, the little drama of history will end in the overthrow of our clumsy Western civilization. . . . In that event, I allow till 1950 to run our race out." This target date, too, is of interest. In fact, when the Twentieth Congress met, Communist China had been for some time engaged in the mass collectivization of its peasants—the kind of human bulldozing that marks the first step in organizing a socialist country into a modern industrial power. It was the fall of China that finally shifted the basic power balance in the world and so gravely complicated the problems of the West.

It is scarcely thirty-five years since Russia's then shaky Communist government convened at Baku, in Soviet Georgia, a great "Congress of Peoples of the East." There the Communist leaders of that day had called on the Far Eastern, Indian and Moslem masses to war against imperialism. The incredible shape of things to come was shadowed forth by a proclamation calling for a "Holy War under the banner of the Comintern."

Even Communists liked to smile at that one in their private gatherings. But they labored unsmilingly to give force to Lenin's strategy on the "Colonial Question." Its end purpose: to strike at the West from the rear, and, by rousing Asia, Africa and Latin America, to add their force to Communism, while depriving the West of overseas markets and sources of raw material which are a foreign base of its economic life. Thus in time, Communism hoped, the rising waters of disaffection might leave the powers of Europe and North America like rooftops, islanded in a flood. The final conflict would then be narrowed to this question: who is to control the rooftops?

No doubt Soviet Foreign Minister Vyacheslav Molotov knew at Geneva that a Soviet arms deal with Egypt would soon lift that flood (in the form of aroused Arab nationalism) against the West. He knew, too, that the rise of the Soviet Union as an industrial power, re-enforced by the production and the scientific and technological brains of half of Germany and all of Czechoslovakia, would enable those Bolshevik businessmen, Khrushchev and Bulganin, to take the road into the colonial markets and initiate a trade competition which must necessarily have a political face. It could all be done, too, under the shield of the atomic bomb. This, grossly oversimplified, was the international power pattern, the new balance of forces, which enjoined the new tactics proclaimed by the Twentieth Congress.

As Secretary of the Communist party, Nikita S. Khrushchev keynoted this tactical shift. His speech runs to several thousand words. Its sense, once pried out of the foam-rubber mufflings peculiar to Communist oratory, spells out the steps of the new tactic: (1) peaceful coexistence; (2) peaceful trade competition with the West; (3) revival of the popular front; (4) collective Communist leadership in contrast to Stalin's one-man rule. Their core meaning can be stripped from thousands of words to four words: no third world war.

How seriously the Communists mean this, how deep-going the zigzag is, can be glimpsed from the fact that to make it at all it was necessary, as Khrushchev expressly noted, to rethink certain of Lenin's conclusions. In *Imperialism,* hitherto a basic Communist text, written by Lenin during World War I, he offered the proposition that capitalism will finally commit suicide in a general war. It is this view that has just been updated.

Three of Khrushchev's points require special notice:

1. He claimed that Communism now spoke for a majority of mankind. He reached this score by counting on the Communist side, in particular, the friendly masses of India. In this he was stretching the elastic only a little thin. It has long been clear that the swing to Communism of one more population mass—Indonesia, for example—would give it something like an even break in any count of the world's noses.

2. Khrushchev was explicit in his popular front come-on. He put it this way: "Here co-operation also with sections of the socialist movement adhering to other views than ours in the question of the transition to socialism [i.e., those differing chiefly about the advisability of violent revolution] is possible and necessary. Today many Social Democrats [i.e., socialists and left liberals in the American sense] are for an active struggle against the war danger and militarism, for closer relations with socialist [i.e., Communist] countries, and for unity of the labor movement. We sincerely welcome the Social Democrats and are ready to do everything possible to unite our efforts," etc. etc.

3. Khrushchev was careful to emphasize that Communism is still militantly revolutionary. There may still remain, he is saying, even after the soughing of the warm peace winds and the disintegrating action of popular fronts, some strongholds of opposition in the West so intractable that they can be brought to reason (i.e., Communism) only by the use of revolutionary violence. The U.S. is chiefly meant.

In effect Khrushchev is saying, "See, the Bomb is not going off. We are now extracting the detonator—a ticklish business. Surely all men of good will want to lend us a hand." To give this tactic force and mass, it is necessary to revive the popular front. To give it a semblance of plausibility, especially in view of the recent past, it is necessary to de-emphasize the cold war. For both it is expedient to liquidate Josef Stalin. For Stalin by his cynical pact with Hitler was not only the destroyer of the old popular front of the 1930's. He showed himself to be also the chief master of cold war.

Let us glance for a moment at cold war. In a sense Communism has always pursued a policy of cold war. It is a specialty of the house. But Communism was able to mount this policy on a world scale only after World War II. Then, the meaning of cold war came home to the incredulous West. Cold war is, in fact, the true brink of war policy, and whoever stands up to it finds himself willy-nilly playing brink of war. For its blackmailing effect depends on crowding an opponent to that brink so that any effort at resistance must make the brink seem more dizzily inevitable. Secretary of State John Foster Dulles was describing the experience with simple literalness in his much-abused phrase. Adlai Stevenson, too, described it more aptly than he knew because he was firing at the wrong target when he called it "Russian roulette."

Cold war, of course, involved a real risk. And the first man in the West who had the hardihood to make a brink of war stand, namely former President Harry S. Truman, took the Communists over the brink. That spoiled the game. The United States lost the Korean war because it was afraid of the threat of a bigger war with which Communism continued to play Russian roulette. The West was afraid. But the Communists must have been terrified, and with much better reasons. The last thing in the world Communism could want was world war.

Thus, the initial American reaction in the Korean war must have brought the Communists to an agonizing reappraisal of cold war policy even before Stalin died, even though his powerful influence may have continued to hold them to that course. For, of course, policies develop an inertia, a momentum, that keeps them going even after their logic is impugned and the risks disclosed. And, of course, the West made a fool of itself in Korea, throwing away almost at once, out of its fear of general war, what its original initiative, General Douglas MacArthur's strategy and the courage of American men had won for it.

How quickly, too, the Communists in the full tide of victory settled for a mere half of Vietnam. What restraint, despite the bloodcurdling war whoops and tossing of stinkpots, has so far characterized Chinese Communist action around the Formosa Strait. No doubt this restraint, like that in Vietnam, reflects China's all-out exertion at collectivization and industrialization. This, in turn, bears directly on the current Communist peace strategy, which, among other items, is buying time for mainland China to emerge as a new Communist industrial massif.

In the mid-1920's chance threw me together with the last military attaché of the czar's Washington embassy. A common love of Russian music sometimes took us together to watch the idiot in *Boris Godunov*. I remember that patient military exile telling me once, from the depths of his longing for the Russian land which he did not live to see again, how, after the interminable winter, the ice begins to break up in the Russian rivers. Then the peasant boys run along the banks, trying to keep pace with the clashing floes; and, as they run, they shout, *"Lyot idyot"*—"The ice is going out!" It is just such an effect that the action of the Twentieth Congress has had upon those minds who have lived, at all deeply, the tragedy of our age wherever Communism has touched it.

I think the West will fail again to measure the full meaning of that effect if it notes only that the men who have brought it about were former collaborators with Stalin in his evil deeds, or supposes that they are merely cynical in their crafty plans, whose guile is not, therefore, questioned. I, for one, do not believe that when Khrushchev wept before Congress delegates those were simulated tears, or that simulated tears could possibly have affected such an audience, or that Khrushchev could have dreamed they could. This is something more: *lyot idyot*—the ice is going out, the ice that froze and paralyzed the messianic spirit of Communism during the long but (in Communist terms) justifiable Stalinist nightmare. Communism is likely to become more, not less, dangerous. It is this that gives us the sensation of passing in a fortnight from one age into another.

Communism has not changed. The dictatorship of the Communist party will not end. (The Twentieth Congress has acted to strengthen it.) It is unlikely that the slave labor camps will go or even shrink much. (Slave labor plays too important a part in the Communist economy and the victims of the reverse purge, or anybody at all who resists, will soon replace such political prisoners as may be released now.) Communist aggression against the West will not end. The Twentieth Congress has acted to give such aggression new, subtler, massive forms whose disintegrating energies are beamed first at specific soft spots around Communism's continental frontiers and far across them—at West Germany, France, Italy, Britain, India, Burma, Indonesia. Yugoslavia is already doing a "slow dissolve" back into the Soviet system—a homecoming which Moscow's official disbanding of the Cominform is intended to promote. For the Cominform, an organization of satellite and West European Communist parties, was used by Stalin chiefly to combat Marshal Tito and his special brand of heresy.

But, above all, it is the smashing of the Stalinist big lie that will change the climate, exerting its influence far beyond mere orthodox Communist lines, upon the internationalist and neutralist opinion of the West. With the smashing of the dark idol of Stalin, Communism can hope to compete again for the allegiance of men's minds, especially among the youth where its influence had fallen almost to zero. What the Twentieth Congress meant to do, and may well succeed in doing, was to make Communism radioactive again.

THE EDUCATED MAN

by Jacques Barzun

OCTOBER 16, 1950

*Modern society is not geared to produce or respect
the educated man, argues Jacques Barzun, educator,
critic, essayist and Dean of Faculties and Provost
of Columbia University. The educated man is still
envied but no longer emulated in an age where the
democratic assumption prevails by sheer force of numbers
and where, he says, "whatever is alarmingly different or
superior is leveled off like the froth on a glass of beer."*

For a writer to express himself publicly about the Educated Man is
perhaps as dangerous as for a lady to bring up the topic of the Virtuous
Woman. In both cases everybody's attention immediately shifts from
the matter in hand to the person who is discussing it. What of his or
her qualifications? If a writer modestly pretends that he does not consider himself an educated man, then what business has he to be
writing on the subject? And if he does allow, again modestly, that he
is educated, then he is suspected of talking down to those less favored
by the gods than he.

Fortunately the present mental state of the world cuts short any shilly-shallying between true and false modesty. Modern society is not geared to produce, receive or respect the educated man, and it is hard to imagine anyone in his senses claiming the title as an honor. The term is in fact seldom used. "Highbrow" has replaced it, and since the new word conveys good-natured contempt, everyone does his best to prove that his own brow is attractively low—a thin line of common sense between two hairy hedges denoting common-manliness. One's intellect or learned profession or habit of self-cultivation is something to hide or live down, and this is true even though more and more people are being schooled and colleged and "educationed" than ever before.

All the purposes and achievements of Western man in the twentieth century conspire, for the time being, to blot out the meaning of education. Looked at globally, today's task is to "educate" the peoples of the earth to mass production and national independence. In this effort the world's work and the world's wealth are now being redistributed among nations, classes and persons, and vast layers of mankind are slowly emerging from ancestral poverty and a sense of wrong. It is a mighty spectacle and one that the highbrow should not scorn, for the ideals and techniques which are at work come straight out of our past culture in the highbrow sense—out of the thoughts and books of educated men, from Jefferson to Bernard Shaw. But it is also true that the pace and scale of this great transformation take the heaviest toll on those best fitted to carry on the work of culture itself. Peace of mind, solitude, long stretches of concentration, have become luxuries almost beyond reach. We express this very inadequately by saying that we are "frightfully busy *just now*." Deep down we know that the condition is permanent for all those who cannot afford the blessed release of a nervous breakdown.

Now the educated man as we have known him in the past has roots in an entirely different soil and breathes a different air. He is a product of leisure and independence, of established institutions and quiet maturing. His destination is a society of his own kind, in which his role is private and his superiority welcome. He does contribute to others' enjoyment of life by sharing with them the pleasures of conversation and friendship and spoken wisdom, but the enrichment of his own mind is his chief concern. He can attend to this, not only because he has the time and the means but also because he does not have to justify his existence nor to issue progress reports on his life-long "individual project." Whatever he does to earn fame or money, from winning battles to farming estates, he is not so bedeviled by it that he lacks time to engage in the fundamental activities of the educated, which are: to read, write, talk and listen.

Actually, everybody would be happier if the plain fact were admitted (as Jefferson admitted it in his plan for public education in Virginia) that no amount of industry or even of acquired knowledge will make an educated man. The specialist knows a great deal and is not educated. The pedant knows more than enough and is not educated. Why then be ashamed of not having what comes mainly from native endowment? Is it sensible to growl about not having absolute pitch or not being a champion billiard player? To resent not being educated is particularly absurd when one considers that education, like virtue, is its own reward, nothing more—nothing, certainly, to brag about. Indeed one test of a true education is that it sits lightly on the possessor. He knows better than anybody else how thin in spots is the mantle which others would pluck from him.

Contrariwise, a frankly aggressive envy of the educated few by the unlettered many is thoroughly justified. It is a fair guess that the solid citizens who put Socrates to death said to themselves: "Why should this outrageously ugly mug spend his days talking with brilliant young men while we wear ourselves out in the fig business?" And to this there is really no amiable answer. Resentment based on democratic equality and patriotism (figs are the cornerstone of empire) is what precipitates the tragedy. Socrates always seems to be saying, "Don't you wish you were like me!" while pointing out that only a chance-selected few can make the attempt. In reality Socrates is not saying or thinking any such thing, but he is the living demonstration of an offensive truth. Hence the accusation which leads to the hemlock cocktail.

With us, the democratic assumption works more gently. It easily prevails by sheer force of numbers. Whatever is alarmingly different or superior is leveled off like the froth on the glass of beer. Go to the friendliest social dinner, and the conversation will run exclusively on current events and common experiences—so much so that after dinner the men and the women form separate groups and talk business in the one, domesticity in the other. The correct mixture of passion and detachment about beliefs, which makes of conviviality something more than eating and drinking together, is less and less attainable.

Despite appearances, the common language of the educated is neither difficult in itself nor overwhelming in extent. The well-read have not read everything, and after a while—as somebody said very wittily—you begin to know things ex officio. In any case facility does not come by grinding away of nights and memorizing obscure facts. Obscurity is the very opposite of culture as it is the opposite of good breeding. But what is required for mastery is a lively and insatiable interest. This is the thing that cannot be faked. And this is also what makes it impossible to "climb" into educated society under false pretenses as people do into snobbish, moneyed or artistic society. The brotherhood of educated men is the one social group which our century cannot open to all by legislative fiat. The irony is that those within have no desire to keep it exclusive—the more the merrier, provided they are the genuine article.

Meantime, from another quarter, the word education has been snatched by business and government to refer to activities ranging from fire drill to political propaganda. The makers of sewing machines have educational departments where you may take lessons in hemstitching, and so have magazines which use alluring pictures to teach how a young lady in the bath should scrub her back. These genteel accomplishments are not to be despised, but they remind us that while the faith in intellect has receded from the high places, the new thing which goes by the name of education has some distance to go before it reaches the head.

For today's young men and women who went to a genuine seat of learning and took their studies seriously, the blind forces of our society act as a barrier to further self-education. At college the chances are that they absorbed just enough to awake their mind and spur its quest for more learning. It is after college that these young people are stymied. The girl, now married, has no help and is too busy in kitchen and nursery to read a book. The man, saddled early with family responsibilities in a competitive world, must by tireless slaving "make good" in the first ten or fifteen years of his career. By taking work home every night he proves to his employers that he cares for nothing in the world but insurance or law or the prospects of natural gas. It remains a mystery how the world's work got done in the old days when college-trained beginners in business worked only from nine to five and were not deemed traitors to the firm if they were seen at a concert.

Today's beginner, it may be said, learns more about the nature of his job and its interconnections with the rest of the "economy." But what he bones up on during those career-building nights is only in part real knowledge. The rest is artificial verbiage and statistics, like so much that we are now compelled to carry in our heads—bunches of initials, trade names and telephone numbers—incoherent facts by the bushel, which are out of date almost before they are learned. Inevitably this essential rubbish soon overlays anything the young man learned to enjoy in college. At the end of a long day which never really shuts down on business, he cannot attend to that other world of which he was given a glimpse in the classroom, the laboratory or the art gallery. And thus, by a queer turn of the wheel, our present equalizing of social and economic rights, which should create a larger sense of community, actually drives people apart by narrowing the contents of their minds. Our hypothetical young couple shows this, sometimes tragically. They married on the strength of common interests, and five years out of college they have nothing to say to each other except what relates to home or office routine.

But there persists a thirst for spiritual refreshment that cannot be satisfied by the glut of "hard facts." There remains one restless want: imaginative experience. To this need our technological age responds with the most lavish provision of organized entertainment, from gambling and sports to radio and the screens. Here at last we are given a chance to be lifted out of our mechanical concerns and to take part in exciting or amusing or awe-inspiring experiences. No doubt the habit of being entertained, of letting the show come in one eye and out the other, may end by destroying one's power to enjoy such thoughts and visions as one may have. But the world owes something to the men and women who lavish their talents for our pastime, twenty-four hours a day, by sink or bedside, in the air, on the road and to the very edge of the grave. It staggers the imagination to conceive what would happen to mankind in its present state if it were left to its own resources like our forefathers, in caves without canasta and tents without television.

For some few mavericks, however, there is no alternative to despair or boredom except the pleasure of making one's life a means to one's education. Young men and women continue to be born with an insatiable desire to know, and among these not all are bent on knowing the things that are negotiable. These marked souls manage somehow, in spite of all they see around them, to make themselves into educated persons. They show a remarkable power to survive unfavorable environments, such as advertising agencies, movie studios and teachers' colleges. But the oddest thing about them is that without any clear guidance from society at large, and in the teeth of all the disturbing forces of the day, they all develop very much the same interests and rediscover for themselves the original humanities. Literature, philosophy and the arts, religion, political theory and history become the staples on which they feed their minds. And with slight variations in diet expressive of different temperaments, they ultimately come into possession of the common knowledge and the common tongue.

Occasionally, of course, they are helped to enter into the Great Conversation, or to keep their footing there, by the presence of other educated men, better entrenched or sufficiently numerous to resist the tides. In one city there is a college truly committed to general education; in another there is an adult reading group; in a third the woman's club actually reads the authors whom it invites to lecture and be stared at. There is no doubt that you could fill Madison Square Garden with educated people. The species is obsolete but not extinct, and you could charge an admission fee without offering them anything to see or hear—except their own well-modulated voices.

Alone though they may be much of the time, they are not so much to be pitied as the sociable creatures who must have "people around" or a movie to go to. For the educated person has appropriated so much of other men's minds that he can live on his store like the camel on his reservoir. Everything can become grist to his mill, including his own misery, if he is miserable; for by association with what he knows, everything has echoes and meanings and suggestions ad infinitum. This is, in fact, the test and the use of a man's education, that he finds pleasure in the exercise of his mind.

Pascal once said that all the trouble in the world was due to the fact that man could not sit still in a room. He must hunt, flirt, gamble, chatter. That is man's destiny and it is not to be quarreled with, but the educated man has through the ages found a way to convert passionate activity into a silent and motionless pleasure. He can sit in a room and not perish.

A DIVIDED SOUTH SEARCHES ITS SOUL

by Robert Penn Warren

JULY 9, 1956

> *Robert Penn Warren, teacher and novelist, is a*
> *Southerner by birth and manner; and some of his*
> *best work, like the Pulitzer prize-winning novel*
> *All the King's Men, has a Southern setting. In the spring*
> *of 1956 LIFE sent him South to explore what the Supreme*
> *Court's order to desegregate schools meant to the*
> *people concerned. Warren traveled through big city*
> *and back country of the Deep South and border states,*
> *talking with hundreds of Southerners, white and colored.*
> *Out of these talks came this eloquent report.*

"I am glad it's you going back," said my friend, a Southerner, long resident in New York, "and not me." But I went back, for going back this time, like all the other times, was a necessary part of my life. I was going back to confront the crisis in Southern life, to look at the faces, to hear the voices, to hear, in fact, the voices in my own blood. A girl from Mississippi said to me, "I feel that it's all happening inside of me, every bit of it."

I know what she meant.

I sat in the tight, tiny living room of an organizer of a new important segregation group (onetime official of the Klan) while he haranged me. He is a fat but powerful man, never genial though the grin tries to be when he has scored a point and folds his hands on his belly. He's out to preserve, he says, "what you might name the old Southern way, what we was raised up to."

He is clearly a man of force, force that somehow has never found its way, and a man of language and leadership among his kind, the angry and ambitious and disoriented and dispossessed. He had been cautious at first, had thought I was from the FBI, but now it seems some grand vista is opening before him and his eyes gleam and the words come.

All the while his very handsome wife has been standing in the deep shadow of the doorway to a room beyond, standing like the proper hill wife while the menfolks talk.

"Excuse me," she suddenly says, addressing me, "excuse me, but didn't you say you was born down here, used to live right near here?"

I say yes.

She takes a step forward. "Yes," she says, "yes," leaning at me in vindictive triumph, "but you never said where you living now!"

Suspicion of the outlander, or of the corrupted native, gets tangled up sometimes with suspicion of the New York press, but the latter may exist quite separately as a calculated judgment, and I was to see a newspaperman of high integrity (an integrationist, by the way) suddenly strike down his fist and exclaim, "Well, by God, it's a fact, it's not in them not to load the dice in the news story!"

It is not merely resentment at real, or imaginary, injustice in the press. There is something else too: the instinctive fear, on the part of black or white, that the massiveness of experience, the concreteness of life, will be violated; the fear of abstraction. I suppose it is this fear that made one man, a subtle and learned man, say to me, "There's something you can't explain, what being a Southerner is."

In the end people talked, even showed an anxiety to talk, to explain something. Even the black Southerners would talk, for over and over the moment of some sudden decision would come: "All right—all right—I'll tell it to you straight."

But how fully can I read the words offered to me in the fullest effort or candor?

It is a town in Louisiana and I am riding in an automobile driven by a Negro, a teacher, a slow, careful man, who puts his words out that way. He says, "You hear some white men say they know Negroes, understand Negroes. But it's not true. No white man ever born ever understood what a Negro is thinking. What he's feeling.

"And half the time that Negro," he continues, "he don't understand either."

Just listening to talk as it comes is best, but there are questions to ask, the old obvious questions, I suppose.

What are the white man's reasons for segregation?

The man I am talking to is a yellow man, about forty years old, shortish, rather fat, with a very smooth, faintly Mongolian face, eyes very shrewd but ready to smile. He gives the impression of a man very much at home in himself. He owns a small business with a few employees.

"What does the white man do it for?" he rephrases the question. He pauses, his smooth yellow face compressing a little. "You know," he says, "you know, years and years I look at some white feller, and I cain't never figure him out. You go 'long with him, years and years, and all of a sudden he does something. I cain't figure out what makes him do the way he does."

Another Negro, a very black man, small-built and intense, leans forward in his chair. He says it is money, so the white man can have cheap labor, can make the money.

"Yeah, yeah," the yellow man is saying, agreeing, "but—"

"But what?" I ask.

"Mongrelization," he says, "that's what a white man will say. He wants to head it off, he says. But"—he grins—"look at my face. It wasn't any black man hung it on me."

The other man doesn't seem to think this is funny. "Yes," he says, "yes, they claim they don't want mongrelization. But who has done it? They claim Negroes are dirty, diseased, but they have Negro nurses for their children. They claim—" and his voice goes on, winding up the bitter catalogue of old paradoxes.

"It's all true," the smooth-faced man says, "what Mr. Elmo here says. But there must be something behind it all. Something he don't ever say, that white feller. Maybe—" He pauses, hunting for the formulation. "Maybe it's just pridefulness," he says, "him being white."

Later, I am talking with the hillman organizer, the one with the handsome wife, and he is telling me why he doesn't want integration. "Hit's agin nature," he says. "The court cain't take no stick and mix folks up like you swivel and swull eggs broke in a bowl. Naw," he says, "you got to raise 'em up, the niggers, not bring the white folks down to nigger level.

"Besides, a nigger ain't got no morals. He don't even know how to treat no wife, not even a nigger common-law wife. He whup her and beat her and maybe carve on her jaw with a pocket knife. When he ought to trick and pet her, and set her on his knee like a white man does his wife."

Then I talk with a Negro grade-school teacher, in the country, in Tennessee, a mulatto woman, middle-aged. She is sitting in her tiny, pridefully clean house, with a prideful bookcase of books beyond her.

"You ought to see the schoolhouse I teach in," she says, and pauses, and her lips curl sardonically, "set in the mud and hogs can come under it, and the privies set back in the mud. And see some of the children that come there, out of homes with nothing, with disease and dirt and no manners. You wouldn't blame a white person for not wanting the white child set down beside them."

Then again the curl of the lips: "Why didn't the federal government give us money ten years ago for our school? To get ready, to raise up a little. It would have made it easier. But now—"

But now, I ask.

"You got to try to be fair," she says.

I am talking with an official of one of the segregation outfits. He is seventy-five years old, bald, sallow-skinned, very clean and scrubbed-looking. He started out to be a lawyer but wound up doing lots of things, finally, for years, a fraternal organizer. He is not the rabble rouser but the persuader, the man who gives the reasons. He is, in fact, a very American type, the old-fashioned, self-made, back-country intellectual—the type that finds apotheosis in Mark Twain and Abraham Lincoln. If he is not one of them, if he says "gondorea" and "enviro-mental" and "ethnolology," if nothing ever came out quite right for him along the way, you can still sense the old, unappeased hungers.

I ask him why the white man wants segregation.

"You got to explain it to him, the ethnolology. How there is just two races, white and black, and—"

"What about the Bible," I ask, "doesn't the Bible say three?"

"Yes, but you know, between you and me, I don't reckon you have to take much stock in the Bible in this business. Nor Darwin in some ways either. He is too enviro-mental, he doesn't think enough about the blood. The point is there's just two races, black and white, and the rest of them is a kind of mixing. Take India. They were a pure white people like you and me, and they had a pretty good civilization too. Till they got to shipping on a little Negro blood. Look at 'em now."

I sit with a lawyer, in another state, an official of another segregation group. He has been talking states rights and I ask him if that is the main issue. "Yes," he says, "in a way. But you've got to fight on something you can rouse people up about." He hesitates, then jerks a drawer open, literally jerks it, and thrusts an envelope at me. "Heck, you might as well see it," he says.

I have seen it before, the handbills showing "Harlem Negro and White Wife" lying across a bed, Negro crooners and white admirers, and so on.

"If there is trouble," I ask, "where will it begin?"

"We don't condone violence," he says.

"But if—just suppose," I say.

He doesn't hesitate. "The red-neck," he says, "that's what you call 'em around here, those fellows—and I'm one of them myself, just a red-neck that got educated—are the ones who will feel the rub. He is the one on the underside of the plank with nothing between him and the bare black ground. He's got to have something to give him pride. Just to be better than something."

To be better than something: so we are back to the pridefulness the yellow man had talked about.

But now, there is more, something else. There is the very handsome lady of forty-five, charming and witty and gay, a totally captivating talker of the kind you still occasionally find among women of the Deep South, but never now in a woman under forty. She is sitting before the fire in the fine room, her brother, big and handsome but barefoot and rigidly drunk, opposite her. But she gaily overrides that small difficulty. ("Oh, don't mind him, he's just had a whole bottle of brandy. Been on a high-lonesome all by myself.") She has been talking about the Negroes on her plantation, and at last, about integration, but that only in one phrase tossed off as gaily and casually as any other of the evening: "But of course we have to keep the white race intact."

But the husband, much her senior, who has said almost nothing all evening, lifts his strong, grizzled old face and in a kind of *sotto voce* growl, not to her, not to me, not to anybody, utters, "In power—in power—you mean the white race in power!"

And I think of another Southerner, an integrationist, saying: "In no county where the Negroes are two to one is the white man going to surrender power. Put a Yankee liberal in the same county and in a week he'd be behaving the same way."

But is it power? Merely power?

I ask a professor in a college in a black section what would happen if a Negro actually enrolled, and he says, "Brother, it would be something."

Yes, he was a segregationist and his reasons were clear, as he leaned happily back in his chair, in the handsome office, a spare, fiftyish man, rather dressy, the voice nasal: "Yeah brother, back in my county there was a long ridge and one side the ridge was good land, and folks put on airs there and held niggers, but on the other side of the ridge the ground so pore you couldn't grow peas and nothing but pore white trash. So when the Civil War came, the pore white trash just picked down the old rifle off the deer horns over the fireplace and joined the Federals coming down, just because they hated those fellows across the ridge. But don't get me wrong, brother. They didn't want any truck with niggers either. To this day they vote Republican and hate niggers. It is just they hate niggers."

I am in another room, the library of a plantation house, in Mississippi, and the planter is talking to me from his high-nosed, command-

218

ing face, propped back at ease, saying, "I'll tell you what I feel. I came out of the university with a lot of ideals and humanitarianism. But I tell you now what has come out of thirty years of experience and careful consideration. I have a deep contempt for the Negro race as it exists here. It is not so much a matter of ability as of character. Character."

He repeats the word. He is a man of character, it could never be denied. He is also a man of fine intelligence and good education. He is a man of human warmth and generosity.

The husband goes on: "It's not so much the hands on my place, as the lawyers and doctors and teachers and insurance men and undertakers—oh, yes, I've had dealings all around, or my hands have. The character just breaks down. They pay lip service to the white man's ideals of conduct. But it is just lip service."

"I don't intend to get lathered up. I believe in segregation but I can always protect myself and my family. I dine at my club and my land is my own and when I travel, the places I frequent have few if any Negroes. Not that I'd ever walk out of a restaurant, I'm no professional Southerner. And I'd never give a nickel to the Citizens Council or anything like that."

Later on, he says, "For years, I thought I loved Negroes. My father —he was a firster around here, first man to put glass windows in for them, first to do a lot to help them toward financial independence— well, my father, he used to look at me and say, son, they will knock it out of you. Well, they did. I learned the grimness and the sadness."

And later, we ride down the long row of the houses of the hands, he points to shreds of screening at windows. "One of my last experiments," he says, dourly. "Three months, and they poked it out of the kitchen window so they could throw slop on the bare ground."

We ride on. We pass a nicely painted house, with a fenced dooryard, flower boxes on the porch, and good, bright-painted porch furniture. I ask who lives there. "One of the hands," he says, "but he's got some energy and character. Has only three children, but when there's work he gets it done fast, and then finds some more to do. Makes $4,500 to $5,000 a year." Some old pride, or something from the lost days of idealism, comes back into his tone.

I ask what the man's color is.

"A real black man, a real Negro, all right. But he's got character."

I look down the interminable row of dingy houses, over the interminable flat of black earth toward the river.

Pridefulness, money, level of intelligence, race, God's will, states rights and the Constitution, filth and disease, morality, power, hate, contempt—but there is another thing. I hear a college student in the Deep South: "You know, it's just that people don't like to feel they're spitting on their grandfather's grave."

Let us, without meaning to be ironical, call this thing piety.

In the Deep South, I sit with an N.A.A.C.P. secretary, another Negro and two white men. I ask the secretary if a staggered system of desegregation would satisfy the Negro. "The law—and Court decision—" he begins. One of the white men breaks in: "Mr. Cranford here doesn't want violence. He knows—we know—that change takes time."

But the white man has said it. Not Mr. Cranford, who sits with his head propped on his hand, brow furrowed, looking away.

Again, it is the Deep South, another town, the bright, new-sparkling living room of the house of a Negro businessman. There are several white men present, two journalists, myself (I have just come along to watch, I'm not involved), some TV technicians, and about ten Negroes, all in Sunday best, at ease but slightly formal.

One of the journalists is instructing a Negro who is to be interviewed, a tall, good-looking, dark brown man in a blue suit. "Now you're supposed to tell them," the journalist is saying, "what a lot of hogwash this separate but equal stuff is."

The interview begins. The dark brown man, very much at ease, is saying: "— and we're not disturbed. The only people disturbed are those who have not taken an unbiased look."

The journalist cuts in: "Make it simple and direct. Lay it on the line."

The tall brown man is unruffled. "Listen," he says, "you all are going back to New York City. But we stay here. We aren't afraid, but we live here. They know what we think, but it's a way of putting it we got to think about."

He says it is going to take some time to work things out, he knows that, but there is a chorus from the Negroes crowded back out of range of the cameras: "Don't put no time limit—don't put any time on it—no ten or fifteen years!"

The dark brown man doesn't put any time on it. All they want, he says, is a biracial committee that will recognize the law and sit down to work out the "how" and the "when." As for the "when": "Well, Negroes are patient. We can wait a little while longer."

The dark brown man gets up and receives the handshakes, the shoulder-slaps, of his friends. They think he did well. He did do well. He looks back over his shoulder at the white men, grins. "When I got to leave town," he says, "who's going to give me that job as chauffeur? I see that nice Cadillac sitting out front there."

There are quick, deep-throated giggles.

I turn to a Negro beside me. "Ten years ago," I ask, "would this have been possible?"

"No," he says.

Then there is another house, and another Negro being arranged for an interview. This one, one of the journalists has told me, is supposed to be the Uncle Tom, just to round out the picture. The Negro elected as Uncle Tom is middle-aged, medium brown, with a balding, rather high forehead. He is wearing a good dark suit. His manner is dignified, slow, a little sad. He had begun life as waterboy on a plantation but a white man had helped him and now he is a preacher. For a voice level he says, "Jesus wept, Jesus wept."

The journalist tells him he is supposed to say some good things for segregation. The Negro doesn't answer directly to that. "If you have some opinions of your own," he says, "your own people sometimes call you a son-of-a-gun, and sometimes the white people call you a son-of-a-gun."

Your own people: and I remember that the Negroes at the last house had said, "Don't tell him you've seen us, don't tell him that or you won't get him to talk."

Is integration a good thing, the journalist asks him, and he says,

"Till Negro people get as intelligent and self-sustaining they can't mix." But he flares up about wage differentials, no good jobs. The N.A.A.C.P. ought to work on that first, that and the ballots. As for the court decision, he says, "it's not something to force, it's something for people to strive for."

I break in—I don't think the machinery is going yet—and ask about humiliation as a bar to Negro fulfillment.

"Segregation did one thing," he says. "No other race but the Negro could build up as much will to go on and do things. To get their goals."

What goals, I ask.

"Just what anybody wants, just anything people can want to be a citizen," he says.

This isn't what the journalist had come for. Uncle Tom is evaporating.

The preacher is a prosegregationist, the journalist suggests, in that he thinks segregation built a will to achieve something.

The mike is lifted on its rod, the slow, sad voice speaks: ". . . segregation has proved that Negroes in the South where it's practiced most have done a fine job of building an economic strength." Therefore he goes along, he says, with the moderate approach. "It is absurd, otherwise it's just foolish thinking for people to believe you can get the South to do in four or five years what the North has been doing for a hundred years. These people are emotional about their tradition, and you've got to get an educational program, and this will be a slow process."

Yes, Uncle Tom is back. Or is he? For the sad voice is now saying: "—has got to outthink the white man—" Is saying: "—not ultimate goal just to go to white schools and travel with white people on conveyances over the country. No, sir, the Negro, he is a growing people and he will strive for all the equalities belonging to any American citizen. He is a growing people."

Uncle Tom is gone again, and gone for good.

The Negro turns to the journalist and asks if he has interviewed other Negroes.

"Oh, some," after a shade of hesitation.

Had he interviewed So-and-So and So-and-So?

"No—why, no. Well, we want to thank you. . . ."

We leave the sad-mannered, slow man and we know that he knows. White men have lied to him before.

I ask my questions of the eminent Negro scholar. His reply is immediate: "It's not so much what the Negro wants as what he doesn't want. He does not want to be denied human dignity."

And I think of a Negro girl, in a shack in the sea of mud, at dusk, who says "It's how yore feelings git tore up all the time. The way folks talk sometimes. It ain't what they say sometimes, if they'd jes say it kind."

I think of another woman, up in Tennessee, middle-aged, a school inspector for country schools, a Negro. "We don't want to socialize. That's not what we want. But I don't want to be insulted."

And in Tennessee again, the Negro at the biracial committee meeting says, "My boy is happy in the Negro school where he goes. I don't want him to go to the white school and sit by your boy's side. But I'd die for his right to go."

The college student, a Negro, says, "The Negro doesn't want social equality. My wife is my color. I'm above wanting to mix things up. That's low class. Low class of both races."

The Negro man in Mississippi says, "Take a Negro man wanting a white woman. A man tends to want his own kind, now. But the white folks make such an awful fuss about it. They make it seem so awful special-like. Maybe that's what makes it sort of prey on some folks' minds."

This is a question for Negroes only. *Is there any difference between what the Negro feels at the exclusions of segregation, and what a white feels at the exclusions which he, any man, must always face at some point?*

"Yes, it is different," the Negro college official says, "when your fate is on your face."

And the Negro lawyer, looking out the window, over Beale Street, "Yes, there's a difference," he says. "A Negro, he doesn't really know sometimes, but he just goes walking pregnant with worries, not knowing their name. It's he has lost his purpose, somewhere. He goes wandering and wondering, and no purpose."

I look out the window, too, over Beale Street. It is late afternoon. I hear the pullulation of life, the stir and new tempo toward evening, the babble of voices, a snatch of laughter. I hear the remorseless juke boxes. They shake the air.

What's coming? "Whatever it is," the college student in the Deep South says, "I'd like to put all the Citizens Council and all the N.A.A.C.P. in one room and give every man a baseball bat and lock 'em in till it was over. Then maybe some sensible people could work out something."

What's coming? The Methodist minister, riding with me in the dusk, in the drizzle, by the flooded bayou, says, "It'll come, desegregation and the vote and all that. But it will be a generation. You can preach law and justice, but it's a slow pull till you get the education." He waves a hand toward the rows of shacks marshaled off into the darkening distance, toward the far cypresses where dusk is tangled. "You can see," he says.

What's coming? I ask the impressive, aristocratic, big gray-haired man, sitting in his rich office, high over the city, a man of exquisite simplicity and charm, and a member of a segregation group. "We shall exhaust all legal possibilities," he says.

Will they win the legal fight?

"No," he says, "but it is just something you have to do." He rolls a cigarette fastidiously between strong, white, waxy forefinger and thumb. "To speak truth," he says, "I think the whole jig is up. I'll tell you why. You see those girls in my office outside. Come from good lower-middle-class homes. Well, a girl comes in here and says to me, a gentleman is waiting. She shows him in. He is as black as the ace of spades. It just never crossed that girl's mind, what she was saying, when she said a gentleman was waiting."

What's coming, I ask the taxi driver in Memphis, and he says, "Lots of dead niggers round here, that's what's coming. Look at Detroit, lots of dead niggers been in the Detroit River, but it won't be a patch on the ole Mississippi."

What's coming, and a man says, "Sure, they aim for violence, coming in here. When a man gets up before a crowd and plays what purports to be a recording of an N.A.A.C.P. official, an inflammatory sex thing, what do you call it? Well, they got him on the witness stand, under oath, and he had to admit he got the record from the Citizens Council. What's going to happen if a guy like that runs things? I ask you."

What's coming, I ask the Episcopal rector, in the Deep South. "The Negro has to be improved before integration," he says. "Take their morals, we are gradually improving the standard of morality and decency."

The conversation veers, we take a longer view. "Well, anthropologically speaking," he says, "the solution will be absorption, the Negro will disappear."

I ask how this is happening.

"Low-class people, immoral people, libertines, wastrels, prostitutes and such," he says.

Does he see the logic of what he has said? Morality delays the "solution."

Out of Memphis, I lean back in my seat on the plane and watch the darkness slide by. I know what the Southerner feels, going out of the South, the relief, the expanding vistas. I think of the new libel laws, of the academic pressures, of the Negro facing the shot-gun blast, of the white man with a hard-built business being boycotted, of the college boy who said, "I'll just tell you, everybody is *scairt.*"

I feel the surge of relief. But I know what the relief really is. It is the relief from responsibility. Yes, you know what the relief is. It is the flight from the reality you were born to.

But what is that reality? It is the fact of self-division. I do not mean division between man and men in society. That division is of course there. But it is not so important, in the long run, as the division within the individual man.

Within the individual there are, or may be, many lines of fracture.

It may be between his social views and his anger at being "forced."
It may be between his own social idealism and his anger at Yankee
Phariseeism. (Oh, yes, he remembers that in the '60's, when federal
bayonets supported black state governments in the South, not a single
Negro held elective office in any Northern state.) It may be between
his social views and his fear of the power state. It may be between his
allegiance to organized labor and his racism—for status or blood purity.
It may be between his Christianity or his sense of democracy and his
ingrained attitude toward the Negro. It may be between his practical
concern at the money loss to society caused by the depressed state of
the Negro and his personal gain or personal prejudice. It may be, and
disastrously, between his sense of the inevitable and his emotional
need to act against the inevitable.

There are almost an infinite number of permutations and combinations, but they all amount to the same thing, a deep intellectual rub,
a moral rub, anger at the irremediable self-division, a deep exacerba-
tion at some failure to find identity. That is the reality.

It expresses itself in many ways. In Tennessee I sit for an afternoon
with an old friend, a big, weather-faced man, a man of good education, of travel and experience. I ask if he thinks we can afford, in the
present world picture, to alienate Asia by segregation here at home.
He hates the question. "I hate to think about it," he says. "It's too deep
for me," he says, and moves heavily in his chair. "My mind just shuts
up."

There are many kinds of rub, but the commonest one is, I suppose,
the moral one—the Christian one. I remember one pastor in Tennessee, a local man, saying, "Yes, I think the decision may have set back
race equality—it was coming faster than any guess because it was
so quiet. But now some people stop me on the street about it. So I
ask about Heaven, what they'll do in Heaven? 'Well,' one woman said,
'I'll just let God segregate us.'

" 'You'll *let* God segregate you?' I said, and she flounced off. You
know, there's just one question to ask: what would Christ do?"

The taxi drew up in front of the house and I ran for the door. I
wanted to write down what the driver had said.

He had been in the war, in Africa and Italy, had bossed work gangs, Arabs first, then Negro troops. Here are the notes:

"It ain't our hate, it's the hate hung on us by the old folks dead and gone. Not I mean to criticize the old folks, they done the best they knew, but that hate, we don't know how to shuck it. We got that hate stuck in our craw and can't puke it up. If white folks quit shoving the nigger down and calling him a nigger he could maybe get to be a asset to the South and the country. But how stop shoving?"

WOMAN, LOVE AND GOD

a LIFE *editorial*

DECEMBER 24, 1956

> LIFE *devoted its special year-end issue of 1956 to*
> The American Woman. *Tucked away among features*
> *showing not only the glamour of U.S. women but*
> *the tremendous variety of useful jobs they do, this*
> *editorial looked more deeply at woman's "central role*
> *in the eternal mysteries of the human spirit and its*
> *relationship to God."*

> This little germ of nuptial love,
> Which springs so simply from the sod,
> The root is, as my song shall prove,
> Of all our love to man and God.
> —COVENTRY PATMORE

The American woman is often discussed as a problem to herself and others. Has she become too dominant in our society, joylessly raising an infantile breed of men? Or is she the prisoner of that unwanted "otherness" forged by the impenetrable egotism of the male? Such questions are important, but less so than the grandest fact about woman: her central role in the eternal mysteries of the human spirit and its relationship to God.

In the Gospels, woman's great role is represented by Jesus' mother, whose joy the Christmas season celebrates. By her free assent to Gabriel's message, the Virgin Mary made it possible for Jesus to be the son of man as well as of God. Her lines in the Gospel are few, but so crucial and beautiful that they earned her the name of Queen of Heaven, "clothed with the sun, and the moon under her feet." As Christianity spread, a special veneration grew around Mary, sweetening the harsh life of the Middle Ages, inspiring whole areas of the Renaissance. Even the American Puritan Henry Adams felt her Gothic power "to the last fibre of his being."

But Protestant America has in the main sought to avoid intercessors between man and God. The Mary of the Bible would scarcely have enjoyed these disagreements among Christians, who have so much to agree on. They can surely agree that if Mary were absent from the Christian story, the meaning of human life would lose half its point and hope, especially in America. For the love the Virgin symbolizes is the love of which Americans stand in most need.

They need, first of all, a clearer concept of the Christian doctrine on sex. Just as the sin of Adam and Eve is vulgarly supposed to have been sexual (it was, as St. Thomas clearly stated, disobedient pride), so the virginity of Mary is vulgarly received as a counsel of lifelong sexual perfection, as though it were the highest Christian calling. Of course it is not. Love is; and Mary represents the human capacity for love at its fullest. She represents that source and nursery of love, the human family, where man and wife, mother and child, father and son, brother and brother first learn the meanings of the great word.

In America the family is in special trouble. But as one psychologist has lately written (Erich Fromm, *The Art of Loving*), psychological understanding, though necessary to love, is no substitute for it; indeed the very popularity of psychology "betrays the fundamental lack of love in human relations today." Many Americans have very inadequate notions of love. They regard it as a happy state one "falls into" (or out of), a state invited by "a mixture between being popular and having sex appeal." But love is an art, and like any art requires discipline and cultivation. And if Americans have failed to pay this tribute to married love, they cannot excel at other branches of the art, for its branches are all related.

Marriage serves many human purposes, from protection of infants to division of labor; but its abiding motive is the fact that every individual is by nature lonely and incomplete. The most obvious aspect of this loneliness is the incompleteness of one's sex. Erotic activity assuages but does not cure this loneliness. Love is the cure, and it cures more than sexual incompleteness; for as it is cultivated, it expands. From a mere egoism *à deux,* married love at its best soon adds the dimension of parental love; and in growing it even transcends the natural exclusivity of the family and takes as its object strangers, enemies, the human race. Who loves his spouse is better able to love his neighbor as himself. But the boundary of love does not stop there.

The bliss of marriage, says the Catholic nuptial prayer, is "a blessing which alone was not removed either in punishment of original sin or by the sentence of the Deluge." It is devoutly called a memory of the earthly Paradise before the Fall, and likewise an anticipation of immortality. Poets of marriage have felt with Paul Claudel that "woman arouses in man a desire which she cannot herself satisfy and which can be satisfied only in God." For as married love is the bliss of earth, so its spiritual counterpart is the bliss of divine love. That is why matrimony is called holy. The loneliness and incompleteness of the individual are most fully cured when man and wife together share the knowledge and love of God.

Women have excelled in every high Christian calling, from the pure mysticism of St. Teresa to the militant patriotism of St. Joan. Early saints were mostly men, those since the Reformation are mostly women; but in every age woman proves the diversity of her genius: the seventh-century abbess of Whitby, St. Hilda, who, by encouraging the peculiar gift of an old man named Caedmon, became the mother of English poetry; the widowed queen St. Elizabeth of Hungary, who fought the famine of 1225 by feeding nine hundred daily at her gate; tough and purposeful Mother Cabrini who left schools and hospitals all over this hemisphere in our own time. And thousands more.

But much as one must praise the diverse accomplishments of saintly women, the inspiration of Jesus' mother is not for saints only and need not lead so far from home. If woman, "the sum and complex of all nature," has one role more important than her others, it is the one symbolized by Mary as a source of love. Only as women guard the art and guide the quest of love can mankind know all the kinds and heights of love of which they are capable. The art and the quest begin in the family and end at God's feet.

THE ARAB WORLD'S ANGRY NATIONALISM

by Keith Wheeler

APRIL 1, 1957

> *Eighty million Arabs are caught up in a surging nationalism which has already led many to a rejection of the West. Soviet influence is becoming stronger, but the West still has ways of countering it. A former newspaperman and a novelist, Associate Editor Keith Wheeler is* LIFE's *Middle East expert.*

For years, Americans working in Arab lands have had to listen to an interminable torrent of anti-Western complaints and threats, the product of what the Arabs consider the West's uninterrupted record of hypocrisy and deceit since World War I. The writer remembers, for instance, an angry Syrian: "You are driving us into the arms of the Russians; look out, we will go Communist." He was Marouf Dawalibi, now a member of the Syrian parliament.

Suddenly, two and a half years ago, the stale old threat became reality. Late in 1954 in Syria, where Communism was illegal, a Moscow-trained party veteran named Khaled Bakdash was elected to

231

parliament. Bakdash was the first acknowledged Communist to hold office in an Arab country. Then the following summer came the event which really shook the West. Egypt's president, Gamal Abdel Nasser, committed Egypt's cotton exports to Russia for a formidable list of weapons including MiG 15's, submarines and T34's and Stalin tanks.

Nasser's explanation for this act, which abruptly turned Egypt's attention from internal development to preparation for war, was that he had failed to get any considerable armament from Western sources. Consequently he had been caught unprepared when the Israeli government staged a big raid on the Gaza Strip on February 28, 1955.

The arms deal made Nasser a hero in the Arab world. He had demonstrated that there was somewhere else to go than to the West, and Arabs looked on this as the beginning of a bright new day.

The size of Nasser's deal has never been fully documented in the West, although there has been plenty of speculation ranging up to and over $200 million. Nasser insists wryly that far from making a massive commitment to the Reds, he was too cautious. "Remember," he said to me not long ago, "I told you last year we hadn't brought in Russian instructors because we didn't want to get involved with foreign uniforms. Now I think that was a mistake; when we needed to fight we were six months behind in training. One of the results of insufficient training was that we had more airplanes than we had pilots. We still have more, including MiG 17's. Supply of aircraft is not a problem.

"And we still have eight hundred tanks, even after those we lost in Sinai. It's a United Nations of tanks, Shermans, Centurions, French AMX's, T34's and Stalins. This was another result of not wanting to be dependent on the Russians. We bought everything we needed at once."

Nasser's decision to turn East for weapons had a sequel that same summer when Syria also decided to buy armament from the Communists. The first weapons to arrive in Syria were World War II German Mark IV tanks mounting a 75-mm gun. The Syrians liked the Mark IV for which, incidentally, they had a good supply of ammunition. However, their new suppliers evidently decided that secondhand German weapons would never make Syria into a guaranteed repeat customer. The supply was cut off and the Syrians were then given Russian-made T34's, a medium-weight tank which is described as simple and easy to operate and mounts an 85-mm main gun.

In Egypt, Nasser himself estimated the local Communists at about five thousand card carriers and told me they "are not strong." American authorities place the figure at fifteen hundred to three thousand, but agree that the party has no prominent or identifiable leader and is split into three quarreling branches. Communist activity appears to consist mainly of distributing tracts, which always attack the West and sometimes Nasser too, and of trying to rally support for the fellow-traveling Peace Partisans or labor fronts. Egyptian newspapermen suspect that some of their colleagues are Communists or fellow travelers, but hesitate to name names or document the charge.

Thus domestically, Egyptian Communism is probably at least as insignificant as Nasser says, perhaps even as insignificant as the U.S. embassy says. Probably far more important is Soviet Russia's appeal to Nasser as a working or potential partner and its appeal to the most vigorously anti-Western among his close associates.

Lebanon, always a restive state because of the religious mixture of its population, is believed to have a sizable party. Membership comes mainly from the printing, masons', carpenters', bakers' and hotel workers' unions and the Greek Orthodox church. Lebanese security officers believe that schools and government offices have been penetrated, "but not much." A high Lebanese official feels that fellow travelers are more dangerous than party members. "The Peace Partisans have done more harm in three years than the Communists have in thirty," he told me.

Iraq's Communists, who once flourished, were thoroughly suppressed in 1949 when Nuri es Said took office for his tenth prime ministry and stepped up an anti-Red drive begun by the previous cabinet. Four leaders were hanged, hundreds jailed and Nuri later claimed that he had located and disposed of the party's central committee and its records. The reputed top leader, Abdel Khader Ismail, was jailed in Lebanon but is now free somewhere in the Middle East.

The Sudan is said to have a sizable party, active largely in the railroad workers' union. Tunisia, where the Communists came in from

France and enjoyed legal standing while the anti-Communist Neo-Destour rebel party was illegal and suppressed, has somewhere between five thousand (an authoritative American guess) and fifteen thousand (an authoritative French guess). Still legal, the Tunisian party operates openly and last November 11 sent a message to Russia's Premier Bulganin congratulating him for his support of Egypt.

"We have to work pretty hard on the youngsters," said Azzouz Rebai, Tunisia's secretary of state for youth and sport. "The French never did much for them. The Communists are after them all the time—lectures, free voyages to Europe, picnics and outings with the sexes mixed." Rebai is countering with Boy Scout groups, summer camps, youth hostels, work and study camps, international exchange programs, organized sports and the Neo-Destour Youth.

Algerian rebel forces at war with the French include at least one Communist-dominated maquis (underground resistance group). The French profess to fear deeper Communist penetration of the rebel National Liberation Front. However, Algerian leaders in Morocco insist, as one said to me, that "the only Communists in Algeria are Frenchmen."

Communism's greatest internal threat may be found in Syria, even though the most pessimistic estimators do not place that country's card-carrying membership much above ten thousand. The problem was succinctly stated by an American observer: "Scarcely anybody accepts Communism as a social, political or economic philosophy. What concerns us here is Russian imperialism. It is not a question of Syrians accepting Communism but of allying themselves with one potential enemy, Russia, against another enemy, Israel."

The most natural field for Communism's burgeoning in Arab lands would seem to be the 900,000 refugees from Palestine. These hordes, increasing at a rapid rate, embittered, living on a meager dole, confined to camps which range from fair to squalid, usually deprived of the right to work and (except in Jordan) to vote, have been described as "a sea of disorder."

"Of course there are Communists here," said an Arab camp director assigned to the sprawling, sun-blistered, mud-walled encampment that harbors more than thirty thousand refugees at Jericho near the Dead Sea. "What else could you expect? But they don't really need agitators. This is a giveaway to the Reds."

Most of the refugees, however, appear to be far more preoccupied with dreams of going home than with political theory. In Beirut, living with his ten children in two rooms whose mud walls he raised under a canvas roof donated by the United Nations, Khalil Mahmoud Halim, once a grocer in Haifa, welcomed me with a cup of Turkish coffee.

"May the next time I see you be in Palestine," he said.

I asked him how he had spent the years since he left.

"I have had three more children," said Khalil. "I built these walls. Every day I go to the camp office to see what is going on. Then I walk into the city and stop at the area welfare office to see if there is anything extra on the ration, such as clothing, although it is not often. I go to the office of the Central Committee of Refugees to see if there is any news about being paid for my property in Haifa. Then I go also to the Arab Higher Committee to see if there is any news about going home. Together with my friends I listen to the radio. We want to know what the world is doing and where we can look for help."

This has been his life for nine years.

It is only outside the camp areas that the refugees have become an active social menace. Israel has felt them for years. No refugee believes that the act of "liberating" anything portable or valuable from across the border is anything more than simply recovering an infinitesimal part of his own. Surreptitious excursions by individuals or small groups of refugees have prompted innumerable Israeli complaints over the years and constitute much of what the Israelis describe as "guerrilla terrorism and provocation."

The refugees have also been used to create civil disorder, though it is sometimes difficult to tell whether their rampaging is self-generated or the result of manipulation. One incident that was probably self-generated was the Jordan rioting in the winter of 1955–56 in which the refugees blocked roads, wrecked autos, looted their own and Point Four properties, burned consulates and caused widespread damage across the entire country. They were out to block Jordan's joining the Baghdad Pact, which they took to be a British trick in Israel's favor, and they succeeded.

Thus far only a few Arab states have recognized the Soviet Union or the satellites diplomatically, and Russian embassies exist only in Egypt, Syria, Lebanon and Libya. But where they are present, the Communist diplomats are very active.

The largest official Communist effort is being made in the same country that harbors the biggest internal threat of Communism— Syria. All the iron-curtain countries except East Germany have missions there and the East Germans have a trade delegation. Within the past year the Russian mission has grown from a legation to the capital's largest embassy with the largest diplomatic list, including not just one but four military attachés. For the last three years the most spendid displays at the Damascus International Trade Fair have been Communist. In 1954 the Russians erected a huge prefabricated building which resembled a New England church except for the red star in the steeple. One entire two-story wall of this structure was lined with champagne and another with potted caviar, and the exhibits included a galaxy of lathes, dental equipment, textiles, earth movers, cameras, Zis limousines and other articles. The Russians would have run off with the fair but for the American ingenuity in bringing in *Cinerama*.

For several years American diplomatic missions have been selecting foreign citizens for observation trips to the U.S. Recently the Communist countries have borrowed the technique, and they have even improved it, reports a Lebanese observer.

"Some years they have taken up to one thousand from Lebanon and Syria," he told me. "If they are taking them to Bucharest they prepare the city and turn it over to them. They furnish everything, even girls. There was a time when our people were afraid to accept Communist invitations. Now they are afraid to decline, even our highest officials."

The Communists have also gone into the scholarship business on a substantial scale. One Syrian youth who received a Russian offer dropped in at the American embassy and reported that the Russian proposal involved six to nine months of preparatory language instruction followed by four years in an engineering school, all free.

The local press, never affluent, receives generous offers too. One publisher who owns an alleged daily and a sometime weekly in

236

Damascus told me that the Russian press attaché had occasionally offered him up to two Syrian pounds (57¢) per line if he would publish innocuous features on such subjects as collective farming or the latest five-year plan.

Even imported Soviet literature is subsidized—and popular. Ahmed Shaibani, a lesser sheik of the Ruwalla tribe which fought for Lawrence of Arabia in World War I, said, "I have the best Communist library in Damascus. I have thirteen volumes of Stalin, eight of Lenin, twenty-one of Marx and six of Engels. The lot cost me $21. But when I wanted a copy of Admiral Leahy's memoirs I wrote to the U.S. embassy and asked if they could help me get it. They sent me a publisher's price list."

The total effectiveness of the Soviet effort in Arab lands will be difficult to measure until it has run more of its course. In a material sense it is probably most dangerous in Egypt and Syria where the arms deals have already made a considerable demand upon the economies and where continued or increased dealings with the East could render those countries economic captives. This danger is more pressing in Egypt, whose one-crop cotton economy is peculiarly vulnerable. Most of the other Arab countries have trade agreements with the East but thus far their commercial relations have been small.

Today the Arabs are receptive to Red blandishments but this seems to be not so much a genuine response to Russian propaganda as it is a way of expressing Arab displeasure with the West. It is true that the Russians have no bad record to hamper their progress in the Middle East—but they have no good record either. If the Arab mood of rejecting the West could change to one of acceptance, Russian influence would probably wither as rapidly as it has grown.

"We need a big friend in the world," said one Lebanese. "But we are also all aware of the danger of going too far with Russia. We are not so naïve about Communism as you think."

One important result the Soviets have already achieved. All Arabs are keenly aware that an alternative exists to Western aid. Even among the nations which are frankly pro-Western there is now a disposition to deliberate over offers of assistance from the West. Foreign Minister Burhanuddin Bashayan of Iraq, a Baghdad Pact nation receiving U.S. military help, said to me, "I understand the arms we are getting are not up to the standards or quantity we require. This does not look well compared with what Nasser is getting from Russia."

A similar view was expressed by Mehdi Ben Barka, president of the Consultative Assembly in Sultan Ben Youssef's pro-Western Morocco: "Our problem here is technique and practical co-operation. If the West refuses it, we in Africa will be forced to the East."

Some countries tried dealing with the U.S. but gave up. Said President Kuwatly in Syria, "We tried to get self-defense arms from you. We tried to make deals; you told us to open credits and then we could have small arms. We did so and waited, and nothing happened except that the Israeli got Mysteres and Sabres. Then Russia came and said, 'We will give you what you require without conditions.' What do you want me to do? Accept this offer or wait until I am killed?"

Egypt's Gamal Abdel Nasser has undergone a subtle hardening of mind toward the West. "He gets impatient with you Americans," said a man who has known him long and about as intimately as anybody does. "He understood how you worked but it didn't make a great deal of sense to him. He could reach an understanding with your ambassador but then the ambassador would have to get it approved by Washington. Sometimes the ambassador would have to go to the Secretary and he to the President and the President to the Congress. Nasser found he could call on the Russian ambassador and get action in twenty-four hours. He knows the system is different but he likes to make a deal that stays made."

Making these deals, Nasser has come to have a warmth not necessarily for Eastern politics but for mechanical things from the East.

"The MiG is a fine aircraft," he told me. "It is very maneuverable. When we had to fight, our pilots discovered that even our old MiG 15's could turn inside the Israeli Mysteres. Later we got the MiG 17's —we only announced that after the fighting, and not announcing it fooled the British who thought our pilots were Russians—and the 17 was even more maneuverable than the 15 and also it is faster than the Mystere. These are good weapons."

Other Arab leaders, however, think that Nasser's flirtations with Russia are far too hazardous. "I don't see how Nasser in Egypt and

Kuwatly in Syria can take help from the Russians and still say they are against Communism," said Tunisia's Bourguiba. "It's irrational. It doesn't make sense."

"Nasser is a patriot," said Abderrahim Bouabid, minister of national economy in Morocco. "He got rid of corruption in Egypt. But he talks too much; his speeches do more harm than his actions. The trouble with Egyptians is they haven't suffered enough. They've been talking about freedom while we fought for it."

There is a widespread supposition that Nasser is a captive of pro-Communist advisers. This may or may not have some truth in it, but Nasser's own personality and background are far more important in analyzing the difficulties of dealing with him. As a youth he was nourished on revolutionary doctrine and on the humiliations imposed on Egypt from outside. His formal education came within the confined framework of a military academy. Except for his trip to Bandung for the Asian-African conference in 1955 and a brief excursion to Brioni (off the Yugoslavian coast) in 1956 to confer with Tito and Nehru, he has never been outside North Africa or his neighboring countries—and only a few times outside Egypt itself. His trip to Bandung made a tremendous impression on him. He has never seen the West and one can only speculate whether a visit to the U.S. soon after he came to power would have proved just as effective. Under the circumstances it is less surprising that his attitudes are narrow and suspicious than that he has acquired as much balance and maturity as he has.

Seldom in the three-thousand-mile stretch of *al Umma al Arabiah* is the voice of a common man raised in doubt or reservation of his leadership. Nasser commands this station because his own nationalistic feelings were shaped by the same forces that shaped most Arabs and because he, almost alone, has reacted to those forces in the ways most Arabs wish they could or dared act.

"It would be possible to get Nasser," said an American who has long been familiar with the Arabs, "but getting him will leave you with a lot of littler, even less responsible Nassers in his place."

Arab nationalism has thus far manifested itself so negatively and destructively that one American on the scene dismisses it angrily as "retrograde xenophobia." Thoughtful Arabs confess this negativism but reply that, except in minor ways, they have not yet been able to evolve into a progressive and constructive phase because until now they have always been on the defensive.

"Nobody wants more than the Arabs to erase the prefix 'un' or 'under' from our development," said Dr. Raif Bellama, acting secretary general of the Arab League. "We have done much in the last ten years but we have much more to do to catch up with the caravan of progress. We can do it in co-operation with the West but we are not going to do it at the expense of our freedom."

For the West the solution seems to lie in reshaping the nature of its necessary impact upon the Arab world in ways that will be unquestionably benign and unobtrusively helpful. Such a course will require great generosity, bottomless patience and, probably more than anything else, a quality of being above suspicion. This last involves the infinitely delicate task of convincing the Arabs, despite their profound belief to the contrary, that they need not fear the continued existence of Israel. The resulting partnership between the Arabs and the West cannot be one-sided; it will require that the Arabs sacrifice a measure of their stiff-necked pride and be willing to accept help.

Optimistic American observers point out that the Arab-West association, now fairly well along in years, has not been a total failure, and some Western educational innovations like the American University of Beirut have been markedly successful. They observe that the Arabs have already adopted many techniques and habits of thought and some of the structures of a new society from the West and have found many of these new ways satisfying. They remember the great and vital Arab past and believe that, with help, the Arab force can be turned toward progress and the Arab nation can once again become a powerful and useful contributor to the family of nations.

"Arab nationalism generates more horsepower than anything else in Africa and Asia," said one American. "It lies at the bottom of today's instability but it is also the best hope for stability in the future. Their effort to get into the twentieth century is desperate and convulsive. But they may make it by 1999—with our help."

LEAD—
OR GET LEFT BEHIND

by John F. Kennedy

MARCH 11, 1957

*If the Democratic party is not to risk the fate of the
Federalists or the Whigs, it must try new ideas, new policies,
new faces, says Senator John F. Kennedy. One of the party's
most dynamic figures, his own intensive campaigning has
already given it new vigor—and some unexpected problems.
Here he calls for a large and definite goal in party
policy, to serve a more lasting purpose than the immediate
issue of one presidential campaign.*

"The tour I lately made with Mr. Jefferson," wrote James Madison to
his father in somewhat disingenuous terms in the fall of 1791, "was
a very agreeable one, and carried us through interesting country, new
to us both." This "new and interesting" country—New York and
the Connecticut River valley—was perhaps more interesting for its
political possibilities than anything else. For the Democratic party of
Messrs. Jefferson and Madison, then in its prenatal stage and using
the Republican or anti-Federalist label, already had growing strength
among the small farmers of the South and what was then called the
West (western Pennsylvania and Virginia). To this nucleus Jefferson

and Madison, astute political organizers as well as scholarly theorists, had added the more aristocratic plantation owners of the South.

Now they were ready to thrust northward, and so between the sessions of the first and second Congresses they took what they insisted was a "botanical excursion" up the Hudson and down the Connecticut rivers. Among the interesting specimens of *homo politicus Americanus* they studied at length were the politically powerful Messrs. Clinton, Burr and Livingston of New York.

The results of this "excursion" were indeed "agreeable." New York in 1800 provided the winning margin for the Jefferson-Burr ticket and the "Grand Alliance" of the Democratic party—today one of the oldest political parties on earth—was thereupon born.

It was, in many ways, a strange alliance: struggling small farmers and wealthy plantation masters, visionary political philosophers and hardened city bosses, unskilled laborers in the East and hardy pioneers in the West. Nearly a century and a half later the alliance, still largely intact under another astute organizer, Franklin Roosevelt, included within its ranks some equally diverse groups: northern Negroes and southern Bourbons, Catholics and Jews, immigrants and veterans, union leaders and farmers, pensioners who wanted higher taxes and small businessmen who wanted them lower. Nevertheless the coalition held and flourished, cemented together by the party's record of accomplishment and brilliance of leadership.

It held and flourished, that is, until it collided with 1952, 1956 and Dwight David Eisenhower.

The man and the name were all-important—the political victories that rocked the "Grand Alliance" were, in a sense, largely his personal victories—but the years were of no small significance. For those election years of 1952 and 1956 climaxed two decades of change in America—economic, social and political change that had gradually corroded and crumbled the foundations of the Democratic coalition.

The South, still largely rural and undeveloped in 1932, had by 1956 witnessed the growth of bustling new industries and cities at a rate that outstripped the rest of the nation. The electoral power of the teeming metropolises of the North, courted by the "botanists" in 1791 and welded by Al Smith in 1928 despite his disastrous electoral vote, had been splintered into ever-increasing clusters of surrounding suburbs. The small farmers who fought on the razor-thin edge of existence—under the banners of Jackson, Bryan and F.D.R.—against mortgage bankers, railroads and insects, had seen their farms disappear at the rate of several hundred a day as mechanization and amalgamation produced larger and larger farm units. The worker without a union, the immigrant without a friend, the Negro without a decent home, the oldster without a pension—these and many others, in years gone by, had found in the Democratic party a champion on issues that in the comfortable prosperity of 1956 no longer burned quite as fiercely. Even the great depression of 1929 was ancient history to a new generation of voters and its scars were no longer deeply felt by its now-contented survivors.

With these changes had come political changes as well. The big-city machines of the North could no longer deliver automatically—as demonstrated by Republican victories in Chicago, Jersey City and a host of other formerly safe Democratic strongholds. The South could no longer be taken for granted as solid—on the contrary, Eisenhower captured an unprecedented majority of its electoral votes.

The Democratic habit—that psychological pull that kept votes coming even after the key issues and personalities had begun to fade —no longer swayed a majority of voters or guaranteed a score of states. Old war horses like Senators George and Lehman were retiring; Harry Truman was in Independence; Franklin Roosevelt and Alben Barkley were in their graves. Across the Senate aisle and down Pennsylvania Avenue, Taft was gone and Ike had come—and however superficial the changes, the Republican party was now sufficiently progressive and internationalist, at least in appearance, to blur the once distinctive position of the Democrats.

In 1956 (as to a slightly lesser extent in 1952) the full impact of these changes upon the "Grand Alliance" became obvious. Young voters, women voters, union families, immigrant families, Negroes, big city voters, independents, Southerners—to name but a few of the pollsters' categories showing great numbers of voters switching Republican—millions who had supported Franklin Roosevelt (or whose fathers had before them) now voted the Eisenhower-Nixon ticket.

A few state Democratic organizations could boast that they had suffered worse losses before, but 1956 clearly represented a disastrous defeat for the Democratic party—and just as Dickens' *A Christmas Carol* began with the fact that "Old Marley was as dead as a door-nail," so any analysis of the Democratic party's status must begin with the inescapable fact that we lost the last election.

To be sure, for a "minority" party, Democrats occupied an extraordinary number of governors' mansions. And true, Democratic majorities were retained in each house of Congress, largely as the result of the party's substantial record of legislative achievement in the 84th Congress. But these majorities do not obscure the party's resounding defeat on the national level and cannot conceal the awesome problems that face us during the next four years.

In 1960 the Democrats will (it now appears) be matched against a tough, skillful, shrewd opponent in Richard M. Nixon. Far from being the pushover some Democrats smugly expect, Mr. Nixon has four well-publicized years ahead in which to increase his public stature, four years of basking in the Eisenhower charm in which to campaign for the favor of previously hostile voters, four years in the spotlight without being required, as his competitors in both parties will be, to go on record (except in rare cases) on controversial issues, four years in which no single Democratic hopeful can possibly receive such a build-up. It will take more than abusive statements to beat Mr. Nixon—*those* he can read riding in the 1961 inaugural parade.

For in addition to a difficult opponent we will in 1960 be up against the party in control of the executive branch, which demonstrated in 1956 its political ingenuity in the utilization of federal appointments, defense contracts, farm relief funds and presidential news conferences. We will be up against our usual disadvantages in terms of campaign contributions and editorial support. And we will be facing an electorate which will not have returned a clear national popular majority for the Democrats in sixteen years. If this seems hard to believe in view of our congressional majorities, let us realize that outside the South the Democrats have not won a clear majority in both houses of Congress since 1936. Indeed, throughout most of the last century the Democrats have been a minority party, able to win nationally only when the people, alarmed or distressed, found it necessary to be "saved" from the Republicans.

Why should the people vote Democratic in 1960? What can we say or do during the next four years to cause them to change?

Certainly, if employment remains high, domestic issues are not likely to be as dramatic or clear-cut as they once were in the days of the great depression and Republican conservatism. The Administration's wholehearted endorsement of internationalism leaves at issue largely day-to-day techniques, judgments and administerial competence rather than broad foreign policy questions. Although a great role for intelligent opposition remains, the political benefit to be reaped must always take second place to responsibility for the national security.

Building a Democratic record, moreover, requires in part opposing a fantastically popular Republican President who is not a candidate for re-election and who has shown marked success in isolating himself from political attack. The Democrats during the last four years have repeatedly drawn the political blood of Messrs. Dulles, Wilson and Benson—but they have rarely, in the public mind, scored a direct hit on the President himself.

Faced with an administration obviously to the left of the traditional Republican position, at least as defined by Republican congressional leadership in the thirties and forties, the Democrats are caught on the horns of a dilemma. We cannot, on the one hand, move to the *right* to oppose (without more progressive alternatives) the President's more constructive measures—on school aid or immigration, for example—without appearing obstructionist or reactionary, appealing only to those already well-represented on the Republican side. But neither, on the other hand, can we move too far to the *left* in order to distinguish the Democratic position without alienating those wayward moderate and independent Democrats whom we are trying to woo back from the Republican column. Indeed, we cannot move either left or right merely to be distinctive, without considering the national interest or the public's feeling. And if we simply stay in the *middle* with a policy of "moderation," we will not—assuming continued good times and

Republican moderation—distinguish our position sufficiently to arouse the much-needed enthusiasm of our more progressive supporters, particularly in the West, and the presidential race will be reduced to largely a personality contest.

How, then, can we continue to be a national party, comprising all elements, with any hope of success? Harry Byrd can continue to carry Virginia as a Democrat, and Wayne Morse can continue to carry Oregon as a Democrat, but can any Democratic presidential nominee ever hope to run on a record that can carry both states?

Finally, hamstringing our efforts to resolve these dilemmas is the chronic and, fortunately for us, bipartisan political virus of factionalism. In too many states Democrats are busy fighting other Democrats—"old guards" versus "new bloods," "ins" versus "outs," liberals versus conservatives. In some communities more Democrats have been read out of the party than are left in. "Whin ye see two men with white neckties, set in opposite corners while wan mutthers 'thraiter' an' th' other hisses 'miscreent,' " said Finley Peter Dunne's Mr. Dooley some fifty years ago, in words that can be applied in some areas today, "ye can bet they're two dimmycratic leaders thryin' to reunite th' . . . party."

Along the Potomac another series of rifts threatens the party, egged on by a press always eager for controversy: Northerners versus Southerners, liberals versus conservatives, congressional leaders versus the national committee. The discordant wings of our party, someone said recently, are held together only by "its debts and its Texans." Without a single titular leader, with prestige and publicity divided among congressional leaders, governors, the national committee and the party's elder statesmen (such as Messrs. Truman and Stevenson and Mrs. Roosevelt), the Democratic party appears at times to speak with many voices and in many accents.

These are sobering problems and prospects, which hopeless pessimism will not eradicate nor blind optimism conceal. They call for a penetrating reappraisal of our party and its course. Personally, I am confident of our party's future. We have an impressive array of able leaders and a host of potential issues. But there are dangers that lurk ahead, dangers that arise largely because of our recent defeats and crumbling coalition. Our chief task, it thus seems to me, is to recognize these dangers, to make certain we do escape the fate of becoming a permanent minority and eventually disintegrating.

Fortunately for us, other parties in earlier times have also stood at this crossroads—particularly the Federalists in 1800 and the Whigs in 1852. Both adopted courses that now tempt the Democratic party, which can plan its own future by recalling their fate. Both frittered away an inheritance of respected leadership and accomplishment. Both died.

The Federalist party's last futile years of life, marked by tirades against its foes and internal bickering, completed the sorry end of a once resplendent and honored ruler.

What lessons does this hold for the Democratic party?

We, too, are in danger of relying upon a glorious past, while fundamental changes transform our nation. "Don't upset the applecart!" or "We have enough troubles as it is!"—these are the supercautious responses that dampen many a new proposal for regeneration of our party. We take comfort in repeating sonorously our traditional slogans—"The party of all the people," "The party of progress," "The party with a heart"—but we dare not measure their validity in concrete terms for fear of admitting some glaring weakness or alienating some entrenched supporter.

Moreover, the same curse of sectionalism that felled the Federalists threatens the Democrats, if in slightly different fashion. In both North and South the pressures to put local popularity ahead of party unity grow greater every day. Unfounded but bitter assertions that go beyond the expression of sectional differences are heard on every side—assertions that the Democratic party is the "captive of the A.D.A." or the "victim of Confederate vengeance," or would do well to cleanse itself of certain elements. Some Democrats—unaware of the fate of the Federalists—may even *prefer* that the Democratic party exist only as a loose confederation of sectional parties, continuing to win locally but never nationally, acquiring patronage but never full responsibility.

Finally, the top echelon of the Democratic party will be hard put to avoid the same excesses of personal and partisan strife that separated the Federalist leaders from the electorate. The first reaction to last fall's disaster was to search for old scapegoats instead of new leadership: whether to blame Stevenson or Kefauver, the volunteers or the professionals, Senator Eastland or Congressman Powell, Lyndon Johnson or Harry Truman or Paul Butler—everyone in fact but Dwight D. Eisenhower. Nor are voters attracted by Democratic factions and personalities struggling in Washington for control of the Congress or the national committee, for public attention or private vengeance. Reckless and unfounded assaults upon the Administration, or cries for a cabinet member's resignation, produce far more headlines in Washington than votes back in the precincts. To be sure, we should not permit the Republicans to take the credit for Stalin's death, but neither should we hold them responsible for how quickly the flooding snows melt in New England.

Such is the lesson of the Federalists. What then can we learn from the passing of the Whigs?

The party's candidates were popular figures but weak fighters. On all the great issues of the day—the extension of slavery westward, the fugitive slave law, even on its own compromise of 1850—the Whig campaign was deliberately ambiguous or silent. The Whig party soon stood for nothing that some other party did not stand for better and the nation, particularly in the critical hour of threatened civil war, could place no confidence in it.

Today the Democratic party must take special care not to go the way of the Whigs. The very nature of our history as a coalition has led to the same kind of special appeals—to the farm vote, the Negro vote, the veterans' vote and all the rest. There is something in our platform or legislative record for everyone (no doubt, if we could, we would devise some inducement for the "suburban vote"—subsidized commuters' cars or tax-exempt lawn mowers). We plot presidential campaigns the same way, not in terms of national issues and trends but in terms of so many Southern electoral votes, so many farm states, so many labor areas, and so on and on. (The temptation to gain power by wooing or misleading each supposed bloc of voters is very great indeed. Example: the secret of one well-known governor's success, I was recently told, is that "the poor think he is a friend of the poor—and the rich know he is not.")

We are in danger, too, of imitating the Whigs in their evasion of controversial issues. We tend, in too many of our party declarations, to offer what the cynics call "straight-from-the-shoulder" generalities or platitudes "without fear or favor" on civil rights, natural gas, clean elections and the treaty-making power. Obviously our consideration of these sensitive issues will divide Democrats and antagonize voters— but to ignore their existence or avoid their solution would, if 1852 is any kind of precedent, forfeit our claim to national leadership.

The Democratic party will never become a radical party, for its nature, its traditions and its good political sense prohibit it, but neither can we replace the Republicans as the nation's conservative party or follow those who would make mediocrity out of moderation. I do not say that our task is to oppose Republicans opportunistically for the sake of opposing Republicans, but neither can we afford to stand still during the Eisenhower reign in a defensive caretaker operation. Our candidates must continue to have more than the colorful personality the Whigs thought to be sufficient.

In failing to substitute for its personal and sectional jealousies a program tailored to the current needs of the nation, the Federalist party stood still. But the Whig party, by going to the other extreme to seek favor by appealing to the current demands of every group in the nation, eventually stood for nothing. The Democratic party must take care not to founder on either shoal.

The only course for the Democratic party, if it is not to join the Whigs and Federalists in political limbo, is to move ahead responsibly, courageously, harmoniously. Under Jefferson, Jackson, Wilson, Roosevelt and Truman our chief claim to the confidence of the nation, North and South, has been leadership.

But leadership for whom and for what? This is not the time or the place to write a Democratic platform or list campaign techniques. Consequently my comments must be confined to a general statement of several guiding principles:

1. The Democratic party must be increasingly willing to embrace new ideas, new policies and new faces, unafraid of controversial issues or candid criticism.

2. Democratic leaders must be increasingly willing to put the party's future ahead of sectional, factional and personal disputes and ambitions. By 1960—or even 1959—it will be too late for a candidate to pull together the diverse elements that can win locally but are at odds nationally or to build a record against the incumbent administration. That task must be begun now.

3. Congressional Democrats must shape a responsible, progressive record with deeds that match our words. For it is precisely this gap between the rhetoric and the record that casts doubt on the new liberalism of the Republicans. It is up to us in Congress, despite the restrictions imposed by the compromises necessary to keep our party intact, and despite the possibility of fighting losing battles, to push forward a progressive program any Democratic candidate in 1960 can run on with pride and hope.

4. Congressional Democrats must demonstrate leadership in the problems of prosperity as they have in the past on problems of poverty. We need not run against Herbert Hoover and the Great Depression. For, New Republicanism or no, the differences in the fundamental approaches of the two parties to the issues will become clearer as we move ahead—and real issues do exist, even in this age of abundance, automation and tranquillity pills.

For example:

Nearly a million boys and girls are deprived of full-time schooling by the classroom shortage, and millions more are held back by unwieldy classes of forty or more as school enrollments continue to increase by more than a million pupils a year. This demands a prompt, imaginative program of federal aid to local school construction.

Untold numbers of the aged and chronically ill need congressional action before they can get decent hospital beds and economical medical care. Pitifully inadequate incomes from inflation-eaten social insurance programs still await many of those who are unemployed, disabled, or "too old to work and too young to die."

An all-time record of over sixty-five million people are at work, but nearly two-thirds of them will continue to have no federal protection against substandard wages unless we can greatly expand the coverage of the Fair Labor Standards Act. Dozens of pockets of chronic unemployment persisting in many states need federal loans and contracts, technical assistance, supplemental jobless benefits and other methods of relief and encouragement.

Businessmen, large and small, concerned about the increasing number of business failures and mergers as money tightens, need old legislation improved to meet these new problems.

Hundreds of thousands of small farmers, foreclosed or merged out of existence as the combined burdens of drought, falling prices and rising costs have proved too much to bear, need new solutions to solve old problems.

The blight, decay and delinquency that plague our aging cities, inequities in taxation, power shortages, fiscal policies, immigration restrictions—these and a host of other problems can be postponed, ignored or swept under the rug, but not for long.

Let it not be said that we are fearful or incapable of solving with fairness and forthrightness the sensitive, complex issue of race relations. The Democratic party is best equipped to provide responsible leadership in this area: first, because we are a national party, including within our membership both a majority of Negroes and a majority of Southerners; and secondly, because we have always, as a party, emphasized human values and human ideals. I, for one, do not share the view that Negro voters are leaving the Democratic party for good. A majority is still with us because it judges the two parties on their records and leadership on a variety of issues rather than on the civil rights statements of a few prominent figures.

5. Democratic spokesmen in and out of Congress must be willing to offer constructive opposition in the field of foreign policy. "Modern Republicanism" has not eliminated all differences between the parties on foreign affairs. Many alarming problems are in need of careful scrutiny. Among them are: the authority of the executive and legislative branches, our policies in the Middle East and Asia, our relations with our Western allies, our neglect of the good neighbor policy carefully nurtured by Cordell Hull, our answer to the challenge of nationalism and colonialism, the questions of disarmament and atomic control, the deterioration of our comparative defense strength.

6. Finally, and perhaps most important of all, Democrats on the

local level must be willing to substitute new life and new leadership for the luxury of petty local factionalism. With a new breed of respected, dynamic professional politicians coming into prominence, we can no longer afford to continue in official party positions tired or tarnished holdovers from another era—men whose stature and activities inspire neither the enthusiasm of volunteer workers nor the respect of their communities—men who keep busy by attending meetings, filing gloomy forecasts and complaints, and fighting zealously to hold on to their positions.

We need another kind of local worker and leader in our party, men and women such as those I met last fall in all regions and particularly in the West—full of enthusiasm, full of new ideas, full of determination, asking nothing in return.

I have offered no single magic formula for a successful Democratic party and I have proposed no candidates for a winning ticket for 1960. For their identity, I believe, is less important than their capacity for wise, progressive, responsible leadership; their methods of campaigning for victory are less significant than the principles that guide their party.

For "the success of a party means little," as Woodrow Wilson said in his first inaugural, "except when the Nation is using that party for a large and definite purpose." The task of the Democratic party during the next four years is to define such a purpose for all the nation; and success, I have no doubt, will then be rightfully ours in 1960 and the years beyond.

EUPHORIA
AND THE SCYTHIANS

a LIFE *editorial*

DECEMBER 16, 1957

> *The U.S. public has shown its loud and justified alarm*
> *about the onset of the Sputnik era, but a more satisfactory*
> *reaction than alarm is called for. A question of values*
> *is involved which is far more basic than the mere problem*
> *of better military hardware—as this modern fable suggests.*

It was the beginning of winter in the Republic of Euphoria. The first snows were melting harmlessly against the panes of the overheated glass houses. The stores were bright with the artificial light at which the Euphorians excelled. The children of Euphoria, healthy, lithe and mobile, rushed about on mysterious four-tired errands, but faithfully came back by evening to cluster around the magic happy screens in every home.

Before screen time, generally, they attended the Euphorians' schools, which were called "Pursuit of Happiness" schools, after an ancient theory. There they were taught principally to get along happily with other Euphorians. A certain amount of learning was required of them, so that they could advance to the level of the popular college, where the smiles were brighter, the cars faster and the happiness possibilities almost without limit.

When they grew older, the Euphorians gave up learning for earning. Earning was a sure path to happiness. The fast return had once performed its alchemies with magic swiftness. Better now was the slow, sure return, with fringe benefits. The comfort and security thus gained made all things possible for Euphorians but, eliminating the necessity of doing most things, made only a few things desirable. Yet the rewards of earning were varied enough to keep the Euphorians from appalling fates like single-mindedness or contemplation or eccentricity.

Most appalling of all were two major failings which the modern Euphorians atavistically called heresies—discontent and curiosity. In this country of smiles, where sophistication was the ability to sit unflinchingly through a play without a happy ending, the true Euphorian did his best to conceal any breach of contentment as quickly as it appeared. This ability grew to be prodigious. The Euphorians were able to apply it, with some success, to facts as well as opinions.

The task of killing curiosity was more difficult, since curiosity had long ago been regarded as a virtual Euphorian patent. But modern Euphorians, with so much done for them, preferred to let curiosity gradually doze off. They still said in their speeches that every Euphorian boy liked nothing better than to take a car apart or explore the sources of a forest river. But the cars grew too complicated for amateur repairmen and everyone knew that all the forest rivers were already carefully mapped.

Critics occasionally questioned whether the happy Euphorians were not destroying their own traditional austerity of mind, valuable in repairing furnaces, inventing nuclear processes, and separating the components of hazy diplomatic situations. The modern Euphorians replied that mental austerity was as uncomfortable, unnecessary and outmoded as a kitchen without push-buttons, or a speech without slogans. Then they would repeat the new national anthem which the children were taught in the happiness schools:

> We are the biggest; we are the best;
> We are ahead of all the rest.

It was at this point in their history, when the winter cruise season lured the mambo-dancing Euphorian vacationist and the school-children in unprecedented numbers were learning how to drive cars and explore their own psyches, that Euphoria found out that it was not ahead.

The latest "ultimate" weapon of destruction had been devised and perfected by the Scythians, a larger but traditionally dumber people whose national symbol, the scowl, had been warring with the Euphorian smile. It was impossible to claim that the Scythians had stolen the weapon from them—a source of curious reassurance in similar cases—for the Euphorians had possessed none themselves. Nor could they pass the discovery off as happenstance. The Scythian schools, not sophisticated enough to give courses in life adjustment, had long been developing a formidable system of study and practice in the newer scientific disciplines.

Their best qualities were strangely effective variants of the two which had long been banished from Euphoria—discontent and curiosity. All the students were chronically discontented. Life in unhappy Scythia made them so. They were also unfailingly curious, if only in the limited tactical pursuit of learning. Under the Scythian system, only the intensive application of curiosity—and hard work—could produce rewards for the student, sufficient to raise him above the common level of discontent.

The cold shock of the Scythian menace was soon translated by the Euphorians into calls for "action." Military emergency measures were taken. Then the Euphorians settled down to do a little thinking. They had obvious alternatives before them. The first—to do business as usual, but a little faster—was made the more palatable as all the soothing resources of the smile country were brought into action. After all, as a well-known Euphorian metalsmith popularly argued, the Scythians were not "nine feet tall." Scholars cited statistics proving that the annual grain and entertainment shortage in Scythia would ultimately decimate the enemy population—if the Scythians had not indeed by that time become crypto-Euphorians through the influence of the happy screen. Prominent earners cited the invincibility of Euphorian "know-how."

The second alternative was far less happy. It not only implied devoting even larger sums of Euphorian happiness money into tangible efforts at security but, even more drastically, it called for a rediscovery of the traditional austerity of mind. For the Euphorians (of all people) had grown so happy, so modern, so integrated in a new age largely of their own creation that they barely realized that another and still newer age was being discovered—right out from under them.

To train their children for the newer age involved a drastic remodeling of the happiness schools and a reinstatement of the heresies, discontent and curiosity, as honored virtues. It demanded that the healthy, lithe, mobile children, whose ancestors had learned Latin and Euclid by the age of twelve, and adjusted later, should relearn some older and exacting habits of mental discipline. For such habits alone could make possible future push-buttons, space ships and the same thinking that might use them well. The second alternative demanded, further, that the teacher, the critic and the discoverer be permanently released from their imprisonment in Euphoria's moated ivy towers and allowed to sit down with the earners at dinner and given money enough to buy a new suit occasionally.

It was of minor concern that the more numerous Scythians would probably still produce more managers, craftsmen and technicians. It was for the Euphorians to produce better and brighter men—discoverers, who were more curious and more divinely discontented than any Scythian ever could be. They could do this only by rediscovering the peculiar individual commitment which the first Euphorians had seen written in their souls—to advance the common Weal by one's single work. In so doing, it would help them to remember that the country of smiles was dedicated to universal life and liberty, as well as to its peculiar pursuit of happiness.

It was quite a choice. There has been a lot of talk about it and the Euphorians are still trying to decide.

THE SUPREME COURT
AT THE CROSSROADS

by John Osborne

JUNE 16, 1958

*The dispute over the judicial power of the U.S. Supreme
Court, its use and its limitations, has brought disorder
in the Court and much confusion in the country at large.
Says* LIFE *Staff Writer John Osborne: the Court is involved
in its most serious crisis since the early 1800's. Osborne,
formerly head of Time Inc.'s London bureau and now
stationed in Washington for* LIFE, *is a long-time reporter
of the political scene.*

In the early afternoon of October 15, 1957, Chief Justice Earl Warren
and Associate Justice Felix Frankfurter were questioning an attorney
at the bar of the U.S. Supreme Court. Dignity and power pervaded
the magnificent courtroom and seemed to envelop the nine Justices,
seated side by side in their black robes.

The lawyer at the bar had been struggling for several minutes with
a series of Warren's rather ponderous questions when Frankfurter
broke in. "If I may restate the question of the Chief Justice," he began with characteristic brashness, and proceeded to restate it. Warren's face reddened and he sat far back in his chair. A little later the

257

attorney was about to answer another question from the Chief Justice when Frankfurter again interrupted. Chief Justice Warren whirled full left in his chair, facing Frankfurter, and began to shout.

"Let him answer *my* question!" the Chief Justice roared. "I want to hear the answer to *my* question!"

Frankfurter, pale and shaking, drew back and mumbled that he was only trying to clear up the attorney's confusion.

"He is confused enough as it is!" the Chief Justice shouted.

Frankfurter's voice, always thin, was reduced to a squeak: "Confused by Justice Frankfurter, I presume!"

The attorney finished his argument as best he could. After the Court had taken its usual half hour for lunch and returned to the bench, Warren and Frankfurter made a show of chatting in cozy whispers. The lawyers who had heard the quarrel were soon trying to forget it, and at least one Justice later denied that it had ever happened. But it did happen, and on a few occasions since then some of the Justices have snarled publicly at each other in a fashion shocking to those who think of the Supreme Court as a row of graven images.

Regrettable though they are, these displays of unjudicial temper serve one good purpose. By comparison with what Americans see of Congress and the Presidency, they see and know almost nothing of their Supreme Court. Brawls on the bench at least make the Court seem more human, and therefore more understandable, than it normally appears to be. As for the friction that is occasionally displayed, it is significant mainly as a measure of the great strain under which the Justices are working at a time of crisis and revolution in the law.

Some measure of both the crisis and the revolution is to be found in the Court's controversial decisions of recent years. By discovering in 1954 that the U.S. Constitution forbids racial segregation in the public schools, the court precipitated the country's deepest social conflict since the Civil War. In a series of decisions interpreting the Smith Act, the Court freed batches of convicted Communist conspirators, made it extremely difficult to convict any others and generally showed a concern for the rights of everybody, including traitors, that seemed to many people to be excessive. The Court also curbed congressional efforts to investigate and expose subversion. It restricted the power of the federal government to fire public employees for security reasons. And, on the ground that federal law had pre-empted the field of national security, it in effect invalidated the antisubversion laws of forty-two states.

Other decisions in ordinary criminal cases have upset policemen, prosecutors and lower court judges with ever-tightening restrictions on the enforcement of the law. The Court has brought into doubt the traditional power of judges to punish criminal contempt on their own authority, without juries, and has created confusion over such questions as whether the federal government can or cannot take away citizenship for reasons provided by law. In handing down twelve individual opinions on this latter question on the same day (in three cases), the Court provided disturbing proof of its own confusions.

Controversial decisions always evoke complaints against the Court, but the present volume of complaint cannot be explained away on this ground. The grave truth is that the Court is involved in a crisis of doubt, possibly the most serious crisis which has confronted it since its power and duty to "say what the law is" were established in the early 1800's.

There is a doubt, widespread and increasingly voiced, that the U.S. Supreme Court is properly fulfilling its function as the supreme interpreter of American law. These criticisms may be summarized in four main points:

1. The Supreme Court has abused and exceeded its immense powers.

2. It has presumed to pass judgment upon the *wisdom* of Congress and state legislatures in their enactments, instead of confining itself to deciding whether they have the *power* to enact certain laws.

3. It has abandoned time-proven precedents without sufficient cause, and in doing so has changed its mind too lightly and too often.

4. It shows insufficient respect for the written law, tending instead to base its decisions upon the personal predilections of its members.

Are these complaints justified? Any arbitrary answer would be both presumptuous and misleading. Consider, for example, a part of the first criticism listed above: has the Court exceeded its powers? The simple answer is that the powers of the U.S. Supreme Court are so immense that it is almost impossible for the Court to "exceed" them. But this fact does not absolve the Court of the duty to use its powers with the greatest care and restraint. Has the Court unduly tended to substitute its own wisdom for that of Congress? Judge Learned Hand of New York recently said that it has—but he would reject any suggestion that he is to be numbered among those now seeking to diminish the Court's power. Has the Court displayed too little regard for the written law, including the precedents set by its own decisions of the past? Retired Associate Justice Stanley Reed clearly thinks that on occasion it has. Yet in 1944 Reed set forth his view that there was nothing sacred about precedent as such and to prove his point cited forty-four instances in which the Court had struck down its own precedents.

One of the difficulties in seeking and offering answers to the present criticisms is that the debate about them is conducted in a public vacuum. The great answers can be intelligently sought by the public, and those offered can be intelligently weighed, only if Americans in general come to know much more than they now do about the simplest aspects of their Supreme Court.

The Constitution says there shall be "one Supreme Court," and there literally has been only one U.S. Supreme Court since Chief Justice John Jay convened the first sitting in 1790. The two hundred page boys, secretaries, law clerks, messengers, guards and charwomen who serve the Justices go about their work as if they, like the Constitution, were intended "to endure through a long lapse of ages. . . ."

In 169 years the U.S. has had 33 Presidents but only 14 Chief Justices. The immortal John Marshall sat as Chief Justice for 34 years, his successor Roger Taney for 28 years, 4 others for 10 years or more.

In the Supreme Court everything is done by rote. The Court convenes its public sessions on the dot of noon and sits exactly four hours (plus thirty minutes out for lunch). Opinions and orders are announced on Mondays, just after noon. The admission of lawyers to the Supreme Court Bar is a solemn ritual. Lawyers may deal with the Court and with individual Justices only through the clerk, according to prescribed forms. Tradition—not always observed in this day of declining judicial manners—requires that the Justices never grant interviews, never discuss politics, never discuss cases before them with anyone except their colleagues.

On days when the Court is not in session, visitors to the marble Supreme Court Building on Washington's Capitol Hill seem to sense a brooding presence—unseen, mysterious, powerful. It is what the august Officers of the Court—the Clerk, the Marshal, the Reporter of Decisions, the Librarian—have in mind when, in a very special tone of reverence, they speak of "The Court." Who hires the principal officers, sets the dockets, prepares the many routine orders, determines whether lawyers will have thirty minutes, an hour or longer to argue their cases? There is just one answer: "The Court." Even attorneys who try to analyze the philosophy of each Justice with microscopic care come to think of the Supreme Court as an impersonal monolith.

But it has never seemed so to the members of the Court. "The fact is," Justice Robert H. Jackson wrote shortly before his death in 1954, "that the Court functions less as one deliberative body than as nine, each Justice working largely in isolation except as he chooses to seek consultation with others." The inner organization and routine of the Court brings all the Justices together on only two occasions: at the public sessions and at their secret conferences, which take place on two or three Fridays of each month when the Court is sitting.

The secret conferences are held in a modest room just off the chambers of the Chief Justice. Only the members of the Court are present. After they enter at 11 A.M. on appointed Fridays the door is locked. The Junior (*i.e.*, most recently appointed) Associate Justice sits by the door, receiving and passing out (via messengers and page boys in an anteroom) any necessary communications and documents. Until 5:30 or 6 P.M., with an hour out for lunch, the Justices do the joint business of the Court in total privacy. No record of the discussions is kept, and the Justices are under a tacit pledge not to disclose the proceedings to anyone, not even to their wives or their law clerks.

Each Justice has in hand a "conference list" of cases already heard, cases the Court has been asked to review and cases due for summary decision without a hearing. The list may include sixty to seventy matters requiring some action by the assembled Justices. Most of the discussion time, however, goes to perhaps ten or twelve cases which have already been argued in open court and are now ready for private debate.

The Chief Justice, who always presides, "states the case" as each item comes up. This is his time of test and opportunity, when all his powers of persuasion are brought to bear in the hope of winning his colleagues over to his view. After the Chief Justice has concluded, the Senior Associate Justice is given his turn—and so on down the line of seniority. Justices may, and often do, "pass" without comment. No Justice may interrupt another and each may talk as long as he likes. A strong Chief Justice may discourage excessive discussion by demeanor and example, but he may not halt it by word or act. On various occasions in recent years Chief Justice Warren has lacked whatever it may take to halt the voluble Justice Frankfurter.

When all who want to talk have had their say, an oral vote is taken. Now the order is reversed: the Junior Justice votes first and the Chief Justice last so that nobody will be influenced by his seniors. Among other things the conference vote guides the selection of the Justice who is to write the majority opinion. If the Chief Justice has voted with the majority, he assigns the opinion either to himself or to a colleague on his side. If the Chief Justice is with the minority, the Senior Justice on the majority side makes the choice. Only the majority opinion is assigned; each Justice decides for himself whether to write a separate opinion in concurrence or dissent, or simply to have his position noted without a written opinion.

Partly because they are not always conclusive, the conference votes as such are never disclosed. Even the cases to be dealt with in published opinions are not finally decided at the conference. The vote on them is merely tentative: it draws initial lines and gets the work on opinions started. Only after this has been accomplished does each Justice get down to what one of them has called "the agony of his duty."

The Justice assigned to write the majority opinion is anxious to "hold his court" and, if possible, to win over one or more of the Justices who took the minority side at conference. Meanwhile, in a hotly disputed case, one or more Justices are working on dissenting opinions with which they hope to confound and riddle the initial majority. The young law clerks, who serve their Justices chiefly as researchers, sweat through mounds of law books in quest of precedents and arguments with which to buttress their man's position. Some Justices may also invite their clerks to try their hands at drafting or revising an opinion, but this aspect of the law clerk's role has been greatly exaggerated. If a clerk influences an opinion at all, it is more often by oral give-and-take than by anything he has written.

When a Justice is at last content with his draft, the manuscript goes to a guarded room on the ground floor of the Supreme Court building. Here the Court's printers, who lock themselves in and carry the only keys to their shop, set up "proofs" of the opinion. It is then circulated to the other eight Justices. Concurring drafts and dissents may be circulated or not, as the Justices who wrote them choose. At this stage the Justices plunge into an orgy of communication, sometimes in marginal notes on the proofs, sometimes by separate memoranda or letters, and often in person. In order to "hold his court" the majority writer may completely revise his draft or accept drastic deletions and insert whole pages of another Justice's work. Occasionally, to the anguish of one Justice and the joy of another, the balance of forces changes during this process as a Justice, swayed by a colleague's opinion, switches his vote. Then the majority opinion becomes the dissent, and the "dissenting" opinion collects the majority. In any event, no case is really decided until what is eventually the majority opinion has gone through the mill and become, in fact as well as theory, the work of all who finally subscribe to it.

The principal purpose of all this activity, and of the institution which engages in it, is to keep the U.S. Constitution alive. "Let us now proceed to the interpretation of the Constitution," Justice Joseph Story said 142 years ago, and the Supreme Court has done so throughout its history. Since the original four thousand words of the Constitution were agreed upon, the nation and its world have changed beyond the imagination of the founders. But the wording of the basic law by which we live still stands with just twenty-two amendments, only eight of them made since 1868. Yet the Constitution today is given meanings and has effects which those who wrote it would find surprising. This is the responsibility and the doing of the U.S. Supreme Court. Despite the Court's trappings of permanence, change has always been its business.

Just why this is so has never been well understood. "This is a court of justice," a lawyer once exclaimed while arguing a case in the Supreme Court. "You are in error," Justice Oliver Wendell Holmes, Jr., instantly replied. *"This* is a court of law." He meant that the Court is primarily concerned with the meaning and constitutionality of law rather than with the fate of individuals who encounter the law.

Most people assume that the Supreme Court is whatever it is "because the Constitution says so." But the Constitution does not "say so." The Constitution, having said that "the judicial power of the United States shall be vested in one Supreme Court" ("and in such inferior courts as the Congress may from time to time ordain and establish"), leaves to the judges the important duty of defining "the judicial power." Among the wonders of our national birth none was more wonderful and astonishing than the way in which the early judges of the Supreme Court performed this duty.

It was not performed in peace. Thomas Jefferson and many other Founding Fathers were surprised and dismayed when the Court, under Chief Justice John Marshall, discovered in its duty to interpret "the supreme law of the land" a further duty—and a resulting power —to "say what the law is." The country rang with denunciations of the Marshall Court's assertions of power to declare acts of Congress and actions of the President unconstitutional "and therefore void."

The Supreme Court is still shaking up the country and causing controversy, but with an enormous difference. President Eisenhower, ordering U.S. soldiers to enforce the integration of a Little Rock school, takes for granted the proposition that the solemn judgment of the Court is "the supreme law of the land." The question is no longer whether the Court has the power to interpret and lay down the supreme law but how it uses its authority.

There is a miraculous and mystic quality in that authority. It rests, fundamentally, upon confidence in The Law—the written law of legislatures and the "declared law" of judges. Beyond this it rests upon the confidence of the American people in the integrity and

264

judgments of the Court or, when the judgments are questioned, upon the universal assumption that they must be obeyed anyhow. This most powerful of courts has no means of its own for enforcing its decisions. The ultimate power of law lies in consent to law, and the special power of the Court will have vanished if its judgment has to be generally imposed by force as it has had to be imposed in Little Rock.

The Court values and enforces a certain amount of privacy, as we have seen. But the notion of many lawyers and judges that the Supreme Court is beyond the view and appraisal of ordinary mortals is mistaken. All of its decisions are announced, and its most important cases are heard at public sessions which everyone is welcome to attend. Yet mystery continues to enshroud the Court, with unfortunate results. Among them are the surprise and consternation which attend the perennial discovery that our highest judges (1) are human and (2) make a lot of law in the course of interpreting the law.

Few people are as well adjusted to these facts as the judges are. Justice Jackson once compared belief in the existence of "dispassionate judges" with the faith of children in Santa Claus. "Judges are men, not disembodied spirits," Justice Frankfurter has said. "Of course a judge is not free from preferences or, if you will, biases."

Chief Justice Marshall was only stating what to him must have been the most obvious of truths when he said in 1803: "It is emphatically the province and duty of the judicial department to say what the law is. Those who apply the rule to particular cases must of necessity expound and interpret the rule." In 1938 when Justice Frankfurter was a professor at Harvard Law School, he summed up the mysteries of "declared law" in cogent terms:

"So the problem is not whether the judges make the law, but when and how and how much. . . . I used to say to my students that legislatures make law wholesale, judges retail. . . . One of the evil features, a very evil one, about all this assumption that judges only find the law and don't make it [is] the evil of a lack of candor. By covering up the law-making function of judges, we miseducate the people and fail to bring out into the open the real responsibility of judges for what they do. . . ."

One of Justice Frankfurter's judicial colleagues remarked recently that the Supreme Court could, if it were foolish enough, declare every law passed by the last Congress unconstitutional and therefore void. Luckily for the Court and the sanity of its members, however, this is an exaggeration: there *are* limits to the Court's power. Many of these limits are subject to the interpretation of the Court and consequently are far from rigid. But they are limits just the same, and the most important one is the least understood. It flows from two words in the Constitution: "cases" and "controversies."

"The Judicial Power shall extend to all Cases. . . ." Section 2 in Article III of the Constitution begins. It uses the word "cases" six times and "controversies" twice in outlining the areas over which the courts are to have jurisdiction. From the beginning, the Supreme Court has concluded it must confine itself to genuine "cases" and "controversies" which have developed between parties with "an immediate, substantial and threatened interest" in the outcome.

This means that the Supreme Court cannot look out upon the U.S. scene, note something amiss and simply decree its correction. For example, even if every Justice on the Supreme Court had come to believe at some point before 1954 that school segregation was both wrong and unconstitutional, the highest tribunal in the land could have done nothing about it until one or more cases fairly presenting the issue came up from "the courts below." And, when such cases do come up on appeal, the decisions reached by the Supreme Court directly and specifically apply only to the particular parties in those particular cases. Whatever the Court says in its decisions becomes "the supreme law" more by consent than by compulsion.

In using its peculiar powers the Supreme Court has never been the haven and exemplar of judicial order that it is traditionally made out to be. Even John Marshall had to put up with vigorous conflicts within his Court. Under William Howard Taft and Charles Evans Hughes, both strong Chief Justices, the Court was torn by philosophical differences and personal antipathies. In the time of Harlan Fiske Stone, who followed Hughes as Chief Justice, a series of personal and professional quarrels brought the Court close to public chaos.

Among those who follow the Court's affairs, Chief Justice Warren has earned great respect on several grounds since he took office in

1953. "My God, he *looks* like a judge, sitting up there!" a lawyer who argues frequently before the Court exclaimed not long ago. With his black-robed bulk and broad, kindly face Warren presides at the public sessions with impressive dignity. He takes his title and responsibilities with passionate seriousness, and he has devoted much time and energy to the federal judiciary as a whole. But, with all respect to the Chief Justice, it must be added that he makes it perfectly clear on the bench that he is not as versed in the intricacies of constitutional law as are Justices Frankfurter, Black, Douglas and Harlan; all too often, he is embarrassed when he gets into public duels with them. Anyone observing the Justices at public sessions is entitled to wonder how the Chief Justice fares during the heated debates over points of law at the private conferences. There the lack of legal scholarship natural to a man who has spent his adult life as a county prosecutor, attorney general and governor of California is bound to be apparent at times. It unquestionably impairs his authority as the presiding Justice and thereby contributes to the Court's occasional disorder.

In discussing disorder it is best not to rely upon that illusory yardstick, "unanimity of opinion." Unanimity on any given case, such as school segregation, is not in itself a sign of a well-ordered Court. Nor is dissent in itself evidence of disorder. Chief Justice Hughes, who displayed the highest possible sense of judicial order, made the classic statement on this subject in 1936 when he said: "How amazing it is that, in the midst of controversies on every conceivable subject, one should expect unanimity of opinion upon difficult legal questions! . . . When we deal with questions relating to principles of law and their application, we do not suddenly rise into a stratosphere of icy certainty."

The unpalatable truth is that the Court for some years has been falling into a swamp of slushy uncertainty. This is principally the result of a process of change in the law—amounting to a profound revolution—which may be ascribed with about equal fairness to the Justices, to the fluid times and to the U.S. Constitution. The law of the land is now at a stage and in a state in which the appearance of judicial order is probably impossible and is certainly not to be expected.

Only yesterday, as judicial time goes, the great question rending the Court was where the power to control the national economy should lie: with the owners and managers of property, or with the national government? After tremendous struggles both inside and outside the Supreme Court the majority, led by Chief Justice Hughes, decided this question in 1937 in overwhelming favor of the national government (or, as people said then, F.D.R.'s New Deal). Today the Court is preoccupied and divided by an infinitely more delicate and difficult problem. To what extent can the U.S. Constitution be stretched to protect human rights—the rights of the individual citizen —against various manifestations of public and private power? Is there a point at which the protection of individual rights may impose upon law and government a greater burden than either one can safely bear?

These are the fundamental questions that Chief Justice Warren and his brethren are thrashing out today, and it is in this area that much of the criticism of the Court is born. The Justices cannot look for sure guidance to the Constitution, to enacted law or to their own "declared law" of the past. Questions of this kind, by their very nature, call powerfully into play the personal philosophies and judgments of the men dealing with them and make for deep differences of opinion. At the same time these questions discourage consistency of judgment, promote uncertainty in the law and utterly defeat the usual efforts to label the Justices as "conservatives" and "liberals."

There are no "conservatives" on today's Court. There are simply two varieties of what many lawyers call "the bleeding hearts." One variety bleeds all the time. The other bleeds part of the time. Chief Justice Warren, who joined the first category soon after he donned the black robe, is described by one of the most eminent attorneys in Supreme Court practice as "a bleeding heart with hemophilia."

Most of the blood is shed over nine of the twenty-two constitutional amendments and a tricky constitutional device called "due process of law." What is going on today can be understood only if these amendments and the meaning of "due process" are examined briefly.

The first ten amendments comprise the Bill of Rights. These are the amendments which guarantee the basic freedoms of religion, speech, the press and assembly, and protect us from such dangers as arbitrary arrest and imprisonment, trial without jury, excessive bail and "cruel and unusual punishments." One of them, the Fifth Amendment, provides that "No person shall be . . . deprived of life, liberty, or property, without due process of law." The Fourteenth Amendment, ratified after the Civil War, greatly broadens the "due process" requirement by applying it to state as well as federal laws and practices.

The requirement that nobody shall be deprived of life, liberty or property "without due process of law" may seem perfectly clear. In fact, however, nothing could be more complex, divisive and unpredictable in its effects. Due process means in application that no person shall be *unreasonably* deprived of his guaranteed rights. And that's the rub. What is reasonable? What is unreasonable? Increasingly since the 1880's the Justices have tended to decide cases in the uncertain terms of due process rather than in the narrower terms of what the Constitution and statutory law actually empower the governments to do.

The key opponents and polar figures of the present Court are Hugo Black, who after twenty years of service is the Senior Associate Justice, and Justice Felix Frankfurter. Many of the differences between them are matters of subtle degree which defy simple and accurate generalization. But the basic difference can be stated as follows:

Justice Black maintains in effect that law and government are inherently strong enough to protect every guaranteed individual right to the utmost, with very few qualifications. He holds that the first business of the Supreme Court is to see that the "human rights amendments" are applied across the board, and he uses the rule of due process to accomplish this end. Justice Frankfurter maintains in effect that there are limits to what law and government can practicably undertake in the field of human rights, as well as in others. He holds that the first business of the Supreme Court is to determine the limits and keep the law within them; and he tries to use the rule of due process to restrain rather than expand the reach of the law.

Any summation of the rival philosophies is open to dispute. Faced with what he regards as an example of "squalid discrimination" in the enforcement of criminal law, for instance, Justice Frankfurter may come to the very kind of conclusion for which he has roundly denounced his brethren. He is the Court's most insistent advocate of orderly and consistent justice, but he has precipitated some of its most disorderly performances and done much to prove that consistency is not to be expected at the summit of the law. Justice Black, for all the fire and force of his beliefs, does recognize some limitations upon the law's capacity. Nevertheless, the only meaningful division to be found on today's Court takes approximately the forms indicated.

With Justice Black when the chips are down stand his staunchest ally, Justice William O. Douglas, and two Eisenhower appointees, Chief Justice Warren and Justice William Brennan. By virtue of his position, the Chief Justice now appears outwardly to lead and speak for the four. But Black remains the dominant figure among them, so much so that lawyers often speak of "the Black court."

Justice Frankfurter's view of the law and its function is supported much of the time by Justices Harold H. Burton and John Marshall Harlan. Justice Tom Clark cries a pox on both houses but often winds up with Frankfurter. Justice Charles E. Whittaker, the most recent appointee, has wavered from one position to the other, perhaps inclining more toward Frankfurter in recent decisions. Justice Brennan has seemed to lean the same way of late, but not often enough as yet to alter his general identification with the Black-Douglas wing.

The important thing is not how individual Justices vote but what the Court as a whole is doing to American law. This, in large part, comes down to what the ever-increasing use of "due process" as a device of judgment is doing to the interpretation of law. Whether a Justice Black invokes "the rule of reason" to extend the reach of the law and the powers of the Court, or a Justice Frankfurter attempts with passionate intensity to apply it as an instrument of judicial restraint, the effect is much the same. The language of enacted law and the precedents of "declared law" come to have less and less weight, while the personal predilections of the individual Justices come to have more and more.

Even in the many cases where no legal question of "due process" is specifically involved, the judicial attitudes fostered by it make for a high degree of instability. As the Justices of today's Supreme Court undertake in more and more of their cases to determine what is reasonable and what is unreasonable, the element of uncertainty in their judgments and in the whole body of the law inevitably increases.

There is no use crying, as many laymen and some lawyers are prone to do, that the judges should simply settle for "what the law says." Often the written law does not "say" at all, or says so many things in so many different ways that only confusion is to be found in it. Whether people like it or not, the judges have to "say what the law is" if they are to function as a court. Their problem is to adapt to their task the means of judgment sanctioned by the Constitution.

Unless the Fifth and Fourteenth Amendments are repealed or superseded, which seems unlikely, the "rule of law" is going to be more and more the rule of reason as judges see it in the light of due process. Critics of the Court must realize that in most cases what they are objecting to is this rule of reason. Justice Holmes, who did as much as anybody to foster the use of due process, could not say today with the old finality, *"This* is a court of law." For better or for worse the U.S. Supreme Court has become a tribunal of law *and* individual justice, with law in the traditional sense running a poor second.

AMERICAN DRAMA IN A TRAGIC AGE

LIFE *Editorials*

DECEMBER 2, 1946 *and*
MAY 18, 1959

> *Why do American dramatists seem unable to write first-rate tragic drama in the tradition of the Greek playwrights and Shakespeare? Is the writing of great tragedy incompatible with American civilization? These two* LIFE *editorials, written thirteen years apart, discuss a problem that goes to the heart of our culture.*

America's failure to create first-rate tragedies may not seem like a national disaster. Yet dramatic tragedy has been the chosen medium of history's greatest artists, and our failure in it may betoken some deeper failure in the American character or scene. A people who cannot witness great reminders of the tragic aspect of their own existence are not getting the most out of life and perhaps cannot be ranked among the greatest civilizations. The people of Athens and of Shakespeare's England were able to suffer vicariously with their tragic heroes in an emotional workout that left them wiser and more serene. That, said Aristotle, is the purpose of tragedy—to purge the emotions through pity and fear. But Americans disapprove of fear and want to free the world of it. Are we an essentially untragic people?

First, a few definitions, necessarily dogmatic. According to Aristotle, the first authority on the subject, tragedy must be "serious, complete and of a certain magnitude," to which Webster's dictionary adds that the hero "is by some passion or limitation brought to a catastrophe," the action as a whole working out as "a manifestation of fate." Strictly speaking, first-rate tragedy has been written in only two eras, by only four men: by Aeschylus, Sophocles and Euripedes in the fifth century B.C. and by Shakespeare. Grade B tragedy (still very fine stuff) has been achieved by Corneille, Racine, Goethe, Ibsen and others, including composers of nineteenth century opera; and you can grade it on down from there. But high tragedy must not be confused with pathos, gloom or a mere unhappy ending.

A key word in Aristotle's definition is "magnitude." The Greek and Shakespearean heroes were princes, kings or generals at least, outsize characters whose fate involved the fate of whole cities or nations with their own. Compare King Oedipus or King Lear with what passes for a tragic hero on the American stage—the clerk-hero of Elmer Rice's *Adding Machine*, significantly named Mr. Zero, or the moronic Lennie in Steinbeck's *Of Mice and Men*. Our heroes appeal not to our awe but to our power of sympathetic identification. Aided by naturalistic settings and dialogue, we are above all made to feel at home, among equals or inferiors. The characters on our stage and screen may be rich and admirable, but we are always reminded of their humble origin, their warts or some other comfortable and exceedingly nontragic flaw. O'Neill's *The Iceman Cometh* carries this democratic snobbism about as far as it can be carried: the characters all start out as a bunch of drunken bums and finish the same.

The requirement of "magnitude," which our drama fails to meet, suggests that great tragedy may be incompatible with American democracy. Except at the Sinatra-fan level, we don't really believe in heroes, and when they appear among us anyway we unfit them for tragedy by cutting them down to size. Just as we reacted to the phenomenon of Hitler by singing *Der Führer's Face*, so we debunk our own heroes, good or bad. American fiction has produced a few characters, such as

273

Ahab in *Moby Dick,* who are of truly tragic magnitude. But the typical American reader tries to get around Ahab by dubbing him a fanatic.

One reason for the greatness of Ahab and for the high seriousness of much Victorian literature in comparison with our own was that our forebears shared a deep Christian sense of sin. This sense of sin was related to a sense of man's cosmic importance, which we seem to have lost. To a Greek, also, man was the center of the universe; his very gods had manlike attributes and were constantly involving themselves in man's affairs, whether guiding him in battle or making love to his wife. But modern man has moved from the center of the universe and reduced himself to a trivial biological specimen. He cannot esteem himself highly enough for high tragedy. He can appraise, analyze, respect and belittle himself, but he cannot regard himself with awe.

Without awe, tragedy cannot achieve its greatest impact. And it may be that our belief that all men are equal, our refusal to admit the very concept of aristocracy, debars us from ever feeling the awe that the Athenians felt toward Oedipus or the Elizabethan groundlings toward Lear. In that case our failure to produce great tragedy may be a virtue, or at least a fair price to pay for our democracy. Maybe we are more like the Romans, who also had great political gifts and never produced any great tragedy either.

Yet democracy does produce heroes, and our history is replete with tragic themes. These themes and heroes may make great American tragedy if we get over our belittling habit and admit to ourselves that the average man is not the measure of all things. But even that won't be enough. For while great tragedy is not necessarily incompatible with democracy, it is incompatible with another habit that lies deep in the American grain.

This habit is an optimistic faith in progress. Professor J. B. Bury, who wrote a history of *The Idea of Progress,* defines it to mean "that civilization has moved, is moving and will move in a desirable direction." This idea is only about as old as modern science, stemming from Bacon and Descartes. But it has as firm a grip on the modern world as the expectation of Judgment Day had on the medieval world. And except among Russian Communists (for Marx swallowed it whole) the idea of progress has nowhere taken deeper root than in America.

Now why is this idea incompatible with high tragedy? Because we have let it replace the old convictions on which tragedy depends, that man is finite (or sinful) and that his destiny does not lie wholly in his own hands. The idea of progress grew from the observable fact of science's increasing conquest of material nature. But Darwin, Herbert Spencer and others stretched this observable fact into certain unprovable assumptions: namely, that "all environments [Darwin's words] will tend to progress toward perfection," that man himself is perfectible through scientific self-knowledge and that evil is not a permanent necessity in the world. Even devout men like Tennyson, whose "Locksley Hall" is the battle hymn of progress, could promote the new faith by assuming God was on its side.

As indeed He may be. But there is increasing evidence to the contrary. There is also evidence that the underpinnings of our faith in progress may be weakening, for the scientists themselves are no longer so sure. The leading physicists have long since regained an almost primitive awe of the universe, and H. G. Wells repudiated a lifelong worship of progress before he left a world for which his final epithet was "doomed formicary." Bury's book was written a generation before the atomic bomb, but the bomb gives these words of his a new point: "If there were good cause for believing that the earth would be uninhabitable in A.D. 2000 or 2100, the doctrine of Progress would lose its meaning and would automatically disappear."

To gain a sense of tragedy, Americans must therefore virtually reverse two of their dearest values: on the one hand, we must recover our awareness of evil, uncertainty and fear; on the other, we must gain a sense of man's occasional greatness (which is quite a different thing from "the dignity of the common man"). For tragedy, in essence, is the spectacle of a great man confronting his own finiteness and being punished for letting his reach exceed his grasp. The Greeks had two words for this—*hybris*, pride, and *moira*, fate—which told them that subtle dangers lurk in all human achievements and that the bigger they are the harder they fall. But if Americans believe that there are no insoluble questions, they can't ask tragic questions. And if they believe that punishment is only for ignorance or inadequate effort, they can't give tragic answers. They can't have the tragic sense.

That sense is to feel a due humility before the forces that are able to humble us, without wishing to avoid the contest where the humbling may take place. We will be a more civilized people when we get it.

⁊ॐ

Concerning Archibald MacLeish's play *J.B.*, we have a question not touched on by our commentators. Does its success indicate any change in America's famous incapacity for great tragic drama?

That incapacity we explored some years ago. We there defined dramatic tragedy (the art of the greatest Greeks, Shakespeare and few others) as the ennobling spectacle of a great man confronting his own finiteness and being punished for letting his reach exceed his grasp. Is significant dramatic tragedy possible in a democratic (*i.e.* egalitarian) society? Even if the audience is ready, don't American efforts to write serious tragedy still somehow fall short of the classical standards? Why? Two recent efforts bear on the point.

One is *The Ballad of Baby Doe,* the Moore-Latouche opera. Less than three years old, this opera is established in many critical minds as a real contribution to the classical tradition. The story is a great love triangle and the setting is Colorado silver mining in the eighties and nineties.

Haw Tabor has the attributes of a tragic hero. He was the richest and most powerful man of his time and place and Baby, his bride, was the loveliest filly. There is a great wedding scene in Washington (Tabor was briefly a senator) attended by President Chester A. Arthur, and a wonderful campaign speech of William Jennings Bryan delivered as an aria. The opera ends when Tabor's silver luck runs out and he dies, old and broke, in 1899. But as no Coloradan needs to be reminded, Baby Doe did not die until 1935, older and broker than Tabor and more truly tragic.

She died still guarding the dead Matchless Mine, faithful to his last words: "Hang on to the Matchless!" It took a three-day blizzard to end her thirty-six-year vigil and freeze her on the floor. But the opera scarcely hints at this fabulous fixation, this heroic dedication to an illusion of perpetual riches. Instead its last words are Baby Doe's farewell song to Tabor, declaring that their love has conquered all. The true story was better art than the opera. Good as it is, *Baby Doe* gets off stage too soon as a mere love story, and is therefore a case of American evasiveness when confronted with a genuinely tragic theme.

Now about *J.B.*? This exciting play deals audaciously with those eternal problems of life, death, the meaning of suffering and the existence of God, which this generation of Americans has become most eager to take seriously. If only for that reason (and there are others) *J.B.* is a welcome enlargement of the dimensions of the American theater.

J.B. can be considered either as a human drama or as a "theodicy" (an explanation of God). As a theodicy, the play requires the fuller explanation, which MacLeish has elsewhere given, of how he sees God's conflict with Satan and man's role therein. "In the struggle between good and evil," says MacLeish, "God stakes his supremacy as God upon man's fortitude and love. . . . Man depends on God for all things; God depends on man for one," that one being man's love freely and unreasoningly given. This might be called a proto-Christian theodicy.

Now consider *J.B.* as a human drama. The hero is denied the one thing he thinks he needs most: a clear explanation of his sufferings from God. The play is therefore a formal tragedy. But it is not a complete tragedy, for the catharsis is blurred by an ambiguous, humanistic ending. Instead of answers, J.B. gets his wife back and a chance at a fresh start. The love they "blow on" is not divine love; it is pathetic, not transcendent. Thus the ending is too biological for good theodicy; and also a little too cozy for good tragedy. Is there a touch of that same escapism that spoils the end of *Baby Doe*?

Ever since Matthew Arnold marked the ebb of faith in "Dover Beach," artists have used romantic love as a handy solvent for man's philosophical dilemmas. But it is not so much a solvent as a way of changing the subject. Our dramatists seem incapable either of sticking to the stark tragic line that withholds this balm, or of transmuting the balm into the genuine solvent of divine love. The reason for this incapacity is perhaps the agnosticism of the age, an age interested in God but still remote from him. The ambiguity of *J.B.* reflects this ambiguity of the age. But by opening the question it may somewhat lessen our remoteness from God, and bring us closer to the day when Americans can confront the tragic aspects of their existence with ennobling humility instead of evasion.

V
MAKERS OF HISTORY

Feliks Topolski

THE RISE
AND DECLINE
OF MUSSOLINI

by G. A. Borgese

OCTOBER 3, 1938

> *More than two decades ago, when Mussolini and Hitler*
> *sounded invincible, G. A. Borgese, the well-known writer*
> *and professor of political science who had fled Fascism*
> *in Italy, analyzed for LIFE the Italian dictator's policies*
> *and their long-term consequences. His article stood then as a*
> *courageous and perceptive judgment. There is no reason*
> *to change a word of it now. This is the concluding section.*

Caught almost unawares under a tightening screw, Italy could not be rescued by heroes and martyrs—though far more numerous in Italy than later in Germany. The Italian nation lost all motion and breath of life, except for muttered, impotent satire. But the fame of Benito Mussolini's Fascism flourished abroad, its misdeeds swathed in half-silence, its whatsoever deeds extolled by Red-scared "haves," nose-led tourists, pitiless literati, power-balancing Britons; by Jews afraid of worse; by Catholics worrying over the Pope—a hostage in unpredictable hands; by strict liberals unwilling to contest the Italians' liberty of choosing bondage; and above all by the nice people loath to concede that anything evil might start from such a fascinating country under so remarkable a ruler.

The goal of his youth had been world-subversion. The goal of his maturity became world-control under the insignia of a Roman Emperor. Whatever the limits of his mind and character, the flight of his imagination always soared sublime. He started early, with the seizure of the Greek island of Corfu in 1923, but Europe, still alive, stopped him short. Preparation thereupon grew relentless. Italy, rightly or wrongly but universally gauged second-rate in military efficiency, was welded by him into one implement of war, and a doctrine of war and death as finest flowers of civilization was drilled into the collectivized mind of the new generation.

The Fascist word, meanwhile, spread over Europe, multiplied by propaganda and bribes aiming at the disruption of the liberal states and at the breeding of future allies for the imperial onslaught. Of all places, however, the black contagion proved most successful in the least desirable—Germany. Fascism was dutifully copied by the Nazi apprentice; but Germany was bigger and better, bigger and worse. To match the German cub's growth to lion-size, mystic faith in Italy's power and Roman Machiavellian virtue were hurriedly drummed up. Ethiopia, a vast land of dubious resources, and world-press headlines were both conquered at amazing speed. Geneva, the last stronghold of international law, was practically razed to the ground. England, blindfolded, assisted in the wreckage. He trod on Spain, a province of the ancient Roman Empire. The rout of Guadalajara in March, 1937, apparently marked the turning point in his career.

A taller Goliath, Hitler, supported by a mightier nation and by his own adamantine loyalty to his own monstrous creed, had stridden to Siegfried's Rhine during the crumbling of the League of Nations, Mussolini-blasted. Two years later the German stalked on Vienna, while tossing to the southern vassal the tough bone of Spain. The Duce gave up Austria, a long tabooed ditch between German leap and Latin skin. And in the ensuing season, to drink "brotherhood" with the frightening neighbor, scourge of the Jews, he also gave up the Jewish race, to which he owed—not indeed his wife although Rachel by name—but Angelica Balabanoff, the candid revolutionary inspirer of his youth now in the U.S., and Margherita Sarfatti (*i.e.* Sephardim), the reactionary Nympha Egeria of his maturity, still in Italy. Anti-Semitism, surreptitious in Italy for long years and censored in the news by Jews and Fascists alike, now had full sway overtopping Hitler's. He wanted thus to show how unflinchingly hand-in-hand the Rome-Berlin brotherhood should proceed toward all goals.

Between consternation and inspiration the Duce still visioned a world war as a chance for dividing the world, too large perhaps for one unsharing will, into the twin empires of Fascism and Nazism. He repeatedly urged Hitler to start the fire—a tail wagging the dog. Hitler, however, as long as possible, was after victories rather than battles. He nodded thanks to the sub-Aryan ally proffering help to crash Czechoslovakia, Nazism's gateway to the flat East and continental hegemony.

Thus, deprived by Lenin of primacy in world-subversion, he also was despoiled by Hitler of real free power in world empire. The sin of naked will to power was meeting its reward. Nobody in the fading summer of 1938 was less free than he on a chain-laden earth, for nobody with passions so huge was caught in so narrow a checkmate: between virtual submission to the German upstart or hasty conversions to Left and West. Such conversions, however, would have been as certainly mortifying as they probably would have been untrue. In either case he was a pawn, stopped at the second row. World cataclysm was the only escape, with its incalculable chances.

Yet, his greatness will be remembered by posterity—not in highroads or swamp-drainings or such other achievements, undifferential features of civilizations and savageries in the machine age—but in the sheer glory of the pathfinder. He it was who, actually and doctrinally, in deed and word, first scouted a new way for history, from Plato's Beautiful-Good or Israel's prophecy or Christ's charity back to the crude natural fact of violence, plunder and death. He it was who, recasting international Bolshevism into the matrix of tribal totemism and extinguishing whatever rays of credible Utopia still gleamed through the totalitarian pall of the Marxian Tzars, invented Fascism —"the first unqualified substitution of the idea of power for the idea of justice in the record of man"—and pointed to an alternate course in evolution, from the ancestral hope of intellectual and individual endeavor to mass instinct in hive or ant-hill.

The Italians, at the close of the sixteenth year of the Fascist Era, all freedom gone, each of them much smaller in an Italy only make-believe taller, saw even the independence of their national state at the mercy of their tyrant's whim or of the German's grip on the Alpine passes. The loveliness of their past tainted by their own cruelties in Africa and Spain, the glow of Roman daydream turning to nightmare, they all ate, in endemic bankruptcy, the gray bread which their master had hated in his boyhood. Garbed in shirts as black as mourning, they paraded, mumbling hushed bewilderment.

His voice still rang and hammered magnificently metallic, though easily outshouted by the howling pitches of the Mastersinger of Nürnberg. With gesticulations and facial twists as unsparing as his anathemas and tally-hos were breath-taking, this quality of voice, on a background of rifles, mounted to irresistible rhetorics. The years, however, had fattened, albeit not satiated, the short but thin stature of his expectant self. Diseases and anxiety neuroses had been bravely checked, but an occasional camera smile would ache on a physiognomy more inamusable than Napoleon's.

Even his shelter at home was saddened with a nepotism of gross Napoleonic style, centering on his daughter Edda and Galeazzo Ciano, son-in-law, Minister of Foreign Affairs, and heir apparent to dictatorship or purple. Nonetheless, the family group, rather numerous and corpulent in its three generations and several branches, shadowed what Mussolini might have been as a school principal and redoubtable grandfather, had not the double deluge of his century shot him to the scum's top. The brother Arnaldo, whom he frowningly liked, had died in 1931. Of friendship around him no scent. Associates as secretaries of state or Fascist hierarchs, even if annuated and paunchy, he would torture in bellicose Neronian divertissements, *e.g.* leaping over crossed bayonets or sprinting into a circle of fire.

Yet, popular compulsory acclaim with *Eia! Eia!* and *Doo-chay! Doo-chay!* and stretched arms, still was available in plenty. On July 22, 1938, he deigned to attend the opera in the imperial Thermae of Caracalla. "Before seeing Him, the crowd felt His presence, and from the depth of its anonymous and immeasurable bosom, surged an oceanic clamor," reported a dervish of the *Giornale d'Italia* whose account the anglicizer is both condensing and softpedaling. "And, lo, uppermost on the furthest tier, a form appeared, unique. HIM the whiteness, near-marmorean, of His garment relieved against the sky. . . ."

Needless to say, it was a Wagnerian soirée in Rome. Cardboard, between limelight and dark, was the plumage of Lohengrin's swan; a Palm Beach suit the Emperor's marble.

JOSEPH STALIN: AN APPRAISAL

by Leon Trotsky

OCTOBER 2, 1939

> *Stalin has long since gone to his niche in history's Hall of Infamy. From his lesser stall, Trotsky no doubt contemplates his archenemy with the cynical eye he reveals in this appraisal of Stalin, written for* LIFE *just after the outbreak of World War II. Stalin died in bed in the Kremlin long after one of his agents had murdered Trotsky in Mexico with an ice pick.*

In 1913 I sat in the Vienna apartment of a fellow exile before the samovar. We drank fragrant Russian tea and we meditated, naturally, on the overthrow of Czarism. Suddenly without a preceding knock the door opened and in it appeared a person unknown to me—of average height and rather thin, with a sallow face on which could be seen pockmarks.

The new arrival held in his hand an empty glass. Uttering a guttural sound which could, had one wished, have been taken for a greeting, he approached the samovar. He silently filled his glass with tea and, as silently, left. I looked questioningly at my friend, who said: "That was the Caucasian, Dzhugashvili, my fellow countryman. He recently entered the Central Committee of the Bolsheviks and is evidently beginning to play an important role."

The unexpected entrance and disappearance, the *a priori* enmity of manner, the inarticulate greeting, and, most importantly, the morose concentration of the stranger made a confused but unusual impression on me. Have later events thrown a shadow back on our first meeting? No, because otherwise I would have forgotten the meeting before these later events took place. Two months or so later, I read in the Bolshevik magazine *Prosveshtchenie* an article on the national question with the signature, strange to me then, of I. Stalin. [In Russian, Joseph is spelled with an I, pronounced "Yosef."—ED.] The article attracted attention mainly because, through the banal monotonous text, there flashed occasionally original ideas and brilliant formulas. Years afterwards I learned that the article had been inspired by Lenin and that in the manuscript of the apprentice there could be seen the hand of the master. At the time, however, I did not even connect "I. Stalin" with the mysterious Georgian who had poured tea into his glass in Vienna in such a discourteous way and who was to become, within four years, the Chief of the Commissariat of Nationalities in the First Soviet Government.

When Stalin became a member of the government, not only the popular masses but even the outer circles of the party itself knew nothing about him. He was a member of the staff of the Bolshevist party and because of this he had a share of power. But even among colleagues in his own Commissariat, Stalin had small influence, and in all important questions he found himself in the minority. There was still, at the time, no possibility of giving commands, and Stalin did not possess the capacity of convincing his young adversaries by debate.

When Stalin failed to get what he wanted and when his patience was exhausted by the resulting frustration, his procedure was simple. He vanished from the meeting. One of his co-workers, Pestkovsky, gave an inimitable account of the behavior of the Commissar. Stalin would say, "I will be back in a minute," depart from the conference room and hide himself in some obscure cranny of the Smolny, or later, of the Kremlin. Pestkovsky said, "It was impossible to find him. At first we used to wait for him. Later on, we merely dispersed."

Sometimes, on such occasions, the faithful Pestkovsky would stay on to wait for his superior and hear, from Lenin's room, the bell calling Stalin. "I would explain that Stalin had disappeared," Pestkovsky recalled, "but sometimes Lenin would insist on seeing him immediately. Then my task became difficult. I began a long walk through the endless corridors of the Smolny, or the Kremlin. Eventually I would find him in the most unpredictable places. Once I discovered him in the apartment of the sailor, Vorontsov. He was lying on the sofa in the kitchen, smoking his pipe."

This story gives us the first key to Stalin's character, in which the chief trait is the contradiction between his extreme will to power and his insufficient intellectual equipment. While puffing his pipe on the sofa in the sailor's kitchen, he doubtless pondered upon the distressing effects of debate, upon the intolerability of disagreement, and how fine it would be to dispense with all such nonsense.

The Revolution of 1905 passed by Stalin—now known by the pseudonym of Koba—without noting him. He spent this year in Tiflis, where the Mensheviks were in control. On the seventeenth of October, when the Czar published the constitutional manifesto, Koba was seen gesticulating on a street lamp. But that day everyone was climbing street lamps, to address the crowds below. No orator, sure of himself only in conspiratorial offices, Koba felt lost in full view of the masses.

In 1912, having at last demonstrated during the years of reaction his firmness and his fidelity to the party, Koba graduated from the provincial to the national arena. The conference of the party did not agree, it is true, to put Koba on the Central Committee but Lenin, who had by this time noticed him favorably, succeeded in persuading the Central Committee to select him as a "co-optive" member. At that time, the Georgian adopted his Russian pseudonym, Stalin ("Steely").

Koba's choice of a new name signified not so much a personal as a party predilection. As early as 1903, future Bolsheviks had been called "hard" and future Mensheviks "soft." Plekhanov, the Menshevik leader, had called his opponents "die hards." Lenin had taken this qualification as praise. One of the then young Bolsheviks adopted the pseudonym Kamenev ("Stoney") for precisely the same reason for which Dzhugashvili began to call himself Stalin. The difference was however that in the case of Kamenev there was nothing stonelike, while the pseudonym of Stalin described his character.

In March, 1913, Stalin was arrested in St. Petersburg and deported to Siberia, under the Arctic Circle, in the little village of Kureika. Stalin was, for his fellow exiles, a difficult neighbor. One of these remembered afterwards, "he occupied himself with hunting and fishing. He was living in almost complete solitude." The hunting was without a gun; Stalin preferred to use traps.

In 1916, Joseph Dzhugashvili was called up for military service. Because of the partial paralysis of his left arm which, like the two connected toes on one of his feet, is an infirmity dating from his birth, he did not enter the Army. Of the eight years which he spent in exile the most astonishing fact is perhaps that he did not succeed in learning a foreign language. In the Baku prison he attempted indeed to study German but rejected this hopeless enterprise and turned instead to Esperanto, consoling himself with the belief that it was the language of the future. In the domain of knowledge, particularly linguistic, the not very lively intellect of Stalin sought the path of least resistance. It is noteworthy that, in the four years he spent in solitude, the years of the World War and a great crisis in world socialism, Stalin wrote not one line which was published afterwards.

Stalin returned from exile in 1917 after the overthrow of the Monarchy. Together with Kamenev, he pushed out of the leadership of the party a group of young comrades, among them Molotov, present President of the Council of the People's Commissars, as too left and oriented himself toward sustaining Kerensky's Provisional Government. But three weeks later Lenin arrived from abroad, set Stalin aside and oriented the party toward the conquest of power. It is difficult to follow Stalin's activity during the months of the Revolution.

More important and capable people occupied the center of the stage and thrust him aside. He had neither theoretical imagination, nor historical perspicacity, nor the gift to grasp future events. In a complicated situation he always prefers to wait. A new idea must create its bureaucracy before Stalin can have any confidence in it.

Revolution, which has its laws and tempos, simply passes by Stalin, the cautious temporizer. It was so in 1905. It was repeated in 1917. And further, every new revolution—in Germany, in China, in Spain —caught him invariably unawares and engendered in him a feeling of dull discontent toward the revolutionary mass, which cannot be commanded by bureaucratic machinery.

Superficial psychologists like Emil Ludwig represent Stalin as a perfectly poised being, as something like a genuine child of nature. In reality, he consists entirely of contradictions. The most significant of these is the discrepancy between his ambitious will and his resources of intellect and talent. What characterized Lenin was the harmony of his psychic forces: theoretical mind, practical sagacity, strong will, endurance. All this was tied up in one active whole. Without effort he mobilized in any suitable moment different parts of his spirit. The strength of Stalin's will is not inferior perhaps to that of Lenin's but his intellectual capacities, as compared to Lenin's, measure only 10 or 20 per cent. Again, in the sphere of intellect there is a new discrepancy in Stalin: extreme development of practical sagacity and cunning at the expense of the ability to generalize and of the creative imagination. The hate for the powerful of this world was always his main driving force as a revolutionary, rather than the sympathy for the oppressed which warmed and ennobled the human image of Lenin, who, however, also knew how to hate.

In the period of the October Revolution, Stalin, more than anybody else, perceived his career as a series of failures. There was always somebody who publicly corrected him, overshadowed him and pushed him into the background. Like an internal ulcer, his ambition gave him no peace and poisoned his relations with eminent persons, beginning with Lenin. In the *Politburo* he almost always remained silent and morose. Only among primitive people without moral prejudices did he become smoother and friendlier. In prison he associated more easily with common criminals than with the political prisoners.

Hardness represents an organic quality in Stalin. But in the course of the years he forged a considerable weapon out of this quality. On ingenuous people hardness often produces the impression of sincerity. "This man does not think slyly, he says openly everything he thinks." At the same time, he is hypersensitive, easily offended and capricious. Feeling himself pushed aside, he turns his back, hides in a corner and smokes his pipe, is morosely silent and dreams of revenge.

In the struggle Stalin never refutes criticism, but immediately turns it against his adversary, giving it a merciless character. The more monstrous the accusation, the better. Stalin's policy, says a critic, violates the interest of the people. Stalin answers: "My adversaries are agents of Fascism." Before Hitler, Stalin had adopted the belief that the people will believe any lie so long as it is big enough. This theory, upon which the Moscow trials were based, might well be immortalized in psychology textbooks as the "Stalin Reflex."

Life in the Kremlin during the first year of the Revolution was very modest. In 1919 I was informed that in the Kremlin's storehouse there was some Caucasian wine and I proposed to have it removed since commerce in spirituous drinks was at that time prohibited. "If the rumor reaches the front that there is drinking in the Kremlin," I said to Lenin, "it will make a bad impression." Stalin was the third person in this conversation.

"How can we Caucasians," he said with irritation, "get along without wine?"

"You see," Lenin replied jokingly, "the Georgians can't do without their wine."

To this argument, I capitulated without a struggle.

In the Kremlin, as in all Moscow, there was an incessant struggle for living quarters, which were insufficient. Stalin wanted to change his apartment for a more quiet one. An agent of the Cheka recommended to him the parade rooms of the Kremlin Palace. My wife, who for nine years was in charge of Russia's museums and historical monuments, objected, since the palace was considered a museum. Lenin wrote her a long, exhortative letter: Would it be possible to remove the precious furnishings from a few rooms of the palace and adopt special measures for the maintenance of the chambers? Stalin needed an apartment in which he could sleep peacefully; in his present apartment it was necessary to establish young comrades who could sleep even under a cannon.

The custodian of the museums didn't give up in this argument. Lenin appointed a commission to examine the problem. The commission reached the conclusion that the palace could not be used for living purposes. Finally Stalin acquired the apartment of the accommodating Serebriakov whom, seventeen years later, he executed.

I never was in Stalin's apartment. But the French writer Henri Barbusse, who shortly before his death wrote two biographies—one of Jesus Christ and one of Joseph Stalin—gave a minute description of the small quarters in the Kremlin, on the second floor where the dictator had his modest apartment. Barbusse's description of the menage is complemented by that of Stalin's former secretary, Bazhanov, who fled abroad in 1928. The door of the apartment is guarded at all times by a sentry. In the little antechamber hang the master's military greatcoat and cap. The three bedrooms and the living room are simply furnished. Stalin's older son slept on a divan.

For a long time it was customary for lunch and dinner to be delivered from the Kremlin's special kitchen. But in the last few years, because of fear of poisoning, the Stalins have begun to prepare their food at home. If the master is not in a good mood and this is quite often the case, everybody remains silent at the table. "With his family," Bazhanov relates, "he conducts himself like a despot. For whole days he observes a haughty silence at home without answering the questions of his wife or son." After lunch, the family chief sits in an armchair near the window and smokes his pipe. The Kremlin inside telephone rings.

"Koba, Molotov is calling you," his wife says.

"Tell him I am asleep," Stalin answers in the presence of his secretary, in order to demonstrate his scorn for Molotov.

Ever since the civil war Stalin has always worn something like a military uniform, as a reminder of his connection with the Army—high boots, greatcoat, khaki trousers. No one ever sees him dressed differently, except during the summer, when he wears white linen.

We accept as authoritative the account of the antechamber, the great-coat, the boots. Automobiles did not allow for much sleep in the Kremlin during the night. The decision was finally made that, after eleven o'clock, automobiles must stop under the arch and everyone must go by foot. However, one automobile constantly broke the rule. Awakened, not for the first time, at three o'clock one morning, I waited at my bedroom window for the car to turn back. I called out to the chauffeur "Don't you know the order?" I asked. "I know, Comrade Trotsky," the chauffeur replied, "but what can I do? Comrade Stalin ordered me to keep going."

Besides his Kremlin apartment, Stalin has a villa in Gorky, the country house in which Lenin once lived and out of which Stalin drove his widow. In one of the rooms there is a motion-picture screen; in another, a valuable instrument which has the function of satisfying the musical wants of the master—a pianola. They tell how delighted Stalin was when, as a child, he was shown for the first time this marvel of marvels. He has another pianola in his Kremlin apartment for he cannot live without art. He spends his hours of relaxation enjoying the melodies of *Aïda*. In music as in politics he wants a docile machine. And the Soviet composers accept as law every preference of the dictator who has two pianolas.

In 1903, when Stalin was twenty-four, he married a young, simple Georgian girl. The marriage, according to a boyhood friend, was happy because the wife had been "raised in the holy tradition which obligated the woman to serve." While her husband was taking part in secret meetings, the young bride passed nights in ardent prayer for his safety. Koba's tolerance of her religious beliefs came only from the fact that he did not seek in her a friend capable of sharing his ideas. The young woman died in 1907 of tuberculosis and they buried her according to the Orthodox rites. She left a little boy named Jasha who, until he was ten, remained in the care of his mother's parents in Tiflis. Later he was taken to the Kremlin. We often found him in our son's room for he preferred our apartment to his father's.

In my papers I find the following note from my wife: "Jasha as a boy of 12 years had a soft, tanned face, and black, glistening eyes. He resembled, I was told, his tubercular dead mother. In bearing and manner he was very graceful. To Sereja [Trotsky's son] who was his friend, he told how his father treated him brutally, beat him for smoking. 'But it is not with blows that he will break me,' he said. 'You know,' Sereja related to me, 'Jasha spent all last night in the corridor with the sentry. Stalin had driven him out of the apartment because he smelled of tobacco.' Once I surprised Jasha in the boy's room with a cigarette in his hand. He smiled with embarrassment. 'Go on, go on,' I said to him soothingly. 'My papa is crazy,' he replied in a tense voice. 'He smokes. But he will not allow me to do it.' "

Today Jasha is separated on not too friendly terms from his father, and lives in a far-away province as an obscure engineer. It is impossible not to relate here another episode, told me by Bukharin in 1924 when, although drawing closer to Stalin, he was still on friendly terms with me.

"I have just come from seeing Koba," he said. "Do you know how he spends his time? He takes his year-old boy from bed, fills his own mouth with smoke from his pipe, and blows it into the baby's face."

"What nonsense," I interrupted.

"By God, it's the truth," Bukharin replied with that impulsiveness which characterized him. "By God, it's the pure truth. 'It will make him stronger,' Koba roars." Bukharin mimicked Stalin's Georgian pronunciation.

"That's barbaric," I said.

"You don't know Koba. He is like that—a little peculiar."

The soft Bukharin was obviously awed by the primitiveness of Stalin. It was, however, easy to agree that the father's behavior was "peculiar." While he tempered the younger boy with smoke, he forbade the older one its use with the help of pedagogical methods employed in earlier times on him by the shoemaker Vissarion.

For his second wife, Stalin married Nadyezhda Alliluieva, a daughter of a Russian father and a Georgian mother. Nadyezhda was born in 1902. After the Revolution she had worked in Lenin's secretariat, and during the civil war at the Tzaritzin front, where Stalin was active. At the time of her marriage she was seventeen and Stalin was forty. She was very reserved and very attractive. Even after having two children, she studied at an industrial college. When a campaign of slander was started against me by Stalin, Alliluieva, when she met my wife, was doubly attentive. She felt herself, apparently, closer to the persecuted than to the persecutor.

On November 9, 1932, Alliluieva died suddenly. On the causes of this sudden death, the Soviet papers remained strangely silent. But in Moscow they whispered that she had committed suicide. One evening, at Voroshilov's house, they asserted, she had allowed herself to make some critical remarks, in the presence of Soviet might, on the peasant policy which doomed the villages to starvation. Stalin had answered her in a raucous voice with the crudest insult in the Russian language. The Kremlin servants noticed Alliluieva's excited manner when she returned home. Sometime later a shot was heard from her room. Stalin received many expressions of condolence and passed on to the business of the day.

In a drama written in 1931 by the popular Russian writer Afinogenov, it is said that, if one observes a hundred citizens, he will see that eighty of them act under the influence of fear. In the years of the bloody purges, fear also seized a great part of the remaining 20 per cent. The mainspring of the policy of Stalin himself is now his fear of the fear which he has engendered.

Stalin personally is not a coward, but his policy reflects the fear of the privileged parvenus for their own future. Stalin never had any confidence in the masses; now he fears them. His alliance with Hitler, which astonished almost everybody, flowed inevitably from fear of the war. It was possible to foresee this alliance, but diplomats should have changed their glasses in time. This alliance was foreseen, particularly by the author of these lines. But Messrs. Diplomats, as simple mortals, prefer probable predictions to true predictions. However, in our insane epoch the true predictions are most often the improbable predictions. An alliance with France, with England, with the United States would be, of course, advantageous to the U.S.S.R. in case of war. But the Kremlin wanted above all to avoid war. Stalin knows that if the U.S.S.R. in alliance with the democracies should emerge from the war victorious, the Russian people would along the way with all certainty debilitate and reject the present oligarchy. The problem for the Kremlin is not to find allies for victory, but to avoid war. It is possible to attain that only by friendship with Berlin and Tokyo. This has been Stalin's goal since the victory of the Nazis.

It is also impossible to close one's eyes to the fact that not Chamberlain but Hitler overawed Stalin. In the Führer, Stalin finds not only what is in himself but also what he lacks. Hitler, for better or worse, was the initiator of a great movement. His ideas, however miserable they may be, succeeded in unifying millions of people. So arose a party which armed its leader with power never before seen in the world.

The personality of Stalin and his career are different. It is not Stalin who created the machine. The machine created Stalin. But a machine, like a pianola, cannot replace human creative power. Bureaucracy as bureaucracy is impregnated through and through with the spirit of mediocrity. Stalin is the most outstanding mediocrity of the Soviet bureaucracy. His strength lies in the fact that he expresses the instinct of self-preservation of the ruling caste more firmly, more decisively, and more pitilessly than anyone else. But that is also his weakness. He sees clearly for a short distance, but on a historical scale he is blind. A shrewd tactician, he is not a strategist. This is demonstrated by his attitude in 1905, during the last war, and in 1917. Stalin carried in himself the consciousness of his mediocrity. Hence, his need for flattery. Hence, his envy of Hitler and a secret deference to him.

According to the account of the former chief of the Soviet espionage in Europe, Krivitsky, an enormous impression was made upon Stalin by Hitler's purge of June, 1934, in the ranks of his own party. "There is a chief," the sluggish Kremlin dictator said to himself. Since that time he has without doubt imitated Hitler. The bloody purges in the U.S.S.R., the farce of "the most democratic constitution in the world" and finally the present invasion of Poland were all inspired in Stalin by the German genius with the mustache of Charlie Chaplin.

The international advocates of the Kremlin—sometimes also its adversaries—attempt to establish an analogy between the Stalin-Hitler alliance and the Brest-Litovsk Peace of 1918. This analogy is a mockery. The negotiations in Brest-Litovsk were carried on openly before all mankind. The Soviet State in those days had not a single battalion capable of fighting. Germany was attacking Russia, seizing

Soviet provinces and military supplies. The Moscow government had no choice but to sign the peace, which we ourselves openly called a capitulation of disarmed revolution before a powerful robber.

And now? The present [Nazi-Soviet] pact was concluded with the existence of a Soviet Army of many millions of soldiers. The treaty's immediate task was to facilitate Hitler's crushing of Poland. Finally, the intervention of the Red Army, under cover of the "liberation" of eight million Ukrainians and White Russians, leads to the national enslavement of twenty-four million Poles. Thus, the two cases are direct opposites. The Kremlin attempts above all, with its occupation of the Western Ukraine and Western White Russia, to give to the population of the U.S.S.R. a patriotic atonement for the hated alliance with Hitler.

The superiority of the strategist Hitler over the tactician Stalin is evident. By the Polish campaign Hitler ties Stalin to his chariot, deprives him of any freedom of maneuver, discredits him and, in passing, kills the Comintern. Nobody will say that Hitler has become a Communist. Everybody says that Stalin has become an agent of Fascism. But even at the cost of a humiliating and traitorous alliance, Stalin didn't retain his principle of peace.

No civilized nation will be able to escape this cyclone, however strict and wise may be the laws of neutrality. Less than any other nation can the Soviet Union escape it. In each new stage Hitler will present to Moscow greater and greater demands. Today he gives to his Kremlin friend for temporary safekeeping the "Great Ukraine." Tomorrow he will raise the question of who is to be master of the Ukraine. Both Stalin and Hitler have little respect for treaties. How long will a treaty between them endure? The "sanctity" of international obligations will definitely dissolve in the clouds of poison gas. "Every man for himself" will become the slogan of the governments of the nations and of the classes.

The Moscow oligarchy, in any case, will not survive the war, by which it is so thoroughly frightened. The fall of Stalin will not serve Hitler, however, who is proceeding with the infallibility of a somnambulist to the brink of the precipice. Hitler will not succeed in rebuilding the planet, even with the help of Stalin. Other people will rebuild it.

THE BATTLE
OF BRITAIN

by Winston S. Churchill

FEBRUARY 28, 1949

> *This chapter from the war memoirs of Sir Winston Churchill tells how the outnumbered Royal Air Force defeated Hitler's Luftwaffe in English skies. It was the climax of that time when, in Churchill's words, "the British people held the fort alone till those who hitherto had been half blind were half ready." The war memoirs were published in fifteen languages in more than fifty countries. LIFE serialized them in the United States.*

Our fate now depended upon victory in the air. The German leaders had recognised that all their plans for the invasion of Britain depended on winning air supremacy above the Channel and the chosen landing-places on our south coast. It was not until July 10, 1940, that the first heavy onslaught began, and this date is usually taken as the opening of the battle.

In the quality of the fighter aircraft there was little to choose. The Germans' were faster, with a better rate of climb; ours more manœuvrable, better armed. One important strategical advantage the Germans enjoyed and skilfully used: their forces were deployed on many and widely-spread bases whence they could concentrate upon us in great strengths and with feints and deceptions as to the true points of attack.

August 15 was the largest air battle of this period of the war; five major actions were fought, on a front of 500 miles. It was indeed a crucial day. In the South all our twenty-two squadrons were engaged, many twice, some three times, and the German losses, added to those in the North, were 76 to our 34. This was a recognisable disaster to the German Air Force.

I was most anxious to form a true estimate of the German losses. With all strictness and sincerity, it is impossible for pilots fighting often far above the clouds to be sure how many enemy machines they have shot down, or how many times the same machine has been claimed by others.

August 21, 1940

Prime Minister to Secretary of State for Air.

The important thing is to bring the German aircraft down and to win the battle, and the rate at which American correspondents and the American public are convinced that we are winning, and that our figures are true, stands at a much lower level. They will find out quite soon enough when the German air attack is plainly shown to be repulsed. It would be a pity to tease the Fighter Command at the present time, when the battle is going on from hour to hour and when continuous decisions have to be taken about air-raid warnings, etc. I confess I should be more inclined to let the facts speak for themselves. There is something rather obnoxious in bringing correspondents down to air squadrons in order that they may assure the American public that the fighter pilots are not bragging and lying about their figures. We can, I think, afford to be a bit cool and calm about all this. . . .

In the fighting between August 24 and September 6 the scales had tilted against Fighter Command. During these crucial days the Germans had continuously applied powerful forces against the airfields of South and South-east England. Their object was to break down the day fighter defence of the capital, which they were impatient to attack. Far more important to us than the protection of London from terror-bombing was the functioning and articulation of these airfields and the squadrons working from them. In the life-and-death struggle of the two Air Forces this was a decisive phase. We never thought of the struggle in terms of the defence of London or any other place, but only who won in the air.

We must take September 15 as the culminating date. On this day the Luftwaffe, after two heavy attacks on the 14th, made its greatest concentrated effort in a resumed daylight attack on London.

It was one of the decisive battles of the war, and, like the battle of Waterloo, it was on a Sunday. I was at Chequers. I had already on several occasions visited the headquarters of No. 11 Fighter Group in order to witness the conduct of an air battle, when not much had happened. However, the weather on this day seemed suitable to the enemy, and accordingly I drove over to Uxbridge and arrived at the Group Headquarters. No. 11 Group comprised no fewer than twenty-five squadrons covering the whole of Essex, Kent, Sussex and Hampshire, and all the approaches across them to London. Air Vice-Marshal Park had for six months commanded this group, on which our fate largely depended. My wife and I were taken down to the bomb-proof Operations Room, fifty feet below ground. All the ascendancy of the Hurricanes and Spitfires would have been fruitless but for this system of underground control centres and telephone cables, which had been devised and built before the war by the Air Ministry under Dowding's advice and impulse. Lasting credit is due to all concerned.

The Group Operations Room was like a small theatre, about sixty feet across, and with two storeys. We took our seats in the Dress Circle. Below us was the large-scale map-table, around which perhaps twenty highly-trained young men and women, with their telephone assistants, were assembled. Opposite to us, covering the entire wall, where the theatre curtain would be, was a gigantic blackboard divided into six columns with electric bulbs, for the six fighter stations, each of their squadrons having a sub-column of its own, and also divided by lateral lines. Thus the lowest row of bulbs showed as they were lighted the squadrons which were "Standing By" at two minutes' notice, the next row those at "Readiness," five minutes, then at "Available," 20 minutes, then those which had taken off, the next row those which had reported having seen the enemy, the next—with red lights—those which were in action, and the top row those which were returning home. On the left-hand side, in a kind of glass stage-box, were the four or five officers whose duty it was to weigh and measure the information received from our Observer Corps, which at this time numbered upwards of 50,000 men, women and youths. Radar was still in its infancy, but it gave warning of raids approaching our coast, and the observers, with field-glasses and portable telephones, were our main source of information about raiders flying overland. Thousands of messages were therefore received during an action. Several roomfuls of experienced people in other parts of the underground headquarters sifted them with great rapidity, and transmitted the results from minute to minute directly to the plotters seated around the table on the floor and to the officer supervising from the glass stage-box.

On the right hand was another glass stage-box containing Army officers who reported the action of our anti-aircraft batteries, of which at this time in the Command there were 200. At night it was of vital importance to stop these batteries firing over certain areas in which our fighters would be closing with the enemy.

After a quarter of an hour the raid-plotters began to move about. An attack of "40 plus" was reported to be coming from the German stations in the Dieppe area. The bulbs along the bottom of the wall display-panel began to glow as various squadrons came to "Stand By." Then in quick succession "20 plus," "40 plus" signals were received, and in another ten minutes it was evident that a serious battle impended. On both sides the air began to fill.

One after another signals came in, "40 plus," "60 plus"; there was even an "80 plus." On the floor-table below us the movement of all the waves of attack was marked by pushing discs forward from minute to minute along different lines of approach, while on the blackboard facing us the rising lights showed our fighter squadrons getting into the air, till there were only four or five left at "Readiness." These air battles, on which so much depended, lasted little more than an hour from the first encounter. The enemy had ample strength to send out new waves of attack, and our squadrons, having gone all out to gain the upper air, would have to refuel after seventy or eighty minutes, or land to rearm after a five-minute engagement. If at this moment of refueling or rearming the enemy were able to arrive with fresh unchallenged squadrons, some of our fighters could be destroyed on the ground. It was therefore one of our principal objects to direct our squadrons so as not to have too many on the ground refueling or rearming simultaneously during daylight.

Presently the red bulbs showed that the majority of our squadrons were engaged. A subdued hum arose from the floor, where the busy plotters pushed their discs to and fro in accordance with the swiftly-changing situation. Air Vice-Marshal Park gave general directions for the disposition of his fighter force, which were translated into detailed orders to each Fighter Station by a youngish officer in the centre of the Dress Circle, at whose side I sat. He now gave the orders for the individual squadrons to ascend and patrol as the result of the final information which appeared on the map-table. The Air Marshal himself walked up and down behind, watching with vigilant eye every move in the game, supervising his junior executive hand, and only occasionally intervening with some decisive order, usually to reinforce a threatened area. In a little while all our squadrons were fighting, and some had already begun to return for fuel. All were in the air. The lower line of bulbs was out. There was not one squadron left in reserve. At this moment Park spoke to Dowding at Stanmore, asking for three squadrons from No. 12 Group to be put at his disposal in case of another major attack while his squadrons were rearming and refuelling. This was done.

The young officer, to whom this seemed a matter of routine, continued to give his orders, in accordance with the general directions of his Group Commander, in a calm, low monotone, and the three reinforcing squadrons were soon absorbed. I became conscious of the anxiety of the Commander, who now stood still behind his subordinate's chair. Hitherto I had watched in silence. I now asked, "What other reserves have we?" "There are none," said Air Vice-Marshal Park. In an account which he wrote about it afterwards he said that at this I "looked grave." Well I might. What losses should we not suffer if our refuelling planes were caught on the ground by further raids of "40 plus" or "50 plus"! The odds were great; our margins small; the stakes infinite.

Another five minutes passed, and most of our squadrons had now descended to refuel. In many cases our resources could not give them overhead protection. Then it appeared that the enemy were going home. The shifting of the discs on the table below showed a continuous eastward movement of German bombers and fighters. No new attack appeared. In another ten minutes the action was ended. We climbed again the stairways which led to the surface, and almost as we emerged the "All Clear" sounded.

It was 4.30 P.M. before I got back to Chequers, and I immediately went to bed for my afternoon sleep. I must have been tired by the drama of No. 11 Group, for I did not wake till 8. When I rang, John Martin, my Principal Private Secretary, came in with the evening budget of news from all over the world. It was repellent. This had gone wrong here; that had been delayed there; an unsatisfactory answer had been received from so-and-so; there had been bad sinkings in the Atlantic. "However," said Martin, as he finished this account, "all is redeemed by the air. We have shot down 183 for a loss of under 40."

Although post-war information has shown that the enemy's losses on this day were only 56, September 15 was the crux of the Battle of Britain. On September 17, as we now know, the Fuehrer decided to postpone "Sea Lion" indefinitely.

Yet the battle of London was still to be fought out. Although invasion had been called off, it was not till September 27 that Goering gave up hope that his method of winning the war might succeed. In October, though London received its full share, the German effort was spread by day and night in frequent small-scale attacks on many places. Concentration of effort gave way to dispersion; the battle of attrition began. Attrition! But whose?

In cold blood, with the knowledge of the after-time, we may study the actual losses of the British and German Air Forces in what may well be deemed one of the decisive battles of the world. No doubt we were always over-sanguine in our estimates of enemy scalps. In the upshot we got two to one of the German assailants, instead of three to one, as we believed and declared. But this was enough.

At the summit the stamina and valour of our fighter pilots remained unconquerable and supreme. Thus Britain was saved. Well might I say in the House of Commons, "Never in the field of human conflict was so much owed by so many to so few."

In the hope that it may lighten the hard course of this narrative I record a few personal notes about the "Blitz," well knowing how many thousands have far more exciting tales to tell. The group of Government buildings around Whitehall were repeatedly hit. During the last fortnight of September preparations were made to transfer my Ministerial headquarters to the more modern and solid Government offices looking over St. James's Park by Storey's Gate. These quarters we called "the Annexe." Below them were the War Room and a certain amount of bomb-proof sleeping accommodation. The bombs at this time were of course smaller than those of the later phases. Still, in the interval before the new apartments were ready life at Downing Street was exciting. One might as well have been at a battalion headquarters in the line.

October 14 stands out in my mind. We were dining in the garden-room of No. 10 when the usual night raid began. My companions were Archie Sinclair, Oliver Lyttelton and Moore-Brabazon. Suddenly I had a providential impulse. The kitchen at No. 10 Downing Street is lofty and spacious, and looks towards the Treasury through a large plate-glass window about twenty-five feet high. The butler and parlourmaid continued to serve the dinner with complete detachment, but I became acutely aware of this big window, behind which Mrs. Landemare, the cook, and the kitchen-maid, never turning a hair, were at work. I got up abruptly, went into the kitchen, told the butler to put the dinner on the hot plate in the dining-room, and ordered the cook and the other servants into the shelter, such as it was. I had been seated again at table only about three minutes when a really very loud crash, close at hand, and a violent shock showed that the house had been struck. My detective came into the room and said much damage had been done. The kitchen, the pantry, and the offices on the Treasury side were shattered.

We went into the kitchen to view the scene. The devastation was complete. The bomb had fallen fifty yards away on the Treasury, and the blast had smitten the large, tidy kitchen, with all its bright saucepans and crockery, into a heap of black dust and rubble. The big plate-glass window had been hurled in fragments and splinters across the room, and would of course have cut its occupants, if there had been any, to pieces.

I could not resist taking Mrs. Landemare and the others from the shelter to see their kitchen. They were upset at the sight of the wreck, but principally on account of the general untidiness!

One day after luncheon the Chancellor of the Exchequer, Kingsley Wood, came to see me on business at No. 10, and we heard a very heavy explosion take place across the river in South London. I took him to see what had happened. The bomb had fallen in Peckham. It was a very big one—probably a land-mine. It had completely destroyed or gutted twenty or thirty small three-storey houses and cleared a considerable open space in this very poor district. Already little pathetic Union Jacks had been stuck up amid the ruins. When my car was recognised the people came running from all quarters, and a crowd of more than a thousand was soon gathered. All these folk were in a high state of enthusiasm. They crowded round us, cheering and manifesting every sign of lively affection, wanting to touch and stroke my clothes. One would have thought I had brought them some fine substantial benefit which would improve their lot in life. I was completely undermined, and wept. Ismay, who was with me, records that he heard an old woman say, "You see, he really cares. He's crying." They were tears not of sorrow but of wonder and admiration. "But see, look here," they said, and drew me to the centre of the ruins. There was an enormous crater, perhaps forty yards across and twenty feet deep. Cocked up at an angle on the very edge was an Anderson shelter, and we were greeted at its twisted doorway by a youngish man, his wife and three children, quite unharmed but obviously shell-jarred. They had been there at the moment of the explosion. They could give no account of their experiences. But there they were, and proud of it. Their neighbours regarded them as enviable curiosities. When we got back into the car a harsher mood swept over this haggard crowd. "Give it 'em back," they cried, and "Let *them* have it too." I undertook forthwith to see that their wishes were carried out; and this promise was certainly kept. The debt was repaid tenfold, twentyfold, in the frightful routine bombardment of German cities, which grew in intensity as our air power developed, as the bombs became far heavier and the explosives more powerful. Certainly the enemy got it all back in good measure, pressed down and running over. Alas for poor humanity!

Another time I visited Margate. A small restaurant had been hit. Nobody had been hurt, but the place had been reduced to a litter of crockery, utensils and splintered furniture. The proprietor, his wife and the cooks and waitresses were in tears. Where was their home? Where was their livelihood? Here is a privilege of power. I formed an immediate resolve. On the way back in my train I dictated a letter to the Chancellor of the Exchequer laying down the principle that all damage from the fire of the enemy must be a charge upon the State and compensation be paid in full and at once. Thus the burden would not fall alone on those whose homes or business premises were hit, but would be borne evenly on the shoulders of the nation.

These were the times when the English, and particularly the Londoners, who had the place of honour, were seen at their best. Grim and gay, dogged and serviceable, with the confidence of an unconquered people in their bones, they adapted themselves to this strange new life, with all its terrors, with all its jolts and jars. One evening when I was leaving for an inspection on the east coast, on my way to King's Cross the sirens sounded, the streets began to empty, except for long queues of very tired, pale people, waiting for the last bus that would run. An autumn mist and drizzle shrouded the scene. The air was cold and raw. Night and the enemy were approaching. I felt, with a spasm of mental pain, a deep sense of the strain and suffering that was being borne throughout the world's largest capital city. How long would it go on? How much more would they have to bear? What were the limits of their vitality? What effects would their exhaustion have upon our productive war-making power?

Away across the Atlantic the prolonged bombardment of London, and later of other cities and sea-ports, aroused a wave of sympathy in the United States, stronger than any ever felt before or since in the English-speaking world. Passion flamed in American hearts, and in none more than in the heart of President Roosevelt. The temperature rose steadily in the United States. I could feel the glow of millions of men and women eager to share the suffering, burning to strike a blow. As many Americans as could get passages came, bringing whatever gifts they could, and their respect, reverence, deep love and comradeship were very inspiring.

In the middle of September a new and damaging form of attack was used against us. Large numbers of delayed-action bombs were now widely and plentifully cast upon us and became an awkward problem. These bombs had to be dug out, and exploded or rendered harmless. This was a task of the utmost peril.

Special companies were formed in every city, town and district. Volunteers pressed forward for the deadly game. Teams were formed which had good or bad luck. Some survived this phase of our ordeal. Others ran twenty, thirty or even forty courses before they met their fate. The Unexploded Bomb (U.X.B.) detachments presented themselves wherever I went on my tours. Somehow or other their faces seemed different from those of ordinary men, however brave and faithful. They were gaunt, they were haggard, their faces had a bluish look, with bright gleaming eyes and exceptional compression of the lips; withal a perfect demeanour. In writing about our hard times we are apt to overuse the word "grim." It should have been reserved for the U.X.B. Disposal Squads.

It seems incongruous to record a joke in such sombre scenes. But in war the soldier's harsh laugh is often a measure of inward compressed emotions. The party were digging out a bomb, and their prize man had gone down the pit to perform the delicate act of disconnection. Suddenly he shouted to be drawn up. Forward went his mates and pulled him out. They seized him by the shoulders and, dragging him along, all rushed off together for the fifty or sixty yards which were supposed to give a chance. They flung themselves on the ground. But nothing happened. The prize man was seriously upset. He was blanched and breathless. They looked at him inquiringly. "My God," he said, "there was a *bloody great* rat!"

One squad I remember which may be taken as symbolic of many others. It consisted of three people—the Earl of Suffolk, his lady private secretary, and his rather aged chauffeur. They called themselves "the Holy Trinity." Thirty-four unexploded bombs did they tackle with urbane and smiling efficiency. But the thirty-fifth claimed its forfeit. Up went the Earl of Suffolk in his Holy Trinity. But we may be sure that, as for Mr. Valiant-for-truth, "all the trumpets sounded for him on the other side."

Very quickly, but at heavy sacrifice of our noblest, the devotion of the U.X.B. detachments mastered the peril.

Towards the middle of October Josiah Wedgwood began to make a fuss in Parliament about my not having an absolutely bomb-proof shelter for the night raids. He was an old friend of mine. His brother was the Chairman of the Railway Executive Committee. Before the war they had had the foresight to construct a considerable underground office in Piccadilly. It was seventy feet below the surface and covered with strong, high buildings. I began to be pressed from all sides to resort to this shelter for sleeping purposes. Eventually I agreed, and from the middle of October till the end of the year I used to go there once the firing had started, to transact my evening business and sleep undisturbed. One felt a natural compunction at having much more safety than most other people; but so many pressed me that I let them have their way. After about forty nights in the railway shelter the Annexe became stronger, and I moved back to it. Here during the rest of the war my wife and I lived comfortably. We felt confidence in this solid stone building, and only on very rare occasions went down below the armour. My wife even hung up our few pictures in the sitting-room, which I had thought it better to keep bare. Her view prevailed and was justified by the event. From the roof near the cupola of the Annexe there was a splendid view of London on clear nights. They made a place for me with light overhead cover from splinters, and one could walk in the moonlight and watch the fireworks. In 1941 I used to take some of my American visitors up there from time to time after dinner. They were always most interested.

On the night of November 3 for the first time in nearly two months no alarm sounded in London. The silence seemed quite odd to many. There had been another change in the policy of the German offensive. Although London was still regarded as the principal target, a major effort was now to be made to cripple the industrial centres of Britain.

On November 15 the enemy switched back to London with a very heavy raid in full moonlight. Much damage was done, especially to churches and other monuments. The next target was Birmingham, and three successive raids from the 19th to the 22nd of November inflicted much destruction and loss of life. When I visited the city a day or two later to inspect its factories, and see for myself what had happened, an incident, to me charming, occurred. It was the dinner-hour, and a very pretty young girl ran up to the car and threw a box of cigars into it. I stopped at once and she said, "I won the prize this week for the highest output. I only heard you were coming an hour ago." The gift must have cost her two or three pounds. I was very glad (in my official capacity) to give her a kiss.

The climax raid of these weeks came once more to London, on Sunday, December 29. All the painfully-gathered German experience was expressed on this occasion. It was an incendiary classic. The weight of the attack was concentrated upon the City of London itself. It was timed to meet the dead-low-water hour. The water-mains were broken at the outset by very heavy high-explosive parachute-mines. Nearly fifteen hundred fires had to be fought. The damage to railway stations and docks was serious. Eight Wren churches were destroyed or damaged. The Guildhall was smitten by fire and blast, and St. Paul's Cathedral was only saved by heroic exertions. A void of ruin at the very centre of the British world gapes upon us to this day. But when the King and Queen visited the scene they were received with enthusiasm far exceeding any Royal festival.

During this prolonged ordeal, of which several months were still to come, the King was constantly at Buckingham Palace. Proper shelters were being constructed in the basement, but all this took time. Also it happened several times that His Majesty arrived from Windsor in the middle of an air-raid. Once he and the Queen had a very narrow escape. I have His Majesty's permission to record the incident in his own words:

Friday, September 13, 1940.

We went to London (from Windsor) and found an air-raid in progress. The day was very cloudy and it was raining hard. The Queen and I went upstairs to a small sitting room overlooking the

Quadrangle (I could not use my usual sitting room owing to the broken windows by former bomb damage). All of a sudden we heard the zooming noise of a diving aircraft getting louder and louder, and then saw two bombs falling past the opposite side of Buckingham Palace into the Quadrangle. We saw the flashes and heard the detonations as they burst about eighty yards away. The blast blew in the windows opposite to us, and two great craters had appeared in the Quadrangle. From one of these craters water from a burst main was pouring out and flowing into the passage through the broken windows. The whole thing happened in a matter of seconds and we were very quickly out into the passage. . . .

The King, who as a sub-lieutenant had served in the battle of Jutland, was exhilarated by all this, and pleased that he should be sharing the dangers of his subjects in the capital. I must confess that at the time neither I nor any of my colleagues was aware of the peril of this particular incident. Had the windows been closed instead of open the whole of the glass would have splintered into the faces of the King and Queen, causing terrible injuries. So little did they make of it all that even I, who saw them and their entourage so frequently, only realised long afterwards when making inquiries for writing this book what had actually happened.

In those days we viewed with stern and tranquil gaze the idea of going down fighting amid the ruins of Whitehall. His Majesty had a shooting-range made in the Buckingham Palace garden, at which he and other members of his family and his equerries practised assiduously with pistols and tommy-guns. Presently I brought the King an American short-range carbine, from a number which had been sent to me. This was a very good weapon.

About this time the King changed his practice of receiving me in a formal weekly audience at about five o'clock which had prevailed during my first two months of office. It was now arranged that I should lunch with him every Tuesday. This was certainly a very agreeable method of transacting State business, and sometimes the Queen was present. On several occasions we all had to take our plates and glasses in our hands and go down to the shelter, which was making progress, to finish our meal. The weekly luncheons became a regular institution. After the first few months His Majesty decided that all servants should be excluded, and that we should help ourselves and help each other. During the four and a half years that this continued I became aware of the extraordinary diligence with which the King read all the telegrams and public documents submitted to him. I was most careful that everything should be laid before the King, and at our weekly meetings he frequently showed that he had mastered papers which I had not yet dealt with. It was a great help to Britain to have so good a King and Queen in those fateful years, and as a convinced upholder of constitutional monarchy I valued as a signal honour the gracious intimacy with which I, as first Minister, was treated, for which I suppose there has been no precedent since the days of Queen Anne and Marlborough during his years of power.

During the human struggle between the British and German Air Forces, between pilot and pilot, between A.A. batteries and aircraft, between ruthless bombing and the fortitude of the British people, another conflict was going on step by step, month by month. This was a secret war, whose battles were lost or won unknown to the public, and only with difficulty comprehended, even now, to those outside the small high scientific circles concerned. Unless British science had proved superior to German, and unless its strange, sinister resources had been effectively brought to bear on the struggle for survival, we might well have been defeated, and, being defeated, destroyed.

Thus the three main attempts to conquer Britain after the fall of France were successively defeated or prevented. The first was the decisive defeat of the German Air Force in the Battle of Britain during July, August and September. Our second victory followed from our first. The German failure to gain command of the air prevented the cross-Channel invasion. The prowess of our fighter pilots, and the excellence of the organisation, which sustained them, had in fact rendered the same service—under conditions indescribably different —as Drake and his brave little ships and hardy mariners had done three hundred and fifty years before, when, after the Spanish Armada was broken and dispersed, the Duke of Parma's powerful army waited helplessly in the Low Countries for the means of crossing the Narrow Seas.

310

The third ordeal was the indiscriminate night bombing of our cities in mass attacks. This was overcome and broken by the continued devotion and skill of our fighter pilots, and by the fortitude and endurance of the mass of the people, and notably the Londoners. But these noble efforts in the high air and in the flaming streets would have been in vain if British science and British brains had not played the ever-memorable and decisive part which this chapter records.

CRUSADE
IN EUROPE

by Dwight D. Eisenhower

DECEMBER 13, 1948

> *Writing about Eisenhower's book* Crusade in Europe, *Fletcher Pratt, U.S. military historian, said: "Unless General Grant objects, it can be set down as the best piece of literary reminiscence by an American." Here, from Eisenhower's book, are some dramatic highlights of World War II as seen through the eyes of the Allied Supreme Commander.*

In January, 1943, before the campaign in North Africa was finished, President Roosevelt came to General Eisenhower's theater for the Casablanca Conference:

In the early evening the President sent word that he would like to see me alone. This was one of several intimate and private conversations I had with Mr. Roosevelt during the war. His optimism and buoyancy, amounting almost to light-heartedness, I attributed to the atmosphere of adventure attached to the Casablanca expedition. Successful in shaking loose for a few days many of the burdens of state, he seemed to experience a tremendous uplift from the fact that he had secretly slipped away from Washington and was engaged in a historic meeting on territory that only two months before had been a battleground. While he recognized the seriousness of the war problem still facing the Allies, much of his comment dealt with the distant future, the post-hostilities tasks, including disposition of colonies and territories.

He speculated at length on the possibility of France's regaining her ancient position of prestige and power in Europe and on this point was very pessimistic. As a consequence, his mind was wrestling with the questions of methods for controlling certain strategic points in the French Empire which he felt that the country might no longer be able to hold.

We went over in detail the military and political developments of the preceding ten weeks; he was obviously and outspokenly delighted with the progress we had made. However, when I outlined some of the possibilities for reverses that the winter held for us, his manner indicated that he thought I took this too seriously. President Roosevelt's estimate of the final collapse was, in my opinion, too sanguine by many weeks. Under his insistence that I name a date I finally blurted out my most miraculous guess of the war. "May 15," I said.*

I found that the President, in his consideration of current African problems, did not always distinguish clearly between the military occupation of enemy territory and the situation in which we found ourselves in North Africa. He constantly referred to plans and proposals affecting the local population, the French Army, and governmental officials in terms of orders, instructions, and compulsion. It was necessary to remind him that from the outset we had operated under policies requiring us to gain and use an ally. He, of course, agreed— but he nevertheless continued, perhaps subconsciously, to discuss local problems from the viewpoint of a conqueror. It would have been so much easier for us could we have done the same!

The President was hopeful of a quick settlement of the French

*Hostilities ended in North Africa on May 12, 1943—ED.

312

political situation through a reconciliation between Giraud and de Gaulle, feeling that he could convince both that the best interests of France would be served by their joining forces. During the conversation, which turned frequently to the personal, I was struck with his phenomenal memory for detail. He recalled that my brother Milton had visited Africa and he told me the reasons why he had assigned Milton to the OWI, which was headed by Elmer Davis. He repeated entire sentences, almost paragraphs, from the radiogram I had sent home to explain the Darlan matter and told me the message had been most useful in calming fears that all of us were turning Fascist.

The surrender of all German troops in North Africa posed a new problem in military protocol for General Eisenhower:

Von Arnim surrendered the German troops, and Field Marshal Messe, in nominal command of the whole force, surrendered the Italian contingent. When Von Arnim was brought through Algiers on his way to captivity, some members of my staff felt that I should observe the custom of bygone days and allow him to call on me.

The custom had its origin in the fact that mercenary soldiers of old had no real enmity toward their opponents. Both sides fought for the love of a fight, out of a sense of duty or, more probably, for money. A captured commander of the eighteenth century was likely to be, for weeks or months, the honored guest of his captor. The tradition that all professional soldiers are really comrades in arms has, in tattered form, persisted to this day.

For me World War II was far too personal a thing to entertain such feelings. Daily as it progressed there grew within me the conviction that as never before in a war between many nations the forces that stood for human good and men's rights were this time confronted by a completely evil conspiracy with which no compromise could be tolerated. Because only by the utter destruction of the Axis was a decent world possible, the war became for me a crusade in the traditional sense of that often misused word.

In this specific instance, I told my Intelligence officer, Brigadier Kenneth Strong, to get any information he possibly could out of the captured generals but that, as far as I was concerned, I was interested only in those who were not yet captured. None would be allowed to call on me. I pursued the same practice to the end of the war. Not until Field Marshal Jodl signed the surrender terms at Reims in 1945 did I ever speak to a German general, and even then my only words were that he would be held personally and completely responsible for the carrying out of the surrender terms.

On his way back to the U.S. from the Teheran Conference, President Roosevelt broke his trip for a stopover in North Africa. General Eisenhower met him when he arrived at Tunis:

The President arrived in midafternoon and was scarcely seated in the automobile when he said, "Well, Ike, you are going to command OVERLORD."

Because I had to discuss with him, at once, details of his next day's plans, we had no opportunity, at the moment, to talk further about the new assignment, but I did manage to say, "Mr. President, I realize that such an appointment involved difficult decisions. I hope you will not be disappointed."

I arrived in England on January 14, 1944, to undertake the organization of the mightiest fighting force that the two Western Allies could muster. The timing of the operation was a difficult matter to decide. At Teheran the President and the Prime Minister had promised Generalissimo Stalin that the attack would start in May; but two considerations combined to postpone the date from May to June. The first and important one was our insistence that the attack be on a larger scale than that originally planned. The second factor was the degree of dependence we were placing upon the preparatory effort of the Air Force. An early attack would provide the Air Force with only a minimum opportunity for pinpoint bombing of critical transportation centers in France, whereas the improved weather anticipated for the month of May would give them much more time and better opportunity to impede the movement of German reserves and demolish German defenses along the coast lines.

After the abandonment of the May target date, the next combination of moon, tide and time of sunrise that we considered practicable for the attack occurred on June 5, 6 and 7. If none of these three days should prove satisfactory from the standpoint of weather, consequences would ensue that were almost terrifying to contemplate. Secrecy would be lost. Assault troops would be unloaded and crowded back into assembly areas enclosed in barbed wire, where their original places would already have been taken by those to follow in subsequent waves. Complicated movement tables would be scrapped. Morale would drop. A wait of at least fourteen days, possibly twenty-eight, would be necessary—a sort of suspended animation involving more than two million men!

During all the months of planning which we hoped would culminate on these three days in June, my personal contacts with the Prime Minister were frequent and profitable. He took a lively interest in every important detail, and was able to lend us an effective hand when some of our requirements demanded extra effort on the part of overloaded British civil agencies.

Visits to the Prime Minister's weekend home at Chequers always had business as their main purpose. But the countryside was so pleasant and peaceful that an occasional hour spent in strolling through the fields and woods was real recreation.

The Prime Minister would usually ask his guests to arrive during the late afternoon. Dinner would be followed by a short movie and then, at about 10:30 P.M., business conferences would begin. These sometimes lasted until three the next morning. Every type of problem was discussed and often definite decisions reached.

Mr. Churchill rarely failed to inject into most conferences some element of emotion. One day a British general happened to refer to soldiers, in the technical language of the British staff officer, as "bodies." The Prime Minister interrupted with an impassioned speech of condemnation—he said it was inhuman to talk of soldiers in such cold-blooded fashion, and that it sounded as if they were merely freight —or worse—corpses! I must confess I always felt the same way about the expression, but on that occasion my sympathies were with the staff officer, who to his own obvious embarrassment had innocently drawn on himself the displeasure of the Prime Minister.

In all our conferences Mr. Churchill clearly and concretely explained his attitude toward and his hopes for OVERLORD. He gradually became more optimistic than he had earlier been, but he still refused to let his expectations completely conquer his doubts. More than once he said, "General, if by the coming winter you have established yourself with your thirty-six Allied divisions firmly on the Continent, and have the Cherbourg and Brittany peninsulas in your grasp, I will proclaim this operation to the world as one of the most successful of the war."

In reply to my insistence that the picture I painted him was not too rosy, even if the Germans continued to fight to the bitter end, he would smile and say, "My dear General, it is always fine for a leader to be optimistic. I applaud your enthusiasm, but liberate Paris by Christmas and none of us can ask for more."

All southern England was one vast military camp, crowded with soldiers awaiting final word to go, and piled high with supplies and equipment awaiting transport to the far shore of the Channel. The whole area was cut off from the rest of England. The southernmost camps where assault troops were assembled were all surrounded by barbed-wire entanglements to prevent any soldier leaving the camp after he had once been briefed as to his part in the attack. The mighty host was tense as a coiled spring, and indeed that is exactly what it was—a great human spring, coiled for the moment when its energy should be released and it would vault the English Channel in the greatest amphibious assault ever attempted.

We met with the Meteorologic Committee twice daily. When the commanders assembled on the morning of June 4, one day before our tentatively chosen D-day, the report we received was discouraging. Low clouds, high winds and formidable wave action were predicted to make landing a most hazardous affair. The meteorologists said that air support would be impossible, naval gunfire would be inefficient and even the handling of small boats would be rendered difficult. Weighing all factors, I decided that the attack would have to be postponed.

The conference on the evening of June 4 presented little, if any, added brightness to the picture of the morning, and tension mounted even higher because the inescapable consequences of postponement were almost too bitter to contemplate.

At three-thirty the next morning our little camp was shaking and shuddering under a wind of almost hurricane proportions and the accompanying rain seemed to be traveling in horizontal streaks. The mile-long trip through muddy roads to the naval headquarters was anything but a cheerful one, since it seemed impossible that in such conditions there was any reason for even discussing the situation.

When the conference started the first report given was that the bad conditions predicted the day before for the coast of France were actually prevailing there and that if we had persisted in the attempt to land on June 5 a major disaster would almost surely have resulted. This they probably told us to inspire more confidence in their next astonishing declaration, which was that by the following morning a period of relatively good weather, heretofore completely unexpected, would ensue, lasting probably thirty-six hours. The long-term prediction was not good, but they did give us assurance that this short period of calm weather would intervene between the exhaustion of the storm we were experiencing and the beginning of the next spell of really bad weather.

The prospect was not bright because of the possibility that we might land the first several waves successfully and then find later build-up impracticable, and so have to leave the isolated original attacking forces easy prey to German counteraction. However, the consequences of the delay justified great risk and I quickly announced the decision to go ahead with the attack on June 6. The time was then 4:15 A.M., June 5. No one present disagreed and there was a definite brightening of faces as, without a further word, each went off to his respective post of duty to flash out to his command the messages that would set the whole host in motion.

A number of people appealed to me for permission to go aboard the supporting naval ships in order to witness the attack. Every member of a staff can always develop a dozen arguments why he, in particular, should accompany an expedition rather than remain at the only post, the center of communications, where he can be useful. Among those who were refused permission was the Prime Minister. His request was undoubtedly inspired as much by his natural instincts as a warrior as by his impatience at the prospect of sitting quietly back in London to await reports. I argued, however, that the chance of his becoming an accidental casualty was too important from the standpoint of the whole war effort and I refused his request. He replied, with complete accuracy, that while I was in sole command of the operation by virtue of authority delegated to me by both governments, such authority did not include administrative control over the British organization. He said, "Since this is true it is not part of your responsibility, my dear General, to determine the exact composition of any ship's company in His Majesty's Fleet. This being true," he rather slyly continued, "by shipping myself as a bona-fide member of a ship's complement it would be beyond your authority to prevent my going."

All of this I had ruefully to concede, but I forcefully pointed out that he was adding to my personal burdens in this thwarting of my instructions. Even, however, while I was acknowledging defeat in the matter, aid came from an unexpected source. I later heard that the King had learned of the Prime Minister's intention and, while not presuming to interfere with the decision reached by Mr. Churchill, he sent word that if the Prime Minister felt it necessary to go on the expedition he, the King, felt it to be equally his duty and privilege to participate at the head of the troops. This instantly placed a different light upon the matter and I heard no more of it.

Nevertheless, my sympathies were entirely with the Prime Minister.

When the Allied armies finally completed their envelopment of the German forces west of the Seine the eventual defeat of the Germans in western Europe was a certainty. Even among the professional leaders of the fighting forces there grew an optimism, almost a light-heartedness, that failed to look squarely in the face such factors as the fanaticism of great portions of the German Army and the remaining strength of a nation that was inspired to desperate action.

Our new situation brought up one of the longest-sustained arguments that I had with Prime Minister Churchill throughout the period of the war. This argument lasted throughout the first ten days of August. One session lasted several hours. The discussions involved the wisdom of going ahead with ANVIL, by then renamed DRAGOON, the code name for the operation that was to bring in General Dever's forces through the south of France.

Coincidentally with this drawn-out discussion, Montgomery suddenly proposed to me that he should retain tactical co-ordinating control of all ground forces throughout the campaign. This, I told him, was impossible, particularly in view of the fact that he wanted to retain at the same time direct command of his own Army group. To my mind and that of my staff the proposition was fantastic. The reason for having an Army group commander is to assure direct, day-by-day battlefield direction in a specific portion of the front, to a degree impossible to a supreme commander. It is certain that no one man could perform this function with respect to his own portion of the line and at the same time exercise logical and intelligent supervision over any other portion. The only effect of such a scheme would have been to place Montgomery in a position to draw at will, in support of his own ideas, upon the strength of the entire command.

A supreme commander in a situation such as faced us in Europe cannot ordinarily give day-by-day and hour-by-hour supervision to any portion of the field. Nevertheless, he is the one person in the organization with the authority to assign principal objectives to major formations. He is also the only one who has under his hand the power to allot strength to the various major commands in accordance with their missions, to arrange for the distribution of incoming supply, and to direct the operations of the entire air forces in support of any portion of the line. The existence, therefore, of any separate ground headquarters between the supreme commander and an Army group commander would have placed such a headquarters in an anomalous position, since it would have had the power neither to direct the flow of supply and reinforcement nor to give instructions to the air forces for the application of their great power.

Modern British practice had been, however, to maintain three commanders in chief, one for air, one for ground, one for Navy. Any departure from this system seemed to many inconceivable and to invite disaster. I carefully explained that in a theater so vast as ours each Army group commander would be the ground commander in chief for his particular area; instead of one there would be three so-called commanders in chief for the ground and each would be supported by his own tactical air force.

After the liberation of Paris in the fall of 1944, SHAEF had to concern itself more and more with the ever-expanding problem of keeping the advancing Allied armies supplied. General Eisenhower became convinced that for this purpose the port of Antwerp must be taken as soon as possible, but British General Montgomery proposed a different strategy:

Montgomery suddenly presented the proposition that, if we would support his Twenty-first Army Group with all supply facilities available, he could rush right on into Berlin, and, he said, end the war. I am certain that Field Marshal Montgomery, in the light of later events, would agree that this view was a mistaken one. But at the moment his enthusiasm was fired by the rapid advances of the preceding week and, since he was convinced that the enemy was completely demoralized, he vehemently declared that all he needed was adequate supply in order to go directly into Berlin.

I explained to Montgomery the condition of our supply system and our need for early use of Antwerp. I pointed out that, without railway bridges over the Rhine and ample stockades of supplies on hand, there was no possibility of maintaining a force in Germany capable of penetrating to its capital. There was still a considerable reserve in the middle of the enemy country and I knew that any pencil-like thrust into the heart of Germany such as he proposed would meet nothing but certain destruction. This was true, no matter on what part of the front it might be attempted. I would not consider it.

It was possible, and perhaps certain, that had we stopped, in late August, all Allied movements elsewhere on the front he might have succeeded in establishing a strong bridgehead definitely threatening the Ruhr, just as any of the other armies could have gone faster and farther, if allowed to do so at the expense of starvation elsewhere. However, at no point could decisive success have been attained, and, meanwhile, on the other parts of the front we would have gotten into precarious positions, from which it would have been difficult to recover. General Montgomery was acquainted only with the situation in his own sector. He understood that to support his proposal would have meant stopping dead for weeks all units except the Twenty-first Army Group. But he did not understand the impossible situation that would have developed along the rest of our great front when he, having outrun the possibility of maintenance, was forced to stop or withdraw.

On the night of March 23–24 General Eisenhower watched artillery prepare the way for the infantry to cross the Rhine:

General Simpson and I found a vantage point in an old church tower from which to witness the gunfire. Because the batteries were distributed on the flat plains on the western bank of the Rhine every flash could be seen. The din was incessant. Meanwhile, infantry assault troops were marching up to the water's edge to get into the boats. We joined some of them and found the troops remarkably eager to finish the job. There is no substitute for a succession of great victories in building morale. Nevertheless, as we walked along I fell in with one young soldier who seemed silent and depressed.

"How are you feeling, son?" I asked.

"General," he said, "I'm awful nervous. I was wounded two months ago and just got back from the hospital yesterday. I don't feel so good!"

"Well," I said to him, "you and I are a good pair then, because I'm nervous too. But we've planned this attack for a long time and we've got all the planes, the guns and airborne troops we can use to smash the Germans. Maybe if we just walk along together to the river we'll be good for each other."

"Oh," he said, "I meant I *was* nervous; I'm not any more. I guess it's not so bad around here." And I knew what he meant.

The next morning I met the Prime Minister with Field Marshal Brooke. Mr. Churchill always seemed to find it possible to be near the scene of action when any particularly important operation was to be launched. On that morning he was delighted, as indeed were all of us. He exclaimed over and over, "My dear General, the German is whipped. We've got him. He is all through."

About noon of March 24 it was necessary for me to rush down to Bradley's headquarters to confer on important phases of his own operations. After I left, the Prime Minister persuaded the local commander to take him across the Rhine in an LCM. He undoubtedly derived an intense satisfaction from putting his foot on the eastern bank of Germany's traditional barrier. Possibly he felt the act was symbolic of the final defeat of an enemy who had forced Britain's back to the wall five years before. However, had I been present he would never have been permitted to cross the Rhine that day.

By March, 1945, the Allies had established themselves on the eastern bank of the Rhine and were proceeding with the encirclement of the Ruhr. The end of the war was in sight, and political aspects of the impending victory were beginning to make themselves felt:

I already knew of the Allied political agreements that divided Germany into post-hostilities occupational zones. This future division of Germany did not influence our military plans for the final conquest of the country. Military plans, I believed, should be devised with the single aim of speeding victory; by later adjustment troops of the several nations could be concentrated into their own national sectors.

A natural objective beyond the Ruhr was Berlin. It was politically and psychologically important as the symbol of remaining German power. I decided, however, that it was not the logical or the most desirable objective for the forces of the Western Allies. I determined that our next major advances would comprise three essential parts. The first would be a powerful thrust by Bradley directly across the center of Germany. The second and third parts of the general plan visualized a rapid advance on each of our flanks. The northern thrust would cut off Denmark; the southern one would push into Austria and overrun the mountains west and south of that country.

Under the arrangement made in January and approved by the Combined Chiefs of Staff, I thought that I was completely within the scope of my own authority and responsibility in communicating

322

this plan to Generalissimo Stalin. However, we quickly found that Prime Minister Churchill seriously objected to my action. He disagreed with the plan and held that, because the campaign was now approaching its end, troop maneuvers had acquired a political significance that demanded the intervention of political leaders in the development of broad operational plans. He apparently believed that my message to the Generalissimo had exceeded my authority to communicate with Moscow only on purely military matters. He was greatly disappointed and disturbed because my plan did not first throw Montgomery forward with all the strength I could give him from the American forces in the desperate attempt to capture Berlin before the Russians could do so. He sent his views to Washington.

The Prime Minister knew, of course, that, regardless of the distance the Allies might advance to the eastward, he and the President had already agreed that the British and American occupation zones would be limited on the east by a line two hundred miles west of Berlin. Consequently his great insistence upon using all our resources in the hope of assuring the arrival of the Western Allies in Berlin ahead of the Russians must have been based on the conviction that great prestige and influence for the Western Allies would later derive from this achievement.

The outcome of all this was that we went ahead with our own plan. So earnestly did I believe in the military soundness of what we were doing that my intimates on the staff knew I was prepared to make an issue of it.

The only other result of this particular argument was that we thereafter felt somewhat restricted in communicating with the Generalissimo and were careful to confine all our communications to matters of solely tactical importance. This situation I did not regard as too serious, particularly because the United States Chiefs of Staff had stanchly reaffirmed my freedom of action in the execution of plans that in my judgment would bring about the earliest possible cessation of hostilities.

April 12, 1945, was a full day for General Eisenhower. He inspected one of the first caches of hidden Nazi treasures discovered by General Patton's Army and saw his first Nazi concentration camp. The day ended with a "dramatic climax":

Bradley, Patton and I sat up late talking of future plans, particularly of the selection of officers and units for early redeployment to the Pacific. We went to bed just before twelve o'clock, Bradley and I in a small house at Patton's headquarters, and he in his trailer. His watch had stopped, and he turned on the radio to get the time signals from the British Broadcasting Corporation. While doing so he heard the news of President Roosevelt's death. He stepped back into the house, woke up Bradley and then the two of them came to my room to tell me the shocking news.

We pondered over the effect the President's death might have upon the future peace. We were certain that there would be no interference with the tempo of the war because we already knew something of the great measures afoot in the Pacific to accomplish the smashing of the Japanese. We were of course ignorant of any special or specific arrangements that President Roosevelt had made affecting the later peace. But we were doubtful that there was any other individual in America as experienced as he in the business of dealing with the other Allied political leaders. None of us had known the President very well; I had, through various conferences, seen more of him than the others, but it seemed to us, from the international viewpoint, to be a most critical time to be forced to change national leaders. We went to bed depressed and sad.

With some of Mr. Roosevelt's political acts I could never possibly agree. But I knew him solely in his capacity as leader of a nation at war—and in that capacity he seemed to me to fulfill all that could possibly be expected of him.

During the Potsdam Conference, which was held after the fall of Germany, General Eisenhower saw President Truman:

While the President was in Germany he expressed a desire to inspect some American troops. I arranged for him to come into the American area and by good fortune the 84th Division was selected as one of those he was to see. In that division his cousin, Colonel Louis Truman, was chief of staff; and so the meeting was not only a pleasant official experience for the President but held a nice personal touch as well.

One day when the President was riding with General Bradley and me he fell to discussing the future of some of our war leaders. I told him that I had no ambition except to retire to a quiet home and from there do what little I could to help our people understand some of the great changes the war had brought to the world and the inescapable responsibilities that would devolve upon us all as a result of those changes. I shall never forget the President's answer. Up to that time I had met him casually on only two or three occasions. I had breakfasted with him informally and had found him sincere, earnest and a most pleasant person with whom to deal. Now, in the car, he suddenly turned toward me and said: "General, there is nothing that you may want that I won't try to help you get. That definitely and specifically includes the presidency in 1948."

I doubt that any soldier of our country was ever so suddenly struck in his emotional vitals by a President with such an apparently sincere and certainly astounding proposition as this. Now and then, in conversations with friends, jocular suggestions had previously been made to me about a possible political career. My reaction was always instant repudiation, but to have the President suddenly throw this broadside into me left me no recourse except to treat it as a very splendid joke, which I hoped it was. I laughed heartily and said, "Mr. President, I don't know who will be your opponent for the presidency, but it will not be I." There was no doubt about *my* seriousness.

Marshal Zhukov accompanied General Eisenhower on his return flight from the Soviet Union to Berlin. The two commanders exchanged views on military procedures:

Highly illuminating to me was Marshal Zhukov's description of the Russian method of attacking through mine fields. Marshal Zhukov gave me a matter-of-fact statement of his practice, which was, roughly, "There are two kinds of mines; one is the personnel mine and the other is the vehicular mine. When we come to a mine field our infantry attacks exactly as if it were not there. The losses we get from personnel mines we consider only equal to those we would have gotten from machine guns and artillery if the Germans had chosen to defend that particular area with strong bodies of troops instead of with mine fields. The attacking infantry does not set off the vehicular mines, so after they have penetrated to the far side of the field they form a bridgehead, after which the engineers come up and dig out channels through which our vehicles can go."

I had a vivid picture of what would happen to any American or British commander if he pursued such tactics. Americans assess the cost of war in terms of human lives, the Russians in the over-all drain on the nation. The Russians clearly understood the value of morale, but for its development and maintenance they apparently depended upon over-all success and upon patriotism, possibly fanaticism.

As far as I could see, Zhukov had given little concern to methods that we considered vitally important to the maintenance of morale among American troops: systematic rotation of units, facilities for recreation, short leaves and furloughs, and above all, the development of techniques to avoid exposure of men to unnecessary battlefield risks, all of which, although common practices in our Army, seemed to be largely unknown in his.

The basic differences between American and Russian attitudes in the handling of men were illustrated on another occasion. While talking to a Russian general I mentioned the difficult problem that was imposed upon us at various periods of the war by the need to care for so many German prisoners. I remarked that they were fed the same rations as were our own soldiers. In the greatest astonishment he asked, "Why did you do that?" I said, "Well, in the first place my country was required to do so by the terms of the Geneva Convention. In the second place the Germans had some thousands of American and British prisoners and I did not want to give Hitler the excuse or justification for treating our prisoners more harshly than he was already doing." Again the Russian seemed astounded at my attitude and he said, "But what did you care about men the Germans had captured? They had surrendered and could not fight any more."

To return the courtesy extended to me by the Russian government, the American War Department, with the approval of President Truman, promptly invited Marshal Zhukov to pay a visit to America. An immediate acceptance was returned and we thought that the marshal would soon depart for the United States.

Unfortunately he soon fell ill. At the time there was some speculation as to whether it was diplomatic illness, but when I next saw him at a meeting of the Control Council in Berlin he gave the appearance of a man who had gone through a serious siege of ill health. In any event this served to postpone his visit until the approach of winter weather and he then expressed a desire to go to our country in the spring. Before that time arrived the Russians had apparently no further interest in sending one of their marshals to spend a week or ten days in America.

I saw Marshal Zhukov for the last time November 7, 1945. It was a Soviet holiday, in honor of which he gave a large reception in Berlin, inviting to it the senior commanders and staff officers of all the Allies. The weather turned bad and flying was impossible. The other two commanders in chief canceled their engagements but, knowing that I was soon to be ordered home, I determined to attend the ceremony, although to do so I had to make a night trip by train, followed by a long automobile trip during the day.

When I arrived Marshal Zhukov, with his wife and a number of his senior assistants, was standing in the receiving line. He greeted me and then promptly deserted the receiving line. He took his wife by the arm, and the three of us, with an interpreter, retired to a comfortable room where were refreshments of all kinds. We talked for two hours.

Americans at that time—or at least we in Berlin—saw no reason why the Russian system of government and democracy as practiced by the Western Allies could not live side by side. Because implicit in Western democracy is respect for the rights of others it seemed natural to us that this "live and let live" type of agreement could be achieved and honestly kept. That was probably the most for which we ever really hoped. But even such a purely practical basis for living together in the world has not been achieved.

What caused the change may possibly never be clearly understood by any of us. But two and a half years of growing tension have shattered our dream of rapid progress toward universal peace and the elimination of armaments. Seriously and soberly, aware of our strengths and our weaknesses, sure of our moral rectitude, we must address ourselves to the new tensions that beset the world.

BITTERNESS ON THE ROAD TO VICTORY

by Field-Marshal Montgomery

OCTOBER 27, 1958

> *Eisenhower's peppery British subordinate tells his side of crucial events in the last stages of the campaign in Europe during World War II. A great commander, Montgomery was never a quiet one. Here, in this excerpt from his war memoirs, his version of the bickering and bitterness in high military places contrasts with the even-tempered narrative of the Supreme Commander.*

On the morning of the 16th December 1944 I felt in need of relaxation, so I decided to fly up to Eindhoven and play a few holes of golf. But my game was soon interrupted by a message that the Germans had launched a heavy attack on the front of the First American Army and the situation was obscure. I flew straight back to my headquarters.

A great bulge or salient was being made in the American line at the Ardennes Forest. The situation deteriorated rapidly and finally General Bradley's 12th Army Group was split in two. At 10:30 A.M. on the 20th December, Eisenhower ordered me to take command at once of all American forces on the northern flank of the bulge. That order put two American armies under my command: the Ninth Army (Lieut. General William H. Simpson) on my immediate right and the First Army (Lieut. General Courtney H. Hodges) to the right of the Ninth Army.

The First Army was fighting desperately. I left at noon for its HQ, where I had instructed the Ninth Army's Simpson to meet me. I found the northern flank of the bulge was very disorganized. Neither army commander had seen Bradley or any senior member of his staff since the battle began, and they had no directive on which to work.

The first thing to do was to see the battle on the northern flank *as one whole,* to ensure that the vital areas were held securely and to create reserves for counterattack. I embarked on these measures.

I put British troops under command of the Ninth Army to fight alongside American soldiers and had that army take over some of the First Army front. I positioned British troops as reserves behind the First and Ninth armies until such time as American reserves could be created. Slowly but surely the situation was held and then finally restored. Similar action was taken by Bradley with the Third Army on the southern flank of the bulge.

I must mention a joke on my part which was not considered funny in Whitehall. The War Office was very naturally worried and I sent a telegram giving the whole story. The last sentence read: "We cannot come out through Dunkirk this time as the Germans still hold that place." My telegram was sent on to the prime minister but with the last sentence cut out!

The Battle of the Bulge may be said to have ended in the middle of January. On the 14th January I sent a letter to General Bradley in which I wrote:

"I would like to say two things:

"First: what a great honor it has been for me to command such fine troops.

"Second: how well they have all done.

"It has been a great pleasure to work with Hodges and Simpson; both have done very well.

"And the corps commanders in the First Army (Gerow, Collins, Ridgway) have been quite magnificent; it must be most exceptional to find such a good lot of corps commanders gathered together in one army.

"All of us in the northern side of the salient would like to say how much we have admired the operations that have been conducted on the southern side; if you had not held on firmly to Bastogne the whole situation might have become very awkward. . . ."

I sent a similar message to Eisenhower.

I was perturbed at this time about the sniping at Eisenhower which was going on in the British press. So I sent a message to the prime minister and said that I proposed to deal with the story of the battle in a press conference. I would show how the whole Allied team rallied to the call and how teamwork saved a somewhat awkward situation. I suggested I should then put in a strong plea for Allied solidarity. The prime minister agreed and said he felt what I proposed would be invaluable.

I held the conference. Many stories have been told about it, and many quotations have been taken out of their context and published. Nobody has ever published the full text of the notes from which I spoke and which were given to the press afterward. Here are pertinent excerpts:

". . . The Germans had broken right through a weak spot, and were heading for the Meuse. . . . As soon as I saw what was happening I took certain steps myself to ensure that . . . they would certainly not get over that river. . . .

"Then the situation began to deteriorate. But the whole Allied team rallied to meet the danger; national considerations were thrown overboard; General Eisenhower placed me in command of the whole northern front. . . . Today British divisions are fighting hard on the right flank of the First U.S. Army. You thus have the picture of British troops fighting on both sides of American forces who have suffered a hard blow. This is a fine Allied picture. . . .

"The battle has been most interesting; I think possibly one of the most interesting and tricky battles I have ever handled, with great issues at stake.

"The first thing to be done was to 'head off' the enemy from the tender spots and vital places. Having done that successfully, the next thing was to 'see him off,' *i.e.*, rope him in and make quite certain that he could not get to the places he wanted. . . . He is now being 'written off,' and heavy toll is being taken of his divisions by ground and air action. . . .

"I shall always feel that Rundstedt was really beaten by the good fighting qualities of the American soldier and by the teamwork of the Allies. . . . I have spent my military career with the British soldier and I have come to love him with a great love; and I have now formed a very great affection and admiration for the American soldier. I salute the brave fighting men of America; I never want to fight alongside better soldiers. . . . It is teamwork that pulls you through dangerous times. . . . Nothing must be done by anyone that tends to break down the team spirit of our Allied team; if you try and 'get at' the captain of the team you are liable to induce a loss of confidence, and this may spread and have disastrous results. . . .

"Let me tell you that the captain of our team is Eisenhower. I am absolutely devoted to Ike; we are the greatest of friends. It grieves me when I see uncomplimentary articles about him in the British press; he bears a great burden, he needs our fullest support, he has a right to expect it, and it is up to all of us to see that he gets it. . . ."

What I said in this conference was skillfully distorted by the enemy. Chester Wilmot says in *Struggle for Europe* that his dispatch to the BBC about it was intercepted by the German wireless, "rewritten to give it an anti-American bias and then broadcast by Arnhem Radio, which was then in Goebbels' hands. Monitored at Bradley's HQ, this broadcast was mistaken for a BBC transmission and it was this twisted text that started the uproar."

Distorted or not, I think now that I should never have held that press conference. So great was the feeling against me on the part of the American generals that whatever I said was bound to be wrong. In contradistinction to the rather crestfallen American command I appeared, to the sensitive, to be triumphant—not over the Germans but over the Americans. This was a completely false picture. But I had also described the battle as "interesting." Those who did not know me well could hardly be expected to share my professional interest in the art of war and were, not unnaturally, aggrieved by this phraseology. They were too sore to find the battle "interesting" as an objective enterprise.

What I could have said but did not say was that, in the Battle of the Ardennes, the Allies got a real "bloody nose," the Americans had nearly 80,000 casualties, and that it would never have happened if we had fought the campaign properly after the great victory in Normandy. Furthermore, because of this unnecessary battle we lost some six weeks in time—with all that that entailed in political consequences as the end of the war drew nearer.

During the Battle of the Ardennes the remorseless march of events had forced Eisenhower to [give me] operational command of the left flank of the Allies, with two American armies under my command. This could not have been very pleasant for my critics at Supreme Headquarters or for the American generals who opposed my ideas.

On the 28th December, Eisenhower visited the northern flank and I had a long talk with him. I again gave it as my opinion that the Ruhr was the immediate objective. All available power must be concentrated to secure it. Operational control of the forces involved must be exercised by one commander.

I reinforced these views in a letter to Eisenhower the next day:

"When you and Bradley and myself met at Maastricht on 7 December," I wrote, "it was very clear to me that Bradley opposed any idea that I should have the operational control over his army group, so I did not then pursue the subject.

"I therefore consider that it will be necessary for you to be very firm on the subject, and any loosely worded statement will be quite useless. . . . I consider that if you merely use the word 'coordination' it will NOT work. . . . One commander must have powers to direct and control the operations. You cannot possibly do it yourself, and so you would have to nominate somebody else. . . ."

After Eisenhower received my letter, he found waiting for him a telegram from General Marshall saying that the appointment of a British officer to hold operational command or control over Bradley would be entirely unacceptable in America.

That finished the issue of operational control as far as I was concerned and I knew it would be useless to open it again.

By the 10th March, the troops of the Ninth American Army and 21st Army Group were lined up along the west bank of the Rhine from Neuss to Nijmegen. Meanwhile, on the 7th March, the First American Army had secured intact the railway bridge at Remagen and at once formed a bridgehead on the east bank. The importance of this bridgehead to our subsequent operations was very great. Not only did it lock up a considerable number of surviving enemy divisions in that area, but more important, it loosened up the whole campaign by providing a bridgehead which could be exploited at will. By the third week in March the Allied armies had closed to the Rhine throughout its length from Switzerland to the sea.

On the 23rd March we began the crossing of the Rhine in strength on a wide front. Once over the Rhine I began to discuss future operational plans with Eisenhower. We had several meetings. I had always put Berlin as a priority objective. It was a political center and if we could beat the Russians to it things would be much easier for us in the postwar years. In his letter to me dated the 15th September 1944 Eisenhower had agreed with me about the great importance of the German capital. But now he did not agree. His latest view was expressed in a message he sent me on the 31st March 1945, which ended with the following words:

"You will note that in none of this do I mention Berlin. That place has become, so far as I am concerned, nothing but a geographical location, and I have never been interested in these. My purpose is to destroy the enemy's forces and his powers to resist."

It was useless for me to pursue the matter further. Anyhow it was now almost too late.

But after the victory in Normandy my point was that the final defeat of the German armed forces was imminent—in a few more months. The important point was therefore to ensure that when that day arrived we would have a political balance in Europe which would help us, the Western nations, to win the peace. That meant getting possession of certain political centers in Europe before the Russians— notably Vienna, Prague and Berlin. If the higher direction of the war had been handled properly by the political leaders of the West, and suitable instructions given to Supreme Commanders, we could have grabbed all three before the Russians. But what happened?

The possibility of seizing Vienna disappeared when it was decided to land in southern France. The troops for the landing were taken from Field Marshal Alexander's force in Italy and that put a brake on his operations. As regards Prague, the Third American Army was halted on the western frontier of Czechoslovakia toward the end of April, for reasons which I have never understood. Berlin was lost to us when we failed to make a sound operational plan in August 1944, after the victory in Normandy.

The Americans could not understand that it was of little avail to win the war strategically if we lost it politically. Because of this curious viewpoint we suffered accordingly from V-E Day onward, and are still so suffering.

With the Rhine behind us we drove hard for the Baltic. By now the Germans had lost so heavily in personnel and territory that they could not again form and equip new divisions. Their cause was lost and the German war had reached its last moments. Hitler's Germany faced utter disaster.

Events now began to move rapidly. On the 1st May we picked up a German broadcast that Hitler had died and that Admiral Doenitz had succeeded him as Führer. On the 3rd May, Field Marshal Keitel, chief of the German high command, sent a delegation to my head-quarters on Lüneburg Heath, with the consent of Doenitz, to open negotiations for surrender. The German officers were brought to my caravan site and were drawn up under the Union Jack, which was flying proudly in the breeze. I kept them waiting for a few minutes and then came out of my caravan and walked toward them. They all saluted, under the Union Jack. It was a great moment: I knew the

Germans had come to surrender and that the war was over.

I said to my interpreter, "Who are these men?" He told me.

I then said, "What do they want?"

Admiral von Friedeburg, a member of the delegation, then read me a letter from Field Marshal Keitel offering to surrender to me the three German armies withdrawing in front of the Russians between Berlin and Rostock. I refused to consider this, saying that these armies should surrender to the Russians. I added that, of course, if any German soldiers came toward my front with their hands up they would automatically be taken prisoner.

Von Friedeburg said it was unthinkable to surrender to the Russians as they were savages, and the German soldiers would be sent straight off to work in Russia.

I said the Germans should have thought of all these things before they began the war and particularly before they attacked the Russians in June 1941.

I then asked if they wanted to discuss the surrender of their forces on my western flank. They said they did not. But they were anxious about the civilian population in those areas and would like to arrange with me some scheme by which their troops could withdraw slowly as my forces advanced. I refused.

I then decided to spring something on them quickly. I said to Von Friedeburg, "Will you surrender to me all German forces on my western and northern flanks, including all forces in Holland, Friesland with the Frisian Islands and Helgoland, Schleswig-Holstein and Denmark? If you will do this, I will accept it as a tactical battlefield surrender of the enemy forces immediately opposing me, and those in support in Denmark."

He said he could not agree to this. I then said that if the Germans refused to surrender I would order the fighting to continue. I next showed them on a map the actual battle situation on the whole western front. They had no idea what this situation was and were very upset. They were convinced of the hopelessness of their cause but they said they had no power to agree to my demands. They were, however, now prepared to recommend to Field Marshal Keitel the unconditional surrender of all the forces on the western and northern flanks of the

21st Army Group. Two of them would go back to see Keitel and bring back his agreement.

I then drew up a document which summarized the decisions reached at our meeting, which I said must be signed by myself and Von Friedeburg, and could then be taken to Keitel and Doenitz.

I was certain Von Friedeburg would return with full powers to sign. I therefore decided to see the press and to describe to the correspondents all that was happening.

Von Friedeburg got back to my headquarters while the press conference was in progress. I saw a staff officer enter the tent and knew he had the answer. I told the correspondents they could all go with me to my conference tent and witness the final scene.

The German delegation was paraded again under the Union Jack, outside my caravan. I gave orders for the surrender ceremony to take place at once in a tent pitched for the purpose. The arrangements in the tent were very simple: a trestle table covered with an army blanket, an inkpot, an ordinary army pen that you could buy in a shop for twopence. The Germans stood up as I entered. They were clearly nervous and one of them took out a cigaret; he wanted to smoke to calm his nerves. I looked at him and he put the cigaret away.

I read out in English the instrument of surrender and then called on each member of the German delegation by name to sign the document, which they did without any discussion. I then signed, on behalf of General Eisenhower. The original of this agreement is in my possession and I will never part with it: it is a historic document. I do not know what happened to the pen we all used. I suppose someone pinched it.

I had ordered all offensive action to cease on the 3rd May when the Germans first came to see me. I now sent out a cease-fire order to take effect at 8 A.M. on Saturday 5th May 1945. Two days later a German delegation signed the final surrender document at General Eisenhower's HQ at Rheims. The Germans in Italy had given up earlier. On the night of the 8th May all firing ended in Europe. The war was now over.

Eisenhower is a remarkable and most lovable man. We did not always agree about the strategy and major tactics of the war in which we were engaged. But history will do no harm in talking about honest differences of opinion between us, provided, as in our case was the fact, it does so under the shadow of the great truth that Allied cooperation in Europe during World War II was brought to the greatest heights it has ever attained. Although it may be true to say that no one man could have been responsible for such an achievement, the major share of the credit goes to Eisenhower, without any doubt.

I would not class Ike as a great soldier in the true sense of the word. He might have become one if he had ever had the experience of exercising direct command of a division, corps and army, which unfortunately for him did not come his way. But he was a great Supreme Commander, a military statesman. I know of no other person who could have welded the Allied forces into such a fine fighting machine in the way he did, and kept a balance among the many conflicting and disturbing elements which threatened at times to wreck the ship.

I have visited Ike regularly since he became President, always staying with him and Mamie, either in the White House or in his home at Gettysburg. Our friendship has grown and developed, and today I have the very greatest admiration and affection for him. I have read a good deal of American history and it is my belief that historians will record that Ike reached his greatest heights as President.

Where does his strength lie? He has a good brain and is very intelligent. But his real strength lies in his human qualities. He is a very great human being. He merely has to smile at you and you trust him at once. He is the very incarnation of sincerity. He has great common sense. People and nations give him their confidence. I am devoted to him and would do anything for him. He is a truly great man, and it is a tremendous honor to have his friendship. He has done a great deal for me, in difficult times and in good, and I can never adequately express what I owe to his personal kindness and forbearance.

Before closing I must make clear my point of view about the future —a sort of final testament. The unity of the West is the goal which has to be reached if the Western Alliance is to flourish. We have a long road to travel before we reach it.

The Western Alliance was brought into being because of fear of aggression from the East. Fear is the basic component of the cement which holds the Alliance together. No alliance based on fear alone has ever lasted because whenever fear recedes the cement begins to crumble.

True unity involves a willingness to make sacrifices for the common cause. An economic cement would be more permanent than one of fear. In any case, an important component of the new cement must be the solidarity of the English-speaking peoples and their determination to help the nations of continental Europe to defend their freedom and maintain their way of life. The hard core of that solidarity must be Anglo-American friendship. If that line breaks, that is the end for each one of us, including the U.S.

The British have been dealing with great world problems for centuries. The U.S. has only the experience of decades. But the Western world must understand that without the United States of America the Western Alliance would collapse. For its part the United States must exercise convincing powers of leadership in the free world. I often think that the United States's foreign policy is inconsistent. She appears to have one policy in the Assembly of the United Nations, and another and different one when her own national interests are involved. These inconsistent policies have played a large part in the weakening of the general strategic position of the West. If continued, they could lead to the breakup of the Western Alliance.

NATO must be strengthened. Now that its main object, the prevention of war, has been achieved, the time has come for a thorough overhaul of the whole organization.

The Western Alliance must be based on unity, hope and courage, cemented together by the joint strength of some 450 million people. The Hungarians have reminded the world what can be achieved by courage alone. If the Western Alliance can have strength *and* courage, there is no limit to what it could achieve, provided that its members also have unity in the true sense.

THE LAST DAYS OF HITLER

by H. R. Trevor-Roper

MARCH 17, 1947

> *At the close of World War II, when the world was*
> *wondering if Hitler was really dead, H. R. Trevor-Roper,*
> *an Oxford historian then serving in British Intelligence,*
> *was instructed to collect every scrap of material he could*
> *find on the subject. After months of research he established*
> *the true facts of Hitler's grisly end. He later wrote a book,*
> The Last Days of Hitler, *from which this article is taken.*

In the spring of 1945 Adolf Hitler was facing the last desperate battle of the war. The Western Allies had crossed the Rhine and the Russians were only sixty miles from Berlin. Now in his underground bunker beneath the Reichschancellery, Hitler was directing the final operations.

The man in the bunker was not the Hitler of prewar days. "Until 1940," says Von Hasselbach, the most reliable of his doctors, "Hitler appeared to be much younger than he actually was (51). From that date he aged rapidly. From 1940 to 1943 he looked his age. After 1943 he appeared to have grown old." In the last days of April, 1945,

339

Hitler had become a physical wreck. The real damage to his health in the last months of his life proceeded from two causes: his manner of life and his doctors.

The most fantastic of the corps of doctors with whom Hitler surrounded himself was Professor Theodor Morell. It is difficult to speak of him in the measured terms and discreet vocabulary proper to the medical profession. Morell was a quack. Those who saw him, after his internment by the Americans, described a gross but deflated old man of cringing manners, inarticulate speech and the hygienic habits of a pig.

Hitler kept Morell in constant attendance for nine years, preferring him above all other doctors and in the end surrendering his person to the disastrous experiments of a charlatan. Morell was totally indifferent to science or truth. He prescribed quick drugs and fancy nostrums and even claimed that a British doctor had stolen from him the secret of penicillin. Actually it was not necessary for Morell to make such ridiculous claims. Hitler himself believed in a kind of mystic medicine, just as he liked magic and astrology. And so when Morell, a former ship's doctor who had set up as a specialist in venereal disease among the artistic demimonde of Berlin, came to Berchtesgaden as a necessary attendant on Hitler's photographer, Hoffman, his fortune was soon made.

A list of the medicines used by Morell upon Hitler, excluding the morphia and hypnotics which were also used, contains the names of twenty-eight different mixtures of drugs, various fake medicines, narcotics, stimulants and aphrodisiacs. For Hitler's stomach cramps Morell prescribed and administered, for at least two years, a proprietary drug called Dr. Koester's Antigas Pills. Dr. Koester's pills contained strychnine and belladonna and the maximum dose which could safely be prescribed was eight pills a day. Hitler was consuming two to four pills with every meal.

Under the combined pressure of such a life and such remedies, only a powerful constitution would have preserved Hitler's health from a much earlier collapse. In 1943 the first symptoms of physical alteration became apparent. Hitler's extremities began to tremble, especially the left arm and the left leg; his left foot dragged on the ground and he developed a stoop. The nature of this tremor was never satisfactorily explained. Some doctors thought that it might be due to Parkinson's disease; others believed the tremor had an hysterical origin, but no certainty could be achieved. By the autumn of 1944 the long-concealed effects of Hitler's declining health were becoming manifest and he was undergoing treatment from a continual series of specialists. Despite their efforts Hitler's health continued to sink. All witnesses of his final days agree in describing his emaciated face, his gray complexion, his stooping body, his shaking hand and foot, his hoarse and quavering voice and the film of exhaustion that covered his eyes.

This then was the condition of the man in the bunker during those last days when Berlin fell. Among the coterie of sycophantic followers still with him, fifty feet underground in the Führerbunker's eighteen cramped and uncomfortable rooms, were the only two creatures whom he regarded as faithful—his Alsatian dog Blondi and Eva Braun.

Eva Braun will be a disappointment to all readers of history for she had none of the colorful qualities of the conventional tyrant's mistress. But then neither was Hitler a typical tyrant. Behind his impassioned rages, his enormous ambitions, there lay not the indulgent ease of a voluptuary but the trivial tastes, the conventional domesticity of the petty bourgeois. It was to this permanent, if submerged, element in his character that Eva Braun appealed, and because she appealed to the triviality, not the extravagance, of his nature, she is herself uninteresting. Pretty rather than beautiful, with a fresh color and slightly high cheekbones, unobtrusive, uninterfering, anxious to please, she soon achieved an ascendancy over Hitler, supplying that idea of restfulness which was so lacking to his political life but for which his bourgeois soul so hankered. She confined her attentions to the intervals between politics, presiding over the teacups.

Thus when Eva Braun arrived in Berlin on April 15, 1945, to share Hitler's fate, she was neither wife nor acknowledged mistress. She came unbidden to the Reichschancellery and had no more right to share in the ritual death of the Führer than Fräulein Manzialy, the vegetarian cook who ate Hitler's meals with him in Eva Braun's absence. Hitler ordered Eva Braun to leave Berlin but she would not go. She had come for her wedding and her ceremonial death.

However, Hitler was not yet determined to die. It seems incredible that in those last days of the Third Reich its leader should have thought the stars or a stroke of subtlety could save him. All the evidence is clear that he never understood the real certainty of his ruin. Deep in the Führerbunker, Hitler sought hope in horoscopes and in Carlyle's *History of Frederick the Great*. One evening while Goebbels was reading aloud to him from the *History*, they came to the passage that tells how the great Frederick, facing certain defeat, decided to take poison if his reverses continued. Carlyle pleads with Frederick in these words: "Brave king! Wait yet a while, and the days of your suffering will be over. Already the sun of your good fortune stands behind the clouds, and soon will rise upon you." When Goebbels read how Frederick was then saved from suicide at the last moment by the death of his enemy, Czarina Elizabeth of Russia, tears came to Hitler's eyes. Hitler and Goebbels discussed Frederick's miraculous change of fortune and sent for two horoscopes that were carefully kept in one of Himmler's research departments: the horoscope of the Führer and the horoscope of the Third Reich. These sacred documents were fetched and examined, and together Hitler and Goebbels brooded hopefully over them. They found that both horoscopes had predicted the outbreak of war in 1939, the German victories until 1941 and then the series of defeats culminating in the worst disasters in the early months of 1945, especially the first half of April. Then there was to be an overwhelming German victory in the second half of April, stagnation until August and, in August, peace. After the peace there would be a difficult time for Germany for three years, but from 1948 she would rise to greatness again.

The horoscopes, which had so accurately prophesied the past, turned out to be much less reliable for the future. Nevertheless a story told by one of the secretaries in Goebbels' Propaganda Ministry shows how much faith Goebbels and Hitler put in them.

"I well remember Friday, April 13," says the secretary. "Every week Goebbels paid a visit to the eastern front to address the troops, taking them supplies of cigarettes, cognac and books. On this day he returned, as usual, very late at night. A heavy bombardment was going on and the chancellery and the Adlon Hotel were burning. We met Goebbels on the steps of the Propaganda Ministry. A reporter said to him, 'Herr Reichsminister, Roosevelt is dead.' Goebbels jumped up out of his car and stood for a moment as if transfixed. I shall never forget the look on his face, which we could see in the light of Berlin blazing. 'Now,' he said, 'bring out our best champagne and let us have a telephone talk with the Führer.' We went into his study, and champagne was served. Goebbels spoke to Hitler on his private line and said, 'My Führer, I congratulate you! Roosevelt is dead. It is written in the stars that the second half of April will be the turning point for us. This is Friday, April 13. It is the turning point.'"

The ecstasy did not last. The evacuation of ministries from Berlin continued but Hitler remained in his bunker, undecided, at least until he had made one further effort to throw the Russians back from the city. On April 21 Hitler ordered a final, all-out attack by the troops in Berlin under SS General Steiner. Every man, every tank, every airplane was to be diverted to take part in it. "Any commanding officer who keeps men back," Hitler shouted, "will forfeit his life within five hours."

So Hitler ordered, but his orders bore no relation now to any reality. He was moving imaginary battalions, making academic plans, disposing nonexistent formations. The Steiner attack was the last, most symbolic instance of Hitler's personal strategy; it never took place.

The facts emerged at the staff conference of April 22, which opened with the usual expositions by Generals Krebs and Jodl. Then came the news that Steiner had failed to attack. In spite of elaborate plans, in spite of ferocious threats the Luftwaffe had not gone into action. And then, following on these negative tidings, came reports of positive calamities. While troops had been withdrawn to support Steiner in the south, the Russians had broken into the suburbs in the north, and their armored spearheads were now within the city of Berlin.

Then came the storm which made the conference of April 22 famous and decisive in the history of Hitler's last days. Hitler flew into a rage. He shrieked that he had been deserted; he railed at the Army; he denounced all traitors; he spoke of universal treason, failure, corruption and lies, and then, exhausted, he declared that the end had come. At last and for the first time he despaired of his mission. All was over; the Third Reich was a failure, and its author had nothing left to do but to die. His doubts were now resolved. He would not go to the south. Anyone else who wished might go. "But," said Hitler, "I will never leave Berlin—*never*."

On the night of April 26, Luftwaffe General Ritter von Greim flew to Berlin. He was accompanied by another exotic character, the celebrated test pilot, Hanna Reitsch. Shrill, vain and voluble, she was well suited to the atmosphere in that last subterranean madhouse in Berlin. An ardent Nazi, she had long worshiped at the shrine of Adolf Hitler.

Below them, in the city, street fighting was in progress; above them Russian planes were in the air. Within a few minutes heavy Russian fire tore the bottom out of the plane and shattered von Greim's right foot. Reitsch leaned over his shoulder to take the controls and, by dodging and squirming close to the ground, brought the plane to rest on the city streets. A passing car was commandeered and von Greim was taken to the chancellery, receiving first aid on the way. In the bunker he was taken to the operating room.

Hitler came into the operating room and welcomed von Greim. His face, says Reitsch, showed gratitude for von Greim's coming. Even a soldier, Hitler said, had a right to disobey orders which seemed futile and hopeless. He asked von Greim if he knew why he had been summoned. Von Greim did not know.

"Because Hermann Goering has betrayed both me and his Fatherland," Hitler explained. "Behind my back he has established connections with the enemy. His action was a mark of cowardice! He has sent me a disrespectful telegram, saying that I once named him as my successor and that now, since I can no longer rule from Berlin, he is ready to rule from Berchtesgaden in my place. He closes the telegram by saying that if he had no answer from me he would take my assent for granted!"

As he spoke there were tears in Hitler's eyes. His head sagged, his face was white, and as he handed Goering's fatal telegram to von Greim to read, it fluttered with the trembling of his hands. As von Greim read, Hitler watched, breathing hard in short, convulsive puffs.

The muscles in his face twitched. Suddenly he screamed:

"An ultimatum! A crass ultimatum! Nothing now remains! Nothing is spared me! No loyalty is kept, no honor observed. There is no bitterness, no betrayal that has not been heaped upon me. And now this! It is the end. No injury has been left undone!"

After a pause Hitler recovered his composure and told von Greim that he had summoned him to declare him commander in chief of the Luftwaffe with the rank of field marshal, in succession to Goering. It was for this formality alone that the lives of German airmen and badly needed machines had been sacrificed to bring von Greim into the bunker. A telegram would have been sufficient, but Hitler preferred this dramatic if expensive method, which incidentally imprisoned von Greim for three days, bedridden and useless, in the bunker.

During the night of April 27 the Russian bombardment of the chancellery reached its highest pitch. To those who cowered in the bunker and heard the shells falling above them, the accuracy seemed deadly, with every shell falling exactly in the center of the chancellery buildings. At any moment they expected the Russian ground troops to arrive and overrun the ruins. During the night, according to Hanna Reitsch, Hitler called his court around him, and in this macabre conclave all rehearsed their plans for suicide and considered, in maudlin detail, the various methods by which their corpses might be destroyed. The first appearance of Russian soldiers, they agreed, would be the signal for the execution of this ritual self-sacrifice. Then everyone made a short speech, swearing perpetual allegiance to the Führer and Germany. Such was the climate of the bunker.

In fact, of course, all this was mostly humbug. Very few of those who thus professed a desire for communal death gave effect to their heroic resolutions. It is interesting to reflect how many who then resolved to die have since been found in continued health and restored sanity, eagerly explaining to their British and American captors that they never really owed any allegiance to Nazi Germany.

Of Hitler at least it can be said that his emotions were genuine. He intended to die if Berlin fell. And yet—such was the extraordinary confidence which still alternated with his despair—even now he still believed that the city might be saved. He regarded himself, it seems, as a kind of palladium, a totem whose presence rendered any citadel impregnable so long as he stayed. "If I leave East Prussia," he once told Field Marshal Keitel, "then East Prussia will fall. If I stay it will be held." Keitel had persuaded him to leave East Prussia and East Prussia had duly fallen. But Hitler did not intend to leave Berlin and Berlin therefore could not fall. Pacing up and down in the bunker, he would wave a road map, fast decomposing from the sweat of his hands, and explain to any casual visitor the complicated military operations whereby they would all be saved. Sometimes he would shout orders, as if himself directing the defenders; sometimes he would spread the map on the table and, stooping over it, with trembling hands he would arrange and rearrange a set of buttons as consolatory symbols of relieving armies.

The most obstinate illusions are ultimately broken by facts. On April 28 the Russians were already fighting near the center of Berlin. Hysterical telegrams began to flow outward from the bunker. "I expect the relief of Berlin," Hitler wired Keitel.

Instead of relief came the news that Himmler was negotiating with the Allies. The scene which followed the delivery of this news was terrible. Hitler stormed with indignation. "He raged like a madman," says Hanna Reitsch. "His color rose to a heated red and his face was almost unrecognizable." This was the last, the unkindest cut of all; *der treue Heinrich*—faithful Heinrich—had betrayed him.

There can be no doubt that to Hitler the treachery of Himmler, as he conceived it to be, was the signal for the end. In the early hours of April 29, after bidding farewell to Field Marshal von Greim and Hanna Reitsch, who managed to escape by plane, Hitler turned to one of the final items of business. He married Eva Braun. For this symbolic ceremony Goebbels had introduced into the bunker a certain Walter Wagner. Wagner, who had an obscure honorary position as an official of Berlin's city administration, was therefore considered a proper person to officiate at this civil ceremony. He appeared in the bunker, where he was completely unknown except to Goebbels, in the uniform of the Nazi party and the arm band of the Volksturm. The ceremony took place in the small conference room in the private part of the bunker. Besides Hitler, Eva Braun and Walter Wagner, Goebbels and Party Leader Martin Bormann were present as witnesses. The formalities were brief. The two parties declared that they were of pure Aryan descent and were free from hereditary disease. In consequence of the military situation and other extraordinary circumstances, they proposed a wartime wedding, by simple word of mouth and without any delay. In a few minutes the parties had given assent, the register had been signed and the ceremony was over. When the bride came to sign her name she began to write Eva Braun, but was checked before completing it. Striking out the initial letter B, she corrected it to "Eva Hitler, nee Braun." The ceremony over, the bride and bridegroom withdrew into their private apartments for a wedding breakfast.

Shortly afterward Bormann, Goebbels, Frau Goebbels and Hitler's two secretaries, Frau Christian and Frau Junge, were invited into the private suite. There they sat for some hours drinking champagne and talking. The conversation was of old times and old comrades, of Goebbels' marriage, which Hitler had witnessed in happier days. Now the position of the parties was reversed and the happiness was reversed too. Hitler spoke of his plans for suicide and a temporary gloom overcame the party. For some time Hitler was absent with his secretary, Frau Junge, in an adjoining room, to which other members of the party were also occasionally summoned. He was dictating his will.

That afternoon Hitler had his dog Blondi destroyed. Professor Haase, his former surgeon, killed it with poison. The two other dogs belonging to the household were shot by the sergeant who looked after them.

In the evening, while the staff was dining in the general dining passage of the Führerbunker, they were visited by one of the SS guard who informed them that the Führer wished to say good-by to the ladies and that no one was to go to bed until orders had been received. At about 2:30 in the morning the orders came. They were summoned by telephone and gathered again in the same general dining passage, officers and women, about twenty persons in all. When they were assembled, Hitler came in from the private part of the bunker, accompanied by Bormann. His look was abstracted, he walked in silence down the passage and shook hands with all the women in turn. Some spoke to him, but he said nothing or mumbled inaudibly. Ceremonies of silent handshaking had become quite customary.

The suicide of the Führer was soon to take place. Thereupon an unexpected thing happened. A great and heavy cloud seemed to roll away from the spirits of the bunker dwellers. The terrible sorcerer, the tyrant who had charged their days with intolerable melodramatic tension, would soon be gone. In the canteen of the chancellery, where the soldiers and orderlies took their meals, there was a dance. The news was brought, but no one allowed that to interfere with the business of pleasure. A message from the Führerbunker told them to be quieter, but the dance went on.

After he had finished lunch the next day, Hitler emerged from his suite, accompanied by Eva Braun, and another farewell ceremony took place. Bormann, Goebbels and twelve members of Hitler's military and immediate household staffs were there. Hitler and Eva Braun shook hands with everyone, apparently in silence, and then returned to their suite. The others were dismissed, all but the high priests and those few others whose services would be necessary. These waited in the passage. A single shot was heard. After an interval they entered the suite. Hitler was lying on the sofa, which was soaked with blood. He had shot himself through the mouth. Eva Braun was also on the sofa, also dead. A revolver was by her side but she had not used it; she had swallowed poison. The time was 3:30.

Shortly afterward two SS men, one of them Hitler's servant Linge, entered the room. They wrapped Hitler's body in a blanket, concealing the bloodstained and shattered head, and carried it out into the passage. Then two other SS officers carried the body up the four flights of stairs to the emergency exit and so out into the garden. After this Bormann entered the room and took up the body of Eva Braun. Her death had been tidier and no blanket was needed to conceal the evidence of it.

In the garden the two corpses were placed side by side, a few feet from the porch, and gasoline was poured over them. A Russian bombardment added to the strangeness and danger of the ceremony and the mourners withdrew for some protection under the shelter of the porch. There Hitler's SS Adjutant Guensche dipped a rag in gasoline, set it alight and flung it out upon the corpses. At once they were enveloped in a sheet of flame. The mourners stood to attention, gave the Hitler salute and withdrew again into the bunker where they dispersed. Guensche afterwards described the burning of Hitler's body as the most terrible experience in his life. Another witness of the spectacle was Hermann Karnau, one of the police guard. Karnau, like others of the guard who were not on duty, had been ordered away from the bunker by an officer of the SS escort and had gone to the chancellery canteen. But after a while, in spite of his orders, Karnau had decided to return to the bunker. On arrival at the door of the bunker he had found it locked. He had therefore made his way out into the garden in order to enter the bunker by the emergency exit. As he turned the corner by the tower he was surprised to see two bodies lying side by side, close to the door of the bunker. Almost at the same instant they burst, spontaneously it seemed, into flame.

Karnau watched the burning corpses for a moment. Only three feet away, they were easily recognizable, though Hitler's head was smashed. The sight, he says, was "repulsive in the extreme." Then he went down into the bunker by the emergency exit. In the bunker he met Sturmbannführer Franz Schedle, the officer commanding the SS escort. Schedle was distracted with grief. "The Führer is dead," he said. "He is burning outside."

Mansfeld, another police guard on duty in the tower, also watched the burning of the bodies. After the mourners had withdrawn, he continued to watch. At intervals he saw SS men come out of the bunker and pour more gasoline on the bodies to keep them alight. Some time afterward he was relieved by Karnau and the two went together to look at the bodies again. By now the lower parts of both bodies had been burned away and the shinbones of Hitler's legs were visible. An hour later Mansfeld visited the bodies again. They were still burning, but the flame was low.

Late that night Brigadeführer Rattenhuber, the head of the police guard, entered the bunker and spoke to a sergeant of the SS escort. He told him to report to his commanding officer and to pick three trustworthy men to bury the corpses.

Shortly before midnight Mansfeld returned to duty in the tower.

Russian shells were still falling and the sky was illuminated by flares. He noticed that a bomb crater in front of the emergency exit had been newly worked upon and that the bodies had disappeared. He did not doubt that the crater had been converted into a grave for them, for no shell could have piled the earth around it in so neat a rectangle.

That is all that is known about the disposal of the remnants of Hitler's and Eva Braun's bodies. Hitler's servant Linge afterward told one of the secretaries that they had been burned, as Hitler had ordered, "till nothing remained," but it is doubtful whether such total combustion could have taken place. The 180 liters of gasoline which were known to have been used, burning slowly on a sandy bed, would char the flesh and dissipate the moisture of the bodies, leaving only an unrecognizable and fragile remainder, but the bones would withstand the heat. These bones have never been found. Perhaps they were broken up and mixed with other bodies, the bodies of soldiers killed in the defense of the chancellery, which were also buried in the garden. The Russians have occasionally dug in that garden, and 160 such bodies have been unearthed there. Perhaps, as SS Adjutant Guensche is said to have stated, the ashes were collected in a box and conveyed out of the chancellery. Or perhaps no elaborate explanation is necessary. Perhaps such investigations as have been made have been somewhat perfunctory. Investigators who left Hitler's engagement diary unobserved in his chair for five months may easily have overlooked other relics which were more deliberately concealed. Whatever the explanation, Hitler achieved his last ambition. Like Alaric the Goth, who sacked Rome in 410 and was secretly buried by his followers beneath the River Busento in Italy, the modern destroyer of mankind is now immune from discovery.

Nevertheless I believe that these facts about the last days of Hitler must be taken into account by even the most extravagant of future mythmakers. Nazism may revive; the ancient froth of Nibelung nonsense, whose exhalations had poisoned German political thought even before Hitler, may well find another vent. A new party may appeal to a myth of Hitler; but if so, it will be to a myth of Hitler dead, not of Hitler living.

THE ROOSEVELT LEGEND

by Hamilton Basso

NOVEMBER 3, 1947

> *The legend of Franklin Delano Roosevelt began when his life ended. The strength of the legend lies in its simplicity, and because of its simplicity it seems likely to endure. This is how novelist and writer Hamilton Basso summed up F.D.R. for* LIFE *in 1947. The passing years tend to confirm his appraisal.*

When some historian of a future era gets around to assessing the character and influence of Franklin Delano Roosevelt he is going to have a troublesome job on his hands. It would be foolish, of course, even to guess what his final verdict will be. Yet, since his segment of history will be simply the present in past tense, it is possible to anticipate at least a few of his conclusions. One of these, certainly, will be that in 1947, nearly three years after his death, the ghost of Roosevelt dominated the American political scene no less forcibly than did his person and presence when he was alive. And another, hardly less inevitable, will be that already, in that same year, a legend of glory had begun to form about him.

To prove these assertions, or to bolster other proof, our hard-working scholar need go no further than the July 1, 1947, issue of the New York *Daily News*, a publication that he may feel tempted to describe, in passing, as a journal of rather inflamed opinion. There, in the department called "Capitol Stuff," which takes the form of a column but more closely resembles a club, he will find this communication: "Dear Sir: . . . You and I, despite years of practical experience to guide us, really do not realize how Americans who cast their first vote for Roosevelt worship him as a god. They never knew any other national leader. . . . This is what the Republicans are really fighting—an invisible faith in a false leader who is practically a saint in memory. . . . A READER."

Certain things about this document may annoy our historian considerably—for instance, the fact that the person who wrote it apparently did not realize that Roosevelt was venerated by large numbers of people in every age group—but he can hardly fail to understand that the letter poses, in its simplest terms, the question that he must try to answer. Saint or false leader, demigod or semidemon? Which was Roosevelt, after all?

Since Roosevelt's death on April 12, 1945, a steady stream of books and magazine articles has appeared that will help our scholar reach his answer; the rush into print has come to resemble the dash into the Cherokee strip. Among the more important of the books are the following—*The Roosevelt I Knew*, by Frances Perkins; *Speaking Frankly*, by James F. Byrnes; *Thank You, Mr. President*, by A. M. Smith; *White House Physician*, by Ross P. McIntire; *As He Saw It*, by Elliott Roosevelt; *Dinner at the White House*, by Louis Adamic; and *Franklin D. Roosevelt*, by Alden Hatch. Of the magazine articles, those published by James A. Farley under the title "Why I Broke with Roosevelt," and the more recent "Morgenthau Diaries," by Henry Morgenthau, Jr., are the most interesting.

Frances Perkins, whose *The Roosevelt I Knew* is by all odds the best book about Roosevelt that has yet appeared [up to 1947], first met the future President in 1910. She was not impressed. Roosevelt was then twenty-eight years old and had recently been elected to the New York state legislature. He seemed to Miss Perkins to be just one more ordinary, respectable, correct young man with an artificially serious expression and little if any concern about social reform. He appeared to have no particular liking or respect for any of his fellow senators nor they for him. He had the habit of throwing his head up and thrusting out his chin, which, in combination with his pince-nez and great height, gave him the rather unfortunate appearance of looking down his nose at the world.

A. Merriman Smith in his *Thank You, Mr. President,* a record of his years of service as the White House correspondent for the United Press, comes to the conclusion that Roosevelt would have made a wonderful actor. The same conclusion has been reached by others, some of whom would insist that Roosevelt was one of the two best actors of his time (Churchill being the other), and there seems but little doubt that during his early years in Albany he was trying to act out his idea of how a young statesman from Dutchess County should look and behave. The performance was not appreciated. Miss Perkins remembers an old-line Tammany politician, Tim Sullivan by name, saying to her, "Awful arrogant fellow, that Roosevelt." She also gives us a snapshot of Roosevelt on the senate floor in Albany, arguing with several of his colleagues. His mouth was pursed, his nostrils were distended and his nose was in the air. "No, no," he said, "I won't hear of it!"

James A. Farley in his "Why I Broke with Roosevelt," which seems to have been written as much out of hurt as anger, tells of hearing the equivalent of that "No, no, I won't hear of it!" many times; so does Henry Morgenthau, Jr. This intransigence, which even his best friends admit was one of Roosevelt's most pronounced characteristics, came to be known as his "Dutch stubbornness." Nearly all those who have written about him, with the exception of Miss Perkins, go out of their way to mention it. But the fact is that Roosevelt was almost 90 per cent English and only about 3 per cent Dutch.

Miss Perkins, when she met Roosevelt in Albany, was already an earnest, serious-minded social worker. She had gone to the New York state capital to fight for the passage of a bill to establish a fifty-four-hour week for women in industry in New York. It was her hope that Roosevelt would get behind the bill, which was a measure of the progressive convictions of the politicians of 1910, but he did nothing to help. Miss Perkins took Roosevelt's indifference hard at the time, but she is now able to see him more objectively. She feels that his early lack of interest in social reform, which might be put down to his background and training, can be traced to the fact that "he really didn't like people very much and because he had a youthful lack of humility, a streak of self-righteousness, and a deafness to the hopes, fears, and aspirations which are the common lot." Roosevelt himself seems to have been at least partially aware of this. Years later, after he became President, he told Miss Perkins, "You know, I was an awfully mean cuss when I first went into politics."

Mean cuss or not, he was certainly a limited one. His whole life had moved in a very narrow range. Roosevelt was born on January 30, 1882. His father, James Roosevelt, was a large, affable man who admired Grover Cleveland, liked to sail, and spent most of his time looking after his large Hyde Park estate. He was one of the leading members of the Hudson River gentry—a self-contained, comfortable, moneyed class that in many ways resembled the Whig aristocracy of eighteenth-century England—and young Roosevelt's playmates and companions were the children of families in similar circumstances. His mother kept sharp watch over him. Instead of being sent to school he was turned over to tutors. He was taken abroad several times and once spent a few months in a school at Nauheim. He enjoyed other vacations at the family summer place in Campobello, New Brunswick. It was not until he was fourteen, when he entered Groton, that he began to mingle with groups of boys his own age.

Roosevelt went to Groton, as Alden Hatch says in his biography of Roosevelt, with a mind "like a jackdaw's nest, full of shiny bits of unrelated knowledge." He had a modest command of French and German, an adequate knowledge of the three R's, the ability to identify birds (there were three hundred stuffed specimens in his collection) and a considerable amount of sailing skill. But, says Mr. Hatch, touching on a point that Roosevelt's enemies often aimed at, "in all Franklin's miscellaneous collection of knowledge there was one significant blank; that was in relation to money. He never heard it discussed, since his parents considered it bad taste to talk of such things in public, even if the public consisted of their son." Franklin's sense of financial security was so strong, Mr. Hatch continues, that he never thought about it at all.

Roosevelt was not much of a student. He kept up his work satisfactorily enough, but neither at Groton nor at Harvard, which he entered in 1900, was he regarded as a scholar. He was more interested in sports than in books. At Groton he went out for baseball, football, track and crew, but his only muscular success came in something known as the high kick, an athletic endeavor later to be featured, en masse, by the Rockettes. Young Franklin's kick of 7 feet 3½ inches enabled him to set a school record. But his special love, and one that he never lost, was for boats. By the time he entered Harvard he was a crack skipper. He knew it, too. Even as President, Miss Perkins observes, he was capable of almost childish vanity about his seamanship.

Drawn to the sea, Roosevelt was also drawn to the Navy. He wanted to go to Annapolis, but his father persuaded him to go to Harvard instead. Not long after he entered Harvard his father died. His mother rented a house in Boston to be near her son. Roosevelt was elected to all the right clubs—Hasty Pudding, Signet Society, The Fly, Institute of 1870 and the Yacht Club, among others—and became editor of the Harvard *Crimson*. He went through the regular liberal-arts course, majoring in government and history, and graduated in 1904. He entered Columbia Law School in the fall of that year and became engaged to a distant cousin, Eleanor Roosevelt, a niece of President Theodore Roosevelt. They were married in the spring of 1905.

At Columbia, as at Groton and Harvard, Roosevelt was an indifferent student. His attendance was irregular and he did not graduate. He was admitted to the bar in 1907 after taking a bar examination. He entered the firm of Carter, Ledyard & Milburn, an upper-bracket organization with upper-bracket clients, but he did not like practicing law any more than he had liked studying it. He spent an increasing amount of time at Hyde Park and in the summer at Campobello. It was a good, easy life, punctuated by trips to Europe and the arrival of children. The financial worries that bother most people were taken care of by a joint income of $10,000 a year.

In 1910, when the Republican party was rocked by the feud between Theodore Roosevelt and William H. Taft, the Democrats swept New York state. John W. Dix was elected governor (the defeated Republican candidate was Henry L. Stimson), and Franklin D. Roosevelt was elected to the state senate. He had gone into politics, it would seem, largely because he did not know what else to do. He was then twenty-eight years old—a well-born, well-off, lackadaisical lawyer who gave the impression of being cool, distant and superior. When Frances Perkins saw him in 1912 at the Democratic National Convention which met in Baltimore and nominated Woodrow Wilson, she found that his habit of looking down his nose, which she had first noticed in Albany, still persisted. Wilson, however, thought well of him. Roosevelt had taken the trouble to visit Wilson while he was governor of New Jersey and, in addition, had worked hard for his nomination.

Wilson, it appears, made a deep impression on Roosevelt; it might even be argued that without the former's New Freedom there would not have been the latter's New Deal. But while Roosevelt was moved by the social and ethical content of Wilson's program, he was more moved by being offered the post of Assistant Secretary of the Navy. "I'd rather have that place than any other in public life," he said. "All my life I have been crazy about the Navy." Roosevelt always thought of himself, then and thereafter, as a Navy man. Elliott Roosevelt recalls that his father, the day after one of the banquets that studded the Teheran conference, asked him if he had heard the final result of the Army-Navy game. Elliott had not, so his father told him the score: Navy, 13; Army, 0. "You *would* join the Army, would you?" the President said, holding out his hand. "That'll be $10, please."

Roosevelt's political education, which was fairly rudimentary when he went to Washington as Assistant Secretary of the Navy, was brought a long way forward during the next few years. One of his jobs during the Wilson administration was to listen to the grievances of state committeemen. The hours were long and the talk interminable, but Roosevelt gained a lasting insight into the average political imagination. "They'd rather have a nice, jolly understanding of their problems than lots of patronage," he told Frances Perkins years later. "A little patronage, a lot of pleasure, and public signs of friendship and prestige—that's what makes a political leader secure with his people and that is what he wants anyhow."

The soundness of this formula is demonstrated by the break between Roosevelt and James A. Farley—without whose help and energy, it should be emphasized, Roosevelt might never have become President of the U.S. The break between the two men seems to have started, judging from Mr. Farley's story, when he was denied the patronage, the pleasure and the public signs of friendship and prestige that Roosevelt stressed as being so important. "Almost before I knew it," Mr. Farley has written, "I was no longer called to the White House for morning bedside conferences, my phone no longer brought the familiar voice in mellifluous familiarity and months dragged between White House luncheon conferences. Soon I found I was no longer being consulted on appointments, even in my own state." Mr. Farley then goes on to say that he was never invited to spend the night in the White House, that he made but two cruises on the presidential yacht and that he was never asked to join intimate White House gatherings. He finally concludes that the reason for this was that the President, according to a remark that he attributes to Eleanor Roosevelt, found it hard to relax in the company of those who were not his social equals.

Mrs. Roosevelt, in her column in *Ladies' Home Journal,* has denied that she ever said any such thing. The rest of the record, as so far written, also indicates that whoever told Mr. Farley that Mrs. Roosevelt said what he says she said (he does not state that he had the remark at first hand) must have been mistaken. Louis Adamic seems to have found Roosevelt a little on the regal side ("A couple of emperors!" he says of Roosevelt and Churchill), and A. Merriman Smith, in his chronicle of the headaches of a U.P. man, says that although Roosevelt loved to associate with royalty, he could be, and usually was, socially democratic. Mary Colum, in her autobiography, *Life and the Dream,* reports that "both the President and Mrs. Roosevelt gave the impression that they regarded everybody as their equals and nobody as their inferiors or superiors; they were completely free from all snobberies." Edward J. Flynn, the former chairman of the Democratic

National Committee, in his book of reminiscences *You're the Boss,* has added his testimony to that of Mrs. Colum and Mr. Smith. "Roosevelt was always human," he said in a recent interview. "He liked to let his hair down. This story about how he couldn't relax with people who weren't his social equals is just silly."

Roosevelt's fondness for all sorts of people, according to Miss Perkins, is traceable in large part to the attack of infantile paralysis that felled him in 1921. He was then thirty-nine and just the year before, as James M. Cox's running mate, had toured the country as the Democratic candidate for Vice President. The campaign of 1920 advanced Roosevelt's political education by several degrees, but it was his illness, in Miss Perkins' opinion (as in the opinion of nearly everyone who has written about him), that was the real educative process of his life.

"Franklin Roosevelt underwent a spiritual transformation during the years of his illness," Miss Perkins feels. "I noticed . . . that the years of pain and suffering had purged the slightly arrogant attitude he had displayed on occasion before he was stricken. The man emerged completely warmhearted, with humility of spirit and with a deeper philosophy. . . . He was serious, not playing now. . . . His viability—his power to grow in response to experience—was beginning to show."

Roosevelt's illness left him an almost helpless cripple. Few people other than those who saw him at close quarters ever realized this. But as A. Merriman Smith has written, his legs were literally lifeless. He walked on his braces. The effort it caused him to get about, even when he was supporting himself on someone's arm, was so excessive that it caused his forehead to become beaded with perspiration even on a cold day. Yet even though he often had to be carried in the arms of his secret servicemen, he did not give the appearance of being a cripple. The crowds that turned out to see and hear him never thought of it, and even in small social gatherings his virtual helplessness was hardly apparent. "That he was physically handicapped," Louis Adamic sums up, "came as a surprised afterthought touched by an instant's disbelief."

The Republican candidate in 1936 was Alfred M. Landon of Kansas. Roosevelt looked upon Landon, according to Miss Perkins, as a nice fellow who was not especially bright—just a figurehead in what

Roosevelt thought the Republicans knew was a hopeless campaign. But Roosevelt liked Landon personally, whereas he did not like Herbert Hoover, whom he looked upon as a solemn defeatist. Wendell Willkie, who apparently caused Roosevelt more worry than anyone else who ran against him, would have made a good Democrat, in his opinion. "Too bad we lost him," he told Miss Perkins.

For Tom Dewey, his opponent in 1944, Roosevelt had neither liking nor regard. He expected Dewey to make a poor campaign and was both surprised and upset when reports from the country showed Dewey was making a rather good one. Roosevelt did not intend to make a real campaign in 1944, but after Dewey began gaining he changed his mind. He also wanted to combat the whispering campaign about his health. One day at a Cabinet meeting he announced his intention of going out to hustle for votes. "There has been this constant rumor that I'll not live if I am re-elected," he said, "and people have been asked to believe that I am all worn out and sick. You all know that is not so, but apparently I have to face them to prove it. Apparently 'Papa has to tell them.' That is the way politics go in this country, and I am going right after Dewey and make a real campaign." When he returned to Washington, he had gained twelve pounds. A few weeks after the election Elliott Roosevelt came home on a temporary assignment. He, too, had heard the rumors about his father's health and was surprised to find him looking so well. "What'd you expect?" Roosevelt asked him. "These campaign trips get a little tougher, but I thrive on 'em!"

Roosevelt's health, as Vice Admiral McIntire points out in his book, was whispered about as early as 1932; even then it was said that if he was elected he could not possibly live. These rumors were silenced by Roosevelt's obvious and apparently inexhaustible vitality, but in 1944, after the passage of twelve years was reflected in thin hair, lost weight and a furrowed face, they revived again. "It became 'common knowledge,'" says Admiral McIntire, "that the President had suffered a paralytic stroke, that he was being treated for cancer of the prostate, that he was the victim of a mental breakdown and, favorite whisper of all, that his heart had played out. Time and again it was specifically asserted that he was in a hospital for some major operation, although there was never any agreement on the city. . . . In not one of these rumors was there a grain of truth. The President never had a stroke, never had any serious heart condition and never underwent other operations than the removal of a wen and the extraction of an infected tooth."

If campaigning was Roosevelt's favorite outdoor sport, as Frances Perkins and others have said, his favorite indoor one was plaguing Winston Churchill. Although Miss Perkins thinks that the way he baited the Prime Minister was a sign that Churchill was "in the family," Elliott Roosevelt takes a different view. His book makes it appear as though the two men were engaged in a sort of mortal ideological wrestling match, with Roosevelt representing the forces of democracy and Churchill the legions of reaction. During the meetings between Churchill and Roosevelt at sea, when the Atlantic Charter was drafted, Roosevelt, according to Elliott, described Churchill as "a real old Tory, of the old school." He felt sure that he and Churchill would get along well, however. "Don't forget one thing," he told Elliott. "Winnie has one supreme mission in life, but only one. He's a perfect wartime Prime Minister. . . . But Winston Churchill lead England after the war? It'd never work." It would appear, nonetheless, that Roosevelt had a genuine affection for Churchill. "It was a feeling," James Byrnes writes in his *Speaking Frankly*, "that was . . . cordially reciprocated. It was the kind of friendship that permitted frankness in their conversations with each other and about each other."

Roosevelt's personal habits and way of life were simple to the point of bareness. As President he used a narrow, white iron bed to sleep in —the same kind of bed that is to be found in boys' rooms all over America. It had a thin, hard-looking mattress, a couple of pillows and a white seersucker spread. On the foot of the bed lay a folded shawl that he used for blanket. "Just the right weight," he once explained. "Don't like those great heavy things." He kept an old gray sweater near his bed and wore it to bed to keep his shoulders warm when he had a cold. A small wooden table, painted white, stood near the bed. On it were aspirin, nose drops, a glass of water, bits of paper with telephone numbers, a few books, a watch, an old prayer book, a package of cigarettes, an ash tray and a couple of telephones. Other than the bed and table, the room contained a heavy dark wardrobe (there are no closets in the White House); an old-fashioned rocker, generally with a piece of clothing thrown over it, and an old bureau covered with a plain white towel. Over a door at one end of the room hung a horse's tail. It used to belong to an animal named Gloucester, which had been raised by Roosevelt's father. Gloucester was regarded by all the Roosevelts as a piece of horseflesh only slightly less superior than Man o' War.

Roosevelt was a moderate drinker and a disinterested eater. He liked to have a cocktail or two before dinner, either Martinis, whisky sours or bourbon old-fashioneds. He rarely drank after dinner. When he did, he preferred Scotch and soda. He liked to make a ceremony of mixing cocktails and, on the evening that Mr. Adamic dined at the White House, served up a mixture that he called "orange blossoms" to Winston Churchill. The Prime Minister made a face but downed it like a man. He did not take seconds, however. Since Churchill's capacity is one of the wonders of modern statesmanship, Roosevelt never tried to match him drink for drink. Whenever he was in a gathering that called for prolonged drinking, he always asked for a "horse's neck," a W.C.T.U.-approved concoction that calls for ginger ale, lemon peel and no alcohol. Up to the day he died he was a chain smoker. When he offered a cigarette to anybody, he always said, "Have a cig."

Judging from what has been written by those who were close to him, Roosevelt was not without a certain amount of religious feeling. He did not go to church as frequently as some people thought he should, but he read the Bible a good deal. He also read the Book of Common Prayer, from which he often quoted, and knew a good many passages from the Bible by heart. He went to church more often when he was away from Washington than when he was in that city. "I can do almost everything in the 'goldfish bowl' of the President's life," he once told Miss Perkins, "but I'll be hanged if I can say my prayers in it. It bothers me to feel like something in the zoo being looked at by all the tourists in Washington when I go to church." Miss Perkins tells a story about a young reporter who once asked Roosevelt, in her presence, if he was a Communist.

"No," Roosevelt answered.

"Are you a capitalist?"

"No."

"Are you a socialist?"

"No," Roosevelt said, with a look of surprise as if he were wondering what he was being cross-examined about.

"Well," the young man said. "What is your philosophy then?"

Roosevelt looked puzzled. "Philosophy?" he repeated. "Philosophy? I am a Christian and a Democrat—that's all."

Miss Perkins, who more than anyone else has attempted to answer the questions that the future historian will have to puzzle over, makes this summation: "Those two words expressed, I think, just about what he was. They expressed the extent of his political and economic radicalism. He was willing to do experimentally whatever was necessary to promote the Golden Rule and other ideals he considered to be Christian, and whatever could be done under the Constitution of the United States and under the principles which have guided the Democratic party." Others, naturally, will disagree.

The future historian will have to take this disagreement into consideration; it is too widespread to be ignored. His job, once he has drawn a portrait of Roosevelt, will have only begun. He will then have to find his way around a tangle of thorny questions. Was the New Deal merely a boondoggler's dream, or did it represent a peaceful, necessary economic revolution? Was Roosevelt so intoxicated with the pomp and privilege of power that he could not bear to delegate authority, or was he so absorbed in all the affairs of government that he simply had to have his finger in every pie? Was he so jealous of those who might be possible political rivals that he either got rid of them or kicked them upstairs? Was his political program composed only of an amorphous mixture of leanings, sentiments and emotions, or did he have a definite end in mind? Was that end the firming-up of the traditional capitalist system or did it seek to transform the U.S. into a socialist state? Did he deliberately provoke the Japanese into attacking Pearl Harbor?

All these and many other questions must be answered, more authoritatively than they can be answered today. But it may be suspected that, as far as the popular image of Roosevelt is concerned, most of this labor will go for nothing. For the truth of history, which is of such rightful importance to historians (and as hard to come by, incidentally, as any other truth), is rarely taken into consideration by the masses. Abraham Lincoln is a case in point. He lives in the popular imagination as Father Abraham—a strong, silent, gentle man who skyrocketed to the presidency from complete obscurity and whose first ambition was to free the slaves. Students of Lincoln know that this is not an accurate picture. Although subject to periods of melancholy and deep introspection, Lincoln was not a silent man; his political buildup was long, well planned and farsighted, and not even in the Emancipation Proclamation did he suggest that the abolition of slavery (although he hated it) was his major purpose. These facts about Lincoln are well known. But as far as the myth of Father Abraham is concerned, they might as well be buried under one of the pyramids.

What has happened to Lincoln has already begun to happen to Roosevelt. He has become a part of our mythology as well as our history. His legend began when his life ended. And we can see in the motion picture, *The Roosevelt Story,* the shape the legend is likely to take. First of all he will be a simple man instead of the complex person he really was, who rose from simple origins (Hyde Park, by the time *The Roosevelt Story* gets through with it, might just as well be Andy Jackson's log cabin). Then, from earliest boyhood, he will be moved by a passion for social justice (instead of coming to an understanding of people and their human problems when he was nearing middle age). His natural wit will serve him in good stead, as when he routed the Republicans with his "Fala speech," and the fact that he was not an intellectual giant will not be held against him (brilliant men never become popular heroes in this country). He will not be a "dresser," as truly he was not, nor will he ever show a trace of vanity or personal arrogance (even though, as Miss Perkins relates, he was pleased when Mme. Chiang Kai-shek told him that she found him a sophisticated person, whereas Wendell Willkie struck her as being a naïve one). But over and above all else, like Jefferson, Jackson, Lincoln and all the other source-springs of our national inspiration, he will be a man of the people. And this, as far as the people themselves are concerned, he was. They believe he was one of them and that he was for them. The Roosevelt legend, in the end, rests solely on this. Its strength lies in its simplicity and because of its simplicity it seems likely to endure.

MY FIRST DAYS
IN THE WHITE HOUSE

by Harry S. Truman

SEPTEMBER 26, 1955

> *When Roosevelt entered the White House in 1933,*
> *Harry S. Truman was a county official in Missouri. After*
> *a remarkable political rise which took him "from precinct*
> *to the presidency," Vice President Truman became the*
> *nation's Chief Executive when Roosevelt died on April*
> *12, 1945. Truman's moving story of his first two days*
> *in the White House is taken from* Years of Decisions,
> *the first volume of his memoirs, which* LIFE *serialized.*

During the first few weeks of Franklin Delano Roosevelt's fourth administration, I saw what the long years in the presidency had done to him. He had occupied the White House during twelve fateful years—years of awful responsibility. It is no wonder that the years had left their mark.

The very thought that something was happening to him left me troubled and worried. This was all the more difficult for me, because I could not share such feelings with anyone, not even with the members of my family.

On February 20, 1945, while I was presiding over the Senate, a rumor that the President was dead swept through the corridors and across the floor. I left my place at once and headed for the office of Les Biffle, Secretary of the Senate. Biffle called the White House and was informed that it was Major General Edwin M. Watson—"Pa" Watson, the Appointment Secretary to the President—who was dead. He had died at sea aboard the U.S.S. *Quincy* while returning with the President from Yalta.

I met with the President a week later and was shocked by his appearance. His eyes were sunken. His magnificent smile was missing from his careworn face. He seemed a spent man.

I tried to think how I could help him conserve his strength. I recalled the expressions of pain I had seen on the President's face as he delivered his inauguration speech. Apparently he could no longer endure with his usual fortitude the physical pain of the heavy braces pressing against him. With that in mind, I urged that he address Congress seated in the well of the House. He appeared relieved and pleased to be accorded this courtesy.

He was to report on the deliberations at Yalta—deliberations that were bound to have a profound effect on the future peace of the world. The speech was arranged for Thursday, March 1, 1945. The chamber was filled as he entered, and Speaker Rayburn and I, together with the others who had met him, followed him in and took our places on the rostrum. I remember looking up into the gallery for Mrs. Roosevelt and daughter, and for Mrs. Truman and our daughter, while the audience, which had risen in honor of the President as he entered, resumed their seats.

Unhappily the famous Roosevelt manner and delivery were not there. And he knew it.

I saw the President immediately after his speech had been concluded. "As soon as I can," he said to me, "I will go to Warm Springs for rest. I can be in trim again if I can stay there for two or three weeks."

He left Washington for the South on March 30, 1945.

I never saw or spoke with him again.

Shortly before five o'clock in the afternoon of Thursday, April 12, 1945, after the Senate adjourned, I went to the office of House Speaker

Sam Rayburn. As I entered, the Speaker told me that Steve Early, the President's press secretary, had just telephoned, requesting me to call the White House. I returned the call and was immediately connected with Early.

"Please come right over," he told me in a strained voice, "and come in through the main Pennsylvania Avenue entrance."

On previous occasions when the President had called me to the White House for private talks, I had used the east entrance to the White House, and in this way the meetings were kept off the official caller list. Now, however, I told Tom Harty, my government chauffeur, to drive me to the main entrance. We rode alone, without the usual guards. The Secret Service had assigned three men to work in shifts when I became Vice President. But on this one occasion I slipped away from all of them.

I reached the White House about 5:25 P.M. and was immediately ushered into Mrs. Roosevelt's study. I knew at once that something unusual had taken place. Mrs. Roosevelt seemed calm in her characteristic, graceful dignity. She stepped forward and placed her arm gently about my shoulder.

"Harry," she said quietly, "the President is dead."

For a moment I could not bring myself to speak.

"Is there anything I can do for you?" I asked at last.

I shall never forget her deeply understanding reply.

"Is there anything *we* can do for *you?*" she asked. "For you are the one in trouble now."

The greatness and the goodness of this remarkable lady showed even in that moment of sorrow.

I was fighting off tears. I had been afraid for many weeks that something might happen to this great leader, but now that the worst had happened, I was unprepared for it. The only indication I had ever had that he knew he was none too well was when he talked to me just before I set out on my campaign trip for the vice presidency in 1944. I told him I intended to cover the country by airplane.

"Don't do that, please," he told me. "Go by train. It is necessary that you take care of yourself."

Some time later, too, Mrs. Roosevelt had seemed uneasy about the

President's loss of appetite. She remarked to me at a dinner shortly after the elections, "I can't get him to eat. He just won't eat."

It seems to me that for a few minutes we stood silent, and then there was a knock on the study door. Secretary of State Stettinius entered. He was in tears. He had been among the first to be notified, for as Secretary of State it was his official duty to ascertain and to proclaim the passing of the President.

I asked Steve Early, Secretary Stettinius and Les Biffle, who now also had joined us, to call the Cabinet to a meeting as quickly as possible. Then I turned to Mrs. Roosevelt and asked if there was anything she needed to have done. She replied that she would like to go to Warm Springs at once, and asked whether it would be proper for her to make use of a government plane. I assured her that the use of such a plane was right and proper, and I made certain that one would be placed at her disposal, knowing that a grateful nation would insist on it.

I went to the President's office at the west end of the White House. I asked Les Biffle to arrange to have a car sent for Mrs. Truman and Margaret, and I called them on the phone myself. I also called Chief Justice Harlan Fiske Stone.

Others were arriving by now.

We were in the final days of the greatest war in history. Yet, now when the nation's greatest leader in that war lay dead, and a simple ceremony was about to acknowledge the presence of his successor in the nation's greatest office, only two uniforms were present, and they were worn by General Fleming, Public Works Administrator, and Admiral Leahy. So far as I know, this passed unnoticed at the time, and the very fact that no thought was given to it demonstrates convincingly how firmly the concept of the supremacy of the civil authority is accepted in our land.

Mrs. Truman and Margaret had not joined me for over an hour after I had called them, having gone first to see Mrs. Roosevelt. They were standing side by side now, at my left, while Chief Justice Stone had taken his place before me at the end of the table.

I picked up the Bible and held it in my left hand. Chief Justice

Stone raised his right hand and gave the oath. With my right hand raised, I repeated it after him:

"I, Harry S. Truman, do solemnly swear that I will faithfully execute the office of President of the United States, and will, to the best of my ability, preserve, protect, and defend the Constitution of the United States."

I dropped my hand.

The clock beneath Woodrow Wilson's portrait marked the time at 7:09.

Less than two hours before, I had come to see the President of the United States, and now, having repeated that simply worded oath, I myself was President.

The ceremony at which I had taken the oath had lasted hardly more than a minute. Then, after most of those present had gripped my hand—often without a word, so great were their pent-up emotions —everyone else withdrew except the members of the Cabinet.

We took our places around the table and as we did so, Secretary Early entered. The press, he explained, wanted to know if the San Francisco Conference on the United Nations would meet, as had been planned, on April 25. I did not hesitate a second. I told Early that the conference would be held as President Roosevelt had directed.

It was the first decision I made as President.

When Early had left, I spoke to the Cabinet. I told them briefly that I would be pleased if all of them would remain in their posts. It was my intention, I said, to continue both the foreign and the domestic policies of the Roosevelt administration. I made it clear, however, that I would be President in my own right, and that I would assume full responsibility for such decisions as had to be made. I left them in no doubt that they could differ with me if they felt it necessary, but that all final policy decisions would be mine. I added that once such decisions had been made, I expected them to support me.

That first meeting of the Cabinet was short, and when it adjourned, the members rose and silently made their way from the room—except for Secretary of War Stimson.

Stimson told me that he wanted me to know about an immense project that was under way—a project looking to the development of a new explosive of almost unbelievable destructive power. That was all he felt free to say at the time, and his statement left me puzzled. It was the first bit of information that had come to me about the atomic bomb.

Many months before, as part of the work of the Special Committee to Investigate the National Defense Program of which I was chairman, I had sent investigators into Tennessee and the state of Washington with instructions to find out what certain enormous constructions were.

At that time Secretary Stimson had phoned me to say that he wanted to have a private talk with me. The subject he had in mind was connected with the installations in Tennessee and Washington. "Senator," the secretary told me as he sat beside my desk, "I can't tell you what it is, but it is the greatest project in the history of the world. It is most top secret. Many of the people who are actually engaged in the work have no idea what it is, and we who do would appreciate your not going into those plants."

I had long known Henry L. Stimson to be a great American patriot and statesman.

"I'll take you at your word," I told him. "I'll order the investigations into those plants called off."

I did so at once, and I was not to learn anything whatever as to what that secret was until the Secretary spoke to me after that first Cabinet meeting. The next day Jimmy Byrnes, who until shortly before had been Director of War Mobilization for President Roosevelt, came to see me, and even he told me few details, though, with great solemnity, he said that we were perfecting an explosive great enough to destroy the whole world. It was later, when Vannevar Bush, head of the Office of Scientific Research and Development, came to the White House, that I was given a scientist's version of the atomic bomb. Admiral Leahy was with me. "That is the biggest fool thing we have ever done," he observed in his sturdy, salty manner. "The bomb will never go off, and I speak as an expert in explosives." Leahy had occupied a unique position in the White House under President Roosevelt. I told him that I would like to have him continue in a similar capacity under me.

"Are you sure you want me, Mr. President?" he asked. "I always say what's on my mind."

"I want the truth," I told him. "You may not always agree with my decisions, but I know you will carry them out faithfully."

The admiral looked at me with a warm twinkle in his eyes.

"You have my pledge," he told me. "You can count on me."

When Leahy left, I reached for the telephone and called Les Biffle. I had asked him to arrange a luncheon with the leaders of Congress.

Shortly after noon we sat down to lunch in Biffle's office—thirteen Senators, four members of the House of Representatives, Les Biffle, and the very new President of the United States.

I was glad to see these congressional leaders. I was deeply touched by the cordial reception they gave me. I had come, I told them, in order to ask that a joint session of the Senate and the House be arranged so that I might address them in person. Some of the group were opposed, and others were doubtful. Most, however, were in agreement. I asked each one for his opinion and listened carefully to what they had to say. I then outlined my reasons for considering it imperative to let the nation know through Congress that I proposed to continue the policies of the late President. I felt that it was important, too, to ask for continued bipartisan support of the conduct of the war.

The points I made appeared convincing, for those who had been doubtful now expressed their agreement.

"Harry," remarked one Senator with whom I had long worked closely, "you were planning to come whether we liked it or not."

"You know I would have," I replied, "but I would rather do it with your full and understanding support and welcome."

As I was leaving the Senate office, a long line of white-shirted page boys gathered outside to greet me. Reporters crowded in as well, and I shook hands with every one of them.

"Boys," I said, "if you ever pray, pray for me now. I don't know whether you fellows ever had a load of hay fall on you, but when they told me yesterday what had happened, I felt like the moon, the stars and all the planets had fallen on me. I've got the most terribly responsible job a man ever had."

"Good luck, Mr. President," said one of the reporters.

"I wish you didn't have to call me that," I told him.

I turned away from that long line of serious faces and entered the Senate cloakroom. I looked into the empty Senate Chamber and entered the silent vice presidential office. These were the surroundings in which I had spent ten active, happy years. But now I was President of the United States, and had to return to the White House.

Messages of sympathy and support arrived in great numbers. The message I received from Senator Arthur Vandenberg stands out in my mind. Arthur Vandenberg was a great American and a highly respected Republican leader. I especially appreciated the message he sent. "Good luck," it read, "and God bless you. Let me help you whenever I can. America marches on."

My desk was piled with papers, and all through the day I had been alternately reading and conferring. I have always been a heavy reader, and it is easy for me to concentrate. Nevertheless, on that first full day as President I did more reading than I ever thought I could. I even selected some papers to take home so that I might study them before retiring and upon waking. This was the first step in a routine of nightly work that I found to be one of the most trying, but also one of the necessary duties of a President.

It was now evening, and I was weary. I picked up the papers I had decided to take with me, and as I left my desk, I heard a loud buzzing. It was the signal to the Secret Service, who now came through the corridors to escort me home. Kind and considerate as the Secret Service men were in the performance of their duty, I couldn't help feeling uncomfortable. There was no escaping the fact that my privacy and personal freedom were to be greatly restricted from now on. I even began to realize, as I rode toward my apartment that evening, that our neighbors were beginning to be imposed upon. They were no longer able to come and go as they pleased. To enter their own homes it was now necessary for them to be properly identified and cleared by the Secret Service men.

They were all very nice about it, but Mrs. Truman and I felt that the sooner we could move to an official residence, the easier it would be on neighbors and friends, from many of whom we hated to part.

I had told Mrs. Roosevelt that Mrs. Truman and I had no intention of moving into the White House until she had had all the time necessary in which to make other arrangements. In the meantime, Blair House, which stands across Pennsylvania Avenue from the White House and which serves as an official guest house for foreign dignitaries visiting Washington, was being made ready for us as our temporary official residence.

On Saturday morning, April 14, I got to the White House at 8:30 A.M. My first visitor was John W. Snyder of St. Louis. He was one of my closest personal friends, and I already knew that I wanted him in my administration in a trusted capacity. There was an important post vacant—that of Federal Loan Administrator—and Snyder was ideally fitted for it. He was an experienced banker who had been executive assistant to Reconstruction Finance Corporation Administrator Jesse Jones, and the Director of the Defense Plants Corporation.

Later, I telephoned Jesse Jones and said "the President" had appointed Snyder as Federal Loan Administrator.

"Did he make that appointment before he died?" asked Jones.

"No," I answered. "He made it just now."

The train bearing the body of Franklin Roosevelt arrived at the Union Station at ten o'clock. I went aboard at once, accompanied by Wallace and Byrnes, and we paid our respects to Mrs. Roosevelt. The body of the late President was to lie in state during the day in the East Room of the White House, and as the funeral procession was formed, I took the place that had been assigned to me. Slowly we moved through the streets that were massed with mourners all the way to the White House.

I shall never forget the sight of so many grief-stricken people. Some wept without restraint. Some shed their tears in silence. I saw an old Negro woman with her apron to her eyes as she sat on the curb. She was crying as if she had lost her son. Others were grim and stoic, but all were genuine in their mourning. It was impossible now to tell who had been for him and who had not.

The procession reached the White House at eleven o'clock, and the flag-draped casket was borne into the East Room. Again I paid my respects to Mrs. Roosevelt, and then returned to the executive offices of the White House.

I had received word that Harry Hopkins had left a sickbed in the Mayo Clinic at Rochester, Minnesota, in order to attend the funeral of his chief and friend. He had already arrived in Washington, and I had sent word that I wanted very much to see him.

Hopkins had been close to Roosevelt throughout his administration. He was a dedicated man who never sought credit or the limelight yet willingly bore the brunt of criticism, just or unjust. He was a rare figure in Washington officialdom and was one of my old friends. I hoped that he would continue with me in the same role he had played with my predecessor.

What I now wanted from Hopkins was more first-hand information about the heads of state with whom I would have to deal, particularly Stalin.

Harry Hopkins had always looked pale and cadaverous, but when he entered my office this time, he looked worse than ever before. He was ill, of course, and the death of Roosevelt had affected him profoundly. If I had not known his great patriotism and his spirit of self-sacrifice, I would have hesitated to tax his strength.

"How do you feel, Harry?" I asked as we shook hands.

"Terrible," he replied, and I knew what he meant.

We talked for over two hours. We did not even take time out for luncheon. Instead, I ordered a tray for each of us from the White House kitchen, and with our minds on other things we ate a bite or two there at my desk.

Hopkins was a storehouse of information and was rarely at a loss for a word or a fact. Furthermore, he was usually able to describe and characterize the many important figures he had met. Certainly he understood the leaders of the Soviet Union.

"Stalin," he told me, "is a forthright, rough, tough Russian. He is a Russian partisan through and through, thinking always first of Russia. But he can be talked to frankly."

He assured me that he would be glad to do all he could, but as he was about to leave, he suddenly asked, "Did you know that I had planned to retire from the government on May 12?"

I told him that I knew nothing of his plans to retire, and if his health permitted, I wanted him to stay. He left without giving me any positive reply, but he promised to give the matter serious thought.

Shortly before four o'clock, I was joined by Mrs. Truman and Margaret, who were to go with me to the Executive Mansion for the service before the flag-draped coffin in the East Room.

At Mrs. Roosevelt's request, there were no eulogies. The late President's favorite hymns were sung by all of us, the first being "Eternal Father, Strong to Save." Mrs. Roosevelt asked Bishop Dun to repeat, as part of the service, the expression of faith which President Roosevelt used in his first inaugural address in 1933—"The only thing we have to fear is fear itself."

The body of President Roosevelt was removed from the White House shortly after 9:30 P.M. and, accompanied by Mrs. Roosevelt and her family, was borne to the Union Station and placed again aboard the funeral train.

Mrs. Truman, Margaret and I arrived at Hyde Park about 9:30 on Sunday morning and soon thereafter went to the Roosevelt garden where the final ceremony took place.

We left for Washington at noon. With us were Mrs. Roosevelt and Anna, James and Elliott and other members of the Roosevelt family. Mrs. Roosevelt, wonderfully in command of herself, broke the tension by talking about some of the household problems of the White House which we would have to face. Elliott and James complained about having been starved by the menus of Mrs. Nesbitt, the White House housekeeper. To which Mrs. Roosevelt replied that Mrs. Nesbitt had been properly trying to keep within the food budget.

The schedule that lay ahead for me was so pressing that I spent a good part of the return journey working on the speech I was to make at the joint session of Congress on the following day.

All presidential messages must begin with the President himself. He must decide what he wants to say, and how he wants to say it. Many individuals and departments of the government are called on to take some part in it in order to maintain full co-ordination of policy. Many drafts are usually drawn up, and this fact leads to the assumption that presidential speeches are "ghosted." The final version, however, is the final word of the President himself, expressing his own convictions and his policy. These he cannot delegate to any man if he would be President in his own right.

Back in Washington that evening I felt that an epoch had come to an end. A great President, whose deeds and words had profoundly affected our times, was gone. Chance had chosen me to carry on his work, and in these two days I had already experienced some of the weight of its unbelievable burdens.

As I went to bed that night, I prayed I would be equal to the task.

THE WAR MACARTHUR WAS NOT ALLOWED TO WIN

by Major General Courtney Whitney

SEPTEMBER 5, 1955

> *There have been many differing interpretations of the events and issues which brought about General MacArthur's recall during the Korean War. Those set forth by General Whitney in this chapter from his book,* MacArthur's Rendezvous with History, *represent the authoritative answer of General MacArthur to his critics.*

The end result of the Korean war for the U.S., we can see now, was an expenditure of $22 billion and the loss of 33,600 young men to little lasting purpose beyond the destruction of American prestige all over Asia. Certainly this was not the intent of President Truman when he made the brave decision, which General MacArthur heartily applauded at the time, to resist the aggression of the North Korean Communists. Yet that was the eventual result of his policies.

It took a little time for the American courage that rolled back the North Korean attack to become transformed into the timidity and abject wheedling with which the U.S. faced the Chinese Communists when they intervened in the war. But some signs of timidity in Washington were early in making themselves apparent, even to MacArthur's headquarters seven thousand miles away.

The first clear indication he had that the U.S. might actually compromise with victory came in the handling of Formosa. MacArthur disagreed with the President's orders to the Seventh Fleet to neutralize the island, thereby protecting the enemy as well as our Nationalist allies on Formosa. MacArthur is still convinced that this policy, which freed the Chinese Reds from the threat of Nationalist raids, made it possible for the Communists to employ large numbers of Chinese troops against his U.N. forces in Korea. But he did welcome the fact that the fleet was at the same time guaranteeing Formosa against seizure by the Communists.

On the night of October 26, a squadron of the Eighth Cavalry Regiment ran into sudden resistance at Unsan, North Korea. The regiment was making an almost uninterrupted advance toward the Yalu River, the boundary between North Korea and Manchuria, when the enemy struck. The regiment was cut off and badly mauled. Simultaneously most of the other U.N. units were feeling increasing enemy pressure. Then came the dread news: prisoners taken in the course of this period indicated for the first time that an estimated minimum of three divisions of Red Chinese had joined the battle.

This was a great deal more than the occasional Chinese "volunteers" who had been showing up at the front from time to time. So the great problem was posed. Were the Chinese finally intervening in force?

There was one weapon MacArthur could use to make sure that this introduction of Chinese troops did not immediately become massive intervention. He ordered his air chief, Lieutenant General George E. Stratemeyer, to employ ninety B-29's on the morning of November 7 to destroy one of the important Yalu bridges and cut off this easy line of entry from Manchuria into North Korea. He advised the Joint Chiefs of Staff of his orders before he retired on the night of the sixth.

He was awakened at 2 A.M. by a messenger bearing an urgent dispatch from the Joint Chiefs. The dispatch countermanded his order to Stratemeyer and directed MacArthur "to postpone all bombing of targets within five miles of the Manchurian border until further orders."

MacArthur jumped out of bed and took the message to his desk, to read it under a stronger light than that provided by his bed lamp. Incredible as it seemed, Washington was extending to the Chinese protection not only for the bridges, which were the only means they had for moving their men and supplies across that wide, natural river barrier into North Korea, but also allowed them a five-mile-deep area in which to establish a bridgehead. It would be impossible to exaggerate MacArthur's astonishment. He took time only to cancel his order to Stratemeyer, pending further instructions, before sitting down to compose his reply.

"The only way to stop this reinforcement of the enemy," he wrote, "is the destruction of the bridges by air attack and air destruction of installations in North Korea which would facilitate the movement. . . . Under the gravest protest I can make, the operation has been suspended. I feel that the operation is within the scope of the rules of war and the resolutions and the directions which I have received. I request that the matter be brought to the attention of the President since I believe your instructions might well result in a calamity of major proportion, for which I cannot accept the responsibility. . . ."

All that resulted from this vigorous protest was a modification of the order to permit the bombing of the "Korean end of the Yalu bridges." At the same time MacArthur was cautioned to exercise extreme care to avoid violation of the Manchurian border and air space, *i.e.*, the privileged sanctuary of the enemy, because of the "necessity for maintaining the optimum position with regard to the United Nations policies and directives, and because it was vital to the national interests . . . to localize the fighting in Korea. . . ."

Thus it was admitted to MacArthur that the attack by the Chinese

Communists was not to be punished except by meek half-measures. Meanwhile, Stratemeyer studied the conditions under which the bombing of the Yalu bridges was to be permitted, compared them with what he knew about the concentrations of Chinese antiaircraft installations and the fact that many of the bridges run east and west, and concluded that knocking out the bridges was virtually impossible.

As we know now, after November 6 there followed twenty days during which massive armies of Red Chinese crossed the Yalu bridges —twenty days during which the near disaster which followed could have been averted.

During this time General Walker, at the Korean front, was making his preparations for coping with the new threat. The disposition of his troops was meticulously planned for a twofold purpose: (1) If the Chinese meant to intervene in great force and had set a trap for the U.N. forces, this drive would spring it before the enemy was fully prepared, *i.e.*, before more thousands of Chinese troops could pour across those bridges which MacArthur was unable to take out. (2) If there were no trap, the drive would finish the Korean war.

So on November 24, 1950, MacArthur gave Walker the signal: advance.

The attack had barely begun when MacArthur received a disquieting message from the Joint Chiefs of Staff: "There is a growing concern within the United Nations," the message read, "over the possibility of bringing on a general conflict should a major clash develop with Chinese Communist forces as a result of your forces advancing squarely against the entire boundary between Korea and Manchuria. . . ." Accordingly, the Joint Chiefs suggested that after advancing to a position at or near the Yalu, MacArthur use ROK forces to "hold the terrain dominating the approaches to the valley of the Yalu."

MacArthur replied on November 25 that "the suggested approach would not only fail to achieve the desired result, but would be provocative of the very consequences we seek to avert." Militarily, he pointed out, "it would be utterly impossible for us to stop upon terrain south of the river as suggested and there be in position to hold under effective control the lines of approach to North Korea."

On the following day the Red Chinese struck in full force. Our troops were hit by seven Chinese field corps. The assault against the ROK forces on the right of the Eighth Army was so strong that the South Koreans broke before it, exposing the right flank of the remainder of the Eighth Army line to possible encirclement.

But the Red trap was sprung and MacArthur and Walker were ready for it. This is a fact which cannot be stated too forcefully. MacArthur's troops did *not* rush blindly north into an ambush as claimed by some detractors. The push had been designed to be effective either as a mopping-up operation or a reconnaissance in force; and now it had unhappily become the latter. Delaying actions had been planned for this development and Walker at once ordered them executed.

MacArthur informed Washington of his necessary decision to "pass from the offensive to the defensive." The Joint Chiefs approved his decision. A new war thus started in Korea.

The new situation called for a new strategy to meet it, and especially new forces. It was patently impossible to stem the enemy advance on such a wide front with the troops MacArthur then had in Korea. He turned to the only other major source available.

At the outbreak of hostilities in Korea five months earlier Chiang Kai-shek had offered his finest corps of thirty-three thousand regulars, with more if needed. At that time MacArthur had been fully occupied integrating South Korean soldiers into his U.N. forces, and he had felt that the Nationalist Chinese soldiers should wait until a more propitious date. Now, however, he cabled the Joint Chiefs of Staff urgently requesting authorization to employ Nationalist troops.

He received a particularly discouraging reply. "We shall have to consider," the Joint Chiefs said, "the possibility that it would disrupt the united position of the nations associated with us in the United Nations. . . . It may be wholly unacceptable to the Commonwealth countries to have their forces employed with Nationalist China. . . ."

Evidently the British preferred sabotaging the U.N. effort in Korea to fighting alongside Nationalist Chinese. Indeed, the British preferred the farcical diplomatic position of officially recognizing a nation and fighting its armies at the same time, as they were with Communist China.

Meanwhile Red Chinese pressure was intensifying. The X Corps was forced to withdraw to the Hamhung-Hungnam area. Not only was the entire corps, consisting of 105,000 men, quickly evacuated through the port of Hungnam in an "Inchon landing in reverse," but almost 100,000 civilian refugees were brought out with the troops. More than 350,000 tons of munitions and supplies were brought out as well.

The Eighth Army disengaged from the enemy in as orderly a fashion as possible in a withdrawal action. The withdrawal was accomplished with such speed that it led to many comments by misguided correspondents that the troops were in full flight. How false these reports were was shown five weeks later when a well-organized Eighth Army turned on the Chinese and slaughtered them in great numbers.

Thus was accomplished one of the most successful military maneuvers in modern history. On October 25, only a few hours after the X Corps' evacuation had been completed, MacArthur received a message from President Truman. "I wish to express my personal thanks . . . for the effective operation," Truman cabled. "It is the best Christmas present I have had." MacArthur had reached up, sprung the Red trap and avoided it. His forces were now ready to regroup and resume the offensive.

But Washington was not ready. In fact, the Joint Chiefs were pondering the possibility of evacuating Korea. "It appears from all estimates available," said one J.C.S. message, "that the Chinese Communists possess the capability of forcing United Nations forces out of Korea if they choose to exercise it." But on the other hand, the same message went on, "we believe that Korea is not the place to fight a major war. Further, we believe that we should not commit our remaining available ground forces to action against Chinese Communist forces in Korea in face of the increased threat of general war. However, a successful resistance to Chinese-North Korean aggression at some position in Korea and a deflation of the military and political prestige of the Chinese Communists would be of great importance to our national interest. . . .

"Your basic directive . . . requires modification in the light of the present situation. You are now directed to defend in successive positions [and] . . . to determine in advance our last reasonable opportunity for an orderly evacuation." The message concluded with a request for MacArthur's views "as to the above outlined conditions which should determine a decision to initiate evacuation. . . ."

MacArthur read the message in dismay. It seemed to argue that, while it would be nice to resist Communist aggression, Korea was not the place to do it if the fighting got too tough. But what shocked MacArthur most was the obvious attempt by the Joint Chiefs to avoid the responsibility for a decision to get out of Korea.

That was clearly a political decision, not a military one. On December 30 MacArthur so reminded Washington and requested clarification. The reply said again: "Should it become evident in your judgment that evacuation is essential to avoid severe losses of men and matériel, you will at that time withdraw from Korea to Japan."

MacArthur tried again to get a straight answer. He could get none. At the height of the bloodiest battles in Korea, he was fighting in a policy vacuum.

Then, suddenly, just as the situation approached the impossible, he received a clear statement of policy—or at least the closest approximation to it that he realized he would ever get under the circumstances. It came on January 14, 1951, in a long dispatch from President Truman.

MacArthur saw in it at last a statement of the aims he and his men were expected to achieve. The national as well as international interest dictated, Truman cabled, that MacArthur should continue "resistance from offshore islands of Korea . . . if it becomes impractical to hold an important portion of Korea itself." Here was no vacillation such as characterized the flurry of messages from Washington in the past two months: ". . . we shall not accept the result [withdrawal from Korea] politically or militarily until the aggression has been rectified." MacArthur quickly scribbled his answer to the President: "We will do our best." He now had his mission.

Accomplishing it was another matter. For two weeks the Red Chinese threw everything they had into an effort to drive the U.N. forces out of Korea. But Lieutenant General Matthew B. Ridgway, who at MacArthur's request had replaced Walton Walker after the latter's death, was fighting as magnificently as Walker had. On January 20 MacArthur flew to Korea to give Ridgway in person the go-ahead for the counteroffensive. In less than a week Ridgway's first probing patrols started north in battalion strength. The Eighth Army was on the way back.

By February 10 Ridgway's men had retaken Kimpo Airfield, just west of Seoul. By March 14 they were nearing the 38th Parallel. But then, in capitals of U.N. countries and even in Washington, the debate started again over whether or not the U.N. forces should cross the 38th Parallel.

To MacArthur the situation was virtually the same as when he had been driving the North Koreans back in this area; militarily the 38th Parallel was meaningless. The question actually was a larger one, and one that could be answered only by policy decisions in Washington and at Lake Success. If the present advance defeated the Chinese, what then? Would the Chinese Communists simply retire into their sanctuary across the Yalu, regroup and flood back again? Could Korea become, by Communist design and U.N. blindness, a bloody open drain into which the best of American manhood was to be poured, perhaps for many years?

MacArthur believed even more deeply than before that Red China's aggression in Asia could not be stopped by killing Chinese in Korea so long as her power to make war remained inviolate. He knew how to destroy this power, but his proposals for doing so had been vetoed in Washington. Even under the restrictions placed upon him, however, he had again evolved a strategy for turning from defense to offense.

First, by employing conventional counterattacks he would secure his base line at the latitude of Seoul. He would then subject North Korea to a series of massive air attacks that would substantially clear it of enemy concentrations. Then he would keep the Chinese from sending in reinforcements by the use of an ingenious new tactic. Because Washington would not permit him to attack the Chinese staging area in Manchuria or even to cut off the bridges over which they were pouring their armies into Korea, he would make their avenues of advance impassable. By plane he would dump across all the major lines of enemy supply and communication a defensive field of radioactive wastes, by-products of atomic bomb manufacture. And then, his armies swelled by reinforcements from Chiang Kai-shek's Formosa troops if permitted, he would sweep "around end" and land, by ship and air, in the enemy's rear on both the east and west coasts.

Washington continued to withhold permission for any effective retaliation against the Chinese. Not until January 12 had the Joint Chiefs of Staff finally overcome their timidity to the point of proposing tentative countermeasures against China, some of which paralleled what MacArthur had already recommended: "Prepare now to impose a naval blockade of China and place it into effect as soon as our position in Korea is stabilized, or when we have evacuated Korea. . . . Remove now restrictions on air reconnaissance of China coastal areas and of Manchuria. Remove now the restrictions on operations of the Chinese Nationalist forces and give such logistic support to those forces as will contribute to effective operations against the Communists."

These recommendations were never approved by the President and so never became U.S. policy. But even if they had, it would have been too late, so far as MacArthur personally was concerned. For the tragedy was moving inexorably into its final act.

At the time they seemed like a series of wholly unconnected incidents. But the relationship of each to the other was important. The first incident occurred on March 20, when MacArthur replied to a note of inquiry from Congressman Joseph Martin, Jr., minority leader of the House of Representatives, asking for the general's views on the question of employing Nationalist troops in Korea.

MacArthur has always felt it a duty to reply frankly to every congressional inquiry into matters connected with his official responsibility. "My views and recommendations," he wrote, ". . . are well-known and clearly understood, as they follow the conventional pattern of meeting force with maximum counterforce. . . . Your view with respect to the utilization of the Chinese forces on Formosa is in conflict with neither logic nor this tradition. It seems strangely difficult for some to realize that . . . here we fight Europe's war with arms while the diplomats there still fight it with words. . . . As you pointed out, **we** must win. There is no substitute for victory."

The next incident occurred on the following day, when MacArthur received a message from the Joint Chiefs of Staff. It read: ". . . Strong U.N. feeling persists that further diplomatic effort toward settlement should be made before any advance with major forces north of 38th Parallel. . . . Recognizing that Parallel has no military significance, State has asked J.C.S. what authority you should have to permit sufficient freedom of action for next few weeks. . . . Your recommendations desired."

MacArthur replied with a strongly urged request that "no further military restrictions be imposed upon the United Nations command in Korea." But in view of the obvious Washington sensitivity to the problem of crossing the 38th Parallel, he did instruct Ridgway not to cross the line in force without previous authority from him. Ridgway replied that he would follow these instructions carefully, and outlined in brief his plan for immediate future operations. To this MacArthur responded, giving his approval and adding, "Will see you at Seoul Saturday."

Before leaving Tokyo on March 24, MacArthur released a statement drawn up to strike at the morale of the enemy. It summed up both the events of the Korean War and the lessons from it. It went on: "The enemy . . . must by now be painfully aware that a decision of the United Nations to depart from its tolerant effort to contain the war to the area of Korea, through the expansion of our military operations to his coastal areas and interior bases, would doom Red China to the risk of imminent military collapse. These basic facts being established, there should be no insuperable difficulty arriving at decisions on the Korean problem if the issues are resolved on their own merits without being burdened by extraneous matters not directly related to Korea, such as Formosa and China's seat in the United Nations. . . ."

Then MacArthur added one more offer to the enemy field commander to talk military terms for possible surrender. "Within the area of my authority as military commander . . ." he said, "it should be needless to say I stand ready at any time to confer in the field with the commander in chief of the enemy forces in an earnest effort to find any military means whereby the realization of the political objectives of the United Nations in Korea, to which no nation may justly take exceptions, might be accomplished without further bloodshed."

MacArthur did not know at the time that this message was to be his valedictory as commander in chief of the United Nations Forces in Korea. For it struck consternation into the ranks of a group of diplomats in Washington.

The charge was made that he was hinting at "enlarging the war." His mention of the possibility of "expansion of our military operations" was of course nothing more than another stroke in a continuing campaign of psychological warfare against the enemy. But the loudest outcry was raised by those who later claimed that in his offer to talk military terms with the enemy commander in the field, MacArthur had disrupted some magic formula for peace on which the U.S. had already secured international agreement and which the President was about to announce. MacArthur has since asked and waited in vain for any record or other proof to indicate that any such plan for restoring peace to Korea had been drafted.

And then came a final development. Without realizing the unfortunate timing, Congressman Martin released the full text of MacArthur's note to him on the subject of fighting Red China to win. Immediately the cry that MacArthur wanted to "spread the war" was redoubled.

The curtain was set to rise on the final act of the tragedy.

On Wednesday, April 11, 1951, the MacArthurs had two luncheon guests, Senator Warren G. Magnuson of Washington and William Stern of Northwest Airlines. The meal was proceeding quietly when from her end of the table Mrs. MacArthur looked over the general's shoulder and through the door at the anguished face of a MacArthur aide-de-camp, Colonel Sidney Huff. She excused herself quietly, rose from the table and left the room. There were tears in Huff's eyes when she came up to him. He told her quickly and simply the news that he had just heard on the radio. The President had abruptly removed MacArthur from command. Mr. Truman had given no other reason for his action than a doubt that MacArthur would be able to "give his wholehearted support to the policies of the United States government and of the United Nations in matters pertaining to his official duties."

The general was laughing heartily at a remark made by one of his guests when she walked into the room behind him and touched his shoulder. He turned and she bent down and told him the news in a voice so low that it was not heard across the table.

Here was the payment of a grateful nation for a longer and more distinguished military service than that of any man in American history. Here was the reward for victory in three wars.

MacArthur's face froze. Not a flicker of emotion crossed it. For a moment he was silent. Then he looked up at his wife who still stood with her hand on his shoulder. In a gentle voice, audible to all present, he said, "Jeanie, we're going home at last."

AN APPRECIATION OF JOHN FOSTER DULLES

by Richard M. Nixon

JUNE 8, 1959

> *"Communism is stubborn for the wrong," the late John Foster Dulles once said. "Let us be steadfast for the right." In this tribute to a famous Secretary of State, Vice President Richard Nixon honors Dulles for his vision and integrity, his basic diplomatic decency.*

I have had the privilege of knowing and working with John Foster Dulles since the time I first met him in 1948. And it was my great fortune that since the fall of 1955 the association between us was particularly close.

In a city where a political leader learns that the number of his friends goes up and down with his standing in the public opinion polls, I found Mr. Dulles' loyalty to his friends was no more affected by the latest poll than was his adherence to his own policies.

He was not unaware of his unique abilities. But he was one of those rare individuals who could accept—and even demand—from his friends constant critical examination of both his policies and his leadership. He was never guilty of that most deadly sin—unreasoned pride and conceit.

I recall at least four occasions when he was under attack when he asked for my advice. His question was not as to his policies, which he believed to be right (a view I shared), but whether he, himself, might have become too controversial to be the best spokesman for those policies.

"I never want to be a burden on the President," he often used to say to me. "As a friend, I want you to tell me whenever you believe that I have become a burden, either politically or otherwise."

He recognized the fundamental truth that a public man must never forget—that he loses his usefulness when he as an individual, rather than his policy, becomes the issue.

This trait was most in evidence on his last arduous journey to Europe when he had to call into play all his superb diplomatic talents in order to help unify the Western position on Berlin. There was seldom a moment on this trip when he was without pain. He was unable to keep down a single meal.

I asked him how he was able to carry on.

He answered, "I told my associates that they were to watch me carefully and that they were to inform me immediately whenever it appeared that my physical condition in any way impaired my ability to carry on the negotiations in which we were participating." But he was never better at the negotiating table than at this most difficult period of his life.

He afterward told me, "I never felt any pain while the negotiating was taking place. Then at the end of the day it would come down on me like a crushing weight."

So much for the quality of the man. His policies will be judged not by his dedication or his skill at the conference table but by what happens in the years ahead, when men like [Secretary of State] Christian Herter build on the foundations Mr. Dulles erected.

But whatever happens there are certain great principles which he advocated which will forever stand as a monument to his memory.

He believed that those who are called to positions of leadership in a democracy have the responsibility to lead, not just to follow public opinion. During the crisis over Quemoy and Matsu the mail, the polls and the opinion makers seemed to be overwhelmingly against the position he advocated. He told me that we had to try to change public opinion by informing the people of facts of which they might not be aware. If, after they learned the facts, the people held the same opinion, theirs of course should be the final judgment. But in this instance, his leadership helped to convince the people and thereby averted a Communist victory that could have destroyed the free world position in Asia.

History will also record that the "inflexibility" and "brinkmanship" for which he was criticized in truth represented basic principles of the highest order.

At a time when the political and intellectual climate in the West appeared to be moving slowly but steadily toward advocacy of short-sighted, opportunistic arrangements with the Soviets, Mr. Dulles' stubborn constancy sometimes appeared like an anachronism. Yet he made an unchallengeable argument for firmness where fundamentals were involved. Speaking before the National Council of Churches of Christ last November, Mr. Dulles said: "Communism is stubborn for the wrong; let us be steadfast for the right. A capacity to change is indispensable. Equally indispensable is the capacity to hold fast to that which is good. So it is that while we seek to adapt our policies to the inevitability of change, we resist aspects of change which counter the enduring principles of moral law."

When he was attacked for "brinkmanship" Mr. Dulles stood on an ancient and honorable principle—that by looking a great danger in the face we may avert it and lesser perils. He was simply taking the same position which Winston Churchill saw so well in 1939: "If you will not fight for the right when you can easily win without bloodshed; if you will not fight when your victory will be sure and not too costly; you may come to the moment when you will have to fight with all odds against you and only a precarious chance of survival."

But it is in a third area in which Mr. Dulles leaves to the free world perhaps his most lasting and valuable legacy. Some of his critics have scoffed at his advocacy of peaceful liberation of the Communist-dominated peoples and at his often reiterated faith in the eventual collapse of Communism.

Yet, what other tenable position can self-respecting free peoples take? The Communists have no hesitancy in proclaiming their faith in the eventual domination of the world by dictators. Can we be less determined in our dedication to the cause of freedom from tyranny for all people?

If we want a foreign policy and a national attitude that bends before every Communist breeze, if we have come to the point where liberty is not worth our lives, if we are becoming convinced that the future is in the hands of dictators rather than in those of free men, then we no longer need the Dulleses or their legacy. But while American greatness and American hope endure, John Foster Dulles will be remembered as one of their most effective and eloquent champions.

VI
ORDEALS

THE SILENCE
OF THE SEA

by Vercors

OCTOBER 11, 1943

> *This long short story, the first piece of fiction to appear
> in LIFE, is perhaps the most remarkable literary product of
> World War II. Written by the famous French author,
> Jean Bruller, who signed himself "Vercors" for safety's
> sake, "Le Silence de la Mer" was printed on French
> Underground presses; proofs were then smuggled out to
> London where the story was republished. It is not only
> distinguished fiction, but a fine piece of reporting on French
> resistance to the German occupation.*

When someone knocked it was my niece who opened the door. She
had just served my coffee, as she did each evening (coffee puts me to
sleep). I was seated at the other end of the room, more or less in the
shadow. The door gives onto the garden, on the same level. A pave-
ment of red brick tiles, which is very convenient when it rains, runs
the whole length of the house. We heard steps, the sound of heels
on the tile. My niece looked at me and set down her cup. I kept mine
in my hands.

It was dark, not very cold; that particular November was not very
cold. I saw the enormous silhouette, the close-fitting cap, the raincoat

thrown over the shoulders like a cape.

My niece had opened the door and remained silent. She had pushed the door against the wall, and herself stood against the wall without looking at anything. I kept on drinking my coffee in small sips.

The officer in the door said, "If you please." He bowed his head slightly. He seemed to measure the silence. Then he came in.

The cape slid down over his forearm, he gave a military salute and took off his cap. He turned toward my niece, smiled discreetly and bent over slightly from the waist. Then he turned to me and made me a deeper bow. He said, "My name is Werner von Ebrennac." I had the time to think, very fast. "The name is not German. Perhaps he is a descendant of a Protestant emigrant?" He added, "I am extremely sorry."

The last word, pronounced in a dragging manner, fell into the silence. My niece had closed the door and remained, her back to the wall, looking straight before her. I had not risen. Slowly I set my empty cup on the harmonium, folded my hands and waited.

The officer resumed: "It was naturally necessary. I would have avoided it if possible. I am sure my orderly will do everything so that you won't be disturbed." He was standing in the middle of the room. He was very tall and very thin. He could have touched the rafters by simply lifting his arm.

The silence lengthened. It became thicker and thicker, like morning fog. Thick and motionless. The motionlessness of my niece, mine too, probably weighted this silence, made it leaden. The officer himself, rather lost, remained motionless, until finally I saw a smile form on his lips. His smile was one of gravity and without a trace of irony. He made a sketchy gesture with his hand, the significance of which escaped me. His gaze settled on my niece, who was still stiff and straight, and I had the opportunity to look unhurriedly at the powerful profile, the prominent, thin nose. Finally he turned and looked at the fireplace and said: "I feel a great respect for persons who love their country," and suddenly, lifting his head, he stared at the sculptured angel over the window. "I could go up to my room now," he said. "But I don't know the way." My niece opened the door giving onto the little stairway and started up the steps, without a glance at the officer, as if she had been alone. The officer followed her. I then saw that he had a stiff leg.

I heard them cross the vestibule; the steps of the German sounded in the hall, alternately loud and faint; a door opened, then closed again. My niece returned. She picked up her cup and continued to drink her coffee. I lighted my pipe. We remained silent for several minutes. I said, "Thank God, he seems to be decent." My niece shrugged her shoulders. She drew my velvet jacket over her knees and finished the invisible patch she had started to sew on it.

The next morning the officer came downstairs as we were having our breakfast in the kitchen. A different stairway leads to the kitchen and I don't know whether the German had heard us or whether he just happened to come that way. He stopped in the doorway and said: "I had an excellent night. I hope that yours was the same." He smilingly looked over the large room.

"Your old Mayor told me I would stay at the Château," he said, pointing with a backward gesture of the hand to the pretentious building that could be glimpsed through the bare trees, a little way up the hill. "I shall congratulate my men on having made a mistake. This is a much nicer château."

Then he closed the door, bowed to us through its glass panes and left.

He came back that evening at the same hour as the day before. We were having coffee. He knocked but did not wait for my niece to open the door. He opened it himself. "I fear I am disturbing you," he said. "If you prefer, I shall pass through the kitchen—in which case you will lock this door." He crossed the room and remained a moment with his hand on the knob, looking at the various corners of the room. Finally he bowed slightly from the waist, "I bid you good night," and he went out.

We never locked the door. I am not sure that the reasons for our not doing so were either very clear or unmixed. By tacit understanding my niece and I had decided to change nothing in our lives, not even the slightest detail; as if the officer didn't exist; as if he had been a ghost. But it is just possible too that another feeling mingled in my heart with that one: I cannot offend a man, even though he be my enemy, without suffering.

For a long time—over a month—the same scene was repeated each day. The officer knocked and entered. He said a few words about the weather, the temperature, or some subject of equal importance. They had this in common, that they did not call for an answer. He always lingered a little on the threshold of the small door, looked around, and then a very slight smile expressed the pleasure that this examination seemed to give him—the same examination each day and the same pleasure. His eyes lingered on my niece's bowed profile, which was unfailingly severe and indifferent, and when he finally turned his gaze away from her I was sure to find there a sort of smiling approbation.

Then, bowing, he said, "I bid you good night," and left the room.

One evening things suddenly changed. Outdoors a fine snow mixed with rain was falling, terribly cold and wet. In the big fireplace I was burning some thick logs that I kept especially for days like this. In spite of myself I pictured the officer outside and the powdery look he would have when he came in. But he did not come. It was well past the time for him to come and I was irritated with myself that he should occupy my thoughts. My niece was knitting slowly and very intently.

Finally footsteps could be heard. But they came from inside the house. From their uneven sound I recognized that it was the officer. I realized that he had entered by the other door, that he was coming from his room. Doubtless he had not wanted us to see him with a wet uniform, his prestige diminished; he had first changed.

The footsteps—one loud, one faint—came down the stairway. The door opened and the officer appeared. He was in mufti. His trousers were of thick gray flannel and his jacket of tweed, steel-blue interwoven with a warm brown tone. The jacket was cut loosely and hung with an elegant casualness. Under his jacket a heavy, natural-colored wool sweater molded the slender, muscular torso.

"I beg your pardon," he said. "I feel a bit cold. I got very wet and my room is quite cold. I shall warm myself a few minutes in front of your fire."

He crouched down with a certain difficulty before the fireplace and stretched out his hands, turning them first one way, then another. "Ah, this is good!" he said. Finally he turned his back to the flame, still crouching with one knee in his arms.

"For me, this is nothing," he said. "Winter in France is a mild season. Where I live it's very bitter. Very. The trees are all pines, the forests are thickly planted, the snow lies heavy upon them. Here the trees are delicate. The snow on them is like lace. At home one thinks of a sturdy, powerful bull that needs its force in order to live. Here, it's the spirit, the subtle, poetic thought."

He remained without moving for a long while, without moving and without speaking. My niece knitted with mechanical vivacity. She did not look at him, not once. I kept on smoking, more or less stretched out in my big cozy armchair. I thought that it would be impossible to lighten the weight of our silence. That the man was going to say good night and leave.

But the muted musical droning started up again. It cannot be said that it broke the silence, it was rather as if it had been born out of it.

"I always loved France," said the officer, without moving. "Always. I was a child during the other war and what I thought then doesn't count. But since then I have always loved it. Only it was from afar. Like the far-off princess." He paused a bit before he said gravely, "Because of my father."

There was an armchair invitingly just beside him. He did not sit down. Until the very last day he never sat down. We did not suggest it to him and he did nothing, ever, that could be considered a familiarity.

He repeated: "Because of my father. He was a great patriot. The defeat caused intense suffering. Still he liked France. He liked Briand, he believed in the Weimar Republic and in Briand. He was very enthusiastic. He used to say: 'He is going to unite us, as husband and wife.' He thought that at last the sun was going to rise over Europe. . . ."

As he spoke he looked at my niece. He did not look at her the way a man looks at a woman, but the way he looks at a statue. And, in fact, she really was a statue. An animated statue, but a statue.

". . . But Briand was defeated. My father saw that France was still led by your cruel ruling class—people like your de Wendels, your Henry Bordeaux's and your old Marshal. He told me: 'You must never go to France until you can go there in boots and helmet.' I had to promise it, for he was about to die. When war came I was acquainted with all of Europe, except France."

He smiled and said, as if it were an explanation:

"I am a musician."

One of the logs fell apart and a few live coals rolled off the hearth. The German leaned over, picked up the coals with the tongs. He continued:

"I am not a performer; I compose music. It's my entire life and, for that reason, I strike myself as rather a comic figure when I see myself as a military man. Still, I don't regret this war. No. I believe great things will come out of it. . . ."

He straightened up, took his hands from his pockets and held them half-raised:

"Excuse me, perhaps I may have offended you. But what I have just said I believe with all my heart: I believe it through love for France. Great things will come out of it for Germany and for France. I believe, like my father, that the sun is going to shine on Europe."

He took two steps, and bowed from the waist. As he did every evening, he said: "I bid you good night." Then he left the room.

I finished my pipe in silence. I coughed a little and said: "It is perhaps inhuman to refuse him the pittance of a single word." My niece lifted her face. She raised her brows very high over shining, indignant eyes. I felt almost as though I were blushing a little.

From that day on his visits took this new form. We saw him only rarely in uniform. He changed first and then knocked at our door. Was it in order to spare us the sight of the enemy uniform? Or to make us forget it—to accustom us to his person? Probably both. He knocked and entered without waiting for the reply which he knew we would not make. He did it quite frankly and naturally, and then came to warm himself before the fire, which was the regular excuse for his coming—an excuse that fooled neither us nor him, and the comfortably conventional nature of which he made no attempt to hide.

One time he said (this was at the beginning of his visits): "What is the difference between a fire in my home and here? Of course the wood, flame and fireplace resemble each other. But not the light. That depends on the objects it lights up—on the inhabitants of this room, the furniture, the walls, the books on the shelves. . . .

"Why do I like this room so much?" he said thoughtfully. "It is not so very attractive—I beg your pardon!" He laughed. "I mean to say, it is not a museum piece. Your furniture, for instance—nobody would say: What marvelous pieces! No. But this room has a soul. This whole house has a soul."

He was standing in front of the shelves of the bookcase. His fingers touched the bindings with a light caress.

". . . Balzac, Barrès, Baudelaire, Beaumarchais, Boileau, Buffon . . . Chateaubriand, Corneille, Descartes, Fénelon, Flaubert . . . La Fontaine, France, Gautier, Hugo—what a roll call!" he said with a light laugh and a lift of the head. "And I've only come to the letter H! Neither Molière, nor Rabelais, nor Racine, nor Pascal, nor Stendhal, nor Voltaire, nor Montaigne, nor all the others!" He continued to glide slowly along the books and from time to time he let out an imperceptible "Ah!" when, I suppose, he read a name he hadn't thought of. "The English," he continued, "make one think immediately: Shakespeare. The Italians: Dante. Spain: Cervantes. And we, right away: Goethe. After that, one has to stop and think. But if one says: What about France? Then, what names immediately spring to mind? Molière? Racine? Hugo? Voltaire? Rabelais? Or which others? They come piling in. They are like the crowd in the entrance of a theater: one doesn't know whom to let in first."

He turned about and said earnestly:

"But music, that's our department: Bach, Händel, Beethoven, Wagner, Mozart—which name comes first?

"And we make war on each other!" he said slowly, shaking his head. He came back to the fireplace and his smiling eyes settled on the profile of my niece. "But this is the last war! We shan't fight any more. We shall get married!" His eyelids crinkled, the hollows under his cheekbones marked two long furrows, his white teeth showed.

Gaily he said: "Yes, yes!" A slight nod of the head repeated this affirmation. "When we entered Saintes," he continued after a silence, "I was happy that the population received us well. I was very happy. I thought: it will be easy. And then I saw that it was not that at all, that it was just cowardice." He had grown serious. "I had contempt for those people. And I was fearful for France. I thought: has France *really* become like that?" He shook his head. "No! No! I saw her later; and now I am happy about her stern countenance."

His glance met mine—which I turned aside—lingered a little on various parts of the room, then returned to the pitilessly indifferent face it had just left.

"I am glad to have found here a dignified old man. And a silent young woman. This silence must be conquered. The silence of France must be conquered. I like that."

He looked at my niece, his fine profile stubborn and reserved, silently and with earnest insistence, in which, however, there still floated the remnants of a smile. My niece felt it. I saw her blush very slightly, and little by little a wrinkle formed between her brows. Her fingers pulled a little too vigorously, too sharply, at the needle, at the risk of breaking the thread.

"Yes," continued the slow, droning voice, "it's better like that. Much better. That makes for a firm union—the type of union in which each grows in nobility. There is a charming tale for children, which I have read, which you have read, which everybody has read. I don't know if the title is the same in the two countries. At home it is called *Das Tier und die Schöne*—Beauty and the Beast. Poor Beauty! The Beast has her at his mercy, powerless and a prisoner; at every moment of the day he forces upon her his implacable heavy presence. . . . The Beauty is proud, dignified . . . she has hardened herself. But the Beast is worth more than he appears. Oh, he isn't very polished! He is awkward, brutal and appears very uncouth beside the fine Beauty! . . . But he has a good heart; yes, he has a heart that aspires to raise itself. If only the Beauty were willing! . . . Yet, little by little, she discovers deep in the eyes of the hated jailer a gleam—a reflection in which prayer and love may be read. She is less conscious of the heavy paw, of the chains of her prison. She ceases to hate him, she is touched by this devotion and she holds out her hand. . . . Immediately, the Beast becomes transformed, the enchantment that had held him in this barbarous hairy skin is dispelled; he is now a knight, very handsome, very pure, refined and cultivated, whom every kiss of the Beauty adorns with ever more radiant qualities. Their union brings about sublime happiness. Their children, who combine the gifts of both their parents, are the most beautiful the earth has ever known! . . .

"Don't you like that story? I have always loved it. I used to read it over and over. It made me cry. I especially loved the Beast, because I understood his suffering. Even today, I am moved when I speak of it."

He stopped speaking, drew a deep breath, and bowed.

"I bid you good night."

One evening—I had gone up to my room to fetch some tobacco —I heard the sound of the harmonium. Somebody was playing the *Eighth Prelude and Fugue,* on which my niece had been working before the debacle. The book had remained open at that page, but until that evening my niece had not brought herself to practice again. That she should have taken it up aroused in me both pleasure and surprise: what inner necessity had suddenly decided her to do it?

It was not she. She had not left her chair or her work. Her glance met mine and sent me a message which I did not decipher. I looked at the tall figure before the instrument, the bent head, the long, slender, nervous hands, the fingers of which moved over the keys like autonomous beings.

He played only the prelude. He rose and went over to the fire.

"Nothing is greater than that," he said in a muted voice which did not rise much above a murmur. "Great? . . . That is not even the word. Beyond man—beyond his flesh. That makes us understand— no; guess—no; feel . . . feel what nature is . . . divine, inscrutable nature—nature . . . divested of the human soul. Yes, it is an inhuman music."

In a dreamlike silence, he seemed to be exploring his own thought. Slowly he bit his lip.

"Bach . . . He could only have been German. Our land has that quality, that inhuman quality. I mean to say: it is not to the measure of man."

A silence, then:

"This music, I love it, I admire it, it overwhelms me, it is in me like the presence of God, but . . . it is not my own.

"I myself want to create music to the measure of man: that, too, is one of the paths toward the attainment of truth. That is *my* path. I would not want to, I could not, follow any other. That, now, is a thing I know. I know it wholly. Since when? Since I have lived here."

He turned his back to us. He pressed his hands on the mantelpiece, holding on by his fingers, turned his face toward the flame, and peered through his forearms as through the bars of a fence. His voice became muted.

"Now I need France. But I ask a lot. I want France to welcome me. It is nothing to be here as a stranger—a traveler, or a conqueror. Then she gives nothing—for nothing can be taken from her. Her richness, her great richness, cannot be conquered. One must have drunk of it at her breast, she must offer you her breast with a maternal gesture and feeling. . . . I know that that depends on us. But it depends on her, too. She must be willing to understand our thirst and be willing to assuage it. . . . She must be willing to unite with us."

He straightened up, his back still turned toward us, his fingers still clutching the stone.

"For myself," he said, a little louder, "I must live here a long while. In a house like this one. As the son of a village like this village . . . I must. . . ."

He grew silent. He turned toward us. His mouth smiled, but not so his eyes, which looked at my niece.

"The obstacles will be surmounted," he said. "Sincerity always surmounts obstacles.

"I bid you good night."

I cannot remember today all that was said during more than a hundred winter evenings. The theme, however, scarcely ever varied. It was a long rhapsody about his discovery of France: the love he had felt for France from afar, before he knew it, and the daily deepening love which he felt now that he had had the good fortune to live there. And really, I admired him. Yes, for not getting discouraged. And for never having tried to break our implacable silence by any violence of language. On the contrary, when occasionally he allowed the silence to invade the room, to saturate its farthest corners like a heavy, unbreakable gas, he, of the three of us, seemed to be the one who was most at ease. On these occasions he would look at my niece with that smiling, yet serious, expression of approbation which he had worn from the first day. And I felt my niece's spirit grow disturbed in its self-constructed prison. I recognized this from many signs, the least of which was a slight trembling of the fingers. And when, at last, Werner von Ebrennac dispelled the silence gently and without a jar, through the filter of his droning voice, it was as though he had allowed me to breathe more freely.

He spoke often of himself.

"My house in the forest, I was born there, I went to the village school, on the other side; I never left it until I went to Munich for my examinations and to Salzburg for music. Since then, I have always lived there. I never liked big cities. I know London, Vienna, Rome, Warsaw and all the big German cities, naturally. I don't like to live in them. I really liked only Prague—no other city has so much soul. And above all Nuremberg. For a German, that is the city that makes his heart swell, because there he finds the phantoms dear to his heart, the memory, in every stone, of those who made the nobility of ancient Germany. I imagine that the French must feel the same thing before the Cathedral of Chartres. They must feel the presence of their ancestors very close to them—the grace of their souls, the grandeur of their faith and their *gentillesse*. Fate took me to Chartres. Truly, when it appears above the ripe wheat all blue with distance, and transparent, incorporeal, that is tremendously moving! I imagined the feelings of those who once went there on foot, on horseback, or in wagons. I shared those feelings and I liked those people, and how I should like to be their brother!"

His face clouded over.

"It must be hard to hear that from a man who came into Chartres in an armored car. . . . Nevertheless, it is true. So many things are stirred up together in the souls of Germans, even the best ones! And things of which they would like to be healed. . . ." He smiled again, a very slight smile which gradually lighted up his entire face.

"Now, fortunately, they are no longer alone: they are in France. France will heal them. And let me tell you something: they know it. They know that France will teach them to be men of real stature and integrity."

He started toward the door. In a repressed voice, as though to himself, he said, "But for that there must be love."

He held the door open for a moment; with his face turned over his shoulder, he looked at the nape of my niece's neck as she bent over her work, that pale, delicate neck from which the hair grew in twists of dark mahogany. In a tone of calm resolution, he added:

"Shared love."

Then he turned his head away and the door shut behind him while he was still rapidly pronouncing his daily words: "I bid you good night."

The long spring days arrived. The officer came downstairs now with the last rays of the sun. He still wore his gray flannel trousers, but with them he wore a lighter jacket of brown wool jersey over a rough linen shirt with open collar.

He said: "I must inform my hosts that I shall be away for two weeks. I am very happy to be going to Paris. It is my turn now to take a leave and I shall spend it in Paris—for the first time. This is a great day for me. It is the greatest day, while awaiting another which I am hoping for with all my heart and which will be an even greater day. I shall know how to wait for years, if necessary. My heart is very patient.

"In Paris I suppose I shall see my friends, many of whom are present at the talks we are having with your statesmen, in order to prepare the wonderful union of our two peoples. In this way I shall be a sort of witness of that marriage. . . . I want to tell you that I am happy for France, whose wounds in this way will heal very quickly; but I am happier still for Germany, and for myself! No one will ever have benefited from a good act as much as Germany will in giving back her greatness and her liberty to France!

"I bid you good night."

We did not see him when he returned.

We knew he was there, because the presence of a guest in the house can be told by a number of signs, even though he remain unseen. But for a number of days—much more than a week—we did not see him.

Shall I confess it? This absence did not leave my mind at rest. I thought about him and I can't say to what extent I did not feel a certain regret, a certain disquiet. Neither my niece nor I spoke of him. But occasionally when evening came and we heard his unequal footsteps indistinctly from upstairs, I saw plainly, from the obstinate attention she suddenly applied to her work, from a few light lines that marked her face with an expression at once obdurate and expectant, that she, too, was not entirely free from thoughts that matched my own.

Finally, one evening, when we had hardly emptied our cups, we heard the irregular beat of the familiar steps, this time coming unquestionably toward us. I suddenly recalled that first winter evening, six months before, when we had heard those steps. I thought: "Today, too, it is raining." It had been raining hard since morning. A regular, persistent rain which soaked everything about and even bathed the inside of the house in a cold, damp atmosphere. My niece had thrown about her shoulders a square of printed silk on which ten disturbing hands, designed by Jean Cocteau, pointed languidly at one another. I was warming my fingers on the bowl of my pipe—and we were in July!

The steps crossed the hall and began to make the stairs creak. The man came down slowly, increasingly slowly, but not as one who hesitates; rather as someone whose will power is going through an exhausting test. My niece had lifted her head and was looking at me; during all this time she fixed me with a transparent, inhuman gaze. And when the last stair had creaked and a long silence followed, my niece's gaze vanished; I saw her lids grow heavy, her head bend over and her entire body wearily seek the back of her chair.

I don't believe this silence lasted more than a few seconds. But they were long seconds. I seemed to see the man behind the door, with his forefinger lifted, ready to knock and yet putting it off, putting off the moment when, just by giving a knock, he would invite the future. . . . Finally he knocked. And it was neither with the lightness of hesitation, nor with the brusqueness of conquered timidity; there were three strong, slow knocks, the assured calm knocks of a decision from which there can be no turning back. I expected to see the door open right away, as it used to. But it remained closed and I was now seized by a mental excitement difficult to master. Should we reply? Why this change? Why did he expect that this evening we would break a silence concerning which he had shown by his serious attitude how much he approved its wholesome tenacity? What did dignity demand this evening—just this evening?

I looked at my niece in order to seek in her eyes some encouragement or sign. But I found only her profile. She was looking at the doorknob. She looked at it with that inhuman stare that had already struck me. She was very pale. I, myself, faced with this suddenly revealed inner drama that went so far beyond the mild torment of my own evasions, seemed to lose what strength was left me. At this moment there were two more knocks—two only, two quick, light knocks —and my niece said: "He is leaving. . . ." in a low voice that was so completely discouraged that I did not wait any longer and said in a distinct voice: "Come in, Monsieur."

I expected to see him appear in mufti, but he was in uniform. I might even say that he was more in uniform than ever, if by that it is understood that it was plain to me that he had put it on with the firm intention of making us look at it. He had thrown the door back against the wall and he stood straight in the doorway, so straight and so stiff that I almost doubted whether I had before me the same man. He stayed like that for several seconds, straight, stiff and silent, his feet slightly apart, his arms hanging expressionless at his sides, and his face so cold, so perfectly impassive, that it did not seem as though the slightest feeling could dwell there.

But seated as I was in my deep armchair with my face on a level with his left hand, my eyes were fascinated by that hand, which gave the lie to the man's entire attitude. That day I learned that a hand, for him who knows how to observe, can reflect emotions quite as well as a face—as well and even better than a face, because it can better escape the control of the will. And the fingers of that hand were engaged in the intensest kind of pantomime while the face and the entire body remained motionless and stiff.

The eyes seemed to revive, they turned for an instant toward me. Then they settled on my niece and they did not leave her again. The hand finally became motionless, and the officer said, his voice more muffled than ever:

"I have some very serious things to say to you."

My niece was facing him, but she lowered her head. She wound the wool from a ball around her finger, while the ball came unwound as it fell on the carpet; this absurd work was doubtless the only kind to which she could still give her distraught attention—and keep her from being ashamed.

"Everything I have said during these six months, everything that the walls of this room have heard," he breathed with effort, "must be—forgotten."

Slowly the young girl let her hands fall in her lap, and slowly she raised her head, and then, for the first time—for the first time—she offered the officer the gaze of her pale eyes.

He said (I hardly heard him): *"Oh welch ein Licht!"* And as if, indeed, his eyes could not stand the light, he hid them behind his fist. Two seconds: then he let his hand fall again, but he had lowered his lids and, from then on, it was he who kept his eyes on the ground. . . .

He said—his voice was muted:

"I have seen those victorious men."

Then, after a few seconds, in a still lower voice:

"I have talked to them." And finally, in a murmur, with bitter slowness: "They laughed in my face."

He raised his eyes toward me and very gravely nodded, almost imperceptibly, three times. His eyes closed, then:

"They said: 'Haven't you understood that we are making fools of them?' They said that. Exactly. *Wir prellen sie*. They said: 'You don't imagine that we are going to be stupid enough to let France rise again right on our frontier? No!' They laughed very loudly. They slapped me gaily on the back looking me right in the face: 'We are not musicians!' "

His voice, as he pronounced these last words, held an obscure contempt about which I am uncertain whether it reflected his own feelings toward the others, or the tone itself of what they had said.

"Then I talked a long while, with much vehemence. They said: 'Politics is not a poet's dream. Why do you suppose we made war? For their old Marshal?' Then they laughed again. 'We are not fools: we have the opportunity to destroy France: she will be destroyed. Not only her power; her soul as well. Especially her soul. Her soul is the greatest danger. That is our task at this moment. Make no mistake, old man! We will make her rotten by our smiles and our attentions. We'll make a cringing bitch out of her.' "

He became silent. He seemed out of breath. He clenched his jaws so energetically that I saw his cheekbones stick out and a thick vein beat under his temple. His eyes clung to the pale, wide eyes of my niece, and in a low, flat tone that was intense and oppressed, he said with exhausted slowness:

"There is no hope." And in an even more muffled, lower voice, and slower, as though to torture himself with this unbearable fact: "No hope. No hope."

Then, silence.

I thought I heard him laugh.

"They blamed me, with a certain anger: 'You see yourself! You see yourself how much you love it! There's the great Danger! But we will cure Europe of this pestilence! We will purge her of this poison!' They explained everything to me. Oh! they didn't let me forget anything. They flatter your writers, but at the same time, in Belgium, Holland and all the countries occupied by our troops, they have already set up the barriers. No French book can get through now—except technical publications, manuals on dioptrics or formulae for cementation—but works of general culture, none. Nothing!"

His glance went over my head, flying and knocking against the corners of the room like a lost night bird. Finally it seemed to find refuge on the darkest shelves—those on which stand Racine, Ronsard, Rousseau. His eyes remained fastened there and his voice resumed, with groaning violence.

"Nothing, nothing, nobody!"

His glance swept once more over the bindings shining gently in the half-light.

"They will put out the flame entirely!" he cried. "Europe will no longer be lighted by this light!"

Silence fell once more. Once more, but this time how much darker and more strained. Certainly, under the earlier silences I had felt—just as, under the calm surface of the waters we sense the mingling of creatures in the sea—I had felt the crawling submarine life of hidden feelings, of desires and thoughts which deny their existence and which struggle. But under this one, ah! nothing but a frightful oppression. . . .

Finally the voice broke the silence. It was gentle and unhappy.

"I had a friend. He was like a brother. We were students together. We shared the same room in Stuttgart. We had spent three months together in Nuremberg. We never did anything without each other: I played my music for him; he read me his poems. He was sensitive and romantic. But he left me. He went to read his poems in Munich, before new friends. It was he who kept writing me to come and join them. It was he whom I saw in Paris with his friends. I saw what they have done to him."

He shook his head slowly, as if obliged to give a sorrowful refusal to some appeal.

"He was the most rabid of them all. He mingled anger and laughter. Sometimes he looked at me with flashing eyes and shouted: 'It's a poison! We must empty the animal of its poison!' Then he would poke me with his forefinger: 'They're scared to death now. Ah! they're afraid for their pocketbooks and their bellies—for their industry and their commerce! That's all they think about! The few others, we flatter them and put them to sleep. Ah! it will be easy!' He laughed and his face grew quite pink. 'We'll exchange their soul for a mess of pottage!' "

Werner took a breath.

"I said: 'Have you thought about what you are doing? Have you *thought* about it?' He said: 'Do you expect to intimidate us with that? Our lucidity is of another variety!' I said: 'Then you will close this tomb—forever?' He said: 'It's a matter of life and death. To conquer, Force is sufficient; but not to dominate. We know well enough that an army is nothing to dominate with.' 'But at the cost of the Spirit!' I cried. 'Not that price!' 'The spirit never dies,' he said. 'It's been through a lot. It is born again from its ashes. We must build for a thousand years: but first we must destroy.' I looked at him. I looked into the depths of his blue eyes. He was sincere, yes. That's the most terrible thing about it."

His eyes were opened very wide.

"They will do what they say!" he cried as though we didn't believe him. "With method and perseverance! I know these tenacious devils!"

He shook his head, like a dog whose ear hurts.

He hadn't budged. He was still motionless, stiff and straight in the doorway, his arms stretched out as though they had to carry hands of lead; and pale—not like wax, but like the plaster of certain dilapidated walls: gray, with whiter spots of saltpeter.

I saw him bow slightly from the waist. He lifted one hand. He held it out toward my niece, toward me. He contracted it, waved it a bit as the expression on his face grew tense with a sort of ferocious energy. His lips half opened, and I thought that he was going to hurl forth God knows what kind of an exhortation: I thought—yes, I thought that he was going to encourage us to revolt. But not a word crossed his lips.

Suddenly his expression seemed to relax. His body lost its stiffness. He bent his face a little toward the floor, then lifted it.

"I have exercised my right," he said simply. "I have asked to join a field division. This favor has finally been granted me; tomorrow I have been authorized to start on my way. . . ."

His arm was raised toward the east—toward those immense plains where the future wheat will be fertilized with corpses.

My niece's face hurt me. It was pale as the moon. Her lips, like the borders of an opaline vase, were apart, and they suggested the tragic pout of the Greek masks. And I saw, at the point where forehead and hair meet, that drops of perspiration were starting forth.

I do not know if Werner von Ebrennac saw it. His pupils, and those of the young girl, linked fast like a boat to a ring on the shore, seemed held by such a taut, stiff cord that one would not have dared pass a finger between their eyes. With one hand Ebrennac had taken hold of the doorknob. With the other he held to the doorframe. Without shifting his gaze a hair's breadth, he drew the door slowly toward him. He said—his voice was strangely stripped of expression—

"I bid you good night."

I thought he was going to close the door and go. But no. He looked at my niece. He murmured:

"Good-by."

He did not move. He remained quite motionless and in his motionless, taut face, the eyes were even more motionless and taut, fixed to the eyes—too wide open, too pale—of my niece. That lasted until finally the young girl moved her lips. Werner's eyes shone.

I heard:

"Good-by."

One had to have listened for this word to hear it, but finally I heard it. Von Ebrennac heard it too and he straightened up, and his face and his whole body seemed to relax.

And he smiled, so that the last picture I had of him was a smiling one. And the door closed and his steps grew fainter and disappeared at the other end of the house.

He was gone the next day when I came down to get my morning cup of milk. My niece had prepared breakfast, as every day. She served me in silence. We drank in silence. Outside, through the fog, a pale sun was shining. It seemed to me that it was very cold.

A CASE
OF IDENTITY

by Herbert Brean

JUNE 29, 1953

> *The newspaper accounts of Manny Balestrero's arrest and trial were terse and buried on inside pages. The sort of thing he was charged with goes on all the time. But when Balestrero was a free man again, LIFE Staff Writer Herbert Brean dug deeply into the story. He found almost an infinity of heartbreak behind the daily headlines.*

At about 5:30 on the evening of January 14, 1953, a forty-three-year-old nightclub musician named Balestrero mounted the steps of his home, a modest stucco two-family house at 41-30 73rd Street in Queens, a borough of the City of New York, and took out his key. As he did so, he heard a hail from across the dark street: "Hey, Chris!" Balestrero turned curiously. His first name is Christopher, but he is known to his family and friends as "Manny," a shortening of his middle name Emanuel. Three men came up to him out of the murky shadows of a winter evening. They said they were police officers and showed him badges clipped to wallets.

Balestrero, experiencing a little quiver of uneasiness, asked what they wanted. The detectives ordered him to come to the 110th precinct station. They were polite, firm and uninformative. Balestrero became alarmed. He is a quiet, mild, family-loving man, who is a first-rate string bass player, never misses a night's work and is content to take the subway home afterward instead of hoisting a few with the boys. His conscience was clear, and the detectives were polite, but their inexorable manner was frightening.

They told him what it was all about. On two occasions last year—July 9 and December 18—an office of the Prudential Insurance Company of America, located in an arcade building at Roosevelt Avenue and 74th Street, had been held up by an armed man. Each time the robbery occurred shortly after noon. The first time the bandit obtained $200, the second time $71. The same man had done both jobs. He, Manny Balestrero, had been identified by witnesses as the bandit.

Up to this point the train of events had had the somnambulistic quality of a bad dream. Now it became a nightmare. The building and insurance office that the cops were talking about were just two and a half blocks from Balestrero's home, where he had lived for twenty years. He was well known in that neighborhood. Below the building was the subway station from which he took the F train each night to Manhattan's glittering Stork Club, where he plays in a rumba band. On the arcade's ground floor is a Bickford's cafeteria where each morning about 4:30 he ate his musician's breakfast of coffee and eggs before walking home. On the second floor is a Household Finance branch where he occasionally negotiated small loans (and had an A-1 credit rating), and the Prudential branch office that had been robbed.

Balestrero knew the Prudential office well—his family held four life insurance policies with the company. Twice when there was illness in the family Balestrero had visited the office to negotiate loans on the policies. The detectives began asking questions, and Balestrero began to be terribly afraid. When was he last in the insurance office? It had been only yesterday. Balestrero's wife Rose had learned that she needed some major dental work. It would cost about $325. At her suggestion Balestrero had walked over to the insurance office to inquire about the size of a loan he could get on her policy.

As he talked with the detectives, Balestrero remembered that the girl behind the counter in the insurance office had kept him waiting a moment while she talked in a low voice with some of the other clerks. The cops asked if he had been in the office on December 18. Balestrero said he had not. Or on July 9? He couldn't remember what he had done on July 9. But he needed money, eh? Of course he needed money (he nets $85 a week, union scale, at the Stork Club), and he had gone yesterday to borrow some. Now, once again, was he sure he had not gone into the insurance office on December 18?

Over and over they repeated the questions, while Balestrero's panic grew. It was not a brutal third degree; the detectives remained polite. But they were obviously skeptical of Balestrero's stumbling answers. They told him two girls from the insurance office were on their way down now to see if they could identify him. Balestrero sat there, helpless and terrified.

The detectives gave him paper and pencil and dictated a note for him to write in block letters. It was the text of a holdup note passed to a girl clerk by the bandit during the second holdup. It read: "This is a gun I have pointing at you. Be quiet and you will not be hurt. Give me the money from the cash drawer." Balestrero printed the note half a dozen times. Each time he spelled the last word correctly, but once he misspelled it: DRAW. That is how it had appeared in the original holdup note. If there had been any thought of mistaken identity in the minds of the detectives it probably vanished with that error.

Balestrero was told to put on his gray tweed overcoat, his hat and his maroon muffler. Presently he became aware that people were looking at him from an adjoining, darkened room. He could not see them but he knew they were there. Then he was placed in a line with some other overcoated men whom he took to be other detectives. Two girls came into the room. They had already identified him from the darkened room. Now to his bewilderment they picked him out again from this informal lineup.

Balestrero is a timid man, by his own admission afraid of his own shadow. He has never been in a fight in his life, never carried a weapon, never been arrested, never even received a traffic ticket. As the net of evidence tightened, his mind spun and he did not know what to do or say. "When things happen like that and you're innocent," he has said since, "you want to shout and scream and you can't. I don't know how many ways I tried to say to them I was innocent. They acted as if I was guilty and wanted me to say so."

Finally Balestrero was led to a detention cell in the station house for the night. He could not sleep. A religious man, he spent most of the night in prayer, much of it on his knees. He wondered what would happen to him, but even more about his family and what his wife was thinking and doing. He worried about his father who had recently had a stroke (what would this do to him?) and about his job at the Stork Club. This was the first night he had missed in two years at the Stork.

By morning he was a famished bundle of nervous fatigue. Two detectives drove him across the Queensborough Bridge to police headquarters in lower Manhattan. There he was photographed, fingerprinted and registered, and was given a roll and a mug of coffee. Then he was driven back to Queens Felony Court for arraignment on a charge of assault and robbery. There, for the first time since the previous noon, he saw his wife.

While the charges against him were read, Balestrero stared across the courtroom at her, wondering what she felt and thought. The hearing took only a few minutes. Balestrero was held in $5,000 bail, which his family could not immediately supply, and he was led back to his cell.

When he was again removed from it, he joined a handful of other prisoners bound for the Long Island City jail. They were handcuffed in pairs and ordered into a van. Being manacled did something corrosive to Balestrero's dignity as a person. He stared at the steel ring encircling his wrist, and he could not look up. He does not know what the man he was handcuffed to looked like.

At the prison he was checked in, stripped, physically examined, given a tin plate and cup and some bedding and led to a cell. This cell had a heavy steel door with only a little window, and once it had crunched shut on him Balestrero felt caged-in and hopeless. About five o'clock he was brought some food—noodles with a kind of sauce over them, hot chocolate, bread and butter, stewed pears. Balestrero looked at the food but could not eat. After a time he heard his name mentioned outside from a distance. Instantly he was on his feet. He flung himself at the door and hammered on it with his tin cup, yelling, "That's me—Balestrero! I'm in here, in this cell! Here!"

Balestrero had now been in custody just twenty-four hours. He had been given every right of the American judicial system. Any professional criminal accustomed to police procedures would say he had been treated with fairness and impersonal consideration. But when he was taken downstairs and saw his brother-in-law Gene Conforti, who had succeeded in obtaining the bail, Balestrero collapsed. His sister Olga went out and got him some coffee. Then they drove him home, and he went quickly to bed and fell into the sleep of utter exhaustion.

When Balestrero awoke the next morning, the nightmare was still upon him. Word was sent that—while the others in the band had vouched for him—it might be better if he did not come to work for a week or so. That was all right. Balestrero did not feel like working, and he had somehow to cope with the incredible problem of finding a lawyer to defend him as an accused robber.

Finally, on the recommendation of friends, the Balestreros decided to ask former State Senator Frank D. O'Connor to take the case. The following Sunday they met with O'Connor after church in his law office. Once he had assured himself of his new client's honesty and repute, O'Connor's assignment was superficially simple. If Balestrero had not committed the two robberies, he had been someplace else at the time. If O'Connor could prove where he had been, then his client would have alibis for each crime.

The first occasion, noon of July 9, 1952, was fairly easy. Rose Balestrero remembered they were in the country. The Stork Club had closed for a week during the summer, from July 3 to 10, and early in the week the Balestreros with their two boys, Robert, twelve, and Gregory, five, had gone to Edelweiss Farm near Cornwall, New York, some fifty miles from New York City. Balestrero's presence there was easy to establish. July 9 was the birthday of the proprietor's wife and

416

he had planned a party for her that was called off when she fell ill. Even so the proprietor could remember that none of the guests, Balestrero included, was missing for that midday meal. Other guests were located and under dint of patient questioning remembered that it had been a rainy day. One of them, Karl Wuechner, had written a letter to his mother in Germany. He recalled that when he started to drive into Cornwall to post the letter, Balestrero had asked if he and his two sons could go along since they had nothing better to do on a rainy day. Later a pinochle game had begun; Balestrero played in it. O'Connor arranged to get the letter back from Germany, obtained weather records and depositions from the pinochle players. That took care of July 9.

December 18 was not so easy. On that day Balestrero had pursued his usual routine, which consists of working until 4 A.M., breakfasting at Bickford's and then coming home, via the Arcade Building's subway station, to sleep until noon or after. Then Balestrero, under the persistent questioning of O'Connor, remembered something else. At about that time he had a great deal of trouble with two abscessed teeth. Records of Dr. August J. Bastien, the family dentist, showed that during the week of December 14 Balestrero's right jaw had been so swollen that the teeth could not be extracted, and he had to be given penicillin. The swelling had not died down by December 22, so Bastien sent Balestrero to Dr. George Long, the family medical man. Both doctors signed statements that Balestrero's jaw could not have returned to normal between the two dates, and members of the rumba band said they recalled that Balestrero's jaw had continued enormously swollen during the week. None of the identifying witnesses had mentioned that the holdup man had a swollen jaw.

The development of these hopeful strategies took days of patient investigation and interrogation, but they did little to buoy Balestrero's morale. In fact it steadily dropped. That was because of his growing concern over his wife. Rose had always been a bustling, hard-working housewife. To other women in the neighborhood she had been a cheerful, amiable friend.

Now she acquired an illogical feeling that somehow she was responsible for her husband's misfortune, because it was to help her that

417

he had gone to the insurance office on January 13. As the days passed she became more and more depressed, said little to her family and found it difficult to perform the daily housework. She stared dry-eyed into space and walked fearfully from room to room.

As one more weapon in his defense, O'Connor had arranged for Balestrero to take a lie detector test. But when the Balestreros appeared for it, it was Rose who interested the psychologist who was to give the test more than her husband. He referred her to a psychiatrist who, after an examination, insisted that she leave at once for a sanitarium. Balestrero had always depended on his wife ("she was my right arm") and her breakdown was the final blow.

His trial opened on April 21 in Queens County Court before Judge William B. Groat. In a carefully calculated gesture of confidence in their case, O'Connor agreed to the first twelve jurors to be approved by the prosecution. Actually, however, he was anything but confident. The months of worry and nerve strain were visibly telling on Balestrero, and O'Connor feared privately that he would suffer a breakdown like his wife's before the trial could end.

The prosecution's opening statement did not help. Assistant District Attorney Frank J. Crisona told the jury that he would show Balestrero had needed money, by his own admission to the police, that he played the horses and was familiar with the location and layout of the insurance office. Four girls in the office would positively identify him as the robber. The holdup note and samples of Balestrero's printing would be introduced and the points of similarity explained.

After the usual preliminaries, the key witnesses took the stand. The first girl was asked if the holdup man was in the courtroom and, if he was, to step down and place her hand on his shoulder. The girl pointed out Balestrero, but when she tried to touch his shoulder she almost fainted from fear. It obviously impressed the jury. After that, the other girl witnesses were asked only to point him out, and one after another they did. Balestrero again was seized with a wild desire to stand up and shout. "It's a horrible feeling, having someone accuse you. You can't imagine what was inside of me. I prayed for a miracle."

And a miracle—of sorts—happened. On the third day of the trial

Juror No. 4, a man named Lloyd Espenschied, rose suddenly in the jury box. The witness on the stand at the time was Yolande Casagrande, whose identification of Balestrero had seemed to O'Connor to be somewhat shaky. O'Connor had been cross-examining for perhaps forty-five minutes when Espenschied got up and irately addressed the bench: "Judge, do we have to listen to all this?" The question implied a presupposition of the defendant's guilt by a juror—a violation of his responsibility to refrain from any conclusion until all evidence is in. It gave the defense an opportunity to move for a mistrial. O'Connor was not sure he wanted one as he felt he had a good case. But after talking it over with his client he made the motion and it was granted.

Yet it was a hollow victory as far as Balestrero was concerned. The defense had not even had a chance to present its case, and now he must go through the whole thing again. He went back to work haunted by the thought that he might once more be seized and jailed. He could not go into Bickford's for breakfast as he always had in the past because it was in that building that all his troubles had begun.

He recalls April 29 as the lowest point in his life. He had visited his wife in the afternoon, found her little improved, and when he returned home from the sanitarium, he received a telephone call from O'Connor saying that the new trial had been set for July 13. Despair flooded him as he made his nightly journey to the Stork. The evening is a half-remembered period of tortured fogginess.

At 1 A.M. the "Latin" band had just gone on the bandstand after a recess and begun to play when Balestrero noticed Jack Elliot, pianist for the Stork's "American" band, coming toward him pointing and grinning. "Put that bass down," called Elliot. "They've caught the guy who did those robberies." Balestrero sensed what that meant, but he kept on playing his string bass. "Don't you understand?" yelled Elliot over the band's din. "They got the holdup man!" Balestrero gripped the neck of the bass fiddle harder. He didn't dare let go. The drummer next to him had heard Elliot. "Will you put that damned bass down?" he growled good humoredly. "Your troubles are over."

Balestrero felt himself begin to tremble. He couldn't believe it. He plucked out a few more measures of music. Then, grinning a little crazily, he put down the instrument and climbed off the bandstand. "You're to call your lawyer right away," Elliot told him.

Balestrero went up to the dressing room. He was shaking so much that he could not fit the nickels into the telephone's slot, and another musician had to do it for him. He reached O'Connor and asked if it it was true. O'Connor said it was. Balestrero doesn't know what he said after that. (It was, "Oh, God! Oh, God! Oh, God!") O'Connor said to come to his office at once. The others crowded around, shaking his hand and thumping his back.

When Balestrero reached O'Connor's office it was thronged with reporters who told him what had happened. Earlier that evening a woman named Frieda Mank, who operates a delicatessen with her husband in Astoria, had noticed a man lurking watchfully outside the store and she had telephoned the police. Soon after, at about 10:30 P.M., the man came in with his hand in his pocket, told her he had a gun and demanded the money in the cash register. Mrs. Mank stamped her foot on the floor, a prearranged signal to her husband who she knew was in the basement. Then Mrs. Mank seized a butcher knife. Her husband charged up from the basement, grabbed the robber from behind and flung him into a corner. That is where he was when detectives arrived from the 114th precinct.

The man was Charles James Daniell, thirty-eight, a jobless plastics molder who at first claimed that this was his only attempt at robbery. But when detectives told him that he would be viewed by victims of a recent wave of stick-ups (as Balestrero had been), he dropped his pose. "Name any stick-up in Jackson Heights," said Daniell, "and I did it." He admitted some forty holdups. "I read in the papers," he said, "they got a guy for holding up the Prudential office. I pulled both those jobs. If this man was convicted, I was going to write the court or the D.A. and try to clear him."

Balestrero, O'Connor and the reporters drove to the 114th precinct station. There Balestrero confronted the man who more than anyone else was responsible for his fifteen weeks of torment. Daniell was handcuffed to a chair. He looked up at Balestrero once and did not look again. There was a fleeting resemblance between the two men, particularly in the set and expression of their eyes.

Balestrero asked, "Do you realize what you have done to my wife?" Daniell did not answer.

It was almost 5 A.M. by the time Balestrero got home. There was a family celebration. He finally went to bed for a half hour's rest, but he was soon up again to see reporters and to make the trip to the sanitarium. He had a wistful hope that if he broke the news suddenly to Rose she would recover immediately. As he told his wife what had happened, a flicker of happiness lighted her face and he knew she understood. But no miraculous recovery occurred, and Mrs. Balestrero is still under treatment although she now spends weekends at home.

The night after his sudden exoneration he was eager to go back to work even though he had had little sleep. He wanted to tell the world about his exoneration. When it came time for the La Rotonda band to go on, the manager of the club detained Balestrero a few minutes in the dressing room. When he finally rushed downstairs, the last member of the band to appear, he discovered that the other members of both orchestras were on the stand. As he walked in they began playing and singing "For He's a Jolly Good Fellow." All the waiters, captains and busboys had been assembled too and they broke into applause. The patrons, forgotten for once, looked up curiously. Balestrero wept. "Oh, I felt so *good*," he says.

A STRICKEN MAN
AND HIS HEART

by Robert Wallace

MAY 9, 1955

Here is the story of a typical heart attack, told in such detail and with such insight into the mind of the sufferer that it reads almost like a personal experience. After the publication of this article, LIFE Staff Writer Robert Wallace rewrote it into a television show which won an award from the American Heart Association. Later, he made it into a movie. Before joining LIFE, Wallace wrote fiction for national magazines.

The pain had begun just before he got on the train. Like most men in middle age he had vaguely considered the possibility that he might someday have a heart attack. His father had died of one. But there was nothing the matter with his own heart, so far as he knew. He was no more of a hypochondriac than any man whose breath comes shorter than it did and whose belt seems tighter than it once was. He had merely considered the possibility and dismissed it.

This account of what happened to him is completely factual except that, at his own request, he is not identified by name.

A specialist might have told him that he was a good candidate for

422

a heart attack. He was 41, 5 feet 8 inches tall, of stocky build and inclined to put on weight; stripped, he weighed 165. He had a nervous stomach. Sometimes, but only sometimes, he worked under pressure and did not readily shake it off when he went home at night. His medical history was undramatic. He had had few illnesses in his life and supposed that he took good care of himself. He rarely drank more than one cocktail a day, smoked about one pack of filter-tipped cigarettes daily and rarely engaged in sudden, violent exercise. He liked to fish, occasionally played golf and puttered gently around the house and garden on weekends.

At 7:55 P.M. on November 10, 1954, having worked a long day, he left his office on 45th Street in Manhattan and started to walk east toward Grand Central Station. He lived in Connecticut and traveled to and from his work in New York on the New Haven Railroad, fifty-eight minutes each way. (He was not a native New Yorker and had not always lived in the atmosphere, sometimes thought to be tense, of a big city.) On this particular evening he was more tired than usual, having worked three eleven-hour days in a row. His company produces commercial films; between Monday morning and Wednesday night he had torn apart and rebuilt a thirty-minute movie for a steel company. He was not worried about the film. He knew it was good. His job had been well done and the pressure was off him.

His train left at 8:09 P.M. He had nearly fifteen minutes to walk five blocks to catch it. He moved rapidly through the huge vaulted lobby of the station, through the train gate and down a flight of twenty-eight steps to the platform where the 8:09 was waiting, already largely filled with passengers. He began to walk up the platform, heading for one of the front cars where he habitually sat. The pain commenced just then.

It arrived full-grown. It was as though a small hot bulb had suddenly started to glow in his chest. It remained constant. The area of pain seemed about the size of a quarter, in the center of his chest, four inches below the knot of his necktie. Never having had a heart pain before, he thought it was indigestion; he often had gas pains and carried a small box of antacid tablets in his pocket.

He had walked halfway up the platform but suddenly did not feel like walking farther toward the head of the train. He stepped into the nearest car and was pleased to find an empty seat on the aisle near the door. If he were going to be sick, he thought, he could get to the washroom quickly without attracting attention.

The pain was severe but he had felt many worse pains at various times in his life. He leaned back in his seat, took an antacid tablet from his pocket and began to chew it. Presently he felt a second ball of pain beside the first one, to the right of it, and then a third, to the left. Soon all three merged into a bar, hot and high up across his chest. He began to wonder whether his heart might not be involved, but he had the conventional notion that the pain of a heart attack would be lower and on the left side of his chest. He thought briefly of leaving the train and trying to find a doctor, even of taking a taxicab to a hospital, but then considered how ridiculous he would feel if he were told that he had indigestion.

For two or three minutes he sat quietly trying not to think, his body simply a container for the little rod of pain. Then he noticed that his left arm was numb. It felt as though he had been carrying a heavy weight for a long distance and had just set it down. He began to knead the arm with his right hand and felt pain running from his left shoulder down to his elbow. He knew then, beyond doubt, what was happening to him.

The train was moving, rumbling through the long tunnel beneath Park Avenue. He looked at the other passengers in the car and saw only a hundred anonymous faces tilted downward toward evening newspapers. He was certain that he was going to die, but was not terrified, and began to say the Lord's Prayer.

When he had finished his prayer he turned to the woman who sat beside him next to the window. He had been twisting in his seat, rubbing his chest and his arm, and he felt that the woman was staring at him out of the corner of her eye. He remembers that she was elderly and had white hair. "Excuse me," he said quietly. "I'm afraid I am very ill."

The woman turned and looked him full in the face. "Lean back and rest," she said in a strong British accent. "You are going to be quite all right."

424

He took enormous, irrational comfort from her remark and repeated it several times to himself. The train emerged from the tunnel and began to roll along the elevated track toward the 125th Street station. For a moment he thought he would try to get off there when the train stopped. Then he was seized by the thought, the conviction, that if he were to stand up he would take only one or two steps and drop dead in the aisle.

He is a practical man and has strong religious faith. He had written his will. It was not terror of death or regret for things undone that disturbed him, but something he describes as an enormous, leaden sense of loss: he would never again see his wife and his three young sons. And he had a faint, struggling feeling of resentment: only forty-one years old.

The conductor entered the car and began to move slowly down the aisle collecting tickets. When the conductor at last reached him he said quietly, "I am having a heart attack. I want to get off the train."

The conductor, a white-haired man with two gold stars on his cap, did not seem much surprised although his eyes widened. "I can stop the train at Mount Vernon," he said. "Can you wait until then?" (Mount Vernon is the first major stop on the commuting line.)

"I'm sorry. I want to get off right away."

"All right. I'll stop the train at Fordham station," the conductor said and walked swiftly away. (Fordham is a small station in the Bronx, still within the New York City limits.) Shortly before the train reached Fordham it began to slow down and switched over onto the outside track. He remembers hearing a man's voice nearby saying irritably, "For Heaven's sake, what are they doing *now?*"

The conductor reappeared, accompanied by a brakeman.

He stood up, wondering whether the motion would kill him. Nothing happened; he felt exactly as before. The brakeman started to reach up in the overhead rack to get his hat and coat.

"No, thanks," he said. "I'll get it myself." It seemed important to him to show the other passengers, who had begun to stare at him, that he could carry his own hat and coat.

Gripping the handrail, leaning on the brakeman, he slowly descended the four train steps and reached the Fordham platform along which a few low-powered bulbs glowed dimly in the dark. The brakeman took his arm. Almost immediately the train pulled away, leaving the two men alone on the platform.

"This is a bad place for you," the brakeman said. "There's a big flight of steps up to the street and no elevator. Do you think you can make it, or—or what?"

"God knows," he said. "I'll have to try." He had decided that death was inevitable. It would come whether he remained on the platform or tried to climb the steps.

Somehow, partly supported by the brakeman, he got to the top of the dark flight of thirty-eight concrete steps, and was still alive. The pain was no greater and no less. There was no one in the station. He and the brakeman walked out into the street.

He leaned against the wall of the station. The brakeman went out into the middle of the street, waving his arms, trying to stop any passing car. None stopped. After perhaps five minutes—here, his recollection of events becomes episodic; he was in fact extremely close to death—a police car suddenly appeared at the curb.

On the way to the hospital he made small talk with the policeman. He chose his words and his thoughts with care, realizing after a while that he was not talking to the policeman at all but to himself. He expected to die momentarily and wanted to have at least a graceful exit line. "I wish my three boys were here," he said. "They'd love to ride in a police car."

The policeman grunted. He was a young man, about thirty.

Within five minutes he was in the emergency room of the Fordham Hospital, an old, overcrowded hospital built in 1907. He remembers that there were half a dozen people sitting along the walls of the room staring at him. They did not seem to be hospital personnel or patients; they were merely there, staring solemnly at him, and he has never made up his mind who they were. He was examined by a woman doctor who spoke with a Middle European accent. She put her stethoscope on his chest, looked at him with narrowed eyes and suddenly slipped a small pill under his tongue. He did not ask what it was. (He was told later that it must have been nitroglycerine, routinely given to relieve the pain of angina pectoris, which, it turned out, he did not have.) Then she injected morphine into his left thigh.

Two hospital attendants, women in blue uniforms, helped him get onto a wheeled stretcher and then began to pull his clothing off him. His small personal belongings and his money were put aside, his suit rolled up into a tight ball held together by a knot tied in the coat sleeves. He remembered that he had paid $90 for the suit.

He could hear someone counting his money. It came to a little less than $7. He was asked if the addition was correct. Then, noticing his cigarette lighter about to be sealed into an envelope with his money, he picked it up. He wanted to give the lighter to the policeman. He held it out saying, "Thanks, I'd like you to have this."

"Sorry, Bud," the policeman said. "I can't accept it."

The attendants wheeled him off to a ward. It was nine o'clock, almost an hour after he had felt the first pain.

The morphine worked quickly. In half an hour he was drowsy, only slightly conscious of the pain, and might easily have gone to sleep. But he expected momentarily to see his wife and his own doctor enter the ward and walk up to his bed, and refused to lose consciousness until they came. Soon the lights in the ward were turned out and suddenly he became aware of all the other human beings in the room with him. In the darkness their breathing and muttering seemed to grow louder and louder. Turning his head slightly he could see the dim white shapes of beds in long rows and realized that there were perhaps fifty men in the ward. They were, as he discovered next morning, all elderly men, many suffering from diseases for which there is no cure. Some of them groaned or wept; some thrashed endlessly upon their beds; one loudly cried out, "Wow!" at regular intervals. The air was warm and thick, full of the smell of antiseptic and of ill old age.

At about 9:30 a male doctor in the white uniform of a resident physician quietly entered the ward and came to his bed. Without a word the doctor took a stethoscope from his pocket and began to listen to his heart. He listened for perhaps a minute, put the stethoscope back into his pocket and then, still bending over him, said tonelessly, "Coronary occlusion."

The Lord's Prayer again. And then from the nearby bed, *"Wow!"*

An old thought that had occurred to him years ago, when he first began to analyze his religion, suddenly bobbed into his mind and he seized it. If one could tell an unborn child that soon it would be forced to leave its only world, the child might struggle frantically against the thought. Birth must be death. But of course it is the other way around.

He lay with his eyes fixed on the door at the end of the ward through which his wife and his own doctor would surely come. All night he stared at it, sometimes dozing for a moment and then snapping awake. They never came.

The New York police had sent a teletype to the police in Connecticut requesting that his friends or relatives be notified. There had been some delay in its transmission and it was long past midnight before a prowl car reached the house where his family was sleeping. His wife, supposing that he was working late in the city, had gone to bed early and had left the porch light burning for him. The policeman could tell her only what was in the teletype—that he was "sick and confined to Fordham Hospital." Having recently moved into the neighborhood, she knew of no one she could ask, at that hour, to come and take care of her children while she went to New York. It was 8 A.M. before she could make arrangements and midmorning before she reached the hospital.

He watched her walk through the ward toward his bed, enormously grateful that he had lived to see her again but unable to think of any words that seemed appropriate. He merely smiled and held out his hand.

Soon his own doctor arrived and an electrocardiogram was taken. The pattern of his heart beat on the long strip of graph paper would show the amount of damage to his heart.

The human heart performs fantastic labor. Every day it pumps about three thousand gallons of blood through thousands of miles of vessels, great and small, in the body. In an average lifetime it beats two and a half billion times and moves seventy-five million gallons of blood. To nourish its own muscular tissue during its terrific effort the heart itself requires a large quantity of blood, which flows through the two coronary arteries and their branches, which encircle the heart, in a vital torrent. In normal individuals the lining of the coronary arteries is clean and smooth. But in those who are likely to have heart attacks the inner layer of the arterial wall is thickened and rough. The thickening is caused predominantly by the slow deposit of a fatty wax called cholesterol, which is found plentifully in the rich diet of most Americans and is also manufactured by the body itself.

In his case, somewhere in one of his coronary arteries, cholesterol had caused an obstruction. For years, perhaps, it had only slightly impeded the flow of blood. But recently the blood had begun to pile up behind it in eddies, and suddenly as he walked down the train platform the eddying had increased. Backed up, some of it unable to pass the obstruction, the blood had begun to seep out through the arterial wall. In a spasmodic, catastrophic reaction the artery had pinched shut. And the heart, deprived of part of its nourishment, had begun to ache. The heart still obtained blood through other coronary artery branches and thus at least a great part of it was still undamaged, but one area of it had actually begun to die.

His was no exceptional case; he had suffered a classic heart attack, of the sort that happens annually to hundreds of thousands of individuals in the U.S. All such attacks result from obstruction or impairment of the flow of blood in the coronary arteries but differ in name and in the exact nature of the catastrophe. In angina pectoris the artery may not be obstructed at any single point but may have sections which have narrowed. Here the flow of blood is not suddenly shut off but is merely restricted. Pain occurs when, as during exercise, the heart does not receive enough blood. In coronary thrombosis there may be a narrowing or obstruction in the artery against which blood congeals to form a clot. But in general, whether the attacks are called coronary occlusion, thrombosis or angina pectoris, cholesterol is thought to be the root cause; if a way can be found to keep the arterial wall free of cholesterol, heart attacks and strokes will be rare.

It should be said here that there is no reason for the average middle-aged American to become a cholesterol hypochondriac. He would be well advised merely to moderate his consumption of fatty foods and await the results of further research in the subject.

At four in the afternoon, the electrocardiogram and other tests having shown that he was not in imminent danger of death, he was wrapped in a firm cocoon of blankets by two muscular but infinitely gentle ambulance attendants and transferred to a hospital in central Manhattan. The ambulance moved silently, with no siren, at an even 20 mph.

There are no miracle drugs, other than emergency, tactical medicines, for cardiac patients. The primary treatment consists of prolonged rest, during which the heart itself makes its own repairs. The obstructed artery is bypassed and new channels are opened, old ones enlarged, through which the blood may flow. It can never restore the damaged area of muscle, which does die and is replaced by scar tissue, but it can make arrangements and compromises in its blood supply for which there is no other word than miraculous. Eight out of every ten individuals who suffer heart attacks survive them and thereafter lead normal and even long lives because of the magnificent vitality of that fist-sized hollow lump of muscle in their chests. Morbid fear of heart attacks is a ridiculous waste of time. The chronic worrier would do better to consider how strong, not how weak, his heart really is.

In the forty-eight hours following his attack the pain gradually subsided. But then in the late afternoon of the third day he awakened from a drugged nap to a new and terrifying sensation. He could not breathe. By good fortune a nurse was standing beside his bed. She realized at once what was happening to him and ran from the room in search of a doctor. He lay very still, struggling to get air into his lungs, but could not. When the doctor reached him he managed to say, "I am only—breathing—on the top half inch of my lungs." He was suffering from pulmonary edema, a disastrous complication that sometimes follows severe heart attacks and fills the lungs with fluid. While an oxygen mask was being connected the doctor gave him an injection which would help clear out the fluid in which he was literally drowning and almost at once he lost consciousness.

For two days he drifted between sleep and wakefulness, burning with a fever that once reached 105°. It was here that he was closest to death and he was not even aware of it. He remembers that once he woke, saw a nurse beside his bed and behind her a screen over

430

which were hung three hospital nightshirts, soaked with his sweat.

Then, as abruptly as it had begun, the fever left him. He awakened one morning feeling completely alive and aware, certain for the first time that he would not die. He was in a semiprivate room; someone else was there, in the other bed, staring at him curiously.

He was overcome with a sense of the freshness of life such as he had not known for many years. He looked at the fabric of the bedclothes and at his own hands, thinking how marvelously they were contrived. Every object on which his eyes fell was remarkable and new. The identity of the other man in the room seemed, as it unfolded, the most remarkable of all. Today it seems to have been only an odd coincidence but then it overwhelmed him.

The other man, whom he had never seen before, was a doctor who had come to the hospital to have a small tumor removed from his thigh. For no reason that he recalls they fell to talking, almost at once, of trout fishing. It developed that in the preceding August they had both gone to Canada to fish. Both had gone to the same township and had fished the same river. Within three days of each other they had stood upon the same rock to cast into the same pool, thinking much the same thoughts, and now they lay side by side, far from summer and the rock.

A well man who has not been close to death would have shrugged it off. But he found the deepest sort of meaning in it, although he is now reluctant to put it into words for fear of being thought foolish. It was a great surging feeling of the kinship and common destiny of men, which came close to overwhelming him. Today he knows that cardiac patients and in fact all men who have gone to the final brink, looked over and drawn back, have such feelings. Children have them as well. It is almost as though these feelings, being found at both extremities of life, seep from outside through the thin walls that enclose life at both ends.

Forty-six days after his attack he went home lying down in the back of a station wagon.

He is still at home, still resting. Occasionally he wonders how he might have lived, what he might have done to avoid the heart attack. He finds some of the answers in the way he must live today; had he always lived so, perhaps he might never have felt the little ball of pain glowing in his chest. Now he is obliged to watch his diet; previously he had known he was fifteen pounds above his normal weight but had never taken the trouble to do much about it. Now he must avoid animal fats which he once consumed in abundance. He must use little salt, which causes the body to retain excess fluid and hence to become overweight. He must not permit himself to become heavily fatigued or emotionally upset; this too he had known previously but had ignored. He must avoid sudden, violent exercise. For years he had heard and read of middle-aged men who suddenly collapsed while shoveling snow, changing automobile tires in a rage, or running anxiously after buses and trains; now he understands that this is a form of suicide.

The other adjustments he must make are small; he may no longer smoke but may drink. Instead of going to bed at midnight he goes to bed at ten; instead of eating large, heavy meals he eats light ones and does not run around the block afterward. He and his wife have taken only one defensive step. For a number of years his wife has had it in mind that she would like to be a schoolteacher, and now she has begun to go to college, three days a week, to get a master's degree.

Much of the time he sits reading in the sun, or only thinking. He will rest another month or two, and then go back to work. He looks quietly at his wife, at his three young sons darting in and out of the house, and watches the grass slowly growing green beside his door. His sense of the extraordinary freshness of life is slowly, and to his deep regret, passing away, but there remains a faint, persistent wonder that will not leave him. To him the sudden flattening of a patch of grass in the wind could be the very footstep of God. To him the coming of spring is not the logical result of the ponderous wheel of earth, an annual occurrence scarcely to be noticed, but an enormous personal gift that can bring tears to his eyes.

AN AGONIZING
ODYSSEY OF LOVE

by William Brinkley

MARCH 5, 1956

> *Pei-Chao Li and Grace Li were married in Shanghai in August, 1946. Two years later, Li went to New York to study at Columbia. In May, 1949, while he was still away, the Communists swarmed into Shanghai. Grace Li fled to Hong Kong. Husband and wife immediately set about the business of reuniting, but seven years later, when* LIFE *Staff Writer William Brinkley wrote this article, Grace and "Chiu," as she called him, were still apart. This excerpt takes up their story after they have been struggling for two years in a morass of British and American immigration restrictions.*

Searching for an opening through the paper wall of immigration restrictions, Li in New York came upon an idea. Perhaps U.S. consular officials in European countries might not be so strict with Orientals as were those in Hong Kong, which was at the Communist border. Several Chinese he had met in New York had got into the U.S. from France.

"Go to Europe," he wrote his wife in 1951. "Go to France. . . ."

Promptly Grace Li went off to the French consulate on Queen's Road in Hong Kong. She applied for a six-month visitor's visa to France. At this point Li in New York did something else. He got

433

Columbia University to admit her as a student, starting in the fall term of 1952. If she could not get to the U.S. as his wife, perhaps she could go as a student.

Grace Li was now twenty-five years old.

On March 19, 1952, Grace Li got her French visitor's visa. It required that she be in France by September 19. She went straight over to a French shipping line. All boats were booked for months ahead, but she had a British travel document which would permit her to set foot in Britain enroute to France. She went to a British shipping line and took the first space available, on the S.S. *Corfu* sailing June 6 for England. Then she bought a teakwood chest lined with camphor wood. It was a big chest, three and a half feet long with beautiful carvings of leaves and birds on the sides. She packed her Chinese dresses and her wedding pictures in it.

At noon on June 6, 1952, her father, who had lately arrived in Hong Kong from Shanghai with her mother, and all her office friends came down to the Star Ferry pier to see her off. The office people brought her great bunches of flowers. Her father cried a little. He wanted her to be with her husband but he was dismayed at the idea of her wandering homelessly around the world. He kept murmuring, "Nur-nur,"—"Little doll"—which had always been his name for her. He said good-by: "Be careful, Nur-nur. And go to church every Sunday and to prayer meeting every Wednesday night."

She walked up the gangplank of the first ship she had ever been on. As the ship backed slowly into the stream she stood at the rail waving down. Her father was shouting something from the pier, but the band was playing and she never heard whatever it was. Then the ship was moving out. "I thought how I didn't know a soul in the world where I was going, France, or have any idea of what was going to happen. . . ." But, as the vessel passed out of the harbor between the ringing mountains, some of her sense of sadness and uncertainty began to disappear. At least she was moving nearer to the husband she had not seen in four years.

After a thirty-two-day passage she arrived at Tilbury, England. "I thought I would like to stay in England a day or two and I asked the immigration officer who came aboard and he said he thought it would be all right but I should report in. I thought I would just have a look before going on to Paris."

It was July 8, 1952. Tomorrow she would be twenty-six years old.

Next day she telephoned the one person she knew in London, a childhood friend from Shanghai. He and his wife immediately invited her out to stay with them. She hesitated, remembering that she had no "status" in England. Then she was saying, "I'm kind of scared here, it's so lonely . . . yes, I'll come." Above all she wanted not to be alone. Why not, she thought, try to get to the U.S. from England rather than from France?

As soon as she was settled with her friends, she went to the Home Office on High Holborn and applied for a visitor's visa. The official said it was not usual to apply for such a visa after one was in a country but they would look into the matter and let her know.

Next she went over to the American embassy on Grosvenor Square and filled out forms for a student's visa to the U.S. She was given an appointment a few days later. When she returned, a vice consul, a good-looking young man, extremely neat and tidy and with nice manners, asked her a number of routine questions of the sort she had been asked so many times: age, place of birth, parents' names, scars if any. . . . Finally he asked, "And where is your husband, Mrs. Li?" "My husband's in the U.S.," she said.

The vice consul looked at Grace Li with what she remembers as a mild smile on his face. "Mrs. Li," he said, "is it your intention to study or is it your intention to join your husband?"

"I do intend to study," she said. "And of course I would like very much to see my husband. I haven't seen him in four years."

The vice consul made notes. Then, smiling, he stood up and held out his hand. "You should be hearing from us in six or seven weeks."

The question about her intentions in going to the U.S. bothered her, but she put it out of her mind. Presently she got a notice to report to the British Home Office. The immigration official reminded her that she had the right to stay only forty-eight hours in England and already she had been there three weeks.

"I have applied for a student visa to the U.S.," she said. "I would very much appreciate it if you would grant me a visitor's visa to remain here until I hear from the U.S. embassy. It shouldn't be long. And I'm enjoying my stay in England so much," she added timidly.

The British immigration official told her he could not give her a visa. However she could stay for a while unofficially.

"Remember, though," the immigration official added, "that your visa to France expires September 19. You'll have to leave by then."

She waited. As the weeks passed and no word came from the U.S. embassy she grew more and more discouraged. Then one day in early September she went to Canada House on Trafalgar Square with a friend who was trying to get into Canada. Suddenly, while she was standing there waiting for her friend to get forms, she thought, well, why not try Canada again?

After filling out still more forms, she was shown into the office of a Canadian visa officer. She was overwhelmed by his courtesy. He asked her the usual questions, which she knew so well by now. Then quite casually, he asked one more question.

"Oh, Mrs. Li. Where is your husband?"

Grace Li hesitated an imperceptible moment. She had a picture of all the past years apart from Chiu. She had a picture of more years of separation to come. She remembered the way the U.S. vice consul had seemed to stick at this same point. Then she visualized being in Canada with nothing but a border separating herself and Chiu, a border he could cross. . . .

"My husband," she said, "is in Hong Kong."

In her desperation the lie was out. She has never ceased to worry about telling it. She knows that if she had not told it, she would probably never have got into Canada. If the Canadian officials had known her husband was in New York and thought she might try to use Canada as a "back door" to the U.S. they might never have let her in. But she felt she *had* to see Chiu, even if she had to go back to Hong Kong right afterward. She felt miserable in her lying and her hands in her lap were trembling. She put them under her purse.

"I'll have to put these papers through Ottawa," the official was saying pleasantly. "We'll let you know."

In New York, Li had begun his third year on his doctorate. His subjects included Psychology of Family Relations.

Meanwhile the deadline on Grace Li's visa to France was fast expiring. She kept hoping that word would come from either the Americans or the Canadians before September 19. But no word came. Finally there was no more time. She had to ask the Americans and Canadians to forward her files to Paris. She went back to her room and packed. The camphor wood chest was still not unpacked and she arranged to have it shipped on.

On September 18, the day before her visa to France expired, she got a 7:45 A.M. plane. She felt no excitement whatsoever about landing in that gayest of all cities of the earth, Paris.

She got a room in a small hotel, a tiny, depressing room with a single window overlooking the Rue Pigalle. Next day she started the machinery all over again at the Canadian embassy and at the American embassy.

She waited, and Paris was the loneliest place she had ever known. One day when she thought she might scream if it had to go on much longer she got a phone call from Holland. It was from a man who had worked for the export-import firm in Hong Kong where she had been a secretary. Now he was a purchasing agent for the same company in Holland and had heard from mutual friends that she was in Paris.

"Look," he said, "why don't you come to Amsterdam and wait? For one thing it's cheaper here. And my fiancée and I are here."

She thought only a moment. "I'd like to," she said.

She went to the Dutch consulate on the Rue de Constantine and got a visa. Then, only a few days before she was due to leave, she received a phone call from the Canadian embassy.

"Mrs. Li," a voice on the other end said, "your application for a visa to Canada has been approved."

Something shot up inside her. She had made an enormous inroad on the miles between her and her husband.

Then, quickly, she was thinking, "If the Canadians will let me come, perhaps the Americans will too." So she decided to wait a while before exercising the Canadian visa. Then if no word came from the Americans she would go to Canada as the next best thing.

"I'm going to Holland right now," she told the Canadian girl on the phone. "Could you please transfer the visa to Holland?"

Again she arranged for her camphor wood chest to be shipped on. On October 26 she flew into Amsterdam where she got a room at a pension not far from her friends. The room was large, bright and spotlessly clean, and overlooked trees and a chapel.

When she was settled she phoned the U.S. consulate in Amsterdam: "This is Grace Li. I applied in England to go to the United States to study. . . ."

She made a long distance phone call to the U.S. embassy in London: "This is Grace Li. Have you any news on my application?"

"I'm sorry, Mrs. Li. Your application is still being processed."

She waited. And then it was 1953.

January passed and by February it had been seven months since she had applied to go to the U.S. as a student, and still she had not heard. Then one day she got a letter from the U.S. consulate, giving her an appointment. With considerable hope she went to the consulate on the Museumplein for an interview. But all the vice consul did was to ask the same questions. He could not tell her how much longer it would take to get an answer. As she sat there she began to get a strange feeling—as if she were watching herself and the official in two mirrors being multiplied into infinity.

Suddenly it came over her that she would wait no more.

"I am going to go to Canada," she said abruptly. "I have a visa for Canada. Could you transfer my file to Montreal?" She knew that this was the nearest large Canadian city to New York.

Her visa to Canada would allow her only two months there. Let happen what will happen after that, she thought. At least Chiu would be able to come see her during those two months.

She booked passage on the *Veendam* of the Holland-America line. She shipped on her camphor wood chest.

After eleven days by boat and by train she arrived in Montreal. It was cold and snow lay along the streets. She got a room in the Y.W.C.A. She had a bath and washed her hair. She put on her flannel pajamas. Then she picked up the phone and asked for long distance.

"I want to speak to Mr. P. C. Li in New York. . . ."

Since it was night she called him at the restaurant where he worked after school hours. In a moment she heard a voice she had not heard in almost five years.

"Yes, yes, Grace? How are you?"

"Chiu." Her voice was unsteady. "I'm all right. How are you?"

"I'm all right. . . . It's been a long time. . . . I can't say too much here. I'm in the restaurant."

"Yes, yes, I understand. I'm at the Y.W.C.A."

"How is it at the Y.W.C.A.?"

"It's very nice."

"Grace," he said. "We're going to *see* each other."

She felt a sort of awe. Then she heard his voice again.

"It's been a long time. . . . Grace, I'm in the restaurant."

"Yes, I know. I'll write. Good night, Chiu."

She sat there looking out the window at the wet, cold-looking street. He sounded the same, she thought, and yet he sounded like a complete stranger. It was curious.

She slept better that night than in a long, long time.

Next day she went to the railway station to check on her camphor wood chest. It had arrived and to save storage charges she asked the help of a social worker, who arranged to have it stored free of cost in the basement of St. James United Church. The chest tucked away, she launched her calls on her fifth U.S. consulate, asking them if they had an answer on her student visa.

At last her file arrived at the consulate. A decision had been reached: "Your application for admission to the United States as a student has been rejected."

A great numbness came over her. All she could think was that after nine months they had finally said no again. She looked out the window. It's April, she thought. It's beginning to be spring.

She phoned her husband. They both stood bent and bewildered before the news that their last avenue of getting together had been blocked off. They were not giving up yet, he said, not when they were only 325 miles apart.

On top of the crushing news of her rejection for entrance into the United States came another blow. It appeared to be impossible for Li to get up to Canada to see her. His trouble arose out of the fact that he was one of those Chinese students who remained in the U.S. as aliens without "status" after the Communist conquest of their homeland. The U.S. immigration office in New York told Li that if he went to Canada, he might not be able to get back to the U.S. Not only that, but there was no telling what Canada might do with him if the U.S. would not let him return.

But Li was unable to stand being only 325 miles from his wife without seeing her. He decided he would just have to take the risk and go. On the night of June 15, 1953, he got on a train out of New York's Grand Central Station. Next morning he got off at the Windsor Station in Montreal. It was 8:40 A.M.

The concourse of the Windsor Station in Montreal is four hundred feet long and overhung by a vast skylight. That morning the June sun poured brilliantly through the glass and held her, almost as in a spotlight, when he walked through the gate and saw her—for the first time in five years.

She was wearing a black Chinese dress with the slits in the sides. She had gone over to the basement of the St. James Church to get it out of the camphor wood chest. She stood there. Carrying his grip, he walked across the twenty feet to her. Then he was touching her. She was trembling almost violently.

"Start asking me questions," she said. "I don't know where to begin. So start asking me questions. Start asking me questions."

He smiled, feeling himself shaking a little, and asked the first one. "Have you had breakfast?"

"No."

"Neither have I. Let's have some."

He remembers that time: "She wanted me to ask questions. So I asked them. I asked big questions and little questions. It was almost, at the start, like the first few times we met. And yet we seemed to be so close. But also we seemed to be so far away."

After breakfast they went out into the June sun and started walking along St. Catherine Street, the main street of Montreal. They bought some chocolate fudge and walked along eating it. Suddenly he said, "Let's take a trip. Let's go to Niagara Falls."

"It would be nice to go there together."

Then he said, "You haven't changed much."

She said, "You haven't changed much either."

They had two weeks together. At Niagara Falls she looked across at that land so near, that land she had heard about since she was a child, that land her father loved, that new land of her husband's, that land she wanted to be hers. She had fought four years and traveled half the globe to come to that land. This was her first look at it.

They talked and they talked. They talked about everything but their problem—they wanted for once to forget that. He told her about his education, and she felt very proud that he was near his doctorate. And she told him of all the cities she had seen.

She remembers those two weeks: "For the first time in five years I felt safe. I hadn't felt safe in five years and we felt closer than we ever had before."

And he remembers: "I think everything is fine when you are with your wife. Anywhere you go. Anywhere we went I liked."

When she saw him off at the Windsor Station they felt unmeasured contentment.

"In time we'll come to some solution about being together all the time," he told her. "And meantime I'll always be able to come up and visit you. I'm just overnight away by train, Grace. Do you realize that?"

Presently she got her visitor's visa to Canada renewed for an entire year.

On the morning of Li's next visit she felt a great surge of anticipation. Waiting under the skylight, she watched the minutes tick off on the big station clock. Then she could see the New York train chugging in. She waited and many passengers came through the gate. She could not see Li anywhere. She wondered if he had missed the train. No, he would have wired.

Then at last she saw him—but walking beside him was a man in a blue uniform. As her husband came up she could see that he was terribly distraught.

"I'm having some trouble with the immigration," he said.

The man in the blue uniform, she realized, was a Canadian immigration officer. She felt suddenly very weak. The officer was escorting her husband into the immigration office at the station. Hurriedly she walked along with them. They went inside and she heard the officer speak to her husband.

"You can't come here without some proof that you can get back into the U.S.," he said. "Otherwise we have no assurance that the U.S. will let you back in. There's a train back to New York in a half hour. I'm afraid you'll have to take it."

"But I was here just recently," Li said. "I was here for a two-week visit."

"I'm sorry," the immigration officer said, "but we have our instructions."

The three of them walked back outside toward the gate. Under the skylight Li stopped and spoke to her.

"Look after yourself," he said. "Perhaps there's some other way. I'll try back in New York."

He turned quickly and went with the immigration officer through the gate. They had not touched.

Back in New York, Li wrote to the Department of Citizenship and Immigration in Ottawa asking for visiting privileges to Canada. Soon he received an answer: "It is regretted we are unable to offer facilities for you to visit Canada."

Apparently it had simply been luck that allowed him to get in on his first try.

Grace Li was twenty-seven years old.

In Montreal her desperation and loneliness grew with the passage of weeks. One day in November she could stand it no longer. She made her way down to the U.S. Consulate on Stanley Street and made a frantic appeal.

"May I go to the United States for one weekend to visit my husband? Let me go for just one weekend. Two days. I will put up bond, any bond you want, to assure you I will return to Canada."

The vice consul was sympathetic. It was just, he said accurately, that such a thing was not allowed for in any of the regulations.

For the first of the many times she had been in a consular or immigration office she felt she might break down crying, and she knew if she did she would never stop crying.

She managed somehow to get out of the consulate. Then she was in her room. She had not the faintest memory of how she had got from the consulate to her room. Then she was sobbing, sobbing violently. It had taken five years for her to break down.

Into this pit of misery there came a hopeful light. From New York, Chiu wrote that he had heard about something called the Refugee Relief Act of 1953, which Congress had recently passed. This law, he explained carefully to her, was designed to help refugees from Communist countries get into the U.S. She was at once hopeful. If there were ever refugees from a Communist country, she thought, it was the Lis.

It is not a simple thing to apply for a visa under the Refugee Relief Act, and still less simple to get admitted under it. One must have as sponsors one or more U.S. citizens who must first give complete financial reports on themselves and then furnish ironclad assurances of personal responsibility for the refugee. One must have documentary proof that he has a specific place to live in the U.S. and that this housing does not displace a U.S. resident. One must have assurance that he will not become a public charge, that he has waiting for him a specified job at a specified salary. And this employment must not displace a U.S. resident. One must, of course, be guaranteed morally and politically and have a thorough security check.

For months the Lis sought out the myriad assurances.

First, the Church World Service in New York City agreed to be the endorsing agency. Two American friends of her father became cosponsors. The Board of Missions of the Methodist Church agreed to employ Grace Li in New York as a stenographer at a salary of $223 a month. The United States Employment Service certified that this employment would not displace any worker in the U.S. The required assurance was given that she would have a place to live in New York —with her husband.

This took numerous visits and scores of letters. In addition Li himself applied for permanent residence under the Refugee Relief Act. These tasks came in a period when Li was in the midst of his hardest work for his doctor's degree. With all this—plus a job outside school hours for support—he worked sixteen to eighteen hours a day, month after month. In Montreal, Grace Li did everything she could to help. She filled out the numerous forms he sent her. She typed his thesis.

At last the mighty battery of forms, assurances and signatures was assembled, and Church World Service mailed them off to the U.S. State Department.

Grace Li was now twenty-eight years old.

Four months passed before, at last, a formal letter precise in its legal language reached Grace Li from the State Department.

As interpreted by the Lis' endorsers, the letter meant that only one slip of paper now barred Mrs. Li's entry into the U.S.: a readmission certificate from the government of Canada. Such a certificate is another requirement under the Refugee Relief Act, as assurance that the U.S. will not get stuck with some undesirable refugee but can always ship him back to the country from whence he came.

Abruptly, as if emerging from some indescribable nightmare, the Lis stood upon a mount of ecstasy. In the most feverish of hopes the Lis had their lawyers approach Canadian officials in Ottawa. Would the government of Canada issue Grace Li a readmission certificate?

Why, no, it would not. A person who was only a visitor to the country obviously could not be given a readmission certificate to the country. In that case Mrs. Li, if deported from the U.S., would become the responsibility of the Canadian government. The Canadian immigration officials also expressed to the Lis' lawyers their sympathy for Mrs. Li, but they pointed out that under the laws of Canada there was nothing they could do to grant the request.

The Lis were caught. They had conquered the mountain of papers that stood between them—all but one paper.

For months the problem was investigated. Brilliant lawyers explored its misty corridors. The U.S. State Department and the Departments of External Affairs and of Citizenship and Immigration of Canada wrote letters back and forth. Agencies and sponsors telephoned, made trips, conferred and wrote from Ottawa to Montreal to New York to Washington. Fourteen months passed.

Last month [February, 1956], after a long period of no news, there came two important developments in the lives of the Lis.

In New York, Dr. Li, who is now doing guidance work with students at the Bernard M. Baruch School of Business and Public Administration of the City College of New York, received the news that the House of Representatives of the U.S. had approved a resolution granting a group of seven hundred aliens, including him, permanent residence in the U.S. under the Refugee Relief Act of 1953.

In Montreal, Grace Li's lawyers received a letter from the Department of Citizenship and Immigration of the government of Canada, the last and pertinent phrases of which read: ". . . it is not considered that we would be justified in granting a further extension of temporary entry to Mrs. Grace Wang Yu-Ching Li. We do not wish to be unreasonable, however, and in order that she may have time to make the necessary departure arrangements, we are willing to allow her to remain until April 30, 1956. It is expected that Mrs. Grace Wang Yu-Ching Li will effect her departure voluntarily prior to that date."

Dr. Li's permanent residence clearance means that he can visit Canada—but only after he has received his official notification and arrangements are made for him to take the required oath. But it will probably take at least four months for all this to happen so that Li will not even be able to get to Montreal in time to see his wife off for Hong Kong.

And so Mrs. Grace Wang Yu-Ching Li sits waiting in her room on the Côtes des Neiges in Montreal in the sovereign state of Canada. Dr. Pei-Chao Li sits in his room on 22nd Street in New York City in the sovereign state of the U.S.A. She is twenty-nine years old. He is thirty-seven.

THE BRUTAL TALE
OF A TEEN-AGE
GANG LEADER

As told to Ira Henry Freeman

APRIL 14, 1958

> *The young Negro who tells this story under the pseudonym
> of "Frenchie" is doubly remarkable. When only thirteen
> he skillfully led to power one of the toughest street
> gangs in Brooklyn, New York. But a few years later, after
> many arrests and a training-school stretch, he completely
> changed his ways. Today at twenty-five he is a graduate
> medical research worker. Ira Henry Freeman, who set
> down his story as Frenchie told it, has expanded this article
> into a book,* Out of the Burning.

I was not yet 14 years old when Gus Gibbons, president of the Little
Bishops, picked me to be president of his new Fifth Division. The
Bishops were then one of the largest street clubs in New York City.
The five divisions had 150 or 200 members between 13 and 18. They
claimed a turf extending for two miles along Fulton Street in Brooklyn
and had brother clubs in Harlem and the Bronx.

I was an important sahib for so young a kid. But I was tall for my
age, a little smarter than most of the other bops, or gang members, and
had the prestige of having already been busted—arrested—twice by
the cops.

My first arrest had been for gang fighting. The second was for firing a zip gun at some kids in John Marshall Junior High School. That is the same school that was in the papers recently because a thirteen-year-old girl was raped there. The principal committed suicide in despair. There were rapes and fights when I went there, too, but our principal did not kill himself. He just left.

I had made the zip gun in shop class out of a toy airplane launcher. Afterward I made more of them for other bops in my division. Our zip guns could throw a .22-caliber cartridge twenty-five yards and were as good as any homemades in Brooklyn.

A few months later, however, I stumbled on a load that made them seem like cap pistols. In an empty lot on Sands Street I found a wooden crate containing two dozen brand new .38-caliber service revolvers and four marine signal flare guns. This was probably a shipment for the Brooklyn Navy Yard that had been hijacked off South Brooklyn piers and hidden temporarily.

I nearly broke my back lugging the crate to Lenny's candy store, where my club hung out. Lenny was a right guy who had been a bop in a street club as a kid and who still hated cops. He let us hide the guns in his cellar. We shook down little kids at school for their lunch money until we had collected $50. With that we bought some ammunition from a fence on the docks.

The sudden haul made a spectacular difference in our division's chances. With our new artillery we might rise to be top club in the city.

Overnight I was no longer afraid of Gus Gibbons, although he was seventeen, much bigger and much meaner than I. I had taken two of the flare pistols for myself and test-fired them on a roof with shot-gun shells. When I let go with both of those cannons at once, I got ideas of becoming the Hitler of all the Little People [junior gang members].

Although Hitler and his Nazis had been wiped out years before, we still looked up to them as the meanest bops in history. Even today some bop gang leaders call themselves Hitler or Goering or Fuehrer, and I know one club—Negro at that—named the Gestapos.

My fellows were always bragging about their new guns. Bo would act out a favorite daydream. "Here a bull walkin' his beat. Here me layin' on the roof with my piece. I take aim. Bam! Scratch one head-beater!"

I told them not to sound off so much about the new pieces. But naturally the news leaked out. So I was not surprised when Calvin, Gus Gibbons' war councilor, arrived at Lenny's one night. A war councilor's main duty is to declare war on rival clubs. And Calvin would rather fight than eat or drink.

"It's on with the Robins," Calvin announced that night as he entered Lenny's.

Jumping off the counter stools, abandoning the pinball machine, jukebox and comics, the fellows crowded around.

"Man, when we goin' down?"

"Lemme get my piece!"

"Cool it a minute," I called above the hubbub. Then to Calvin I said, "What's shaking?"

Calvin said the Robins had stuck one of our Little People in the Second Division. But he couldn't give me any details.

"Gus says every division goin' down tomorrow night and hit 'em outside the Wynne Center," Calvin said. "Come packin' all you got. Gus says bring some pieces for him and the others too."

That was it. I figured that Gus, hearing rumors about new guns, wanted to see what we had. If we had anything good, he wanted a share. At the same time, he might as well show off our guns so as to build up his rep as headman with the most firepower. The show would be spectacular enough since the Thomas Wynne Center of the Police Athletic League was only one block away from the 79th Precinct.

"Well, I don't know about that," I said. I was not eager for us to take all the risk just for Gus Gibbons' benefit.

But my fellows begged for trouble.

"Aw, dig, Frenchie. Calvin says it's on. We can't punk out." I supposed it did not make much difference if Gus were jiving us up about an attack by the Robins. Clashes have been turned on for less than that. Something was bound to give soon anyway. You could not leave two dozen .38's in a hole in the floor for long with kids like us around.

"Okay, it's on," I agreed, setting off a chorus of war whoops.

The following night, forty-three bops showed up at Lenny's in uniform—black leather battle jackets, green Army fatigue pants starched and pressed sharp, boots and black bleeckers with silver bands. The bleecker was a felt hat creased low in front that we bought from a shop in Bleecker Street for $5.

As we loaded up, you could feel the tension. None of us had yet fired a real gun with live ammo at anybody. Just to wrap our fingers around the grip of a businesslike, blue-black .38 gave us a charge down to our toes.

At 8:30 we took off. "Bishops goin' down!" the fellows sung out.

"Take it easy," Lenny called after us enviously.

We walked eastward on Fulton Street and on the parallel Atlantic Avenue, the main stems in our turf. It was a half hour's hike to the Wynne Center at Gates Avenue near Marcy. But we were in no hurry, and it is traditional to walk down to a turn-on.

We cruised down the avenues in threes, keeping a half-block interval so as not to attract attention. We kept our jackets zipped up to cover the heats stuck into our waistbands, and we tried to look as though we were not going anywhere in particular. This was no time to get picked up.

The headbeaters would stop any group of five or more boys on suspicion of unlawful assembly. If they found a heat on us, they would take us in and beat our heads off. We hated those headbeaters worse than anybody in the world.

I was leading a column with Red, my vice president, and Chukker, the war councilor. Although it was a clear, cool night in February, I could feel sweat trickling down from my armpits. This was a big clash for a kid not yet fourteen to lead.

Along the way we drank sneaky pete—as we called the strong, sweet, cheap wine—out of pint bottles, and we paused outside the candy stores to kid the babes in their car coats and kerchiefs. The Fifth Division did not yet have real debs or an organized girls' auxiliary. Of course, many of us had bams, as we called our steadies. These were schoolgirls, sometimes as young as thirteen, but we thought of them as women and made the old valentino when their parents were not home. Usually the bams would try to talk us out of a fight, although afterwards they never failed to boast of what we had done. If they had been real debs, on the other hand, they would have walked down with us, carrying the heats in case a bull padded the boys down. During the clash, the debs would wait at a candy store nearby.

As we passed the headquarters of the other four divisions in candy stores, quick-and-dirtys and cellar clubs, I thought it funny there was nobody there.

"It figures," Red said reassuringly. "They went down ahead."

"Maybe," I said, "unless they went to prayer meeting."

I was more leery than ever. Gus was planning on us being his expendables. We met him in a hallway just this side of Robin turf. With him were only Tattoo, his vice president; Calvin; and three or four officers of the other divisions.

Gus asked me, "How many guys you brung?"

"Forty-three," I said. "How many you brung? I didn't see anybody on the way down."

"They be here," Gus said.

"Don't jive me up. We're the farthest division out. How come we the first to show?"

"If I tell you they be here, they be here," Gus said.

I was not ready to challenge him for the boss job just yet. I had seen him fight, and you could see in his eyes he hated the whole world. Besides, he still had a majority on his side.

"Your guys got their pieces?" Gus wanted to know.

"Sure, what you think?"

"You ought to give us some of them pieces," Gus said.

"Well, we gotta hold a council on that," I said.

Of course I was unwilling to give up a single piece. Gus squinted at me in his mean way, but he was in no position to dicker. My guys were piling up, and we had him five to one.

He decided to skip it for the moment. "Let's get goin' on the strategy."

Gates Avenue is lined with rundown, four-story brick tenements and a few stores. The Wynne Center is a fairly large recreation hall of dirty white stone with windows screened against breakage. A sign on the façade reads: "Helping Our Boys and Girls Become Good Men and Women."

I took a command post with my officers in a hallway opposite the center, where the Solid Rock Baptist Church is now. There are many storefront churches with crudely painted windows like that in our neighborhood, but they don't seem able to do much about bad kids. Gus and his staff hid in a basement nearby.

The rest of the boys were stationed in hallways, on cellar stairs and on roofs facing the center. I could see the red dots of their cigarettes glowing as we waited for the Robins to come out after their basketball game. We shivered in the cold, talking in whispers, fingering our guns.

At one point I slipped into Gus's hiding place to ask if his guys had arrived yet. "All set," he whispered. "Get back to your post." I had seen no sign of them, but it was too late to argue about it now.

Every time the door of the center was opened, we could hear yelling from the gym. It was ten o'clock before the game ended, and a dozen Robins in their brown bleeckers appeared in the lighted doorway.

I had given orders to hold fire until they came out a way, but some trigger-happy jerks couldn't wait.

"Here they come!"

"Give it to them!"

"Burn! Burn! Burn!"

The firing began too soon while the Robins were still clustered on the stoop with the door open behind them. They fell over each other trying to scramble back into the center.

But Dick Forbes, their president, and one or two others chose to run. I ran out after Forbes. The whole street was echoing with gunfire. Slugs were pinging against the sidewalk and steps near me. I heard a window crash and people hollering from their apartments.

I caught up with Forbes. He snatched an ashcan cover to shield himself, but it was chained short to a railing. Grabbing his collar with one hand, I held a flare gun to his head with the other.

He grabbed my wrist to get the gun away. Gus, Tattoo, Calvin, Red and Pete leaped to help me. We dragged Forbes into an areaway and beat him. He went down, screaming, with blood on his face. Then we stomped him with our boots. I had nothing against him personally, but the meaner you act, the bigger your rep.

Meanwhile three Robins had been shot on the stoop of the center.

Two were helped inside by their friends. Bo and Youngblood jumped the other one left moaning on the cement. Bo rolled him for cash. But Youngblood, who was clothes-happy, began wrenching off the wounded boy's gray suède shoes.

A siren wailed. Cops in fleets of cars and on foot were pouring into the street.

"Headbeaters!"

We scattered. A prowl car screeched around the corner of Marcy Avenue on two wheels and blocked Red and me off. We ducked into a hallway and pounded up the stairs. As we tore up the dark stairwell we could hear footsteps drumming behind us. At a landing a tenant came out and cried, "Here!" spreading his arms. I chopped him aside with the flare gun.

Bursting out onto the roof, we could hear police whistles shrilling and people shouting in the street below. We sprinted over the roof-tops, vaulting the parapets. Glancing back, I saw the silhouette of a head in a police cap against the skyline.

"Fire escape," Red gasped. We tiptoed down the iron ladders, taking care not to pant noisily as we passed lighted windows.

In the back yard we scrambled over a fence. We scurried through a cellar and finally crept out onto Monroe Street. Red had a reefer and we smoked it, puff for puff, as we zigzagged home through dark side streets.

Youngblood and eight others of the Fifth Division were busted by the cops that night, and we lost nine pieces. Youngblood was grabbed with his gun on him. The others were able to throw their pistols away before being nabbed, but we never recovered them.

Afterward Youngblood said Musclehead Ahearn worked him over in the station house that night and the next day. "Where'd you get that gun?" Whack! "Who else has 'em?" Whack! "Who was with you?" Whack! Youngblood never sang even though his nose was broken. Since he was over sixteen, Youngblood was arraigned in Adolescent Court on the felony of carrying a gun. He copped a plea and got off with a suspended sentence.

The others, being under sixteen, were sent to Youth House, where they played cards and shot the bull for a day or two before appearing in Children's Court. Only two were "adjudicated" juvenile delinquents and both were released on probation.

The judge said he was being lenient because of their good family situation. That was a laugh. Youngblood and I were the only boys in the club whose homes were not broken. Red's father lived in Harlem with another woman and Red had threatened to kill him if he set foot in the house. Chukker never knew who his father was and maybe his mother, who worked in a Chinese laundry, didn't either. Bo was one of five children by different fathers. He didn't see much of his mother, who worked nights in a hospital.

The real reason the judge released the boys was that all the state institutions for bad kids were bursting at the seams already.

The clash built up our rep. But it also grounded us. Prowl cars rolled through our turf once an hour, and the bulls checked Lenny's like night watchmen.

So much police protection kept our turf smooth for a while. This situation was intolerable and we blamed Gus Gibbons for it.

So when Calvin paid us another visit, saying, "It's on again with the Robins," we didn't cheer this time.

"Says who?" Chukker demanded.

"Says me and says Gus, is who. Gus says go down and hit 'em tomorrow night in the Sweet Shop. And, Frenchie, this time don't forget those pieces you promised us."

"Now hold time," I said. "You tell Gus go find some other jive cats. Only the Fifth Division showed last time and only Fifth Division guys got busted. It's us, not you, the headbeaters are running. From now on this club goes down when I say go down."

My guys thumped my back. "Tell him, Frenchie."

Calvin shrugged. "Gus won't be happy," he said threateningly as he left.

We wasted no time in preparing our defense against the invasion we figured Gus was planning. At six o'clock every night the whole division mustered with pieces loaded. Our sentries lay out in Fulton Street and Atlantic Avenue to signal when Gus's columns appeared. The rest of us hung around Lenny's and waited for the alarm to take our stations.

"If my windows get busted," Lenny warned me, "you gotta pay for it, no matter whose fault."

"Don't worry, Lenny," I reassured him.

"What makes you think I worry?" he said with a grin. I think he was delighted to see a big clash coming.

On the third night, clear and mild, the eight o'clock relief of sentries had just gone out when we heard a whistle being passed down Fulton Street. We tumbled out of Lenny's like firemen. Little Man came up panting: " 'Bout forty Bishops cruisin' down Fulton."

Then Moose loped toward us, shouting that another column was advancing up Carlton Avenue.

"Everybody take your post and wait for the signal to burn."

Pete took half a dozen guys with .38's onto the roof of a hardware store on the northwest corner. Boston led a similar squad of gunmen to the top of a four-story tenement on the northeast corner.

Red, our best close-combat man, took a big assault party into an empty lot on the southeast corner. They smashed out the lights of an advertising billboard so they could crouch there in darkness behind piles of rubbish. They had previously collected mounds of rocks, empty bottles and half bricks.

Chukker was in charge of a fourth party of in-fighters similarly armed inside Lenny's. Chukker himself had "borrowed" a .22 rifle from a friend's father.

As soon as the head of the enemy columns came into view, I walked out alone to the middle of the intersection. Waving both arms, I yelled, "Frenchie's here, have no fear!" I drew both flare pistols and crouched there, like Richard Widmark in a commando movie.

As they charged me from both directions, I heard them firing. But from the sound of the reports I knew their guns were just homemades. I recognized Gus leading the bunch in Fulton Street. He fired at me without effect and then had to stop to reload. I let go with one flare gun. The range was long, but the birdshot must have peppered him because he howled and grabbed his ear. I fired the other gun toward Calvin's crowd approaching from the other direction. Then I ducked for cover, fast.

The snag was on. Our artillery opened up on the invaders under the street lights on the corner. We had the intersection under cross-fire from all four corners. "Burn! Burn!" And we poured it down.

The enemy broke. Red's team swarmed out of the lot, hurling bottles and bricks after them. Swinging bats, Chukker's squad rushed from Lenny's, and Chukker let go a round or two from the rifle.

During the hullabaloo, traffic continued in Fulton Street almost as if everything were normal. The windshield of one taxi was shattered accidentally. The outraged driver got out, but when he saw the melee he jumped back into the cab and took off.

We faded away as the police cars began to arrive, and we took care not to reassemble in Lenny's or the Ritz Bar that night. The head-beaters made a pass at searching Lenny's. They said they had a complaint he had pushed narcotics to boot us up for the clash.

"You don't search no place without a warrant." Lenny talked right up to bulls. "I never pushed junk to no kids or nobody else."

Shows you how much cops know. None of us, except Rat, began on junk until much later. We never even smoked a reefer before a clash because drugs slowed us down. Before a clash we drank pete to get high. It was only after a fight that we smoked reefers.

Meeting the next night on the corner, we decided unanimously to jump independent. We chose Deacons for a new name because the record "Deacon's Hop" was virtually our theme song. For years now church titles have been popular among Brooklyn street clubs—Bishops, Apostles, Chaplains and so on. I don't know why. We never paid church much mind.

I selected Red and Chukker, Moose and Pete to walk with me through Gus's turf and nail down our victory. We knocked off a pint of pete each, filled the chambers of our pieces with six shells and went down.

When we reached Gus's hangout at Marcy Avenue and MacDonough Street we lined up, ready for hell, with our right hands on our heaters in our side pockets. Some Big People [older gang members] loafing on the stoop stared at us.

"Where's Gus?" I said.

"What's shakin'?" one of them asked.

"Nothing shakin' but the leaves, and they ain't shakin' cause ain't no breeze. I want to see Gus."

They didn't know what we were up to, but by now they knew what we had in our pockets. We didn't explain but just stared them down until Gus appeared. I couldn't help smiling when I saw his ear wrapped up.

"We jumped independent," I told Gus. "We're the Deacons, and we're taking over the turf of the Fifth Division as of now. Stay out of Deacon Square until you're invited."

If they were going to jump us, this was the moment. We five stood there ready with our fingers on the triggers. The Bishops looked at us, then at Gus.

"We supposed to be brother clubs," he said to me. "You tried to kill me last night."

Relax, I said to myself, he's licked. Out loud I answered, "Was you turned it on, not us."

"Was only a sham," he said.

"Didn't look like it to me," I said. "But, anyway, as far as we're concerned, it's off."

"Call it cool if you want," Gus said sullenly.

We hung around a while, yakking friendly with the fellows and kidding their debs. Then we went home, horsing around all the way. We could have beat each other up out of sheer happiness. With only my fourteenth birthday coming up, I was already president of the club with the hardest rep in Brooklyn.

THE LAST DAYS
OF ANNE FRANK

by Ernst Schnabel

AUGUST 18, 1958

*Anne Frank's "Diary" symbolized the triumph of
childhood innocence over organized brutality. As a book, the
diary became a world-wide best seller in many languages;
as a play it made German audiences weep; as a movie,
it was one of Hollywood's finest efforts. Anne Frank's
diary ends abruptly when she and her family were captured
by the Nazis in 1944. The rest of the story was largely
unknown until the record of her sad, courageous last
days was set forth by Ernst Schnabel in his book* Anne
Frank: A Portrait in Courage, *from which this article was
drawn.*

Last year in Amsterdam I found an old reel of movie film on which
Anne Frank appears. She is seen for only ten seconds and it is an
accident that she is there at all.

The film was taken for a wedding in 1941, the year before Anne
Frank and seven others went into hiding in their "Secret Annexe." It
has a flickering, Chaplinesque quality with people popping suddenly
in and out of doorways, the nervous smiles and hurried waves of the
departing bride and groom.

Then, for just a moment, the camera seems uncertain where to look.
It darts to the right, then to the left, then whisks up a wall, and into

view comes a window crowded with people waving after the departing automobiles. The camera swings farther to the left to another window. There a girl stands alone, looking out into space. It is Anne Frank.

Just as the camera is about to pass on, the child moves her head a trifle. Her face flits more into focus, her hair shimmers in the sun. At this moment she discovers the camera, discovers the photographer, discovers us watching seventeen years later and laughs at all of us, laughs with sudden merriment and surprise and embarrassment all at the same time.

I asked the projectionist to stop the film for a moment so that we could stand up to examine her face more closely. The smile stood still, just above our heads. But when I walked forward close to the screen the smile ceased to be a smile. The face ceased to be a face, for the canvas screen was granular and the beam of light split into a multitude of tiny shadows, as if it had been scattered on a sandy plain.

Anne Frank, of course, is gone too, but her spirit has remained to stir the conscience of the world. Her remarkable diary has been read in almost every language. I have seen a letter from a teen-aged girl in Japan who says she thinks of Anne's Secret Annexe as her second home. And the play based on the diary has been a great success wherever it is produced. German audiences, who invariably greet the final curtain of *The Diary of Anne Frank* in stricken silence, have jammed the theaters in what seems almost a national act of penance.

Last year I set out to follow the fading trail of this girl who has become a legend. The trail led from Holland to Poland and back to Germany, where I visited the moss-grown site of the old Bergen-Belsen concentration camp at the village of Belsen and saw the common graves shared by Anne Frank and thirty thousand others. I interviewed forty-two people who knew Anne or who survived the ordeal that killed her. Some had known her intimately in those last tragic months. In the recollections of others she appears only for a moment. But even these fragments fulfill a promise. They make explicit a truth implied in the diary. As we somehow knew she must be, Anne Frank, even in the most frightful extremity, was indomitable.

The known story contained in the diary is a simple one of human relationships, of the poignant maturing of a perceptive girl who is thirteen when her diary begins and only fifteen when it ends. It is a story without violence, though its background is the most dreadful act of violence in the history of man, Hitler's annihilation of six million European Jews.

In the summer of 1942 Anne Frank, her father, her mother, her older sister Margot and four others were forced into hiding during the Nazi occupation of Holland. Their refuge was a tiny apartment they called the Secret Annexe, in the back of an Amsterdam office building. For twenty-five months the Franks, the Van Daan family and later a dentist, Albert Düssel, lived in the Secret Annexe, protected from the Gestapo only by a swinging bookcase, which masked the entrance to their hiding place, and by the heroism of a few Christians who knew they were there. Anne Frank's diary recounts the daily pressures of their cramped existence: the hushed silences when strangers were in the building, the diminishing food supply, the fear of fire from the incessant Allied air raids, the hopes for an early invasion, above all the dread of capture by the pitiless men who were hunting Jews from house to house and sending them to concentration camps. Anne's diary also describes with sharp insight and youthful humor the bickerings, the wounded prides, the tearful reconciliations of the eight human beings in the Secret Annexe. It tells of Anne's wishes for the understanding of her adored father, of her despair at the gulf between her mother and herself, of her tremulous and growing love for young Peter Van Daan.

The actual diary ends with an entry for August 1, 1944, in which Anne Frank, addressing her imaginary friend Kitty, talks of her impatience with her own unpredictable personality. The stage version goes further: it attempts to reconstruct something of the events of August 4, 1944, the day the Secret Annexe was violated and its occupants finally taken into a captivity from which only one returned.

What really happened on that August day fourteen years ago was far less dramatic than what is now depicted on the stage. The automobiles did not approach with howling sirens, did not stop with screaming brakes in front of the house on the Prinsengracht canal in

Amsterdam. No rifle butt pounded against the door until it reverberated as it now does in the theater every night somewhere in the world. The truth was, at first, that no one heard a sound.

It was mid-morning on a bright summer day. In the hidden apartment behind the secret bookcase there was a scene of relaxed domesticity. The Franks, the Van Daans and Mr. Düssel had finished a poor breakfast of ersatz coffee and bread. Mrs. Frank and Mrs. Van Daan were about to clear the table. Mr. Van Daan, Margot Frank and Mr. Düssel were resting or reading. Anne Frank was very likely at work on one of the short stories she often wrote when she was not busy with her diary or her novel. In Peter Van Daan's tiny attic room Otto Frank was chiding the eighteen-year-old boy for an error in his English lesson. "Why, Peter," Mr. Frank was saying, "you know that *double* is spelled with only one *b*."

In the main part of the building four other people, two men and two women, were working at their regular jobs. For more than two years these four had risked their lives to protect their friends in the hideout, supplied them with food and brought them news of a world from which they had disappeared. One of the women was Miep, who had just got married a few months earlier. The other was Elli, a pretty typist of twenty-three. The men were Kraler and Koophuis, middle-aged spice merchants who had been business associates of Otto Frank's before the occupation. Mr. Kraler was working in one office by himself. Koophuis and the two girls were in another.

Elli, now a mother whose coloring and plump good looks are startlingly like those of the young women painted by the Dutch masters, recalled: "I was posting entries in the receipts book when a car drove up in front of the house. But cars often stopped, after all. Then the front door opened, and someone came up the stairs. I wondered who it could be. We often had callers. Only this time I could hear that there were several men. . . ."

Miep, a delicate, intelligent, still young-looking woman, said: "The footsteps moved along the corridor. Then a door creaked, and a moment later the connecting door to Mr. Kraler's office opened, and a fat man thrust his head in and said in Dutch: 'Quiet. Stay in your seats.' I started and at first did not know what was happening. But then, suddenly, I knew."

Mr. Koophuis is now in very poor health, a gaunt, white-haired man in his sixties. He added: "I suppose I did not hear them because of the rumbling of the spice mills in the warehouse. The fat man's head was the first thing I knew. He came in and planted himself in front of us. 'You three stay here, understand?' he barked. So we stayed in the office and listened as someone else went upstairs, and doors rattled, and then there were footsteps everywhere. They searched the whole building."

Mr. Kraler wrote me this account from Toronto: "A uniformed staff sergeant of the Occupation Police and three men in civilian clothes entered my office. They wanted to see the storerooms in the front part of the building. All will be well, I thought, if they don't want to see anything else. But after the sergeant had looked at everything, he went out into the corridor, ordering me again to come along. At the end of the corridor they drew their revolvers all at once and the sergeant ordered me to push aside the bookcase and open the door behind it. I said: 'But there's only a bookcase there!' At that he turned nasty, for he knew everything. He took hold of the bookcase and pulled. It yielded and the secret door was exposed. Perhaps the hooks had not been properly fastened. They opened the door and I had to precede them up the steps. The policemen followed me. I could feel their pistols in my back. I was the first to enter the Franks' room. Mrs. Frank was standing at the table. I made a great effort and managed to say: 'The Gestapo is here.' "

Otto Frank, now sixty-eight, has remarried and lives in Switzerland. Of the eight who lived in the Secret Annexe, he is the only survivor. A handsome, soft-spoken man of obviously great intelligence, he regularly answers correspondence that comes to him about his daughter from all over the world. He recently went to Hollywood for consultation on the movie version of *The Diary of Anne Frank*. About the events of that August morning in 1944 Mr. Frank told me: "I was showing Peter Van Daan his spelling mistakes when suddenly someone came running up the stairs. The steps creaked, and I started to my feet, for it was morning when everyone was supposed to be quiet. But then the door flew open and a man stood before us holding his pistol aimed at my chest.

"In the main room the others were already assembled. My wife and the children and Van Daans were standing there with raised hands. Then Albert Düssel came in, followed by another stranger. In the middle of the room stood a uniformed policeman. He stared into our faces.

" 'Where are your valuables?' he asked. I pointed to the cupboard where my cashbox was kept. The policeman took it out. Then he looked around and his eye fell on the leather brief case where Anne kept her diary and all her papers. He opened it and shook everything out, dumped the contents on the floor so that Anne's papers and notebooks and loose sheets lay scattered at our feet. No one spoke, and the policeman didn't even glance at the mess on the floor as he put our valuables into the brief case and closed it. He asked us whether we had any weapons. But we had none, of course. Then he said, 'Get ready.' "

Ironically enough, the occupants of the Secret Annexe had grown optimistic in the last weeks of their self-imposed confinement. The terrors of those first nights had largely faded. Even the German Army communiqués made clear that the war was approaching an end. The Russians were well into Poland. On the Western front Americans had broken through at Avranches and were pouring into the heart of France. Holland must be liberated soon. In her diary Anne Frank wrote that she thought she might be back in school by fall.

Now they were all packing. Of the capture Otto Frank recalled: "No one wept. Anne was very quiet and composed, only just as dispirited as the rest of us. Perhaps that was why she did not think to take along her notebooks, which lay scattered about on the floor. But maybe she too had the premonition that all was lost now, everything, and so she walked back and forth and did not even glance at her diary."

As the captives filed out of the building, Miep sat listening. "I heard them going," she said, "first in the corridor and then down the stairs. I could hear the heavy boots and the footsteps, and then the very light footsteps of Anne. Through the years she had taught herself to walk so softly that you could hear her only if you knew what to listen for. I did not see her, for the office door was closed as they all passed by."

At Gestapo headquarters the prisoners were interrogated only briefly. As Otto Frank pointed out to his questioners, it was unlikely, after twenty-five months in the Secret Annexe, that he would know the whereabouts of any other Jews who were hiding in Amsterdam.

The Franks, the Van Daans and Düssel were kept at police headquarters for several days, the men in one cell, the women in the other. They were relatively comfortable there. The food was better than the food they had had in the Secret Annexe and the guards left them alone.

Suddenly all eight were taken to the railroad station and put on a train. The guards named their destination: Westerbork, a concentration camp for Jews in Holland, about eighty miles from Amsterdam. Mr. Frank said: "We rode in a regular passenger train. The fact that the door was bolted did not matter very much. We were together and had been given a little food for the journey. We were actually cheerful. Cheerful, at least, when I compare that journey to our next. We had already anticipated the possibility that we might not remain in Westerbork to the end. We knew what was happening to Jews in Auschwitz. But weren't the Russians already deep into Poland? We hoped our luck would hold.

"As we rode, Anne would not move from the window. It was summer outside. Meadows, stubble fields and villages flew by. The telephone wires along the right of way curved up and down along the windows. After two years it was like freedom for her. Can you understand that?"

Among the names given me of survivors who had known the Franks at Westerbork was that of a Mrs. de Wiek, who lives in Apeldoorn, Holland. I visited Mrs. de Wiek in her home. A lovely, gracious woman, she told me that her family, like the Franks, had been in hiding for months before their capture. She said: "We had been at Westerbork three or four weeks when the word went around that there were new arrivals. News of that kind ran like wildfire through the camp, and my daughter Judy came running to me, calling, 'New people are coming, Mama!'

"The newcomers were standing in a long row in the mustering square, and one of the clerks was entering their names on a list. We looked at them, and Judy pressed close against me. Most of the people in the camp were adults, and I had often wished for a young friend for Judy, who was only fifteen. As I looked along the line, fearing I might see someone I knew, I suddenly exclaimed, 'Judy, see!'

"In the long line stood eight people whose faces, white as paper, told you at once that they had been hiding and had not been in the open air for years. Among them was this girl. And I said to Judy, 'Look, there is a friend for you.'

"I saw Anne Frank and Peter Van Daan every day in Westerbork. They were always together, and I often said to my husband, 'Look at those two beautiful young people.'

"Anne was so radiant that her beauty flowed over into Peter. Her eyes glowed and her movements had a lilt to them. She was very pallid at first, but there was something so attractive about her frailty and her expressive face that at first Judy was too shy to make friends.

"Anne was happy there, incredible as it seems. Things were hard for us in the camp. We 'convict Jews' who had been arrested in hiding places had to wear blue overalls with a red bib and wooden shoes. Our men had their heads shaved. Three hundred people lived in each barracks. We were sent to work at five in the morning, the children to a cable workshop and the grownups to a shed where we had to break up old batteries and salvage the metal and the carbon rods. The food was bad, we were always kept on the run, and the guards all screamed 'Faster, faster!' But Anne was happy. It was as if she had been liberated. Now she could see new people and talk to them and could laugh. She could laugh while the rest of thought nothing but: Will they send us to the camps in Poland? Will we live through it?

"Edith Frank, Anne's mother, seemed numbed by the experience. She could have been a mute. Anne's sister Margot spoke little and Otto Frank was quiet too, but his was a reassuring quietness that helped Anne and all of us. He lived in the men's barracks, but once when Anne was sick he came over to visit her every evening and would stand beside her bed for hours, telling her stories. Anne was so like him. When another child, a twelve-year-old boy named David, fell ill, Anne stood by his bed and talked to him. David came from an Orthodox family, and he and Anne always talked about God."

Anne Frank stayed at Westerbork only three weeks. Early in September a thousand of the "convict Jews" were put on a freight train, seventy-five people to a car. Brussels fell to the Allies, then Antwerp, then the Americans reached Aachen. But the victories were coming too late. The Franks and their friends were already on the way to Auschwitz, the camp in Poland where four million Jews died.

On the third night the train stopped, the doors of the car slid violently open, and the first the exhausted passengers saw of Auschwitz was the glaring searchlights fixed on the train. On the platform *Kapos* (criminal convicts who were assigned to positions of authority over the other prisoners) were running back and forth shouting orders. Behind them, seen distinctly against the light, stood the SS officers, trimly built and smartly uniformed, many of them with huge dogs at their sides. As the people poured out of the train, a loudspeaker roared, "Women to the left! Men to the right!"

Mrs. de Wiek went on calmly: "I saw them all as they went away, Mr. Van Daan and Mr. Düssel and Peter and Mr. Frank. But I saw no sign of my husband. He had vanished. I never saw him again.

"'Listen!' the loudspeaker bawled again. 'It is an hour's march to the women's camp. For the children and the sick there are trucks waiting at the end of the platform.'

"We could see the trucks," Mrs. de Wiek said. "They were painted with big red crosses. We all made a rush for them. Who among us was not sick after those days on the train? But we did not reach them. People were still hanging on to the backs of the trucks as they started off. Not one person who went along on that ride ever arrived at the women's camp, and no one has ever found any trace of them."

Mrs. de Wiek, her daughter, Mrs. Van Daan, Mrs. Frank, Margot and Anne survived the brutal pace of the night march to the women's camp at Auschwitz. Next day their heads were shaved; they learned that the hair was useful as packing for pipe joints in U-boats. Then the women were put to work digging sods of grass which they placed in great piles. As they labored each day, thousands of others were dispatched with maniacal efficiency in the gas chambers, and smoke rising from the stacks of the huge crematoriums blackened the sky.

Mrs. de Wiek saw Anne Frank every day at Auschwitz. "Anne seemed even more beautiful there," Mrs. de Wiek said, "than she had at Westerbork. Of course her long hair was gone, but now you could see that her beauty was in her eyes, which seemed to grow bigger as she grew thinner. Her gaiety had vanished, but she was still alert and sweet, and with her charm she sometimes secured things that the rest of us had long since given up hoping for.

"For example, we each had only a gray sack to wear. But when the weather turned cold, Anne came in one day wearing a suit of men's long underwear. She had begged it somewhere. She looked screamingly funny with those long white legs, but somehow still delightful.

"Though she was the youngest, Anne was the leader in her group of five people. She also gave out the bread to everyone in the barracks and she did it so fairly there was none of the usual grumbling.

"We were always thirsty at Auschwitz, so thirsty that at roll call we would stick out our tongues if it happened to be raining or snowing, and many became sick from bad water. Once when I was almost dead because there was nothing to drink, Anne suddenly came to me with a cup of coffee. To this day I don't know where she got it.

"In the barracks many people were dying, some of starvation, others of weakness and despair. It was almost impossible not to give up hope, and when a person gave up, his face became empty and dead. The Polish woman doctor who had been caring for the sick said to me, 'You will pull through. You still have your face.'

"Anne Frank, too, still had her face, up to the very last. To the last also she was moved by the dreadful things the rest of us had somehow become hardened to. Who bothered to look when the flames shot up into the sky at night from the crematoriums? Who was troubled that every day new people were being selected and gassed? Most of us were beyond feeling. But not Anne. I can still see her standing at the door and looking down the camp street as a group of naked gypsy girls were driven by on their way to the crematorium. Anne watched them going and cried. And she also cried when we marched past the Hungarian children who had been waiting half a day in the rain in front of the gas chambers. And Anne nudged me and said, 'Look, look! Their eyes!' Anne cried. And you cannot imagine how soon most of us came to the end of our tears."

Late in October the SS selected the healthiest of the women prisoners for work in a munitions factory in Czechoslovakia. Judy de

Wiek was taken from her mother, but Anne and her sister Margot were rejected because they had contracted scabies. A few days later there was another selection for shipment from Auschwitz. Stripped, the women waited naked for hours on the mustering ground outside the barracks. Then, one by one, they filed into the barracks where a battery of powerful lights had been set up and an SS doctor waited to check them over. Only those able to stand a trip and do hard work were being chosen for this new shipment, and many of the women lied about their age and condition in the hope that they would escape the almost certain death of Auschwitz. Mrs. de Wiek was rejected and so was Mrs. Frank. They waited, looking on.

"Next it was the turn of the two girls, Anne and Margot," Mrs. de Wiek recalled. "Even under the glare of that light Anne still had her face, and she encouraged Margot, and Margot walked erect into the light. There they stood for a moment, naked and shaven-headed, and Anne looked at us with her unclouded face, looked straight and stood straight, and then they were approved and passed along. We could not see what was on the other side of the light. Mrs. Frank screamed, 'The children! Oh, God!' "

The chronicle of most of the other occupants of the Secret Annexe ends at Auschwitz. Mrs. Frank died there of malnutrition two months later. Mr. Frank saw Mr. Van Daan marched to the gas chambers. When the SS fled Auschwitz before the approaching Russians in January, 1945, they took Peter Van Daan with them. It was bitter cold and the roads were covered with ice and Peter Van Daan, Anne Frank's shy beloved, was never heard of again.

From Auschwitz, Mr. Düssel, the dentist, was shipped to a camp in Germany where he died. Only Otto Frank remained there alive until liberation. Anne Frank and Mrs. Van Daan and Margot had been selected for shipment to Bergen-Belsen.

The train that carried Anne from Auschwitz to Belsen stopped at every second station because of air raids. At Bergen-Belsen there were no roll calls, no organization, almost no sign of the SS. Prisoners lived on the heath without hope. The fact that the Allies had reached the Rhine encouraged no one. Prisoners died daily—of hunger, thirst, sickness.

The Auschwitz group had at first been assigned to tents at the Bergen-Belsen heath, tents which one survivor recalls gave an oddly gay carnival aspect to the camp. One night that fall a great windstorm brought the tents crashing down, and their occupants were then put in wooden barracks. Mrs. B. of Amsterdam remembered about Anne: "We lived in the same block and saw each other often. In fact, we had a party together at Christmastime. We had saved up some stale bread, and we cut this up and put onions and boiled cabbage on the pieces. Over our feast we nearly forgot our misery for a few hours. We were almost happy. I know that it sounds ghastly now, but we really were a little happy in spite of everything."

One of Anne Frank's dearest childhood friends in Amsterdam was a girl named Lies Goosens. Lies is repeatedly mentioned in the diary. She was captured before the Franks were found in the Secret Annexe, and Anne wrote of her great fears for the safety of her friend. Now the slim and attractive wife of an Israeli Army officer, Lies lives in Jerusalem. But she was in Bergen-Belsen in February, 1945, when she heard that a group of Dutch Jews had been moved into the next compound.

Lies said, "I waited until night. Then I stole out of the barracks and went over to the barbed wire which separated us from the newcomers. I called softly into the darkness, 'Is anyone there?'

"A voice answered, 'I am here. I am Mrs. Van Daan.'

"We had known the Van Daans in Amsterdam. I told her who I was and asked whether Margot or Anne could come to the fence. Mrs. Van Daan answered in a breathless voice that Margot was sick but that Anne could probably come and that she would go look for her.

"I waited, shivering in the darkness. It took a long time. But suddenly I heard a voice: 'Lies? Lies? Where are you?'

"I ran in the direction of the voice, and then I saw Anne beyond the barbed wire. She was in rags. I saw her emaciated, sunken face in the darkness. Her eyes were very large. We cried and cried as we told each other our sad news, for now there was only the barbed wire between us, nothing more, and no longer any difference in our fates.

"But there was a difference after all. My block still had food and clothing. Anne had nothing. She was freezing and starving. I called to her in a whisper, 'Come back tomorrow. I'll bring you something.'

"And Anne called across, 'Yes, tomorrow. I'll come.'

"I saw Anne again when she came to the fence on the following night," Lies continued. "I had packed up a woolen jacket and some zwieback and sugar and a tin of sardines for her. I called out, 'Anne, watch now!' Then I threw the bundle across the barbed wire.

"But I heard only screams and Anne crying. I shouted, 'What's happened?' And she called back, weeping, 'A woman caught it and won't give it to me.' Then I heard rapid footsteps as the woman ran away. Next night I had only a pair of stockings and zwieback, but this time Anne caught it."

In the last weeks at Bergen-Belsen, as Germany was strangled between the Russians and the western Allies, there was almost no food at all. The roads were blocked, the railroads had been bombed and the SS commander of the camp drove around the district trying unsuccessfully to requisition supplies. Still, the crematoriums worked night and day. And in the midst of the starvation and the murder there was a great epidemic of typhus.

Both Anne and Margot Frank contracted the disease in late February or early March of 1945. Margot lay in a coma for several days. Then, while unconscious, she somehow rolled from her bed and died. Mrs. Van Daan also died in the epidemic.

The death of Anne Frank passed almost without notice. For Anne, as for millions of others, it was only the final anonymity, and I met no one who remembers being with her in that moment. So many were dying. One woman said, "I feel certain she died because of her sister's death. Dying is easy for anyone left alone in a concentration camp." Mrs. B., who had shared the pitiful Christmastide feast with Anne, knows a little more: "Anne, who was very sick at the time, was not informed of her sister's death. But a few days later she sensed it and soon afterward she died, peacefully."

Three weeks later British troops liberated Bergen-Belsen.

Miep and Elli, the heroic young women who had shielded the Franks for two years, found Anne's papers during the week after the police raid on the Secret Annexe. "It was terrible when I went up there," Miep recalled. "Everything had been turned upside down. On the floor lay clothes, papers, letters and school notebooks. Anne's little wrapper hung from a hook on the wall. And among the clutter on the floor lay a notebook with a red-checked cover. I picked it up, looked at the pages and recognized Anne's handwriting."

Elli wept as she spoke to me: "The table was still set. There were plates, cups and spoons, but the plates were empty, and I was so frightened I scarcely dared take a step. We sat down on the floor and leafed through all the papers. They were all Anne's, the notebooks and the colored duplicate paper from the office too. We gathered all of them and locked them up in the main office."

Miep and Elli did not read the papers they had saved. The red-checked diary, the office account books into which it overflowed, the 312 tissue-thin sheets of colored paper filled with Anne's short stories and the beginnings of a novel about a young girl who was to live in freedom, all these were kept in the safe until Otto Frank finally returned to Amsterdam alone. Thus Anne Frank's voice was preserved out of the millions that were silenced. No louder than a child's whisper, it speaks for those millions and has outlasted the raucous shouts of the murderers, soaring above the clamorous voices of passing time.

A FAMOUS LADY'S INDOMITABLE FIGHT

by Margaret Bourke-White

JUNE 22, 1959

> "I've always taken on the toughest challenge," Margaret
> Bourke-White has said, and it sums up her fame as
> photographer, lecturer and author. Here, in a personal
> epic, she tells of the toughest challenge she ever faced
> —her seven-year battle against Parkinson's disease. Miss
> Bourke-White took LIFE's first cover picture (1936)
> and for nineteen years ranged the world with her cameras
> for the magazine. Some time ago she put in her bid to be
> the first LIFE photographer to fly to the moon and make
> pictures there. And she wasn't kidding.

The mysterious malady began so quietly I could hardly believe there
was anything wrong. There was nothing strong enough to dignify
with the word pain, nothing except a slight dull ache in my left leg
when I walked upstairs. I did not dream it was the stealthy beginning
of a seven-year siege during which I would face a word totally new to
my vocabulary—incurable.

For half a year the dull ache wandered haphazardly to other parts
of my leg, my arm, my back—always on my left side. Then came

something small but very peculiar. I was in Tokyo at the time (1952) and I discovered that when I arose after sitting for an hour, at lunch for instance, my first three steps were grotesque staggers.

Highly embarrassed by these staggers, I thought up little concealing devices such as dropping my gloves and retrieving them—any brief delaying action helped, because on the fourth step I could walk normally again. I consulted doctors but found that my wisp of a symptom meant as little to them as it did to me.

Over the next three years I found there were a good many diseases I did not have. I did not have cancer, heart trouble, infantile paralysis or arthritis. When I thought back over my experiences during two wars, I was amazed at the notion that a mere disease could catch me. In the Mediterranean during World War II, I had been aboard a transport that was torpedoed and had escaped in a lifeboat. I had flown over Cassino in Italy with German fighters following our little Piper Cub. I had been through too many bombings and shellings to count them, and once I was even dropped into the Chesapeake Bay by a helicopter. I had always been arrogantly proud of my health and durability. The strong might fall by the wayside but I was indestructible.

Then a friend suggested I talk to Dr. Howard Rusk. I already knew Dr. Rusk, whose Institute of Physical Medicine and Rehabilitation at New York University's Medical Center has done so much for the physically disabled, but it was a shock to think of myself as a cripple.

Dr. Rusk took me to his staff neurologist, Dr. Morton Marks, to whom my malady was no mystery.

"But," he said, "I'm not going to give it a name, because some day you may see an advanced case, and it might discourage you." He asked the chief physical therapist to draw up a program of exercise for me, "to help save what you've got."

To save what I've got! He can't mean me! Soberly he explained. "You can do a great deal to control your disease. From now on, exercise is more important to you than rest. You must exercise. If you skip one day you'll fall back two. If you skip three days you'll lose six."

Jack Hofkosh, the therapist, a short powerful man with a large head, began telling me ways to strengthen my hands.

"Crumpling pages of newspaper into a ball, using all four fingers and thumb, would be excellent," he said. "And for the wrist, nothing could be better than mixing up cake batter."

I was as cross as a petulant child. "I don't make cake," I snapped.

He suggested that I twist and squeeze out wet clothing under a warm-water tap. Foolishly I scolded him: "I don't wash my own clothes."

But a few weeks later something frightened me out of all this nonsense. I found I could not type, not even on my electric typewriter, for my fingers were stiffening. I went back to Mr. Hofkosh, determined to master whatever he could teach me.

Beginning in 1955, everything I did became an exercise. Wherever my photographic assignments took me I tried to walk, run, climb, fly. My great dread was that editors would try to spare me, but when I said I was under doctor's orders to walk at least four miles a day, they understood. They sent me to Pittsburgh, to Colorado, to the edge of the Yukon. Wherever I was I rose half an hour early to crumple newspapers into popcorn-ball size. The space under my seat in any plane, train or bus overflowed with these popcorn balls. Every motel room I stayed in was soon knee-deep in them, and any well-appointed hotel bathroom was an invitation to me to wring out all the Turkish towels in water.

I clung to such routines as I clung to my work, and both strengthened my spirit. The more impossible an assignment looked, the more savage I was about doing it. In British Columbia in 1957 I flew low over icy crusts of glaciers, photographing some of the wildest country in the world. It thrilled me to find I could work easily in the air, swinging my heavy airplane cameras, because each step on earth was becoming labored now. I could not hide from myself the knowledge that each year left me a little worse than it found me.

When I opened some medical insurance papers one day and learned I had Parkinson's disease, the name did not frighten me because I did not know what in the world it was. Then slowly a memory came back, of a description Edward Steichen once gave at a photographers' meeting of the illness of Edward Weston, "dean of photographers," who was a Parkinsonian. I remembered the break in Steichen's voice: "A terrible disease . . . you can't work because you can't hold things . . . you grow stiffer each year until you are a walking prison . . . there is no known cure. . . ."

Parkinsonism is Hydra-headed. Push it down in one form and it rears up in another. Its two main symptoms are rigidity in various parts of the body and arm and leg tremors. But to know what Parkinson's is you must know the surprise of finding yourself taking sudden, involuntary backward steps. You must know the surprise of finding yourself sloping forward as though you were trying to impersonate the tower of Pisa. You must discover the awkwardness of taking eleven cautious steps to get around your own kitchen when one swift pivot used to do the job. You must live with the tight anxiety whenever you walk into a roomful of people, and the near-panic of the questions you ask yourself:

Do I just imagine it that I can't seem to turn over in bed any more? Why does everyone ask me to repeat on the telephone? If I stand or walk near other people how will I keep from knocking them down? How will I cut my meat? Do people notice anything wrong?

As I look back, however, I recall that somehow this was not an unhappy period. Finding that I could accomplish so much by my own will and by concentration was one of the many heartening things that were making my life over into a new pattern. Vividly I remember the pursuit of my left pocket. I had made the melancholy discovery that I could not put my left hand in the pocket and retrieve or place anything there. So I began studying the right hand, the well hand, and tried to teach its little sequence of movements to the left hand. Some time later, delighted, I realized my effort had paid off. Without thinking I had put my left hand in my pocket and pulled something out. This was an achievement I wore like an invisible jewel.

I was amazed to see what the body will do for you if you insist. Walking is an unbelievably complex matter. To keep your balance your arms must swing, but mine had grown rigid and would not do it naturally. I had to keep a straight back or my chest would contract still more and make me grotesquely round-shouldered.

And every day I walked. In snow or rain or sun I walked and walked, trying to remember all these things at once. *See that bush ahead? I'm going to swing my left arm till we reach it. . . . I'll think only about straightening my back until we come to the first mailbox. . . .* For weeks in my neighborhood dogs barked and children stared at the solitary walker with the unreal gait. They've long since stopped staring—they are used to me now.

I never suffered from the crashing falls which are the curse of most Parkinsonians, nor was I afflicted with the terrible tremor which is characteristic. I think my determination not to have these helped fend them off. Whenever I noticed the slightest trembling I stopped whatever I was doing and instantly did exercises. But I knew this could not go on forever. I knew only too well I was on an escalator which was moving down while I was trying to run up. I could not shout down the fact that Parkinsonism is a progressive disease.

In the spring of 1958 I went to the Pisgah Mountains of North Carolina after a lecture date, to see the azaleas brilliant on the mountaintop and to write and walk. I was too early; the inn was lost in rain clouds and it was chill and dark. But there was an isolated road there, and down the middle of that empty road ran a white line that seemed to stretch from me to infinity. Here was my fogbound gymnasium where, all alone, I could practice the "Hofkosh pace." Every day I did my four miles. I did deep knee-bends, touched my toes—and walked. If anyone had asked me why, I would have been hard put for a reply. The chances seemed one hundred to zero against my getting back my health. But I could not imagine laying down my weapons in the middle of the fight. And somehow I had the unshakable faith that if I could just manage to hang on, somewhere a door would open.

And then this door did, indeed, open.

Last summer I learned that a young surgeon, Dr. Irving S. Cooper of New York University and St. Barnabas Hospital, had made an exciting discovery seven years previously while operating on a middle-aged man with Parkinsonism. Dr. Cooper had expected—because then it was all that surgeons could expect—to relieve his patient's trembling only at the terrible cost of replacing it with semiparalysis. But a small artery in the man's brain suddenly hemorrhaged. Dr. Cooper tied off the artery, thus cutting the blood supply to an area deep in the brain tissue called the thalamus. Next day to his amazement the man's tremors ceased and his limbs functioned normally.

With this clue to work on, Dr. Cooper began an intensive study of the nerve centers in the brain that seem to govern Parkinsonism. He has refined his technique until now, after more than a thousand operations, he can expect genuine improvement in 80 per cent of his patients. His method is to deaden permanently a part of the thalamus by an injection of tiny drops of alcohol. Such surgery cannot aid all Parkinsonians since age and physical condition are limiting factors. Few over sixty-five can qualify, but for many in a lower age group it can hold out hope.

I redoubled my exercising, determined to bring to the operation the strongest body I could make. Some medical opinion goes contrary to Dr. Cooper, holding that surgery for Parkinsonians should be used only as a last resort, usually when the patient is old and almost bed-ridden. But Dr. Cooper feels that the cases should be caught early, while the sufferer is still strong. I agreed. I could not wait on the sidelines for a shambling old age. I wanted to face it while I was as strong as possible. I was playing to win.

This was my first operation, and it never occurred to me I would not walk to it under my own steam. When the morning arrived I found myself flat on my back with the long, narrow corridor ceiling sweeping over me. I had a childish urge to catch at something to slow me down. And then I realized: *I am in it now. I have made the decision, and there is nothing more to think about.*

The ceilings stopped racing and an X-ray technician came and stood at my side. He chatted with me and asked, as people do, "What distant part of the globe are you going to next?"

I was thinking of another "globe," much smaller, and of the very personal and remarkable journey that was about to begin inside it.

Dr. Cooper came and the operation began. A local anesthetic is used so that surgeons can keep checking on the patient's reactions. I was conscious all during the operation and I was glad of it. I heard a grinding noise and thought it sounded like someone sawing into lime-stone. The surgeon was making a hole the size of a dime in my skull. (Absurd as it sounds, I found myself thinking it was not such a bad time to have one's head shaved: wigs are all the rage!) As the team worked I knew they were probing slowly, carefully toward the thala-mus, the troublemaker. And they talked to me. They knew my nick-names.

"Maggie, can you raise your arm?"

"Now clench your fist, Peggy."

They tested constantly for flexibility in my wrist and mobility in my fingers. I never knew so much hand-holding could go on during an operation, but it was strangely comforting.

I do not know what phase the operation had reached when I was suddenly aware of an extraordinary feeling. I just knew the doctors were doing the right thing. I could tell by a kind of inner harmony, almost an ecstasy. And soon, answering my instinctive thoughts, Dr. Cooper was saying, "Maggie, everything's fine."

At that instant I wanted terribly to take a deep breath. I was floating in a dream world, suspended, hesitating to move even a fraction without instructions—and the breath hovered, light as a bird's wing. Then I accepted the gift and breathed deeply.

The next few weeks were one continuous Christmas, every second or third day bringing its own gift. First, my left arm swung and swung and swung from the socket as if it wanted to take off on its own, like an animated baseball bat. Then my back began to straighten up as the iron-stiff muscle bands gradually freed themselves. Walking again became a happy thing; I had always known it could be a pleasure, but in the long months of my illness it had been such an effort that rhythm and joy of motion had been forgotten.

Not all the gifts were pleasant ones. There was an invisible magnet which seemed to be dragging my hands down to earth. In retrospect I think this downward drag was a reaction to the spectacular release which had freed me, but at moments I lay in my criblike hospital bed fighting off grief and fright. The worst sensation was that a floating chunk of fog, about the size of a suitcase, seemed to block my arms. When I found this slab of fog a barricade between me and my typewriter, I was bitterly disappointed.

What was happening was that the cells and fibers in my brain were slowly readjusting from the effects of the operation. I did not know this then, but I did know from my long months of physical therapy that if I kept hammering doggedly at one difficulty, time would reward me, and that a day or so later I would find serenity in a small success, a small but increased ability.

Then came a morning when I was given, as usual, a fresh hospital gown to put on and I discovered that without even thinking I had tied the little laces at the back of my neck. A friend came to take me for an outing in her car and before I realized it I had opened the door and jumped in. In the days which I now thought of as B.C.— before Cooper—it might have taken me half a morning to tie those laces, and it surely would have taken two strong-armed friends to help me into that car.

Dr. Cooper sent me back to the Institute to complete my rehabilitation, and my procession up the corridors there felt to me like a welcoming parade up Broadway. The therapists, doctors and elevator boys ran after me as I walked heel-toe, heel-toe with arms swinging like a metronome, and there was Jack Hofkosh waiting for me with a beaming face. At the Institute I was again stretched and flexed. I lifted weights. I learned to tango and do a cha-cha-cha.

About that time I met Donald Grazier, who also was battling to win over his typewriter keys. From birth, Donald had malformed arms too short to reach the typewriter keys—but one weekend he typed seventeen flawless pages of a thesis for a fellow student. I thought of an old saying: "I cried because I had no shoes, and then I saw a man who had no feet." And I kept banging away at the typewriter keys, and finally conquered them. My fingers remembered old movements, and the fogbank before my eyes slowly floated away.

Even today, at my home in Connecticut, I keep reminding myself dutifully of Dr. Cooper's sober warning that although he had relieved Parkinsonism in my left side, my right side was also lightly involved and that this may some day require a second operation. No one can say with certainty how the disease starts or stops, how slowly or how swiftly it progresses; doctors agree that my best insurance is to keep up my resolute exercising every day. But nowadays my fingers are more and more often loading my cameras, changing their lenses, and turning their winding buttons as I practice the simple blessed business of living and working again. For me—and for hundreds like me—the light is falling into dark places, the world is beating at my windows.

VII
MEMORIES

Richard Kool

THE NORMAN CONQUEST

by Winston S. Churchill

MARCH 26, 1956

> *Nine hundred years ago, England was conquered for the last time when William of Normandy vanquished Harold the Saxon at the Battle of Hastings. This account of the conquest is taken from Sir Winston Churchill's A History of the English-Speaking Peoples, serialized in the U.S. by* LIFE. *Sir Winston had almost completed the History by 1940 when he laid it aside to assume direction of Britain's war effort. In that year, England faced the prospect of another invasion, as total as William's in its intent, planned by Hitler's Nazis, who also used Norman ports. Happily, Adolf proved to be no William.*

William the Conqueror's invasion of England was planned like a business enterprise. The resources of Normandy were obviously unequal to the task; but the Duke's name was famous throughout the feudal world, and the idea of seizing and dividing England commended itself to the martial nobility of many lands. The barons of Normandy at the Council of Lillebonne refused to countenance the enterprise officially. It was the Duke's venture, and not that of Normandy. But the bulk of them hastened to subscribe their quota of knights and ships. Brittany sent a large contingent. It must be remembered that some of the best stocks from Roman Britain had found refuge there, establishing a strong blood strain which had preserved a continuity with the Classic Age and with the British race. But all France was deeply interested. Mercenaries came from Flanders, and even from beyond the Alps; Normans from South Italy and Spain, nobles and knights, answered the advertisement. The shares in this enterprise were represented by knights or ships, and it was plainly engaged that the lands of the slaughtered English would be divided in proportion to the contributions, subject of course to a bonus for good work in the field. During the summer of 1066 this great gathering of audacious buccaneers, land-hungry, war-hungry, assembled in a merry company around St. Valéry, at the mouth of the Somme. Ships had been built in all the French ports from the spring onwards, and by the beginning of August a considerable fleet and about seven thousand men, of whom the majority were persons of rank and quality, were ready to follow the renowned Duke and share the lands and wealth of England.

But the winds were contrary. For six whole weeks there was no day when the south wind blew. The heterogeneous army, bound by no tie of feudal allegiance, patriotism, or moral theme, began to bicker and grumble. Only William's repute as a managing director and the rich pillage to be expected held them together. At length extreme measures had to be taken with the weather. The bones of St. Edmund were brought from the church of St. Valéry and carried with military and religious pomp along the seashore. This proved effective, for the very next day the wind changed, not indeed to the south, but to the southwest. William thought this sufficient, and gave the signal. The whole fleet put to sea, with all their stores, weapons, coats of mail, and great numbers of horses.

On September 28 the fleet came safely to anchor in Pevensey Bay. There was no opposition to the landing. The local "fyrd" had been called out this year four times already to watch the coast, and having, in true English style, come to the conclusion that the danger was past because it had not yet arrived had gone back to their homes. William landed, as the tale goes, and fell flat on his face as he stepped out of the boat. "See," he said, turning the omen into a favorable channel, "I have taken England with both my hands."

He occupied himself with organizing his army, raiding for supplies in Sussex, and building some defensive works for the protection of his fleet and base. Thus a fortnight passed.

Meanwhile Harold and his housecarls, or bodyguard, sadly depleted by the slaughter of the battle of Stamford Bridge in the north (where they had repulsed a Scandinavian invasion), jingled down Watling Street on their ponies, marching night and day to London. They covered the two hundred miles in seven days. In London the King gathered all the forces he could, and most of the principal persons in Wessex and Kent hastened to join his standard, bringing their retainers and local militia with them. Remaining only five days in London, Harold marched out towards Pevensey, and in the evening of October 13 took up his position upon the slope of a hill which barred the direct march upon the capital.

King Harold had great confidence in his redoubtable axmen, and it was in good heart that he formed his shield wall on the morning of October 14. There is a great dispute about the numbers engaged. Some modern authorities suppose the battle was fought by five or six thousand Norman knights and men-at-arms, with a few thousand archers, against eight to ten thousand ax- and spearmen, but the numbers on both sides may have been fewer. However it may be, at the first streak of dawn William set out from his camp at Pevensey, resolved to put all to the test; and Harold, eight miles away, awaited him in resolute array.

As the battle began Ivo Taillefer, the minstrel knight who had claimed the right to make the first attack, advanced up the hill on horseback, throwing his lance and sword into the air and catching them before the astonished English. He then charged deep into the English ranks, and was slain. The cavalry charges of William's mail-clad knights, cumbersome in manoeuver, beat in vain upon the dense, ordered masses of the English. Neither the arrow hail nor the assaults of the horsemen could prevail against them. William's left wing of cavalry was thrown into disorder, and retreated rapidly down the hill. On this the troops on Harold's right, who were mainly the local "fyrd," broke their ranks in eager pursuit. William, in the center, turned his disciplined squadrons upon them and cut them to pieces.

The Normans then reformed their ranks and began a second series of charges upon the English masses, subjecting them in the intervals to severe archery.

It has often been remarked that this part of the action resembles the afternoon at Waterloo, when Ney's cavalry exhausted themselves upon the British squares, torn by artillery in the intervals. In both cases the tortured infantry stood unbroken. Never, it was said, had the Norman knights met foot soldiers of this stubbornness. They were utterly unable to break through the shield walls, and they suffered serious losses from deft blows of the axmen, or from javelins or clubs hurled from the ranks behind. But the arrow showers took a cruel toll. So closely were the English wedged that the wounded could not be removed, and the dead scarcely found room in which to sink upon the ground.

The autumn afternoon was far spent before any result had been achieved, and it was then that William adopted the time-honored ruse of a feigned retreat. He had seen how readily Harold's right had quitted their positions in pursuit after the first repulse of the Normans. He now organized a sham retreat in apparent disorder, while keeping a powerful force in his own hands. The housecarls around Harold preserved their discipline and kept their ranks, but the sense of relief to the less trained forces after these hours of combat was such that seeing their enemy in flight proved irresistible. They surged forward on the impulse of victory, and when halfway down the hill were savagely slaughtered by William's horsemen.

There remained, as the dusk grew, only the valiant bodyguard who fought round the King and his standard. His brothers, Gyrth and Leofwine, had already been killed. William now directed his archers to shoot high into the air, so that the arrows would fall behind the shield wall, and one of these pierced Harold in the right eye, inflicting a mortal wound. He fell at the foot of the royal standard, unconquerable except by death, which does not count in honor. The hard-fought battle was now decided. The last formed body of troops was broken, though by no means overwhelmed. They withdrew into the woods behind, and William, who had fought in the foremost ranks and had three horses killed under him, could claim the victory. Nevertheless the pursuit was heavily checked. There is a sudden deep ditch on the reverse slope of the hill of Hastings, into which large numbers of Norman horsemen fell, and in which they were butchered by the infuriated English lurking in the wood.

The dead King's naked body, wrapped only in a robe of purple, was hidden among the rocks of the bay. His mother in vain offered the weight of the body in gold for permission to bury him in holy ground. The Norman Duke's answer was that Harold would be more fittingly laid upon the Saxon shore which he had given his life to defend. The body was later transferred to Waltham Abbey, which he had founded. Although here the English once again accepted conquest and bowed in a new destiny, yet ever must the name of Harold be honored in the Island for which he and his famous housecarls fought indomitably to the end.

The Conquest was the supreme achievement of the Norman race. It linked the history of England anew to Europe, and prevented forever a drift into the narrower orbit of a Scandinavian empire. Henceforward English history marched with that of races and lands south of the Channel.

Once the secular conquest had been made secure, William turned to the religious sphere. The key appointment was the Archbishopric of Canterbury. In 1070 the Saxon Stigand was deposed and succeeded by Lanfranc. A Lombard of high administrative ability, Lanfranc rapidly infused new life into the English Church. In a series of councils such as had not been held in England since the days of Theodore, greatest of Rome's seventh-century missionaries, organization and discipline were reformed.

The spirit of the long-vanished Roman Empire, revived by the Catholic Church, returned once more to our Island, bringing with it three dominant ideas. First, a Europe in which nationalism or even the conception of nationality had no place, but where one general theme of conduct and law united the triumphant martial classes upon a plane far above race. Secondly, the idea of monarchy, in the sense that Kings were the expression of the class hierarchy over which they presided and the arbiters of its frequently conflicting interests. Thirdly, there stood triumphant the Catholic Church, combining in a strange fashion Roman imperialism and Christian ethics, pervaded by the social and military system of the age, jealous for its own interests and authority, but still preserving all that was left of learning and art.

Two decades of anarchy followed the death of William's son, Henry I (1135), as Stephen and Maud (also known as Matilda) warred for the throne, and a starved and pillaged people groaned "that Christ and his saints were asleep." Strikingly, however, the horror of those years, far from discrediting the monarchy, convinced the people that only a strong monarchy could secure life and property. The need of the hour found the man: Henry II, first of the Plantagenets, son of Maud and Geoffrey of Anjou. Although his dominions in France were extensive and he was actually more a French than an English king, he gave the Island "one of the most pregnant and decisive reigns in English history."

The new sovereign ruled an empire, and, as his subjects boasted, his warrant ran "from the Arctic Ocean to the Pyrenees." England to him was but one—the most solid though perhaps the least attractive—of his provinces. But he gave to England that effectual element of external control which was indispensable to the growth of national unity. He was accepted by English and Norman as the ruler of both races and of the whole country. The memories of Hastings were confounded in his person, and after the hideous anarchy of civil war between robber barons all due attention was paid to his commands. Thus, though a Frenchman, with foreign speech and foreign modes, he shaped our country in a fashion of which the outline remains to the present day.

After a hundred years of being the encampment of an invading army and the battleground of its quarrelsome officers and their descendants, England became finally and for all time a coherent kingdom, based upon Christianity and upon that Latin civilization which recalled the message of ancient Rome. Henry Plantagenet first brought England, Scotland, and Ireland into a certain common relationship; he re-established the system of royal government which his grandfather, Henry I, had prematurely erected. He relaid the foundations of a central power, based upon the exchequer and the judiciary, which was ultimately to supersede the feudal system of William the Conqueror.

The King gathered up and cherished the Anglo-Saxon tradition of self-government under royal command in shire and borough; he developed and made permanent "assizes" as they survive today. It is to him we owe the enduring fact that the English-speaking race all over the world is governed by the English Common Law rather than by the Roman. By his Constitutions of Clarendon he sought to fix the relationship of Church and State and to force the Church in its temporal character to submit itself to the life and law of the nation. In this endeavor he had, after a deadly struggle, to retreat, and it was left to Henry VIII, though centuries later, to avenge his predecessor by destroying the shrine of St. Thomas at Canterbury.

A vivid picture is painted of this gifted and, for a while, enviable man: square, thick-set, bull-necked, with powerful arms and coarse, rough hands; his legs bandy from endless riding; a large, round head and closely cropped red hair; a freckled face; a voice harsh and cracked. Intense love of the chase; other loves, which the Church deplored and Queen Eleanor resented; frugality in food and dress; days entirely concerned with public business; travel unceasing; moods various. It was said that he was always gentle and calm in times of urgent peril, but became bad-tempered and capricious when the pressure relaxed. "He was more tender to dead soldiers than to the living, and found far more sorrow in the loss of those who were slain than comfort in the love of those who remained." He journeyed hotfoot around his many dominions, arriving unexpectedly in England when he was thought to be in the South of France. He carried with him in his tours of each province wains loaded with ponderous rolls which represented the office files of his day. His Court and train gasped and panted behind him. Sometimes, when he had appointed an early start, he was sleeping till noon, with all the wagons and pack horses awaiting him fully laden. Sometimes he would be off hours before the time he had fixed, leaving everyone to catch up as best they could. Everything was stirred and molded by him in England, as also in his other much greater estates, which he patrolled with tireless attention.

But this twelfth-century monarch, with his lusts and sports, his hates and his schemes, was no materialist; he was the Lord's Anointed; he commanded, with the Archbishop of Canterbury—"those two strong steers that drew the plough of England"—the whole allegiance of his subjects. The offices of religion, the fear of eternal damnation, the hope of even greater realms beyond the grave, accompanied him from hour to hour. At times he was smitten with remorse and engulfed in repentance. He drew all possible delights and satisfactions from this world and the next. He is portrayed to us in convulsions both of spiritual exaltation and abasement. This was no secluded monarch: the kings of those days were as accessible to all classes as a modern President of the United States. People broke in upon him at all hours with business, with tidings, with gossip, with visions, with complaints. Talk rang high in the King's presence and to His Majesty's face among the nobles and courtiers, and the jester, invaluable monitor, castigated all impartially with unstinted license.

Few mortals have led so full a life as Henry II or have drunk so deeply of the cups of triumph and sorrow. In later life he fell out with Queen Eleanor. When she was over fifty and he but forty-two he is said to have fallen in love with "Fair Rosamond," a damosel of high degree and transcendent beauty, and generations have enjoyed the romantic tragedy of Queen Eleanor penetrating the protecting maze at Woodstock by the clue of a silken thread and offering her hapless supplanter the hard choice between the dagger and the poisoned cup. Tiresome investigators have undermined this excellent tale, but it certainly should find its place in any history worthy of the name.

When Henry had named his intimate friend and counselor, Thomas Becket, to be Archbishop of Canterbury, he had counted on having a conveniently malleable ecclesiastical colleague. Henry deceived himself: pious, proud and stubbornly independent, Becket fought every attempt by Henry to tighten royal authority on Church policies and offices.

So—500 years after the Synod of Whitby bowed to Rome and almost 400 years before Henry VIII would finally make the fate-

ful break with Rome—there came this battle between two friends to dramatize and to sharpen the thousand-year conflict.

Henry Plantagenet, first of all his line, with all the fire of his nature, received the news of Becket's defiance when surrounded by his knights and nobles. He was transported with passion. "What a pack of fools and cowards," he cried, "I have nourished in my house, that not one of them will avenge me of this turbulent priest!" Another version says "of this upstart clerk." A council was immediately summoned to devise measures for reasserting the royal authority. In the main they shared the King's anger. Second thoughts prevailed. With all the stresses that existed in that fierce and ardent society, it was not possible that the realm could support a fearful conflict between the two sides of life represented by Church and State.

But meanwhile another train of action was in process. Four knights had heard the King's bitter words spoken in the full circle. They traveled fast to the coast. They crossed the Channel. They called for horses and rode to Canterbury. There on December 29, 1170, they found the Archbishop in the cathedral. The scene and the tragedy are famous. He confronted them with Cross and miter, fearless and resolute in warlike action, a master of the histrionic arts. After haggard parleys they fell upon him, cut him down with their swords, and left him bleeding like Julius Caesar, with a score of wounds to cry for vengeance.

This tragedy was fatal to the King. The murder of one of the foremost of God's servants, like the breaking of a feudal oath, struck at the heart of the age. All England was filled with terror. They acclaimed the dead Archbishop as a martyr; and immediately it appeared that his relics healed incurable diseases, and robes that he had worn by their mere touch relieved minor ailments. Here indeed was a crime, vast and inexpiable. When Henry heard the appalling news he was prostrated with grief and fear. All the elaborate process of law which he had sought to set on foot against this rival power was brushed aside by a brutal, bloody act; and though he had never dreamed that such a deed would be done, there were his own hot words, spoken before so many witnesses, to fasten on him, for that age at least, the guilt of murder, and, still worse, sacrilege.

The immediately following years were spent in trying to recover what he had lost by a great parade of atonement for his guilt. He made pilgrimages to the shrine of the murdered Archbishop. He subjected himself to public penances. On several anniversaries, stripped to the waist and kneeling humbly, he submitted to be scourged by the triumphant monks. Under this display of contrition and submission the King labored perseveringly to regain the rights of State and in 1172 he made his peace with the Papacy on comparatively easy terms. To many deep-delving historians it seems that in fact, though not in form, he had by the end of his life re-established the main principles of his authority in Church affairs, which are after all in harmony with what the English nation or any virile and rational race would mean to have as their law. Certainly the Papacy supported him in his troubles with his sons. The knights, it is affirmed, regained their salvation in the holy wars. But Becket's somber sacrifice had not been in vain. Until the Reformation the Church retained the system of ecclesiastical courts independent of the royal authority, and the right of appeal to Rome, two of the major points upon which Becket had defied the King.

It is a proof of the quality of the age that these fierce contentions, shaking the souls of men, should have been so rigorously and yet so evenly fought out. In modern conflicts and revolutions in some great states, bishops and archbishops have been sent by droves to concentration camps, or pistoled in the nape of the neck in the well-warmed, brilliantly lighted corridor of a prison. What claim have we to vaunt a superior civilization to Henry II's times? We are sunk in a barbarism all the deeper because it is tolerated by moral lethargy and covered with a veneer of scientific conveniences.

Through all such struggles whirling around the throne, one historic work steadily progressed: the Law. Now, a century after William the Conqueror, his great-grandson daringly elaborated and advanced what the Norman Conquest had begun.

Henry II threw open to litigants in the royal courts a startling new procedure—trial by jury. *Regale quoddam beneficium*, a contemporary called it—a royal boon; and the description illuminates both the origin of the jury and the part it played in the triumph of the Common Law. Henry did not invent the jury; he put it to a new purpose. The idea of the jury is the one great contribution of the Franks to the English legal system, for, unknown in this country before the Conquest, the germ of it lies far back in the practice of the Carolingian kings. In origin the jury was a royal instrument of administrative convenience: the King had the right to summon a body of men to bear witness under oath about the truth of any question concerning the royal interest. It was through this early form of jury that William the Conqueror had determined the Crown rights in the great Domesday survey. The genius of Henry II, perceiving new possibilities in such a procedure, turned to regular use in the courts an instrument which so far had only been used for administrative purposes.

Only the King had the right to summon a jury. Henry accordingly did not grant it to private courts, but restricted it to those who sought justice before the royal judges. It was an astute move. Until this time both civil and criminal cases had been decided through the oath, the ordeal, or the duel. The court would order one of the litigants to muster a body of men who would swear to the justice of his cause and whom it was hoped God would punish if they swore falsely; or condemn him, under the supervision of a priest, to carry a red-hot iron, or eat a morsel of bread, or be plunged in a pool of water. If the iron did not burn or the bread choke or the water reject him so that he could not sink, then Divine Providence was adjudged to have granted a visible sign that the victim was innocent.

The duel, or trial by battle, was a Norman innovation based on the modern theory that the God of Battles will strengthen the arm of the righteous, and was at one time much favored for deciding disputes about land. Monasteries and other substantial landowners took the precaution however of assisting the Almighty by retaining professional champions to protect their property and their rights.

All this left small room for debate on points of law. In a more rational age men were beginning to distrust such antics, and indeed the Church refused to sanction the ordeal during the same year that Magna Carta was sealed. Thus trial by jury quickly gained favor.

But the old processes were long in dying. If a defendant preferred to take his case before God, man could not forbid him, and the ordeal therefore was not abolished outright. Hence a later age was to know the horrors of the *peine forte et dure*—the compulsion of the accused by slow pressure to death to agree to put himself before a jury. Time swept this away; yet so late as 1818 a litigant nonplused the judges by an appeal to trial by battle and compelled Parliament to abolish this ancient procedure.

The jury system has come to stand for all we mean by English justice, because so long as a case has to be scrutinized by twelve honest men, defendant and plaintiff alike have a safeguard from arbitrary perversion of the law. It is this which distinguishes the law administered in English courts from Continental legal systems based on Roman law. Thus amidst the great process of centralization the old principle was preserved, and endures to this day, that law flows from the people, and is not given by the King.

It was in these fateful and formative years that the English-speaking peoples began to devise methods of determining legal disputes which survive in substance to this day. A man can only be accused of a civil or criminal offense which is clearly defined and known to the law. The judge is an umpire. He adjudicates on such evidence as the parties choose to produce. Witnesses must testify in public and on oath. They are examined and cross-examined, not by the judge, but by the litigrants themselves or their legally qualified and privately hired representatives. The truth of their testimony is weighed not by the judge but by twelve good men and true, and it is only when this jury has determined the facts that the judge is empowered to impose sentence, punishment, or penalty according to law.

All this might seem very obvious, even a platitude, until one contemplates the alternative system which still dominates a large portion of the world. Under Roman law, and systems derived from it, a trial in those turbulent centuries, and in some countries even today, is often an inquisition. The judge makes his own investigation into the civil wrong or the public crime, and such investigation is largely uncontrolled. The suspect can be interrogated in private. He must answer all questions put to him. His right to be represented by a legal adviser is restricted. The witnesses against him can testify in secret and in his absence. And only when these processes have been accomplished is the accusation or charge against him formulated and published. Thus often arise secret intimidation, enforced confessions, torture, and blackmailed pleas of guilty.

These sinister dangers were extinguished from the Common Law of England more than six centuries ago. By the time Henry II's great-grandson, Edward I, had died, English criminal and civil procedure had settled into a mold and tradition which in the mass govern the English-speaking peoples today. In all claims and disputes, whether they concerned the grazing lands of the Middle West, the oilfields of California, the sheep runs and gold mines of Australia, or the territorial rights of the Maoris, these rules have obtained, at any rate in theory, according to the procedure and mode of trial evolved by the English Common Law.

MAINE WINTER

by Robert P. Tristram Coffin

FEBRUARY 12, 1945

> *In these poems, the late Robert P. Tristram Coffin describes the winter moods of Maine as he saw them through a LIFE photographer's lens. To point out the scenes he wanted to write about, Mr. Coffin spent a subzero week tramping around Brunswick, Maine, with Photographer Kosti Ruohomaa. Then, with the photographs before him, he wrote for LIFE these poems about his native state. Novelist and teacher as well, Coffin was one of the foremost poets in the U.S. He won the 1936 Pulitzer Prize for poetry.*

THE COAST

Maine in winter is a fishing-shack
With the stovepipe sticking through a pane,
Slatted lobster traps picked out by snow
Like ribs on some starved martyr of old Spain.

The largest farms of all in Maine are blue,
They curve up from the South Pole and Cape Horn,
White codfish swim through them like nebulae
And lobsters with their claws built out of thorn.

Where the old world's granite bones show bare,
The farmers fish and double up their labors,
They plow the icy sea in little boats
With sudden death and beauty next-door neighbors.
They make a friend of blue eternity
And write their brave names on the nameless sea.

THE LAND

This home of winter is the black and white
Euclid land, all angles and right lines,
A country made of ivory and light,
Snow-fences and the point-lace of the pines.

The steep road slanting down to the dark sea
Smokes with long fires of the drifting snow,
Green blazes of the balsams lick the sky,
And islands climb the ocean, row on row.
The wind's a pillow that a man can lean on
As he goes down to white boats on the bay,
It has the whole Atlantic to come clean on,
Maine seems a bright place made but yesterday.
Here are cut crystals with the jet between
Where snowsqualls blossom on the evergreen.

THE PEOPLE

Six out of twelve months of the Maine State year
The farmer lives in his kitchen, very near
Heaven, with his spruce and beechwood heat,
His thoughts and talk, the news, hot things to eat.
The long nights, high winds, and sub-zero weather
Bring love and lamp, bring man and wife together.
Joined by the cookstove, John and Mrs. Hummer
With wide smiles and warm work make indoor summer.

Of course, the farmer has some chores outside.
Likely there he builds for a giant's bride

Cubistic wedding-cakes of new-sawn boards.
Out in the breezes cutting like blue swords
Horses and he join breaths and heap up clear
White-pine ribs for houses of next year.

THE TOWN
Brunswick had bright citizens long ago:
Longfellow, Hawthorne, Harriet Beecher Stowe.
It still has bright ones; elm trees tall and old
And engines breathing high in winter cold.

The shade trees after ice-storms are entire
Laces made of filigrees of fire;
Folks come out of movies to their cars
And find a town of crystals and crushed stars,
They say good evening on the shopping street
With diamonds ankle-deep around their feet.
Winter is no dark time in our town,
It is angels shaking feathers down,
And windows blazing like the wind-blown coal,
A constant Christmas halfway to the Pole.

ITALY'S MYTH OF AMERICA

by Carlo Levi

JULY 7, 1947

> Among the poor peasants of southern Italy, the impression
> of America as the enchanted land of big cities, untold
> riches and gold teeth is so fanciful and imaginative that it
> constitutes a modern myth. It is here described by Carlo
> Levi, author of the best-selling Christ Stopped at Eboli,
> who lived among the peasants of Lucania after he was
> banished from Rome by Mussolini in 1935 for his
> anti-Fascist writings.

Everywhere people think they know Italy, and indeed no other
country in the world is better known, none more open and welcoming. Everyone knows Rome's baroque sunsets, with golden clouds
hanging over the pine trees and the sensual fountains of Bernini; the
amorous Oriental marbles of Venice; the intellectual grace of Florence;
the Persian colors of medieval Siena; the classical Bay of Naples, home
of dolphins and tritons; the monotonous Arab enchantment of Sicily.

Yet far from the illustrious cities and the Roman roads there lies
another Italy, the Italy of the peasants. Everywhere south of the Alps
this Italy may be found—just beyond the dusty suburbs. Here is an-

other nation. This peasant civilization is found in untouched, original form in the interior wastelands of the south, where there is no commerce from the sea, and the barren mountaintops of the lower Apennines seem to repel outsiders.

This is one of the poorest regions of Europe. Here there is little room for joy or hope. The melancholy loneliness of the peasant world results not only from the physical isolation of the villages, the bad roads, the impassable mountains, the climate, the malaria but also from the psychological atmosphere of this region. It is the sad but noble loneliness of a people richly endowed with the ancient virtues of patience, hospitality, human understanding and natural justice, but rudely shocked by "man's inhumanity to man," locked up in a world remote from time and history, behind a wall of ancient customs and usages, surrounded by magic and pantheism. In this solitude, peopled by archaic pre-Christian divinities, by animal and earthly spirits and magic influences, man feels estranged from himself, hopelessly banished from impossible paradises. Upon such concepts the peasants have built a whole world of fancy and fable—myths of bygone days, stories of treasure hidden in caves and tree trunks and under solitary boulders.

Among the hundreds of myths cherished by the peasants one stands out among the rest by providing the perfect avenue of escape from grim realities. It embodies fable and fact, concrete existence and romance, necessity and imagination. It is their version, magical and real at the same time, of an earthly paradise, lost and then found again: the myth of America.

This myth of America has always been one of the chief incentives to emigration. And the myth, in turn, has been strengthened, enriched and modified by the experiences of the emigrant in his actual contact with the New World. Because the peasants are steeped in magic, there is an overlap of reality and imagination in their minds. Together they make a dual superreality which is to them very simple but which cannot easily fit into the unimaginative thinking of a rational modern man. America has come to be an essential part of the daily life of the south Italian village, a social and economic element mingled with their concepts of bread, work, family and sentiment of every kind, and at the same time a mystical sustenance and the basis of a magical religion.

In its time Italian emigration was a revolutionary phenomenon, a massive effort to break up the "farm bloc." An entire people left their native land for unknown shores. Most of them stayed there. But a few came back, and a new class arose in the unchanging villages—the "Americans."

Italian mass emigration dates from the 1880's, a period of economic and political upheaval in Italy and of large-scale demand for manual labor in the U.S. It is significant, however, that the Italian peasants had begun long before 1880 to think of America as a dream-refuge from their woes. In 1853, for instance, the inhabitants of the village of Vasto sent a petition to the Bourbon minister of the interior, asking for an end to deforestation, couched in these terms:

> Your Excellency: His Majesty's faithful subjects beg to inform Your Excellency that the woods belonging to both charitable institutions and private individuals are being cut down and the land cleared for ˜ultivation, to the detriment of our pastures. For lack of firewood the undersigned and all other inhabitants of the Abruzzi region will be compelled to emigrate to California.

It never occurred to the peasants of Vasto that they might emigrate to a more prosperous district of the Kingdom of Naples or to some other European country. Their minds were filled with the image of a faraway promised land in California although mass emigration had not yet begun and America was still out of reach. But once emigration started, it increased steadily and reached its peak between 1903 and 1908. Then came a brief letup—and then a second wave, lasting right up to the beginning of World War I. In 1913, for instance, there were almost four hundred thousand Italian emigrants to America. Entire sections of Italy were emptied. Eventually a good many emigrants came back home, though between the two wars this happened only rarely (except around 1929 when the crash in the U.S. and the rosy promises of Fascist propaganda caused some emigrants to return to Italy, where they found themselves stuck).

Emigration has had a tremendous effect on many towns. San Fele, for example, is a little Italian village of twelve thousand inhabitants. Yet sixteen thousand former natives of San Fele have emigrated to America and have never come back except for brief visits. The chief ice-cream dispenser of San Fele came home and stayed for four years, but then he finally left again for the country of his adoption. There are streets in San Fele where the emigrants' houses remained empty and roofless in order to avoid the payment of taxes. Other streets are lined with houses belonging to "returned Americans," well kept and comfortable, with shiny doorknobs and green shutters.

American influence on everyday life is apparent everywhere in southern Italy. The language of the peasants is strewn with words coined in the U.S. that are a queer mixture of English and Italian. The oldest is *ticchetto* (ticket), symbol of the first stage of the great adventure. The shovel, commonest tool of the Italian highway- and railroad-builder in America, became in Italian *la sciabbola*. American place names took on a softened and familiar sound like Massaciusette and Broccolino. I have often asked old "Americans" to tell me about the places they had seen over there, but they are often very vague on the subject. It seems almost as if, after all their struggle to attain the promised land, they had never actually looked upon its face or really entered it but had been content to linger on the threshold and feel its existence around them. They gave me only the most general descriptions: "a big, big city" or "a big bridge between New York and Broccolino." They have more distinct memories of the street where they lived, the store kept by their relatives and the limited circle of friends from their own village. They have brought back with them from this narrow world, where they were at last free from fear, all sorts of souvenirs. Many of them have returned with their mouths sparkling with gold teeth. Others have brought back calendars, photographs, newspaper clippings and advertisements, which were pinned up on the walls of their homes and their shop windows and turned yellow with age, covered with flies in the sun. The baker of Avigliano still keeps calendars advertising the bakery of his cousin in New York. The peasants' thoughts and aspirations came to be centered in faraway, friendly America rather than in Naples and Rome.

America is present not only in the language and memories of the peasants but in the objects of everyday life and the tools of their trades: razors, scissors, armchairs. These importations from the other side are the outward signs of the peasants' religious devotion to all that is American. They very often use American weights and measures—inches, feet and pounds—instead of the European metric system. Many village streets, even during the Fascist regime, were called "Via Washington." In fact this is a popular street name all over the regions of Apulia, Basilicata and Calabria.

Family life, relations between the sexes and religion have all been influenced by the journey to America. Strict, old-fashioned morals have been considerably modified; crimes of passion and jealousy have become infrequent; women have cast off many of their shackles; free love and illegitimate children are on the increase. A rather practical reason for such changes is the large number of men who emigrated, leaving their brides at home. In 1901, when the peak of emigration had not yet been reached, there were in Calabria alone 42,963 women with husbands overseas, and this number increased in the following years. At first the men sent back letters and money. The women began to buy new clothes and shoes and to sit in the front pews of the village church beside the gentry. There was, indeed, a certain snobbery about the "Americans." Later some of the husbands returned and built white stucco houses for their families on the main square of the village. Others never came back, and they gradually stopped writing letters and sending money:

> My husband doesn't write from America;
> What can I have done to offend him?

says the deserted bride in an Italian song. She must either sink back into poverty or else acquire a new husband and children.

Some former emigrants, particularly in Apulia and Sicily, have kept their American ways. They are quick-witted and enterprising and in many cases have contributed to the modernization of local life. When I recently revisited Matera, after many years, I found a new public swimming pool built with the savings of a returned "American." But most of the peasants who have come back even after a lapse of many years are exactly the same as they were when they left. While they were away they remained a part of the old community and its civilization. When they return, they soon forget what little English they have learned on the other side, sink their savings into a piece of barren land, pick up their former trade, recover the age-old way of life. The only explanation of their total relapse lies in the nature of the myth of America; indeed the relapse is a conclusive proof of the myth's existence.

The myth of America is no such romantic invention as the "South Sea Islands." It is not a creation of the intellect, such as that last of the myths of Western Europe, "Paris, City of Light," nor is it a social and political myth like that of Soviet Russia. It is a true, a magical myth, the expression of a peasant world, where magic has real power and every object has, in consequence, a dual nature. Because it is my most directly experienced comprehension of the peasants' feeling for America, I refer to a passage in my own book, *Christ Stopped at Eboli*:

> The Kingdom of Naples has perished, and the kingdom of the hopelessly poor is not of this world. Their other world is America. Even America, to the peasants, has a dual nature. It is a land where a man goes to work, where he toils and sweats for his daily bread, where he lays aside a little money only at the cost of endless hardship and privation, where he can die and no one will remember him. At the same time, and with no contradiction in terms, it is an earthly paradise and the promised land. . . . As a place to work, it is indifferent to them; they live there as they would live anywhere else, like animals harnessed to a wagon, heedless of the street where they must pull it. But as an earthly paradise, Jerusalem the golden, it is so sacred as to be untouchable; a man can only gaze at it, even when he is there on the spot, with no hope of attainment.

It is because the peasants see in America the magical vision of both an earthly paradise and a promised land that the myth has its dual nature. So does every image and object belonging to it; for instance, the pictures of Franklin Delano Roosevelt in the peasant houses. This, too, I have tried to comprehend in my book:

> . . . The eyes of the two inseparable guardian angels that looked at me from the wall over the bed. On one side was the black, scowling

face, with its large, inhuman eyes, of the Madonna of Viggiano; on the other a colored print of the sparkling eyes . . . and the hearty grin of President Roosevelt. I never saw other pictures or images than these: not the King nor the Duce, nor even Garibaldi, no famous Italian of any kind, nor any one of the appropriate saints; only Roosevelt and the Madonna of Viggiano never failed to be present. To see them there, one facing the other, in cheap prints, they seemed the two faces of the power that has divided the universe between them. . . . Sometimes a third image formed, along with these two, a trinity: a dollar bill, the last of those brought back from across the sea, or one that had come in the letter of a husband or relative, was tacked up under the Madonna or the President or else between them, like the Holy Ghost or an ambassador from heaven to the world of the dead.

This is the mythical value of the dollar, the *pezzo* of the emigrant's money order to his family at home: it is at one and the same time a bank note with concrete purchasing power in the village, a factor in the national budget because it can purchase foreign imports and, by virtue of its dual magical nature, a gift from the powers above. The dollar bill is chiefly used to honor the Madonna. The peasants pin it to the clothing of religious statues and burn it during the display of fireworks on the feast days of the major saints. In other words the dollar is a sacred object—not in the worship of financial success but in the peasants' magic conception of paradise. Just after the Allied invasion, when the exchange value of the dollar began to fluctuate wildly, the peasants of southern Italy underwent an almost religious crisis. What? The dollar had lost its value. Ten dollars would no longer buy a sheep? This actually weakened the myth of America. The newest official exchange threatens to undermine the faith of the peasants and to have its effect on religious feasts and fireworks, on the worship of the Madonna and the saints.

The Statue of Liberty in the harbor of New York is to the peasants an image of the Madonna, not a black, earthly Madonna but a shimmering white Madonna with a light-bearing torch in her hand that gleams with the most precious and magical of metals—gold. Politicians have been quick to see possibilities in this mythical identification and to play them up to their advantage. During recent local elections the left-wing parties in Apulia joined together on the ballot under the sign of the Statue of Liberty. They won a substantial victory over the conservative barons and landowners, partly because peasants voted for the Madonna of Liberation.

The mythical America, both real and unreal, rooted in fact and fancy, appears in popular songs and poems in a variety of guises: as a definite place where men work for a living, as a place of refuge or escape, as a fairyland, as a land, even as the very edge of the known world. Many songs of family love have America for a background:

> "Mother, give me a hundred lire
> And to America I shall go. . . ."
> "A hundred lire you shall have,
> But to America—no, no, no!"

America enters into the vicissitudes of life in this Calabrian lament for the great earthquake of 1908:

> The beautiful city of Reggio,
> Known as the "fairy queen,"
> Reggio, beautiful Reggio,
>
> Is pitiful to be seen. . . .
> From faraway America
> There came a telegram,
> Asking for our dear mother. . . .

And these lines from a song portray the dual nature of America:

> Here's America for you:
> Hard work and money;
> A cross of gold, but all the same a cross. . . .

After World War I American quotas and Fascist policy in Italy combined to stem the flow of emigration. The bonds between the two countries weakened steadily until the war cut them entirely. Then two unexpected events revived the myth of America. First, the arrival of the American Army on Italian soil. The inhabitants of the promised land had come; these must be messengers from heaven. Certainly they were not as other men, even when they had Italian names because they were the sons and grandsons of emigrants. They were liberators, with powerful weapons, with money jingling in their pockets, and they swept through the villages south of Naples without stopping, like visitors from another planet.

The second event was the arrival, after years of silence, of packages of food and clothing. Communications with the other world were resumed, and there was proof that the lost paradise still existed beyond the seas. An essential and sorely missed part of the peasants' life was restored to them. In the precious packages from America they rediscovered the capital city of their souls. They heard from relatives and friends who had dropped completely out of their ken. At last they had something to talk about besides the gossip of their own village, and they could learn from America how to build themselves a new form of government. The peasants of southern Italy have often shown more interest in American politics than in their own. The election of William Howard Taft, who was considered a friend of the Italians, was greeted with band music and fireworks. When the peasants were called upon to choose between the monarchy and a republic, they had the example of the U.S. in mind. The millions of votes cast that turned Italy into a republic were due in considerable measure to the myth of America.

Since the war a new spirit has grown up among the south Italian peasants. For the first time in history they feel close to their government and ready to take part in the experiment of democracy. With time the myth of America may undergo a change; it may lose its magical character and become rather an inspiration to action. Even then it will remain deeply rooted in two realities: the very old civilization of the peasants and the modern civilization of the New World.

There is in southern Italy a song about America, a lament filled with sorrow but also with patience and resolution:

> America is very long and very wide,
> Surrounded by mountains and the sea.
>
> We came, then, to America,
> We built towns and cities;
>
> We slept on the bare ground,
> Taking our rest like beasts of burden. . . .

The emigrants who built these "towns and cities" have shared in the making of America, not a mythical or magical America, but an immense reality. Where they came from there are still the same ancient villages perched on stony mountains, with all their old problems: poverty, malaria, backward agricultural conditions and, on top of all these, the ravages of war. There, too, Italians must build new "towns and cities." To them the myth of America might prove a realistic inspiration.

COMEDY'S GREATEST ERA

by James Agee

SEPTEMBER 5, 1949

> *In the good old days of the silent screen, some great comedians made action both louder and funnier than words. There has never been anything like them and their droll beauties of comic motion since the movies turned into "talkies." There never will be again. The late James Agee, a distinguished American writer who was concurrently motion-picture critic of* TIME *and* The Nation, *wrote this article for* LIFE *after spending months studying the movie comedy of the great silents.*

In the language of screen comedians four of the main grades of laugh are the titter, the yowl, the belly laugh and the boffo. The titter is just a titter. The yowl is a runaway titter. Anyone who has ever had the pleasure knows all about a belly laugh. The boffo is the laugh that kills. An ideally good gag, perfectly constructed and played, would bring the victim up this ladder of laughs by cruelly controlled degrees to the top rung, and would then proceed to wobble, shake, wave and brandish the ladder until he groaned for mercy. Then, after the shortest possible time out for recuperation, he would feel the first wicked tickling of the comedian's whip once more and start up a new ladder.

The reader can get a fair enough idea of the current state of screen comedy by asking himself how long it has been since he has had that treatment. The best of comedies these days hand out plenty of titters and once in a while it is possible to achieve a yowl without over-straining. Even those who have never seen anything better must occasionally have the feeling, as they watch the current run or, rather, trickle of screen comedy, that they are having to make a little cause for laughter go an awfully long way. And anyone who has watched screen comedy over the past ten or fifteen years is bound to realize that it has quietly but steadily deteriorated. As for those happy atavists who remember silent comedy in its heyday and the belly laughs and boffos that went with it, they have something close to an absolute standard by which to measure the deterioration.

When a modern comedian gets hit on the head, for example, the most he is apt to do is look sleepy. When a silent comedian got hit on the head he seldom let it go so flatly. He realized a broad license, and a ruthless discipline within that license. The least he might do was to straighten up stiff as a plank and fall over backward with such skill that his whole length seemed to slap the floor at the same instant. Or he might make a cadenza of it—look vague, smile like an angel, roll up his eyes, lace his fingers, thrust his hands palms downward as far as they would go, hunch his shoulders, rise on tiptoe, prance ecstatically in narrowing circles until, with tallow knees, he sank down the vortex of his dizziness to the floor, and there signified nirvana by kicking his heels twice, like a swimming frog.

Startled by a cop, this same comedian might grab his hat brim with both hands and yank it down over his ears, jump high in the air, come to earth in a split violent enough to telescope his spine, spring thence into a coattail-flattening sprint and dwindle at rocket speed to the size of a gnat along the grand, forlorn perspective of some lazy back boulevard.

Those are fine clichés from the language of silent comedy in its infancy. The still more gifted men, of course, simplified and invented, finding out new and much deeper uses for the idiom. They learned to show emotion through it, and comic psychology, more eloquently than most language has ever managed to, and they discovered beauties of comic motion which are hopelessly beyond reach of words.

To put it unkindly, the only thing wrong with screen comedy today is that it takes place on a screen which talks. Because it talks, the only comedians who ever mastered the screen cannot work, for they cannot combine their comic style with talk. Because there is a screen, talking comedians are trapped into a continual exhibition of their inadequacy as screen comedians on a surface as big as the side of a barn.

We will discuss here what has gone wrong with screen comedy and what, if anything, can be done about it. But mainly we will try to suggest what it was like in its glory in the years from 1912 to 1930, as practiced by the employees of Mack Sennett, the father of American screen comedy, and by the four most eminent masters: Charlie Chaplin, Harold Lloyd, Buster Keaton and the late Harry Langdon.

Mack Sennett made two kinds of comedy: parody laced with slapstick, and plain slapstick. The parodies were the unceremonious burial of a century of hamming, including the new hamming in serious movies, and nobody who has missed Ben Turpin in *A Small Town Idol,* or kidding Erich von Stroheim in *Three Foolish Weeks* or as *The Shriek of Araby,* can imagine how rough parody can get and still remain subtle and roaringly funny. The plain slapstick, at its best, was even better: a profusion of hearty young women in disconcerting bathing suits, frisking around with a gaggle of insanely incompetent policemen and of equally certifiable male civilians sporting museum-piece mustaches. All these people zipped and caromed about the pristine world of the screen as jazzily as a convention of water bugs. Words can hardly suggest how energetically they collided and bounced apart, meeting in full gallop around the corner of a house; how hard and how often they fell on their backsides; or with what fantastically adroit clumsiness they got themselves fouled up in folding ladders, garden hoses, tethered animals and each other's headlong cross-purposes. The gestures were ferociously emphatic; not a line or motion of the body was wasted or inarticulate. The reader may remember how splendidly upright wandlike old Ben Turpin could stand for a Renunciation Scene, with his lampshade mustache twittering and his sparrowy chest stuck out and his head flung back like Paderewski assaulting a climax and the long babyish back hair trying to look lionlike, while his Adam's apple, an orange in a Christmas stocking, pumped with noble emotion. Or huge Mack Swain, who looked like a hairy mushroom, rolling his eyes in a manner patented by French Romantics and gasping in some dubious ecstasy. Or Louise Fazenda, the perennial farmer's daughter and the perfect low-comedy housemaid, primping her spit curl; and how her hair tightened a good-looking face into the incarnation of rampant gullibility. Or snouty James Finlayson, gleefully foreclosing a mortgage, with his look of eternally tasting a spoiled pickle. Or Chester Conklin, a myopic and inebriated little walrus stumbling around in outsize pants. Or Fatty Arbuckle, with his cold eye and his loose, serene smile, his silky manipulation of his bulk and his satanic marksmanship with pies (he was ambidextrous and could simultaneously blind two people in opposite directions).

The intimate tastes and secret hopes of these poor ineligible dunces were ruthlessly exposed whenever a hot stove, an electric fan or a bulldog took a dislike to their outer garments: agonizingly elaborate drawers, worked up on some lonely evening out of some Godforsaken lace curtain; or men's underpants with big round black spots on them. The Sennett sets—delirious wallpaper, megalomaniacally scrolled iron beds, Grand Rapids *in extremis*—outdid even the underwear. It was their business, after all, to kid the squalid braggadocio which infested the domestic interiors of the period, and that was almost beyond parody. These comedies told their stories to the unaided eye, and by every means possible they screamed to it. That is one reason for the India-ink silhouettes of the cops, and for convicts and prison bars and their shadows in hard sunlight, and for barefooted husbands, in tigerish pajamas, reacting like dervishes to stepped-on tacks.

The early silent comedians never strove for or consciously thought of anything which could be called artistic "form," but they achieved it. For Sennett's rival, Hal Roach, Leo McCarey once devoted almost the whole of a Laurel and Hardy two-reeler to pie-throwing. The first pies were thrown thoughtfully, almost philosophically. Then innocent bystanders began to get caught into the vortex. At full pitch it was Armageddon. But everything was calculated so nicely that until late in the picture, when havoc took over, every pie made its special kind of point and piled on its special kind of laugh.

Sennett's comedies were just a shade faster and fizzier than life. According to legend (and according to Sennett) he discovered the sped tempo proper to screen comedy when a green cameraman, trying to save money, cranked too slow. Realizing the tremendous drumlike power of mere motion to exhilarate, he gave inanimate objects a mischievous life of their own, broke every law of nature the tricked camera would serve him for and made the screen dance like a witches' Sabbath. The thing one is surest of all to remember is how toward the end of nearly every Sennett comedy, a chase (usually called the "rally") built up such a majestic trajectory of pure anarchic motion that bathing girls, cops, comics, dogs, cats, babies, automobiles, locomotives, innocent bystanders, sometimes what seemed like a whole city, an entire civilization, were hauled along head over heels in the wake of that energy like dry leaves following an express train.

"Nice" people, who shunned all movies in the early days, condemned the Sennett comedies as vulgar and naïve. But millions of less pretentious people loved their sincerity and sweetness, their wild-animal innocence and glorious vitality. They could not put these feelings into words, but they flocked to the silents. The reader who gets back deep enough into that world will probably even remember the theater: the barefaced honky-tonk and the waltzes by Waldteufel, slammed out on a mechanical piano; the searing redolence of peanuts and demirep perfumery, tobacco and feet and sweat; the laughter of unrespectable people having a hell of a fine time, laughter as violent and steady and deafening as standing under a waterfall.

The silent-comedy studio was about the best training school the movies have ever known, and the Sennett studio was about as free and easy and as fecund of talent as they came. All the major comedians we will mention worked there, at least briefly. So did some of the major stars of the twenties and since—notably Gloria Swanson, Phyllis Haver, Wallace Beery, Marie Dressler and Carole Lombard. Directors Frank Capra, Leo McCarey and George Stevens also got their start in silent comedy; much that remains most flexible, spontaneous and visually alive in sound movies can be traced, through them and others, to this silent apprenticeship. Everybody did pretty much as he pleased on the Sennett lot, and everybody's ideas were welcome. Sennett posted no rules, and the only thing he strictly forbade was liquor. A Sennett story conference was a most informal affair. During the early years, at least, only the most important scenario might be jotted on the back of an envelope. Mainly Sennett's men thrashed out a few primary ideas and carried them in their heads, sure that better stuff would turn up while they were shooting, in the heat of physical action. This put quite a load on the prop man; he had to have the most improbable apparatus on hand—bombs, trick telephones, what not—to implement whatever idea might suddenly turn up. All kinds of things did— and were recklessly used. Once a low-comedy auto got out of control and killed the cameraman, but he was not visible in the shot, which was thrilling and undamaged; the audience never knew the difference.

Sennett used to hire a "wild man" to sit in on his gag conferences, whose whole job was to think up "wildies." Usually he was an all but brainless, speechless man, scarcely able to communicate his idea; but he had a totally uninhibited imagination. He might say nothing for an hour; then he'd mutter "You take . . ." and all the relatively rational others would shut up and wait. "You take this cloud . . ." he would get out, sketching vague shapes in the air. Often he could get no further; but thanks to some kind of thought-transference, saner men would take this cloud and make something of it. The wild man seems in fact to have functioned as the group's subconscious mind, the source of all creative energy. His ideas were so weird and amorphous that Sennett can no longer remember a one of them, or even how it turned out after rational processing. But a fair equivalent might be one of the best comic sequences in a Laurel and Hardy picture. It is simple enough—

simple and real, in fact, as a nightmare. Laurel and Hardy are trying to move a piano across a narrow suspension bridge. The bridge is slung over a sickening chasm, between a couple of Alps. Midway they meet a gorilla.

Had he done nothing else, Sennett would be remembered for giving a start to three of the four comedians who now began to apply their sharp individual talents to this newborn language. The one whom he did not train (he was on the lot briefly but Sennett barely remembers seeing him around) wore glasses, smiled a great deal and looked like the sort of eager young man who might have quit divinity school to hustle brushes. That was Harold Lloyd. The others were grotesque and poetic in their screen characters in degrees which appear to be impossible when the magic of silence is broken. One, who never smiled, carried a face as still and sad as a daguerreotype through some of the most preposterously ingenious and visually satisfying physical comedy ever invented. That was Buster Keaton. One looked like an elderly baby and, at times, a baby dope fiend; he could do more with less than any other comedian. That was Harry Langdon. One looked like Charlie Chaplin, and he was the first man to give the silent language a soul.

When Charlie Chaplin started to work for Sennett he had chiefly to reckon with Ford Sterling, the reigning comedian. Their first picture together amounted to a duel before the assembled professionals. Sterling, by no means untalented, was a big man with a florid Teutonic style which, under this special pressure, he turned on full blast. Chaplin defeated him within a few minutes with a wink of the mustache, a hitch of the trousers, a quirk of the little finger.

With *Tillie's Punctured Romance*, in 1914, he became a major star. Soon after, he left Sennett when Sennett refused to start a landslide among the other comedians by meeting the raise Chaplin demanded. Sennett is understandably wry about it in retrospect, but he still says, "I was right at the time." Of Chaplin he says simply, "Oh, well, he's just the greatest artist that ever lived." None of Chaplin's former rivals rate him much lower than that; they speak of him no more jealously than they might of God. We will try here only to suggest the essence of his supremacy. Of all comedians he worked most deeply and most shrewdly within a realization of what a human being is, and is up against. The Tramp is as centrally representative of humanity, as many-sided and as mysterious, as Hamlet, and it seems unlikely that any dancer or actor can ever have excelled him in eloquence, variety or poignancy of motion. As for pure motion, Chaplin would have made his period in movies a great one singlehanded, even if he had never gone on to make his magnificent feature-length comedies, even if he had made nothing except *The Cure,* or *One A.M.* In the latter, barring one immobile taxi driver, Chaplin plays alone, as a drunk trying to get upstairs and into bed. It is a sort of inspired elaboration on a soft-shoe dance, involving an angry stuffed wildcat, small rugs on slippery floors, a Lazy Susan table, exquisite footwork on a flight of stairs, a contretemps with a huge, ferocious pendulum and the funniest and most perverse Murphy bed in movie history—and, always made physically lucid, the delicately weird mental processes of a man ethereally sozzled.

Before Chaplin came to pictures people were content with a couple of gags per comedy; he got some kind of laugh every second. The minute he began to work he set standards—and continually forced them higher. Anyone who saw Chaplin eating a boiled shoe like brook trout in *The Gold Rush,* or embarrassed by a swallowed whistle in *City Lights,* has seen perfection. Most of the time, however, Chaplin got his laughter less from the gags, or from milking them in any ordinary sense, than through his genius for what may be called *inflection*—the perfect, changeful shading of his physical and emotional attitudes toward the gag. Funny as his bout with the Murphy bed is, the glances of awe, expostulation and helpless, almost whimpering desire for vengeance which he darts at this infernal machine are even better.

The finest pantomime, the deepest emotion, the richest and most poignant poetry were in Chaplin's work. He could probably pantomime Bryce's *The American Commonwealth* without ever blurring a syllable and make it paralyzingly funny into the bargain. At the end of *City Lights* the blind girl who has regained her sight, thanks to the Tramp, sees him for the first time. She has imagined and anticipated him as princely, to say the least; and it has never seriously occurred to him that he is inadequate. She recognizes who he must be by his shy, confident, shining joy as he comes silently toward her. And he recognizes himself, for the first time, through the terrible changes in her face. The camera just exchanges a few quiet close-ups of the emotions which shift and intensify in each face. It is enough to shrivel the heart to see, and it is the greatest piece of acting and the highest moment in movies.

Harold Lloyd worked only a little while with Sennett. During most of his career he acted for another major comedy producer, Hal Roach. He tried at first to offset Chaplin's influence and establish his own individuality by playing Chaplin's exact opposite, a character named Lonesome Luke who wore clothes much too small for him and whose gestures were likewise as unChaplinesque as possible. But he soon realized that an opposite in itself was a kind of slavishness. He discovered his own comic identity when he saw a movie about a fighting parson: a hero who wore glasses. He began to think about those glasses day and night. He decided on horn rims because they were youthful, ultravisible on the screen and on the verge of becoming fashionable (he was to make them so). Around these large lensless horn rims he began to develop a new character, nothing grotesque or eccentric, but a fresh, believable young man who could fit into a wide variety of stories.

Lloyd was even better at the comedy of thrills. In *Safety Last,* as a rank amateur, he is forced to substitute for a human fly and to climb a medium-sized skyscraper. Dozens of awful things happen to him. He gets fouled up in a tennis net. Popcorn falls on him from a window above, and the local pigeons treat him like a cross between a lunch wagon and St. Francis of Assisi. A mouse runs up his britches-leg, and the crowd below salutes his desperate dance on the window ledge with wild applause of the daredevil. A good deal of this full-length picture hangs thus by its eyelashes along the face of a building. Each new floor is like a new stanza in a poem; and the higher and more horrifying it gets, the funnier it gets.

In this movie Lloyd demonstrates beautifully his ability to do more than merely milk a gag, but to top it. (In an old, simple example of topping, an incredible number of tall men get, one by one, out of a small closed auto. After as many have clambered out as the joke will bear, one more steps out: a midget. That tops the gag. Then the auto collapses. That tops the topper.) In *Safety Last* Lloyd is driven out to the dirty end of a flagpole by a furious dog; the pole breaks and he falls, just managing to grab the minute hand of a huge clock. His weight promptly pulls the hand down from IX to VI. That would be more than enough for any ordinary comedian, but there is further logic in the situation. Now, hideously, the whole clockface pulls loose and slants from its trembling springs above the street. Getting out of difficulty with the clock, he makes still further use of the instrument by getting one foot caught in one of these obstinate springs.

A proper delaying of the ultrapredictable can of course be just as funny as a properly timed explosion of the unexpected. As Lloyd approaches the end of his horrible hegira up the side of the building in *Safety Last,* it becomes clear to the audience, but not to him, that if he raises his head another couple of inches he is going to get murderously conked by one of the four arms of a revolving wind gauge. He delays the evil moment almost interminably, with one distraction and another, and every delay is a suspense-tightening laugh; he also gets his foot nicely entangled in a rope, so that when he does get hit, the payoff of one gag sends him careening head downward through the abyss into another. Lloyd was outstanding even among the master craftsmen at setting up a gag clearly, culminating and getting out of it deftly, and linking it smoothly to the next. Harsh experience also taught him a deep and fundamental rule: never try to get "above" the audience.

Lloyd tried it in *The Freshman.* He was to wear an unfinished, basted-together tuxedo to a college party, which would gradually fall apart as he danced. Lloyd decided to skip the pants, a low-comedy cliché, and lose just the coat. His gag men warned him. A preview proved how right they were. Lloyd had to reshoot the whole expensive sequence, build it around defective pants and climax it with the inevitable. It was one of the funniest things he ever did.

If great comedy must involve something beyond laughter, Lloyd was not a great comedian. If plain laughter is any criterion—and it is a healthy counterbalance to the other—few people have equaled him, and nobody has ever beaten him.

Chaplin and Keaton and Lloyd were all more like each other, in one important way, than Harry Langdon was like any of them. Whatever else the others might be doing, they all used more or less elaborate physical comedy; Langdon showed how little of that one might use and still be a great silent-screen comedian. In his screen character he symbolized something as deeply and centrally human, though by no means as rangily so, as the Tramp. There was, of course, an immense difference in inventiveness and range of virtuosity. It seemed as if Chaplin could do literally anything, on any instrument in the orchestra. Langdon had one queerly toned, unique little reed. But out of it he could get incredible melodies.

Like Chaplin, Langdon wore a coat which buttoned on his wishbone and swung out wide below, but the effect was very different: he seemed like an outsized baby who had begun to outgrow his clothes. The crown of his hat was rounded and the brim was turned up all around, like a little boy's hat, and he looked as if he wore diapers under his pants. His walk was that of a child which has just gotten sure on its feet, and his body and hands fitted that age. His face was kept pale to show off, with the simplicity of a nursery-school drawing, the bright, ignorant, gentle eyes and the little twirling mouth. He had big moon cheeks, with dimples, and a Napoleonic forelock of mousy hair; the round, docile head seemed large in ratio to the cream-puff body. Twitchings of his face were signals of tiny discomforts too slowly registered by a tinier brain; quick, squirty little smiles showed his almost prehuman pleasures, his incurably premature trustfulness. He was a virtuoso of hesitations and of delicately indecisive motions, and he was particularly fine in a high wind, rounding a corner with a kind of skittering toddle, both hands nursing his hat brim.

He was as remarkable a master as Chaplin of subtle emotional and mental processes and operated much more at leisure. He once got a good three hundred feet of continuously bigger laughs out of rubbing his chest, in a crowded vehicle, with Limburger cheese, under the misapprehension that it was a cold salve. In another long scene, watching a brazen showgirl change her clothes, he sat motionless, back to the camera, and registered the whole lexicon of lost innocence, shock, disapproval and disgust, with the back of his neck. His scenes with women were nearly always something special. Once a lady spy did everything in her power (under the Hays Office) to seduce him. Harry was polite, willing, even flirtatious in his little way. The only trouble was that he couldn't imagine what in the world she was leering and pawing at him for, and that he was terribly ticklish. The Mata Hari wound up foaming at the mouth.

Langdon came to Sennett from a vaudeville act in which he had fought a losing battle with a recalcitrant automobile. The minute Frank Capra saw him he begged Sennett to let him work with him. Langdon was almost as childlike as the character he played. He had only a vague idea of his story or even of each scene as he played it; each time he went before the camera Capra would brief him on the general situation and then, as this finest of intuitive improvisers once tried to explain his work, "I'd go into my routine." The whole tragedy of the coming of dialogue, as far as these comedians were concerned— and one reason for the increasing rigidity of comedy ever since—can be epitomized in the mere thought of Harry Langdon confronted with a script.

Langdon's magic was in his innocence, and Capra took beautiful care not to meddle with it. The key to the proper use of Langdon, Capra always knew, was "the principle of the brick." "If there was a rule for writing Langdon material," he explains, "it was this: his only ally was God. Langdon might be saved by the brick falling on the cop, but it was *verboten* that he in any way motivate the brick's fall." Langdon became quickly and fantastically popular with three pictures, *Tramp, Tramp, Tramp, The Strong Man* and *Long Pants*; from then on he went downhill even faster. "The trouble was," Capra says, "that highbrow critics came around to explain his art to him. Also he developed an interest in dames. It was a pretty high life for such a little fellow. He never did really understand what hit him. He died broke [in 1944]. And he died of a broken heart. He was the most tragic figure I ever came across in show business."

Buster Keaton started work at the age of three and a half with his parents in one of the roughest acts in vaudeville ("The Three Keatons"); Harry Houdini gave the child the name Buster in admiration for a fall he took down a flight of stairs. In his first movies Keaton teamed with Fatty Arbuckle under Sennett. He went on to become one of Metro's biggest stars and earners; a Keaton feature cost about $200,000 to make and reliably grossed $2 million. Very early in his movie career friends asked him why he never smiled on the screen. He didn't realize he didn't. He had got the dead-pan habit in variety; on the screen he had merely been so hard at work it had never occurred to him there was anything to smile about. Now he tried it just once and never again. He was by his whole style and nature so much the most deeply "silent" of the silent comedians that even a smile was as deafeningly out of key as a yell. In a way his pictures are like a transcendent juggling act in which it seems that the whole universe is in exquisite flying motion and the one point of repose is the juggler's effortless, uninterested face.

Keaton's face ranked almost with Lincoln's as an early American archetype; it was haunting, handsome, almost beautiful, yet it was irreducibly funny; he improved matters by topping it off with a deadly horizontal hat, as flat and thin as a phonograph record. One can never forget Keaton wearing it, standing erect at the prow as his little boat is being launched. The boat goes grandly down the skids and, just as grandly, straight on to the bottom. Keaton never budges. The last you see of him, the water lifts the hat off the stoic head and it floats away.

No other comedian could do as much with the dead pan. He used this great, sad, motionless face to suggest various related things: a one-track mind near the track's end of pure insanity; mulish imperturbability under the wildest of circumstances; how dead a human being can get and still be alive; an awe-inspiring sort of patience and power to endure, proper to granite but uncanny in flesh and blood. Everything that he was and did bore out this rigid face and played laughs against it. When he moved his eyes, it was like seeing them move in a statue. His short-legged body was all sudden, machinelike angles, governed by a daft aplomb. When he swept a semaphorelike arm to point, you could almost hear the electrical impulse in the signal block. When he ran from a cop his transitions from accelerating walk to easy jogtrot to brisk canter to headlong gallop to flogged-piston sprint— always floating, above this frenzy, the untroubled, untouchable face— were as distinct and as soberly in order as an automatic gearshift.

Keaton was a wonderfully resourceful inventor of mechanistic gags; as he ran afoul of locomotives, steamships, prefabricated and over-electrified houses, he put himself through some of the hardest and cleverest punishment ever designed for laughs. In *Sherlock Jr.*, boiling along on the handlebars of a motorcycle quite unaware that he has lost his driver, Keaton whips through city traffic, breaks up a tug-of-war, gets a shovelful of dirt in the face from each of a long line of Rockette-timed ditchdiggers, approaches a log at high speed which is hinged open by dynamite precisely soon enough to let him through and, hitting an obstruction, leaves the handlebars like an arrow leaving a bow, whams through the window of a shack in which the heroine is about to be violated, and hits the heavy feet-first, knocking him through the opposite wall. The whole sequence is as clean in motion as the trajectory of a bullet.

Keaton worked strictly for laughs, but his work came from so far inside a curious and original spirit that he achieved a great deal besides, especially in his feature-length comedies. (For plain hard laughter his nineteen short comedies—the negatives of which have been lost—were even better.) He was the only major comedian who kept sentiment almost entirely out of his work, and he brought pure physical comedy to its greatest heights. Beneath his lack of emotion he was also uninsistently sardonic; deep below that, giving a disturbing tension and grandeur to the foolishness, for those who sensed it, there was in his comedy a freezing whisper not of pathos but of melancholia. With the humor, the craftsmanship and the action there was often, besides, a fine, still and sometimes dreamlike beauty. Much of his Civil War picture *The General* is within hailing distance of Matthew Brady. And there is a ghostly, unforgettable moment in *The Navigator* when, on a deserted, softly rolling ship, all the pale doors along a deck swing open as one behind Keaton and, as one, slam shut, in a hair-raising illusion of noise.

Perhaps because "dry" comedy is so much more rare and odd than "dry" wit, there are people who never much cared for Keaton. Those who do cannot care mildly.

As soon as the screen began to talk, silent comedy was pretty well finished. The hardy and prolific Mack Sennett made the transfer; he was the first man to put Bing Crosby and W. C. Fields on the screen. But he was essentially a silent-picture man, and by the time the Academy awarded him a special Oscar for his "lasting contribution to the comedy technique of the screen" (in 1938), he was no longer active. As for the comedians we have spoken of in particular, they were as badly off as fine dancers suddenly required to appear in plays.

Harold Lloyd, whose work was most nearly realistic, naturally coped least unhappily with the added realism of speech; he made several talking comedies. But good as the best were, they were not so good as his silent work, and by the late thirties he quit acting.

Up to the middle thirties Buster Keaton made several feature-length pictures (with such players as Jimmy Durante, Wallace Beery and Robert Montgomery); he also made a couple of dozen talking shorts. Now and again he managed to get loose into motion, without having to talk, and for a moment or so the screen would start singing again. But his dark, dead voice, though it was in keeping with the visual character, tore his intensely silent style to bits and destroyed the illusion within which he worked.

The only man who really survived the flood was Chaplin, the only one who was rich, proud and popular enough to afford to stay silent. He brought out two of his greatest nontalking comedies, *City Lights* and *Modern Times,* in the middle of an avalanche of talk, spoke gibberish and, in the closing moments, plain English in *The Great Dictator,* and at last made an all-talking picture, *Monsieur Verdoux,* creating for that purpose an entirely new character who might properly talk a blue streak. *Verdoux* is the greatest of talking comedies though so cold and savage that it had to find its public in grimly experienced Europe.

Good comedy, and some that was better than good, outlived silence, but there has been less and less of it. The talkies brought one great comedian, the late, majestically lethargic W. C. Fields, who could not possibly have worked as well in silence; he was the toughest and the most warmly human of all screen comedians, and *It's a Gift* and *The Bank Dick,* fiendishly funny and incisive white-collar comedies, rank high among the best comedies (and best movies) ever made. Laurel and Hardy, the only comedians who managed to preserve much of the large, low style of silence and who began to explore the comedy of sound, have made nothing since 1945. Walt Disney, at his best an inspired comic inventor and teller of fairy stories, lost his stride during the war and has since regained it only at moments. Preston Sturges has made brilliant, satirical comedies, but his pictures are smart, nervous comedy-dramas merely italicized with slapstick. The Marx Brothers were sidesplitters but they made their best comedies years ago. Jimmy Durante is mainly a nightclub genius; Abbott and Costello are semiskilled laborers, at best; Bob Hope is a good comedian with a pleasing presence, but not much more, on the screen.

There is no hope that screen comedy will get much better than it is without new, gifted young comedians who really belong in movies, and without freedom for their experiments. For everyone who may appear we have one last, invidious comparison to offer as a guidepost.

One of the most popular recent comedies is Bob Hope's *The Paleface*. We take no pleasure in blackening *The Paleface;* we single it out, rather, because it is as good as we've got. Anything that is said of it here could be said, with interest, of other comedies of our time. Most of the laughs in *The Paleface* are verbal. Bob Hope is very adroit with his lines and now and then, when the words don't get in the way, he makes a good beginning as a visual comedian. But only the beginning, never the middle or the end. He is funny, for instance, reacting to a shot of violent whisky. But he does not know how to get still funnier (*i.e.,* how to build and milk) or how to be funniest last (*i.e.,* how to top or cap his gag). The camera has to fade out on the same old face he started with.

One sequence is promisingly set up for visual comedy. In it, Hope and a lethal local boy stalk each other all over a cowtown through streets which have been emptied in fear of their duel. The gag here is that through accident and stupidity they keep just failing to find each other. Some of it is quite funny. But the fun slackens between laughs like a weak clothesline, and by all the logic of humor (which is ruthlessly logical) the biggest laugh should come at the moment, and through the way, they finally spot each other. The sequence is so weakly thought out that at that crucial moment the camera can't afford to watch them; it switches to Jane Russell.

Now we turn to a masterpiece. In *The Navigator* Buster Keaton works with practically the same gag as Hope's duel. Adrift on a ship which he believes is otherwise empty, he drops a lighted cigarette. A girl finds it. She calls out and he hears her; each then tries to find the other. First each walks purposefully down the long, vacant starboard deck, the girl, then Keaton, turning the corner just in time not to see each other. Next time around each of them is trotting briskly, very much in earnest; going at the same pace, they miss each other just the same. Next time around each of them is going like a bat out of hell. Again they miss. Then the camera withdraws to a point of vantage at the stern, leans its chin in its hand and just watches the whole intricate superstructure of the ship as the protagonists stroll, steal and scuttle from level to level, up, down and sidewise, always managing to miss each other by hair's-breadths, in an enchantingly neat and elaborate piece of timing. There are no subsidiary gags to get laughs in this sequence and there is little loud laughter; merely a quiet and steadily increasing kind of delight. When Keaton has got all he can out of this fine modification of the movie chase he invents a fine device to bring the two together: the girl, thoroughly winded, sits down for a breather, indoors, on a plank which workmen have left across sawhorses. Keaton pauses on an upper deck, equally winded and puzzled. What follows happens in a couple of seconds at most: air suction whips his silk topper backward down a ventilator; grabbing frantically for it, he backs against the lip of the ventilator, jackknifes and falls in backward. Instantly the camera cuts back to the girl. A topper falls through the ceiling and lands tidily, right side up, on the plank beside her. Before she can look more than startled, its owner follows, head between his knees, crushes the topper, breaks the plank with the point of his spine and proceeds to the floor. The breaking of the plank smacks Boy and Girl together.

It is only fair to remember that the silent comedians would have as hard a time playing a talking scene as Hope has playing his visual ones, and that writing and directing are as accountable for the failure as Hope himself. But not even the humblest journeymen of the silent years would have let themselves off so easily. Like the masters, they knew, and sweated to obey, the laws of their craft.

THE FATEFUL
ONSLAUGHT
OF THE STORM

by Alan Moorehead

JANUARY 27, 1958

> *In the tumultuous month of April, 1917, Lenin was returned to war-weary Russia with German connivance, and the die was cast for Soviet Communism. Forty years later, with new research which reveals the extent of German intrigues against Czarist Russia, a history of the Russian Revolution was written by Alan Moorehead on commission from* LIFE. *After being serialized in the magazine, it was published in book form. Moorehead, an Australian of international reputation, has written many books, including a definitive account of the World War I battle at Gallipoli.*

One could draw a simple graph to illustrate the years 1906 to 1914 in Russia. It would show two lines, one representing the fortunes of the Russian government and the other those of the revolutionaries—and as the one line went up so the other would go down. After 1906 the government's reputation rises steadily until it reaches its peak during the prime ministership of Peter Stolypin in 1909. At the same time the revolutionary movement comes almost to a standstill. Thereafter the government's fortunes fall again (with a short recovery in 1914 and early 1915) into the final and fatal chaos brought on by World War I. This is the point at which the revolutionary movement emerges from the depths and breaks through permanently into the open.

It is the Duma, Russia's first parliament, which is the touchstone of these events, and in the whole Russian tragedy there is nothing sadder or grimmer than the way in which this one white hope of the situation was sabotaged and beset from all sides. It had enemies everywhere: Czar Nicholas II and the court, who loathed the whole idea, the revolutionary parties, most of whom boycotted the elections, and the bureaucracy, which would have preferred to go on running the country in its own autocratic way without any outside criticism or interference.

There is, however, one brief and important respite from this dismal round, and it comes with the appointment of Peter Stolypin as Prime Minister. Stolypin was a remarkable man, the best Prime Minister Russia ever had. His program of agrarian reform was admirable and it was desperately needed: it permitted peasants to own their land outright instead of sharing it with others on a communal basis. Immediately there was an improvement. Men began to take a pride in their farms and worked hard to buy more land and to increase the yield. Lenin, ever a realist, saw great danger in this, the danger that the revolutionary spirit might die out among the peasants. But it was not Lenin or any of the revolutionaries who made the most difficulties for Stolypin during this hopeful time. As early as 1909 the Prime Minister's most insidious opposition came from a most unexpected quarter, from Empress Alix herself.

Since the birth of her son in 1904 the empress had retired more and more from public life. She was obsessed about the health of the little czarevich, who suffered from hemophilia. The threat that at any moment the slightest knock could bring on fatal internal bleeding had caused the empress herself to develop a nervous heart disease. The 1905 disturbances had naturally added to her neurosis. She had one ruling thought in her mind—the defense of the royal family against the mob, and it was not a passive defense. Let any politician threaten or disturb her husband and she rose up in a perfect blaze of rage and contempt.

Meanwhile, within the palace walls and the gardens of Czarskoe

Selo outside Petrograd, the young imperial family was growing up entirely insulated from the ordinary life of Russia. Few intimates were admitted to this closed circle. Of those that were, the most prominent of all—and the direct cause of the empress's newly found hate for Stolypin—was Rasputin.

Gregory Efimovich Rasputin has been so blackened and discredited in the forty-odd years since his death that it is almost impossible to see him any more. He appears as the pure quintessence of wickedness. Rasputin seldom washed and he smelled vilely. At the table he plunged his greedy hands into his favorite fish soup. He was the kind of drunkard who smashes the furniture. He was blasphemous, vicious and obscene. His lechery had a barbaric Mongolian quality that made him more like a beast than a human being.

Rasputin was three years younger than Nicholas, a year younger than Lenin. He began life in a small village in the Tobolsk province of Siberia and until the age of thirty he loitered in the absymal backwater of Russian peasant life, known only to the local people as a horsestealer and as a wild eccentric with erotic appetites and immense physical strength. Somewhere around the turn of the century he abandoned his wife and three children and went wandering off as a kind of holy man or "starets." Though not an ordained priest, he felt he had seen the true light of God. At the end of 1903 he turned up in Petrograd, a ragged peasant of average height, with a long tangled beard and dirty hair falling over his shoulders. There was a cult of mysticism in Petrograd at this time, and Rasputin's fanatical eyes and outlandish appearance obviously helped his reputation. Through admirers he gained entry to the imperial court.

He must have impressed himself directly on Nicholas and his wife from the beginning. But the bond between them was absolutely sealed when it was discovered that Rasputin had strange powers over the czarevich. He had only to gaze into the child's eyes murmuring soothing words—or even speak over the telephone—and all would be well. The pains would subside and the boy would go to sleep.

Given the empress's highly religious nature, it was enough to convert her into a blind follower of this grubby prophet. She adored him. Nothing he did, nothing that was proved against him disturbed her confidence in the least. Soon Rasputin's influence spread to politics and Empress Alix begged Nicholas to listen to her mentor.

Stolypin, on his side, was quite aware of this new breeze blowing and he did not like it. He ordered Rasputin out of the city.

So now in the summer of 1911 Stolypin had enemies on every side. Lenin and the revolutionaries were against him, the Duma was against him and Nicholas was already quarreling with him. Now, with Rasputin's banishment, he had acquired in the empress his bitterest opponent of all.

Stolypin was ill, tired and disillusioned. He wanted to resign but was kept in office as the only possible man for the job. He was drifting into another breach with the czar and the Duma when, on September 14, 1911, the thing that they may all have half-wished for in their hearts actually happened. He was murdered.

Although Stolypin's successor kept the same policies going through the last few years of European peace, Russia's great chance for orderly progress imposed from above had come and gone. Already there were signs that the revolutionary movement was beginning to revive. With every month that went by the number of strikes steadily increased.

The czar did not seem concerned in the slightest. In 1914 Nicholas had been twenty years on the throne, and still the steely mildness remained, the same adamant dream of the divine right of kings. So far as he was concerned, Lenin and the other scheming exiles might just as well have been living on the moon.

It is Lenin's resilience—his ability by sheer persistence to wear the others down—which in the end astonishes one more than anything else about him. The year 1911 finds him apparently at the nadir of his career. But in 1912 things begin to change. Before long he is once again at the front of his party.

Lenin's return to power among the Bolsheviks was helped to a large extent by unrest in Russia. The attempt of the liberals in the Duma to find a remedy in democracy had been sabotaged. Again, as in 1905, it was the emotions and the feelings of the mass of the Russian people which were now starting to take charge. Between January and July, 1914, more than a million workers went out on strike in the big cities. That summer a strange heaviness, a sense of apathetic dread, pervaded the Petrograd scene.

When war came on August 1 this dismal atmosphere abruptly evaporated. The workers abandoned their strikes at once and the churches were filled with vast congregations who could think of nothing but self-sacrifice and victory. This was no phenomenon confined to Petrograd. All over Russia the peasants and the workers responded willingly to the first army call-up; something like 96 per cent answered the summons to serve.

The war worked a wonderful change on the royal family as well. The empress threw herself into hospital and Red Cross work. The czar too was transformed. He was furious with his cousin, Kaiser Wilhelm of Germany. He was on fire to take personal command of his armies in the field and was only with difficulty persuaded to appoint his uncle, the Grand Duke Nicholas, instead. With emotion he saluted the regiments as they went off, and they answered him with cheers. Finally after twenty bitter years Nicholas was at one with his people.

With a front of 550 miles to control and the Army not yet prepared for major action it was quite obvious that at the outset Russia should remain on the defensive. But the Russians wanted to use up the fuel of their enthusiasm by attacking at once, and almost from the first day the French were urging them forward. Gallantly, hastily and mistakenly the grand duke went onto the offensive when only a third of his soldiers were deployed.

The result was the calamitous Battle of Tannenberg at the end of August, 1914. That disaster was followed in September by the Battle of the Masurian Lakes, which resulted in the Russians being swept entirely out of German territory. In January, 1915, a second Battle of the Masurian Lakes was fought and, with this third defeat, the Russian offensive in the north was broken. The Army never recovered.

The exuberance with which the people had first gone to war was now replaced by a steadily mounting resentment against the government. Suddenly there was a hysterical anti-German outburst in Moscow. For three days on end German shops, banks and factories were looted and set on fire. Anyone with a German name was hunted down and some were lynched. It was one of the most ferocious pogroms ever carried out in Russia and it was the clearest of all possible warnings that a crisis was on the way. Next time the mob would strike at the czar and the government itself.

Meanwhile the empress was in a blaze of patriotic and religious energy. Her thesis was very simple. Russia must be saved. Nicholas alone can save her and only Rasputin can show him the way.

In particular the empress reserved her real enmity for those who dared to attack Rasputin and presently she declared that Grand Duke Nicholas, who had shown contempt for Rasputin, must be removed. The czar himself must take command.

Through August, 1915, Nicholas hesitated, pulled one way by the empress and the other by his ministers, who knew that if the czar left the capital there was nothing to stop the empress and Rasputin from taking charge of the government. But in September the grand duke was packed off to a command in the Caucasus and the czar took over at the front. The only reassuring aspect about the change was that Nicholas proposed to be more or less a figurehead: the actual control of the Army was given to General Michael Alekseev, an uninspired man but still a professional soldier of some ability. In Petrograd people waited to see what the empress and Rasputin were going to do.

They did not wait long. Eleven days after the czar's departure the Duma was prorogued and there began now a series of government dismissals and reshuffles, of intrigues and underhand dealings that were to bring Russia to the very edge of the revolution.

By the last week of December, 1916, the situation had become like nothing so much as one of the horrendous Mongol tragedies playing at the opera house. It was an extreme confusion and hopelessness. Just one thing was lacking: some act of high dramatic violence. And this presently was supplied by the murder of Rasputin.

Rasputin's death of course was a profound blow to the empress, and Nicholas hurried back from the front to comfort her. One of the most significant reactions to the murder, however, came eight hundred miles away in Berlin, where the Kaiser saw in the event a great hope for getting Russia out of the war. German planners and Russian revolutionaries alike waited in equal ignorance to see what the aftermath was going to be.

But no demonstrations occurred and the government did not fall.

When, after a few days, it was seen that there was to be no change—that Nicholas and the empress meant to continue precisely as they had before—a mood of utter despondency began to spread throughout Russia. Few now could see any hope of winning the war or of bringing Nicholas to his senses and it became common talk around Petrograd that revolution was now inevitable. With the revolution would certainly come starvation, chaos, the end of Russia.

Nicholas was less approachable than ever. Rasputin's death seemed to have left him in a kind of fatalistic and resentful daze. On January 12 the British ambassador, Buchanan, went to Nicholas to express the anxiety that Britain and France were feeling about the situation. The czar received him standing up and it was during this interview that Nicholas made the celebrated remark, "You tell me, Ambassador, that I must deserve the confidence of my people. Isn't it rather for my people to deserve *my* confidence?"

Still revolution did not strike and no one party or group of parties had the power to make it strike. On March 1, 1917, bread rationing was introduced and there was a run on the bakeries. But it was the sort of thing that had happened often before and there was no real alarm in Petrograd.

Nicholas had been planning to return to his military headquarters. Now he saw no reason to delay his departure any longer and on March 8 he left. On that day the Russian Revolution began.

Looking back now on the events of March, 1917, reading the accounts of the people who were there, looking at the old photographs, one finds oneself immediately struck by the absence of spectacle, the ordinariness of it all. There ought to be some thunderclap, some highly charged act of drama that announces that a new age has begun. But nothing of the sort occurs. There before you lie the familiar streets, the cobblestones, the tramlines running up the center, the shops, the office where you go to work and the restaurant where you eat. It is a surrealist and inexplicable thing that now there should be dead bodies slumping in the gutters and on the open roadway.

There was another aspect to the March days in Petrograd which also made them seem unnatural and unreal: it was hard to find out who had started the rising or just what force there was behind it. For the first few days of the revolt the demonstrators did not know where they were going to go or what they were going to do. They only wanted to protest. But then, as more and more people came into the streets, the crowds took confidence from their own numbers. They accepted the leaders who appeared, and in the absence of personal enemies they attacked symbols. The policeman in his uniform was a symbol. So was the rich man in his car. So was the Winter Palace. And so were the law courts, the police stations, the jails, the fortress of St. Peter and St. Paul, the arsenal. All these were symbols of the corrupt and hated authority and they were attacked.

It was the attitude of the soldiers which counted most. When mutinies and uprisings had occurred in the past, military detachments like the Cossacks and the Imperial Guards had always been willing to fire on the crowd. Now, however, it was different.

The Petrograd garrison, for example, numbered over 160,000 men. They were armed with rifles, machine guns, armored cars and even artillery. For a long time socialist agitators had been quietly active among them. From the first there was a definite sympathy between the garrison and the striking factory workers. They did not immediately throw in their lot together, there were many hesitations and backslidings, but after the first few days of rioting the bulk of the soldiers did go over to the workers' side, and there developed then—to borrow a phrase from nuclear physics—a critical mass, an explosive force strong enough to blow the Romanovs out of existence. It was the soldiers who really made the revolution.

On March 3 a branch of the Putilov works in Petrograd's Moscow-Narva district had come out on strike as a protest against the dismissal of some of the men. When the strikers' demands were refused other branches of the works joined them. They staged an "Italian strike"— a sitdown strike. The management's answer to this was to impose a general lockout on all employees at the works, a total of more than twenty thousand workers. Deputations of strikers at once went off to the factories on the Viborg side asking for their support.

And now a new and unusual factor entered the situation. March 8 had been chosen as "Women's Day." This was to be a citywide demonstration by the working women of the capital. Their presence in a street demonstration was not only a gesture of solidarity but also deterred the police from breaking up the processions too roughly. And so on the eighth most of the textile factories, which were staffed with women, came out on strike, and they soon joined hands with the men who had been locked out of the Putilov works. A major political upheaval was on the way.

In the course of the afternoon two attempts were made by the demonstrators to cross the Neva River into the main part of the city. Each time the police came out and drove them back. Later a third attempt was made and a column made up chiefly of women succeeded in breaking through to the Nevsky Prospekt, Petrograd's principal thoroughfare. They marched as far as the Kazan Cathedral, rhythmically singing "Give us bread" and looting the bakeries.

March 9 was largely a repetition of the previous day except that this time the strikers came across the Neva in much greater strength. Then everyone suddenly began to act. The Mezhrayonka—a Social Democratic group composed of intellectuals who hoped to reunite the Bolsheviks and Mensheviks—were the first in the field. They issued a strike order halting all of the street cars—always an effective way to foment disorder—and followed this up later that night with a call for a three-day general strike.

The government on its side was also beginning to realize that this was no ordinary demonstration. Quite apart from the size and the vehemence of the mob, there was at least one ominous sign that a fundamental break with the past was occurring: the Cossacks had not charged upon the crowds as they had been ordered to do. The czar was urged to return to Petrograd and to enter into negotiations for the formation of a popular government. Late on March 10 Nicholas replied by issuing a strangely incongruous command to Petrograd's military governor: "I order that the disorders in the capital shall be stopped tomorrow."

But on Sunday, March 11, huge crowds were out in the streets again. This time they were met by soldiers, and troops of the Volynsky regiment were ordered to open fire. They fired but they aimed their rifles at the sky. It was the first sure sign of defection in the garrison, though it was a premature one. In the afternoon a serious clash took place in Znamenskaya Square and this time the Volynsky soldiers shot directly into the mob. Some sixty people were killed and as many wounded.

By now the crowd was running amok. Everywhere police stations were being attacked, looted and burned. The law courts were stormed and rioters ran through the building hurling documents out onto the frozen canal below. When night fell many fires were burning throughout the city.

The soldiers had been shocked and confused by the events of the day. In the Volynsky regiment in particular there was a sense of revulsion at what they had done: to shoot at armed Germans was one thing but to murder their own people was another. After a night of debate the Volynsky regiment marched out of its barracks to fight for the revolution. With the band playing the soldiers proceeded to the quarters of the Preobrazhensky and the Litovsky regiments and these too came out against the czar. A snowballing movement had begun and it meant the end of the imperial army in Petrograd.

The Duma meanwhile had become the real center of events, and all through the day of March 12 there was a continuous stream of people pressing on toward its meeting place, the Tauride Palace. They thrust themselves into the building, shouting, arguing, waving red banners and singing the "Marseillaise." The deputies themselves had spent the first four days of the revolution in a state of great uncertainty. It was only now, under the extreme pressure of the mob outside, that they forced themselves to admit that the czar's government had collapsed and that there was no alternative but to take over the power themselves. After much wrangling a group of moderates led by the Cadets—the Constitutional Democratic Party—formed an Emergency Committee of the Duma, and in the next few days, in a confused and erratic way, this body began to act as the new government of Russia.

Petrograd's socialists in turn were constructing an emergency committee of their own, essentially a re-creation of the Soviet which had appeared in Petrograd twelve years before in the rising of 1905. It was the result of an intricate network of influences and pressures that came from all the socialist parties, from the mutinous garrison and from the mob itself. Yet its formation was a haphazard and hastily contrived affair. A few men gravitated together: N. D. Sokolov, the socialist deputy, was one of them and Sukhanov was another. They were soon joined by other Social Democrats and Social Revolutionaries. Their first meeting, at 9 P.M. on March 12, was attended by some fifty workers and twenty soldiers, who formed an Executive Committee (henceforth to be known as the Ex Com). The Ex Com from the start was the real center of the Soviet's power, just as the Emergency Committee was the real source of power in the Duma. Irakli Chkheidze, a Menshevik, was made chairman, and among the members were a young Duma deputy named Alexander Kerensky (who was respected by both camps), Steklov (who subsequently became editor of *Isvestiya*) and later several Bolsheviks who emerged either from hiding or from prison. Predominantly, however, the Ex Com was a Menshevik group and it continued to be so until the bitter end in November.

So from March 12 on there were two rival groups in the Tauride Palace to whom the striking workers and the soldiers could come for leadership: the Emergency Committee (of the Duma) and the Soviet's Ex Com. From the start each side maneuvered against the other. The Duma's Emergency Committee, which had control of the treasury, temporarily refused a demand of ten million rubles from the Ex Com. The Ex Com, for its part, started issuing proclamations and orders to the Army and the workers over the head of the Duma. Yet neither side at this critical moment could ignore the other. There was chaos in the streets of Petrograd and it was spreading fast throughout the country. More important still, there was a great fear in both camps that the revolution would fail, that Nicholas would rally forces for a counter-revolution and return to Petrograd to crush them all.

Indeed, Nicholas at last announced that he would return to Petrograd. But he never arrived. Orders went out from the Duma to stop him, and the imperial train was diverted to Pskov.

We have now reached March 14. In the streets of Petrograd things were somewhat quieter but the Tauride Palace was in a state of headlong commotion. Here, in circumstances of the utmost confusion, with impromptu meetings going on in every part of the building, the Emergency Committee and the Ex Com were meeting simultaneously and hammering out their rival programs. Kerensky was acting as a go-between and it is Kerensky that eyewitnesses seem particularly to remember in these days. Pale-faced, impassioned, his eyes blazing, he rushed from place to place, now arguing with the Emergency Committee, now with the Ex Com members, now pausing to harangue the crowd outside. The mob greeted him with cheers: he appeared to be the very embodiment of the revolution at this moment.

Somehow a provisional government had to be formed. By the early morning of March 15 Paul Milyukov, the Emergency Committee's leader and a co-founder (back in 1905) of the Constitutional Democratic Party, was ready with a list of ministers.

It remained now to decide on a policy and a series of meetings began between the new ministers and the Ex Com. There was a fairly large area of agreement. Both sides felt that the Provisional Government should give way eventually to a constituent assembly elected by a universal and secret vote and that the assembly should decide what kind of government Russia was to have. Both wanted the czar to abdicate.

But the Ex Com wanted a good deal more too. It wanted not only the abdication of Nicholas but the abolition of the monarchy as well. It wanted an entire reorganization of the Army. This last question—the control of the Army—was the real issue between the two sides. Already the Ex Com had stolen a march on the Provisional Government in this matter. On its own authority it had issued its famous Order No. 1, which stated that in all political matters the members of Russia's military forces were to be under the command of the Petrograd Soviet. The soldiers were to obey the orders of the Duma only if they did not contradict the orders of the Soviet. Further, soldiers' committees were to control all weapons and were not to deliver weapons to officers.

But upon one other matter Milyukov was prepared to fight the Ex Com to the last ditch. If Nicholas were to abdicate, he said, the monarchy at least should be preserved. It was not through any great admiration of the Romanov family that Milyukov pressed this matter. It was simply that he did not believe that any government would survive unless it had the traditional weight of the monarchy behind it. Without consulting the Ex Com he sent a delegation to the czar to urge abdication.

Nicholas received the Duma's representatives aboard his train at Pskov and listened very patiently while they explained the situation at length. Presently he stated his wish that his brother, the Grand Duke Michael, rather than the sickly czarevich, should succeed to the imperial throne. This was agreed to by the Duma delegates and before midnight the document was signed. It ended with the words, "May the Lord God help Russia!"

It was sincere, this last exhortation, not merely a ceremonial phrase, and the moment was a historic one. The two Duma delegates found themselves very much moved when they came to say good-by. One of them related later that he burst out with, "Your Majesty, if you had done all this earlier, even as late as the last summoning of the Duma, perhaps all that . . ." He was unable to finish. The czar looked at him and said simply, "Do you think it might have been avoided?"

Early the following morning, March 16, the two delegates got back to Petrograd to find the streets much quieter but the Tauride Palace, where the Duma was meeting, still in an uproar. The feeling against the Romanovs had hardened considerably while they were away. The Ex Com members were making it clear they were not content with Nicholas' abdication. They wanted the end of the whole dynasty and the formation of a republic. Milyukov was forced to give way. He and other members of the Provisional Government, including Kerensky, paid a call on Grand Duke Michael and outlined the situation. The grand duke listened quietly and then very sensibly said he wished to withdraw into the next room while he considered. He returned in five minutes and announced that he would accept the throne only if it were offered to him by a constituent assembly. Pending the election of such an assembly, he would abdicate.

"Monseigneur," Kerensky cried out, "you are the noblest of men."

In a short while a second instrument of abdication was typed out and signed, and for the first time in more than three centuries Russia found herself without a czar. In his place she had two exhausted and mutually suspicious groups of politicians struggling for power in the Tauride Palace, a mob in the streets and no certainty in the future anywhere. Dark heavy clouds had begun to roll over Petrograd from the Gulf of Finland and snow fell so thickly along the Neva it was impossible to see the icy course of the river, even from twenty paces away.

Throughout these hectic days the conflicting groups had very little idea of just what backing the revolution had through Russia. The news was not long in arriving and it was both encouraging and alarming. Moscow rose and formed a Soviet of its own, and presently most of the other cities followed suit. The Army too declared for the revolution and acknowledged the new government. So did the foreign minority states inside the Russian Empire. Meanwhile, Soviet Order No. 1 was being interpreted at the front by some of the soldiers as an invitation to do pretty much what they liked and what they liked was not war but peace. At places along the line they fraternized with the Germans and the Austrians. Then the desertions began. Within a few weeks of the March rising about a million soldiers had deserted and were making their way home in trains, in carts and on foot, and there was no authority capable of holding them back.

In the Navy the Provisional Government did not even get political support. The Kronstadt base with twenty thousand sailors mutinied against its officers, and after butchering some held about two hundred of the rest as hostages whom they forced into the heaviest and most degrading work. And now they were running a semi-independent camp of their own. At first they refused to recognize even the Soviet in Petrograd.

In some ways the picture was not so dark. Somehow or other, perhaps because of the prodding of the Ex Com itself, the trams, the factories, the banks and the arsenals started up again and the bureaucracy returned to work. And help came to Russia from another quarter: America, France, Britain and Italy promptly recognized the Provisional Government so that it had at least a standing in the eyes of the outside world. Much more important than this, America was not only about to come into the war herself, she also was prepared to back the Provisional Government both with supplies and money.

Just when the Emergency Committee's prospects seemed to be brightening, however, the revolutionary leaders who in time would work its undoing were beginning to arrive back in Petrograd. During the first weeks of the rebellion no really front-ranking Bolsheviks had been on the scene. The Ex Com, while it contained a few of Lenin's followers, was basically a Menshevik organization. The Bolshevik party was a second-rate organization. On March 25, however, things began to change. Kamenev arrived back from exile in Siberia under the terms of the amnesty issued by the Provisional Government and he was accompanied by Stalin, who had also spent the war years in exile, hunting and fishing on the edge of the Arctic Circle. They at once took charge of the Bolshevik committee. Other exiled leaders now began to arrive in the capital with every week that went by.

One man of particular importance was lacking, and that was Lenin. And now in mid-April word was received in Petrograd that he was on his way back from Switzerland. He was crossing Germany in a sealed train, due to arrive at the Finland Station in Petrograd on the night of April 16.

The Germans had not expected the rising in Russia to happen so swiftly. Through January and February they knew that the atmosphere in Petrograd was becoming increasingly tense, but the Foreign Office in Berlin seems to have been more preoccupied with the possibility of coming to terms with the czar than with the plans for destroying him by revolution. Certainly few of the German leaders had any notion of getting Lenin and his friends back into Russia.

Could these revolutionaries really be trusted? Lenin soon made it clear he could. He was going to attack the Provisional Government tooth and nail, he said, and would sue for peace. Furthermore he was going to promote civil war in Russia. This satisfied the Germans, who sent word that they had no objection to the revolutionaries traveling through Germany.

Two weeks passed while the details were ironed out, but on April 9 the party was at last ready to set off. The train left Zurich at 3:15 P.M.

There were wild scenes on the platform before the train drew out, for by now the news of the departure had got out and a fiercely divided crowd had gathered. There were thirty-two revolutionary passengers in all, including nineteen Bolsheviks, six members of the Jewish Bund, three internationalist Mensheviks and one four-year-old boy. The most important were Lenin, his wife Krupskaya, Gregory Zinoviev, Inessa Armand and Gregory Sokolnikov. Karl Radek, who was an Austrian citizen, joined the train at the German border. It is also said that there was a British secret service agent on board, and that he was subsequently removed in Germany, but upon this point the German records are silent.

After two days in Germany the train pulled into the Baltic seaport of Sassnitz and the party proceeded by boat to Stockholm. A Swedish train took them to the Finnish border at the top of the Gulf of Bothnia. The border itself was crossed on sledges. Another train took them southward through Finland and into Russia proper. A few miles outside Petrograd the train was boarded by Lenin's sister and a group of supporters from the Bolshevik party.

In the evening of April 16 they steamed into the Finland Station in Petrograd. Ten years had passed since Lenin had seen Russia and he had serious doubts about the way he would be received. But he need not have worried.

The arrival had been brilliantly organized. A vast crowd blocked the square in front of the station and innumerable red banners were waving everywhere. Troops with military bands were drawn up near the side entrance through which Lenin was expected to emerge, and a mounted searchlight kept moving its bright beam across the faces of the crowd onto the buildings beyond. On the platform itself more soldiers were standing ready to present arms and more banners were displayed, more printed slogans and triumphal arches of red and gold. At long last the train arrived.

"A thunderous *Marseillaise* boomed forth on the platform," wrote Sukhanov, a practiced and ironical observer who was there with Chkheidze, the chairman of the Ex Com. "We stayed in the imperial waiting rooms while the Bolshevik generals exchanged greetings. Then we heard them marching along the platform, under the triumphal arches. . . . "

There were cries of "Please, comrades, make way," and in the midst of a throng of people Lenin came hurrying in.

"He wore a round cap," says Sukhanov, "his face looked frozen and there was a magnificent bouquet in his hands. Running to the middle of the room, he stopped in front of Chkheidze as though colliding with a completely unexpected obstacle. . . ."

Chkheidze got in first with a welcoming speech which urged the Bolsheviks to join in a defense of the revolution from any encroachments either from within or from without.

"Lenin plainly knew exactly how to behave," writes Sukhanov. "He stood there as though nothing taking place had the slightest connection with him—looking about him, examining the persons round him and even the ceiling of the imperial waiting room, adjusting his bouquet (rather out of tune with his whole appearance), and then, turning away from the Ex Com delegation altogether, he made his 'reply.'

" 'Dear comrades, soldiers, sailors and workers! I am happy to greet in your persons the victorious Russian revolution, and greet you as the vanguard of the worldwide proletarian army. . . . The piratical imperialist war is the beginning of civil war throughout Europe. . . . The worldwide Socialist revolution has already dawned. . . . Germany is seething. . . . Any day now the whole of European capitalism may crash. The Russian revolution accomplished by you has prepared the way and opened a new epoch. Long live the worldwide Socialist revolution!'

"Suddenly," Sukhanov goes on, "before the eyes of all of us, completely swallowed up by the routine drudgery of the revolution, there was presented a bright, blinding, exotic beacon. . . . There had broken in upon us in the revolution a note that was . . . novel, harsh and somewhat deafening."

THE QUIET DEATH
OF AN AMERICAN ERA

by Bruce Catton

AUGUST 20, 1956

> *When the last veteran of the Grand Army of the*
> *Republic was buried and "the last notes of the bugle*
> *hung against the sky," Bruce Catton, distinguished*
> *Civil War historian, wrote this grave piece in memoriam.*
> *A lingering chapter in our history had quietly*
> *and forever closed. Let there be a muffled roll for the*
> *Grand Army as the last flag is furled, and the last survivor*
> *marches into the shadows.*

The greatest parade in American history has finally come to an end.
The Grand Army of the Republic has marched off to join the shadows,
and no matter how long the nation exists there will never be anything
quite like it again. This chapter in our history has been closed. Something deeply and fundamentally American is gone forever.

For the Grand Army of the Republic was the living link that bound
us intimately to the great morning of national youth. As long as the
Army existed—even though it was at last embodied in one incredibly
old man, who stood alone without comrades—the great day of tragedy
and of decision was still a part of living memory. There was an open

door into the past, and what we could see through that opening was magically haunted, because everything that was visible there was strangely touched by the light of the future.

Taking a look at what we had been, we could also glimpse what we must someday be. The Civil War, the greatest single experience we ever had, was both an end and a beginning. But when the final handful of dust drifted down on Albert Woolson's casket, and the last notes of the bugle hung against the sky, the door swung shut. It cannot be reopened.

In the beginning, of course, the Grand Army was simply a collection of old soldiers—very youthful old soldiers, mostly, for the organization was founded in 1866, when the average veteran was just ripening into full voting age. But eventually, like the Civil War itself, it came to mean a great deal more than the men who started it ever intended.

What it originally meant was nothing very good. It came into being partly because various ex-soldiers wanted to keep alive the comradeship of Army days, but mostly because clever politicians realized that great things could be done with a solid phalanx of war veterans. In no time at all it became an effective action arm for the dominant Republican party.

The Grand Army offered a forum at which vindictive orators could indulge in "waving the bloody shirt," inviting all patriots who revered the heroes of Chickamauga and Gettysburg to maintain high tariffs, keep the carpetbaggers in power and vote steadfastly against all candidates for office who ran under the banner of the Democratic party. It fought vehemently to win pensions, first for disabled veterans and at last for all men who had ever worn the Union blue. And for two or three decades it had prodigious power.

But the country matured, and so did the members of the Grand Army of the Republic, and around the turn of the century it began to move down the sunset slope. It got away from politics and self-interest and devoted itself, quite simply, to remembering the war—the great days that had been lived, the great things that had been done, the mysterious dedication that had enabled hundreds of thousands of young men to serve something greater than themselves. And at this point a strange change took place.

As the G.A.R.'s political influence died, its moral and emotional influence increased. It became the keeper of a great tradition, and at last it became the tradition itself, the incarnation of the tragedy and the truth that lay behind the shadowed years of the 1860's.

The old age of the Grand Army must have been rather lonely. The Grand Army belonged to a simple, unsophisticated time, and as simplicity departed and sophistication arrived it moved in something like a vacuum. Its home was the small town, the Odd Fellows Hall and the village park, the shaded cemetery with faded little flags waving forlornly among the headstones. When the Army marched it moved slowly to the ragged, inexpert rhythm of the amateur band, and as the ranks thinned year after year it became evident that the men were not so much parading past an observer as moving on toward some mystic goal of fulfillment and reunion in which no one else could share.

The life of the Grand Army men became a series of silent farewells, of Decoration Day observances in the warm May sunlight, of painfully recited tributes "to our departed comrades." A haze of unreality lay across the present, and only the faraway past spoke with an authentic voice. The men lived in memories and yet in a queer way they seemed almost to live in the future as well, for implicit in all of their observances was some unimaginable get-together over on the other shore. And the younger generation, looking on with tolerant inattention, began to consider these men well-intentioned old bores.

How could it have been otherwise? These old soldiers lived under the strangest conditions men can know. They had reached the very pinnacle of human experience before they were out of their teens.

No matter what they might do, once they left off soldiering to become civilians again, nothing could hapen to them that would be as stirring and as meaningful as what they had already had. To a man who has lived through a Pickett's charge—on whichever side of the field—anything else is going to be anticlimax. These men were set apart not merely from their fellows but from life itself by the terrible and unforgettable days of their early youth.

They spent all of their adult lives in a pathetic isolation. As the

Army grew older it came to seem like a mute and oddly unreachable survival of the olden days, forever passing in silent review, forever cut off from real communication with those who were reviewing it.

The change came, along toward the very end, when the past that spoke through these men began to get through to people once more. Here, on the seventy-fifth anniversary of the great battle, almost two thousand Northern and Southern veterans camped once again, as they had twenty-five years before on the slanting fields around the historic little Pennsylvania town, shook hands across the chasm of the dead years and for a few days brought back to life a little of the history they had made.

It was about then that the country began to realize that it possessed in these old men a living tradition that was inexpressibly significant and precious. North and South, they stood for something: something more than just the memory of far-off battles and youthful valor, something that went to the very heart and center of the American experience.

This living tradition, obviously, was all-inclusive. When the old men in blue and gray clasped hands over the low stone wall that runs across Gettysburg's famous high-watermark ridge, they were not simply winner and loser exchanging sportsmanlike words after a stirring game of tennis. They were men who, seventy-five years earlier, had tried their level best to kill one another, meeting now in the final twilight with a new perspective on the meaning of their old enmity.

The Grand Army had been wrong, in the old bloody shirt days; whatever the high comradeship of the Civil War meant, whatever the war itself meant, with all of its heartbreak and suffering, the United Confederate Veterans belonged in it along with the G.A.R. They were part of the same tradition.

Which was the beginning of wisdom. For it began to be apparent that something more than a romantic swords-and-roses drama lay back of these aging veterans. The Civil War had not been just an incident. In a compelling way it was somehow a continuous process, a permanent possession of the American people, an unlimited experience which had added the enlightening and ennobling element of tragedy to American life. The heritage that derived from it went so far beyond victory or defeat that the words ceased to mean anything. Out of that gigantic struggle the nation had gained a commitment to the future, a commitment which made the old lines of sectional antagonism insignificant.

And as the long parade moved on toward its end the nature of that commitment began to be clear. By fighting the Civil War the nation had unconsciously dedicated itself to two lofty, almost unattainable ideals: to the notion that there must be a unity in human society—that no man is finally an island, that we are members one of another, that our salvation must eventually lie in the striving toward brotherhood—and to the idea that human freedom is something that goes all across the board.

That dual goal will not be reached for a very long time, but the effort to reach it is what gives American life its deepest significance. The obligation to make the effort, and to keep on with it in spite of doubt and discouragement, is the strongest moral force in the world today. It is not by accident that America during the last decades has stood as the world's great bulwark against a rising tide of dictatorship and oppression. The ability to stand so—the built-in quality that compels us to stand so, and leads free people everywhere to gain new hope and courage because of our stand—was bought in the Civil War. If something was won then, that is what it was. Be it noted, too, that, North and South together, we did not win this from each other; perhaps we won it *for* each other.

To all of which the last files of the Grand Army might have assented. As the final shadows lengthened and deepened, the old men learned something, and the notion that there had been something in the war that could not be expressed in the simple words "victory" and "defeat" finally came to them.

They would at least have subscribed to the proposition that the Civil War was something to be felt rather than something to be fully understood; and it was in the realm of the emotions that their bannered parade had its greatest impact.

For the Grand Army of the Republic (precisely like the United Confederate Veterans) was above everything else a carrier of emotion. Back of it were the watchfires of a thousand circling camps, the crowds that had lined unpaved streets to cry and cheer as young men went off to war, the swift disillusionment that training camp and route march brought to adolescent innocents who had followed drums and fifes and waving flags, and the bleak boredom of comfortless bivouacs and the quick terror of battle.

What was gained and lost in all of this, and what was paid for it by the young men who lived through it, could never really be totaled up and explained; it could only be felt, and the generations which witnessed the parade of the old soldiers were touched by something beyond the bounds of their own experience. Moved by some inkling of what these old men had felt, and moved even more by the men themselves, we who looked on learned a little more about what America meant, learned to understand at least a little of the tragedy and the incomprehensible splendor of human life.

Now the parade is finished. It began in 1861 and it stopped just the other day, and in one way or another all America moved with it. The last flag has been furled and the last drum-tap has died away, and we have lost something we can never regain. One very old man died, and all of us are made a little more lonely.

THE MEANING
OF THE WEST

by A. B. Guthrie Jr.

APRIL 13, 1959

> *Every year wagons lumbering through the grim grandeur*
> *of Death Valley re-enact an episode from California's past.*
> *In similar varieties of civic whoopdedo—pageantry,*
> *fiestas, costumery, mock gunfights—the West*
> *commemorates its history. This piece by A. B. Guthrie Jr.,*
> *who lives in Montana and whose novels are among the best*
> *ever written on the early West, reaches to the heart of the*
> *U.S. fascination for the West—apparently an endless one.*
> *Thoreau once put it this way: "Eastward I go*
> *only by force: but westward I go free."*

Americans east and west are a sunset people. From the Atlantic sea-board, over the Appalachians, through the wooded valleys, past the flatlands, on to the high plains, the Rockies and the Pacific, there goes our course, and somewhere along the western way lies heart's desire.

Millions of us have made the trip in fact and, settled, keep making it, in association with travelers before our time and through episodes and over trails outside our experience. Others, not so lucky as to have made the actual journey, travel altogether by way of illusion, on page or screen becoming one with Lewis and Clark, with buckskinned beaver hunters, with home-seekers on the Oregon Trail, with Wild

546

Bill Hickok and Calamity Jane, with the panners of gold at the grass roots and the cowmen to whom grass was gold, with the men good and bad of Dodge City and Tombstone. It doesn't matter for our purposes that true characters have been altered often and real situations falsified or that some presentations are downright silly and others endlessly repetitious. Somehow they still are the West.

The direction was pointed a long time ago by one whose words roll down the centuries. That was Cabeza de Vaca, sixteenth-century Spanish adventurer. In his search for the golden Seven Cities he had endured much, and now, as before, he was lost, this time near the present dividing line between Texas and New Mexico, but still he could say of that summer of 1535, ". . . We ever held it certain that going toward the sunset we must find what we desired."

Some three hundred years went by before another man so well expressed the sentiment. From his little vantage point in New England, Henry David Thoreau wrote, "When I go out of the house for a walk, uncertain as yet whither I will bend my steps, and submit myself to my instinct to decide for me, I find, strange and whimsical as it may seem, that I finally and inevitably settle southwest. . . . The future lies that way to me, and the earth seems more unexhausted and richer on that side. . . . Eastward I go only by force; but westward I go free."

Though he was a native and lifelong resident of the Atlantic coast, Walt Whitman, too, felt the pull of sun. "These States," he said, "tend inland and toward the Western sea, and I will also."

The feeling is in a majority of us still. It helps to account for our fascination with American history, since all parts of our country inland from the Atlantic shore once were west and we chose with Thoreau— as if the choice were hard!—to "walk toward Oregon, and not toward Europe." It helps particularly to account for our fascination with the present West and its history.

This fascination reveals itself in a multitude of ways.

With the state centennial coming up, a man hitches oxen to a cart and slow-wheels from northern Minnesota to Minneapolis. Old buildings are preserved and restored, as in the early gold camps of Columbia, California, and Virginia City, Montana. A wagon train re-enacts the first Death Valley pilgrimage. Billy the Kid makes his last escape again. Every year there dangles from a rope the body of Joe Slade, the mean drunk up from Colorado for whom Montana Vigilantes held a necktie party, perhaps with less than justice. Lake City, Colorado, retries Alfred Packer on charges of murder and cannibalism. The Pony Express renews operations. An old locomotive pants as it panted before. Collectors are hot after old Western paintings, old Western firearms, old Western books.

Individuals still travel the Oregon Trail, from the Missouri to the Kaw to the Platte, to Courthouse and Chimney Rocks, to Scotts Bluff, to Fort Laramie and over South Pass to Fort Bridger, and here now is Bear River and yonder, somewhere across the long miles, the Blue Mountains and, beyond them, the new home in the West.

Every summer at flood tide a random flotilla of small boats leaves Fort Benton, Montana, the old head of navigation on the unruly Missouri. For most of them terminus is Fort Peck, Montana, but some get around the dam and go on, on to St. Louis and sometimes even farther. Between Benton and Peck the voyagers roll back the decades. They become Lewis and Clark, camping on or near the sites the two captains chose. Or they are Prince Maximilian of Wied, the German savant who came this way in 1833, or fellows of the fur-trade officials on keelboats that had to be wrestled upriver. Or they are Captain Joe La Barge or Captain Grant Marsh, who could pilot their paddle-wheel steamers on dew. No matter. They see the Walls of the Mountains and the Coal Banks and the White Castles, and in country so grim as to prohibit population and so grand as to flutter the heart they develop the look of wonder that stares at you from old reports.

Along the California Trail, the Mormon Trail, the Santa Fe Trail, beside or atop Independence Rock, in the vicinities where members of the Donner party traveled and starved and with rare exception subsisted—a pitiful few of them—on the corpses of the less hardy, the tourist stops for a minute, for an hour, for a day or maybe more. With him are the gold-seekers, the travelers to the New Jerusalem, the chiselers in stone of names long since forgotten, the crews of caravans to the rich Spanish Trade. And one of the Donner party toasts on a stick a human heart that just has quit pulsing. History is here, Western history, and it beats in the blood; and the visitor knows that there is no past: the past is now.

We are captivated by sheer adventure, by the rediscovery of adventure, by the hard simplicities of loneliness, privation, danger, the elemental contests of man versus nature and man versus man.

We are caught up in admiration for the men who went before, as courageous and hardy as we wish to be and never can or shall be.

We are atavistic, in rebellion against the conventions and limitations and order and tameness of what we call civilization. Give us the good old raw days! The South has always taken pride in gracious living. Almost from the start the North has had its gods of culture, government, shipping and finance. Both sections celebrate aspects of civilization. But more important in our whole thinking and inclination is the old and uncivilized West, the West of rugged individuality, of lawlessness, hardship, license, dispute and resolution by revolver and rifle, the West whether in legend or fact that opposes propriety.

We watch motion picture and TV Westerns because they give us the simple choices of good and bad and don't tax our minds.

We like the West because it underscores our ancient and vestigial dislike of things European, like wiggery on the bench and the anti-democracy of caste.

These reasons apply east and west, though eastern critics keep asking why actual Westerners buy the myth of the West when they know better. Why do they read and write formula Western fiction, which takes a germ of fact and by artificial insemination procreates a whole colony? Why do they go to Western movies? Why do they sit hypnotized when the gunman of legend comes on the TV screen? Why do they affect big hats, jeans or frontier pants and cowboy boots when most of them never bridle a horse, can't harness a team and live by virtue of commerce in oil or insurance or underwear?

Because the "becauses" are common to all of us. Because the state of knowing better never has been fatal to fantasy. That a time never quite was, that a represented thing never happened, that hero and "heavy" in actual life weren't that way, all these detractions grow niggling against gallop and gunshot. And except for the plainly functional, all styles of dress are affectations anyway, made popular by custom, designers, whim or whatever. Think of the Homburg or Ivy League suits, or the vaunted variations of old Congress gaiters. (It can be thrown in here that the cowboy boot with its high heel, though fashioned for the foot in the stirrup, is in fact a great comfort to the foot on the throttle.)

The foregoing explanations are all true but do not constitute the whole truth. Other and deeper ones hit closer home.

The greatest value in the West, if not the first reason for our fascination with its history, actual and exaggerated, is the specialty of space. Though the great open spaces is a term turned comic, its appeal abides. While thronging the earth with his offspring, man still hankers for room for himself, room, as the late Joseph Kinsey Howard of Montana put it, to swing his elbows and his mind. He not only hankers for it; he insists on having it, whether in fact or vicariously.

Early in our national experience that compulsion was recognized. Writing in 1786, Thomas Jefferson expressed the belief that a density of ten persons to the square mile was about the limit of endurance. "Wherever we reach that," he wrote, "the inhabitants become uneasy as too much compressed, and go off in great numbers to search for vacant country." His opinion is kinder and truer than the postulation that misfits and neurotics populated the West, which served the happy function of a safety valve for the pressures of social and economic conflict in the East.

Space, then.

By Jeffersonian standards a sizable portion of the old West still qualifies, if not as vacant, then as generally agreeable. Consider the Rocky Mountain states. Colorado with its great and growing city of Denver numbers only about thirteen people to the square mile. A hundred and fifty years and more after Jefferson, the states of Utah, Idaho, Arizona, New Mexico, Montana, Wyoming and Nevada are well under his limit. Today he might revise his maximum and include border and Pacific states—Texas, Kansas, Nebraska, Oregon and Washington—which count far fewer than forty people to the mile. (California, with the population of its crowded cities spread by average into still-existent space, would have to be excluded.)

Massachusetts, by contrast with her Western sisters, can count 596.2 noses per unit, New York 309.3.

The West, the thinly peopled West, thus satisfies a basic desire, in actuality or image, as does the larger West of history and fiction. A man still has room to gallop a horse, unequipped with rear-vision mirror. He can look across the miles without being reminded that the continent is infested with his kind.

Space breeds its own type of man, and here again is a reason for the general leaning. The true Westerner is not necessarily better or worse than the product of congestion, but he is very likely to be different. He is commonly freer and friendlier. He hasn't learned to be suspicious. He appraises a man for his worth, not his wealth and for sure not his ancestry. Weather and work and the demands on himself alone have shaped him, and chance has taught him to take fortune as it unfolds. Ordinarily he has a stout sense of humor. He can dismiss an adversity with a shrug or a wisecrack.

Perhaps above all, he is democratic. In him lingers the old liberalizing effect of free land. No class system could develop where acres were to be had for the asking, and the lines that exist today are few and faint. In all probability the penniless Westerner wouldn't know what you meant by "proletarian." Broke, he's still as good as the next man.

These attitudes, these ways will pass and are passing now, but while they endure we can think, all of us, that life can be different and good and refreshing, and when they are gone, we shall keep digging them up for page and screen and festival, and somehow we shall feel renewed.

The West is our youth, the youth of our nation and, by translation, the youth of us all. Beyond the beckoning vestige, it is a harking back to simpler and more vigorous and buoyant—yes, and more violent— days. Its history, like our green years, is right there, or just was. We can almost catch it by the coattails. The fragrance of its leaving lingers in the still unsettled dust of departure. We reach for it, for the stout heart and muscles of yesterday, for the great and exciting pastures of innocence, for the young simplicities of right and wrong, for the vanished opportunities to do our stuff.

It doesn't matter too much that our hands come back empty. They were close, so close that for a moment we hunted furs with the mountain men and caught the firelight playing in the eyes of Indian girls.

Or we traveled the Oregon Trail with old Joel Palmer and fought the muscled waters of the Snake. Or we panned the gleaming gold from the placer mines of California, Colorado, Idaho. Or we helped string up Henry Plummer, the murderous sheriff of the Montana gold camps, or walked with Doc Holliday to the fight at the O.K. Corral. Or we stood stout with Captain Benteen against the circling Sioux after Custer had fallen.

We were young for that moment, and the land was young, and the old westering was fresh in our blood. And maybe, despite the immediate toil and excitement, we thought *America, America,* from the pygmy beginnings of Jamestown and Plymouth across the unimagined miles to the bar and balm of the Pacific. Farms are chopped out along the way. Cabins rise. Ferries start up. Here's a fort or a cross-trail tavern, germ of a city to be. Out of the woods, then, to the new land, to the strange and bare land, to the Great American Desert, where undreamed-of herdsmen and tillers and armed contestants soon will add to knowledge and legend. On toward the still brief-storied mountains, on toward Oregon, California, maybe Washington, and the hell with Indians, Mexicans, British, the hell with weather and windfall and river and range. Men drop out along the way to try their luck here and there, but wheels roll on, hoofs plod, and other men won't turn or tarry.

Furs. Fish. Small crops. Lumber. Gold in the mountains. Fat grass on the plains, fertile soil in the desert. Ranches. Irrigation. Dryland farms. Cities and towns. Industries. Today.

It all happened almost under our eyes. Two long lifetimes span much of it. Seeing it again on the screens of our minds, we think how happy is that hard phrase, Manifest Destiny. And we know that, more than journey's end, it is the journey itself that enchants us. The fresh and free years. The years of youth.

If there is a prime reason less than mystic for our enduring attachment to the West of fact and story, it can now perhaps be capsuled. The West freed and frees us. It emphasized and emphasizes us as individuals—this in an elsewhere and nowadays world which at its freest and best still dwarfs individuality by congestion and restricts high adventure to a Sunday afternoon picnic. The West still makes the blood sing as it used to sing when hearts were stout and vistas inviting and the limit of hope in each of us was the far-western sea.

The West is an adventure of the spirit.

Each passing generation of actual inhabitants loses the West, and each succeeding one rediscovers it. For mountain men like Jim Bridger and Tom Fitzpatrick the end came when beaver thinned out and Londoners ruined the market, to boot, by quitting fur hats in favor of them newfangled silk ones. It came for the hide-hunter when he had killed all the buffalo and put himself out of business. In Montana a bunch of them named a place Belly Ups. It came for the placer miner when the placers played out. With the wolves gone, the West was gone for the wolfer. The cowpuncher rode high, wide and handsome, but not for long after some fool invented barbed wire. Fences, internal combustion and the increasing number of pilgrims finished the good life for Charlie Russell, the famous Western painter, himself once a pilgrim. His later years were years of lament. Owen Wister married the West, only to divorce it when it turned false. Today's aging homesteaders, destroyers of one West, pine for their own good old days.

Out of informed imagination, sympathy and perhaps a touch of the same personal sentiment, Walter Prescott Webb, the Texas historian, speaks eloquently in his study, *The Great Frontier:*

"The period of fusion is about over, the loom is about full, the tapestry of an epoch is almost finished. . . . The imagination cannot play any more with the mystery and uncertainty of a half-known world, for there is no such thing. The map is finished, the roads are surveyed, and all the paths to that kind of adventure are plainly marked and tended. . . . The end of an age is always touched with sadness for those who lived it and those who love it. . . . The people are going to miss the frontier more than words can express. For four centuries they heard it call, listened to its promises, and bet their lives and fortunes on its outcome. It calls no more, and regardless of how they bend their ears for its faint whisper they cannot hear the suggestion of a promise."

Admit the broad position but take some exception. All is not lost. They come season after season, the new finders of the West: tourists, dude-ranch guests, members of the military, chain-company transplantees, traveling men who have not been this way before. After

New York or Chicago or St. Louis here is virgin land, here is the real thing, the unpossessed and pristine property. They look with wonder and delight, many of them do, feeling within themselves the cozy excitement of discovery. This foot may be the first that trod here. These lungs breathe air no others ever breathed. *Space is mine. I am filled, I flow with it, and so at last am free.*

An astonishing number of these new discoverers stay in the West. An astonishing number return whenever they can. An astonishing number hate the necessity of leaving. But were they all to settle, the last vestige of the West would vanish.

I have made the trip west many times, and never with a lessening of old elation. Once, flying, I went instantly from Courthouse Rock to Chimney Rock, a whole day's journey on the trail to Oregon, but I could see them underneath me there in present-day Nebraska, the laden wagons, the patient oxen, the striving men, the anxious and long-suffering women, all wheeling out our history. The pistons pounded and the props tore air, but above the din came "Gee" and "Haw."

By car I approach or reach or pass the 98th meridian, the rough dividing line between woodland and plain. I come to Tulsa or Topeka or Fargo or Fort Worth or Sioux Falls, and I can smell home. Even eastward along the Mississippi, at Dubuque or Davenport or Burlington or St. Louis or Minneapolis, its scent blows in the wind. When I attain the Missouri, if my route lies that way, I'm in full chase. From here all ways lie west. The Black Hills. The Little Bighorn. The Sweetwater and the Wind River range. The Colorado Rockies and the mountain parks where wintered mountain men. Virginia City and the Comstock Lode. Taos and old Santa Fe. The Grand Canyon. Between me and them the fields of truth and story. And always beyond, the golden shore.

In these directions, any of them, the roads will straighten and traffic thin. The land will shine, the long and young yet memoried land of wish, and distance will expand my chest. Here, now, looking westward, I've got the whole world in my hand, and going toward the sunset I shall find what I desire.

554

VIII
RELIGIONS

Rembrandt

WHAT THE JEWS BELIEVE

by Rabbi Philip S. Bernstein

SEPTEMBER 11, 1950

> At the beginning of Judaism's 5,711th year, Rabbi Philip
> Bernstein explained in LIFE the ancient teachings of the
> Jews that start with a drop of honey on the first page the
> child is to learn to read. Dr. Bernstein has been Rabbi of
> Temple B'rith Kodesh at Rochester, N.Y., since 1926.
> He was president of the Central Conference of American
> Rabbis from 1950 to 1952. So great was the response to this
> article that Dr. Bernstein expanded it into a book.

The Jew has no single organized church. He has no priests. The concept of salvation by faith is alien to his mind. Yet he has deep religious convictions which run like golden threads through all Jewish history. For him Judaism is a way of life, here and now. He does not serve his God for the sake of reward, for the fruit of the good life *is* the good life. Thus his answers about the nature of his religious beliefs are profoundly different from the answers made by Christians.

Judaism around the world is marked by diversity of practice and latitude of faith. But for all the degrees of divergence on detail, a great common denominator of faith unites most American Jews. This unique agreement is not imposed from the top down upon the congregations because the Jew acknowledges no supreme ecclesiastical authority, but rather it wells up from the depth of the Jewish heart, nourished in the long history of an ancient people.

In the days of ancient Israel the priesthood at Jerusalem laid down the law for all Jews. Then, in 586 B.C., Nebuchadnezzar besieged Jerusalem, demolished Solomon's Temple and carried the Jews into exile in Babylon. With their Temple and their priesthood gone, the Jews in the strange new communities where they found themselves formed voluntary assemblages for common worship and study of the law. These congregations were called synagogues, quite free and independent of one another. This institution proved so valuable that it has been continued to this day as the method of Jewish worship. It also provided the basic pattern for the churches which, after Paul, the Christians set up and developed along more unified lines. Among the Jews, however, the synagogue has survived in its pristine form. Any ten adult male Jews today can establish a congregation.

In the central fortress of Jewish spirituality, the Torah is the repository for the Law of Judaism. Torah embraces a triple meaning. Primarily it is the Sacred Scrolls found in every synagogue. These are contained in an ornamental ark which, whenever possible, is built into the wall of the structure so that when the congregation faces it they look toward Jerusalem's Holy Temple. This is an abiding reminder of the Biblical Ark of the Covenant in which the Tablets of the Law were carried. The Torah scrolls are written by hand on parchment, fastidiously and often beautifully done by one who is usually a descendant of generations of scribes. In 1908 when the synagogue of which this writer is now minister burned down, an Irish policeman dashed to the ark and seized the Torah. He handed it to the rabbi who was rushing up to the building. "Here," he said, "I saved your crucifix." Well, the Jews have no crucifix, but the policeman had the right idea: the scrolls are the most sacred symbols of Judaism.

Torah has a second meaning: the Pentateuch, the first five books of the Bible: Genesis, Exodus, Leviticus, Numbers, Deuteronomy.

These books are the acknowledged foundation of Judaism, containing the principles of the faith, the Ten Commandments, the golden rule, the laws of holiness. The Pentateuch is at once the biography of the greatest Jew of all time—Moses—and the history of the formation of the Jewish nation and the development of its faith. It runs the whole gamut of Jewish spiritual experience from the sublime poetry of the creation narrative to the minutiae of the dietary laws. So precious is the Pentateuch to the Jews that they divide it into fixed weekly portions and read them on every Sabbath and holy day in the year. When the sacred round is completed, there is the gay festival of Simchas Torah ("rejoicing in the law") at which the last verses of Deuteronomy are followed by the first verses of Genesis, symbolizing the eternal cycle of the law.

Finally, Torah means teaching, learning, doctrine. If a Jew says, "Let us study Torah," he might be referring to the Pentateuch or to the Prophets or to the Talmud or any of the sacred writings. He is certainly referring to the first obligation of the Jew to study God's ways and requirements as revealed in Holy Writ.

For a Jew the educational process begins at the age of five. According to tradition, a drop of honey is placed on the first page the child is to learn to read; he kisses it, thus beginning an association of pleasantness which is expected to last through life. When most of the world was illiterate, every Jewish boy could read and by thirteen was advanced in the study of a complex literature. Thus arose the love of learning, the keenness of intellect to be found among so many Jews.

For all his love of learning for its own sake, the religious Jew finds much more in the Torah than burdensome legalism. It is an unending source of inspiration and practical help to him. He begins and ends the day with prayers. He thanks God before and after every meal, even when he washes his hands. All his waking day the traditional Jew wears a ritual scarf beneath his outer garments as a reminder of God's nearness and love. There are prescribed prayers for birth, circumcision, marriage, illness, death. Even the appearance of a rainbow evokes an ancient psalm of praise. In effect, law means the sanctification of life.

Jews never regarded the codification of law as a strait jacket. One basic device keeps it fluid: the oral law which supplemented the written law and was subject to emendation, interpretation, adaptation. For example, the ancient Torah says, "An eye for an eye." In itself this was an advance over the laws of the surrounding tribes which usually prescribed death for the taking of an eye. Nevertheless the sages were not content to let this law stand. They said that the intent of the law was to compel the offender to pay in damages the accepted equivalent for the loss of an eye. Thus the written law was not repudiated but became the basis of a sensible adaptation to the realities of human society. As another example, the Torah proclaimed, "Remember the Sabbath day to keep it holy." Jews observed this commandment with the greatest seriousness, but in the oral law the rabbis evolved a whole series of necessary exceptions. They said the Sabbath could be violated to bring help to the sick or to defend oneself against attack. They formulated it into a principle, stating long before Jesus was born that the Sabbath was made for man, not man for the Sabbath.

The central prayer of Judaism is the Shema: "Hear, O Israel, the Lord our God, the Lord is One." This is the heart of every Jewish service. More, it is recited by the Jew when he believes death is approaching. Together with "Thou shalt love the Lord thy God with all thy heart," it is to be found in printed form in the Mezuzah, the little tubed case placed on the doorposts of the homes of observant Jews, a constant reminder of God's presence and a sign of the Jewishness of the inhabitants.

Following Paul, the Shema took on a new significance. Although Jews are able, if they wish, to understand Jesus, the Jew of Nazareth, they have never been able to understand or accept the idea of the Trinity. Thus from the beginning of the Christian era to this day, the Shema has been the rallying point of Jewish loyalty confronting the persecution or the blandishments of a daughter religion.

For the modern American Jew two meanings have emerged which, while not new, are current in their emphasis. The first, suggested by the writings of Albert Einstein, is, in effect, the scientific confirmation of the unity of God which binds the atom to the stars in universal law. The advances in human knowledge, always welcomed by the

Jew, seem to vindicate his basic belief in the oneness of the universe.

From God to man, from His Fatherhood to our brotherhood—this is the second meaning of the Shema to modern Jews. The concept of human oneness has always been an integral element in the Jewish religious outlook. Frequently this has been misunderstood because of the Jews' insistence on remaining a distinctive group. The Jew has never believed that brotherhood means regimentation, the elimination of differences or the stifling of minorities. Loving your neighbor as yourself, he believes, requires respect for differences. One of the great rabbis who lived more than two thousand years ago said that the most important statement in the Bible was not the Ten Commandments nor the golden rule but "This is the book of the generations of man." To the Jews themselves the Scriptures were not the heritage of a single people but of all humanity.

The prayer which after the Shema has the deepest hold on all Jews is the Kaddish. In actual practice it is the prayer honoring the dead, recited for a year after the death of a loved one and on the anniversaries thereafter. Its solemn phrases exalt the name of God and pray for the coming of His Kingdom. "Exalted and hallowed be the name of God throughout the world. . . . May His Kingdom come, His will be done." There is no doubt that Jesus spoke this ancient prayer in the synagogue and that it became the basis for the Lord's Prayer.

Though honoring the dead, the Kaddish does not make specific the Jewish attitude toward immortality. For the Jews have never agreed on what happens after death. Most Jews of recent centuries have recited the Credo of Maimonides, the twelfth-century physician-philosopher who affirmed the physical resurrection of the dead. But the hearts of many stricken Jews have also echoed the lament of Job: "As the cloud is consumed and vanisheth away so he that goeth down to the grave shall come up no more." Modern Jews have tended increasingly less to believe in physical resurrection. This probably accounts for the increasing trend toward cremation which is found among non-Orthodox Jews. Among American Jews the Kaddish is returning more to its original meaning, our acknowledgment of God's rule and readiness to leave our ultimate fate in His hands.

"The catechism of the Jew is his calendar," said Samson Raphael Hirsch, nineteenth-century German rabbi. One can learn more about the mainsprings of the Jew's spirituality from the cycle of year-round observances than from any formal statement of faith. In these are revealed his habits of thought and feeling, his historic memories and patterns of religious conduct.

In the annual cycle of religious observances followed by American Jews, the new year begins in the early fall—this year [1950] on September 12. According to traditional Biblical chronology, this week begins the 5,711th year since creation. The advent of the new year is greeted in a spirit far removed from the festivities of January 1. It ushers in a ten-day period of penitence, culminating in the fast of Yom Kippur and dedicated to spiritual stock-taking. What is man? What is our life? What will be our fate? Some Jews have believed literally, others metaphorically, that on the new year the books of life are spread open before the Great Judge. In this period of judgment it is determined "who shall live and who shall die, who shall be at rest and who shall wander, who shall be tranquil and who shall be harassed, who shall become poor and who shall wax rich, who shall be brought low and who shall be exalted."

This holy-day period is pervaded with a solemn appraisal of the facts of our frail human existence. No attempt is made to gloss over the evils of life. God's ways may be inscrutable, but ultimately they are accepted as just. Therefore the fear of the Lord is the beginning of wisdom. Judaism offers no easy way to God. No son has been sent down to lead us to Him. No mediator intercedes for us. In the final accounting there is a purely personal relationship between the individual and his God. This is an awesome responsibility. Need we wonder, then, that this penitential period is known as the Days of Awe? Even the blowing of the Shofar, the ram's horn, which from Biblical times has announced the New Year, penetrates into the heart of the modern Jew and causes it to tremble.

The climax is reached on Yom Kippur. Like all Jewish holidays it begins at sundown, for Jews follow the Biblical pattern of creation: "There was evening and there was morning, one day." The service opens with the Kol Nidre chant. This is the most stirring, the most haunting melody in the entire religious experience of Jews. The words are a plea for the absolution of vows made under duress the preceding year—a plea that was poignantly meaningful at the time of forced conversions of Jews to Christianity during the Middle Ages.

The spiritual concern of Yom Kippur is with our human sinfulness —but what is sin? To answer this question we must go back to Judaism's balanced interpretations of the nature of man. On the one hand there are no perfect saints in the Jewish tradition. Even Moses, the greatest Jew of all time, was denied admittance to the promised land because he disobeyed God. But Judaism, on the other hand, does not regard man as inherently sinful or depraved. Our instinctive drives are considered good because God gave them to us. There is no asceticism in Judaism, no retreat to monasteries. Celibacy is not required of the rabbis. The rabbis of the Talmud maintain that much good has come from our so-called "evil desires." They say that our sex drive has produced love, marriage, the family, the perpetuation of the race. Without the acquisitive instinct, they claim, homes would not be built, fields would not be tilled.

In its Hebrew origin the most commonly used word for sin means "missing the mark"—the repudiation of God's commandments. There are, it must be added, various formulations of God's requirements. While the Torah lists 613 commands, Micah reduced them to three: "To do justly, to love mercy and to walk humbly before God." How do we walk in God's way? The answer is given in the climactic moment of the Yom Kippur morning service, when the rabbi stands before the ark and, about to remove the scrolls, prays in words proclaimed of old to Moses: "God, merciful, gracious, long-suffering, abundant in goodness and ever true." Such are God's ways, and such must be ours. Atonement must include not only rapprochement with God but also expiation toward our fellow men.

On Yom Kippur, God forgives our sins against Him but not the wrongs we have done our fellow men. Only the penance of restitution can clear the way for God's grace. The rabbis go beyond this and say, "Whoever has a sin to confess and is ashamed to do so, let him go and do a good deed and he will find forgiveness."

Jews, like other religionists, have been troubled by the paradox of man's sinfulness. Why, if we were created by a good and omnipotent God, do we have and use the capacity to do evil? Judaism has no general theological explanation of "sin" such as Christianity offers in the doctrine of man's fall. In the Jewish religion sinning is simply a wrong which the individual may or may not commit, depending upon his character and free choice. As the rabbis say, everything is in the hands of God but the fear of God. To free men and women, then, the Yom Kippur service brings this great challenge: "Behold, I set before thee this day life and good, death and evil . . . therefore choose life that ye may live."

In the atonement process there is a profound mystical element. God meets us halfway. First, we must acknowledge our waywardness. He who recognizes his sin has already begun to loosen its hold on him. Then, where possible, there must be expiation, restitution. Now the Jew is ready for penitent prayers. Many of them are in the plural form, "*We* have sinned, *we* have done perversely." Thus it is recognized how deeply we are involved in one another's weaknesses and failures. Then, worn with fasting and humble in penitence, the worshiper may be ready for God's forgiveness. But God's forgiveness does not come easily. He searches the innermost recesses of the heart; no secrets are hidden from Him. His probings make His task of forgiveness even more difficult. So on Yom Kippur, say the rabbis, even God Himself must pray:

> May my mercy conquer my wrath
> So that I may treat my children with love.

Jews leave Yom Kippur with a great sense of exaltation. This is tempered by a sense of relief, for no one can live continuously on that high and exacting level. Again the sense of balance asserts itself. After a lapse of only four days the Festival of Tabernacles begins. This is a happy fall holiday of thanksgiving.

With winter come two holidays which dramatize a distinctive feature of Jewish experience. Chanukah and Purim tell with colorful ceremony of attempts to destroy the Jewish people and of the defeat of the persecutors. This recurring emphasis on oppression and its overthrow represents a people's choice of what it wishes to remember. In this sense, as Thomas Mann has said, character is fate. The inner nature of the people leads it to select from its past that which is necessary for survival and for the perpetuation of its specific values. Thus memory shapes its destiny. So Jews have chosen to remember that always their faith and God's justice have prevailed against oppressors —from the age of the pyramids of ancient Egypt to the gutted Reichschancellery in Berlin.

Chanukah, which comes in December, is historical and deeply spiritual, commemorating the Jewish people's successful struggle against the persecution of Antiochus IV, less than two centuries before the birth of Jesus. Antiochus desecrated the Jews' sacred Temple, in the year 168 B.C., by the erection of Greek idols, before which he ordered the Jews to bow down. Old Mattathias, the priest, aroused his people. Shouting "Whosoever is zealous of the Law, let him follow me," he and his son, Judah the Maccabee, led the outnumbered and ill-equipped Jews to victory—and to the rededication (Chanukah) of their Temple. They found a cruse of oil which, according to the account in the First Book of Maccabees, lasted eight days. Ever since, the Jews have lit candles in their homes for eight days, one the first night, two the second, etc.

Purim, which usually falls in March, is a folk tale almost devoid of religious meaning. In ancient Persia a vizier named Haman sought to exterminate the Jews for being "different." His wicked designs were thwarted by Queen Esther and her uncle, Mordecai. He who plotted to kill the Jews was himself hanged.

Perhaps even more than Chanukah and Purim, Passover is a festival of freedom, celebrating the liberation of the ancient Hebrews from Egyptian bondage. This first great mass emancipation in recorded history has always inspired not only the reverent memory of Jews but the imagination of all free mankind. On the American Liberty Bell are words not of Washington but of Moses: "Proclaim liberty throughout the land to all the inhabitants thereof." It may be safely said that after this first great liberation men were never content again to be in chains.

Each Jew is taught to feel as if he personally had been liberated from Egypt. This feeling is imparted chiefly through the Seder, the loveliest and most moving of all Jewish ceremonies. For this home observance of the first two evenings of Passover, the families gather from near and far. The atmosphere is festive. The service includes ancient gay songs and games for the children. At a dramatic moment during it, the door of the house is thrown open for the return of Elijah, the prophet, to bring news of the coming of the Messiah.

The profoundest meaning of Passover is something which sets Judaism apart from all other religions, for it marks the birth of a nation. Out of a mass of slaves Moses fashioned a nation and gave them a faith. From that day, Jews have never ceased to be a people. They have not been a sect or denomination.

Nationhood was the natural state of the ancient Hebrews in their own land. But what held them together as a people through the nineteen centuries from the time Titus drove them out until their return to Israel in 1948? Certainly their faith was the principal binding force. By the time of the dispersion their faith was surrounded by a whole rubric of laws and customs which set them apart—and was afflicted with a persecution only strengthening their sense of solidarity. Beyond this was the sense of mission: Jews believed they were the chosen people.

This doctrine has lent itself to much misunderstanding. It has been compared with the German Nazi or the Russian Communist sense of mission. But it has nothing to do with conquest, power, glory. Its classic definition was that of the prophet Isaiah, a "suffering servant." When the Jews were chosen, they received not a crown but a yoke. "You alone have I known; therefore will I punish you for your iniquities." Their burden was the acceptance of exacting responsibility, their goal the realization of God's justice—first in their own nation and then in the life of all humanity. A people that is so chosen (or, as some Jewish modernists believe, so chose) to be witnesses of the living God must live with a sense of special mission that sets them apart. They discourage intermarriage; by belief and custom they remain a distinctive group. This exacts a price, often a terrible one, for many men do not understand those who seem determinedly different. What they do not understand, they fear; what they fear, they hate. Out of this fear and hate have ever come persecution and pogroms—ever making service and suffering one for the Jews.

Why did the Jews reject Jesus? The answer is that they have never done so. We do not know from any contemporary Jewish sources what the Jews thought about the young carpenter from Galilee who died on a hill overlooking Jerusalem. There is not a single reference to him in any existing Jewish document of that period.

Only later when Paul fashioned a new religion around Jesus, the Christ, did Jews take cognizance of him. Then they rejected not Jesus, the Jewish teacher, but Christ, the Messiah. There were, for them, definite criteria for the advent of the Messiah. He was to usher in the Messianic Kingdom of justice, truth and peace—but after Jesus wars, oppression, corruption continued as before. The Jews were also especially repelled by the claim that Jesus had fulfilled the law, which thenceforth could be disregarded.

Finally, Jews have rejected Christianity because of the concepts with which the Church fathers buttressed and embellished the new faith as they spread it through the pagan Roman world. Completely alien to Jewish thought were such ideas as Immaculate Conception, virgin birth, the Trinity, the Holy Ghost, vicarious atonement, the "fall." The religion *of* Jesus was understandable to them; it was Jewish. The religion *about* Jesus was beyond their recognition.

Over the centuries the Jewish attitude toward Jesus has been conditioned by another factor: Christian persecution. The stubborn intransigence of the Jews in their faith has always seemed to many Christians a challenge crying for some kind of retaliation or at least retort. But, as anti-Semitism in recent times has become less religious than political, Jews in turn have felt more able to accept Jesus' role in their own history. Jesus' basic teachings have been found to be Jewish. His stature is that of the Hebrew prophet, fearless fighter for righteousness. As with Isaiah and Amos before him, he did not merely echo his people's convictions. Passing through the alchemy of his sensitive soul, the ancient beliefs found a new emphasis; they received the immortal impress of his luminous, loving personality.

None of this, however, reflects any readiness of Jews to accept Jesus as Christ—for, by history and conviction, the Jews have their own concepts revolving around the Messianic idea. Here one must distinguish between traditional and modernist Jews. The Orthodox still believe in the coming of a personal Messiah and pray each day for his advent. A large segment of the liberal Jewish community has discarded the notion of a single Messianic personality who is to save mankind. In its place they affirm their faith in a Messianic Era to be achieved by the co-operative work of good men of all nations, races and religions. With few exceptions religious Jews today believe in the restoration of Israel and the ultimate redemption of mankind. To most liberal Jews the solution of the historic Jewish problem through the founding of the commonwealth of Israel is a step toward the fulfillment of the democratic and Messianic aspirations of prophetic Judaism. This return to Zion is essentially religious in its motivation, for it is charged with a profound mystic conviction that thus will the Jews again make a contribution to mankind. Nearly four thousand years ago a tribe emerged from the desert and attached itself to the soil of Palestine. This union of land and people received a divine blessing. From it came Moses and Jesus, Judaism and Christianity, the Ten Commandments and the Sermon on the Mount. Is it too much to hope that the return of this courageous people to that sacred soil may again yield new insights, new healing and hope, to the troubled children of men?

The Jews are, in the prophet's arresting phrase, "Prisoners of Hope." The Jewish outlook is deeply and abidingly optimistic, progressive, forward-looking. A people that has endured so much knows that it can survive more. Hope wells from faith in a good God whose ways may sometimes be obscure but whose justice and goodness are ultimately triumphant. It inspires Jews constantly to strive for a better world, to be in the thick of movements for social reform. Even the non-religious Jewish radical, who may ignore his Jewishness, is the product of its Messianic fervor.

Until the modern world emancipated the Jew from the ghetto, the Torah was the established basis of his life. He lived in a world of his own where the law could be observed without complications. Once he emerged into modern society, however, the whole foundation of his life was shaken, and the observances of his beliefs seemed in ever sharper conflict with the world about him. Some Jews accordingly became indifferent to the demands of their faith, and this process was abetted by the steady secularization of life in America. Some have outspokenly repudiated it; others sought to disappear as Jews, simply to melt into the general environment. Still others, a small number, chose to go to Palestine, where one can live, they believe, a completely uncomplicated life as a Jew. But the great majority of the American Jews continue to be loyal to Judaism in principle, see no reason for surrendering their distinctive beliefs and observances, and plan to live their lives out in this land which they love and where their roots are deep. What about them?

They give a threefold answer—Orthodox, Reform and Conservative. Orthodox Jewry still maintains in principle the absolute authority of the revealed Torah. Adaptation there may be, but the basic law is unchangeable and inviolable. Nevertheless Orthodox Jews face the same problems in the modern world as do the others.

Reform Jews follow an entirely different line. They maintain that Judaism is the sum of the evolving religious experience of the Jewish people. It is and always has been subject to change. By their views, for example, the observance of ancient dietary laws is optional. The Reformers permit men and women to sit together in the synagogues; men may shave their faces; the New Year is observed for one day, not two.

Conservative Judaism is a midway house. Arriving later on the American scene, it sought to avoid the extremes of the Reformers, reconciling tradition to American conditions without compromising its integrity. Of late the difference in observance between many Conservative and Reform Jews has narrowed very much, and there have been proposals advanced for merging the two groups.

All the modern debate concerning Jewish law and its application is related to the final holiday, Shavuos, the Feast of Weeks. Observed in the late spring, it was originally a festival celebrating the gathering in of the first harvest. In the course of time, like most Jewish holidays, it came to be associated with an historic event—in this case the giving of the Torah on Mount Sinai. The poetic imagination of the Jew has embroidered this scene with haunting beauty and with universal meaning.

For Reform Jews, Shavuos has become the logical occasion for confirming Jewish youth in the faith of their forefathers when, after eight to ten years of study, they are deemed worthy of standing before the sacred ark and being accepted into the company of adult Jews. With the traditional Bar Mitzvah ceremony the boy is henceforth to be held responsible for living a Jewish life.

At this ceremony of confirmation the whole great heritage of Judaism is summoned to mind, with a poignant sense of immediacy evoked by the Jews' ever keen sense of history and memory of suffering. It is, for both the old and the young generations, a moment at once of sorrowful reflection and sober dedication.

For my son Stephen and myself, this moment and ceremony came January 25, 1947, in Frankfurt, Germany. It was a singularly provocative place for such a ceremony—the ruins of one of the most battered cities of Germany, but a city whose centuries, long before the Nazis, were enriched by the traditions of a great Jewish community, bright with names like Rothschild, Speyer and Ehrlich. Here, in the charge which I delivered to my son, I summed up the spirit which animates my beliefs:

". . . The oppressor may triumph for a moment, but his house is built on sand. It cannot withstand the irresistible moral laws of history. And Israel survives.

"The Lord says: 'Fear not, for I am with thee.' That is a magnificent promise and an imperishable source of hope. It makes me proud I am a Jew. Despite the misfortunes of my people, I would not exchange that heritage for anything in the world.

"It is this heritage which we formally transmit to you today, Stephen. When I place my hands upon your head in benediction, I will be the humble instrument through which will flow the stream of history and memories of the great and the good in Israel, the ideals and the aspirations of our people, the strength and the lift of our faith. It is something which places upon you a solemn responsibility to be worthy of its precepts, to be loyal to its ideals, and to express them in a life of service.

" 'So be the Lord with you as I will let you go.' "

THE ONWARD MARCH
OF CHRISTIAN FAITH

by Paul Hutchinson

DECEMBER 26, 1955

> *Through the centuries, devoted men have taught the*
> *gospel of Jesus, building Christianity into the world's*
> *most widespread religion. This sketch of the history of*
> *Christianity and the meaning of the Church was written*
> *by the late Dr. Paul Hutchinson for* LIFE's *special*
> *issue on Christianity and later expanded for* LIFE's *book,*
> The World's Great Religions. *As a writer on religious*
> *subjects and editor of The Christian Century, Dr.*
> *Hutchinson wrote hundreds of articles during his lifetime.*
> *He regarded this as his best writing on a religious subject.*

Among all the religions by which men seek to worship, Christianity
is the most widely spread, has the most adherents and makes the
most stupendous claims for the divinity of its Founder and the finality
of its teaching. Of the two and a half billion human beings on earth,
about 850 million—one out of every three—are listed as Christians.

The churches in which Christians worship have, during their nearly
two thousand years since Christ lived and died, developed such an
astonishing diversity of belief and ritual that it is sometimes difficult
to recognize that they all acknowledge the same Lord. The glittering
spectacle of an Easter Mass in St. Peter's, the stillness within the bare

walls of a Quaker meetinghouse, the squatting circle of Congo tribesmen around the white-haired medical missionary, the chanting monks cut off from the world on the forbidden peak of Mount Athos, a hundred thousand Mar Thoma devotees gathered in a dry river bed to join their prayers under the blazing sun of South India, thousands pressing forward in Wembley Stadium at the appeal of an evangelist, wraithlike figures kneeling in perpetual adoration before the altar in a Quebec convent, a sea of dark faces swaying while the tide of the spiritual rolls across them: "It's me, O Lord, standin' in the need of prayer"—how can these, and hundreds of other differing manifestations, all be accounted parts of the whole to which we give the name of Christianity?

Some will deny that they are. But there is justification for the habit of including all such diversities in the reckoning. For all, under whatever form, acknowledge one God; all declare their loyalty to one Lord; all find in one Cross the symbol of their faith. The differences they present to the world are endless, confusing even to themselves, often enfeebling. It is not true, as one of their most sung hymns affirms, that "We are not divided / All one body we / One in hope and doctrine / One in charity." But in their ultimate allegiance, they are one. They are Christians.

Inevitably the questions rise: Where did this Christian religion come from? How did it spread? Why has it taken so many forms? The answers make up one of the most dramatic and, in some parts, romantic stories known to history. From the days of St. Luke, who wrote his account of the Acts of the Apostles some time in the first Christian century, down to the present, thousands of scholars have labored to tell this story. Within the limits of such a sketch as this, one can name only a few of the men and women who bore leading parts in making Christianity what it is today, trying to catch them in characteristic moments which suggest their importance to the record.

A recent cartoon showed a matron asking at a bookstore for "an impartial history of the Civil War written from the Southern point of view." Accounts of the way in which Christianity has developed are usually impartial in much the same sense. No matter who writes them —Protestant, Catholic, Marxist or agnostic—the author's background shows through. So it will be here, in a sketch written by a Protestant who believes that his Protestant heritage preserves vital spiritual values while it respects the values embodied in other traditions.

Christianity is the religion which springs historically from Jesus of Nazareth. The first followers of Jesus believed that He traveled about Palestine as a preacher and teacher; that He healed and worked wonders; that He ran afoul of the conservative religious and political forces in that land, was crucified and rose from the dead. They declared that, in a resurrected and glorified form, He appeared to many of them. They *must* have believed it, for within forty days after Jesus had been executed, what had been a despairing and disintegrating band of disillusioned dreamers was transformed into a company of zealots ready to dare any fate to proclaim that this resurrected Jesus was in fact God's promised Messiah, or, in Greek, the Christ. The Christian religion is founded on the fact that He rose from the dead.

In the company of Jesus' twelve specially chosen disciples—reduced to eleven by the treachery of Judas Iscariot—the one who stands out is Simon, better known as Peter, a name derived from the Greek *petros* meaning "rock." In Matt. 16:18, 19, Jesus is reported to pun on the name and its meaning: "Thou art Peter, and upon this rock I will build my church. . . . And I will give unto thee the keys of the kingdom of heaven. . . ."

The other apostles, as this band of Jesus' intimates came to be known, are shadowy figures. But Peter, headstrong, blundering, violently temperamental, easily influenced by his surroundings or by the words of others, yet always ardent and—after one terrible experience while Jesus was on trial—always courageous, Peter is unforgettable. It is Peter to whom the Gospels accord the honor of first openly saluting Jesus as the Messiah. And when, fifty days after the Resurrection, the followers of the new faith made their first attempt to win a public hearing, it was Peter who preached the sermon on that first Pentecost. In his subsequent career he preached and taught in many places, finally reaching, in some unknown fashion, Rome, where he is generally believed to have suffered martyrdom under Nero about A.D. 65.

Besides Peter, the outstanding figure in Christianity's formative first century was the man who has been credited—though with some scholarly dissent—with having written most of the Epistles, which form such an important part of the New Testament, St. Paul. In his fine study on early Christianity, Dr. J. W. C. Wand has explained its rapid expansion from a Jewish sect into a world-wide religion by the fact that "the Christian society was born at the place where two worlds met, the East and the West, the Semitic and the Graeco-Roman, the Jew and the Gentile." This mingling of cultures was very nearly incarnated in this one man, St. Paul.

In Peter and Paul the Christian religion can be seen beginning to develop along both the great avenues which give it permanent importance. It develops as an institution (the Church) and as a teaching, a theology, a faith. The institution is named first because the theology came out of it, not the institution out of the theology. The New Testament—Gospels, Epistles, Apocalypse—is a product of the Church. Little of it was written until there was a flourishing Church all over the Roman world. It was not gathered in its finally agreed-on form until 692.

With Peter the rudimentary original nature of the Christian institution and the Christian teaching stands out. The early chapters of Acts show Peter rushing about to set up emergency forms of organization in the first Christian community in Jerusalem. They were improvisations, and some did not work out well. Peter's teaching, as shown in the long report of his sermon on the first Pentecost and in I Peter, was just as rudimentary. Jesus was the Messiah, sent by God, rejected by His nation but certified by His Resurrection, Who was soon to return to lift into a glorious and eternal state of bliss all who acknowledged Him as Lord and were baptized in His name. The tremendous questions regarding the nature of Christ and His relation to God and to humanity, which were to rend later generations and still torment men's minds, seem scarcely to have occurred to Peter.

Paul was of a different stripe. He was no Galilean fisherman being carried to immortality by the intensity of his devotion to a Master with Whom he had lived on terms of personal intimacy. Paul was a sophisticated Roman citizen and a product of the Greek-Hebrew culture.

He was an indefatigable founder of churches, and in these churches he had to deal with all sorts of competing interpretations of what Christian teaching was. So he wrote letter after letter to straighten out the thinking—and at times behavior—in these churches. Many of these letters have not survived, but those that have are the real beginning of the attempt to formalize, rationalize, put down in logical argument the Christian faith. So much so that it has been charged that Paul, not Jesus, is the true author of what we know today as Christianity—that differences and divisions among Christians have resulted from the obscuring of the simple moral precepts of the Galilean by the sophisticated metaphysical speculations of this man from Tarsus.

One trouble with this interpretation is the increasing realization that what Jesus taught was by no means confined to simple moral precepts. Along with the Beatitudes and the rest of the Sermon on the Mount, along with His assurances of God's fatherly love and care, must be set His prediction of impending catastrophe, of coming judgment and punishment—and only after these the coming of a new age. When Paul, writing twenty to thirty years later, tried to give a satisfying interpretation of these teachings to the Gentile converts in his churches, naturally the first question he had to answer was: Who was this Jesus Christ? By what authority did He make His tremendous declarations about the relationship of God to the world and man, and about what was to be the ultimate outcome of their relationship? When Paul attempted to answer those inescapable questions—inescapable if Christianity was to survive—the theology which was to take hard-and-fast form in the later creeds was born.

For 250 years after the martyrdoms of Peter and Paul the Christian Church continued to spread steadily over the Mediterranean world. By A.D. 287, it was the state religion of Armenia, and its expansion was generally unaffected by eras of official repression and persecution.

The second and third centuries witnessed an accelerating decline of the Roman Empire. A rough-handed old soldier, Diocletian, who became emperor in 284, stopped the retreat for a time and even reconquered most of Britain and Persia. But for reasons not entirely clear, Diocletian's reign also brought the most terrible of all the persecutions of Christians. For two ghastly years the old emperor did his best to drown Christianity in blood. One legend says that when the emperor's order to destroy churches was affixed to the palace gate at Nicomedia, a high-ranking officer tore it down and was immediately executed—to become St. George, patron saint of England. If he ever fought a dragon, it must have been imperial Caesar.

In 305 Diocletian gave up his effort to destroy the young religion and abdicated. A struggle for the imperial power between two "Caesars" and two "Augusti" began at once, but it was speedily decided in favor of Constantine, who led his troops from York, in England, first to victory in Italy, and later to control of the eastern portion of the empire as well. It is said that Constantine, before a decisive battle at the Milvian Bridge outside Rome, saw a vision of a lighted cross in the afternoon sky and the words *"In hoc signo vinces."* After that his legions bore standards with *Chi Rho*, the first Greek letters of Christ's name, above a cross.

Constantine was not then an avowed Christian; indeed, he was not baptized until on his death bed. But his political sagacity told him that he required some strong cultural cement to hold together his sprawling, multicultured empire, and he believed that he could find that binding element in Christianity. He began, in the so-called Edict of Milan of 313, by extending complete toleration to Christians. As emperor in his new capital of Constantinople, he became the great patron of the Church. Theodosius I, who became emperor only forty-two years after the death of Constantine, made Christianity the only official religion of the empire.

But Constantine must have begun to wonder whether Christianity was the unifying force he had believed. From all quarters came reports of the bitterness with which Christians were disputing over theological issues, excommunicating and denouncing each other. These disputes came to a focus in Alexandria, where the elderly and popular presbyter of a fashionable church, Arius, had challenged the teaching of his bishop, Alexander, on the Trinity. The issue was whether Christ was of the *same* substance as God the Father, or, as Arius held, of *like* substance. Because the two Greek words involved, *homoousion* and *homoiousion,* were so similar, Gibbon later passed on a sneer that in the struggle which followed for more than a century, Christians fought each other over a diphthong. But that diphthong carried an immense meaning. This battle raged and spread until finally the emperor, who was not capable of understanding the theological subtleties involved but was determined to have internal peace, summoned all Christian bishops to a council at Nicaea in 325. The first great Christian historian, Eusebius, who participated in that historic meeting, tells how some three hundred bishops—all but ten from the eastern section of the empire—rushed with their attendants to Nicaea in a frenzy of excitement, many scarred by what they had undergone in Diocletian's persecutions, with eyeless sockets, disfigured faces, twisted limbs, paralyzed hands. Constantine himself presided, and out of an assembly which partook more of the characteristics of a political convention than a religious convocation there came finally that Nicene Creed which declares Christ was of the *same* substance as God and still remains a standard of orthodoxy for Roman, Eastern Orthodox, Anglican and some other churches.

For a thousand years after Rome's fall, Europe was one vast welter of fighting and political anarchy. Emperors in Constantinople from time to time tried to assert their shadowy claim to monarchy over the West, but like the grin of Alice's Cheshire cat, their authority faded and faded until nothing was left. On Christmas Day, 800, the Bishop of Rome crowned in St. Peter's the German chieftain Charlemagne, who had conquered Germany, France, northern Spain and most of Italy, bestowing on him the title of Roman Emperor. Charlemagne, who admired St. Augustine, tried to rule by Christian principles.

G. A. Studdert-Kennedy once remarked that no miracle in the Bible begins to equal in incredibility the miracle that Europe's warlike tribes should have chosen Jesus of Nazareth for their God. Yet they did, sometimes because tribal kings were converted by daring missionaries and then ordered their subjects to accept baptism, and sometimes as a consequence of more gradual and deep-going social transformations brought about by missionary labors. As an illustration of the sort of thing that happened, recall the young Patrick born in a Christian family in Britain late in the fourth century. Raiders carried him off to six years of slavery in Ireland. From there he seems to have escaped to a monastic life in France. Eighteen years later he responded to voices which he said sounded constantly in his ears: "We beseech thee, holy youth, to come and walk again amongst us as before." He was consecrated a bishop and started back to convert the people among whom he had suffered as a slave. He not only converted Ireland, but covered it with churches for worship and missions in which many pupils were taught. It is notable that St. Patrick, unlike many Church leaders of later centuries, gave women an important part in the work of evangelizing Ireland. So thoroughly was Ireland evangelized that the impulse carried Irish priests to the conversion of Scotland, parts of England and even Switzerland. Wherever they went, they carried Irish learning.

While the territorial extension of Christianity thus continued, the institutional authority of the Western Church came steadily to center in the bishops of Rome. By the middle of the fifth century, these bishops were asserting that, as successors of St. Peter in that office, they outranked other patriarchs. When the see of Constantinople refused to acknowledge that claim, as well as to concur in some of Rome's doctrinal decisions, there began the schism between Western and Eastern Churches, a great Christian tragedy which directly led to the crusaders' sacking of Christian Constantinople.

When Charlemagne conquered most of western Europe, he gave the harried common people almost the only extended period of order they experienced from the fall of Rome to the end of the Napoleonic wars. Feudalism—the social system in which every person from serf upward was expected to render service in some form to an owner or superior—grew amid the constant guerrilla warfare of the period, and gradually the Dark Ages merged into the Middle Ages. As feudalism grew, Popes struggled with monarchs over the question whether, because of the ghostly powers of the pontiffs, kings were vassals of the heads of the Church. This contest reached its dramatic climax when Gregory VII, one of those short men who stand tall in history, forced Henry IV, the German ruler, to stand for three successive days in the snow, barefoot and clad in penitent's garb, at the castle of Canossa in Tuscany, while he besought the Pope to lift his excommunication. Henry later captured Rome and Gregory VII died in exile. But history has never forgotten that picture of the barefoot king waiting in the courtyard in Canossa.

The issue on which Gregory VII and Innocent III carried the Papacy to its greatest secular power continues to this day and crops up in many forms. It is the issue of church and state relations, the effort to draw a dividing line between the powers of ecclesiastical and secular authorities. Specific issues change with the centuries, and modern totalitarianism has added its special complications. But every branch of the Christian Church has, at one time or another, been troubled by that issue. The attempts made by Popes and Protestant reformers to settle it by appeal to the words attributed to Christ, "Render therefore unto Caesar the things which be Caesar's, and unto God the things which be God's," have settled nothing, for this leaves unanswered who is to say what is Caesar's and what God's. Modern Popes, patriarchs and theologians have advanced many theoretical answers, but in actuality the relations of church and state are being fixed in our time, whether in the United States, Spain or the Soviet Union, on a basis of pragmatic workability.

While the medieval Church in the West was building up its power, that in the East, under the immediate shadow of the corrupt Byzantine court, was passing through a sad period when servility to the throne, incessant intrigues against the Church and too frequent scandalous conduct by clergy and laity were undermining its spirituality. Yet this Church also had its missionaries, who converted the Bulgarians, the Moravians in what is today Czechoslovakia, and finally the Russians. When Russia was overrun by the Mongols, the Orthodox Church was not disturbed. By the end of the sixteenth century, with the country again free and unified, Moscow was declared a patriarchate. When Peter the Great ascended the throne, one of his first moves to "modernize" Russia was to place the Church under control of the czar. So it remained until the Communist revolution of 1917. Today it lives, no longer "established" but not actively suppressed, under a Communist government officially atheist, to which it renders as obsequious political obedience as in former days it did to the Romanov czars. Even so, the Orthodox Church in both of its major groupings, Greek and Russian, is significant. Its many patriarchates are, in effect, all part of one large, loosely knit ecclesiastical federation, of which the senior partner is the Ecumenical Patriarch in Constantinople. They include eighteen self-governing churches with a total of 150 million communicants, about 2.4 million of them in the U.S.

The medieval period, especially as it flowered in the early thirteenth century, has been held by many the apogee of the Church's glory. It was "the age of faith," an age when the authority of the Church was accepted almost without question. Marvelous monuments to the religious devotion of that time are in the cathedrals, which can still enthrall even such an agnostic mind of our time as Henry Adams.

That was also the age which could produce world-renouncing piety that reached its highest attainment in St. Francis of Assisi. In his figure, as appealing to our own as to his world, medieval Europe saw the embodiment of its religious ideals. Francis, one might say, "had everything." His was a life of wealth voluntarily renounced for extreme poverty, of humble identification with the poor, the sorrowing and the loathsomely afflicted, of consecration to the service and discipline of the Church, of founding a large monastic order, of readiness to court death in missionary ventures, especially to the infidel, and of a sweetness and exhilaration of spirit which found expression in companionship with all living creatures and all the facets of nature.

Another aspect of medieval religion that commands respect was the intellectual subtlety of monkish schoolmen which reached its highest expression in St. Thomas Aquinas. Born into the nobility in 1225, Thomas, who early entered the Dominican Order, had one of the most logical, integrating minds in the history of philosophy. His *Summa Theologica* is still the greatest compendium of Roman Catholic theology. Aquinas remains a living influence in Western thought, as well as a reminder that the "age of faith" could produce discriminating, rigorous minds dedicated to the service of God.

Out of the medieval era were emerging the modern kingdoms of Europe. As the kings slowly established their rule over their great vassals, they found galling the claims of Popes that they were themselves vassals to whoever might be on the throne of St. Peter. In the fourteenth century, Philip the Fair of France determined to elect a Pope he could control. A French archbishop was elevated and moved the papal court to Avignon in southern France, where he and his successors lived for seventy years as French puppets. Two remarkable women, St. Catherine of Siena and St. Bridget of Sweden, played important roles in stirring up popular demand which finally brought the Popes back to Rome from what has been called their "Babylonian captivity" in Avignon. But this return served only to expose the Papacy to other secular ambitions.

If France could control the head of the Church for almost three generations, why not the fiercely rival dukedoms of Italy or the "Holy Roman" emperor of Germany? The consequence was the most melancholy forty years in papal history, with rival Popes hurling anathemas at each other and, in the end, three Popes, each claiming to be the legitimate successor of Peter, while the nations divided their allegiance among them according to what seemed their political interest. "The miserable truth has to be faced," says the Catholic historian Philip Hughes, "that no pope, on either side, was at all worthy of his office. They were, all of them, little better than partisan leaders of rival factions."

Not until 1417 did the Council of Constance straighten out this scandalous state of affairs and a single Pope reign again. However, two legacies had been left by this century of division which were to have profoundly disturbing effects. On one hand, the Popes were determined to surround themselves with such power and pomp in Rome that there could never be another "captivity." And on the other hand, the decisive part of the Council of Constance in cleaning up the mess spread widely the idea that the ultimate seat of decision in Church affairs was not the Pope but the general councils of the Church. It is time for the curtain to go up on the Reformation, and the modern history of Christianity.

When Martin Luther, an Augustinian monk serving as professor of theology at the University of Wittenberg in Saxony, posted his historic ninety-five theses on the door of the castle church on October 31, 1517, he had no inkling of the dimensions of the Church schism which was to follow. But his study of the Pauline Epistles, as interpreted by St. Augustine, had already caused him to reject the conception of salvation as being earned partly by human works of righteous living, penance and appropriation of the merits of the sacraments and the saints. Salvation, he believed, was the unmerited gift of God to sinful man, gained by faith in the divine promise that Christ by His atoning death had paid the penalty for sin. When man experienced the inner transformation achieved through God's mercy, he then had access to God and assurance of salvation without the need of any intermediary—church or sacrament, priest or saint. Pushed to its logical conclusion, as the theologians who met Luther in debate quickly forced him to push it, Luther's declaration of salvation by faith alone and of the priesthood of all believers led to denial of the Pope's infallibility as a source of doctrine, thence to denial of the inerrancy of general Church councils, and finally to affirmation that the Bible is the sole and sufficient source of the Christian's spiritual guidance.

How could a monk guilty of such defiance of churchly authority not only escape the extreme penalties pronounced against him, but carry a large part of Germany into revolt with him? History contains few more dramatic scenes than that at the Diet of Worms, with Luther facing Charles V, the Holy Roman emperor, and the papal legate, his life hanging in the balance as he was bidden to repudiate his books: "I cannot revoke anything, nor do I wish to, since to go against one's conscience is neither safe nor right. Here I stand. I cannot do otherwise. God help me. Amen." Why did this not lead to the same end that befell John Hus? It was not because Luther came to Worms under safe conduct. Hus had gone to Constance under safe conduct, where he was burned at the stake.

Very largely the answer lay in the political situation of that time. The shift from feudalism to territorial monarchies, with paid armies (and soon navies) instead of feudal levies, required heavy taxes and forced the monarchs to build up their treasuries. At the same time, the Papacy, building St. Peter's and maintaining the most extravagant court in Europe, found it increasingly difficult to draw large revenues from the strong new monarchies of Spain, France and England; it looked much easier to levy on divided Germany. But many of the German princes were fed up with the sight of revenues from their states going south over the Alps. They were thus in a mood for political rebellion, and when the monk from Wittenberg raised a doctrinal and ecclesiastical rebellion which sparked an immense popular response, some of these German princes stepped forward to champion the Lutheran revolution. To see how inextricably these political strands run through the Reformation, one need only note the peace finally made at Augsburg in 1555, after the fighting which swept over Germany in the wake of Luther's defiance. It was a peace of princes which established the rule that the religion of a territory would be that of its prince, thus fastening the system of state churches as firmly on Protestant as on Catholic Europe.

The other "father of the Reformation" was about as different from Luther as a mortal could be. John Calvin was a wispy French intellectual with an introspective, syllogistic mind. Forced to flee from France for his heretical views, he settled in Geneva. There he set up a theocratic city-state with such relentless care for the morals and beliefs of its citizens that on one occasion they drove him into a three-year banishment. Calvin's great contribution was to reduce the Protestant revolt to theological coherence. This he did in his *Institutes of the Christian Religion*. To this day, this presentation of Christian doctrine, based on the absolute sovereignty of God and the omnipotence of His inscrutable will, remains the greatest of all Protestant theological volumes. It is as remorselessly logical as Aquinas' *Summa*, pursuing the Pauline-Augustinian doctrine of predestination to the conclusion that those whom God has chosen for salvation cannot resist nor fall from that choice, but that those who are chosen for damnation are doomed to everlasting hell, even though they be infants who die before they are capable of conscious acts. The Presbyterian and Reformed Churches, which regard themselves as the spiritual heirs of Calvinism, today handle with extreme reticence John Calvin's views on predestination.

Shocked by the revolt in Germany, which spread rapidly to other parts of Europe, the Roman Catholic Church wasted no time in embarking on that period of internal correction and external opposition to the Protestant advance that is usually called the Counter Reformation. The Council of Trent, which met intermittently for eighteen years, ended many abuses and laid down a body of Catholic doctrine that is still definitive. Its recognition of the legitimacy of tradition as well as of the Scriptures as a source of truth has had an immense influence on later dogmatic declarations, especially those defining papal infallibility and the Immaculate Conception and Assumption of the Virgin. At the same time, the Inquisition was revived to suppress heresy wherever the civil authorities favored its operations.

A main glory of the Counter Reformation, from the Catholic point of view, was the organization and spread of the Society of Jesus—the Jesuit order which stopped Protestantism in its tracks in Hungary and Poland, won back to papal allegiance much of Germany and most of France, all but wiped out the feeble beginnings of Protestantism in Italy, spread excellent schools over Europe and thrust Catholic missions into India, Japan, China and the New World.

From the years of the Reformation down to the present, the history of Christianity becomes inextricably interwoven with the history of national states. It was partly nationalism—manifesting itself in a determination to be sole ruler of his realm—that led King Henry VIII to denounce the Pope's authority and proclaim himself the "head of the church" in England. Thus the Church of England, with its Anglican affiliates throughout the world, including the Protestant Episcopal Church in the U.S., still claims a succession of bishops from the apostles and considers that it is Catholic as well as Protestant.

Discovery of the New World brought a race between the three most robust monarchies, as they were suddenly faced with the dazzling prospect of expanding their small European kingdoms into world empires. Political and economic motives dominated in the building of the French, Spanish and British empires—in Asia as well as in the Americas—but the religious motive was a not inconsiderable factor. Settlers in New England felt its influence more directly than those in the southern colonies, but from Florida to the St. Lawrence the scattered settlements along the Atlantic seaboard, as W. E. Garrison has written, "were not allowed to forget that they were holding a Protestant 'rampart' (the word was often used) against an otherwise solidly Roman Catholic New World."

At the start the American colonies accepted the European pattern of church establishment almost without question. By 1776, however, there was a fast-growing conviction that a Church establishment was a prolific source of political and religious evils. The revolution, during which the ministers of the Anglican establishments largely supported the crown, produced swift changes in the legal picture. Finally, the adoption by the young republic of the First Amendment to its Federal Constitution, providing "Congress shall make no law respecting an establishment of religion," completed the federal process of giving legal status to the principle of separation of church and state.

Establishment of this principle has been the most important contribution of American churches to the development of Christianity. It has not meant that there has been no contact between the American churches and the American state. On the contrary, the churches time and again have exerted great moral influence on decisions of the state, while the state has repeatedly acknowledged its indebtedness to religion: "In God We Trust." But there has been no "establishment of religion," no state church with tax support, no interlocking of the official machinery of the church with the official machinery of the government. The churches have been on their own, growing by their own efforts—which largely accounts for that interest in revivalism and "activism" that has exposed them to criticism from European churches under no need to support themselves.

This had not been heard of in organized Christianity since the edict of Theodosius I in A.D. 380 made political loyalty and membership in the Christian Church virtually synonymous. For fourteen hundred years after that, membership in the church and in the state was regarded as two aspects of the same thing—which was one reason for brutal treatment of the Jews. This was as true in the Protestant countries which emerged from the Reformation as in the Catholic monarchies. But the United States, from its infancy as a nation, turned back to the concept of the Christian Church as it was held before Constantine, when men joined of their own free will and supported it of their own voluntary desires, and the church in consequence was a free institution. Judged by what has followed, the American adoption of the principle of church and state separation has been a godsend for the churches, Protestant, Roman Catholic and of every sort. The voluntary principle has gained, in the friendly American climate, an impressive pragmatic sanction.

Here, then, is organized Christianity as it now appears after almost two thousand years. Missionary labors have planted churches in almost every nation. The 850 million Christians fall into four great branches —the Roman Catholic, Eastern Orthodox, Anglican and Protestant— with the last designation including an amazing array of denominations and sects. In the U.S. alone 255 Protestant sects are recognized. But most American Protestants are in a half-dozen denominational families; 173 of the Protestant churches reporting membership figures contain less than 2 per cent of the 59 million Protestant total. To an outside observer, the most striking fact about Christianity in the U.S. today is likely to be its numerical force—nearly 100 million adherents in a population of 168 million—and its divisions. Why these divisions?

Usually it is answered that these represent differences in doctrine. But this is true to a limited extent only. As Christianity has spread around the globe in recent centuries, differences in local customs have also notably affected it. Roman Catholicism in the U.S. has been rather more puritanical than in the Latin countries, while Protestantism in the U.S. has been rather more concerned with social questions—such as slavery, liquor, the eight-hour day—than has its European counterpart. In the field of doctrine a few churches eschew all creedal affirmations, but most of them recite that ancient formulation of Christian belief known as the Apostles' Creed. As for the divisions among American Protestants, Professor H. Richard Niebuhr of Yale has conclusively shown that they more frequently represent differing national origins in Europe or differing social groupings in the U.S. than differing theologies. Of course there is theological and dogmatic division between Protestant and Protestant, as well as between Protestant and Roman Catholic and Eastern Orthodox. But there are other divisions which the ordinary American churchman encounters far more frequently.

What are these intimately, emotionally experienced divisions? One concerns the nature of the Church. What is the Church? Until recently, Protestants have tended to ignore that question. Today, as they strive to end some of their debilitating divisions by co-operating in bodies like the World Council of Churches or America's National Council of Churches, they find the question lying right across the line of advance. Moreover, this is a question which has a direct bearing on the attitudes of individual Christians, as truly as on the deliberations of great Church councils.

To a Roman Catholic, Orthodox, or high-church Anglican, the Church is a body divinely instituted and with a priesthood which is primarily ordained to re-enact at the altar the miracle of the Mass, by which in a symbolic manner, through the consecration of the two elements of bread and wine into the veritable Body and Blood of the Lord Jesus Christ, the Son of God made man is really present, offering Himself as the "food of souls." The Catholic, therefore, also the Orthodox or Anglican, when he enters a church of his persuasion, enters a place of mystery. His devotion focuses on the altar, where the miracle of his redemption is re-enacted, with Christ Himself mysteriously present. But if a Protestant finds himself in this sanctuary, he is bewildered by this mystery and repelled by the notion of a sinful man, even though he be an ordained priest, having the power to change bread and wine into the true flesh and blood of Christ.

When, however, the Protestant enters his church, while there may be quite an elaborate ritual centering on the service of Holy Communion, most typically he is waiting for that moment in the service which was the highest of moments to Luther, Calvin, Knox and all the other great Reformers—the moment when the minister enters the pulpit for the preaching of the Word in the form of the sermon. The sermon is the climax of Protestant worship, though often the feeble capacities of the preacher make it the anticlimax. The congregation is there to hear, not to see. But if a Roman Catholic, risking rebuke from his confessor, finds himself in this service, the chances are that he will be repelled by its verbalism, by its refusal to point him to the very spot where he may meet God.

From this it follows that a second great line of division between the Churches is drawn by their antagonistic conceptions of the sacraments. The difficulty is not only that the Catholics, Orthodox and many Anglicans say there are seven sacraments and the Protestants only two (with the Quakers, Unitarians and Universalists recognizing none as such), but that the sacrament itself, for whatever end administered, is differently conceived. The familiar definition of a sacrament is that it is "an outward and visible sign of an inward and spiritual grace." But there is a wide gulf between Protestant and Catholic use of the word "sign." The latter holds that the sign itself accomplishes what it stands for; the former that the effects follow only from the faith of the believer. The gulf here is as wide, for example, as that between those who consider baptism a saving rite and those who reject that belief.

And yet again, these worshipers who profess "one Lord, one faith, one baptism" find themselves sundered by their differing conceptions of the nature of religious authority. Most Protestants will say that the final authority to which they appeal is that of the Word of God—not simply the text of the Bible, but that text as interpreted either by the Church through its ordained ministry or by the spirit of the individual Christian. Protestants, Anglicans and Orthodox differ widely among themselves, however, as to how this access to the Word is to be sought and, when found, safeguarded. Some Churches look for authority to a historical succession of episcopally ordained bishops, priests and deacons; some to ministers chosen by congregations; some to rule by elders.

The Roman Catholic position is clear-cut. Spiritual authority is centered in a priesthood hierarchically organized in a great pyramid, at the apex of which stands the Pope, direct successor of St. Peter as Bishop of Rome and head of the visible Church, endowed by virtue of his exalted office to guide his Church infallibly in all matters of faith and morals. From him the power of the keys descends to bishops, and from the bishops to the humblest priest. The priest, accordingly, is clothed with the authority of his Church to bind and free from sin. The role of the laity in doctrine and sacraments is to receive the spiritual gifts that come through the priest all the way from the Pope.

Christ's birth, which happened so inconspicuously so long ago, marked the greatest watershed in history. The religion which was born out of that event developed mankind's most enduring and world-encompassing institution, the Christian Church. The Church has taken many forms; its divisions go back to the very beginning of the record in the Acts of the Apostles, and they appear more implacable as the centuries pass. At present an "ecumenical" (*i.e.*, all-embracing, universal) sentiment calls for bridging some of the chasms, but it is hardly attempting to close the great divisions between East and West, between Catholic and Protestant. Yet despite the fragmentation of institutionalized Christianity into innumerable churches, there is a fact —the Christian Church—which men everywhere must take into their reckonings, and do. The whole is greater than the sum of its parts.

Today the Churches of the West are well into the most productive intellectual period they have known since the sixteenth century. From the proclamation of *Rerum novarum* (1891) to the present, they have spoken with more insight and prophetic ardor on the ills of a social order in the revolutionary flux than since the collapse of feudalism. The defensive note, so strong in Christian preaching during the half century before the outbreak of the world wars, has nearly died away. The Churches have a renewed confidence in the relevance and adequacy of their gospel. The confidence is assuredly not unrelated to the renewed seriousness and respect with which our storm-tossed generation regards the religious approach to life's problems and the Christian explanation of its meaning.

What, then, is the outlook for Christianity and its Churches? It is not one to sustain a boundless optimism, but it is by no means hopeless. Thoughtful Christians see the weaknesses of the Churches. If Christianity is responsible for the character of civilization, then its task is hardly more than begun. Nevertheless, the prevalent sense of unsatisfied spiritual needs among men, and of the insufficiency of other answers to their problems, makes this an hour of opportunity for religion. Freud and the neo-orthodox theologians are one in locating man's ills far below the outer layers. Can the Christian Churches now help man to realize that the grace of God can penetrate deeper, and with more saving power, than any analyst's probing?

Never has the figure of Christ risen higher or in more compelling majesty over the debris of human failure.

Never has the Cross stood out more clearly as the symbol of man's ultimate hope.

Never has the prayer for the Church used in ecumenical conferences seemed more timely or pertinent:

"O Gracious Father, we humbly beseech Thee for Thy holy Catholic Church, that Thou wouldest be pleased to fill it with all truth, in all peace. Where it is corrupt, purify it; where it is in error, direct it; where in any thing it is amiss, reform it. Where it is right, establish it; where it is in want, provide for it; where it is divided, reunite it; for the sake of Him Who died and rose again, and ever liveth to make intercession for us, Jesus Christ, Thy Son, our Lord. *Amen.*"

THE PAPACY'S AWESOME TASK

by Emmet John Hughes

OCTOBER 20, 1958

> *Published in the interregnum between the death of Pius XII and the election of John XXIII, this article gives insight into the problems that are inseparable from the heritage of the prelate who is called to the throne of St. Peter, problems which moved some predecessors to pray in agony of spirit: "Have mercy upon me, O God." A Roman Catholic, Emmet John Hughes was head of Time Inc.'s Rome and Berlin newsbureaus and, later, text editor of* LIFE. *He is now senior adviser on public policy to the Rockefeller brothers.*

The world watched, millions prayed, some wept, with the coming of death to Eugenio Pacelli, Pius XII, Bishop of Rome, Vicar of Jesus Christ, Successor of the Prince of Apostles, Supreme Pontiff of the Universal Church, Patriarch of the West, Primate of Italy, Arch-

590

bishop and Metropolitan of the Roman Province, Sovereign of the State of the City of the Vatican. Such magisterial titles did little to obscure, in the sight and mind of a whole generation, the vivid presence of the frail and graceful man who bore them for almost twenty years. Gentle in gesture, slender in form, the man seemed to wear life itself rather like a cloak, assumed lightly and casually, serving but to fold around the soul.

Quite apart from the man, his unique office now summons again the attention of men and nations. It is an office that pitilessly summons, often exhausts all the vigor of those who hold it. Its fate is increasingly linked to the final destiny of the Christian, or pseudo-Christian, West. In an age that appears to be testing Western civilization itself, even the least compassionate critic of the Roman Catholic Church finds it impossible to be indifferent to the story of Western civilization's oldest institution.

Thus do both the man and the institution of the Papacy invite some understanding of the specific and immediate problem besetting the Vatican under *any* pontificate of this mid-twentieth century. For no matter who sits upon this oldest throne in the world, he can know but one heritage, one purpose and, in G. K. Chesterton's words, "one scheme . . . bestriding lands and ages with its gigantic arches, and carrying everywhere the high river of baptism upon an aqueduct of Rome."

History and chance, the choice of Peter and the Church's doctrine have conspired to lean the weight of the world-wide Church heavily upon Italy, specifically upon Rome, ultimately upon the Papacy.

The city of Rome, age upon age, has affected the destiny and trials of the Church in profound and ever new ways. In the early centuries Rome meant the majestic heritage of the empire, bringing a matchless prestige to the Popes as they became statesmen-saviors and warrior-defenders of the West. In the fifth century, Leo I could mysteriously persuade by speech the retreat of Atilla and his Huns from the river Po. Four centuries later another Leo, with the less mysterious persuasiveness of a well-equipped navy, could save Italy from the Moslems. But by this time Rome also meant something else. It meant misfortune to the Papacy to be situated among the most lawless people of Italy. The head of Christendom lived in the heart of a mob equally ready to bully conclaves, to loot the Vatican, to profit from corruption or to toss the corpse of the late pontiff into the Tiber.

The present is no exception: Rome still has its eternal impact. Italy, since World War II, has borne the curious distinction of displaying the Western world's most massive Communist party. The struggle against this party has sharpened not only the Church's fear of Communist purposes but also its knowledge of Communist methods. At the same time it has impelled leaders of the Church to engage in political action that most of them would shun.

Such an obvious instance offers some hint of the size and weight of the papal burden. For many years the task of combatting Italian Communism taxed and strained all the resources of the Italian state: its men, its moneys and its allies. But to the Pope and the Church, this combat could never be more than a skirmish upon the kind of battlefield where they are committed to fight for all time.

As a state or institution, the Vatican seems singularly small for the huge labor it assumes. It boasts an area of only 108.7 acres, a population of little more than a thousand. Yet it maintains its own complete official hierarchy, from armed forces to gardeners. It has its own legal system and wears all the common emblems of sovereignty: flag, seal, stamps, currency. The actual "government" of the world-wide Church, under the Pope, is divided among twelve congregations, comparable to the ministries of a secular government.

The most crucial of these congregations is the Supreme Congregation of the Holy Office. It is charged with the defining and guarding of all the Church's teaching. By far the largest congregation is that of the Propagation of the Faith, charged with all missionary territories, but even this congregation numbers slightly less than two hundred officials.

It is the Consistorial Congregation, however, that most directly touches the labors of the bishops of the world. The bishops, proconsuls of the empire of the faithful, constantly report in writing and are required to report in person every five years to the Consistorial Congregation, whose sweeping authority is officially defined in the simple phrase of the Vatican annual: "it presides over the affairs of

592

the dioceses." To all bishops and archbishops this congregation bears some resemblance to a secular nation's foreign office in its relations with its own ambassadors. When a bishop in some distant diocese notes the arrival of a sharp-eyed Vatican monsignor, coming as an apostolic visitor, he need not be told that the Consistorial Congregation is inspecting some not quite satisfactory phase of his diocesan affairs. But over them all—bishops, cardinals and congregations alike —remain the ceaseless watch, the matchless authority, of the Pope.

Solemn, total command, be it of armies or states, imposes a notoriously lonely vigil, and no man is so alone as he who sits upon the papal throne. A few prelates in history have feverishly coveted and pursued the awesome title, but their number is surpassed by those who have dreaded it, even fled from it. Gregory the Great tried to flee Rome in 590 when he learned of his election. Only by force was he carried to St. Peter's to become the first of the great medieval Popes. A thousand years later Sixtus V, on his deathbed, sighed a lament that he had not been able to remain "a dishwasher in my Franciscan monastery." In March of 1939, as the cardinals of the Sacred College kneeled to kiss his hand and foot, Pius XII murmured softly, over and over, *"Miserere mei, Deus!"* (Have mercy on me, O God!). From that instant there was no one else to whom such words could be spoken.

From the humble and imposing figure of the great Gregory, more than thirteen centuries ago, dates the noble phrase, *Servus servorum Dei* ("Servant of the servants of God"), perhaps the most splendid of all titles used by Popes to the present day. Over the years of Pius XII's pontificate, such service, as always, dictated an almost bewildering variety of lofty and humble duties: from countering Nazi persecution and Communist aggression to serving as a self-assigned "lightning rod" to discourage World War II bombers over the city of Rome; from immense wartime relief and refugee labors to the theological mysteries of of the doctrine of the Assumption; from patient reception of ministers of the world's great nations to idle chatter with visiting U.S. congressmen—or the acceptance of honorary membership in the fire department of Newark, New Jersey. Even the good servant must enjoy an occasional smile of wry amusement.

Through the centuries the awesome range of papal duties has been matched by the astonishing variety of men called to bear them, to master them or be cruelly crushed by them. Sons of peasants and tailors have succeeded sons of nobles and statesmen. The celibacy that the Church struggled so long to enforce has saved it from the curse of inherited power and has kept the high office, for all its incense and pageantry, remarkably close to the people. The resulting procession of pontiffs has included scores of saints and a few rakes, as well as able warriors, scholarly humanists, skilled theologians, adroit diplomats, vigorous aggrandizers, reformers both feeble and fiery, octogenarians of startling steel and stamina. Upon the man, again and again, the chemistry of the office has wrought surprising change. In the fifteenth century young Silvio de Piccolomini could write brisk stories in the style of Boccaccio and deplore clerical celibacy, then become a Pope of formidable rectitude and reforming zeal. In the last century Pius IX could enter office as the favorite of the liberals of the Western world —only to convert his, the longest pontificate in the Church's history, into a monumental record of belligerent conservatism. And the Pius who was renowned in the world in 1939 as a diplomat, essentially a man of international political action, may well enter his Church's history as one far more to be remembered for his personal piety and his doctrinal proclamations.

Of all changes in the Papacy wrought in the memory of living men, none is more striking—and few are less recognized—than the quite new appreciation of the Papacy itself by all Western nations. So powerful has been the impact of the personalities of Pius and his immediate predecessors, so manifest their integrity and dignity of purpose, that the respect won is almost universally accepted as unremarkable. Yet it was only ninety years ago, merely yesterday on any Church calendar, that the triumphant armies of Italian nationalism were smashing papal forces at the gates of Rome, while the New York *Herald* matter-of-factly said, "The Papacy has lived out its time. It has had the full thousand years of the life of a nation, a government or a system, and it must die."

As it was ninety years ago, as it ever has been, so it is today: the most solemn problems of Church and Papacy are, in the deepest sense, timeless, changeless, quite without historic answer. These problems are born of a single, simple cause: the mere existence of the Church. To be *in* the world, yet not *of* the world: no other institution of man is dedicated to so solemn and sweeping a commission. Its life is its burden.

This strange but simple fact is the essential source of all the conflicts that have racked the Church in all ages: the rude clash with current intellectual fashion, the stubborn denial of what often to the world seems rational or obvious or inevitable, the occasional division and confusion within the Church itself. For the Papacy, every age rings with ever-echoing questions. What are the respective claims of piety and polity? What are the respective virtues and rewards of devout passivity and of temporal action? To survive and to flourish—with what weapons? To guard and defend—against the threat of what ideas, what nations? Again and again, such questions are asked and answered, only to be asked again in the next generation, the next century. The perilous dialogue knows no pause.

It is inevitable that Church and Papacy shall invite, at any and all times, a ceaseless cross fire of criticism, attack or hate. From this, Church and Papacy can never hope to escape. They must forever endure the onerous weight of contradictory criticism. Their religious teaching is deplored both for its appalling rigidity and for its presumptuous proclamation of new doctrine. Their political practices are attacked, again and again, for being at once too stubbornly traditional and too opportunistically inventive. Their saints are derided for their remoteness from the worldly problems and perils of "real life" while their diplomats find their worldly skills and practical labors cited as unbecoming signs of a lack of saintliness.

All such charges serve merely to underline the cares and costs of a mission dedicated, in a quite unusual sense of the words, to making the best of two worlds. All the institutional labor of the Church and all its striving for worldly safety and strength are but the beginning of the great task.

Beyond this beginning lies the second, ceaseless task of defining, defending and propagating what the Church holds to be the truth of God and of man. This labor, too, is never finished. For though the enunciated truths may be held to be whole and final, from the beginning and for all eternity, every theologian knows the endless newness and thus the infinite variety to be found in error. The determined defense of yesterday becomes irrelevant to the attack of today or the threat of tomorrow. In this sense the changeless teaching can always change.

These are the ever-present problems that the Papacy must face in all ages and in all circumstances. But there are also the particular problems of the current moment. Many of these are obvious. Others are scarcely glimpsed outside Rome itself.

The plainest and harshest, of course, has come with the challenge of Communism. At times it has seemed, at least for the Church in Rome, like a thunderous echo of the onetime threat of Islam to overrun Christendom. But one critical fact of history distinguishes the present from that earlier conflict: to meet this twentieth-century threat the Church must depend largely upon non-Catholic nations.

In terms of military might, political prestige or economic resources, the Church and Papacy face everywhere the same truth: without the United States, without Great Britain, without Germany, all the force of the preponderantly Catholic world would be as nothing against the massive weight of Communism. Thus in myriad ways are summoned all the resources of persuasion, of imagination, of diplomacy, of political action, to achieve in the twentieth century what a Leo IV could accomplish eleven centuries ago by the simple act of throwing a chain across the Tiber to guard its waters from Moslem ships.

In Europe the problem of the Church in Soviet-occupied areas is plain enough in its most obvious and tragic aspects, but a most tormenting and little-known aspect is what some in Rome crisply call "the problem of the ambitious canon." As Communist authorities have removed or jailed many bishops in eastern Europe, they have found a remarkable number of the bishops' own clerical aides, the canons, ready and happy to accept the Communist offer of the office so rudely vacated.

The swift-rising concern of the Papacy for non-European areas has been a striking mark of the pontificate of Pius XII. He gave to the Far East its first cardinals in history. In China, long known principally as a missionary area, he raised the hierarchy and gave the Church increased stature—although now there seems no way to avoid, for a generation or more, almost total loss of all that was wrought by missionaries over the centuries.

In terms of continents the greatest challenge to the next pontificate almost certainly will be neither Europe nor Asia but Latin America. "Above all," says one of the men who has been closest to Pius XII, "the next Pope must look to this area—an area predominantly Catholic, an area likely to double in population and wealth in a generation and, unhappily, an area where the Church already has grave troubles." The Latin American Church is in serious disorder. It lacks both seminaries and priests. It also lacks the financial sinews for effective organization. Huge labor lies ahead if all this is to be repaired before the Church faces again, as on occasions in the past, the tragedy of too little done too late.

Such are but a few of the matters and dilemmas with which Church and Papacy live daily. Awesomely varied—conventionally routine or appallingly global—they suggest the living paradox of the intricate, ceaselessly moving institution that so deceptively seems a fixed and simple monolith.

As it is with issues, so it is with the men of the Church. Serving a single cause, each may conceive of his service in a different sense. Confronting common enemies, each may favor distinct strategy and tactics. Wedded solemnly to a common life, each knows that this, like all marriages, is imperfect. Daily and without cease, the search continues for the greatest service, the wisest decision, the truest response.

Thus the next Pope may be a mystic, passionately dedicated to the proposition that the prayer is mightier than the sword. (If so, he will most certainly have counselors to suggest to him, at appropriate times, that the quite important struggle of the nations is not likely to be wholly resolved within the walls of his private chapel.) Or he may be a pontiff of most sensitive conscience in matters social and political, deeply convinced that the knowing of justice in this world encourages faith in it for the next. (If so, he will quite probably number among his advisers a few to note, from time to time, that the good life in either

597

world is unlikely to be completely assured by act of congress or parliament.) He may be a man of great scholarship or a man of stern practicality. He may be the son of wealth or a child of poverty. He may prove to be a weak leader or one whom history will thank and honor.

Whoever the next Pope may be, the chances are that his hand will tremble when the Fisherman's ring is put upon his finger. Then, as best he can, by the devices he knows and trusts most, he will proceed with the ancient and endless business of serving the servants of God.

THE WORLD, THE FLESH AND THE DEVIL

by John K. Jessup

DECEMBER 26, 1955

> *This editorial from LIFE's special issue on Christianity discusses how the main challenges to the Christian faith in America may be surmounted, unless one of them— the possibility of the H-bomb putting an end to man's terrestrial adventure—suddenly makes further discussion academic. John K. Jessup has been a senior editor of TIME, chairman of the board of editors of FORTUNE, and is now chief editorial writer of LIFE.*

A recurrent pattern in the stormy history of Christianity is of advance and retreat, vigor and lassitude, whose tidal sweeps have nevertheless enlarged the net area of Christendom. The number of baptized is now at an all-time high. If the pattern holds good as it has for nineteen centuries, the next great movement would seem to be another retreat, perhaps before the root-and-branch challenge of Communism. On the other hand, the long internal crisis of Christianity that began with seventeenth-century rationalism is now being superseded by a religious revival, especially in the U.S., which may well herald another great expansion. So instead of speculating whether Christianity's immediate future is bright or bleak, we here summarize the main challenges to the faith in America, judging not whether but how they may be surmounted.

Christian thinkers and theologians are deeply aware of these challenges. They have doubted whether the American religious revival is real or phony, and also whether, even if it is real, the Christian churches will prove an adequate channel for it. Our religious boom has many bizarre features, and may even be based on a profound misunderstanding of what it means to be a Christian. The National Council of Churches has voiced its concern that "the average church member is not conspicuously different from the average nonmember." Tolerant, well-behaved America has the defect of its virtues; it is not good democratic form to assert unconditional beliefs of any kind. As Monsignor Ronald Knox once put it,

> . . . Suave politeness, temp'ring bigot Zeal,
> Corrected "I believe" to "One does feel."

This "vaporized Christianity" is not the kind of faith that spread the Gospel in the great missionary eras.

Besides its own attenuation, Christianity in America faces a number of other challenges, from the secularism of our prosperous democracy to the possibility of an H-bomb finis to the human adventure. Most of these challenges seem to us unprecedented; whether or not Christianity is making progress, its enemies seem to have made a good deal. Yet, since Christianity does not change with its conditions, and the change in its conditions is also somewhat illusory, the "unprecedented" challenges of our day can be read as the same that have faced the Church since it was born.

In the fourth century, St. Cyril, then Bishop of Jerusalem, encompassed all the foes of Christ in a triple renunciation which has stood as a warning to neophytes in the baptismal service ever since. This is "the World, the Flesh and the Devil." Let us see what novel forms these three old foes have taken today. Because it is common to all men, Christian or not, we begin with the challenge of the flesh.

The flesh has received plenty of attention from the genius of our age. Like modern science, Jesus Christ was also a miracle-worker in fleshly healing. There is nothing un-Christian about the pleasure of health, nothing specifically Christian (despite saintly examples) about the mortification of the flesh. But as the Apostles were tempted to, and perhaps did, overexploit Christ's miracles at the expense of his message, so American Christianity is tempted to redefine salvation itself in terms the secular healers use: wholeness, the integrated personality, adjustment to the environment of this life. The stated clerk of the Presbyterian Church, Eugene Carson Blake, has even warned against a new kind of idolatry here: we may be turning God into Astarte and Apollo, the givers of children and health.

The true health of the Christian soul is not measured by a bovine "adjustment" to life. The sign of Christian health is Christian joy, which can include the lesser pleasures of the here and now but is more than pleasure, more even than happiness, because (in Paul Tillich's words) it also includes a sense of "the inner aim of life, the meaning of creation." The challenge of the flesh to Christianity today is the temptation, amid so much health and comfort, to settle for less than this inner aim. The sign of our danger is the absence of interest in the question of life after death.

Anthropologist Geoffrey Gorer, in a recent article on "The Pornography of Death," points out that death has become as unmentionable to us as was procreation to the Victorians. "Our great-grandparents were told that babies were found under gooseberry bushes or cabbages; our children are likely to be told that those who have passed on (fie! on that gross Anglo-Saxon monosyllable) are changed into flowers, or lie at rest in lovely gardens."

Are Americans trying to evade the fact of death, the natural climax of existence? Christians may well take concern for the false sense of reality in our suppressed hostility to death and in our embarrassed incuriosity about what lies beyond. If our human need for immortality is driven underground, it will probably erupt into idolatry or superstition. St. Francis, who could say "welcome!" to "our sister the death of the body, from whom no living man can escape," and Walt Whitman, who could hymn "sane and sacred death," were in far closer touch with reality than America's eupeptic sunbathers who never talk of these things.

"In the last days," wrote Paul to Timothy, "men shall be lovers of their own selves . . . ever learning, and never able to come to the knowledge of the truth." It is the essence and glory of Christianity that it has this truth. Only the love of God, and no lesser love, can put this pleasant life of flesh in a despair-proof relationship to the fact of death and the hunger for immortality—and give these their "inner aim and meaning." If Christianity should become a religion of the flesh only, however healthy that flesh and however broadly defined, Christianity will make a lovely corpse.

The challenge of the world has always been its power to preoccupy the Christian's mind and corrupt his aim. It still has that power, as is shown by the grip of secularism on American life, whose urgent trivialities crowd the hours of the soul as the advance of science crowds faith's realm in the mind. But the challenge of the world today is a magnificent assertion. It asserts that man, science and altruism can by combined effort turn the globe into a material near-Eden. It backs this assertion with the evidence of success, notably in America. In our time, instead of the lifelong hunger and hard work to which most men have been condemned since Adam, there has arisen at least one country—our own—where abundance is, or is rapidly becoming, the norm of life.

To make this assertion a global reality, the world seems to stipulate only two conditions, neither of which the Christian can object to. First, the world asks that we refrain from atomic slaughter of civilization. Second, it asks that we keep on doing what we're doing, or a little more, in the way of technical and economic progress; and that little more involves an effort of altruism which comes from our better nature. Our best men, not our worst, will lead us into the new Eden—men of imagination, who preach constructive aid to less fortunate peoples abroad and the final extermination of poverty and prejudice at home; men of character who want democracy to work and believe in the human race.

This modern Western notion, that men by reasoned behavior and mutual aid can define a world-shared goal and achieve it, is rapidly becoming an article of world faith. It is not only a good notion, it can call itself a Christian notion. Millions of good Christians and twenty

Christian centuries have brought it to birth. Christianity, "stretched between earth and heaven," has always set itself worldly tasks and fought the visible and quantitative evils around it, including poverty and ignorance.

As to the world's promise of an attainable quasi-Eden, the Christian conditions are not easy. The temptation in this Eden is not so much of evil as of partial goodness; not so much of materialism as of spiritual mediocrity; not so much of false idols as of idle falsities and second bests. Paul Tillich has warned that "if Christianity ever dies in America, it will die in the American suburban church . . . not under attacks from without, but of its own respectability." The social and organizational work of many American churches has already so domesticated the Gospel of Jesus as almost to rob it of its point and its power. Altruism may create a quasi-Eden, but it is far from a definition of the Christian life.

Nor can it even create the kind of Eden that Christians will want to live in. For example, take the problem of work. To make work easier, as an economy of abundance does, is not to make work meaningful; the shorter working hours become, the more insistent grows the question, why work at all? It will need a better answer than economics can give. At a recent conference held under Church auspices on this subject, Toynbee declared that work must become "consecrated" once more, as agricultural labor was consecrated during most of human history. And the Harvard Business School, seeking an answer to the same problem, is now concerned in its executive training program with what its dean calls "the great truths of the Sermon on the Mount." A strange back door for Christian joy to re-enter the world's work! But they must re-enter if the economy of abundance is to be tolerable, and Christians are its logical guides.

Thus the Christian is deeply involved in our civilization, none more so; and in its golden promise. But if the world's optimistic assertion implies that the world is man's best hope, the Christian must respond with an unqualified no. None of the promises the world has made to the spirit of man has deserved that kind of confidence. If Christianity is the soul of Western civilization, that soul is nevertheless dedicated by its own doctrine to a world beyond this world. The Christian's very value to our civilization is his detachment from it. The firmer in his faith, the better he knows that neither war nor peace, civilization nor catastrophe, prosperity nor adversity, are for him the end of life or hope or responsibility. "This world is not his home."

Few educated Westerners have taken the Devil seriously for many years. Among those few, however, are some of Christianity's best minds, and they have a simple explanation for the Devil's disappearance from common consciousness: he planned it that way. But although the Devil offends reason, it is not therefore unreasonable to recognize his existence. He simply dwells in a different dimension of reality.

The Devil's challenge to American Christians is, first, that they should complete the unmasking of his pretended nonexistence; and second, that they should do their best to anticipate his next major disguises. Some clue to the latter problem may be gained from his two most famous Biblical appearances, in the Garden of Eden and on the "exceeding high mountain."

To Jesus on the mountain, the Devil was what W. R. Bowie calls "the voice of the plausible lower choice." He offered Jesus a great career as the George Washington of the Hebrew nation, which badly wanted one at the time. But Jesus knew how much greater than that was His mission. So to all churches, including America's, comes at some time the temptation to embrace great worldly causes which are nevertheless not great enough. It seems pretty clear that Communism is a form of Satan in action, to be resisted by all means at all times. But Satan's also is the temptation to invest the countervailing virtue and power of America, or democracy, or Western civilization, or the U.N., or the processes of history, with the hope and faith that Christianity owes only to God. Such "plausible lower choices" can scarcely be recognized, let alone resisted, except by a continuous rededication to the Christian life.

As for the Devil in the Garden of Eden, he was not the sole guilty party (as Eve claimed), any more than Eve was (as Adam claimed). Nor ever since; the sterile Devil can work only through the materials of Another's creation, and those materials include the crucial fact of mankind's free will. The American's experience is that he can do something about evil, both within himself and in the world; and he has. The Devil's final challenge to American Christianity is that we should not falter in this fight.

Theologians dispute whether the fight does any good. Is evil a constant, and man's capacity for sin and error unchanged by centuries of trying to overcome them? Ever since the Pilgrims identified themselves with the followers of Moses and this continent with the Promised Land, the perfectibility of human life and even of human nature has been part of the American dream. But even if that were a false dream, no change of signals is in order. For whether or not man is infinitely perfectible, Christian man is infinitely responsible, both for his own soul and his neighbor's. His responsibility varies with his opportunities, which were never greater than the modern American's. And his reward for discharging them is incalculable even if he fails; for it is God's infinite love.

IX
WARS

Richard Gangel

EUROPE
IN THE SPRING

by Clare Boothe Luce

JULY 29, 1940

> *When Clare Boothe Luce returned to the United States from Europe a month after Hitler's blitzkrieg began slashing and tearing through Holland, Belgium and France, she wrote a best-selling book,* Europe in the Spring. *It contained some of the most striking and authoritative reporting of early World War II. Mrs. Luce has been at various times editor, writer, columnist and playwright* (The Women). *She has also been a U.S. Congresswoman from Connecticut and the United States Ambassador to Italy.*

If you had been in England and France in March and April and early May you probably would have seen many of the same people that I saw, asked many of the same questions I asked and gotten most of the same answers that I got. And on the strength of them you probably would have reached the same conclusions I reached. (In early May they were still quite optimistic.) But, being an American, when the bombs began to fall uncomfortably close to you (as they did to me in Brussels and Paris) you would have thought first of yourself and then of your family and both thoughts would have counseled your hasty departure from Europe. Whereupon you'd have clutched your dear red American passport firmly to your breast, gathered together your remnants of luggage and—your curiosity about "what was going to happen in Europe" quite satisfied for the time being—you'd have gotten back as best you could to your native country, revising rapidly in transit many of your optimistic conclusions. But once at home in physical security but mental torment you'd then have begun to ask yourself: what is going to happen to America? Because if you'd been there you'd surely feel what I feel now: the background of the blitzkrieg in democratic France, in democratic England, was the same background we are all living in here today in America.

The first thing I found out in Paris in early March was that everybody's *morale* was excellent. There was one phrase on everybody's lips, *"Il faut en finir"* (We must put an end to it). People said it on the streets, waiters told you so in cafés, dressmakers embroidered the motto into the corners of gay chiffon handkerchiefs, jewelers made gold charm bracelets spelling it. It was on the urgent honeyed lips of every radio commentator, it began the editorials in every paper, every politician rounded his peroration with it, and the soldiers sang it lustily in the canteens to music. We'll put an end to it! Anyone who didn't believe *that* was a defeatist or pro-German. (The words "Fifth Columnist" did not come into popular usage until after the invasion of Norway.)

Sometimes the French spoke of their morale as though it were something *tangible*: the "morale" of the French *poilu*, they said, "made him impervious to the longest coldest winter France has ever had." Or something negotiable like money: "The morale of the home front was such that it supplied our poilus, on short notice, with millions of blankets." Or functional, like an antitank gun, or a bomb shelter: "the morale of our troops will really begin to operate when faced with the menace of German tanks;" "the morale of French civilians will protect them against any amount of the bombing of open cities." French morale was regarded as not only different in quality but in kind from German morale. "When we bomb Berlin," everybody said, "you will see how German morale will break." But: "if they bomb Paris, our morale will be hardened."

Sometimes the French café-pessimists and the English weekend spoil-sports said, "But suppose Hitler *really* has . . . some secret weapon?" "Now," the logical Frenchmen said, "what secret weapon could he have—besides those nose-dive bombers and tanks he used in Poland, which was a weak unprepared country and couldn't take it?" Then everybody freely speculated about gases, which might humanely put you to sleep or horribly peel you alive like a banana, and flame throwers and giant liquid air bombs, but even while they shuddered as people do always shudder at well-told horror tales, they were quickly consoled, discounting at once such Martian horrors. Hitler would have to get through the French Maginot (or Belgian Maginot) first, and by that time the British Navy's blockade would have starved him, etc.

Now everybody knows what Hitler's secret weapon was: efficiency. The iron efficiency which coldly co-ordinated military strategy, economics, domestic politics, foreign diplomacy, propaganda, espionage and the will of the people to his one increasing purpose—to conquer or die.

Our real problem, nearly everybody in France said, is how to keep our boys in uniform warm and contented throughout the summer and another hard winter. (In a way, you see, they thought even of their troops as accidentally uniformed civilians.) So they told you about the "foyers" and "canteens" and *"théâtres des Armées"* that the celebrated actresses and elegant duchesses and all the poor but patriotic French and English women were organizing and financing behind the Maginot and right on the Belgian border to keep the boys smiling. And they showed you the Red Cross rooms where there were pile upon pile of *colis* or bundles with writing paper and Chinese checker boards and sweaters and cigarettes and footballs and light reading matter waiting to go to the soldiers. And then that made them think, too, of the boredom and the discontent and misery which "might grow" on the home front. In eight months of "war" they had still managed to do wonders for the 500,000 evacuees from the Rhineland. They had found them schools and food and employment and shelter. They had even found sewing machines for evacuated prostitutes of Strasbourg who were now being taught the more social if less popular profession of seamstress. They pointed with pride to the facts that Daladier had not enforced the totalitarian "decrees" conscripting male and female labor, that everybody was being allowed plenty of gas to motor to the Bois or to the races at Longchamp, that the three days-without-coal law was being "held over" to the following winter to avoid discontent, that Schiaparelli and Chanel and Balenciaga and Lelong were showing and exporting collections made of the fine silks still being made in French factories, which were being "gradually" turned into munition plants in order not to bring about too sudden unemployment among the silk weavers, and also because the continued export of silk was one factor in keeping a "favorable trade balance."

After the invasion I saw a French soldier in a base-line hospital. He had a great many German bomb fragments in his thigh and shoulder. Among his other souvenirs of the war he had a piece of French silk from a German parachute which he kept in his pajama pocket. He caressed it with a bitter wonder. "Look at it," he said, "how fine! You only see silk like *that* in *this* country on the backs of models in dressmakers' salons."

I remember M. Herriot one night in late April made a long, impassioned and really brilliant analysis of the German metaphysical mind, how from Hegel to Hitler Germany had *logically* sought to prove "might is right." (Nothing about how Germany had always managed to implement this metaphysical monstrosity with shell and strategy.) "*Bien, il faut en finir,*" said M. Herriot at long last, brushing the cigar ashes off his rotund vest wearily. And for the first time that evening all the other politicians in that drawing room agreed with him enthusiastically, almost tearfully. Their morale, you see, was also excellent. They were all really very patriotic gents. Now I see in the papers, there is a tendency to "smear" them . . . to say *they* "betrayed France." I deny it. It's too happy and easy an explanation. And it is not, as the French say, "*raisonable.*" They knew, and the bankers knew, and the financiers and the manufacturers knew, that if France was beaten, Hitler would give them no quarter and no profits. They were stupid and blind and egoistic and mean and human—all too human perhaps. But alas, they were not "traitors." I say alas, because if "treachery" were the key to the Fall of France, then, to be safe, all America need do never to fall is watch for and weed out "traitors."

. . . It was not what these gentlemen *did* before or during the war; it's what they didn't do. "The price of Liberty is eternal vigilance." They were simply asleep at the switch: they didn't even appoint *soldiers* to watch the switch while they slumbered. Much cynical postmortem, some idealistic prognostications, a little clever opportunism and the irreducible minimum of performance. Hasn't that always been the portrait of a politician? But believe me, they, too, were patriotic and confident.

I complained one day to M. Leger, who was then Permanent Secretary of Foreign Affairs, that I wished that France had a more eloquent, American-wise propagandist for an Ambassador in Washington than Count René de Saint-Quentin—somebody like Lord Lothian, for instance. He was indignant. "M. Saint-Quentin gets everything for France he asks," he said haughtily. I said, "Then your demands are very much more modest than America fears they might be." And he said with gentle slyness: "You don't know what M. Saint-Quentin asks or gets! He may not be very popular with Americans, but he is a most intimate friend of your President, which is better." "Oh, I know about five thousand of Mr. Roosevelt's most intimate friends," I said and let it go at that. I think it made many Americans in France angry and unhappy and uneasy to see how everybody loved Mr. Roosevelt and despised America. M. Leger was no exception. Like every other politician in France, he didn't care a hoot what Americans thought, only about what Mr. Roosevelt said, personally. Everybody in France trusted Mr. Roosevelt implicitly.

I never met a single man on the streets or a single man in high authority who wasn't utterly convinced that if France ever should be on the verge of defeat, Roosevelt would bring a recalcitrant America quickly to heel and pour all its enormous resources into the breach. I know that in those last awful days of early June, it was a bitter, bitter shock to them and to little M. Reynaud that not only Mr. Roosevelt couldn't bring America into war, but that he could not even send what it turned out rather suddenly we didn't have, and which nobody apparently had told them (or us) before we didn't have, "clouds of airplanes."

It was the loveliest crystal-clear spring Europe had had in many years. There was not a little drop of rain, not a faintly mottled sky until mid-June. In Europe, that spring, like an ethereal army with blossom-strewn banners, seemed to come on forever. Before the invasion, the English called it "King's Weather." After that the English didn't talk much about the weather because they knew that in Germany everybody was calling it "Hitlersvetter," and that in Flanders and Picardy this heavenly boon to mankind, a perfect spring, had become a hideous evil. In such a spring tanks could push up faster than flowers. . . .

Now, in April, chestnuts burst into leaf on the lovely avenues of Paris, sunlight danced off the opalescent gray buildings, and the sunsets, glimpsed through the Arc de Triomphe at the end of the long splendid vista of the Champs-Elysées, brought a catch of pain and pleasure in your throat. Paris was Paris in April! There were not many children in the parks but the cafés were thronged with old men and women sipping aperitifs and reading the thin confident papers, with pretty girls, many of them in Red Cross ambulance-driver uniforms, with little dark-eyed, khaki-clad, sloppy, tough-looking permissionaires. The shops were open and "doing business," and there was plenty of traffic in all streets. It was a ghost war, in the skeleton of peace, but it wasn't as unpleasant looking as that simile. The worst that it was, in Paris, was boring. British war correspondents, week-ending in Paris, groused about the "phony war," the dearth of readable dispatches to send, and told how they had written letters to their editors asking to be sent to the "trouble spot of the Balkans," to Turkey or to the U.S. to report the political situation in America.

"The trouble is," an English colonel said to me at a big luncheon at Versailles, "we are gentlemen. There are so many *nasty* things they can do and we simply can't and won't be nasty." His mustache bristled fiercely. "We've got to . . . bomb Baku—bomb Batum! Extreme, of course," he said, "but by cutting off Germany's oil supply from Russia it will end the war quickly." A Rumanian diplomat, anxious to remove the seat of war a little further from his doorsteps, suggested the English might instead take Narvik to cut off Hitler's iron-ore supply—but nobody at luncheon seemed to know where Narvik was, so we all dropped the subject.

On April 6, at the invitation of the French G.H.Q. (and as an

enormous concession to foreign "propaganda"), I was allowed to go up
to the Maginot Line. . . . Now let me be honest. By that time, I had
begun to believe, like the English (and the French), that the answer
to victory was simply morale: sticking it, and that in the end the
slow inexorable grinding of democracy's productive machinery would
bring about the almost bloodless collapse of Germany. And then I
went into *"la zone des armées."* I saw Alsace and Lorraine in April.
How beautiful they looked, how rich, how fair the fields were in the
spring sunshine. And then, speeding through this sweet countryside,
when you looked closer, you saw that innocent golden haystacks concealed ugly guns, half-built cottages housed machine-gun nests and
on the slopes of tender hills nestled many a camouflaged pillbox. All
this lovely, lovely part of budding France, *bristled with hidden death,*
like a beautiful woman with a dread disease. Woe, I thought, to the
men who sought to embrace her! (I had a fleeting thought . . . why
should they try it?) Then we came to the Maginot forts—those
machine-gun-manned, tank-trapped, barbed-wired, small ugly entrances into the vast deadly ouvrages, the cement catacombs, the row
on row of sunken earthbound battleships—*La Ligne Maginot!*

You weren't in a Maginot fort very long before you realized that
it *was* impregnable from the enemy's side. I thought, the Germans
are smart, they know everything. Either they have some secret weapon
or they won't try to come through this way. I—even I—suddenly
figured out that one. Now, I was in the Mont des Welshes. (Oh,
my fort, the Mont des Welshes, of which I was the marraine. I had
sent them their cigarettes, their champagne, their brave flag embroidered in gold with the Maginot motto: *Ils ne passeront pas.* What
comfort it is now that they *didn't* pass—that way?) I said to the little
commander of my fort, "Why should they try to come this way?"
"Ah, Madame, of course they can't get through, but you don't understand the Germans—*ils sont bêtes*—They *will* try. Imagine if they
didn't? How foolish we would look—France would look . . . *Madame,
c'est pas raisonable,*" said the commander. "But," I persisted, "can't
they get through some *other* way?" "What other way?" the commander
laughed and all the lieutenants laughed quickly. "Holland? Belgium?"
I said timidly. They laughed even louder. "First," they said, "they

don't want to take on three million more Dutch and Belgian soldiers —second, we are reliably informed the Dutch have a flood system, and the Belgians a small Maginot Line, and third, the Germans are stupid but not that stupid. . . ."

On April 9 I was the guest of honor at an officers' mess of the 164th Regiment in the Maginot Line. Suddenly a pale-faced radio operator brought the commander a small piece of square lined paper covered with delicate penciled French handwriting. He looked at it gravely and then with a blank face read it aloud.

Bulletin

New York: "Communications being cut off between the Scandinavian nations and the other countries, we can not have confirmation of the news from New York according to which the Norwegian Minister declares that his country is in a state of war with Germany.

Paris: "According to the news from Norway, the German troops have occupied Bergen, the Norwegian Government has left Oslo.

Amsterdam: "About fifty German war boats left German ports yesterday going north. At 11 o'clock the German forces were in the Kattegat towards the northwest."

There was a silence. We all looked solemn and utterly bewildered. The general said, after a long pause: "*Bien*, this is the affair of England. They have the Navy." And because, as it turned out, very few of the French officers knew except in a general way where Olso was and certainly not where the Kattegat was, they found they couldn't talk very brightly about the German invasion of Norway. As they bade me adieu they gave me a little bouquet of red roses. Heavens knows where they found red roses in the Maginot—but that's what's so wonderful about the French. They know that even in the Maginot red roses must be given to ladies.

A French colonel said, "Yes, now we are really comrades. . . . Not since the affair of Jeanne d'Arc have the English and the French so well understood each other." Everybody thought this Norway was the beginning of the end for Hitler, that at last a front had been found, and that, as Chamberlain said in Commons the first day, "Hitler had missed the bus," and as Churchill said, "made the worst military blunder since Napoleon's Spanish peninsular campaign."

So I was jubilant. I decided to go to England, which was going to be closer now to the war and victory.

That's when I met our military attaché, Colonel Horace Fuller, in the hall of the American Embassy where I had gone to get my exit permit to England. "Isn't it wonderful," I said. He looked very sour. "Oh, yes," he said, "Hitler's missed the bus, but he's caught a transport plane." I looked bewildered, so he said, "Innocent, come with me." And in his office he showed me the maps of Norway, and explained what it meant in ships, in men, in guns, to face an armed fjord, and how Norway of all countries was the kind of country which if you "got there fustest with mostest men" you couldn't be got out in a year or a day. And Hitler had got there fustest. And then he showed me other maps, of the Belgian and Dutch frontiers, and how many Panzer divisions he figured (at minimum) the Germans had there and near Luxembourg. And then he called in Lieutenant Colonel George Kenney, assistant air attaché who told me how many planes he thought the Germans had. The colonel was in a great hurry and wouldn't talk much, because he was going back to the U.S.A. with an urgent report based on a study he had made, in the face of violent political and military and diplomatic obstruction and red tape, of French aviation production and of German sample planes brought down behind the French lines. "Gee," he said, "I've got to get home to make the politicians see that we might as well throw our whole Air Force into the ashcan—it's so out of date for the kind of war the Germans are going to have here!" I said, "Is there no hope for—for France?" Colonel Fuller said, "You want me to say something vague and comforting. O.K. The English never know when they're licked. *They'll* always keep on fighting. That's the only hope." I wanted to cry. I think I did. I said, "Oh, you don't really *believe* the Germans are going to win do you?" Colonel Fuller said, "Yes, if some miracle doesn't happen, they've got the guns, and the tanks and the planes and the men, and a plan, and the initiative." And I said, "Oh, dear!" He said, "Come have a drink."

On April 25, armed with the sore knowledge about Norway provided me by the only two men in France who had talked war facts to me, I went to London. London was lovely in that late April, lovely beyond belief. There were masses of blue hyacinths and tulips in Hyde Park, and bright azaleas in the window boxes of hotel windows. The little barrage balloons like silver toys disported themselves innocently high up against the blue sky twinkling in the warm sunlight. Traffic tooted and jostled in the crowded thoroughfares, and in spite of the pitch blackouts, which you didn't notice much on the bright moonlit nights, London was altogether much gayer than Paris. Good Hungarian music in Claridge's, fine Italian food at Quaglinos, no rationing there, no gloom—not even a little sign of "grim determination." Paris was Paris in April, but looking back on it, I saw now everybody was *secretly* gloomy because, after *all*, a "long war" with an enormous army kept mobilized was bound to be severer on France than on England. The triumphant progress (in the newspapers) of the Norwegian campaign was lifting every Englishman's spirits.

England, the English said in early May, "always loses every battle but the last one." Perhaps they are so proud of that tradition, so proud that they have subconsciously allowed it to become their blueprint of military strategy. They were also proud of "muddling through." So they made that their political policy. Now I remembered an Italian Fascist in Rome saying to me in March about the English: "A nation which is overripe with tradition is overripe for ruin."

They were willing to bury the Norwegian thing. They also began very openly to "venture to suggest" to one another that it's "a rotten shame we can't bury Chamberlain with it." " 'E's dead, but 'e won't lie down," somebody quoted a Gracie Fields music-hall song. "We certainly will get rid of him when we have a real crisis," a British undersecretary said to me at an English weekend luncheon. "A real crisis," I said, feeling sick down inside of me again, "what do you call a *real* crisis? By that time it may be too late."

Now at this luncheon there was an old, untidy, distinguished Gladstonian-looking gentleman called J. L. Garvin at the table. Right then to the astonishment of all the conservative lords and ladies and old politicians there assembled, he made a magnificent speech. In it, he said he now saw clearly all that was wrong with England, its inertia, its smugness, its fatal unpreparedness. Eloquently, with many a quotation from the classics to trim a point, and point a dart, he begged everyone at lunch to help get rid of Chamberlain *now*. This was the great crisis, he said. How do you know, they said, half-convinced. Mr. Garvin quoted Johnson—" 'When a man knows he's to be hanged in a fortnight, it concentrates his mind wonderfully.' We're going to be hanged at any minute now," he said. "Hitler has warned us in Norway."

The next day the great debate on the conduct of the Norwegian campaign began in the House of Commons. I remember it was a Tuesday, May 7. Now since my talk with Colonel Fuller, I had had a strange desire to see the Low Countries. In fact faced with the only other alternative, a long Whitsuntide weekend in the English country, playing bridge or golf, and "talking politics," I decided on a short look-see at Holland and Belgium. "One last look," I told someone, and they said you were very brave to go to a *neutral* country. Because it was standing joke in both France and England that the only *safe* place in Europe was one of the three belligerent countries. So on the day Mr. Chamberlain was defending himself as a military strategist, I flew on KLM, and landed at the Schiphol Airport at Amsterdam.

At dinner that night I sat next to Mr. Snouck Hurgronje, the permanent Secretary General for Foreign Affairs. Naturally I asked him about the crisis. "The Germans are making troop movements which suggest an invasion," said Mr. Snouck placidly. "Oh," I said, "are you sure?" "Yes," he said cheerfully. "The same sources have informed our government so, which informed it so five days before the German invasion of Norway." I said aghast, "You *knew* five days before that the Germans were going to invade Norway?" "Yes," he said, "our sources of information are excellent. You see a good Dutchman often can pass as a real German." (I thought "and vice versa.") "Oh," I said, "you knew five days before. Did you . . . (I held my breath) tell the English and French about it?" "Certainly not," he said indignantly. "Why should we? They're not *our* allies!" (Mr. Snouck ten days later was in London, a member of Her Exiled Majesty's belligerent government.) I said, "If your sources are reliable, aren't you—er—uneasy? . . ." He went on eating. "Well, you can never tell," he said, cheerfully. "We've had three crises like this. This may also pass. One does one's best, one waits, one accepts the inevitable."

I guess he noticed the rather amazed expression on my face at so much stolidity, so much fortitude. "It's a wonderful thing," he said, "to be a neutral—*if* you are strong like America." I said severely, "Mr. Snouck, if you really fear Germany . . . why don't you throw in with the Allies?" He smiled patiently. "We don't want to be invaded like Poland and Norway," he said. "On the other hand we are in no hurry to precipitate the 'assistance' the Allies gave Norway and Poland." The argument seemed unanswerable, so I let it pass.

The crisis passed too, in Holland. In Amsterdam on May 9 a prominent journalist explained it to me neatly: "Just Germany jacking up Holland a bit so she wouldn't get too friendly tradewise with the Allies." A second newspaperman had another explanation. "Created," he said, "by the Dutch government itself" as an excuse for its projected roundup of thirty thousand (30,000!) listed fifth columnists. "Yes," he said, "the jails are already bursting with them." A third had another explanation. "Bet you," he said, "the government has made a secret military alliance with the French and the Belgians and the English. They've whipped up this little scare to test out their mobilization power in an emergency." An English newspaperman said: "The *Germans* probably arranged it for one of two reasons. First, to see where Dutch troops would be deployed, if they do get desperate and have to come in, in the summer or next spring; or second, to distract everybody's attention from other troop movements on the Siegfried or in the Balkans." So that was the "crisis" and I left Amsterdam for Brussels on the train, chugging peacefully over that flat pretty flower-painted dinner plate of a country, feeling very happy that it was safe, at least for the moment.

I reached Brussels at 11 P.M. on the night of the ninth of May and because I was very tired, I went right to bed in a pleasant, wide-windowed room in our embassy. I had no time in Brussels to find out how the Belgians felt about neutrality or the Americans or the English or the French or the Dutch, because six hours later in a lovely dawn, clouds of bombers came out of the sky from the east, and began to drop their lethal offal all around me, and on the Belgians. From that moment on I never talked or thought of politics. Neither did the Belgians. This was WAR now. These were the Germans. . . .

AMERICA
GOES TO WAR

by the Editorial Staff of LIFE

DECEMBER 22, 1941

> *Here is a typical* LIFE *news roundup, put together from the dozens of dispatches, wires, telephone and teletype reports that stream into the magazine's editorial offices every week from its news bureaus across the country. This one, published a few weeks after Pearl Harbor, describes in terse, spare prose how the United States was reacting to the sudden all-out demands of war.*

In the nation's capital and in cities on both continental coasts the lights of peace flicked off. Troops in steel helmets bared bayonets before the gates of military establishments and areas of arms production. Congress prepared to muster a gigantic pool of manpower—ten million men between nineteen and forty-five for military service, thirty million men up to sixty-five for defense activities of all kinds. The ban on overseas duty for selectees was lifted. Air-raid alarms sounded in Seattle, San Francisco, Los Angeles, New York.

At long last two-ocean war had come to America. It had spanned the Pacific treacherously and with catastrophic effect December 7.

It roared across the Atlantic in harsh Hitlerian tones December 11. Now all the battles of the hemispheres were fused into one titanic war of the world without parallel in time. Men were fighting and dying in the frozen lightless Arctic and all around the warm girdle of the Equator. Into this stupendous struggle the U.S. marched without indecision or fear.

At first all the news was bad. No one knew precisely what happened at Pearl Harbor, but rumors of unprecedented disaster spread and magnified across the land. The Philippines and intermediate U.S. outposts in the Pacific shivered under savage and recurrent assaults. Britain's mighty *Prince of Wales* and *Repulse* went down off Malaya. Singapore faced mortal danger. But at week's end the Stars and Stripes still waved over all of America's Pacific establishments except Guam, U.S. fliers had sunk at least three Japanese warcraft, including the battleship *Haruna.* Dutch submarines blasted four Jap troopships off Thailand. And Nazi armies in Russia were fleeing before a great resurgent Red wave of attack.

Americans took the news, good and bad, with admirable serenity. Initial incredulity changed quickly to fierce determination that the Axis nations would pay enormously for the cataclysm they had brought on the earth's free people. Politics were suspended. America First announced it would dissolve. Prophets who had accurately foreseen the course of events refrained from recrimination. Ideologically the nation was united as it had never been at any other military crisis in all its history. U.S. industry made ready to operate 24 hours a day, 365 days a year and to produce $1,000,000,000 in arms weekly. The civilian populace prepared to do without new motorcars, new tires, and the encyclopedic news coverage to which a free press had made it long accustomed. Significantly, it stopped using the word "defense." The ultimate goal had become "Victory." And for its battle cry America had a fine fighting slogan, "Remember Pearl Harbor!"

From the tragedy at Pearl Harbor, from the blood spilled and the ships lost and the treachery of the foe, came the U.S. battle cry of World War II. Divided and dubious on the morning of December 7, the American people arose the morning of December 8 united by a common enemy and a common hurt. Never before in history had the

U.S. been attacked by surprise. Some 130,000,000 Americans would remember Pearl Harbor as long as they lived. The phrase, "Remember Pearl Harbor," stirred Americans in 1941 as "Remember the *Maine*" had stirred their fathers forty-four years ago.

Within a few hours of the Pearl Harbor attack, the face of America began to undergo a swift transformation. First came a rush of uniforms as men on leave reported back to their posts and all officers up to the Chief of Naval Operations and the Army's Chief of Staff switched from mufti to uniform.

To prevent possible sabotage, soldiers and police immediately took up guard outside the chief office buildings at Washington and outside all the important war factories. The plants themselves began switching to a total output schedule: twenty-four hours a day, seven days a week.

Meanwhile the FBI was making a swift roundup of enemy aliens, by week's end had some 2,541 in custody. On the West Coast, where Japanese are thickest, misguided mobs beat up a number of slant-eyed citizens including not a few Chinese. Reporters trying to interview the head of the Japanese School at Seattle were told: "So solly. No school today. FBI have principal." To head off a foolish persecution by local authorities, Attorney General Biddle urged citizens to recognize that most aliens are loyal, leave roundups to the FBI.

Many thousands of young men did not wait to be drafted under the new and tighter draft regulations. The rush to get into uniform was such that long lines soon piled up outside recruiting offices. One young New Yorker, finding the Army line too long, impatiently switched to the Navy line. One young Bostonian named Tom Mahoney pinned a note to the wall of the New Haven Railroad engine house where he had been working: "To my buddies at the roundhouse . . . The liberty we enjoy will never be destroyed while boys like you and I can prevent it. That is why I left my job here and enlisted in the United States Marines."

With swift, decisive action the U.S. declared its war on Japan, Italy and Germany. From the moment the Japanese attack was announced by the White House, there was no division of opinion in America. The armed forces struck back at once, with all their might.

623

And in Washington there was enacted the impressive drama of a people's government voting itself at war with its sworn and mortal enemies.

The first declaration, against Japan, came on Monday, December 8, twenty-seven hours after the first bombs fell. Through most of the night President Roosevelt had been receiving military reports, conferring with his Cabinet, Senators and Congressmen. Precisely at noon Monday he emerged from the White House, wrapped in a big, dark naval cape. He was grim, angry, unsmiling. Carloads of heavily armed secret service men whisked him to the Capitol, where the Congress waited in joint session. At 12:30 he began his brief, historic message, ending: "I ask that the Congress declare that since the unprovoked and dastardly attack by Japan . . . a state of war has existed. . . ." Eighty million Americans, listening to radios, heard his voice.

The Senate and House raced to pass the declaration first, the Senate winning while a lone female dissenter voted "Nay" in the House. At 1:10 o'clock Congressional action was completed, and at 4:10 P.M. President Roosevelt signed the nation's declaration of war. Three days later, when Fascist Italy and Nazi Germany announced that they were at war with the U.S., Congress slapped right back with declarations in kind. This time the President simply sent his message. And there was no dissenting vote.

In no time at all, the civilians got a taste of war. Air-raid alarms shrieked on both coasts. Big cities blacked out, or tried to. There were dozens of casualties, mostly from auto accidents in the darkened streets. The tests showed that the citizens had very little idea of what to do when bombers come. But they also showed that the country was quick and eager to learn.

Monday night, air-raid alerts startled the West Coast. Enemy planes were reported coming in over San Francisco. Searchlights could not find them and they dropped no bombs. If they were enemy planes, as the Army insisted they were, they would have had little trouble finding the metropolis because blackout hardly dimmed it. Alcatraz Island was lit up like a gay ocean liner. A rosy neon glow bathed the downtown sky. A big insurance company sign on Market Street placidly spelled out its traditional message: "S-A-F-E."

Seattle had practiced blackouts last spring, went at the problem with a comparatively professional air. First blackout night two thousand citizens went on a window-smashing spree, broke the fronts of twenty-six stores which did not turn their lights off.

The eastern U.S. had its air-raid alarm on Tuesday when news came that enemy planes were coming in at New York from the Atlantic. Some Army men afterward classed the news as a "phony tip," others as a test alert. Interceptors whirred up to meet the enemy. But the people of New York waited curiously in the streets to see what would happen. Nothing stopped—traffic, business, lunch, conversation. The fire sirens wailed but their sound did not carry very far and nobody heeded them. A million delighted school kids were sent home and a few frightened elevator girls ran their cars down to the basement and refused to come up again. Mayor Fiorello LaGuardia, Director of the Office of Civilian Defense, was in Seattle when he heard about the shameful way his own citizens behaved. "Am I embarrassed?" he proclaimed. "Am I humiliated? And won't somebody catch hell about this when I get home!"

TORPEDO SQUADRON 8
GOES INTO ACTION

by Sidney L. James

AUGUST 31, 1942

> *Winston Churchill wept when he heard of the exploit*
> *of Torpedo Squadron 8. The story touched the hearts of*
> *people who thought themselves already numb to*
> *the pain and heroism of war. LIFE reported the full story for*
> *the first time when Ensign George H. Gay, the squadron's*
> *only survivor (he is now a TWA pilot), told it to Sidney*
> *L. James. Before he joined the staff of Time Inc. in*
> *1936, James was a reporter with the St. Louis Post-Dispatch.*
> *He has been head of Time's newsbureaus in Chicago and*
> *Los Angeles and assistant managing editor of LIFE. He*
> *is now publisher of Sports Illustrated.*

. . . Fifteen torpedo planes from this group, therefore, located the
enemy to the westward and proceeded to attack at once without
protection or assistance of any kind. Although some hits were re-
ported by radio from these airplanes and although some enemy fighters
were shot down, the total damage inflicted by this squadron in this
attack may never be known. None of these 15 planes returned. The
sole survivor of the 30 officers and men of this squadron was Ensign
G. H. Gay, Jr., U.S.N.R., who scored one torpedo hit on an enemy
carrier before he was shot down.

Thus, in Communiqué No. 97, the U.S. Navy wrote the terse
official epitaph of Torpedo Squadron 8. That might have been all that
the world ever knew, were it not for the one young officer who sur-

vived. Ensign Gay, saved by some whim of fate while all his comrades perished, has come back to tell a story of sacrifice and gallantry that deserves to live forever in American history.

The actual achievement of Torpedo Squadron 8, in a military sense, was important but not crucial. It took place on the second day of the Battle of Midway, when the Japanese attacking force was still almost intact. Squadron 8 found the Japanese force, which had been lost for several hours, recklessly attacked one of the enemy carriers and disrupted the whole force for the dive bombers which delivered their attack a few minutes later.

The real importance of the story of Torpedo Squadron 8 is not the damage it did to a Japanese carrier but the reckless heroism with which it carried out its mission. It is a story of a veteran U.S. Navy pilot who welded a group of relative youngsters from the four corners of his country into a fighting unit to defend it, in a time that was all too short and under conditions that were none too favorable. It is the story of young Americans, brought up in a world of peace and safety, who sought the danger of battle and, when they found it, flew unflinching into what they knew must be for most of them certain death. This is the story that Ensign Gay has to tell. It is at once an inspiration to all America and eloquent proof that American manhood has the stuff of which heroes are made and victories won.

Torpedo 8 had its beginning in Norfolk, Virginia, in the fall of 1941, when Lieutenant Commander John Charles Waldron was ordered to organize a torpedo squadron. Lieutenant Commander Waldron, a seamy-faced, square-jawed native of Fort Pierre, South Dakota, received his appointment to Annapolis before most of the group that later became his boys were born. To start with he had some Navy-made SBN's, turned out in 1932 and long ago obsolete. His boys were sent to him from Navy training bases at Miami and Pensacola as fast as they finished their flying lessons. Few were as experienced as Lieutenant J. C. Owens, Jr., son of a Los Angeles lumber dealer, who had been a Navy pilot for six years, or Lieutenant Raymond A. Moore of Petersburg, Virginia, who had entered the Navy as a seaman and worked his way into Annapolis. Jimmy Owens, quiet, easygoing and serious, became Waldron's executive officer. Moore, whose nose earned him the nickname of "Moose," was gunnery and engineering officer, jobs that would have been given to two men had there been two to handle them.

There was Ensign Grant W. Teats, the biggest man in the outfit, who came from Sheridan, Oregon, and had worked in lumber camps all over the Northwest after leaving Oregon State, where he was a crack trackman. Called "Teatso" at first, Ensign Teats later acquired "Plywood" as a nickname. Once, after the war was going on in earnest and Torpedo 8 was traveling on its carrier through the battle zones of the Pacific and undergoing the tedium of standing by in daily readiness during the critical dawn hours, Ensign Teats stepped to the front of the room and brought them to attention in their reclining leather chairs by smartly tapping his pencil. "Gentlemen," he said, "I have been informed that this organization is ignorant of the fine art of manufacturing plywood." Then he continued for two hours with a lecture on the art, from the felling of the trees to the final product. This started an institution of regular dawn lectures.

Ensign William R. Evans of Indianapolis, who entered the Navy after leaving Harvard Law School, gave a learned lecture on the law, comparing its circuitousness with Navy red tape. Ensign William W. Abercrombie, who had worked in the packing plants of Kansas City, spoke long and earnestly of the packing business. "Abbie" was proud of Kansas City and his invariable query, when he scanned the chart and determined the position of the carrier, was: "How far are we from Kansas City?" He maintained that he wanted to be transferred some day to submarine patrol duty in Missouri.

Ensign Evans was the learned member of the group and, though his parents called him plain Bill, the boys called him "the Squire." A true product of Harvard, he dutifully took the weight of the world on his shoulders. On December 7, when the news of the Jap attack reached Norfolk, he sat down and soberly wrote to his parents as follows: "People will not realize, I fear, for some time how serious this matter is. The indifference of labor and capital to our danger is an infectious virus and the public has come to think contemptuously of Japan. And that, I fear, is a fatal mistake—today has given evidence of that. Let us hope tonight that people, big people, little people, all people throughout this great country have the faith to once again sacrifice for the things we hold essential to life and happiness. Let us defend these principles to the last ounce of blood. But then, above all, retain reason enough to have 'charity for all and malice toward none.' If the world ever goes through this again, mankind is doomed. This time it has to be a better world."

The Squire kept his crew haircut to the end and he was reluctant to lay aside his stovepipe-legged, high-cut Harvardian trousers after the Japs hit Pearl Harbor.

Ensign Harold J. ("Elly") Ellison, handsome, slender and fidgety, had left a white-collar job in an insurance office in upper New York State. Ensign Ulbert M. Moore, called "Whitey" because of the silk down he had for hair, was a cherubic half-pint who became the virtual mascot of the outfit. It was said of Whitey that he could sleep on a picket fence. When he wasn't sleeping he wore a perpetual smile and enjoyed hugely the razzing he got for his love of slumber.

Ensign George H. ("Tex") Gay hailed from Houston and had spent three and one-half years at Texas A. & M., where any student can tell you the number of officers his institution has sent to the armed forces. In true Texas A. & M. tradition, Tex Gay quit school in 1940 to join the Army Air Corps, but the Air Corps medical officers decided that his heart did not score high enough in the Schneider test. They told him he had apparently spent too much time at a desk. After six months of work in the field with a construction gang he took another examination, but he was told he would never make a pilot. A year later, however, the Navy decided he was pilot-officer material and he entered the Navy's flying school at Miami. In October, 1941, he was commissioned, and a month later he joined Torpedo 8.

Such were the flying members of Torpedo 8. The Skipper, as they invariably called Lieutenant Commander Waldron, treated them like a father and, in turn, they gave him everything they had. They used to say of him that he apparently had been flying torpedo planes while the Wright brothers were still "batting the breeze." When he yelled at them, "Don't sit there fat, dumb and happy—do something," they moved. He made them fly four hours in the morning and four hours in the afternoon and had them on four hours of duty after that. He never failed to impress upon them that there was a job to be done and little time to do it in. When things went bad, he and his lively brunette wife, Adelaide, would throw a tremendous binge for them. If they had to get into Norfolk and lacked transportation, they could use the Skipper's Lincoln Zephyr. When the Skipper spoke of severe difficulties in his last message to them, the boys knew what he meant. He meant red tape, delays, insufficient equipment, lack of ammunition and even torpedoes to practice with. He meant the farmers of the Norfolk countryside who, thoughtless of what the boys were being trained for, complained that their low flying on practice torpedo run-ins was causing their cows to give sour milk, as though the sweet state of their milk had to be preserved along with democracy. Several months later, though, they put these petty annoyances behind them when they steamed off, ultimately to join the enemy in battle.

But in the timetable of war, schedules are flexible and Torpedo 8's first taste of battle was still months away. Each dawn and each dusk they spent hours in the ready room aboard the carrier, hoping that the enemy would appear. The afternoons they spent at lectures, cramming in more tactical knowledge. They were ready, their planes were ready. Let the enemy show himself.

On the evening of June 3, as the carrier snaked its way through a starry Pacific night, the pilots of Torpedo 8 filed into the ready room. Several days out from their base, they had every reason to feel that on this trip they were at last going to see the action the Skipper had trained them for. That morning, patrol planes had sighted a strong Japanese force approaching Midway in five columns, and during the day Army Flying Fortresses from Midway had attacked it, setting two ships afire.

In the ready room the Skipper handed his boys a mimeographed plan of attack and to it he appended his own final message. It ran as follows:

"Just a word to let you know that I feel we are all ready. We have had a very short time to train and we have worked under the most severe difficulties. But we have truly done the best humanly possible. I actually believe that under these conditions we are the best in the world. My greatest hope is that we encounter a favorable tactical situation, but if we don't, and the worst comes to the worst, I want each of us to do his utmost to destroy our enemies. If there is only one plane left to make a final run-in, I want that man to go in and get a hit. May God be with us all. Good luck, happy landings, and give 'em hell."

The boys felt proud of the confidence the Skipper expressed in them. They, too, felt they were ready, and they were determined that, whatever the action, there would be more than one plane left to make the final run-in for a hit.

At 3:30 the next morning, June 4, the pilots of Torpedo 8 again gathered in the ready room, there to sit through a critical dawn. As they entered the low-ceilinged, white-walled steel room, their practiced eyes turned first toward the illuminated three-foot-by-three-foot screen above the teletype machine. Projected from the machine below was the last message that had been received: four PBY patrol planes had made a moonlight torpedo attack on a Japanese occupation force near Midway at 1 A.M. As they settled in their comfortable leather chairs they hauled out their flight charts and copied off the data that had been chalked in the neat columns on the blackboard up front: wind, course, speed, visibility, dew point, nearest land, etc. But the teletype remained silent, and soon most of them had pushed the arm button on their chairs so that they could spend the remainder of their watch in their usual semireclining position. Whatever tension there was relaxed with them.

After daybreak, when it was announced that the ship was secure and they were dismissed by the Skipper, Abbie, as usual, moaned, "I'm hungry," and they went to the ward room for breakfast, where Rusty Kenyon ordered his usual plate of beans, for which he got his usual ribbing from the rest of the boys. By eight, the sun was up in a brilliant sky and most of them were back in their quarters. Scarcely had they got themselves settled for their after-breakfast rest, when the loudspeaker barked for their attention: "All pilots report to ready room." When they got to the ready room they found a new message on the teletype screen: "Midway was attacked this morning by Japanese aircraft and bombers." There was a scraping of wood on wood as each man jerked open the drawer built into the bottom of his chair, and a flurry of commotion as they hauled out helmets, goggles, gloves, and the pistols and hunting knives which the Skipper had made "must" equipment for them against a forced jungle landing. Then they began to copy off the latest flight data from the blackboard.

Presently the teletype began tapping again. The pencils stopped. And all eyes turned up to the screen to read the message, letter by letter, as it was projected: "E-N-E-M-Y N-A-V-A-L U-N-I-T-S S-I-G-H-T-E-D W-I-T-H-I-N S-T-R-I-K-I-N-G D-I-S-T-A-N-C-E. E-X-P-E-C-T-E-D S-T-R-I-K-I-N-G T-I-M-E o-9-o-o." Then, after a pause of almost breathless silence: "L-O-O-K-S L-I-K-E T-H-I-S I-S I-T."

Pencils began to scratch again as the pilots put every last bit of information onto their flight charts. Ellie Ellison leaned over toward Tex Gay with a broad grin. "Good luck," he whispered, as he extended his hand across the aisle to meet Gay's. "Pilots man your planes," ordered the loudspeaker. As the boys rose in silence, the Skipper addressed them: "I think they'll change their course. If you check your navigation, don't think I'm getting lost, just follow me. I'll take you to 'em." As they hurried from the room and climbed up the ladder to the flight deck, not another word was spoken.

Their silence was the grim silence of a football team that has been given the next play by the quarterback and is moving up from the huddle to the line of scrimmage. Before stepping onto the ladder, Tex Gay sidestepped to the sick bay nearby and picked up a tourniquet, which he stuffed into his pocket. When they got on deck, their planes were already there in neat rows. The mechanics were busy and the whine of the inertia starters drowned out the clatter of their trotting feet on the deck. Tucked neatly under the belly of each Douglas Devastator was a white-nosed torpedo—a pickle, as the boys preferred to call them. When they saw the pickles, the boys forgot about the Japs for a split second, for never before had they wheeled their Devastators off the deck with a live pickle in tow. One after the other the signalman waved off the scouts, the fighters and the dive bombers. Finally, Torpedo 8 was waved up and Tex Gay took his plane off with no difficulty.

After they rendezvoused in the sky, the Skipper took the lead and the fifteen planes of Torpedo 8 fell into the prearranged formation in which the Skipper had chosen to take them on their first adventure. Flying in six sections of two and a seventh section of three, with Gay bringing up the rear, the Skipper led them on a course south of west at three hundred feet.

After an uneventful hour, the Skipper's voice broke the radio silence: "There's a fighter on our tail." What he saw proved to be a cruiser plane flying at about a thousand feet. It flew by without paying any apparent attention, but the Skipper and boys knew it had probably radioed an alarm back to the Jap fleet and that they would doubtless be met by a reception committee of fighters.

They kept to their course and the flight continued uneventful until the motor of the plane Plywood Teats was flying, in the last section, began to spurt oil. When the windshield was obscured, Plywood reached outside with a rag to wipe it off. As he did so, he transferred the stick to his left hand. Unwittingly, his thumb pressed the trigger button on the stick and sent eight or ten rounds whizzing past Abercrombie's plane. Quick to understand what had happened, Abbie mopped his brow in mock panic and then grinned broadly at Plywood, who appeared to be roaring with laughter.

Almost another hour had passed since they had seen the Jap plane when two columns of smoke were sighted beyond the horizon. The Skipper dropped down low and the boys followed. Now they roared forward at torpedo-attack level, barely skimming the waves. When they burst over the horizon, it looked as if the entire Jap fleet was before them. They identified the carrier *Soryu* and a cruiser as the burning vessels set afire the day before, and counted in all three carriers, about six cruisers and ten destroyers. The ships were moving away from Midway, as the Skipper had guessed, and the carriers were loaded with planes which apparently were being refueled and rearmed. The Skipper immediately broke radio silence to send his contact report back to the U.S. carrier, giving position and strength.

Then the action the Skipper and the boys had been waiting for began. Antiaircraft fire went up from the ships and the surface guns began hurling explosive shells. Some thirty Zero fighters that had been circling high above the fleet, awaiting their arrival, began to dive. But the Skipper paid no attention to them. He wiggled his wings, as a signal for the boys to follow, and opened up the throttle.

As the Zeros swooped down on them, the Squadron's rear gunners opened up, making a terrific racket of machine-gun fire, punctuated by the louder, less rapid explosions of the cannon on the Zeros. By the time they were within eight miles of the Jap fleet they were caught in a barrage of fire from the ships.

When the first plane plunged into the water the Skipper, apparently forgetting to press his intercockpit communication button, was heard asking his radioman, Dobbs, in the rear seat: "Was that a Zero?" If Dobbs answered his voice was not heard, but in any case it was not a Zero. It was the first plane of Squadron 8 to go down.

When the second went down, Radioman Bob Huntington spoke from the back of Gay's plane. "Let's go back and help him, sir," he said. "To hell with that," Gay blurted, "we've got a job to do." Then the Skipper got it. His left gas tank hit, his plane literally burst into flame. Tex Gay could see him stand up and try to get out but it was no use. The waves that had been lapping at his undercarriage claimed him and Radioman Dobbs. Dobbs, a veteran enlisted man, had been ordered back to San Diego to become a radio instructor for the duration, after this engagement.

The barrage from the Jap ships grew deadlier. Surface shells, aimed to hit the ocean just ahead of them, were throwing up spouts of water which licked the bellies of the planes. Antiaircraft filled the air with acrid black smoke. One by one, the planes of Torpedo 8 went down. Flying so close to the water, they might as well have been crashing into a stone wall when they hit it. Tex Gay's mind flashed back to his childhood for a comparison with what was going on around him. There was a far-off day when he had tossed orange peelings in the water from a speedboat. It reminded him of that. The planes hit the water and they were gone, as though they were moving in the opposite direction.

There was one plane to Gay's left, close by, and another in front of him and below the nose of his plane. He lowered the nose to see what plane it was and it was gone. When he looked to the left, that plane was gone too. Now there was only Gay's plane left. The Skipper had lost his hope of "a favorable tactical situation." "The worst" had "come to the worst," and there was "only one plane left to make a final run-in." Tex Gay doesn't remember whether at the moment the Skipper's message actually flooded through his mind again, but he had seen the Skipper die and he was determined "to go in and get a hit."

Then the voice of Radioman Bob Huntington came into his ears over the intercom from the rear seat. "They got me," it said. "Are you hurt bad?" asked Gay. "Can you move?" There was no answer. Tex took his eyes off the waves long enough to see that Huntington was lifeless, his head limp against the cockpit. As he turned back, he felt a stab in his upper left arm. The hole in his jacket sleeve told him what had happened. He shifted the stick to his left hand, ripped his sleeve, pressed a machine-gun slug from the wound with his thumb. It seemed like something worth saving, so he sought to put it in the pocket of his jacket. When he found his pocket openings held shut by his safety belt and parachute straps and life jacket, he popped it into his mouth.

He kicked his rudder to make his plane slip and skid so as to avoid the Zeros. He was heading straight for the carrier that the Skipper had picked out. The ship turned hard to starboard, seeking to put its bow forward and avoid his torpedo. He swung to the right and aimed for the port bow, about a quarter length back. When he pushed the button to release his torpedo nothing happened. Apparently the electrical releasing equipment had been knocked out. Since his left arm was practically useless from the bullet and a shrapnel wound in his hand, he held the stick between his knees and released the torpedo with the emergency lever. By now he was only eight hundred yards from the ship and close to the water. He managed to execute a flipper, turning past the bridge of the carrier and clearing the bow by about ten feet. As he passed over the flight deck he saw Jap crewmen running in all directions to avoid his crashing plane. He zoomed up and over but as he sought to turn back, four Zeros dived on him. An explosive bullet knocked out his left rudder pedal and he careened into the sea, a quarter of a mile from the Jap carrier.

The impact slammed his hood shut tightly and the plane began to sink. He opened the hood and rose to the surface. As he reached the surface, he heard the explosion of his torpedo striking home on the Jap carrier. Floating beside him was a black rubber seat cushion and a deflated rubber boat. Apparently the Jap bullets had broken the straps which held them secure. Afraid that the Zeros would dive again and machine-gun him, Tex held the seat cushion over his head. Two cruisers steamed close by him and a destroyer all but ran him down. The white-clad sailors on the destroyer saw him and ran to the deckside to point him out. However, he was unmolested. In about ten minutes the dive bombers from his carrier, apprised of the Jap fleet's location by the Skipper's contact report, swooped in. As they exhausted their bomb loads, more came in. The Jap fleet was in utter confusion, with most of its air arm trapped on the decks of the carriers where they had been refueling. For two hours the bombers dived, sending their destructive loads into ship after ship.

Thus, with all of its fifteen planes destroyed and all but one of its pilots killed in its first engagement, Torpedo Squadron 8 had done its part to rout, for the first time in the war, a Japanese fleet. It had also kept the planes which were refueling on the carrier's deck from taking off in time to meet the attack. Had the Skipper not played his hunch with his faithful boys following in his wake, the planes that were caught refueling on the decks of the Jap carriers might have had time to take the air again to reverse the tide of battle.

When the next dawn came, the ships of the Jap fleet that had not sunk had limped away, leaving telltale oil slicks behind. Gaunt and sick from swallowing salt water, Tex Gay floated idly in his rubber boat, heedless of his badly burned leg, a shrapnel-torn left hand and bullet-punctured arm. At 6:20 a PBY patrol boat roared over the horizon. Spying the oil slicks, its pilots swooped down, waved to the figure in the lifeboat and flew on out of sight. Tex didn't mind. He knew the PBY had a patrol mission to execute. At 2:30 that afternoon, the PBY returned and he was flown to Midway for hospitalization.

Ensign Gay, thirty pounds lighter and slimmer and harder, is back in the U.S. He has had a furlough and time to tell his story to friends who knew him before he became a warrior. He has done his best to console the widows, mothers and fathers of his lost pals, and he is now back in San Diego [1942] with a new torpedo squadron that is being formed. He knows he is probably going back into the Pacific again to fight the Japs and he is certain that he knows who is going to win. If it should be his fate to die, he is ready to join the boys of Torpedo 8 who, when put to the test, proved they were just what the Skipper said they were—"the best in the world."

"ALL HANDS, AIR RAID! THIS IS NO DRILL!"

by Walter Lord

DECEMBER 10, 1956

> *For twenty-seven years, off and on, Walter Lord worked
> singlehandedly on research for* A Night to Remember, *the
> story of the sinking of the Titanic. Here is an excerpt
> from his book,* Day of Infamy, *commissioned by* LIFE.
> *In this case, with the help of* LIFE *newsbureaus, the
> research was completed in only a year. Walter Lord and*
> LIFE *correspondents interviewed or sent questionnaires to
> 850 Japanese and Americans who had lived through Pearl
> Harbor. From the mass of material thus made available,
> Lord wrote this unique and compelling account.*

Lieutenant Commander Logan Ramsey jumped up from his desk at
the Patrol Wing 2 Command Center on Ford Island when a single
dive bomber screamed down on the seaplane ramp at the southern
tip of the island. It looked like a young aviator "flathatting," and both
he and the duty officer tried to get the offender's number. Then a blast.
A column of dirt and smoke erupted from the foot of the ramp. "Never
mind," said Ramsey, "it's a Jap."

The plane pulled out of its dive and veered up the channel between
Ford Island and 1010 dock. It passed less than six hundred feet from
Rear Admiral William Furlong on the deck of the ancient minelayer

638

Oglala. The admiral took one glance at the orange-red circle on the fuselage and shouted for general quarters. Then, as SOPA (senior officer present afloat) Admiral Furlong hoisted the signal, "All ships in harbor sortie."

The time was 7:55 A.M.

Two more planes screeched down. Parts of the big PBY hangar at the head of the ramp flew in all directions. Seaman Second Class Robert Oborne, member of a utility plane squadron based on the island, was sure it was an Army snafu. "Boy," he thought, "is somebody going to catch it for putting live bombs on those planes."

Ensign Donald Korn of the cruiser *Raleigh,* moored on the northwest side of Ford Island, was turning over his deck watch when he noticed planes flying from the valley leading up the center of Oahu. Ensign Korn had already alerted the antiaircraft battery when a torpedo struck opposite the *Raleigh's* second funnel.

The *Utah* shuddered under two solid blows.

A torpedo fired at the *Oglala* and *Helena,* moored side by side, passed completely under the *Oglala* and barreled into the *Helena* amidships. The concussion burst the seams of the old *Oglala* alongside and hurled Musician Second Class Don Rodenberger from his upper bunk. He thought that the ancient boilers had finally exploded.

On the *Nevada* Musician First Class Oden McMillan waited with his band to play morning colors at eight o'clock. His twenty-three men had been in position since 7:55. As they moved into formation McMillan saw a lot of dirt and sand go up at the other end of Ford Island and thought it was a drill. Now it was 7:58 and planes started coming in low from southeast Loch. Heavy muffled explosions began booming down the line, and then it was eight o'clock.

The band crashed into "The Star-Spangled Banner." A Japanese plane skimmed across the harbor, dropped a torpedo at the *Arizona* and peeled off right over the *Nevada's* fantail. The rear gunner sprayed the men standing at attention, but he succeeded only in shredding the flag which was just being raised.

Not a man broke formation until the final note died. Then everyone ran for cover. Ensign Joe Taussig, officer of the deck, sounded the alarm. The ship's bugler got ready to blow general quarters but Taussig impulsively grabbed the bugle away from him and tossed it overboard. Somehow it seemed too much like make-believe at a time like this. Over the PA system Chief Boatswain's Mate Adolpho Solar shouted again and again, "All hands, general quarters! Air raid! This is no drill!"

Ship after ship began to catch on. The executive officer of the destroyer *Castor* shouted, "The Japs are bombing us! The Japs are bombing us!" On the submarine *Tautog*, the topside anchor watch yelled down the forward torpedo hatch, "The war is on, no fooling!"

On the *Oklahoma* there was first an air-raid alert and then general quarters a minute later, after which the voice on the PA system added a few words, which one crew member recalls as follows: "Real planes, real bombs, this is no drill!" Other witnesses have a less delicate version of the last part. The language, they say, convinced them that this was it.

Down corridors, up ladders, through hatches the men ran, climbed, milled and shoved toward their battle stations. One and all they accepted it now, some with a worldly grasp of affairs, some with almost ingenuous innocence. Captain Mervyn Bennion, skipper of the *West Virginia*, calmly remarked to his Marine orderly, "This is certainly in keeping with their history of surprise attacks." A seaman on the destroyer *Monaghan* told Boatswain's Mate First Class Thomas Donahue, "Hell, I didn't even know they were sore at us."

In the confusion many of the ships, unlike the *Nevada*, never carried out morning colors. Others did, but in somewhat unorthodox fashion. On the sub alongside the oil barge *YO-44*, a young sailor popped out of the conning tower and ran to the flagstaff at the stern. Just then a torpedo plane roared by, its guns firing. The sailor scurried back to the conning tower, hugging the flag. Next try, he clipped it on before another plane sent him diving back to shelter. Third time, he got it up, just before another plane sent him ducking for cover again. The men on *YO-44* laughed and clapped and cheered.

In the Navy housing areas around Pearl Harbor, people couldn't imagine what was wrecking Sunday morning. Chief Petty Officer Albert Molter, puttering around his Ford Island flat, thought a drill was going on until his wife Esther called out to him, "Al, there's a battleship tipping over."

As eleven-year-old Don Morton scuffed back to his house in Pearl City for more fishing bait, an explosion almost pitched him on his face. He scrambled home and asked his mother what was happening. She told him to go back and fetch his brother Jerry from the pier where they had been fishing. He ran out to find several planes gliding by at housetop level. Don was scared to go any farther. As he ran back to the house he saw his next door neighbor, a Navy lieutenant, standing on the grass in his pajamas, crying like a child.

Up on the hill at Makalapa, where the senior officers lived, Admiral Kimmel was waiting in his yard for a car to take him to HQ. He stood there for a few moments as the planes made their first torpedo runs. Near him was Mrs. John Earle, wife of Admiral Bloch's chief of staff. She remarked quietly, "Looks like they've got the *Oklahoma*."

"Yes, I can see they have," the admiral answered.

In a house directly across the street Mrs. Hall Mayfield, wife of Admiral Bloch's district intelligence officer, heard the noise and glanced through a window. She saw her husband in pajamas standing on the back lawn. He was leveling binoculars on the harbor, which lay below the house. Seconds later she joined him. Mrs. Mayfield's first words were a bit of wifely advice: "Hall, go right back inside and put in your teeth."

When two planes flashed by with the rising sun insignia, they turned and dashed back to the house. Captain Mayfield began pawing about his closet, hurling clothes and hangers in every direction. "Why," Mrs. Mayfield asked him, "don't the Navy planes do something?"

The captain's glare showed that her question was treason. "Why," he yelled back, "doesn't the *Army* do something?"

Less than ten minutes had elapsed since the attacks began, but the unprepared ships in the harbor were already firing back.

Up in the *Maryland*'s foretop, where he had climbed to address Christmas cards in peace and quiet, Seaman First Class Leslie Vernon Short looked twice at the planes diving on Ford Island, dropped his cards, loaded the ready machine gun and was hammering away when the first torpedo planes glided in from Southeast Loch.

On the *Sacramento*, Watertender Second Class Gilbert Hawkins found himself carefully untying each knot on the canvas awnings that stretched over the decks and guns—he just couldn't shake off the peacetime way of doing things. Finally a cook ran up and slashed the lines with a butcher's knife.

They used fire axes on the *New Orleans* to smash open the ammunition ready boxes. The *Pennsylvania* locks were knocked off by a gunner's mate who walked around swinging a big hammer: he had been bombed by the Japanese on the gunboat *Panay* in 1937, he announced, and he wasn't going to be caught again. On the *Monaghan* Boatswain's Mate Thomas Donahue, captain of No. 4 gun, slung wrenches at low-flying planes while the ammunition-box locks were sawed off. Somebody called up from the magazine and asked what he needed. "Powder," he called back. "I can't keep throwing things at them."

Frantically the gun crews were moving into action. On the afterdeck of the *Detroit* men banged their three-inch shells against the gun shields to get the protector caps off the fuses and Aviation Metalsmith First Class George Dormeister wondered why the whole ship didn't blow up.

One torpedo bomber had tried to get the *Nevada* and had been shot down. Now another plane glided toward her. The machine guns in her foretop blazed away. The men were wild with excitement as the plane plowed into the water. The pilot frantically struggled clear and floated face up past the ship. But they got him too late. Marine Private Payton McDaniel watched the torpedo's silver streak as it headed for the port bow. He remembered pictures of torpedoed ships and half expected the *Nevada* to break in two and sink enveloped in flames. It didn't happen that way at all. Just a slight shudder, a brief list to port.

Then she caught a bomb by the starboard antiaircraft director. Ensign Joe Taussig was at his station there when it hit. Suddenly he found his left leg tucked under his arm. Almost absently he said to himself, "That's a hell of a place for a foot to be," and was amazed to hear Boatswain's Mate Second Class Allen Owens, standing beside him, say exactly the same words aloud.

Ahead of the *Nevada* a torpedo struck the *Arizona* almost right away and steel rained down from the horizontal bombers. A big bomb shattered the boat deck between No. 4 and No. 6 guns. It came in like a fly ball, and Seaman First Class Russell Lott, standing in the antiaircraft director, had the feeling he could reach out and catch it.

The *West Virginia* was taking a terrible beating. Down in the plotting room, well below the water line, Ensign Victor Delano looked up through an overhead hatch and saw that the third deck was starting to flood. The list grew steeper. Tracking board, plotting board, tables, chairs, cots, everything slid across the room and jumbled against the port bulkhead.

Soon oily water began pouring through the exhaust trunks of the ventilation system. Delano led his men forward to central station, the ship's damage control center. Before closing the watertight door behind him, he called back to make sure no one was left. From nowhere six oil-drenched electrician's mates showed up: they had somehow been hurled through the hatch from the deck above.

Then Warrant Electrician Charles T. Duvall called to please wait for him. He sounded in trouble and Delano stepped back in the plotting room to lend a hand. He slipped on some oil and slid across the linoleum floor, bowling over Duvall in the process. The two men ended in a tangled heap among the tables and chairs now packed against the "down" side of the room. The oil was everywhere. They couldn't get back on their feet. Even crawling didn't work—they still got no traction. Finally they grabbed a row of knobs on the main battery switchboard which ran all the way across the room. Painfully they pulled themselves uphill, hand over hand, along the switchboard. It was almost like scaling a cliff.

In central station at last, they found conditions almost as bad. The lights dimmed, went out, came on again for a while as the auxiliary circuit took hold. Outside the watertight door on the lower side the water began to rise. Delano could hear the pleas and cries of the men trapped on the other side, and he thought with awe of the decision Lieutenant Commander J. S. Harper, the damage control officer, had to make: let the men drown, or open the door and risk the ship as well as the people now in central station. The door stayed closed.

The *California* caught her first torpedo at 8:05 and another shortly after. Water poured in and surged freely through the ship. It swirled into the forward air compressor station, where Machinist's Mate First Class Robert Scott was trying to feed air to the five-inch guns. The other men cleared out, calling Scott to come with them.

He yelled back, "This is my station. I'll stay here and give them air as long as the guns are going." They closed the watertight door and let him have his way.

On the *Oklahoma*, which took five torpedoes, hundreds of men who had no air defense stations trooped down to the third deck, where they would be protected by the armor plate that covered the deck above. The water rose, the emergency lights went out, the ship listed. Everything was breaking loose. Big thousand-pound shells rumbled across the handling rooms, sweeping men before them. Eight-foot reels of steel towing cable rolled across the second deck, blocking the ladders topside. The door of the drug room swung open, and Seaman First Class George Murphy watched hundreds of bottles cascade over a couple of seamen hurrying down a passageway. The boys slipped and rolled through the broken glass, jumped up and ran on.

Men battled grimly on the few remaining ladders to get to the main deck. Yeoman Third Class L. L. Curry and some mates were still in the machine shop on third deck amidships when the list reached 60°. Someone spied an exhaust ventilator leading all the way to the deck, and one by one the men crawled up. As they reached fresh air, an officer ran over and tried to shoo them back inside, where they would be safe from bomb fragments. That was the big danger, he explained: a battleship couldn't turn over.

But she kept listing and around the harbor all eyes were now glued on the sight. From his bungalow on Ford Island, Chief Albert Molter watched her gradually roll over on her side, "slowly and stately, as if she were tired and wanted to rest." She kept rolling until her mast and superstructure jammed in the mud, leaving her bottom up. Only eight minutes had passed since the first torpedo hit her.

On the *Maryland*, Chief Electrician's Mate Harold North recalled how everyone had cursed on Friday when the *Oklahoma* tied up alongside, shutting off what air there was at night.

Inside the *Oklahoma*, Storekeeper Third Class Terry Armstrong found himself alone in a small compartment on the second deck. As it slowly filled with water, he dived down, groped for the porthole, squirmed through to safety. Seaman First Class Malcolm McCleary escaped through a washroom porthole the same way.

Nearby Lieutenant (j.g.) Aloysius Schmitt, the Catholic chaplain, started out too. But a breviary in his hip pocket caught on the coaming. As he backed into the compartment again to take it out, several men started forward. Chaplain Schmitt had no more time to spend on himself. He pushed three, possibly four, of the others through before the water closed over the compartment.

Some men found themselves gasping, swimming, trying to orient themselves to an upside-down world in the air pockets that formed as the ship rolled over. Seaman George Murphy splashed about the operating room of the ship's sick bay, wondering what part of the ship had a tile ceiling, never dreaming he was looking up at the floor.

Topside the men had it easier. As the ship slowly turned turtle, most of the men simply climbed over the starboard side and walked with the roll, finally ending up on the bottom. Ensign Bill Ingram climbed out the high side just as the yardarm touched the water. He stripped to his shorts and slid down the bottom of the ship.

As Ingram hit the water, the *Arizona* blew up. A huge ball of fire and smoke mushroomed five hundred feet into the air. There wasn't so much noise—most of the men say it was more a "whoom" than a "bang"—but the concussion was terrific.

For an instant the whole ship seemed to rise bodily out of the water, then settled back, a sagging hulk. Far above, Commander Fuchida's bomber trembled like a leaf. On the fleet landing at Merry's Point a Navy captain wrung his hands and sobbed that it couldn't be true.

Over one thousand men were gone.

Incredibly, some still lived. Radioman Third Class Glenn Lane was blown off the quarterdeck and found himself swimming in water thick with oil. He looked back at the *Arizona* and couldn't see a sign of life.

But there were men there. On the third deck aft Coxswain James Forbis felt skinned alive, and the No. 4 turret handling room was filling with smoke. He and his mates finally moved over to No. 3 turret where things were a little better, but soon smoke began coming in around the guns there too. The men stripped to their drawers and crammed their clothes around the guns to keep the smoke out. When somebody finally ordered them out, Forbis took off his newly shined shoes and carried them in his hands as he left the turret. The deck was blazing hot and covered with oil. But there was a dry spot farther aft near No. 4 turret, and, before leaving the ship, Forbis carefully set his shoes there. He lined them neatly with the heels against the turret—just as though he planned to wear them up Hotel Street again that night.

A number of heavy bombs smashed into the *Tennessee* and scattered splinters in all directions. One hunk ripped the bridge of the *West Virginia* alongside and cut down Captain Mervyn Bennion. He slumped across the sill of the signal bridge door on the starboard side of the machine-gun platform. Soon after the captain fell, Ensign Delano arrived on the bridge.

Captain Bennion had been hit in the stomach and it took no medical training to see that the wound was fatal. Yet he was perfectly conscious and at least he might be made more comfortable. Delano opened a first-aid kit and looked for some morphine. No luck. Then he found a can of ether and tried to make the captain pass out. He sat down beside the dying man, holding his head in one hand and the ether in the other. It made the captain drowsy but never unconscious. Occasionally Delano moved the captain's legs to more comfortable positions, but there was so little he could do.

Captain Bennion prodded Delano with questions. He asked how the battle was going, whether the ship and the men were badly hit. Delano did his best to answer, resorting every now and then to a gentle white lie. Yes, he assured the captain, the ship's guns were still firing.

The attack had now been on for thirty-five minutes and the backbone of the fleet was gone or immobile: *Arizona, Oklahoma* and *West Virginia* sunk, *California* sinking, *Maryland* and *Tennessee* bottled up by the wrecked battleships alongside, *Pennsylvania* squatting in drydock. Only the *Nevada* was left, and she seemed a forlorn hope with one torpedo and two bombs already in her.

Twelve B-17's which had set out from California the day before under Major Truman Landon were now approaching Hawaii. It was a long flight for those days—fourteen hours' flying time. To save gas the planes were flying separately instead of in formation. They also were stripped down: no armor or ammunition, their guns in cosmoline.

Lieutenant Karl Barthelmess' plane got to Oahu around 8 A.M. He was suddenly overtaken by about fifteen light planes marked with large red circles. They flew above, under and alongside the B-17, apparently escorting the big plane in. The bomber's crew sighed with relief and removed their life belts. They waved their thanks, but the pilots of the other planes were apparently too preoccupied to respond.

As Major Landon approached the island, a flight of nine planes came straight at him, flying north. For an instant he too thought it was a reception committee. Then a burst of gunfire and a quick glimpse of the red circles told him the truth. He pulled up into the clouds and shook off any pursuit.

Now some of the planes were asking for landing instructions from the tower at Hickam Field. A calm flat voice gave wind direction, velocity, the runway on which to land, as though it were any other day. Occasionally the voice observed without emotion that the field was under attack by "unidentified enemy planes."

From her anchorage off Pearl City the old destroyer-minecraft sighted a conning tower turning up the west side of Ford Island just after 8:30. The *Medusa* and *Curtiss* saw it a few minutes later, and signal flags fluttered from all three yardarms.

The destroyer *Monaghan* caught the warning right away as she headed down the west channel. A signalman turned to Commander Bill Burford: "Captain, the *Curtiss* is flying a signal that means 'Submarine sighted to starboard.' "

Burford explained it was probably a mistake, that such a thing could easily happen in all the confusion of gunfire and burning ships.

"Okay, Captain—then what is that thing dead ahead of us that looks like an over-and-under shotgun?"

The skipper squinted through the smoke and was amazed to see a small submarine moving toward them on the surface several hundred yards ahead. In its bow were two torpedo tubes, not side by side as usual, but one directly above the other. They seemed to be pointed directly at the *Monaghan*.

By now everybody was firing. The *Curtiss* pumped a shell right through the conning tower at 8:40—decapitating the pilot, according to her gunners; clipping off his coat button, according to *Monaghan* men. The *Medusa* was firing too. The *Monaghan*'s own guns were blazing as she rushed at the sub, but her shots missed and hit a derrick along the shore.

The *Monaghan* rushed on and everybody else held fire as Burford tried to ram. He grazed the conning tower. It was not really a square blow but hard enough to spin the sub against the *Monaghan*'s side as she surged by. Chief Torpedoman's Mate G. S. Hardon set his depth charges for thirty feet and let them go. They went off with a terrific blast, utterly destroying the sub and knocking down nearly everybody on deck. Fireman Second Class Ed Creighton thought the ship had blown up her own fantail.

But she hadn't. Instead, the *Monaghan* rocketed on, now too late to make her turn into the main channel leading to sea. She drove ashore at Beckoning Point, piling into the derrick already set on fire by her guns. Burford backed off, turned and steamed out to sea, while the nearby ships rang with cheers.

In their excitement men performed astonishing feats. On the *Tennessee* Seaman First Class Woodrow Bailey chopped a ten-inch line in half with one stroke. Yeoman Third Class Kenneth Carlson ran up vertical ladders on the *Selfridge* with two bandoleers of .50-caliber machine-gun shells slung over his shoulders—normally he could handle just one of the seventy-five-pound belts. A man on the *Phelps* adjusted a blue-hot 1.1 gun barrel by twisting it with his hands—didn't even notice the heat.

At the moment all anybody cared about was keeping the guns going.

At 1010 dock tugs towed the sinking *Oglala* clear of the *Helena* to a new berth farther astern. As the lines between the two ships were cast off, Admiral Furlong appeared on the *Oglala*'s bridge and wandered into the line of fire of a *Helena* five-incher. A very young boatswain's mate called out: "Pardon me, Admiral, sir! Would you mind moving from the wing of the bridge so we can shoot through there?"

Off Ford Island a flotilla of all sorts of small craft continued dodging Japanese strafers, darting in and out of the burning oil, picking up the men still swimming. They were all types. When Seaman Second Class James Albert Jones idled his motor for a second to spread sand for better footing on the floorboards of his whaleboat, a sailor in the water screamed hysterically—he was sure he would be forgotten. Another man swam over and did his best to help. It wasn't easy, for he had just lost his own arm.

Ensign Maurice Featherman of the *West Virginia* lay exhausted on the deck of a harbor tug and didn't care whether he lived or died. His shipmate, Ensign John Armstrong, appeared from nowhere in starched whites, looking as if he had just stepped out of the Harvard Club. Kneeling at Featherman's side, he set about injecting his friend with the will to live: "Mo, history is being made now, and you and I are in the middle of it, and our actions might affect the outcome."

THE BIG DAYS
IN NORMANDY

by Charles C. Wertenbaker

JUNE 19, 1944

> *Many books have been written about D-Day and the Allied invasion of France in World War II. All have benefited from intensive research after the event. But this dispatch to* LIFE *was written with the noises of the battle for the Normandy beaches ringing in the writer's ears. It is a fine example of cool observation and news reporting under extreme difficulties. The late Charles C. Wertenbaker was chief of foreign correspondents for Time Inc. and head of the Paris newsbureau before he retired to write.*

D-day minus three was a clear, mild day with a fresh breeze blowing in the Channel from the west. Aboard this ship, the U.S.S. *Acamar* (a false name), there were quiet, intense preparations for directing the battle ahead. AA and machine-gun crews were briefed; there was a general-quarters drill during the afternoon. Ship's officers collected signatures on brand-new hundred-franc notes which, with luck, would be their mementos of the invasion.

At midnight General Eisenhower and his staff were studying the weather reports. For some days they had known that a low-pressure area was moving eastward in the Atlantic but the weather experts had expected it to turn north before it reached the Channel. Instead, the gale had come straight on, with another slighter blow behind it. This was probably the hardest decision General Eisenhower ever had to make. Perhaps he remembered the Spanish Armada and the disaster that overtook it. At any rate, sometime before dawn he chose the cautious course. At 5:45 the *Acamar*'s radio buzzed: "stand by for important message." Just before six the message came: the invasion is postponed for a minimum of twenty-four hours.

The landing boats scurried back. A brace of destroyers went barking after the thousand-ship convoy that was bearing toward Normandy with its radio sealed. All around the coast of England ships, big and little, on missions, big and little, had to slow up or turn around. The greatest armada in history broke up before it was assembled.

All day Sunday, June 4, it blew a gale, churning up the water even where the *Acamar* and the command ship of Admiral Alan G. Kirk and Lieutenant General Omar Nelson Bradley were sheltered. At 1:30 that afternoon General Bradley visited his headquarters ship to check reports and plans. The naval officers at the meeting wanted forty-eight hours to reassemble their forces. General Bradley was in a hurry. Finally Admiral Kirk agreed that he could be ready for Tuesday. The British were also ready. H-hour was moved back by half an hour in the new tentative plan. General Eisenhower promised a tentative decision by evening, a final decision by six in the morning.

By evening the new plans were worked out. By evening it was pouring rain. The wind whipped spray over the open boats and the rain blotted out the faces of the men in them. Some of them were ending their fifth day in the boats. "They're pretty tough by now," said an officer watching them through glasses, "but I'll bet they'll be glad to hit the beach." "The poor sons of bitches," said another, "they're lucky to be where they are."

Around nine o'clock the gale had blown itself out and the smaller one following it was not so much feared. The forecast: clear Tuesday morning, with weather closing in by evening. That would be good for the airborne landings, for the air bombardment, for observation for the naval bombardment.

Monday morning at six o'clock the final confirmation came. The day was cloudy and cold. The staff officers looked at the sky, shrugged and put their trust in the weatherman. A sleepy colonel said: "Win, lose or draw—and there ain't no draw—they can't call it off now, thank God."

Tuesday, June 6, the invasion began almost exactly on schedule at thirty minutes past midnight. That was the time when airborne troops began landing by parachute at six hours before H-hour, the actual moment of land attack. At the instant the first parachutist lowered his head and fell toward the earth of Normandy, U.S., British and Canadian armies had afloat or in the air some thousands of men and thousands of vehicles.

Landing on the western beach in the target area went well; by 7:30 A.M., one hour and a half after the sixth hour of the sixth day of the sixth month of the year 1944, two regiments of infantry and some tanks were ashore. On the eastern beach waves were higher, obstacles more stubborn and the enemy prepared; a fresh division had been rushed there a few hours earlier. On this beach all tanks were swamped. The entire beach was under enemy fire and on most parts of it boats could not unload. Not until early afternoon did the first waves get off the beach and begin to spread out in the high ground beyond the bluffs.

At two places where landing parties had found exits from the beaches, destroyers standing in close to the shore were pouring fire into the valleys beyond the exits and enemy guns were firing in the valleys themselves. On either side of the valley heavier ships crashed broadsides deep into the interior. Their guns spat orange flame. The air seemed to tremble as they fired.

On into the night destroyers stood inshore firing intermittently. From the enemy also came sporadic shelling while the engineers on the beach worked to clear some of the wreckage. On the beach, fires flared and died down. Out beyond the line of destroyers hundreds of ships lying at anchor were dark and silent under a cloudy sky. At 11:30 that night enemy raiders came and the night was lit with bomb bursts and with tracers firing into the clouds. One ship, hit, flared brilliantly for no more than five minutes, lighting the whole eastern sky, then suddenly went out. Shortly after midnight three raiders fell slowly flaming into the sea.

After less than five hours of sheer night, lighter streaks low in the sky showed where the moon was. The horizon appeared again and by ones and twos and dozens and scores the great flotilla appeared. Warships made black silhouettes like those printed in *Jane's Fighting Ships*, and the smaller craft were at first mere blobs of black. Then all became clearly visible, down to the guns of the warships and the men aboard the landing craft nearby waiting for the moment of landing. The first Flying Fortresses appeared and, as the light grew, the obstacles on the beaches stood out sharply in the queer predawn pink that made dark things darker. From the shore still came the sounds of shelling and of rifle and machine-gun fire as the first twenty-four hours of the invasion ended.

In the full light of day you could look down from a bluff through the opening of the river valley at the beach spread out below. It looked like a great junk yard. From the water's edge at low tide to the high-water mark were landing craft, some impaled on obstacles, blown by mines, shattered by shellfire and stranded by the ebbing of the tide. Among them, following a narrow path from the water to the valley's edge, moved a line of sound vehicles and a company of men just landed. As they passed, some of the men turned to look at the wreckage through which they moved: there was a bulldozer with its guts spattered over the sand, and another with its occupants spattered, an arm here, a leg there, a piece of pulp over yonder. There were discarded things all over the beach: lifebelts, cartridge clips, canteens, pistol belts, bayonets, K-rations. Behind the beach, across a wide, deep tank ditch half full of water was the casemated German 88 that had caused much of the wreckage. A clean shell hole through the steel shield of its narrow opening showed how it had been put out of action.

By the afternoon of D-day plus one, the battle of this beachhead was already the most desperate of the invasion. The Germans had set up machine-gun positions atop the bluffs; and these, with ingeniously concealed batteries, had raked landing parties. Casualties of some of the assault forces had been high. Now most of the beach was still under shellfire. The intermittent hammer of machine guns made another sector untenable and only in two places could forces be brought ashore. They were needed quickly—especially artillery and artillery observation planes—for it was inland from here that Rommel was expected to make his first counterattack.

A narrow, dusty road twisted up from the beach to the bluff. Up it wound a column of men and vehicles. They moved slowly over the steel road and past signs saying "*Achtung, Minen*," keeping to the road, to the top. There, overlooking the beautiful seascape with its twinkling balloons, was a cluster of large mass graves, and near them were men digging fresh ones. Beside the road a single soldier lay full-length on his face, his arms stretched above his head in an attitude of repose, a bullet hole through the top of his steel helmet. Behind the bluff to the right was a field hospital, where the slightly wounded were lying on the ground before the tents. The smell of ether crossed the road. There were several Frenchwomen working in the hospital, but they were too busy to talk.

There were bright red poppies and some yellow flowers in the field near the hospital but dust was beginning to cover them over. Behind the hospital was a barbed-wire enclosure already packed with prisoners of war. Nearly five hundred had come in by Wednesday afternoon, and more were on their way down from the forward units. Most of them were under twenty or over forty; they were well-fed, well-shod and fairly well-clothed; and all wanted water. A captain explained to a guard that they had been drinking local water for two or three years and they saw no reason to wait for the chlorinated water the Americans drank. The guard gave the captain a drink. Many of the men were not Germans but Poles and Balts and Russians who had been put there to die in the first assault while the crack German divisions assembled farther behind. But the officers were German. All of them looked stolid and resigned, and even the youngest ones seemed to have lived longer than their captors.

Along the road inland from the bluff, columns moved forward in the dust. About a mile and a half inland was a regimental command post, on a road at the edge of a thicket. This regiment had come ashore at two o'clock of the previous afternoon, D-day, and so far had seen only light fighting. The worst things were snipers and mines, said the regiment's colonel. Those machine guns which had moved up to the bluff just before the attack had slipped back into the thickets and into farmhouses and were sniping at the roads. There were also many concealed riflemen, and another officer said he had found snipers in a house all dressed like Frenchmen and speaking French. Mines were small antipersonnel mines that blew off a leg, and they were everywhere. The colonel wanted to know if there was any news from the Russians and looked disappointed when there was not.

Late in the afternoon a regiment that had been resting beside the road moved up to attack with the rest of its division. But the battle of this beachhead was still being fought on the beach itself, and the battle was now as much against time as it was against the Germans. Troops and tanks and artillery moved ashore slowly through the wreckage and mines and shelling, and for miles offshore landing craft were waiting to get into the beach. Just before sunset warships increased the tempo of their shelling and bombers dropped load after load on the places where the enemy artillery was thought to be, but still the enemy shells found their targets. Engineers fought all night against time and by dawn had cleared two more exits from the beach. More forces moved ashore. Whether they would be in time to meet the expected counterattack, no one knew.

THE DEFEATED LAND

by Sidney Olson

MAY 14, 1945

> *This graphic account of an enemy in collapse and chaos
> was written by Sidney Olson, a Time Inc. war
> correspondent with the good fortune to get into Germany
> just a few days after the Nazi surrender. Since then he
> became a senior editor of* Time *and is now a vice-president
> of J. Walter Thompson Company.*

The collapse of the Nazi Empire is a fantastic show. Germany is a
chaos. It is a country of crushed cities, of pomposities trampled on the
ground, of frightened people and also glad people, of horrors beyond
imagination.

In the ruins the Germans stand, cooking their meals on open-hearth,
improvised brick ovens, readying the food to take down below into
the innumerable caves and cellars they have been living in so long.
Many of them have had no electric light or running water for a long,
long time. They live like people will, perhaps, when the ice returns
over the earth, huddled together for warmth and comfort and against

loneliness, with someone outside in the night guarding the hole that leads down to their caves. In those caves life is exactly what you would imagine it to be: foul and pitiful, but at least warm and safe against the bombs and the terror outside.

But the ones who move with cocky assurance through the ruins are the thousands of DP's (the Army initials for displaced persons) who are now thronging out of Germany in a phantasmagoric pilgrimage, an endless wave of thousands of vengeance-minded slaves and war prisoners, pillaging and raping and burning their way through the towns and cities, hopelessly out of hand for days after their liberation, as the fighting troops move rapidly on and the expert but pitifully undermanned staffs of the Military Government strive desperately to cope with them somehow.

Into the cities have poured thousands of the liberated from the environs. The greatest number were Russians—virile, short, stocky, happy, and the vast majority of them beautifully drunk with liberated champagne, cognac, vermouth and even beer. For two days you would see them fighting and clawing, tearing the clothes from each other's back in an effort to crowd into an already jam-packed underground warehouse where the Nazis kept food and especially liquor. An American soldier would order them away but the happy, drunken DP's would merely give him the old Bronx cheer with a flutelike tone. Scores of them would thumb their noses at the lone soldier, who could only grin helplessly. If he fired a shot in the air they merely clapped their hands admiringly and crowded around him to offer him bottles of their stolen schnapps.

There are no cities left in Germany. Aachen, Cologne, Bonn, Koblenz, Würzburg, Frankfurt, Mainz—all gone in one sweeping reach of destruction whose like has not been seen since the mighty Genghis Khan came from the East and wiped out whole nations all the way from China to Bulgaria.

Nürnberg, once a city symbolizing German culture, then Hitler's symbol of Nazi *Kultur,* is now no symbol of anything. Today Nürnberg looks like all the rest of the shells of cities, a great waste of broken bricks. From the burg on the hill in the inner walled city the vista is much like that looking down into Bryce Canyon in southern Utah, a stretching pink labyrinth of stone broken in fantastic shapes in canyons that wind about senselessly.

We went in with a man who had lived in Germany many years, who knew Nürnberg well and had often attended Hitler's party congresses. He had his Baedeker guidebook with him to refresh his memory. From the start he was utterly bewildered. There were no landmarks to guide him: the huge railway station, the Grand Hotel, his favorite restaurants, all of them turned out to be heaps of rubble when he finally, uncertainly, identified them.

Very gingerly we entered the shell of the St. Sebaldus-Kirche, one of Nürnberg's famous churches whose construction spread over the thirteenth, fourteenth and fifteenth centuries. A strong wind was blowing and from time to time big stones fell from the shreds of the vaulted roof far above. The whole church is gone except for one huge mass of reinforced concrete in the center where the Germans had bricked over the priceless shrine of Saint Sebald. From the top of a rickety sixty-foot ladder you could see that this modern brick sarcophagus had held firm against the years of bombings and the days of shelling, with only a few cracks in the concrete. In the St. Lorenz-Kirche one such shrine also is safely walled up, guarded by a stone crucifix with the left arm shot away. The Liebfrauen-Kirche is utterly smashed and the famed entrance, which had also been walled over, suffered a direct shell hit that broke the reinforced concrete into powder. Above it there is no trace of the world-renowned Männlein Kraft clock, where every day at noon the seven electors came out of the clock jerkily and nodded their little metal heads in a stiff bow to the seated figure of Emperor Karl IV and filed back into the clock to await another noon.

The massive *Rathaus*, or city hall, is entirely gone except for the shrapnel-chipped groups of caryatids at one end. The Bratwursthaus is obliterated; only a leaning, dusty poplar tree marks where it stood. The famous fountains are destroyed. The Hans Sachs house is gone, although the statue of the cobbler immortalized by Wagner in *Die Meistersinger* is there in the rubble. The house of Albrecht Dürer, the artist, has vanished. The Germanisches Museum and the tower near Burgberg, which held the "iron maiden" in whose spiky embrace many a victim of the Inquisition perished, are mere shells. The crown jewels of the ancient German emperors, which for centuries reposed in the city, are in some vault, perhaps.

Over all this sickening desolation hangs the pall of a city not yet done burning, with dark smoke where some old smoldering wood has been fanned up again and pink clouds of fine dust, brick dust that has been pulverized finer than sand, almost into talcum powder.

And throughout the city is the smell of all such cities as they are conquered, a smell compounded of many smells—of death first, of offal, of wood smoke, of gunpowder, and a sick-sweet smell that comes from thousands of opened bottles of wine and spirits half-drunk and then smashed on the ground.

The ruins in the cities are not nearly so horrifying as the ruins of humanity which you find in the prison and concentration camps. When all the other names of prison camps are forgotten, the name of Dachau will still be infamous. I entered the camp with the first American troops. Beside the main highway into the Dachau camp there runs a spur line off the main Munich railroad. Here a soldier stopped us and said, "I think you better take a look at these boxcars."

The cars were filled with dead men. Most of them were naked. On their bony, emaciated backs and rumps were whip marks. Most of the cars were open-top like American coal cars. I walked along these cars and counted thirty-nine of them which were filled with these dead. The smell was very heavy. I cannot estimate with any reasonable accuracy the number of dead we saw here, but I counted bodies in two cars and there were fifty-three in one and sixty-four in another.

As we walked back down to our jeeps a soldier suddenly shrilled, "Look, for Christ's sake, one of them's alive!" Out of the mass of bony, yellow flesh a figure sat up feebly. One of us jumped up in the freight car and lifted the skinny thing out. The only way you could tell he was any more alive than the dead was that he could still move slightly. He could not even smile. But he was semiconscious. From the patch with capital letter *P* on his coat we knew he was a Pole. He weighed about eighty pounds, but was fairly tall. He was wearing only a short coat. We wrapped him in blankets, put him in a jeep and drove him back to a field hospital.

Now we began to meet the liberated. There were several hundred Russians, Frenchmen, Yugoslavs, Italians and Poles, frantically, hysterically happy, many of them in blue-and-white-striped pajamalike uniforms. They began to kiss us and there is nothing you can do when a lot of hysterical, unshaven, lice-bitten, half-drunk, typhus-infected men want to kiss you. Nothing at all.

In the smaller towns the chaos is no less chaotic; only the scale is smaller. Lauda is a little town on the Tauber River in southern Germany. Each of its three tiny stone bridges over the Tauber is barely wide enough for cart traffic and big American trucks could barely squeeze past the ancient statues of Christ on the main bridge, a bridge constructed in the year 1378. The little town slumbers in the sun in a cloud of apple blossoms and smells richly of cow manure. A middle-aged German woman did my laundry in one of the little houses that cluster together behind masses of lilacs. She did a great bag of laundry for me three times, and each time charged me what she obviously regarded as the maximum: three marks, which equals 30¢. She did it beautifully, too. The last time I went there, when she knew we were moving out of town, she gathered her young daughter and her grandson close behind her and nerved herself to ask the big question that had obviously preyed on her mind for some weeks: "When are you going to send us all to Siberia?"

We drove into Aichach, some thirty miles south of the Danube, just as the last snipers were being cleared from the far end of town by troops of the 42nd Division.

A small riot was going on in and around the town's main shoestore. We crowded our way in to find the whole store had been stripped almost completely of its stock while the frantic Germans ran around wailing and wringing their hands. The proprietor, a middle-sized, balding German about forty, was especially frantic and was outraged that the Americans would permit such things. We asked him if he had not heard that the German Army itself had done such things in France, Belgium, Greece, etc., etc. He drew himself up proudly and said, "Sir! The German Army would never stoop to such things!" We asked him mildly how he knew and he said, "I was a soldier myself." Still mildly we asked to see his *Soldbuch,* the little service-record book all German soldiers must carry. This was most interesting; it showed that he had been discharged from the Army that very morning, Sunday, April 29. He had gone to his commanding officer, told him that he was in his own home town and that the war was over and that he wanted to go back into the shoe business. This seemed sound to his CO, who discharged him honorably. He had then changed clothes and played his violin for the first time in several years, getting ready for Monday's shoe trade. We escorted him outside to the lone GI who had arrived to guard the place and the GI took him off to the prisoner-of-war cage.

The last two weeks of April and the first days of May have been very cold in Bavaria, with occasional snow and sleet storms driven by high winds. Down the superb *Autobahn* marched a column of German soldiers several miles long, plodding steadily into the driving sleet. These were the defenders of Munich. Each company was guarded by only two doughboys, and one American jeep moved slowly at the head and one at the tail of the column. The Germans had that disheveled look that all soldiers get the moment they become prisoners, weaponless, often hatless, unbuttoned and beltless. Despite their obvious fatigue most of them seemed happy. Many were smiling; many waved at our jeep as it passed. Some were women, but these were the equivalent of our Wacs. Many of these prisoners had been clerks in the equivalent of our SHAEF until a few days ago and had never fired a gun in anger. Most of them looked as if they didn't have a care in the world now that their greatest care—the fear of death—had been removed. They slogged off into the sleet. They looked as if they would gladly have sung a song if it had been permitted.

In Munich an officer in charge of counterintelligence referred to his latest secret sheet of information. His unit had moved in only a few hours before. He riffled the pages to the latest report on the condition of Hitler's famed Brown House. The sheet said "apparently intact." We rushed over to the spot that was so sacred to the Nazis; it was only a few blocks away. All that was left were parts of three walls and a fine pile of rubble from which some radio correspondents were making broadcasts, surrounded by embarrassed GI's.

Munich is gay, almost Parisian. Here the people welcomed the Americans as liberators, and they really meant it. Again and again and again the Germans said, "We have waited so long for you to come," or "You have taken so long to come!" Somewhat fed up, the Americans usually answered, "Well, we had a long way to come."

In Munich the tankers carried lilacs on their tanks. The women were very numerous, very accessible and often very attractive. In Munich it was astonishing to find how many women came up to you with little notes, saying in effect, "Please take good care of Fräulein Anna Blank. She was very good to me and helped me in my escape and is a friend to all Americans. Signed by an American prisoner of war." In Munich the famed Munich beer was very poor. But the warehouse cellars were so full of champagne that the soldiers and the liberated prisoners were still hauling it out days after Munich fell.

Six days before Munich was taken, two American prisoners escaped to the 42nd Division. They told us that the camp commandant, a Nazi named Captain Mulheim, spoke good American slang and was a nice guy. They said he made a speech to them several times in almost exactly these words, "Now lots of you guys are going to try to escape. Lots of you are going to make it. I just want to impress on you one thing; when you escape, make it good and keep on going. Stay in the woods and travel by night and go toward the Rhine. We will probably catch you all right. But what I mean is this: that kind of escape is honest and I won't be hard on guys that really are trying. But for God's sake don't just go into Munich and shack up with those Munich whores. They'll just turn you in after a while. I'll be rough on any guys we catch who've been shacked up with those girls." The escapees said he was as good as his word. They also said that cigarettes were the real money of the camp at Munich. They swore that for one cigarette you could get a bar of soap, for twenty cigarettes you could get a woman, for fifty cigarettes you could get plenty of liquor and for two thousand cigarettes you could meet a man in Munich who would conduct you safely all the way to the Swiss border. They insisted this was true and gave the name of one American Air Force officer who had a standing offer: he would give $500 for five hundred cigarettes, which was all he needed to complete the necessary two thousand for his escape. The PW's got their cigarettes from their Red Cross packages twice a week.

The conflict now seething within American soldiers between their hatred of Germans and Germany and Nazism, and their natural Christian upbringing and kindness and susceptibility to beautiful children and attractive women and poor old ladies, is one of the great stories of today. The same doughboys who went through Dachau's incredible horrors were the very next day being kissed and wreathed in flowers by the German women of Munich. Some doughboys say they hate all the Germans, and they obviously do; and yet others who have been through just as much bitter fighting and obvious trickery will tell you that they hate only the Nazis and they like many Germans.

Few Germans in the ruined great cities, which are so close to plagues of typhus and where the Germans get thinner every day unless they move to their friends in the country, can yet realize the place of Germany at the bottom of the list of civilized nations. They learn with shock and shame of the American nonfraternization policy. Many of them simply cannot understand it. They thought they were fighting in an honorable war. When parents realize that they lost all their sons in a cause unspeakably dirty they are filled with a despair that will mark the rest of their lives. Of course they should have realized it years ago when they were heiling the Führer. But they lived two lives, they say, one of exaltation at his great political promises of the wonderful new Germany to come, and one of terror that the Gestapo might knock on their door that night. And yet it is clear that Josef Paul Goebbels did the job he set out to do all too diabolically well. But the over-all, inescapable fact is that the German people are so solidly, thoroughly indoctrinated with so much of the Nazi ideology that the facts merely bounce off their numbed skulls. It will take years, perhaps generations, to undo the work that Adolf Hitler and his henchmen did.

JOE IS HOME NOW

by John Hersey

JULY 3, 1944

This is the story of a discharged soldier of World War II trying to readjust to civilian life. Told in fictional form, it is in fact based on the actual experiences of forty-three discharged soldiers. John Hersey's piece attracted widespread notice because it drew attention to the problems of human reconversion, about which little or nothing had been done at the time it was published. A war correspondent for LIFE, *John Hersey is now a novelist. Among his books are the best-selling* A Bell for Adano *and* The Wall.

The boy with one arm stood in the Rochester station and looked around. He was on his way to Onteoga, New York, and he was full of going home.

He glanced up at the iron clock—5:15, it said. Above the clock he saw the service flag showing that the railroad had sent 25,602 men to the wars. Jeepers, the boy thought, more than a division.

When he got off the train, his sisters Anna and Mickey were waiting for him in the old car. Joe was very excited and he said, "Well, after so long a journey I'm almost home, I only got nine miles to go. How's the car run? It still running? Those girls you taught driving lessons to ruin it? Can we get any gas?"

Anna said, "We waited a long time for this. You've gone a long time from home. We've been praying every day you'd come home. You did, Joe."

Mickey said, "We hated to hear about the arm."

They all started out with a crying jag and wound up laughing.

They drove out to Onteoga and as they crossed the tracks into town, Mickey said, "I'm sorry we don't have the brass band out for you."

Joe said, "Let the band go to hell; I don't need the band. Riding up Genesee Street, that's all the welcome I ever wanted. This is my homecoming, the streets are out to greet me." And he said not very loudly, "Hello, streets."

The first stop was home, naturally, 143 Front Street. He walked up to the front door and banged on it. His father shouted from bed upstairs, "Who is it?"

Joe Souczak shouted, "Does Joe Souczak live here?"

His father shouted, "He ain't home yet."

Joe shouted, "Who you think this is, dad, it's me."

Right away Joe's father and mother came downstairs together in their night things. The two kid brothers, Anthony and Sam, came crashing down after.

Joe's mother went straight to him and took him. All she said at first was, "My boy."

She held him and moved her hands up and down his back. She said, "You're all one piece, I'm so glad they didn't molest your face at any point, you're very thin, my Joey." She did not speak of the arm.

Joe's father stood by smiling and said to Anna, "Looks like mother took first choice at embracing the boy."

Finally Joe's mother let go. Joe's father stepped up and said, "Son, a good many days I wished Our Lord that if you could only come back, Our Lord could take me then, only I wanted to see you just one time." Joe's father was fifty-three, he was a railroad worker, he had his wish now.

Joe could not think of anything except to reach out a bottle to his father and say, "Take a drink." His father took the bottle and drank. That only made the mother cry.

Joe broke into a temper in spite of himself and said to his mother savagely, "What's the sense of crying, for God's sake, I'm home now, ain't I?"

His father said, "Come in the house, son."

They turned on the lights and sat in the living room formally.

The father said, "How was it in this war, son?"

Joe said, "I don't know but it's rougher than the last."

Joe's young brother Anthony said, "How many Germans you kill, Joe?"

Joe said, "Nobody who is a soldier answers that, Tony. You don't like to talk about it, mostly you don't even know, the range is big."

Anthony went over and touched Joe's empty left sleeve and said, "What happened, Joe?"

Joe said, "I remember it was nighttime, doing a patrol action, well, that's when I got hit. It was a rifle bullet."

"Sniper, son?"

"That I couldn't say, maybe it could've been a sniper. They took me to the 38th Evac, that's a hospital. They took the arm in Algiers. . . . Could I have something to eat?"

Anna asked, "What you want?"

"Could I have some eggs, plenty of eggs anyhow? Then they started bringing me home, see."

When it was day Mrs. Souczak stopped crying and went to the telephone. She dialed a number and said, "Joe is home now," and hung up. She dialed many numbers and all she would say was "Joe is home now." Then she would hang up.

Pretty soon the people she had called started coming, uncles, cousins, Mrs. Souczak's neighbors, friends of the family. Mr. Shaughnessy, president of the Onteoga Knitting Mills, where Joe worked before the war, came. He said never to worry about a job, just worry about getting well. "The factory is there waiting for you, Joe," he said. "Come over this afternoon and see us." Joe agreed to go at two o'clock.

At each knock at the door, Joe jumped up and went to see who it was. It was about ten o'clock before Mary Ellard, his girl, came.

Joe reached out his hand. She couldn't seem to say anything. Joe had decided to be cold toward her, for defensive reasons. He just said,

"Hello, Mary," and led her right into the living room. They couldn't kiss because of all the company.

Everyone talked busily, but Mary just sat there looking at Joe. He pretended not to see her. After a while she stood up and said, "My brother, he's in from the Pacific only he has to go back this afternoon, his leave's up. Three o'clock. I better go see him."

Joe went out onto the porch with her.

Mary said, "Our first meeting wasn't too personal together, Joey."

Joe said coldly, "It couldn't be. Didn't you see all those people?"

Mary said, "I'm so excited, I been biting my fingernail right off."

Joe said, "I'll be seeing you," and he went back in the house. He was trembling all over. He ran upstairs and looked at himself in the mirror; the sleeve was quite neat in his pocket, but his face looked sickly and the uniform was too big.

At about two o'clock Joe reached the factory. He went up on the second floor, where he found the whole mill waiting for him in a large room. Mr. Shaughnessy said, "We've shut off the wheels of progress for thirty minutes, we want you to make us a little speech."

Then Mr. Shaughnessy and Joe presented each other with gifts. The factory gave Joe a 21-jewel Lord Elgin wrist watch, plus $161 purse. Joe gave Mr. Shaughnessy a green French pocketbook. "On here," Joe said, "is the inscription in silver thread made by the Ayrabs, it says ORAN. I carried this through all the battles, even the worst ones. I had you in mind, Mr. Shaughnessy."

Afterward Joe went out and shook hands around the town. Everyone wanted to shake his one hand, and he felt like quite a hero. He stopped in at the barbershop and was very glad to see Charley the barber again, his old friend. When he got home late in the afternoon his mother asked him what he had been doing and he said, "People been patting me on the back and offering me lifetime jobs."

After a couple more days of callers at 143 Front Street, a crowd of fellows came after Joe and said, "Let's hit the road and do some hell-raising. Let's have a doings amongst ourselves."

So the boys began going out. The first night they planned to make all the rounds, but the first place was as far as they got. Joe had such a good time that he persuaded the crowd to repeat, night after night.

When he reported back to Walter Reed the doctor said, "You look better. Want thirty days more?"

Joe said, "No, thanks. My friend told me, he said, 'Joe, I seen you twenty-seven days and I seen you drunk twenty-seven days.' I could use thirty days to rest, doctor."

After a few days they brought an artificial arm and strapped it on. From the first, Joe disliked it. He told the nurse, "It hurts my—the upper part of my arm that's left." He never could learn to say stump. But they taught him to use the arm.

In January his honorable discharge came. This time Joe got a uniform that fit better and he thought he looked pretty well as he started out on the train. He had left off his fake arm, because he liked the empty sleeve in his pocket. The arm was in his suitcase. He had on his ribbons—African Theater, Purple Heart, Before Pearl Harbor.

When he first got home, Joe found that it was not at all easy to get out of uniform. He was authorized to wear the uniform for ninety days. He felt better in uniform. The khaki sleeve in the khaki pocket was very neat. His stump felt a lot better in a uniform sleeve.

For a long time Joe just lay around the house. He told his parents he figured he'd earned a month's vacation, and that when the month was up he would choose one of these high-paying defense jobs. "In the meantime," he said, "don't bother me, I'm all geared up ahead of everyone else around me, I'm looking for a slowdown."

But the more Joe tried to rest, the more restless he got. He got feeling disgusted with himself. He began to think he was not worth anything and never would be again. He tried walking out in the town, but he felt like a beaten dog; he would not speak to a civilian.

He tried working around the house but whatever he did, he ended in a rage. His father had been a frequent fisherman once, and Joe got out some of his tackle one day. But trying to oil the reel and feed the line through the little leader holes on the rod with one hand got him more and more nervous, and he wound up putting his fist through his closet door. That was the way it went.

"You better get a job," Charley said. "And I know just the one, if we could only work it. You know Seraviglia's Bakery? Well, the old man died a couple months ago and the shop's idle. You'd make a good baker, Joe." Joe said, "With one arm?" Charley said, "Why not?"

He decided to try a war job. Out in the field he had heard all about the high wages in defense industries. Now it was his turn for some of the gravy. No more Onteoga Knitting for him.

He went first to the Principo Company—small makers of safety razors before the war, aircraft self-starters now. He was introduced to a Mr. Fenner in the personnel department.

Fenner said, "We'd be glad to take you on, Mr. Souczak, any day you can start."

Joe said, "What do I get?"

Fenner said, "We'll start you at 73¢ an hour, that'll come to about $48.50 if you work a good week."

Joe said, "That don't sound like a lot of tin to me. I read in *Stars & Stripes* over the other side about these $150 a week positions in defense plants. I don't go for that $48.50."

Fenner said, "That's our starting rate, Mr. Souczak."

In the following days Joe tried three other small war shops and got the same story at each. Then one afternoon he came home and found a telegram waiting for him. It was from Mr. Shaughnessy of Onteoga Knitting. It said: HEAR YOU ARE LOOKING FOR JOB. REPORT TOMORROW MORNING FOR PHOTOGRAPH AND INTERVIEW PLANT NEWSPAPER AND GO TO WORK EIGHTY CENTS HOUR PLUS FIVE CENTS EXTRA FOR NIGHT WORK. REGARDS.

Joe knew he would take his old job back but he did not bother to show up the next morning, nor for four mornings after it. "Let the damn job wait for me," he said, as if it were an imposition to ask him to go to work.

On the fifth morning he strapped his artificial arm on for the first time in two weeks and reported at the plant. All the people there were very kind to him. The personnel manager said, "We start most at 65¢ an hour and 5¢ extra for night work. We're going to make an exception in your case and start you at 80 and 5."

Joe said, "I don't want any personal favors."

The personnel man said, "It's not because of your handicap, Mr. Souczak. After all, you're one of our old hands around here." He gave Joe an advance on his first week's wages.

Joe could not handle his previous job at the yarn-winder with one arm, so they put him on oiling and cleaning the machines.

At the end of the first day's work Joe was very tired but also happier than he had been for a long time. The advance payment felt nice and crisp in his pocket. He joked at supper and his family were glad to see him perked up.

The job seemed to go well and day by day Joe felt more and more like himself. He went to work in khaki pants and shirt, with an old basketball sweater on top. After a few days he left off his artificial arm. The men in the plant fixed up a special harness for him to carry the oil can and waste around with, so he could leave off the arm.

He felt like going out with Mary again, and he did. They went the rounds and ended up at The Siding. It was like old times for a change. They laughed all night.

On the way home Joe stopped the car. He said, "I don't know what to say, Mary, I'm kind of stumbling in my words."

She said, "That's all right, Joe." Then she added, "In case you've been wondering, it doesn't matter to me."

He knew that she meant about the arm. And his tongue was free and he was able to say, "I'm not much use to a girl, I only got one hand."

She said, "Love comes from the heart, not from the hand, Joe."

"Yeah," Joe said, "that's right, I never thought of that."

She said, "Everything's the same."

Joe put his arm around her and kissed her. After a while he said, "I don't want to rush into anything."

Mary said, "You haven't been in any rush so far. I been waiting so long for this."

"Hugging you with the one arm is kind of strange," Joe said, "but the kissing is just the same as it ever was."

She said again, "Everything's the same."

Joe said, "Yeah."

After that it was one good day after another. The days just flew.

Joe got all his appetites back. He couldn't seem to get caught up on food. He was always buying an ice-cream cone on the way home from work or stopping for a hamburger late at night. He found he wanted to do many of the old things, and found he could do them. He joined the plant bowling team. He went roller skating. He even went swimming in an indoor pool and found he could pull himself along lying on his right side in the water.

One night he walked with Mary down to Seraviglia's Bakery. They put their faces against the plate glass and looked in. They saw the mixer, a long table, some racks, a roll-top desk and in the back, the big oven.

"Looks nice, don't it, Joey?" Mary said.

"Yeah," Joe said, "but not for a one-arm man."

Three weeks after he went to work he heard about a badge for honorably discharged soldiers—a little gold-plated plastic button with an eagle on it, for the lapel buttonhole. He went over to Camp Prestley with his discharge certificate and got one. That helped with getting out of uniform and for a while he wore khaki pants and shirt and a civilian coat with the badge on it. No one knew what the badge meant but he was glad to explain.

Then he bought a whole new set of civilian clothes. He blew a lot of money on the outfit: a suit for $42, topcoat for $50, shoes for $10.50 and a hat for $10. The things were just made to his taste. Everybody made remarks about his showing up in civilian clothes. His brother Tony said he looked like a preacher. Charley the barber said he looked like an undertaker. Mary said, "You look like Joey." Joe passed off the remarks with a joke which was only half a joke: "I got me a spruce outfit in case opportunity comes my way."

Joe and Mary discovered the countryside together. They would drive out in the Souczak car and then leave it and walk across the farmlands. They would take off their shoes and socks and wade in streams, and Mary would pick bunches of violets, snowdrops and arbutus. They would lie on their backs in the grass and play cloud games and funny-name games. And Joe would point at a blossoming tree and say, "What's that? I forget the name of that one." Mary would say, "That's the shad tree, Joey. That's the one the farmers say, 'When the shad blows, bullheads will bite and time to plant corn.'" They went fishing a couple of times, and Mary was very good about hooking the bait and taking the bullheads off the barb. And sometimes they kissed until it was hard to stop. Those were very happy days.

But then one night they went to the movies. The picture was *Bombardier,* and everything was fine until a bomb came down on a Japanese, the Japanese was running toward the camera, the bomb went off, the concussion exploded a big oil drum, blew the Japanese to Jap-hell. Joe felt the blows and the pain all through his body and his heart began pounding. He said, "Excuse me," to Mary and got up abruptly and left. She followed him out as quickly as she could but he had already hurried home.

Joe felt sick and upset all that night, and from the next day on things seemed to go badly. Joe began to be touchy all the time. People bothered him.

A veteran of the first war came into the barbership one day when Joe was talking with Charley, and began shooting his face off. He said, "It's going to happen the same thing in this war that it did the last—after the war England will take all the gravy."

Joe got angry and said, "We are American citizens, we give a square deal and we get back a square deal, save criticisms till after."

The veteran said, "I think it's rather stupid sending lend-lease to Russia. Russia will declare war on us, she'll be looking for us in the future."

Joe was very angry. "Those Russians can fight," he said. "Let 'em win this war first. There's no way whatsoever that she has any intentions to declare war."

Very soon afterward he was riding out to the plant on a bus and an elderly woman sat down next to him and said, "You poor boy." Joe's face got red. She asked, "Where did you get maimed like that?"

Joe said, "Tunisia."

The sympathetic lady said, "Dear me." Then she added with genuine interest, "Are those little Japs as bad as people say?"

Joe lost his temper wildly. "Dammit, lady," he said, "they don't have Japs in Africa."

She was alarmed at his outburst, and she said, "My goodness, son."

Joe said, "I'm sorry, lady, but you people get me all nerved up. A person has gambled with their life, it's wrong soldiers should have to listen to such ignorance."

Each day Joe seemed to get more and more out of control. Someone made a perfectly innocent remark in the drugstore about rationing, and Joe turned and said: "We should all have our food cut in two by 50 per cent and we'd still be in luxury compared with those occupied countries, hell, they was eating grape leaves over there." And when a girl at the mill, thinking she was kidding Joe, called him a privileged character, he said loudly, "I don't ask for any privileges. I can take care of myself."

He grew increasingly irritable. In the mill one day his foreman, who had some kind of inferiority complex about not having been to the war, told Joe he was spending too much time in the toilet.

Joe said: "I can't handle these little gidgets and gadgets. It makes my hand nervous. I have to have a smoke."

The foreman said something about not having to smoke all day, and Joe blew up and quit.

A couple of days later he moved out of his family's house into an unfurnished room. He said he didn't want to sponge any longer. He also said: "I don't like this neighborhood, too many trucks and buses, it's just like before an action, they're all going somewhere, you never know where but they're all going like hell. You can't sleep."

Joe's family loaned him an iron bed. He found it just as hard to sleep in the bare room as it had been at home. One night he would lie awake reliving his experiences, the next night he would do the same thing, only imagining himself more heroic than he had actually been: he would save his battalion, he would capture slews of Germans, he would end up walking the floor and smoking.

It was at this period that Joe joined both the Veterans of Foreign Wars and the Disabled American Veterans. Joe took comfort from the meetings, where members talked over all the problems of returned soldiers.

But all through his unhappy days, Mary was Joe's greatest support. She went walking with him every evening; they must have walked a hundred miles in those days. She sided with him in almost everything he did. She kept saying he ought to go into business for himself. He asked how she expected him to do that, when he had no money and was no use.

She urged him at least to go and inquire about the bakery. Joe went to Seraviglia's cousins and they said the bank owned the bakery now. Joe went to the bank and they told him there that the bakery was for sale, but there was a $4,900 mortgage on it. Joe told Mary it was hopeless. She said to take a job—but not to forget that someday he would he his own boss.

He took a job as a clerk in a local grocery store, Maturo Brothers. It was hard on his feet and all the reaching with his right arm made his stump hurt. He quit after three days. He signed on with John B. North, riggers and haulers, supposedly doing desk work in the office. On the fourth day the company fell shorthanded and Mr. North asked Joe if he'd mind riding out on a job. The job involved moving an upright piano down some porch steps. That was no work for a one-armed man; Joe quit on the spot. He took a job with Moley, the line contractor, as a lineman's assistant. He understood he would merely be handling tools and cutting and unreeling wire, and he thought he would enjoy the outdoor work. But they made him help set up poles, lifting and tugging at the heavy logs, propping them into deep holes. He quit there, too.

The night after he quit Moley's he went out with Mary. He talked about his jobs. He said, "Is that what we laid in slit trenches for? Is this what we stood those bullets for? I'm going around talking to myself, Mary, I tell myself everything's going to be okay, then I get the real picture, I can't do much at all, there's no hope for me here in this valley."

Mary said, "It's not that bad."

Joe said, "I tell you how bad it is: sometimes I think I'd rather be out there fighting again, that's how bad."

Mary asked, "What seems to be the trouble, Joey?"

"It's a lot of things," Joe said. "One thing, out there a man is proud, he's in the best damn unit in the whole United Nations, he's got buddies who would gladly die for him, he's got something to do all day, a routine. He's got responsibility. If he flops, somebody's going to die. Back here, I'm not busy, I got no buddies, nobody's interested in giving me responsibility. I'm just burning up my days."

Mary said, "God doesn't punish people, Joe. People punish themselves. You got to do something about this."

Joe said, "You're a good girl, Mary, and there's nothing to keep a man on the track excepting a good girl."

Mary said, "Would you be fed up if I gave you some advice?"

Joe said, "I've took so much advice and orders for two years, I'm still in the habit."

Mary said, "Don't try to earn a million dollars the first job you take."

Joe said, "I don't care if King Solomon himself advised you along those lines. Out in the field you've heard all these stories about the gravy train back home, you get so you believe them."

Mary said, "Don't try to be a bank president, Joe. Don't try to earn a thousand bucks a week. Be satisfied with what's coming to you."

Joe thought a little, then said, "I guess you're right, Mary, I got thousand-buck ambitions and forty-five-buck ability."

"It's all right to have ambitions," Mary said, "and maybe when you have a chain of bakery shops you'll get a thousand a week."

Joe said, "That bakery again."

Mary said, "I just thought of something, Joe. Why don't you go see Mr. Shaughnessy about the bakery?"

Joe said, "What would I say to him? What use he got for a guy who quit his mill?"

Mary said, "He likes you, Joey, maybe he could figure out some way for you to acquire the property."

After a couple days of getting up his courage, Joe did go to see Mr. Shaughnessy. He told Mr. Shaughnessy about the bakery, how nice it looked from the outside. He spoke of the mortgage. He asked, "What can a man do to beat a mortgage?"

Mr. Shaughnessy was noncommittal. He said he'd think it over, and asked Joe to leave his address. Joe couldn't figure out whether Mr. Shaughnessy was still sore at him for having left the knitting mill. Joe was discouraged by the conversation.

Four days later a messenger from the knitting mill came to Joe's room and told Joe to report to Mr. Shaughnessy's office. When Joe got there Mr. Shaughnessy had a lawyer with him. He told Joe to come with them, and they went out to Mr. Shaughnessy's Packard and drove off. Joe didn't know what it was all about.

Mr. Shaughnessy pulled up in front of the bakery. He and the lawyer and Joe got out. Mr. Shaughnessy went up and unlocked the door and motioned the others in.

Joe said, "How come you got the key to the bakery?"

Mr. Shaughnessy said, "It's yours, Joe."

Joe said, "You wouldn't pull my leg, Mr. Shaughnessy."

Mr. Shaughnessy said, "We got together in a small syndicate of men here in Onteoga who have confidence in you, Joe. We've bought out the mortgage on the bakery and we want you to run it."

Then the lawyer went into a long song and dance about common stock, 40 per cent for Joe, 60 per cent for "the syndicate," a lot of stuff Joe didn't understand. All he could think about was that he wanted to tell Mary. He hurried off to tell her as soon as he could get away.

Mr. Shaughnessy had arranged to send Joe to a bakery in Binghamton to learn the trade. Joe spent three weeks there as an apprentice and then came back to be his own boss.

In those first days Joe Souczak was a proud baker. He worked like a slave. He loved the smell of the dough in the proofing box as the bread came up, and his one hand, growing strong now, soon became expert at knocking the gas off and rounding the loaves. He kept his oven at exactly 400°, he pinched off his loaves and scaled them at exactly eighteen ounces. He reached the peel into the deep oven and scooped out the loaves like an old hand. He ruined some loaves, but they had told him in Binghamton that the only way to learn is to have a few bad batches.

One night he borrowed the family car and took Mary to Charter's. They had a fine meal and quite a few drinks. Joe was not particular about drinks; he would toss off anything that passed under his nose. The evening was fast and happy, and on the way home Joe stopped the car.

"I'm on the up-and-up," he said. "We taken in $64.85 this week." He always said "we" when he talked with Mary about the bakery.

"That's wonderful, Joe,"

"Of course," Joe said, "we're not going to have as much in our pocket while we're building up our stocks of ingredients and things as we would have."

676

"That doesn't matter, Joey."

"I got a pension coming," Joe said. "A 60 per cent disability means $60 a month, plus $35 because I lost the arm. I'm grabbing that mustered-out pay: I'm expecting a check for $300 any day from the Army. I'm doing fine."

Mary said, "You're doing very good, Joe."

Joe said, "You understand, I won't ever be rich. I'm too good-hearted, I could never get rich."

Mary said, "Who wants to be rich?"

He said, "I don't know how it is with you."

Mary said, "It's the same as it always was, Joe."

Joe paused. He pulled out a cigarette and said, "I'm great stuff for this smoking. I got started heavy on that invasion over there." He paused again.

Mary hurried in, "I want to marry you in spite of the arm, Joe. I like your strong right arm."

Joe was quiet for a long time. He just sat there. He wanted to cry. Finally he said, "How's June? June okay?"

She said, "June would be good, Joe. June would be very good."

For a couple of days Joe was wildly happy. He had now what Charley had said he needed: the right job and the right girl. Everything, he thought, was going to be hunky-dory. But then Joe found out that his serenity was neither permanent nor automatic.

It rained on the third day after he and Mary got engaged. On the way to the bakery, walking through the rain, Joe saw a new war poster in a store window. It was a lurid picture of death on a battlefield, with a young man pointing an accusing finger at passers-by. The young man looked like one of Joe's friends in Company G who had been killed. The poster shocked Joe. He felt a little dizzy as he went to the bakery. Joe forgot to put flour on the cloths in the proofing box, so when the bread came up it was all stuck to the cloth. The dampness crept into his stump and it began to ache; then his head did too.

Mary came into the bakery at about noon and found Joe slumped at the roll-top desk with his hand over his eyes. She said, "What's the matter, Joe?"

He looked up and said, "I thought everything was going to be good now that I was my own boss and I got you."

Mary said, "The only person who can help Joe Souczak is Joe Souczak."

Joe said, "Mary, I don't want to be a wreck, nobody wants to be a wreck from this war."

Mary said, "You're no wreck, you're going good, Joey, look at this bakery."

Joe said, "You're the only thing that keeps me going any good at all."

Then he thought about the war again. He frowned and said, "I got to concentrate on my business, therefore concentrating my mind and I'd rather forget a lot of these past incidents. That's the way I'd like to do if I could only do it. If I could only."

Joe leaned forward and put his hand back over his face. "If I could only," he said.

Mary said, "You can't do it overnight, Joe, you can't do everything all at once. It takes a little time to get happy."

THE ATOM BOMB AND FUTURE WAR

by Hanson W. Baldwin

AUGUST 20, 1945

> *In a world where the science of mass destruction has been incredibly furthered by the H-bomb and the ICBM, this article, written a few weeks after the first atom bomb in history was dropped on Hiroshima, might appear to be dated. But now or then, it would be hard to quarrel with Hanson Baldwin's perceptive analysis of this new kind of war, still less with his conclusion that "man must establish a common brotherhood or die in droves beneath the atomic bombs." Baldwin is the distinguished writer on military affairs for* The New York Times.

In a fraction of a second on August 5, 1945, American scientists not only destroyed Hiroshima, Japan, but with it many human concepts —chief among them our ideas of how to wage war. We are opening today a fresh page in military history and our first scribblings on it will be cramped and difficult, for what is to come far transcends all man's experience of what has gone before.

Major General J. F. C. Fuller, the British military historian, has written of the First World War, "God now marched with the biggest industries rather than with the biggest battalions." This remark is even more fundamentally true of the Second World War than of the

First. Our victories have been based on material superiority, upon mass production. Tomorrow the big factories, but with the big laboratories beside them, will dominate war and will make it—in its most virulent form, at least—the business of the big and wealthy nations, not of the small and the weak. The two A1 priorities in our postwar national defense program must be: superiority in research and development (something we have not always enjoyed by any means in this war, despite our "first" with the atomic bomb) and continued superiority in mass production—in other words a coupling of quality with quantity—never an easy mating.

Atomic energy explosives, revolutionary though they are in concept and effect, cannot be considered alone. There have been many other revolutionary weapons and techniques in this war—rockets, for instance—and it is only when they are considered together that the impact of the technological revolution in warfare is fully apparent.

Well before the development of the atomic bomb and the rocket, it was clear that the pendulum which in all past history has swung between offense and defense was in this war heavily weighted toward the offense. Man always has sought in his weapons for the ultimate in range and in destructive power. If he could hit the enemy first and hit more of him, he won the battle. The javelin, the arrow, the catapult, the cannon and now the plane have been man's successive solutions of this problem. The plane gave man great range, gave him the ability to leap over terrain barriers and seas, to pass above the struggling surface forces and to strike directly the enemy's cities, industries, communications and will to resist. But the plane was a vulnerable and expensive instrument. Tremendous destructive power could be obtained only by the use of tremendous numbers, and heavy bombers, with all their appurtenances, are among the most expensive and complicated instruments of war ever invented. Moreover, they could be intercepted and shot down.

But the coupling of atomic energy explosives (destructive power) with rocket propulsion (range) provides the world potentially with the most terrible weapon ever known. The V-2 stratosphere rocket, as used by the Germans, looped sixty to seventy miles into the skies, moving at a speed of thousands of miles an hour, and could not be intercepted by any means now known. These rockets were inaccurate and their range was limited, but science has it in its power to correct inaccuracy and increase range to transoceanic distances. In the foreseeable future science does not appear to have it in its power to stop the rocket, once launched. This suggests the ultimate triumph of the offense over the defense—"ultimate," that is, insofar as one can foresee the future. If rockets, whether propelled by chemicals or by atomic energy engines, can span the Atlantic and if their atomic warheads can destroy cities at one breath and if man can do nothing to prevent this, man has unleashed a Frankenstein monster.

This thought can be carried to what may seem fanciful extremes, but who dares use that adjective after August 5, 1945?

Rockets and atomic bombs may reverse social and economic urbanization processes of past centuries, for cities (area targets) could not live (even conventional bombs have demonstrated this) under a hail of atomic charges unless built deep underground or decentralized. Serious attention must be paid in the postwar period to dispersion of our industries and to new ideas for city planning.

Where does any such "push-button" war as this leave the military man? Is there need in this fantastic world of tomorrow for piloted planes, ground armies, surface navies?

General of the Army H. H. Arnold has predicted that this is the last war of the pilots. The inference is obvious. Robot planes, rockets, television and radar bombing and atomic bombs will do the work today done by fleets of thousands of piloted bombers.

This may well be. Indeed it seems likely that the bulk of area bombing may be done in the future by robots controlled or directed from the ground. But this will not replace the piloted plane for specialized tasks—pin-point visual bombing of rocket-launching sites, photo and visual reconnaissance, airborne operations. The pilot will still have a place in the world of tomorrow for the very simple reason that man has not yet invented a machine endowed with all the brains of man.

Partly for the same reason, partly because of the inherent limitations of bombardment in any form—even in this terrific combination of rocket and atomic warfare—there will be, as far as we can see now, use for ground armies. This use will probably be more limited and specialized than exists today. The plane, the robot, the rocket, long-range artillery and the atomic bomb can destroy and devastate, kill and maim, but cannot occupy, hold and organize the earth on which men live and from which they have their being. Men on the ground must do this; hence, even if those men are transported by air as airborne armies, some sort of an occupying and organizing ground force will be needed. Perhaps it will have to be an army of moles, specially trained in underground fighting, for man may well burrow into the earth, as the Japs have done in this war, to escape insofar as it is possible the terrible effects of the atomic bomb. Certainly it will have to be an army trained in wide dispersion rather than in close concentration and possessing tremendous mobility, an army whose principal transport may be aircraft.

The atomic bomb has wrenched us violently from the moorings of the military past. It appears to have invalidated, technologically, the concept of peacetime conscription and mass armies, of giant warships and tremendous bombers. It underscores and re-emphasizes the primary need for research, particularly research to control and defend against atomic energy and long-range rockets.

Even before Hiroshima there was major need for a comprehensive, all-embracing, judicial and nonpartisan study of our postwar military problems and the requirements of national defense, as tied to foreign policy. Today that need is imperative, or the future extraordinary needs of our defense may be judged by partisan and conventional minds. A commission of the nation's leading citizens should be appointed at once by the President and Congress to study the technological revolution in warfare.

It would be a happy day if such a commission concluded and could persuade its fellow men that this is One World and that man must establish a common brotherhood or die in droves beneath the atomic bombs.

THE BRAVE MEN
OF NO NAME RIDGE

by James Bell

AUGUST 28, 1950

> *It was a bloody and brutal skirmish during the Korean War in which the Marines captured an enemy-held ridge so insignificant that it has no name. James Bell's account of the action is a gem of news reporting. A veteran* Time Inc. *foreign correspondent, now stationed in Johannesburg, Bell has covered the news for* LIFE *in many parts of the world.*

This little ridge was hardly worthy of the term. It ran north and south, paralleling the Naktong River ten miles west of Yongsan. It was the southern end of an enemy salient in the Changnyong area where for ten days U.S. troops had been trying to shove a North Korean bridgehead back across the sluggish stream. It was just a little hump three quarters of a mile long and less than three hundred feet above the green valley floor. But this ridge with no name, undignified even by a primitive trail, will not be forgotten by the U.S. Marine Corps.

What historians will call it I have no idea. Perhaps it will be known simply as "Objective One," as it was designated on the map Brigadier

General Edward Craig, commander of the 1st Provisional Marine Brigade, held in his lap as he sat in a bean field. But no one is going to forget it any more than he will forget Bloody Nose Ridge at Peleliu or Mount Suribachi at Iwo Jima or the sand dunes at Tarawa. Here took place the most brutal battle in the first two months of the Korean campaign.

"This," said one of Ed Craig's senior officers as he watched the long line of litters coming out of the valley below No Name Ridge, "is the toughest we've hit. This is like Iwo."

The Marines, having won the objective assigned them south of Chinju, were thrown into the Changnyong bulge after one night's rest. With the 19th Regiment and a regimental combat team they set out to drive an estimated twelve thousand Commies from positions which were a menace to Pusan. No Name Ridge was the first assault point. The Marines had to take it before the combat team could move ahead in the center. Intelligence figured the enemy had around six hundred troops well dug in along the ridge.

During the night of Wednesday, August 16, the Marines moved into position on another ridge just east of there. Early on Thursday morning American artillery hammered No Name Ridge for five minutes. Then for fifteen minutes Marine Corsair fighters raked it with bombs, rockets and machine guns. Then came another ten minutes of artillery. Finally, as the 8 A.M. jump-off hour neared, the Corsairs moved back in for their final strafing runs, and No Name Ridge was smoking with dust and cordite.

Then the Marines started down into the valley, and the seemingly lifeless ridge suddenly became alive with the enemy. From the left rear of the assault force came the angry eruption of a machine gun. Another machine gun opened up from the valley floor to the right. From the top of the hill came more machine-gun fire, interlaced with bursts from automatic weapons and mortars. Hell burst around the leathernecks as they moved across the valley and up the ridge. Everywhere along the assault line men fell.

But, glory forever to the bravest men I ever saw, the line did not break. It went forward in spurts. The casualties were unthinkable, but the assault force never turned back. It moved, fell down, got up and moved again.

"God!" exclaimed a veteran Marine Officer as he watched. "How brave can men be?"

"I never saw men with so much guts," said General Craig watching through glasses. His hand shook slightly, but his mouth was a firm line and his cold blue eyes did not cloud.

For more than an hour the assault force stumbled and struggled forward. The enemy mortar was knocked out by artillery, but the machine guns and automatic weapons never let up. As the Marines neared the crest, their line ripped apart, the North Koreans came out of their positions throwing grenades. They were cut down, but the grenades did terrible work.

The Marine line wavered, paused, withdrew a bit and waited. Then, with a final thrust, an estimated ten Marines reached the crest of the ridge. They never came back.

The rest were ordered to withdraw. Men too exhausted to cry crawled back down the ridge. For all the terrible sacrifice the position stayed in enemy hands.

The ridge became quiet. Corpsmen, leading stretcher teams of South Koreans, who never flinched at sniper fire which raked their trail, began crossing the valley to pick up the wounded. They took them to an aid station just beyond the bean field where General Craig sat sweeping the ridge with his field glasses. I sat beside him all choked up and wondered if the stream of litter bearers would ever stop coming up out of that damned valley.

Craig, a kind and sensitive man, tried not to look at his torn kids. Finally he said, with sad pride, "I haven't heard one of the wounded cry. We'll take this piece of real estate, but the cost is going to be terrible."

Artillery began plastering the Communist positions. Then the Corsairs came roaring out of the sky with a terrible anger. They seemed to be live creatures mad for revenge. Their gull wings almost touched the tops of the low bushes as they screamed in on all sides. Their rockets hardly left their wings before they blasted into the targets with searing orange flame. The pilots, knowing the kids down there had had a horrible time, jerked their planes out of dives and pulled away in turns that were almost too tight, eager to make another run.

The wounded on the litters were carried past their general, who sat with a terrible calm waiting for his second assault wave to come up the winding mountain road. Near General Craig the bearers gently lowered the litters and rested for a brief moment. Troops nearby and correspondents watching the battle gave the wounded water.

The new assault wave moved up and they watched the wounded going in the other direction. They were unsmiling, and there was fear in their faces. The faces were so young.

As they got ready to jump off, the last of the wounded were coming out of the valley. General Craig came down from the edge of the bean patch and watched. Finally he walked to a litter and touched a badly wounded boy on the shoulder.

"Nice work, son," he said very softly. "Thank you." Then he returned to the bean patch. The boy did not hear what the general said. It is probably just as well.

It is nice to report that the second assault wave carried the ridge with no name and that the Marines continued their advance. But it will never be nice to remember those kids who were being carried out of that valley. The only good of it all is the wonderful knowledge that there are good, brave Americans still about.

WHAT KOREA WAS REALLY LIKE

by Lt. John W. Harper, USMCR

DECEMBER 3, 1951

> *During what was officially described as a "quiet" period on the Korean battlefront, John W. Harper, a Marine lieutenant in a line company, wrote this letter to his father, a Marine lieutenant-colonel in World War II. It was not intended for publication, but LIFE was given permission to publish it, unedited, as a small masterpiece of reporting on life in the front lines at a time when nothing was supposed to be happening.*

October 14, 1951

DEAR PAW,

Please excuse the delay in writing. It was not caused by anything more serious than natural laziness and inconvenience. I regained the 3rd Battalion on October 1. I discovered that H Company had been assigned a sector on the battalion left which extends down to the base of the hill and into a valley. My platoon sergeant had taken over the platoon after I was hit and carried it right on through to the conclusion of the assault and then set it up in a very good defensive position. He did a fine job then—in fact from the time I took over

687

the platoon—and I have recommended him for a meritorious promotion to the next higher grade although he has only been a sergeant for about five months. I also discovered that one of the squad leaders —the Indian boy named Yellowhead—conducted a wild one-man banzai charge during the assault, killing a number of gooks and collecting four or five prisoners. For this, he was recommended for the Silver Star Medal by the other platoon leader present. After getting back to the company, I found a new C.O. The former exec had been sent to Regt. having served four months on line and also the second lieutenant in charge of the 2nd platoon, having been five months on line, had been given a job at battalion. The 60-mm mortar officer, too, was rotated rear-ward to the 4.2 mortars leaving three vacancies. Then the 1st platoon commander was given an emergency leave home.

I ended up with the 60-mm mortar section in the company. The other day we caught four gooks cooking rice outside their bunker. I won't say that we splashed it right into their bowl, but all four were in a state of collapse when we ceased firing.

To go back to when I first got back to the line, the minute I arrived I could tell that morale was fair. From a quarter of a mile back, I could hear whooping, laughing, cursing, trees being felled, holes being dug, trails being hacked out, word of one kind or another being passed up and down the line from bunker to bunker with yells the gooks across the way could surely hear and probably understood. The boys all had unnecessarily big grins for me when I trooped the platoon line to see how they were set in. Light wounds remain a big joke and excellent luck, it seems, especially for rank of any kind.

That night was the last of the very active nights as far as infiltrators were concerned. The whole company line is interconnected with telephones so that the nightly frights and jitters can be communicated from one end of the line to the other with maximum speed. As soon as darkness settles there is a wait of about a half an hour before the first man gets rattled and heaves the first grenade. Then someone else hears the bushes shake and heaves two or three, then he gets to a phone and wants a flare so he can see the charging hordes. If a parachute flare is shot over his head, the hard white light of the burning magnesium coming from the falling and drifting parachute throws jet black shadows through the trees which move, creep and jump from side to side just like a gook. The only satisfaction they give is that they fail to reveal the imagined charging phalanx. One night on the platoon phone watch went something like this when my platoon sergeant was on the phone.

(Crash of a grenade)

PLT. SGT.: Who threw that last grenade, that you first squad?

PHONE (whispered trembling voice): Yea—there's something in the wire!

(Crash of a second grenade)

PLT. SGT.: Did you get him? You better have!

PHONE: Yea—heard his pants rip on the wire!

PLT. SGT.: Never mind pantsing him. Did you kill him?

(Wild confusion on the other end of the line followed by another grenade crash)

PLT. SGT.: OK! 60-mm fire coming up.

(A delay of five or ten minutes while the mortar crew is woken up, gotten to the gun and the rounds pooped out. They crash into the hillside close in to our lines.)

PLT. SGT.: How does that look to you?

PHONE: Fine! Fine! Only now it sounds—sounds like somebody chokin' a pheasant!!

PLT. SGT.: Choking a pheasant! How do you know—go back to sleep!

PHONE: OK, OK. Thanks for the mortar fire.

(Half an hour passes)

PHONE: Platoon CP!! Platoon CP! Cee Pee!!

PLT. SGT.: Yea?

PHONE: They're blowin' a bugle!!

PLT. SGT.: Oh?—Well—What are they playing?

PHONE: I dunno—I can't make it out. I tell you they're blowin' bugles!!

PLT. SGT.: Who's blowing bugles?

PHONE: The GOOKS!!

PLT. SGT.: How far away are they—can you tell?

689

PHONE: I guess about across the valley on the other side of the ridge. (Fully nine hundred yards)

PLT. SGT.: Well—can't you tell what tune they're playing? Listen close and see if it's on the hit parade—

PHONE (squawks and rattling noises, then very calmly): I don't know what they're playing. All I know is they're blowin' a bugle.

PLT. SGT.: Roger. OK. But if you hear a piano and violin accompaniment, let us know and we'll come and help you get back to the rear.

PHONE: Yes. Sgt. (Followed by sputtering noises)

Later on, one of the boys heard noises in front of him and screamed for a parachute flare. When he got it, he could see the squirrels which made the noise.

In another hole, having heard a noise, a rifleman prepared to toss a grenade and roused his buddy in doing so. As he wound up to make the throw the buddy sat up and the grenadier smacked the grenade into the buddy's teeth, knocking him cold. This threw his aim off and the grenade flew out, hit a tree, bounced back and exploded just a few feet from the bunker. The grenadier thought that a gook had tossed it back at him, so he threw another half dozen grenades in all directions to defend himself. When his panic subsided, he realized what had happened and helped his buddy look for his teeth in the dark.

Yesterday the 7th Marines on our left, under orders from X Corps, had to run a combat patrol (pronounced "Probing Attack" by the press, I believe) onto the ridge to our front. They trundled up fourteen tanks, ran an air strike, and fired artillery and mortars (mine included) in battery and battalion salvoes all morning and early afternoon. In mid-afternoon they were moved through our lines and minefield and on out into the wide open valley.

From my own OP, I had a fifty-yard-line seat of the whole show —just like a football game only the other team not only fought our team, but they shot at the spectators as well. The infantry was preceded by the tanks which drew fire from a 76-mm up on a high ridge about three miles to the front. The long rounds from the 76-mm landed all around my bunker because the tanks thoughtfully parked right to my front. The first round hit three men in the 3rd platoon to my right.

Another, a dud, missed the new company commander by about four feet. Another cut my telephone line to the mortars in effect putting them out of the fight because I couldn't shift their fire as the infantry advanced. So we watched. The tanks took up positions out in the open and began to whack away with their 90-mm at point blank range (about six hundred yards) at the little ridge. The 76 gun put round after round within yards of them. But they nonchalantly stood their ground firing 90's and machine guns whenever the infantry radioed for it.

I finally spotted the 76 by its peculiar muzzle blast. It took about seventeen seconds for the rounds to hit after being fired—seventeen seconds to ponder a misspent life and swear never to drink more than three Martinis at a sitting again as long as-I-live-*crash*—shooting at the tanks that time. Serves them right for moving out in front of us —*crash*. Speaking of Martinis—and so on until the infantry broke cover to run across the valley to go up the ridge. No sooner had they begun their dash when a gook 82-mm mortar splashed a fountain of dust and smoke right at the feet of one of them. A Navy Corpsman who must have nerves of steel and ice water for blood, whoever he is, rushed to the fallen Marine, in full view of the enemy, in an obviously "zeroed-in" spot, opened his pack, pulled out his bandages and went to work. In a few minutes a South Korean stretcher team was coaxed out to pick him up and carry him back.

Another 82 went to work on our lines, joining the 76. They kept firing and we kept firing, both close support and counter battery on the ridges and ravines of the big hill, 951, to the front.

The attack patrol regrouped under the little ridge to the front and moved up onto it as rapidly as their equipment would permit. They climbed to a level just under the sky line on our side and moved quickly toward the known bunkers. The tanks by now were blazing away and were joined by a 75-mm recoilless higher up on our ridge. A gook popped out of one of the bunkers to see how close the attackers were moving and the 75-mm slammed one right into him. Another trotted up from somewhere underground and took his place. When the patrol got to within about seventy-five yards of the bunker position, he fired a shot with his rifle and the patrol took cover. Round after round of 90-mm and 75 burst on and near the position and the ridge from the bunker on up to the right was raked back and forth by tank and infantry machine gun fire, plus 75 recoilless. But every time the patrol tried to move, the little gook, clearly visible in his new green quilted winter uniform, would pop up, fire a few rounds and duck back underground before a fresh storm of TNT and steel broke over his head. One gook with a bolt-action rifle stopped the platoon cold in its tracks.

For some reason, the gooks didn't drop mortars on the patrol while it was on the ridge. All the fire seemed to fall on the spot where its route crossed our lines. As the sun went down, the patrol was ordered to pull back under cover of a heavy white phosphorus smoke screen. Then all the gook fire shifted to our lines and rear. They dropped a few within fifty feet of the 60-mm section area, but no one in the section was hurt. Aside from that, today was a beautiful, quiet Indian Summer day.

The surrender propaganda leaflets in another envelope are dropped impartially from airplanes—half to the gooks—half for us. They seem to work, as the company picks up one or two deserters a day. One of my agents conned the red bills off one of the deserters who said he had been told that the Russian Army was coming through here any day now. We also use a loudspeaker set up on a hillside to broadcast propaganda. It pulled twenty-eight deserters in two nights. So much for the war news.

Thanks again for your fine services, and thanks to Carrie for her "get well" note. The wound causes *no* inconvenience and is closing nicely. I've been on a patrol (no shooting) and am doing everything else I am supposed to do and it causes no trouble whatever. My rugby knee injury will cause me much more grief in the future than the wound ever will.

Will write again much sooner.

Regards,
YOUR SON

X
WORLDS

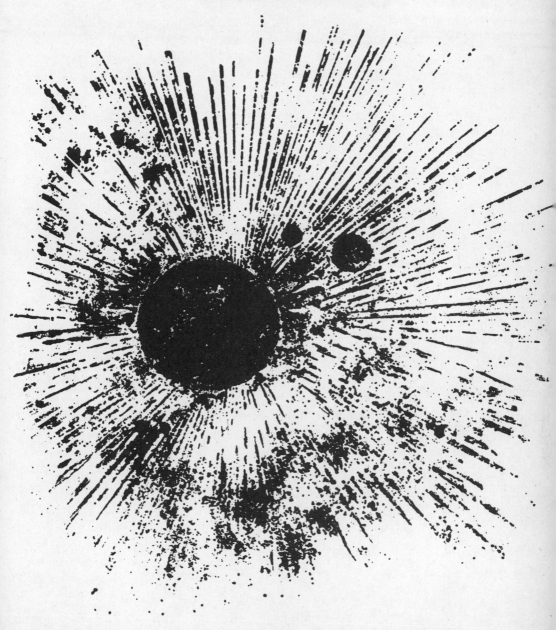

Nicholas Musi

THE EARTH IS BORN

by Lincoln Barnett

DECEMBER 8, 1952

Spawned in a whirl of cosmic dust and forged in elemental fire, the earth spins toward destruction by the sun. This excerpt from the first of a series of articles about the world we live in by Lincoln Barnett, a LIFE writer, conveys the grandeur and sweep of the subject in language easily understandable to the layman.

Earth! Thou mother of numberless children, the nurse and the mother,
Sister thou of the stars, and beloved by the Sun, the rejoicer!
Guardian and friend of the moon, O Earth, whom the comets forget not,
Yea, in the measureless distance wheel round and again they behold thee!
SAMUEL TAYLOR COLERIDGE, *Hymn to the Earth*

Prisoned in his paved cities, blindfolded by his impulses and necessities, man tends to disregard the system of nature in which he stands. It is only at infrequent moments when he finds himself beneath the stars, at sea perhaps, or in a moonlit meadow or on a foreign shore, that he contemplates the natural world—and he wonders.

Yet it is his essence to wonder. On some primeval hilltop half a million years ago the first man raised his eyes to the sky and wondered. At that instant, transcending himself and nature, he left behind the animal forebears from which he sprang: the questioning spirit of man was born, and with it the initial spark of his philosophy, religion and science. His earliest graves, in caverns of age-old rock, bespeak his awareness of the mystery of existence and of realities beyond immediate space and time. In the regularities of nature—the march of days and seasons—and in the irregularities—the caprices of lightning and volcanoes—he saw the will of supernatural beings. Only yesterday, as his own brief history is computed, did he win the key to nature's outer ramparts. This was the idea of causality, telling him to seek in natural causes the explanation of natural events.

Today it seems incredible he ever penetrated the disguises of the visible world at all. To his eye the vistas of earth are flat; the ground on which he walks seems stationary. How did he find himself clinging to the surface of a sphere—spinning about its axis at a thousand miles an hour, whirling around the sun at twenty miles a second, riding through space on the rim of the Milky Way at 170 miles a second, slipping, sliding, wobbling, dipping among the stars in a half dozen other intricate, eccentric motions? What could he think of this strange craft bearing him he could not know where—how explain the awful vibrations of its deck, or the alarming sounds and vapors that recurrently issued from below?

It is the apparent loneliness and singularity of our planet in a hostile universe that evoke the deeper questions: How was the earth created? When did it come into being? What is its fate? The concept of a random universe, existing without origin or destiny, is meaningless to the human animal who lives in a dimension of time. Man has always postulated a Creation, and Genesis speaks with universal accents in its mighty opening phrases: *"In the beginning God created the heaven and the earth. And the earth was without form, and void; and darkness was upon the face of the deep. . . ."* In its assault on these uttermost questions modern cosmogony impinges on the ancient realm of religion. The striking fact is that today their stories seem increasingly to converge. And every mystery that science resolves points to a larger mystery beyond itself.

696

By the turn of the nineteenth century a few lonely pioneers were creating a new science: geology. Chipping away at hillsides and in valleys where streams had cut deep gorges exposing antique strata of rock, they soon noted a relation between the separate layers and the fossils they contained. Each level held its own characteristic plant and animal remains, and they differed strikingly from layer to layer. And so they began dimly to sense vast vistas of time, punctuated by profound changes of climate, topography and life. How else could one explain the bones of whales on Vermont hilltops, marine deposits on the plains of Kansas, palm trees in England or glacial debris in Australia and Brazil? In 1858 Darwin's epic work not only revealed that terrestrial life had undergone an irreversible evolution but had supplied a coherent system of geologic chronology: the calendar of fossils pushed back the time of creation untold millions of years.

However, the reading of the rocks remained a formidable task. All across the scarred, pitted, folded face of the earth, the record of the past has been obscured or obliterated by the scouring of glaciers, repeated outpourings of volcanic lava, and eons of erosion by rain and frost. It was not until the discovery of radioactivity around 1900 that the age of the earth could be fixed with approximate precision. For the radioactive elements, such as uranium, thorium and radium, decay at fixed rates that are independent of heat, pressure or any external influence. Each loses in a given period a certain proportion of atoms which then undergo a long series of transformations at a fixed, known rhythm, ending up eventually as atoms of lead. One gram of uranium, for example, yields 1/7,600,000,000th of a gram of lead per year. So it is possible to weigh the amount of uranium in any bit of radioactive rock against its residue of lead and thus calculate how long ago the deposit was formed.

Careful analyses of radioactive rocks in all parts of the world have failed to disclose any older than two and a half billion years—these are in South Africa—thus pointing to the conclusion that the earth's crust solidified about three billion years ago. Other approaches to the problem—calculations of the ratio of salt in the ocean to the amount of salts annually conveyed by rivers to the sea, as well as recent studies of stellar combustion and galactic movements—all indicate a beginning, a creation fixed in time. The date always falls within certain crude limits, never less than two billion years, never more than four or five. And so the earth did not exist always. Yet it is older far than man from his brief temporal perspective ever surmised till now.

In the morning of time the earth was a featureless ball of anarchic matter, hurtling down the dusty corridor of its orbit. Some theorists think its substance was cold and wet, like snow. But most agree that as it grew it must have been heated to incandescence by the squeeze of gravitation and the friction of its passage through the solar cloud. While in the molten state the heaviest elements sank to the core, the lightest floated to the surface and the others arranged themselves between. Great jets of water vapor and carbon dioxide, pent in the interior, welled up and away to form the primal atmosphere. Slowly the crust cooled.

It may have taken a few centuries for the surface rocks to freeze, or a few thousand years, or, as some say, a million years. For as fast as heat radiated from the surface into space, new streams of hot matter rode upward on convection currents, only to cool and settle again toward the center. And so it is probable that the first crystallization took place in the interior, that the olivine mantle hardened before the outer crust, sealing in the core the primeval heat that remains undiminished to this day.

It was in this epoch of convection currents that the first continents took shape amid the wildest scenes of geologic time. All across the savage face of the earth smoke and flame arose incessantly, and fierce fountains of fluid rock spewed to the surface, spreading new layers of lava on the plutonic plain. As years became centuries, island blocks of granite and basalt began to harden in the molten mass. Many dissolved or foundered, but here and there granitic masses loomed like icebergs on the fiery sea, expanding outward and downward by crystallization until at last they rested on the basalt basement. These were the protocontinents of earth—continents in process of formation. No one knows for certain when the map acquired its present lineaments. One theory has it that the continents congealed exactly where they rest today; another that they crystallized in a single mass, then separated and floated around the globe—impelled by the earth's rotational force —until the basalt basement froze them to their present sites. (A glance at the map shows that the eastern coastlines of the Americas fit those of Western Europe and Africa like the pieces of a jigsaw puzzle.) A third theory holds that the process of continent building is still going on today, as globs of matter continue to rise from the furnacelike interior.

After the land cohered, the seas were made. As the rocks hardened, water vapor and carbon dioxide released in the process of crystallization rose into the cooler atmosphere and collected in enormous cloud masses that shrouded the earth in perpetual darkness. Sometimes in the upper reaches of the cloud canopy rain started to fall—only to boil and turn again to steam. For possibly one thousand years sunlight never penetrated this dense, self-renewing pall of gloom. It must have taken at least that long for the new-formed crust of the earth to cool from the freezing point of rocks (1,000°–2,000°) to the boiling point of water (212°). But at last the day came when rains fell and did not boil away. And the falling rains hastened the cooling process and quickened the condensation of the clouds. No one can say how long this greatest deluge of all time went on—perhaps for centuries. But when at last the clouds thinned, the primeval oceans glittered in the rays of the bright new sun. Many eons elapsed before the sea basins became brimful as they are today. Since that first great flood the level of the earth's waters has risen and fallen many times; coastlines have changed; the seas have crept inland and receded; and the profile of the continents has been repeatedly revised.

As the earth's interior continued to cool, it contracted, shrinking away from its outer crust as a dried apple shrinks within its skin. And like the apple skin the earth's crust wrinkled. The wrinkles were mountains. How many mighty ranges rose and fell in the first eon of prehistory no one can assert; their roots lie buried miles deep in the earth, strewn in the sediments of the sea, lost in the ruins of time.

Throughout geologic time violent periods of mountain building, when the earth's crust readjusted itself to thermal contraction and the changing stresses of its load, have alternated with longer periods of calm, when the implacable rains drilled away at the mountaintops, leaching out their minerals, carving canyons and gorges, sweeping the substance of the mountains down to the insatiable sea. Then for millions of years the earth lay flat and the oceans rose from their basins and encroached on the continents, and the land was level and featureless, save for slow rivers and shallow inland seas—until once again the crust revolted and new mountains arose.

Somewhat more than one billion years ago there came an age of prodigious upheaval which geologists call the Laurentian Revolution, because the roots of some of the great mountains that were reared then still lie embedded in the Laurentian Hills of eastern Canada. All over the world the earth's crust revolted, warping upward and downward to form oceanic deeps and vast mountain chains. Here and there the process of crustal uplift was accompanied by earthquakes and volcanic outbursts. The Laurentians, in particular, were born amid such a fury of volcanic activity as the earth has not known since— a stupendous upwelling of molten rock that engulfed two million square miles of the region around Hudson Bay in a cover of lava two miles thick. It is still there today—the great granite floor of the Canadian Shield. The Appalachian Chain came into existence two hundred million years ago, a range then splendid as the modern Alps but now long since leveled by erosion, so today only its underlying folds remain to suggest the snow-crowned peaks that once marched unbroken from Newfoundland to Alabama. All the high mountains of the earth today—the Himalayas, Rockies, Alps, Andes—came into existence within the last sixty million years. Scarcely one million years ago the youngest of all, the Cascade Mountains of our own West Coast, arose out of the sea accompanied by outbursts of volcanism whose traces are everywhere visible in the West. Nor has it ceased yet. All around the Pacific, from Alaska to the Indies, volcanoes form a ring of fire. There is evidence that the Himalayas and other mountains are still growing. For we are living even now in a revolutionary age of mountain-building. All of human history has been enacted during one of the earth's brief interludes of splendor when mountains transfigure the planet's ordinarily flat countenance. There have been perhaps ten mountain-building epochs since the beginning.

We live moreover in a glacial age. Wherever tall mountains stand there is snow and ice; and geology reveals that many epochs of mountain-building have been accompanied by one of glaciation.

The last and possibly greatest series of all ice ages began one million years ago, at about the time the curtain rose on man. Glaciers covered more than one-fourth of the earth's land surface. In our hemisphere they extended south as far as Louisville, Kentucky. Sheets of ice two miles thick bestrode the mountains of New England, hollowed out the Great Lakes, shaped the Mississippi and Missouri river valleys, stripped the soil from eastern Canada and deposited it in the rich farmlands of our Midwest. At least four times the glaciers advanced and retreated during the million years of this last epoch of refrigeration. Today we are just emerging from the last great advance which reached its climax about twenty thousand years ago. About one-tenth of the earth's surface is still permanently glaciated. Greenland and Antarctica, where in other ages vegetation thrived, lie capped beneath five million cubic miles of ice. Glaciers still armor the mountains of Alaska, New Zealand and Scandinavia as well as the loftier Himalayas, Andes and Alps. Yet in the last two hundred years there has been a marked retreat. Hotels in Switzerland, built at the turn of the century to command scenic vistas of ice, today have no glaciers in view. The Arctic and Antarctic ice packs recede yearly. According to present calculations the earth's climate will become increasingly warmer until A.D. 20,000; the next ice age will begin about A.D. 50,000. The profoundest consequence of the melting of the present icecaps will be the raising of sea level by more than a hundred feet—enough to submerge New York, London, Paris and most of the great seaports and coastal areas of earth.

"The created world," wrote Sir Thomas Browne, "is but a small parenthesis in eternity." On a lesser scale man's world is but a small parenthesis in terrestrial time. In the ages ahead the earth's great recurring rhythms will repeat themselves. Each day the rains and running waters will sweep eight million tons of the land's substance into the sea, until all the towering peaks we know lie crumbled on the ocean floor. But new summits will arise. And again, at intervals so vast as to be meaningless in man's meager dimension of time, the earth's face will buckle, volcanoes will roar, glaciers will abrade the plains and forests, leaving new lakes and rivers in their wake, and the seas will rise and fall.

For the earth is still young. Though man has known less than a thousandth part of the time since living things first stirred in Paleozoic seas, though life itself is but the most recent chapter of geologic time —yet the earth is still young. Its existence will probably continue as long as the sun's, and the sun is a young star. The best testimony of astrophysics suggests that the solar fuel supply will last for many billions of years. Barring some rare catastrophe, like a stellar collision, the earth should continue to wheel in its orbit so long as the sun remains unchanged. Astronomers used to believe that in the end the sun would fade, like a dying ember, and that as its brilliance dimmed, terrestrial life would succumb to the chill of space, the oceans would freeze, the continents revert to barren rock. But they know more today about the processes that keep the stars alight. And they suspect that stars do not die peacefully. It appears that man, or whatever he may become, is destined to perish not of cold but by fire, and that the earth itself will return, as Heraclitus believed, to primordial flame.

Perhaps three to ten billion years from now the hydrogen that lights our sun will begin to run low, and as it dwindles certain dynamic processes will come into play to make the sun grow brighter and hotter. Slowly but steadily, millennium by millennium, the temperature on earth will rise until life shrivels and the oceans boil away. Yet for countless ages more the scorched and lifeless planet will still turn on the grill of the dying sun. Its final immolation may come in one of several ways. In its death throes the sun may swell, at first slowly, then more and more rapidly, evolving finally into what astronomers call a "red giant," somewhat like Betelgeuse or Antares—diffuse, distended stars so huge that if one were substituted for the sun it would fill the entire orbit of the earth. So one by one the nearer planets—Mercury, Venus, Earth and perhaps even Mars and Jupiter —would be engulfed in the monstrous, swollen body of the expiring sun.

But it is also possible that the sun, in its final paroxysm, may explode. If it blows up all at once in a single catastrophic explosion— *i.e.*, if it becomes a "supernova," like the Star of Bethlehem—the surface of the earth would be vaporized in a matter of minutes. But for technical reasons astronomers believe that the sun is more likely to become a "nova," disintegrating in a series of partial explosions, each temporarily increasing its luminosity ten thousand times. Although only about thirty supernovae have been observed since the dawn of astronomy, at least thirty novae appear in our local galaxy each year.

When the fatal day arrives the sun will hurl forth the outer layers of its incandescent atmosphere, disclosing the fearful white fires of its core. The first flare of light and heat will bathe the earth in deadly radiation just eight minutes after the initial explosion. Two days later the atmospheric gases blown from the sun's surface and tumbling outward in all directions at a speed of 2,000,000 mph will envelop our doomed planet in veils of fire, melting the rocks and enkindling the very air. The end is best pictured in Revelation in another of the striking parallels between Biblical and modern scientific prophecy: *"And the fourth angel poured out his vial upon the sun. . . . And men were scorched with great heat . . . and the cities of the nations fell. . . . And every island fled away, and the mountains were not found. . . ."*

THE EDGE
OF THE SEA

by Rachel Carson

APRIL 14, 1952

> *This description of the living things to be observed on the*
> *shores of the sea, an extraordinary combination of the lyric*
> *and the scientific, is taken from Rachel Carson's first book,*
> Under the Sea Wind, *which established her reputation*
> *as an aquatic biologist of the first rank. Her best-known*
> *book,* The Sea Around Us, *gave her a wide new fame.*

The island lay in shadows only a little deeper than those that were
swiftly stealing across the sound from the east. On its western shore
the wet sand of the narrow beach caught the same reflection of palely
gleaming sky that laid a bright path across the water from island
beach to horizon. Both water and sand were the color of steel overlaid with the sheen of silver, so that it was hard to say where water
ended and land began.

With the dusk a strange bird came to the island from its nesting
grounds on the outer banks. Its wings were pure black, and from tip
to tip their spread was more than the length of a man's arm. It flew

steadily and without haste across the sound, its progress as measured and as meaningful as that of the shadows which little by little were dulling the bright water path. The bird was called Rynchops, the black skimmer.

At the last spring tide, when the thin shell of the new moon brought the water lapping among the sea oats that fringed the dunes of the banks, Rynchops and his kin had arrived on the outer barrier strip of sand between sound and sea. They had journeyed northward from the coast of Yucatan where they had wintered. Under the warm June sun they would lay their eggs and hatch their buff-colored chicks on the sandy islands of the sound and on the outer beaches. But at first they were weary after the long flight and they rested by day on sand bars when the tide was out or roamed over the sound and its bordering marshes by night.

About sunset the tide had been out. Now it was rising, covering the afternoon resting places of the skimmers, moving through the inlet and flowing up into the marshes. Through most of the night the skimmers would feed, gliding on slender wings above the water in search of the small fishes that had moved in with the tide to the shelter of grassy shallows. Because they fed on the rising tide, the skimmers were called flood gulls.

On the south beach of the island, where water no deeper than a man's hand ran over gently ribbed bottom, Rynchops began to wheel and quarter over the shallows. He flew with a curious, lilting motion, lifting his wings high after the downstroke. His head was bent sharply so that the long lower bill, shaped like a scissor blade, might cut the water.

The blade or cutwater plowed a miniature furrow over the placid sheet of the sound, setting up wavelets of its own and sending vibrations thudding down through the water to rebound from the sandy bottom. The wave messages were received by the blennies and killifish that were roving the shallows on the alert for food. In the fish world many things are told by sound waves. Sometimes the vibrations tell of food animals like small shrimps or oar-footed crustaceans moving in swarms overhead. And so at the passing of the skimmer the small fishes came nosing at the surface, curious and hungry. Rynchops, wheeling about, returned along the way he had come and snapped up three of the fishes by the rapid opening and closing of his short upper bill.

Ah-h-h, called the black skimmer. Ha-a-a! Ha-a-a-a! Ha-a-a-a! Ha-a-a-a! His voice was harsh and barking. It carried far across the water, and from the marshes there came back, like echoes, the answering cries of other skimmers.

In the waters bordering the island many creatures besides the skimmers were abroad that night, foraging in the shallows. As the darkness grew and the incoming tide lapped higher and higher among the marsh grasses, two diamondback terrapins slipped into the water to join the moving forms of others of their kind. These were females, who had just finished laying their eggs above the high-tide line. They had dug nests in the soft sand, working with hind feet until they scooped out jug-shaped holes not quite so deep as their own bodies were long. Then they had deposited their eggs. These they had carefully covered with sand, crawling back and forth to conceal the location of the nest. There were other nests in the sand, but none more than two weeks old, for May is the beginning of the nesting season among the diamondbacks.

The terrapins nibbled at the marsh grasses and picked off small coiled snails that had crept up the flat blades. Sometimes they swam down to take crabs off the bottom. One of the two terrapins passed between two slender uprights like stakes thrust into the sand. They were the legs of the solitary great blue heron who flew every night from his rookery three miles away to fish from the island.

The heron stood motionless, his neck curved back on his shoulders, his bill poised to spear fish as they darted past his legs. As the terrapin moved out into deeper water she startled a young mullet and sent it racing toward the beach in confusion and panic. The sharp-eyed heron saw the movement and with a quick dart seized the fish crosswise in his bill. He tossed it into the air, caught it headfirst and swallowed it. It was the first fish other than small fry that he had caught that night.

The tide was almost halfway to the confused litter of sea wrack, bits of sticks, dried claws of crabs and broken shell fragments that marked high-water level. Above the tide line there were faint stirrings in the sand where the terrapins had lately begun to lay their eggs. The season's young would not hatch until August, but many young of the year before still were buried in the sand, not yet roused from the torpor of hibernation. They were weak and emaciated, moving feebly in the sands where the old terrapins were laying the eggs of a new generation of young.

About the time the tide was midway to the flood, a wave of motion stroked the tops of the grasses above the terrapin egg bed, as though a breeze passed. A rat, crafty with the cunning of years and filled with the lust for blood, had come down to the water along a path which his feet and his thick tail had worn to a smooth track through the grass. The scent of terrapin and of terrapin eggs, fresh laid, was heavy in the air. Snuffling and squeaking in excitement, the rat began to dig and in a few minutes had uncovered an egg, had pierced the shell and bit out the yolk. He then uncovered two other eggs and might have eaten them if he had not heard a movement in a nearby clump of marsh grass—the scrambling of a young terrapin struggling to escape the water that was seeping up around its tussock of tangled roots and mud. A dark form moved across the sand and through the rivulet of water. The rat seized the baby terrapin and carried it in his teeth through the marsh grasses to a hummock of higher ground. Engrossed in gnawing away the thin shell of the terrapin, he did not notice how the tide was creeping up about him and running deeper around the hummock. It was thus that the blue heron, wading back around the shore of the island, came upon the rat and speared him.

There were few sounds that night except those of the water and the water birds. The wind was asleep. From the direction of the inlet there came the sound of breakers on the barrier beach, but the distant voice of the sea was hushed almost to a sigh, a sort of rhythmic exhalation as though the sea, too, were asleep outside the gates of the sound.

It would have taken the sharpest of ears to catch the sound of a hermit crab dragging his shell house along the beach just above the waterline: the elfin shuffle of his feet on the sand, the sharp grit as he dragged his own shell across another; or to have discerned the spattering tinkle of the tiny droplets that fell when a shrimp, being pursued by a school of fish, leaped clear of the water. But these were the unheard voices of the island night, of the water and the water's edge.

The sounds of the land were few. There was a thin insect tremolo, the spring prelude to the incessant chitin fiddles that later in the season would salute the night. There was the murmur of sleeping birds in the cedars—jackdaws and mockingbirds—who now and again roused enough to twitter drowsily one to another. About midnight a mockingbird sang for almost a quarter of an hour, imitating all the bird songs he had heard that day and adding trills, chuckles and whistles all his own. Then he too subsided and left the night again to the water and its sounds.

There were many fish moving in through the deep water of the channel that night. It was a run of spawning shad, fresh from the sea. For days the shad had lain outside the line of breakers beyond the inlet. Tonight with the rising tide they had moved in past the clanging buoy that guided fishermen returning from the outer grounds, had passed through the inlet and were crossing the sound by way of the channel.

Some of the migrating shad were three years old and were returning to spawn for the first time. A few were a year older and were making their second trip to the spawning grounds up the river. These were wise in the ways of the river and of the strange crisscross shadows it sometimes contained.

By the younger shad the river was only dimly remembered, if by the word "memory" we may call the heightened response of the senses as the delicate gills perceived the lessening saltiness of the water and the changing rhythms and vibrations of the inshore waters. Three years before they had left the river, dropping downstream to the estuary as young fish scarcely as long as a man's finger, moving out to sea with the coming of autumn's chill. They roamed widely in the sea, feeding on shrimps and amphipods. So far and so deviously did they travel that no man could trace their movements.

The shad roamed the sea paths known and followed only by fish while the earth moved three times through the cycle of the zodiac. In the third year, as the waters of the sea warmed slowly to the northward-moving sun, the shad yielded to the promptings of race instinct and returned to their birthplaces to spawn.

Most of the fish coming in now were females, heavy with unshed roe. It was late in the season and the largest runs had gone before. The bucks, who came into the river first, were already on the spawning grounds, as were many of the roe shad. Some of the early-run fish had pressed upstream as far as a hundred miles to where the river had its formless beginnings in dark cypress swamps.

Each of the roe fish would shed in a season more than a hundred thousand eggs. From these perhaps only one or two young would survive the perils of river and sea and return in time to spawn, for by such ruthless selection the species are kept in check.

The fisherman who lived on the island had gone out about nightfall to set the gill nets that he owned with another fisherman from the town. About midnight, as the tide neared the full, the cork line bobbed as the first of the migrating shad struck the net. The line vibrated and several of the cork floats disappeared under the water. The shad, a four-pound roe, had thrust her head through one of the meshes of the net and was struggling to free herself. The taut circle of twine that had slipped under the gill covers cut deeper into the delicate gill filaments as the fish lunged against the net; lunged again to free herself from something that was like a burning, choking collar; something that held her in an invisible vise and would neither let her go on upstream nor turn and seek sanctuary in the sea she had left.

The cork line bobbed many times that night and many fish were gilled. Most of them died slowly of suffocation, for the twine interfered with the rhythmic respiratory movements of the gill covers by which fish draw streams of water in through the mouth and pass them over the gills. Once the line bobbed very hard and for ten minutes was pulled below the surface. That was when a grebe, swimming fast five feet under water after a fish, went through the net to its shoulders and in its violent struggles with wings and lobed feet became hopelessly entangled. The grebe soon drowned. Its body hung limply from the net, along with a score of silvery fish bodies with heads pointing upstream in the direction of the spawning grounds where the early-run shad awaited their coming.

By the time the first half-dozen shad had been caught in the net, the eels that lived in the estuary had become aware that a feast was in the offing. Since dusk they had glided with sinuating motion along the banks, thrusting their snouts into crabholes and seizing whatever they could catch in the way of small water creatures.

Almost without exception the eels of the estuary were males. When the young eels come in from the sea, where they are born, the females press far up into rivers and streams, but the males wait about the river mouths until their mates-to-be, grown sleek and fat, rejoin them for the return journey to the sea.

As the eels poked their heads out of the holes under the roots of the marsh grasses and swayed gently back and forth, savoring eagerly the water that they drew into their mouths, their keen senses caught the taste of fish blood which was diffusing slowly through the water as the gilled shad struggled to escape. One by one they slipped out of their holes and followed the taste trail through the water to the net.

The eels feasted royally that night, since most of the fish caught by the net were roe shad. The eels bit into the abdomens with sharp teeth and ate out the roe. Sometimes they ate out all the flesh as well, so that nothing remained but a bag of skin, with an eel or two inside. The marauders could not catch a live shad free in the river, so their only chance for such a meal was to rob the gill nets.

Although there was as yet no light in the east, the blackness of water and air was perceptibly lessening, as though the darkness that remained were something less solid and impenetrable than that of midnight. A freshening air moved across the sound from the east and, blowing across the receding water, sent little wavelets splashing on the beach.

Most of the black skimmers had already left the sound and returned by way of the inlet to the outer banks. Only Rynchops remained. Seemingly he would never tire of circling the island, of making wide sorties out over the marshes or up the estuary of the river where the shad nets were set. He passed upstream about a mile, flying low to the water, then turned by circling widely over the marshes and came down to the estuary again. There was a strong smell of fish and of water weeds in the air which came to him through the morning mists, and the voices of the fishermen were borne clearly over the water. The men were cursing as they worked to raise the gill net, disentangling the fish before they piled the dripping net on the flat bottom of the skiff.

The next time Rynchops flew up the estuary he met the fishermen coming downstream on the ebbing tide, net piled in the boat over some half-dozen shad. All the others had been gutted or reduced to skeletons by the eels. Already gulls were gathering on the water where the gill net had been set, screaming their pleasure over the refuse which the fishermen had thrown overboard.

The tide was ebbing fast, surging through the gutter and running out to sea. As the sun's rays broke through the clouds in the east and sped across the sound, Rynchops turned to follow the racing water seaward.

Now there came days when the sky was gray as a mullet's back, with clouds like the flung spray of waves. The wind, that throughout most of the summer had blown from the southwest, began to veer toward the north. On such mornings large mullet could be seen jumping in the estuary and over the shoals of the sound. On the ocean beaches fishermen's boats were drawn up on the sand. Men stood on the beach, with eyes on the water, patiently waiting. The fishermen knew that mullet were gathering in schools throughout the sound because of the change in the weather. They knew that soon the schools would run out through the inlet before the wind and then would pass down along the coast. So the fishermen waited, confident in their generations of tested lore.

Other fishers besides the men awaited the runs of mullet. Among them was a fish hawk, or osprey, whom the mullet fishermen watched every day as he floated, a small dark cloud, in wide circles in the sky. To pass the hours as they stood watch on the sound beach or among the dunes, the fishermen wagered among themselves when the osprey would dive.

The fish hawk sailed on set wings, riding the mounting columns of warm air that shimmered upward from the water. Far below him the water was like green silk rippling in a breeze. The terns and skimmers resting on the shoals of the sound were the size of robins. The amber eyes of the osprey flickered as a whipper ray leaped three times from the water, coming down with a sharp spat that was carried away on the wind and lost.

A shadow took form on the green screen beneath the osprey and the surface dimpled as a fish nosed at the film. In the sound two hundred feet below the fish hawk, a mullet gathered his strength and flung himself in exhilaration into the air. As he was flexing his muscles for the third leap a dark form fell out of the sky and viselike talons seized him. The mullet weighed more than a pound, but the osprey carried him easily in his taloned feet, bearing the fish across the sound and to a nest in a loblolly pine tree three miles away.

Flying up the river from the estuary the osprey carried the mullet headfirst in his talons. As he neared the nest he relaxed his grip with the left foot and, checking flight, alighted on the outer branches of the nest with the fish still gripped in his right foot. He lingered over his meal of fish for more than an hour, and when his mate came near he crouched low over the mullet and hissed at her. Now that the nesting was done, every bird must fish for itself.

Later in the day, as he returned down the river to fish, the osprey swooped low to the water and for the space of a dozen wing beats dragged his feet in the river, cleansing them of the adhering fish slime.

On his return he was watched by the sharp eyes of a large brown bird perched in one of the pines on the west bank of the river, overlooking the marshes of the estuary. The bald eagle lived as a pirate, never fishing for himself when he could steal from the ospreys of the surrounding country. When the fish hawk moved out over the sound the eagle followed, mounting into the air and taking up a position far above him.

For an hour two dark forms circled in the sky. Then from his high station the eagle saw the body of the osprey suddenly dwindle to sparrow size as he fell in a straight drop, saw the white spray mount from the water as the fish hawk disappeared. After the passing of thirty seconds the osprey emerged from the water, mounting straight for fifty feet with short, heavy wing beats and then leveling out into straight flight toward the river's mouth.

Watching him, the eagle knew that the osprey had caught a fish and was taking it home to the nest in the pines. With a shrill scream the eagle whirled in pursuit, keeping his elevation of a thousand feet above the fish hawk.

The osprey cried out in annoyance and alarm, redoubling the force of his wing beats in an effort to reach the cover of the pines before his tormentor should attack. The speed of the hawk was retarded by the weight of the catfish that he carried and by the convulsive struggles of the fish, held firmly in the strong talons.

Between the island and the mainland the eagle gained a position directly over the hawk. On half-closed wings he dropped with terrific speed. The wind whined through his feathers. As he passed the osprey he whirled in air, back to the water, presenting his talons to the attack. The osprey dodged and twisted, eluding the eight curved scimitars. Before the eagle could recover himself the hawk had shot aloft 250 feet. The eagle hurtled after him, mounted above him. But even as he began the stoop, the fish hawk, in another upward soaring, surmounted the position of his enemy.

By turns rising and swooping, hawk and eagle rose to a great height. A dozen white feathers ripped from the hawk's breast as he barely evaded the eagle's talons on the last swoop fluttered earthward. Of a sudden the osprey bent his wings sharply and dropped like a stone toward the water. The wind roared in his ears, half blinded him, plucked at his feathers. It was his final effort to outwit a stronger and more enduring enemy. But from above, the relentless dark form fell even faster, gained on him, passed him, whirled and tore the fish from his grasp.

The eagle carried the fish to his pine-tree perch to rend it, muscle from bone. By the time he reached the perch the osprey was beating out heavily over the inlet to new fishing grounds at sea.

The north wind was tearing the crests off the waves as they came over the inlet bar, so that each was trailing a heavy smoke of spray. In the shallow river estuary and over the many shoals of the sound the fish sensed the sudden chill and began to seek the deeper waters which held the stored warmth of the sun.

The wind blew down the river and across the sound to the inlet, and the fish ran before it to the sea. Past a dozen sandspits of the sound, each with its little colony of resting gulls, the tide took the mullet past the big inlet buoy that was leaning toward the sea with the press of the water. The channel widened and the pale green water grew murky with the wave scourings of loose sand. The mutter and rumble of the surf grew. With their sensitive flanks the fish perceived the heavy jar and thud of sea vibrations. The changing pulse of the sea was caused by the long inlet bar, where the water foamed to a white froth as the waves spilled over it. Now the mullet passed out through the channel and felt the longer rhythms of the sea—the rise, the sudden lift and fall of waves come from the deep Atlantic. Just outside the first surf line the mullet leaped in these larger swells of ocean. One after another swam upward to the surface and jumped into the air, falling back with a white splash to resume its place in the moving school.

The lookout who stood on a high dune above the inlet saw the first of the mullet running out of the sound. With practiced eye he estimated the size and speed of the school from the spurts of spray when the mullet jumped. Although three boats with their crews were waiting farther down the ocean beach, he gave no signal at the passing of the first mullet. The tide was still on the ebb; the pull of the water was seaward and the nets could not be drawn against it.

The tide turned, and one of the boats was launched between the breakers to be ready for the fish. Just outside the surf line the men waited at the oars. The captain stood in the bow, arms folded, leg muscles flexing to the rise and fall of the boat, his eyes on the water, looking toward the inlet.

Half a dozen gulls mewed above the water. That meant the mullet were coming. The gulls didn't want the mullet; they wanted the minnows milling about in alarm as the larger fish moved through the shallows. The mullet came down just outside the breakers, traveling about as fast as a man could walk on the beach. The lookout marked the school. He walked toward the boat, keeping opposite the fish, signaling their course to the crew by waving his arms.

The men braced their feet against the thwarts of the boat and strained to the oars, pulling the boat in a wide semicircle to the shore. The net of heavy twine spilled silently and steadily into the water over the stern, and cork floats bobbed in the water in the wake of the boat. Ropes from one end of the net were held by half a dozen men on shore.

A shadow loomed in the green, sun-filled water in the path of the mullet. From a dim, gray curtain the shadow resolved itself into a web of slender, crisscross bars. The first of the mullet struck the net, backed water with their fins, hesitated. Other fish crowded up from behind, nosing at the net. As the first waves of panic passed from fish to fish they dashed shoreward, seeking a way of escape. The netting wall extended into water too shallow for a fish to swim. They ran seaward, but met the circle of the net as it grew smaller, foot by foot.

Of a sudden the whole school surged upward. In a turmoil of flying spray and splashing water, mullet by the hundred leaped over the cork line and pelted against the fishermen, who turned their backs to the fish raining about them. Two piles of slack netting were growing on the beach, and the net took on the shape of a huge, elongated bag, bulging with fish. The fishermen worked quickly to take the mullet from the net and toss them into the waiting boats. By a dexterous shake of the net they tossed on the beach the small fish of other species that had become gilled in the seine.

Soon the bodies of the young fish—too small to sell, too small to eat—littered the beach above the waterline, the life oozing from them for want of means to cross a few yards of dry sand and return to the sea. Some of the small bodies the sea would take away later; others it would lay up carefully beyond reach of the tides among the litter of sticks and seaweeds, of shells and sea oats stubble. Thus the sea unfailingly provides for the hunters of the tide lines.

After the fishermen had made two more hauls and then, as the tide neared the full, had gone away with laden boats, a flock of gulls came in from the outer shoals, white against the graying sea, and feasted on the fish. As the gulls bickered among themselves over the food, two smaller birds in sleek, black plumage walked warily among them, dragging fish up on the higher beach to devour them. They were fish crows, who took their living from the edge of the water. After sundown the ghost crabs would come in legions out of their holes to swarm over the tide litter, clearing away the last traces of the fish. Already the sand hoppers had gathered and were busy at their work of reclaiming to life in their own beings the materials of the fishes' bodies. For in the sea, nothing is lost. One dies, another lives, as the precious elements of life are passed on and on in endless chains.

THE STARRY
UNIVERSE

by Lincoln Barnett

DECEMBER 20, 1954

> *Beyond our planet lies an endless sea of space jeweled*
> *with galaxies and cloaked in mysteries that man has only*
> *begun to fathom. Here it is poetically described by Lincoln*
> *Barnett, who first came into literary prominence with a*
> *nontechnical book on a vastly technical subject:* The
> Universe and Dr. Einstein. LIFE's *series of articles entitled*
> *"The World We Live In," of which this is the concluding*
> *chapter, was published as a book in 1955 and overnight*
> *became one of the great nonfiction best sellers in the history*
> *of publishing.*

Let there be lights in the firmament of the heaven to divide the day from
the night; and let them be for signs, and for seasons, and for days, and
years.

GENESIS 1:14

Steadfastly through the ages men of science have sought to strip nature
of its disguises and lay bare the hidden order that underlies the
diversity of the visible world. Their quest has taken them to the depths
of the sea and the highest fringes of the atmosphere, to deserts, jungles
and the frozen lands that engird the terrestrial poles. With the slow
enlargement of human knowledge, man's perspectives of space and
time have correspondingly expanded. He has learned to count himself
as one in the endless succession of living things that have populated
the surface of the earth since life appeared. And he has reluctantly
recognized his dependency on the system of nature in which he

stands—his ineluctable need for air, water and sunlight and for all the substances he must exploit to assuage his implacable hungers.

In no realm of science has new understanding so operated to disclose man's humbling situation in the natural world as in the advance of astronomy. However strong his conviction that he is overlord of earth, his self-image shrinks to insignificance when he lifts his eyes to the star-strewn vault of night and contemplates the dark and fathomless depths of space within which his petty domain is less than a grain of sand. This revelation was slow in coming and not easy to accept; it has always been man's nature to envisage himself at the center of the universe. From where he stands on the apparently stationary pedestal of earth, the sun and moon regularly wheel westward from horizon to horizon, and the whole nocturnal sky seems like a great rotating bowl, carrying with it the bright diamonds of the fixed stars. It is only natural that for most of his brief span of existence, man has believed his earth to be static, a solidly anchored object in a world of moving lights.

As the centuries passed and telescopes improved, astronomers probed deeper into space, and slowly there dawned a sense of the immensity of the cosmos and the profusion of its quenchless fires. On a clear night some five thousand stars can be seen with the naked eye. But a small telescope discloses over two million and the great Palomar telescope sucks in the light of billions. Yet for all their spangled myriads the distances between them are so vast that on another scale they might be envisaged as lonely lightships, a million miles apart, floating in an empty sea. The nearest star to earth, save the sun, is Alpha Centauri, 4.4 light years away. (A light year is the distance light travels in a year, or roughly six trillion miles. The sun is only eight light minutes away.) Betelgeuse, the giant red star in the shoulder of Orion, is 300 light years away. The light from Rigel, the blue giant in Orion's knee, takes 540 years to reach our eyes.

Yet even these stars are close neighbors, and their distances are inches in the cosmic scale. It is only in recent decades that the terrifying dimensions and complexity of the universe have been dimly discerned. We know now that our solar system is actually but an infinitesimal unit on the outer rim of the great galaxy of stars that compose the Milky Way. And in turn the Milky Way, which once was thought to constitute the entire universe, is but one unit in a cluster of galaxies linked by gravitation and wheeling together through space. Yet it is not merely the size of the universe that dismays the cosmologist when he reaches the frontiers of vision two billion light years, or 12,000,000,000,000,000,000,000,000 terrestrial miles, away. For here he encounters enigmas that warn him not to assume—as man tends to do—that he can apply the simple physical laws that govern his earthly domain to the deeps of space and time. There is evidence that all his systems of measurement break down when he tries to fit them to the exterior vistas of the cosmos. And there is doubt that his ordinary notions of geometry and form, derived from his limited senses, can be used to understand a universe in which space may have no bounds. Staring into the void, he faces concepts like infinity and eternity, where science and imagination stand together on the brink of darkness, and he can perhaps but echo the words of the philosopher Schiller, "The universe is a thought of God."

The first watchers of the sky, beside the Euphrates and the Nile, noticed that five bright stars changed their positions swiftly from night to night, drifting among the constellations in apparently capricious paths. The Greeks named them πλανῆται, the wanderers. Today we know that they are not true stars, burning in distant space, but merely cold companions of the sun, like the earth, shining by reflected light. We know too that in addition to the five visible to the naked eye, three others may be seen by telescope. Because of their kinship to earth, man has often wondered if any of these neighboring worlds might support life comparable to his own.

All answers to this question rest on a basic postulate of science: the principle of the uniformity of nature, which asserts that the elements found on earth persist throughout the universe and obey the same physical laws. For this reason the possibility of life on the five outer planets must be ruled out. They are far too cold: their surface temperatures range from $-170°$ F. on Jupiter to $-380°$ on distant Pluto. All save Pluto are heavily enshrouded in dense clouds of poisonous gases. Neither do the two inner planets offer any friendlier abode. Airless Mercury turns one face perpetually toward the sun. On this side the temperature reaches 670°; on the other the temperature is near absolute zero (−460°). Venus lies mantled beneath dense clouds containing much carbon dioxide, a gas whose insulating properties are such that the surface temperature of the planet may approximate that of boiling water.

Of all the planets, only Mars remains a possible domain of life. Although its maximum temperature barely reaches 50°, seasonal color changes analogous to those of Earth can be observed over large areas. All one can say is that conditions on Mars are such as to render possible the growth of primitive vegetation. If higher forms of life exist elsewhere than on earth, they must be found outside the solar system, in the starry fields of the Milky Way or the distant galaxies beyond.

From the platform of the apparently stationary earth, the planets appear to wheel across the heavens within a narrow belt which the ancients called the zodiac. Today we know that the avenue of the zodiac is the flat plane of an enormous disk-shaped system in which our earth and all the planets are forever imprisoned by gravitation, destined to revolve around our central star, the sun, so long as they exist. Infinitely complex, our solar system encompasses not only the nine planets, but also thirty-one moons or smaller satellites of the planets, thirty thousand asteroids or minor planets, thousands of comets, and incomputable numbers of meteors which burn their way into the earth's atmosphere every day.

For all its apparent complexity, the solar system also reveals an order that has ever impressed scientists contemplating the harmonious laws that govern the motions of the skies. The planets revolve in elliptical orbits, varying their distances and velocities—moving fastest when closest to the sun, more slowly when farther away. Their movements are governed by a delicate balance between their inertia (*i.e.*, their tendency to keep moving in a straight line) and the gravitational pull of the sun. It is this tenuous equilibrium that keeps them from flying away into space on the one hand or falling into the flaming mass of the sun on the other. The same laws rule the comets: as they reach the outer ends of their elongated orbits the gravitational tug of the sun slows their speed and pulls them back; as they reach the inner ends of their orbits their inertia and increasing speed impel them past the sun rather than into it.

To earth-bound man the dimensions of the solar system seem stupendous. He himself lives 93 million miles from the sun. His small planet has a diameter of 7,900 miles, less than one-tenth that of massive Jupiter and less than one-hundredth that of the sun. In terms of volume it would take 1,300,000 building blocks the size of the earth to make one sun—and the sun is but an average-size star. If the sun were imagined as a ball six inches in diameter, Earth would then be about 55 feet away and Pluto would be about half a mile away—but the nearest stars would be about 3,000 miles away. And even these are but near neighbors in the vastness of the Milky Way.

"Like a great ring of pure and endless light," the Milky Way girdles the heavens from pole to pole. Throughout the ages its pearly luminescence and intimations of fathomless distance have provoked the awe and imagination of man. It was not until recent times, however, that the Milky Way came to be recognized for what it is: a mighty river of suns, star fields, clusters and clouds composing the visible part of the galaxy in which our solar system moves. The difficulty in envisaging the architecture of the Milky Way is that we are *inside* it. Yet in the last century astronomers have broken through the confining perspective of earth and ascertained that what we see of the Milky Way is actually the interior arc of a stupendous lens-shaped aggregation of stars similar to the galaxies of outer space. From the Earth, situated some 30,000 light years from the center of our galaxy, we can discern only a fraction of the billions of stars it contains, only a segment of its over-all diameter of 100,000 light years.

Most of the matter in our galaxy—stars, dark clouds of gas and dust —lies within the main disk of the Milky Way and its tightly coiled spiral arms. The galaxy rotates, completing one revolution every 200 million years and carrying earth and sun with it at a velocity of about 600,000 miles an hour. In its flight through space the great disk is accompanied by an outer swarm of globular clusters, each containing hundreds of thousands of stars, each revolving at random around the center of the galaxy. Together, the Milky Way and its aureole of globular clusters makes up what astronomers refer to as The Galaxy.

In the stupendous perspectives of the cosmos, however, our galaxy is but one member of a still larger cosmic aggregate, called the Local Group, which includes seventeen or more systems held by gravitational force within a radius of 1.5 million light years. Near one end of this vast supersystem rides the glowing wheel of the Milky Way, at the other end the great spiral of its sister galaxy, Andromeda.

The Local Group also embraces six small elliptical galaxies, possessing no spiral arms and little dust or gas, four structureless veils of stars like the Magellanic Clouds, and perhaps three distant spirals, sparsely distributed through the immense void. Remote as they are, they are nevertheless united by the mysterious force of gravitation and revolve around an unknown center somewhere between Andromeda and the Milky Way.

As the eye of the telescope peers outward, past the familiar constellations, past the more distant star clouds and clusters of the Milky Way, it discovers an ever increasing number of hazy luminous patches suspended like cobwebs in the void. These are the outer galaxies, the so-called "island universes," each composed of billions of stars but so deeply sunk in the abyss of space that the light by which they disclose themselves required millions of years to traverse the distance to the earth. Within the bowl of the Big Dipper alone, a rectangle enclosing only 1/2000 of the whole sky, faint glimmers of enfeebled light reveal a cluster of more than three hundred galaxies. By comparison, our Local Group, with its seventeen members, is a dwarf cluster. In general the galaxies of outer space tend to congregate into communities of about five hundred—into galaxies of galaxies—united by gravitation, often interpenetrating one another in their huge wanderings.

Astronomers estimate that about one trillion galaxies lie within range of our largest telescopes. Three main categories are recognized: elliptical galaxies, representing 17 per cent of those catalogued; spirals, comprising 80 per cent; and irregulars, composing 3 per cent. Because they rotate at various speeds the ellipticals range from perfectly symmetrical spheres to flattened saucer-shaped disks. For the same reason, the spirals range from the tightly coiled through the more loosely coiled like the Milky Way to wide-open pinwheels with small nuclei and arms thrown out by the centrifugal force of rapid rotation. Most spirals have round centers, but about 30 per cent of them are "barred spirals" with elongated nuclei. The third main group of galaxies, the irregulars, are like the Magellanic Clouds, formless, without nuclei or systematic rotational movement.

A few modern astronomers try to fit the various types of galaxies into an evolutionary sequence, suggesting that the turbulent irregular galaxies are newborn systems that will form into fast-spinning spirals, and then in time evolve into slower-moving ellipticals. But most astronomers insist that all galaxies are of about the same age. They assert that the various types of galaxies were shaped by their various rotational speeds at creation and that these speeds determined how much of their primordial matter should coalesce into stars and how much should continue to drift freely in clouds of gas and smoke.

Of all the mysteries of the universe the darkest surround inchoate masses of matter that drift in space in clouds of gas and dust. Floating between the stars in the arms of all spirals and large areas of irregular galaxies, this material reveals itself either by catching the light of adjacent stars or by obscuring it behind opaque shrouds. Its density is so inconceivably low—sixteen atoms per cubic inch—that it surpasses the most perfect vacuums that can be produced on earth. Yet in regions near the sun these diffuse clouds are so vast that they equal in mass the total substance of the stars in these regions.

The cosmic clouds are significant because they are the raw material of creation. Some five billion years ago, according to present theory, our galaxy consisted of a stupendous mass of swirling hydrogen gas rotating invisibly in starless space. As the cloud spun, turbulence developed and eddies formed, and within the eddies gravitational force began to weld particles into ever greater bodies. Then as the enlarging masses felt the squeeze of gravitation their internal temperatures rose. Eventually, in the hot centers of each mass, atomic nuclei began to react; hydrogen changed to helium (as in the H-bomb), and so lit up the first stars. In this way the Milky Way and all other galaxies are thought to have formed. Among the immense dim clouds that can be seen hanging in the depths of the sky, astronomers believe the same slow processes of stellar creation may still be going on.

The history of astronomy has been a record of receding horizons. In the beginning the retreat was slow; many centuries passed between the dim age when man believed that the sky—"this majestical roof fretted with golden fire"—hovered only a few miles above the earth and the dawn of his apprehension of cosmic distances. Indeed it was not until the beginning of our century that the focus of astronomy shifted from planets to stars. Only within the last twenty-five years has it comprehended the galaxies of outer space.

The astronomer most responsible for this change in perspective was the late Edwin Hubble of the Mount Wilson Observatory, who in 1924 published photographs proving once and for all that the far, hazy patches of light which astronomers had called nebulae and believed to be inchoate masses of gas and dust were actually huge systems of stars like the Milky Way. Thereafter he devoted himself to studying the galaxies, measuring their distances, charting their distribution in space and, most important, analyzing their movements. The curious feature of these movements was that they did not seem to be random, like the aimless drifting of molecules in a gas, but highly systematic: each galaxy, wherever it rode in space, appeared to be rushing away from our solar system at a velocity directly proportional to its distance; that is, the greater the distance, the greater the speed. Hubble and his associate, Milton L. Humason, proceeded to work out the ratio, and in 1929 published an equation destined to be of supreme importance in cosmology and known today as the Hubble-Humason Law. It reads: $V_m = 38r$. In the shorthand of science V_m stands for the velocity of the receding galaxies in miles per second, and "r" expresses the present distance from earth in units of one million light years. Hence a galaxy one hundred million light years away is found moving at a speed of 38x100 or 3,800 miles per second; galaxies one billion light years away flee outward at 38x1,000 or 38,000 miles per second, about one-fifth the speed of light.

The universe thus appears to be expanding about us in all directions. Yet this does not mean that modern astronomy has reverted to the old anthropocentric picture of the cosmos; it does not imply that our earth stands at the center of the universe any more than it does at the center of the solar system, Milky Way or Local Group. If one thinks of the universe as a balloon covered with inelastic spots representing galaxies, then as the balloon inflates each spot must recede from every other spot. Or to take another analogy, one can envisage the universe as a giant cloud of rarefied gas in which each individual galaxy is an individual molecule. If the cloud expands uniformly, each molecule doubles its distance from every other molecule in a given interval of time. And so, if sensate observers exist in the galaxies that we see hurrying away from us, they also see us hurrying away from them— at velocities proportional to distance.

The concept of an expanding space, however, has presented cosmological problems of enormous subtlety. For example, when an astronomer looks outward in space he looks backward in time. The dim, distant galaxies whose antique light swims to our vision through two billion years of terrestrial time do not actually exist where we see them now. The light by which we discern their images started its immense journey when life on earth was barely stirring in the primordial seas. While it has come to us, they have traveled another one and one-third billion light years farther away. It is thus that in any conception of the universe space and time become inseparable and cosmologists speak of a space-time continuum—which means that to describe the position of a galaxy one must fix it not only in three dimensions of space but also in one of time. In this sense the universe is four-dimensional, and the fourth dimension is time.

The cosmologist cannot therefore think of the universe as here and now in the way that one can think of New York City or the earth as here and now. For every object in the heavens has two positions: (1) where we see it, and (2) where it is. Even in the case of the nearest star, Alpha Centauri, we cannot say that we see it "now," for its light takes a little over four years to reach our eyes. So what we actually see is the ghost of a star that was shining back in 1956. Whether or not it is still shining in 1960 we cannot know until 1964. The situation becomes vastly more complicated, however, in the case of the flying galaxies, not only because of their immense distance but because of their incredible velocities.

If one assumes that all the galaxies we see today have been traveling outward through eons of cosmic time in the same relative directions and at the same relative velocities—the farthest galaxies most swiftly, the nearer ones at lesser rates of speed—the startling corollary emerges that all started from the same place at the same time. Calculations made from present measurements of their rate of recession indicate that their cosmic journey began about five billion years ago. The extraordinary fact about this figure is that it coincides with recent findings as to the probable age of radioactive substances found in the earth's crust, and the age of the oldest stars derived from modern theories of stellar evolution. All the clues of science point to a time of creation when the cosmic fires were ignited and the vast pageant of the present universe brought into being. And this time was five billion years ago.

Profound as the problems of the expanding universe are when one looks back in time, enigmas no less deep arise in any attempt to guess what lies beyond the reaches of telescopic vision. It is here that cosmology leaves behind the ordinary realm of human experience. For in trying to separate appearance from reality it has invaded domains of abstraction whose concepts stand utterly removed from the visible, tangible world perceived by man's senses. Yet abstractions, however difficult to comprehend, are necessary if one is to penetrate the mysteries of the cosmos. For example, would greater and greater telescopes disclose wider oceans of space and new myriads of galaxies, hurtling at ever greater speeds? The question leads to one of the great paradoxes of cosmology. For the galaxies we can see two billion light years away (actually three and a third billion light years away at the present time) are traveling at two-thirds the speed of light. If mightier telescopes extended man's vision to two and a half billion light years (to galaxies which would now be five billion light years away) he would then be in range, according to the Hubble-Humason Law, of galaxies whose speed equals that of light. But would he see them? For if they are rushing away from him at the speed of light, then by Newtonian physics the light they emit would never get back to earth. At this point the astronomer has to abandon simple logic and introduce the subtler rationalizations of Einstein's theory of relativity.

In 1905 when Einstein was twenty-six years old he published the Special Theory of Relativity, which opened a new world of physical thought. If the velocity of light is constant with respect to earth, he argued, it must be constant with respect to any galaxy in the universe. Since the speed of light cannot be increased by the motion of the source or receiver, Einstein assumed that nothing in the universe can travel faster than light.

From these premises Einstein formulated a series of equations that have become an integral part of modern physics and cosmology. Specifically, his equations make all measurements of distance and time vary with the velocity of the observer. For example, we may see two galaxies on opposite sides of the earth, each one moving away from us at two-thirds the speed of light. Do they then see each other moving away at four-thirds the speed of light, as the simple addition of velocities would assert? According to relativity, observers in both galaxies would measure time and distance differently from observers here on earth and would compute their combined velocities at somewhat less than that of light.

Strange as its concepts appear to the layman, relativity has been repeatedly validated by observation and experiment. In cosmology the principle of the constant velocity of light has been confirmed by studies of double stars which show that the light from an approaching star in these revolving systems reaches earth at the same speed as that from a receding star. But relativity also warns the cosmologist never to forget that his observations are limited by his situation in the universe, and that he can never be certain of what he measures in the vast drowned depths of space and time.

With these warnings in mind, modern cosmology has attempted warily to speculate on the possible size and architecture of the universe. Special Relativity plus the Hubble-Humason Law suggest that its radius cannot be greater than five billion light years, for: (1) The universe apparently began to expand five billion years ago; (2) The outermost galaxies have been flying into space since then at a constant velocity close to the speed of light; (3) Relativity asserts that no moving object can exceed the speed of light. Hence the swiftest galaxies can have traveled, at the most, a little less than five billion light years since creation. Since our observations encompass but two-thirds of that distance, we can only assume that invisible galaxies are there, and that their farthest outrushing echelons mark the present limits of the universe.

The human mind recoils from the notion of a universe that somewhere terminates, just as it falters at the opposite concept of a space that never ends. We tend to think of space, however, in the familiar images of our experience—or else more abstractly in the terms of Euclid's plane geometry, where a straight line is the shortest distance between two points and the area of a circle is always πr^2. But in the immensity of the cosmos where so many of our familiar terrestrial concepts fail, it may be that our simple Euclidean geometry is delusive too. Just as man believed till recently that his earth was flat, perhaps we now are misled by our short perspectives into believing that the space of the universe must be like the space we see in our immediate neighborhood. Ultimately man discovered the curvature of the earth —by observation and deduction. By analogous techniques cosmologists are now endeavoring to discover whether or not the space of the universe is curved.

Here again the first clues were provided by Einstein when, in 1915, he proposed his General Theory of Relativity, putting forth a new concept of gravitation. Instead of treating gravity as a "force," as Newton had, Einstein pointed out that the space around any celestial body represents a gravitational field akin to the magnetic field around a magnet. He concluded further that the presence of any gravitating body must warp or bend the region of space in which it lies, and hence that light rays passing through a gravitational field must travel not in straight lines but in curves. Four years later during an eclipse of the sun astronomers confirmed his theory by establishing that the light from stars passing through the gravitational field of the darkened sun was deflected precisely as Einstein had forecast.

Since the triumphant validation of Einstein's prediction concerning the bending of starlight, theorists have been speculating as to the curvature of the universe as a whole. They foresee three main possibilities: (1) The universe is Euclidean—it has no curvature and within it a straight line is the shortest distance between two points; (2) It has positive curvature—within it the shortest distance between two points is a closed curve, like the great circles that form the meridians of longitude on the surface of the earth; (3) It has negative curvature—analogous to a saddle-shaped surface and within it the shortest distance between two points is some type of open curve such as a parabola or hyperbola. The expectation of the cosmologist is that he will be able to choose among these possibilities by counting and analyzing the apportionment of the galaxies in space. At present, according to the most recent observations, the greatest likelihood is that space either curves negatively or not at all.

These concepts, though difficult to envisage, are inextricably entwined with the phenomenon of expansion and with the ancient philosophical debate as to whether space is infinite or finite. If it is Euclidean, it is by definition infinite. If it is negatively curved, it must also be infinite for its outer reaches would then curve away from each other indefinitely. But if it has positive curvature, it would then have the strange property of being at once finite and boundless, like the surface of our earth which, though finite, has no boundaries.

At this present interval in the march of human knowledge, cosmology thus finds itself drawn ever farther from the familiar world of sensory impressions. Its theorists are constantly tormented by uncertainty as to the choice of their concepts, and beset by doubts as to the accuracy of their interpretations. The whole phantasmagoria of the outrushing galaxies and expanding space so assails the imagination as to make even cosmologists question the intricate framework of observation and deductive reasoning on which it rests. And yet there appears no other way to explain the faint glimmers of light which the great telescopes receive, and the undeniable reddening of that light which the spectrographs disclose.

Less than a century ago scientists felt confident that little remained for them to do but perfect more accurate systems of measurements. There seemed to be no process of nature that could not be described in terms of mechanical laws and accurately defined by Newton's beautiful equations. And the conviction grew that, given the immediate position and velocity of every particle in the universe, its past and future could be perfectly revealed. The events that shattered this assumption were the development of relativity and the swift advance of atomic science. For all the tremendous insights that modern physics has provided in its separate realms, it has also added to the enigma of man's existence, introducing new paradox, uncertainty, duality into his vision of the world he inhabits.

Today we can no longer distinguish clearly among the old entities by which the universe used to be described. In the new science it has become clear that mass and energy are the same thing. And similarly space and time grow indistinguishable in the vast, veiled depths of the outer cosmos. Handicapped by his inadequate conceptions, confined in the prison house of his senses, man can only grope through the twilight that dims both of his ultimate horizons—on the one hand the inscrutable universe of the elementary particles, on the other the illimitable universe of space and time. Whether he will ever penetrate them more deeply is a question that can be answered only with hope, not assurance. For in the words of Paul, "We know in part, and we prophesy in part. . . . Now we see through a glass, darkly."